D0148211

The Antitrust Revolution

Economics, Competition, and Policy

Third Edition

John E. Kwoka, Jr.
Lawrence J. White

New York   Oxford
OXFORD UNIVERSITY PRESS
1999

Oxford University Press

Oxford   New York

Athens   Auckland   Bangkok   Bogotá   Buenos Aires   Calcutta
Cape Town   Chennai   Dar es Salaam   Delhi   Florence   Hong Kong   Istanbul
Karachi   Kuala Lumpur   Madrid   Melbourne   Mexico City   Mumbai
Nairobi   Paris   São Paulo   Singapore   Taipei   Tokyo   Toronto   Warsaw

and associated companies in

Berlin   Ibadan

Published by Oxford University Press, Inc.,
198 Madison Avenue, New York, New York 10016

Oxford is a registered trademark of Oxford University Press

Library of Congress Cataloging-in-Publication Data
The antitrust revolution : economics, competition, and policy / John
E. Kwoka, Jr., Lawrence J. White. — 3rd ed.
p.   cm.
Includes bibliographical references (p.   ).
ISBN 0-19-512014-0 (cloth : alk. paper). — ISBN 0-19-512015-9
(pbk. : alk. paper)
1. Trusts, Industrial—Government policy—United States—Case
studies.   2. Antitrust law—Economic aspects—United States—Case
studies.   I. Kwoka, John E.   II. White, Lawrence J.
HD2795.A64   1998
338.8'5—dc21   97-52203

2 4 6 8 9 7 5 3 1

Printed in the United States of America
on acid-free paper

To Margaret,
the best of all daughters.
J. E. K.

To the two most important people in my life:
Martha and David.
L. J. W.

Contents

PART 2: Horizontal Practices

PART 3: Vertical and Complementary Market Issues

Contents

Preface

The first edition of *The Antitrust Revolution* was motivated by our belief that economic analyses of recent antitrust cases would fill an important need in the classroom. The motivation for this third edition is in one sense no different: the role of economics in the antitrust process continues to grow and evolve in new ways that deserve examination. But we have found ourselves even more committed to this project as a result of another consideration: the enthusiasm of students, instructors, and others for economics-oriented case studies of antitrust and for the type of material that comprises *The Antitrust Revolution* in particular.

We have experienced firsthand, and heard from others, the potential for these case studies to stimulate the interest of students in economics, business, public policy, and law. We have learned from many sources the diverse ways that this material lends itself to classroom and other uses. We have encountered virtually unanimous approval for having economists who worked on cases describe the issues that were actually addressed by themselves and by other parties. And we are constantly reminded of additional antitrust cases that raise new issues and affect major industries. These whet the appetites of students, instructors, and antitrust observers alike, who ask us if such cases will appear in "the next edition."

Our hope is that this third edition answers this question "yes" and in so doing piques further interest in antitrust economics. To accomplish this, we have significantly altered this edition. We have included many more cases than in past volumes—a total of nineteen. This larger number of cases is designed to allow coverage of recent cases while retaining many that appeared previously. These are divided, roughly as before, into three topic areas: horizontal structure, horizontal practices, and vertical and complementary market issues. The focus of the last group has been broadened to reflect the increasing importance of issues arising from vertical and complementary markets.

There are eleven new case studies, by themselves nearly as many as the total number in past editions. These reflect the numerous new issues raised by networks and dominant firms (Microsoft), mergers in deregulated industries (Baltimore Gas & Electric, Union Pacific-Southern Pacific), joint venture access (Visa-Discover Card), unilateral effects theories (Staples-Office Depot), defense industry consolidation (Lockheed-Martin), potential competition (Bell Atlantic-NYNEX), related market practices (Kodak, Time Warner-Turner), and pricing coordination (MIT financial aid, Airline Tariff Publishing). The present edition includes many cases for their insights into modern economic analysis as well as for their importance as antitrust precedents.

And finally, we have shortened the average case discussion to approximately twenty-five pages. This was simultaneously the result of reader suggestions and the desire to include more cases without having the book grow in length.

While this edition is novel in all these respects, we have maintained the key pedagogic features: these are important recent cases that reveal the role (or limitations) of economic analysis in antitrust. All are written by economists involved in the particular proceedings. All authors have presented a balanced picture of the issues and evidence, thereby allowing readers to make their own assessment. All provide an evaluation of the economic and legal significance of the cases. And of course, each sets out an economic analysis of a major industry and provides insights into the process that governs antitrust policy in the United States.

For this third edition, we want to express our gratitude to many people who provided assistance. These include Ken MacLeod, our editor at Oxford University Press, for his encouragement and support for this project; Bill Burnett, who provided many suggestions and assistance; and Charlene Kalenkoski, our editorial assistant based at George Washington University, for the innumerable things that ensured completion of our task. In addition, we should acknowledge our numerous authors—in addition to ourselves, now twenty-six in total—for their interest in participating in this project, for their willingness to write balanced accounts of cases about which they feel very strongly, and—not least of all—for their adhering to our tight deadlines.

Most of all, however, we want to thank our students, students elsewhere, instructors, and all others who have used our book. Your enthusiasm, encouragement, and suggestions have been critical to the past success and to the continuation of *The Antitrust Revolution.* We hope this volume meets your expectations.

May 1998

J. E. K.
L. J. W.

Contributors

Gustavo E. Bamberger is a Principal, Vice President, and Senior Economist at Lexecon, Incorporated.

Kenneth C. Baseman is a Principal at Microeconomic Consulting and Research Associates. He previously served as Staff Economist in the Antitrust Division, U.S. Department of Justice.

Stanley M. Besen is a Vice President of Charles River Associates. He has been Co-director of the Network Inquiry Special Staff at the Federal Communications Commission, Allyn M. and Gladys R. Cline Professor of Economics and Finance at Rice University, Senior Economist at the Rand Corporation, and Co-editor of *The Rand Journal of Economics.*

Severin Borenstein is a Professor of Business Economics at the Haas School of Business, University of California at Berkeley, and Director of the University of California Energy Institute. He is also North American editor of *The Journal of Industrial Economics* and a research associate of the National Bureau of Economic Research.

Steven R. Brenner is a Vice President in the Washington, D.C., office of Charles River Associates. He previously was a Senior Economist at the Federal Communications Commission and Assistant Professor of Economics at Grinnell College.

William B. Burnett is a Vice President in the Washington, D.C., office of Charles River Associates. He previously held a number of positions in the Bureau of Economics of the Federal Trade Commission.

Dennis W. Carlton is Professor in the Graduate School of Business at the University of Chicago and President of Lexecon, Incorporated. He has been a member of the Economics Department of MIT and the University of Chicago, as well as the Law School and Graduate School of Business at the University of Chicago. He is the co-editor of *The Journal of Law & Economics.*

Serdar Dalkir is an Associate at Microeconomic Consulting and Research Associates. He has served as a consultant to the World Bank.

David M. Eisenstadt is a Principal at Microeconomic Consulting and Research Associates. He was formerly an economist with the Antitrust Division of the Department of Justice.

Kenneth G. Elzinga is Professor of Economics at the University of Virginia. He was one of the first Special Economic Assistants at the Antitrust Division of the Department of Justice and more recently was Thomas Jefferson Visiting Scholar at Cambridge University.

David S. Evans is Senior Vice President of National Economic Research Associates. He was previously Adjunct Professor of Law and Associate Professor of Economics at Fordham University.

Richard J. Gilbert is Professor of Economics and Business Administration at the University of California at Berkeley. He served as Deputy Assistant Attorney General for Antitrust in the U.S. Department of Justice and has also been on the faculty at Stanford University.

George A. Hay is the Edward Cornell Professor of Law and Professor of Economics at Cornell University. He has served as Chief Economist in the Antitrust Division of the U.S. Department of Justice.

Ira Horowitz is a Graduate Research Professor in the College of Business Administration at the University of Florida, and is periodically a Visiting Professor at the City University of Hong Kong.

Paul L. Joskow is James and Elizabeth Killian Professor of Economics in the Department of Economics at Massachusetts Institute of Technology. He is a Fellow of the Econometric Society and the American Academy of Arts and Sciences.

John E. Kwoka, Jr., is Professor of Economics and Columbian College Distinguished Professor at George Washington University. He has previously served in the Federal Trade Commission, the Antitrust Division of the U.S. Department of Justice, and the Federal Communications Commission, and been on the faculty of the University of North Carolina at Chapel Hill.

William J. Lynk is Vice President and Senior Economist at Lexecon, Incorporated. He previously served as Director of Economic Analysis at the National Blue Cross and Blue Shield Association.

Jeffrey K. MacKie-Mason is a Professor of Economics and Information in the Economics Department and in the School of Information at the University of Michigan. He is also a Research Associate at the National Bureau of Economic Research.

John Metzler is a Ph.D. candidate in Economics at the University of Michigan specializing in industrial organization and an economist working with Resource Economics.

E. Jane Murdoch is a Principal in the Palo Alto office of Charles River Associates.

Philip B. Nelson is a Principal with Economists, Incorporated. He has previously been an Assistant Director of the Bureau of Economics of the Federal Trade Commission.

Daniel P. O'Brien is a Principal with Charles River Associates. He has previously been an Assistant Professor of Economics at the University of Michigan, an Adjunct Professor of Law at Georgetown University, and a staff economist with the Antitrust Division of the U.S. Department of Justice.

Steven C. Salop is Professor of Economics and Law at the Georgetown University Law Center and a Special Consultant at Charles River Associates. He has previously served as Associate Director, Bureau of Economics, at the Federal Trade Commission, and also at the Civil Aeronautics Board.

Richard L. Schmalensee is the Gordon Y. Billard Professor of Economics and Management at the Massachusetts Institute of Technology and a Special Consultant for National Economic Research Associates, Inc. He has served as a member of President Bush's Council of Economic Advisers.

Robert D. Stoner is Vice President with Economists, Incorporated. He has been a Deputy Assistant Director of the Bureau of Economics of the Federal Trade Commission.

Frederick R. Warren-Boulton is a Principal of Microeconomic Consulting and Research Associates. He served as Chief Economist and Deputy Assistant Attorney General in the Department of Justice, and has been a Resident Scholar at the American Enterprise Institute, and Associate Professor of Economics at Washington University, and a Research Associate Professor of Psychology at American University.

Lawrence J. White is the Arthur E. Imperatore Professor of Economics at the Stern School of Business, New York University. He has served as a Board Member on the Federal Home Loan Bank Board, as the Chief Economist in the Antitrust Division of the U.S. Department of Justice, and on the Senior Staff of the Council of Economic Advisers.

John Woodbury is currently a Vice President at Charles River Associates. He has served on the Network Inquiry Special Staff and in the Common Carrier Bureau of the Federal Communications Commission, at the Federal Trade Commission, and as Research Vice President at the National Cable Television Association.

Introduction

Antitrust policy in the United States is now more than a century old. Since the passage of the Sherman Act in 1890, the nation has undergone an Industrial Revolution, a Great Depression, and now an Information Revolution. Along the way additional antitrust laws and enforcement practices evolved into an antitrust policy—or somewhat more accurately, a succession of antitrust policies. Each era seemed to have its own unique policy, the product of distinctive judicial interpretation, popular sentiment, and economic perspectives of the time. Thus, early in this century antitrust boldly broke up monopolies and dominant firms. Somewhat later, it challenged vertical integration among companies and then aggressively attacked horizontal mergers. Throughout, it diligently pursued what it perceived to be predatory conduct by large companies against smaller rivals and new entrants.

Given this history—not all of which has brought credit to antitrust— it is important to recognize that over the past twenty years, there has been a revolution in U.S. antitrust policy. This revolution has involved the ascendence of economics in antitrust policymaking, with repercussions throughout the institutions and enforcement practices of antitrust.

Economic analysis now plays a crucial role in determining what cases the Antitrust Division of the U.S. Department of Justice and the Federal Trade Commission actually pursue. Economics frames the central issues for investigation and, on the basis of data analysis and theory, structures the examination of the likely competitive effects of various practices or structural changes in companies and the industries in which they operate. Courts have endorsed a central role for economics in rendering their own decisions.

Inevitably, economists themselves have become heavily involved in the process. Each antitrust agency has a large economics staff that plays a crucial role in internal deliberations. Outside academic and nonacademic economists advise companies and the antitrust agencies, act as expert witnesses in cases, analyze and write about the economic soundness of agency and court decisions, and are sometimes appointed to the most senior policymaking positions at the antitrust agencies.

The leading edge of the economic revolution in antitrust—but, as we shall see, not its only manifestation—has been so-called "Chicago School" economics. That school has emphasized the use of basic microeconomic theory for evaluating the effects of industry structure and conduct on economic performance. Mergers are analyzed in terms of their likely price effects versus plausible cost savings and the trade-off between the two. Price increases, it claims, are not so easy to achieve, either because of the inherent difficulty of tacit cooperation or because of ease of entry by new competitors. On these key questions, market shares and concentration are therefore poor indicia. In addition, cost savings much more typically flow from mergers and easily outweigh likely price effects, so that mergers are almost always procompetitive.

On other issues, the Chicago School has spoken equally strongly. Price cuts almost invariably reflect lower costs and are therefore procompetitive. For price cuts to be predatory, by contrast, requires various stringent conditions that are unlikely to be met, and hence predation is unlikely to occur. Similarly, efforts by manufacturers to establish retail prices or to constrain the behavior of independent retailers most likely represent efforts to control certain aspects of the sale in which the manufacturers have a legitimate interest. They do not reflect an interest in higher downstream prices and hence are not anticompetitive.

Partly as a result of this methodological emphasis, the Chicago School also has developed a distinctive perspective on the *purposes* of antitrust. It has argued long and strenuously that antitrust should be guided solely by the economic efficiency consequences of structural changes and firm conduct. Efficiency, this school has maintained, is what the plain language of the law implies and in any event is the only objective that can sensibly be pursued. And it has documented numerous instances in which the pursuit of other objectives has actually imposed costs on consumers rather than enhanced the competitiveness of markets.

The result of these challenges to both the methodology and to the objectives of antitrust has been a fundamental change in antitrust policy itself. Evidence of this can be found in a simple comparison of antitrust policy as recently as thirty or forty years ago with that of the 1980s and 1990s. Policy in the earlier period often reflected the populist objective of protecting small business and that prohibited mergers between companies with small market shares. By the 1980s, by contrast, megamergers of petroleum companies were approved with only minor modification. Mergers in the steel and airline industries won approval despite large market shares. All of these decisions were said to be based on new economic learning about market structure and competitive effects.

Similar accommodations to business conduct have been made in the area of firm conduct. Whereas earlier Supreme Court cases held that virtually any tampering with market price was illegal per se, by the late 1970s the Court admitted the possibility of procompetitive justifications even for price fixing by horizontal competitors. In the area of predatory pricing, the traditional view seemed to be that price cuts injuring competitors were evidence of predation, but later cases have adopted a more permissive view of what is acceptable pricing behavior by an incumbent firm.

Perhaps no area underwent more fundamental revision than vertical mergers, vertical pricing practices, and nonprice vertical restraints. In contrast to the hostility toward most vertical arrangements up through the mid-1970s, the antitrust agencies now challenge few vertical mergers or vertical pricing restrictions. Court decisions have adopted the same laissez faire attitude toward nonprice vertical restraints. These judicial and enforcement attitudes reflect changing economic views of structural and nonstructural relationships between vertically related companies.

Other traditional concerns of antitrust have been subject to vigorous criticism by economists and others, virtually disappearing from the agenda of the antitrust agencies. Price discrimination, with its generally ambivalent economic effects, is no longer the subject of agency action. Cases in which mergers eliminate potential competitors are rarely pursued, partly because the judicial standard of proof is so high and partly because of the popular—but not unanimous—view that potential entrants are numerous. Conglomerate mergers, previously challenged on potential competition grounds (or on the basis of their sheer size), have ceased to be even the subject of serious debate in the antitrust community.

The magnitude and significance of these changes in antitrust economics and policy can hardly be overstated. Chicago School economics permanently altered the debate over the purposes and methods of antitrust. Regardless of how much of it one agreed with, the Chicago School view raised a series of fundamental questions, provided its answers to those questions, and made clear that any other answers would be held to an intellectually rigorous standard.

And there *were,* and are, other answers. While few advocated a return to the antitrust posture of the 1960s, not all economists ever subscribed to the Chicago School doctrine. Many continued to believe that market shares and concentration were informative about competitive conditions and that entry was rarely so quick, cheap, and easy as alleged. Serious reservations were raised about the permissive policy toward price cutting and other dominant firm practices, since many believed that predation (or its close cousin, disciplining behavior) does indeed occur. A significant number of economists were unwilling to go so far as to absolve vertical relationships of any anticompetitive potential. And many were distinctly uncomfortable with the argument that strict economic efficiency was or should be the essential purpose of antitrust.

3

Apart from those who never accepted this new learning, theorists and applied economists have more recently been drawn to the intellectual challenges of antitrust economics. They have revisited traditional issues and put Chicago School formulations under the same intense scrutiny as that school gave earlier views. Those formulations have not always held up. The new analyses have involved more powerful theory, which is better adapted to specific issues and more capable of identifying conditions under which various practices might have procompetitive versus anticompetitive effects. The result has been demonstrations of the potential competitive harm from actions that the Chicago School exonerated. In addition, techniques of empirical analysis have become much more sophisticated, with data better suited to its task, models well grounded in theory, and superior econometric tools. The return to empirical inquiry has helped counterbalance the near-exclusive reliance on theory that characterizes the Chicago approach.

Out of this has emerged an alternative approach to antitrust economics. Sometimes called "post-Chicago economics," it argues that many formulations of the past twenty years are *too* reliant on theory—and simplistic theory at that—with the result that important issues are overlooked and incorrect conclusions are drawn. It contends that many practices must be evaluated in light of facts specific to the case, rather than being pigeonholed into some tidy theoretical box. And it is far more skeptical of the ability of the market to discipline firms and thereby negate the anticompetitive potential of mergers and various practices.

Post-Chicago economics is not—or at least not yet—a unified alternative paradigm. It certainly has not displaced the Chicago approach in many quarters. And some have expressed concern that its more fact-based approach will make determinations of antitrust violations more difficult. But it has gained acceptance as an intellectually rigorous alternative approach to antitrust. It represents a significant counterweight to the views that have dominated the past twenty years, with fundamentally different policy implications and with increasing impact on antitrust enforcement and court decisions.

And significantly, post-Chicago antitrust economics is very much a part of the "antitrust revolution." Economics constitutes its foundation just as much as economics did for the new learning—indeed, its advocates would argue, more so. These new views simply represent another step in that revolution. And there will be many more such steps, as economics strives to clarify the effects of structural changes and various business practices on market performance.

While the outcome of that process cannot be foretold, two predictions can safely be made. The first is that the paramount importance of economics in the antitrust process is firmly established. Enforcement policy and court decisions seem virtually certain to be grounded in economic analysis at least as much as they are at present. Even critics of antitrust policy have come to debate it in terms of competition and efficiency, clearly conceding the central role that economics plays.

Second, advances in economic understanding set the stage for improvements in the rationality and consistency of antitrust policy. As these advances gain acceptance, they progressively narrow the range within which policy decisions are made. That is, by demonstrating that some propositions are incorrect, lack generality, or suffer from other defects, they limit the degree to which future policy can ever revert to them. It is therefore difficult to imagine that mergers of firms with small market shares will again be prohibited, or that allegations of predation will be so routinely accepted, or that vertical restraints will be treated with such hostility.

That does not imply complete agreement about the proper course of antitrust. A considerable range of acceptable policy remains, and there is—and will be—legitimate disagreement over goals and strategies within that range. But to an increasing extent, that range is defined by economics. Policy outside that range bears an increasing, even unsustainable, burden. The antitrust revolution is secure.

PART 1

Horizontal Structure

The Economic and Legal Context

The economic theory of horizontal structure of firms in a market falls logically into two categories: pure monopoly, or a dominant firm with market power; and oligopoly, in which a comparative handful of leading firms may be able explicitly or implicitly to coordinate their behavior and jointly achieve or enhance market power. Antitrust concerns about horizontal structure have largely focused on the same two areas. Section 2 of the Sherman Act is concerned with monopolization, which is usually given a joint behavioral and structural interpretation. Section 7 of the Clayton Act forbids mergers and acquisitions, the effects of which "may be substantially to lessen competition, or to tend to create a monopoly."

Five of the six cases in this section discuss mergers and antitrust concerns about oligopolistic coordination and market power, as well as allegations (and denials) that monopolies would be created and strengthened; the sixth case discusses a joint venture that converted a duopoly into a monopoly. (Two additional merger studies, which involved substantial vertical elements, are presented in Part 3.) Since the monopoly model is clearly at the heart of any analysis involving market power, we first turn our attention to monopoly.

MONOPOLY

Economic Theory

The microeconomic theory of monopoly is straightforward: a single firm, selling a product for which there are no good substitutes and where entry by other sellers is not likely, will be able to charge a higher price (at a reduced sales volume) and earn higher profits than would an otherwise similar competitive group of sellers.[1] Most economists would agree that the social loss from this pricing behavior is related to the output reduction: the deadweight loss "triangle" created by the forgone net value received by consumers because of the reduced output. Some economists, and most politicians, would also count the monopolist's excess profits (above competitive levels) as social loss, whereas efficiency theory considers these excess profits as neutral transfers from consumers to the owners of the monopoly enterprise. Some would claim that at least part of the monopolist's potential excess profits are likely to be dissipated either through socially wasteful efforts to defend the monopoly[2] or through inefficiency that arises because of the absence of competitive pressures.[3]

Instances of pure monopoly in the U.S. economy can be commonly found, although collectively they account for only a modest fraction of aggregate economic activity. Examples include (for many geographic areas) local residential telephone, electricity, natural gas, water, and cable television distribution; postal service for first-class and bulk mail; the single hardware store, pharmacy, or gasoline station in an isolated crossroads town; and firms producing unique products protected by patents (e.g., those patented pharmaceuticals for which there are no good substitutes). Over time, technological advances tend to erode existing monopolies but also to create new ones.

It is a short leap from the single seller to a dominant firm that has a fringe of smaller competitors. Though technically not a monopoly, this dominant firm is also likely to be able to exercise and enjoy the fruits of market power. The extent of this enjoyment will depend on the elasticity of demand, the elasticity of supply by the fringe, and the ease or difficulty of entry.[4] Historical examples of dominant firms would include Alcoa in aluminum, IBM in mainframe computers, Xerox in photocopy machines, and Kodak in cameras and film, at least for some time periods. More recent examples would include Microsoft in personal computer operating systems,[5] Intel in microprocessors, and United Parcel Service for small package delivery.

Monopoly can arise in three basic ways. First, economies of scale, interacting with the size of the market, may dictate that only one firm can efficiently serve the market. In essence, the technology of production may be such that average costs decline over the entire range that the market demand encompasses, so that the lowest unit costs are achieved when only one seller serves the market. (Note that this is a market-size-dependent concept; for a given technology, small markets may be served by a monopolist, whereas

---

[1]A similar argument applies to monopsony: a single buyer in a market, who may be able to buy at a lower price than if competition among buyers prevailed.

[2]See Posner (1975).

[3]See Leibenstein (1966).

[4]See Stigler (1965) and Landes and Posner (1981).

[5]See Case 17 by Richard Gilbert in Part 3 of this book.

larger markets may be more competitive. Railroad city-pair markets appear to be a good example of this.[6]) Thus the local telephone and other services mentioned appear to be instances of technology-driven monopoly, as is the single retailer in the isolated crossroads town. Whether, and the extent to which, market power can be exercised by these structural monopolies is dependent on the elasticity of demand and the ease of potential entry.

The second path to monopoly is through a merger of all the producers to yield a single entity or a dominant entity. Such consolidations were common during the merger wave of 1887–1904, which produced monopolies or dominant firms in petroleum (Standard Oil), steel (U.S. Steel), tin cans (American Can), cigarettes (American Tobacco), explosives (DuPont), cameras and films (Kodak), and over sixty other major industries.[7]

The third way to monopoly is through government regulation and restriction. Airline routes between some city-pairs prior to the late 1970s, taxicab franchises in some cities, intrastate long-distance telephone service in some states prior to the mid-1990s, and the U.S. Postal Service's monopoly on first-class and bulk mailing are examples. Patents are a special case. A government-granted patent in essence creates a property right for an idea, which prevents others from copying the idea and thereby free-riding without the permission of the idea's originator. The justification for the patent system is that it encourages invention by allowing inventors to exploit their inventions and earn returns on their investments, which free-riding would otherwise prevent or discourage.[8] Most patents probably offer their holders little in the way of monopoly rents, since the inventions frequently have close substitutes. Over 200,000 U.S. patents are granted each year; it is unlikely that all or even most are conveying real monopoly power. But some inventions (e.g., Polaroid's early patents on self-developing film, Xerox's early patents covering photocopying, pharmaceutical companies' patents on unique drugs, Intel's patents on its microprocessors) do involve unique products and create true monopolies. Many economists would argue, however, that the social costs of the market power exercised by these infrequent monopolies are probably a worthwhile price to pay for the incentives for invention and innovation created by a patent system.

A monopoly or a dominant firm may be able to entrench or enhance its position by raising the barriers to entry or raising the costs of its rivals.[9] These actions may involve measures aimed directly at its rivals, for example, predatory practices, which will be discussed in Part 2; or they may involve restraints in vertically related markets involving customers or suppliers, which will be discussed in Part 3.

---

[6] See Case 3 by Kwoka and White in Part 1 of this book.

[7] See Markham (1955), Nelson (1959), and Scherer and Ross (1990, ch. 5).

[8] The patent system also encourages public disclosure of the technology to implement the idea.

[9] See Salop and Scheffman (1983, 1987).

Antitrust

Government economic regulation (through formal commissions or other bodies) and government ownership have been the most frequent way in which public policy in the United States has tried to deal with monopoly. But from its beginnings in 1890, antitrust law has also tried to address monopoly problems. Section 2 of the Sherman Act creates a felony offense for "every person who shall monopolize, or attempt to monopolize, or combine or conspire with any other person or persons, to monopolize. . . ."

The antitrust approach, however, has not been especially successful. In the *Standard Oil*[10] and *American Tobacco*[11] cases of 1911, the Supreme Court declared that a "rule of reason" should apply to monopolization cases: the courts must look beyond just structural conditions and consider also behavior and intent, as well as the efficiencies of size (economies of scale and scope). As a consequence, "big" government cases alleging monopolization have been infrequent, victories have been rare, and structural remedies— that is, breaking up a monopoly into two or more competitive firms—rarer still.[12] The last major horizontal monopolization case[13] brought by the U.S. Department of Justice—the IBM case[14]—was in 1969, and the Department dropped the case in 1982. The Federal Trade Commission brought joint monopolization cases against a group of breakfast cereal manufacturers[15] and a group of integrated petroleum companies[16] in the early 1970s, but both actions were dropped by the agency in the early 1980s. Only slightly more common have been "smaller" monopolization cases that have not aimed at structural remedies but instead have focused on practices by a dominant firm that may make entry more difficult or that raise the costs of smaller rivals.[17] Private antitrust suits alleging monopolization are more common, but they almost always involve heavy doses of alleged predatory behavior and intent (see Part 2) or involve vertical restraints (see Part 3), and private plaintiffs are not able to obtain structural relief from the courts.[18]

---

[10]*United States* v. *Standard Oil Co. of New Jersey et al.*, 221 U.S. 1 (1911).

[11]*United States* v. *American Tobacco Co.*, 221 U.S. 106 (1911).

[12]A survey can be found in Scherer and Ross (1990, ch. 12).

[13]The *AT&T* suit was largely a case involving vertical structural relief; see Noll and Owen (1994).

[14]*United States* v. *International Business Machines Corporation,* complaint filed January 17, 1969.

[15]*In the matter of Kellogg Co. et al.,* docket no. 8883, complaint filed January 24, 1972.

[16]*In the matter of Exxon Corporation et al.,* docket no. 8934, complaint filed January 24, 1973.

[17]These cases often have vertical restraint elements; see Case 17 in Part 3 by Richard Gilbert. In yet another variant, the Justice Department prosecuted American Airlines and its CEO Robert Crandall under Section 2, for his 1982 invitation to a rival to raise prices, as an attempt to monopolize airline markets where American was the dominant carrier; see *U.S.* v. *American Airlines,* 743 F.2d 1114 (1984).

[18]See *International Telephone & Telegraph Corp.* v. *General Telephone & Electronics Corp. et al.,* 518 F.2d 913 (1975).

In sum, antitrust has not played a large role in dealing with monopoly market structures through horizontal structural relief. In the absence of major changes in judicial interpretations of Sherman Section 2 and in enforcement policies by the two antitrust enforcement agencies, this characterization will continue to hold true.

OLIGOPOLY

Economic Theory

If we leave the world of monopoly or of the dominant firm but continue to focus on a relatively small number of sellers in the market, we are in the world of oligopoly. The essence of the oligopoly market structure is that the number of sellers is few enough so that each seller is aware of the identities of its rivals and recognizes that its output and price decisions affect their decisions (and that the others probably have similar perceptions). This condition is frequently described as conjectural interdependence.

Because of this mutual awareness among oligopolists, there is no definitive solution or outcome to an oligopolistic market structure (unlike the outcomes that can be predicted for monopoly and perfect competition). Instead, additional assumptions about the oligopolists' expectations or behavior must be made before a solution can be predicted.

One branch of oligopoly theorizing has focused on "noncooperative" behavior and outcomes, that is, situations in which each seller makes a specific assumption about the likely response by its rivals to its own strategic actions and then attempts to maximize its own profits. One common example of noncooperative oligopoly is the Cournot model, in which each firm assumes that its rivals will hold their outputs constant and adjust their prices only in response to any price and quantity changes by that firm. The popularity of this model among economists is due at least as much to its mathematical tractability as to the extent to which its predictions comport with economists' intuitions about outcomes in oligopoly markets. Other assumptions, of course, can and have been made about oligopoly behavior, with differing consequences for model outcomes.[19]

Another branch of theorizing has focused on "cooperative" behavior and outcomes among oligopolists, that is, situations in which a group of oligopolists will jointly try to coordinate their behavior so as to achieve the monopoly market outcome (which yields the largest aggregate profits), but in which also they individually may be tempted to "cheat" on any common agreement or understanding (explicit or implicit) for their own

[19]For an overview, see Shapiro (1989) and, especially for relevance to horizontal mergers, Jacquemin and Slade (1989).

extra gain and at the expense of the others.[20] As is discussed further in Part 2, this approach focuses attention on the structural conditions that would make coordination among oligopolists, and mutual policing of any understanding among them, easier or more difficult. These conditions include the number of sellers and their relative sizes (i.e., seller concentration), since coordination is likely to be easier among a few sellers with large market shares; conditions of entry and of expansion by small firms in the market, since easy entry can eliminate the ability of even a monopolist to exercise market power; the nature of the product, since pricing coordination and policing among oligopolists may be easier for simple products with comparatively few quality dimensions or variations; the number and relative sizes of buyers, since a few large buyers may be able to shop around and induce price cutting by the oligopolists; the sociology and history of the industry; and the legal rules (e.g., antitrust) that may make easier or more difficult the formal or informal communications among sellers that aid them in reaching and policing understandings.

Antitrust

Antitrust law has had at least four approaches to oligopoly markets. First, in a handful of cases (e.g., the cereals and petroleum cases mentioned before) oligopolistic market structures have been attacked directly, sometimes under the rubric of joint monopoly. Second, as will be discussed in Part 2, practices and arrangements that facilitate coordination among sellers have been attacked. Third, vertical structures and arrangements that enhance market power have come under antitrust scrutiny, as will be discussed in Part 3. Fourth, and most relevant for the discussion here, under Section 7 of the Clayton Act, mergers that would increase concentration and thereby increase the likelihood of coordinated behavior among oligopolists have been challenged.

Though the Clayton Act was passed in 1914, Section 7 remained largely a dead letter until 1950 because of an unintended loophole in the original act.[21] In the latter year, however, the Celler-Kefauver Act closed the loophole, and Section 7 gained life. A series of government challenges to mergers in the 1950s and 1960s yielded a set of important Supreme Court decisions, beginning with *Brown Shoe* in 1962,[22] which indicated that the Court was ready to prohibit both horizontal mergers and vertical mergers (i.e., between a customer and a supplier) between firms with even relatively

---

[20]Theoretical support for these arguments, and the propositions that follow, can be found in Chamberlin (1933), Fellner (1949), Bain (1956), and Stigler (1964). See also Scherer and Ross (1990).

[21]The 1914 act forbade mergers that were effected through one company's purchase of the stock of another. Merger candidates quickly realized that they could easily evade this restriction through the one company's purchase of the underlying assets of the other.

[22]*Brown Shoe Co. v. United States,* 370 U.S. 294 (1962).

modest market shares and even in industries with relatively easy entry. The Court expressed concern about competition but also opined that Congress had intended to halt mergers so as to preserve market structures with large numbers of firms, even at the sacrifice of some efficiency that might be achieved by a merger. The Court backed off somewhat from this quite tough, semipopulist position in a few merger decisions in the 1970s,[23] and decisions by the enforcement agencies and by the lower courts since then have further modified the legal climate surrounding mergers.

Flushed by the favorable Supreme Court decisions of the 1960s, the Department of Justice's Antitrust Division developed its *Merger Guidelines* in 1968. The *Guidelines* indicated the circumstances (described primarily in terms of four-seller concentration ratios and the sales shares of the merging firms) in which the Department of Justice (DOJ) would be likely to challenge mergers, so that the private antitrust bar could provide better guidance to their clients.

The 1968 *Guidelines* were largely scrapped and a new set issued in June 1982. Economists at the DOJ played a large role in the development of the new guidelines, and the Assistant Attorney General for Antitrust at the time (William Baxter) was well versed in and sympathetic to the teachings of microeconomics. The 1982 *Guidelines* were revised modestly in 1984 and again, somewhat more substantively, in 1992. In this latter year, the economics and legal staffs of the Federal Trade Commission (FTC) also participated in the revisions, and the FTC became a coauthor of the guidelines. In 1997 a modest revision was made to the *Guidelines*' evaluation of efficiencies that might arise as a consequence of a merger.

The *Guidelines* have proved influential in shaping antitrust lawyers' and economists' approaches to mergers; indeed, they shaped many of the economic arguments that were developed in the cases described in this section. Accordingly, we next turn to a more detailed discussion of the *Guidelines*.[24]

THE *MERGER GUIDELINES*

The *Merger Guidelines*[25] start from the fundamental premise that the antimerger provisions of the Clayton Act are intended to prevent the exercise or enhancement of market power that might arise as a consequence of

---

[23]See *United States* v. *General Dynamics Corp. et al.*, 415 U.S. 486 (1974); and *United States* v. *Marine Bancorporation et al.*, 418 U.S. 602 (1974).

[24]More discussion of the specifics of the *Merger Guidelines* and their application can be found in Fox (1982), Werden (1983), Fisher (1987), Schmalensee (1987), White (1987), Scherer (1989), Denis (1992), Willig (1992), and Yao and Arquit (1992).

[25]Unless otherwise indicated, the following discussion refers to the common elements of the 1982 *Guidelines* and its subsequent revisions.

a merger.[26] They take as their analytical base the microeconomics monopoly and oligopoly propositions briefly discussed above.[27]

Proceeding from this analytical base, the *Guidelines* address six crucial issues: (1) the delineation of relevant markets for merger analysis, so as to determine whether the merger partners compete with each other and what their (and other relevant sellers') market shares are; (2) the level of seller concentration in a relevant market that should raise antitrust concern about a merger; (3) the possibility that the merging firm might unilaterally be able to affect prices and output; (4) the extent and role of entry into the market; (5) other characteristics of market structure that might make coordinated behavior among sellers easier or more difficult; and (6) the extent to which cost savings and efficiencies that arise from the merger should be allowed as a defense to a merger that appears to increase the likelihood of the exercise of market power. Each will be discussed in turn.

Market Definition

Since the prevention or inhibition of the exercise of market power is the goal of merger enforcement, the *Guidelines* define a market as a product (or clump of products) sold by a group of sellers who, if they acted in concert, could raise their prices by a significant amount for a significant period of time. This is equivalent to defining a relevant market as one that can be monopolized.[28] The *Guidelines* indicate that a 5-percent increase sustained for one year is the likely value that the antitrust agencies will use in their market definition determinations. The smallest group of sellers that could exercise market power is generally selected as the relevant market for analysis. That is the group that can most readily raise prices if its buyers would not switch away to sellers of other products and/or sellers located in other geographic areas in sufficient quantities so as to spoil the profitability of and thus thwart the price increase. These principles apply to the determination of product markets as well as geographic markets.

The market definition paradigm largely focuses on groups of sellers (rather than buyers), since it is sellers who might exercise market power. But if a group of sellers could practice price discrimination and raise prices significantly for a group of customers in a specific geographic area,

---

[26]The *Merger Guidelines* thus reject a populist approach that the pure sizes of the merging entities should be a consideration in the evaluation of a merger. Though the earlier versions devoted modest attention to mergers with vertical aspects, the 1992 version was silent on the topic, as its title—*Horizontal Merger Guidelines*—indicates. Nevertheless, where vertical issues can have horizontal consequences, the *Guidelines'* principles come into play, as will be discussed in Part 3.

[27]The 1982 and 1984 versions focused primarily on the "cooperative" oligopoly theory framework, much influenced by Stigler (1964); the 1992 version added "noncooperative" and "unilateral effects" (for differentiated products) frameworks.

[28]Or, in instances in which one or more firms are already exercising market power, the relevant market would be one in which their market power could be significantly enhanced.

that group of customers (beyond some de minimus size threshold) should also be treated as a market.

Seller Concentration

With the market boundaries determined (and the presence of the two merger partners in that market ascertained), the focus turns to a post-merger standard of seller concentration that should trigger antitrust concern. The *Guidelines* use the Herfindahl-Hirschman Index (HHI) for this measurement. The HHI for a market is computed by summing the squared market shares (expressed as percentages) of all of the sellers in the market. Thus, an atomistic market would have an HHI very close to zero; a pure monopoly would have an HHI of 10,000 ($100^2 = 10,000$); and a duopoly consisting of, for example, two firms with 70-percent and 30-percent market shares, respectively, would have an HHI of 5800 ($70^2 + 30^2 = 5800$).

The *Guidelines* specify two nominal decision points: for a market with a postmerger HHI below 1000, the merger will rarely, if ever, be challenged; for a market with a postmerger HHI above 1800, and the merger itself causing an increase in the HHI of 100 or more, there is a presumption that the merger could be anticompetitive and should be challenged,[29] but the merger partners' lawyers (and economists) could nevertheless convince the agencies not to challenge by providing convincing evidence of easy entry or of other market characteristics that would make the exercise of enhanced market power in the postmerger market unlikely. For mergers in between, the *Guidelines'* presumption that the merger could be anticompetitive is weaker (and the merger partners' representatives can succeed with weaker supporting evidence).

In practice, the enforcement agencies have been considerably more lenient than the nominal HHI thresholds would indicate. Rarely have mergers with postmerger HHIs of less than 2000 been challenged, and some mergers with substantially higher HHIs have also not been challenged.[30] In essence, the agencies have been willing to consider the other characteristics (discussed below) of the market and/or the merger itself in reaching conclusions that some mergers with comparatively high HHIs do not pose competitive problems.[31]

---

[29]There are two ways of translating the HHI decision points of 1000 and 1800 into more familiar terms. An HHI of 1000 would be yielded by a market with ten equal-size firms each having a 10-percent market share; an HHI of 1800 would be yielded by a market with between five and six equal-size firms. Alternatively, since most markets do not have equal-size firms, the two decision points translate empirically (on the basis of simple correlations) to four-firm concentration ratios of roughly 50 percent and 70 percent, respectively. See Kwoka (1985).

[30]See Leddy (1986).

[31]Of course, many potential mergers that would create high HHIs without extenuating circumstances are never proposed, because the merger partners' legal counsel advise them that the merger would be likely to be challenged.

Unilateral Effects

Although coordinated behavior by oligopolies is the primary "story" of concern with respect to horizontal mergers, the *Guidelines* also recognize that for some mergers the merged firm might be able unilaterally to raise prices and reduce output, even in the absence of coordinated interactions among its rivals. One such possibility that has attracted increasing attention arises in markets with differentiated products. Firms may sell products that substitute to varying degrees for each other, so that any attempt by a single firm to raise price results in so much consumer switching that the attempt fails. A merger between two of these firms, however, may be profitable to the extent that the merger includes the firm to which enough of the customers switch. Since the price rise is initiated by a single firm, the competitive problem with such a merger is not coordinated behavior but rather is characterized as "unilateral effects."

Another possibility, even for markets with undifferentiated products, is simply that the merger itself would create a firm that was of sufficient size that the characteristics of the "dominant firm" model discussed above would apply. The *Guidelines* identify a combined market share of 35 percent for the merging firms as the point when such concerns about unilateral effects would be triggered.

Entry

Since easy entry by new firms could thwart efforts to exercise market power by sellers even in highly concentrated markets, the *Merger Guidelines* recognize entry as an important component of merger analysis. They indicate that, for entry to be characterized as "easy" (and hence obviating concerns about the potential for postmerger exercise of power), it must be "timely, likely, and sufficient in magnitude, character, and scope. . . ." The *Guidelines* acknowledge that a significant barrier to entry can be high levels of "sunk costs": the acquisition costs of tangible and intangible assets that are "uniquely incurred to serve the relevant . . . market" and that cannot be completely recouped by redeploying them elsewhere. (Examples include specialized production equipment, marketing costs, training costs, research and development, etc.) The *Guidelines* ask specifically whether, despite the presence of sunk costs, sufficient entry would be likely to occur (in response to a merger-induced price increase) within two years[32] so as to cause prices to return to their premerger levels.

---

[32]Firms that could enter easily (i.e., without the expenditure of significant sunk costs) within one year are considered to be in the market, as part of the market delineation process.

Other Market Characteristics

Sellers always have an incentive to "cheat" on any implicit (or explicit) understanding among themselves to temper their competition, especially if they believe that such cheating (e.g., price cutting) can go undetected for a considerable period. Accordingly, the ability of sellers to detect and "punish" (e.g., through severe price cutting) deviations from any understanding is important for the success of any sustained period of noncompetitive behavior. The *Guidelines* discuss the major market characteristics that oligopoly theory recognizes as important determinants of the ability of sellers to detect and punish deviations and thus to coordinate their behavior: the availability to all sellers of key market information about market conditions and individual transactions; typical pricing or marketing practices by firms in the market; the level of concentration on the buyers' side of the market; the degree of complexity in the quality and service dimensions of the product or products at issue; and the antitrust history of the sellers in the relevant market.

Cost Savings and Efficiencies

In principle, the cost efficiencies achieved by a merger could yield social savings that would more than compensate for the social loss created by the exercise of market power.[33] A continuing dilemma of antitrust policy is whether the promises of such savings should be allowed to count as an offset and thus permit an otherwise objectionable merger to be completed.

The 1982 version of the *Merger Guidelines* took a skeptical view of these promises. Such efficiencies are easy to promise; they are often difficult to achieve in practice. The 1984 and 1992 revisions to the *Guidelines*, however, took a more tolerant view of such promises; and the 1997 revision expanded on this latter view, stating that the agencies "will not challenge a merger if cognizable [i.e., merger-specific and verifiable] efficiencies are of a character and magnitude such that the merger is not likely to be anticompetitive in any market." One consequence of current policy is that most merging firms advance claims of efficiencies, and the antitrust agency must undertake the challenging task of evaluating their admissability.

MERGER ENFORCEMENT PROCEDURES

Under the provisions of the Hart-Scott-Rodino Act of 1976,[34] the parties to all prospective mergers that exceed specified thresholds[35] must notify

---

[33]See Williamson (1968).

[34]The act was a response to complaints by the enforcement agencies that they sometimes found out about mergers late or even only after the event and that legally "unscrambling the eggs" of a completed merger created an unnecessary extra burden on merger enforcement.

[35]The thresholds for notification are, basically, that the acquiring firm must have at least $100 million in sales or assets and the acquired firm must have at least $10 million in sales or assets. An

the FTC and the DOJ of their intentions to merge and provide a basic set of information about their companies. Within a few days the FTC and the DOJ decide which agency should take responsibility for reviewing the merger. The basis for this allocation is usually the presence of expertise about the industry in the agency (although political "horsetrading" among the agencies when prominent cases arise is not unknown). Most mergers receive a quick screening and are found to be innocuous. In the instances where the potential for anticompetitive effects seems to be present, a group of lawyers and economists within the relevant agency will be assigned to undertake further analysis.

The agency has thirty days (15 days if the merger involves a hostile takeover) from the initial notification during which the merger cannot be consummated (unless the agency's quick screening reveals an absence of problems and the agency so notifies the parties). At the end of that period the parties can consummate their merger unless the agency makes a "second request" for more information. In this latter event, after the parties deliver the requested information,[36] the agency has an additional twenty days (10 days for a hostile takeover) to indicate its decision. If the agency has potential concerns but has not quite made a final decision, it usually asks the parties to delay consummation, and the parties almost always accede.[37] Because of delays in the information responses to second requests and then specific requests for further delays by the agency, the elapsed consideration time for a controversial merger—from the initial notification to an agency decision—can stretch considerably beyond the minimum fifty days, often running four to five months or longer.

If the agency concludes that a merger does pose a potential problem, the parties and the agency will try to determine if there is an acceptable remedy or "fix" that would remove the agency's competitive concerns and still allow the merger partners to gain the efficiency or other advantages that they seek from the merger.[38] Typically, solutions can be found whereby the merger partners sell off facilities (for some product lines and/or in some geographic areas) to smaller rivals or to new entrants, so as to reduce the relevant HHIs to acceptable levels. For example, in mergers between large banks with widespread branch networks that encompass many metropolitan

---

enforcement agency is still free to challenge a merger involving smaller parties that comes to its attention if it believes the merger to be anticompetitive.

[36]The parties' lawyers often request meetings with agency officials to present their case for the absence of competitive harm, to which they typically bring company executives and economics consultants/experts.

[37]The agency is saying to the parties, in essence, "If you try to consummate immediately, you will force us to go to court to try to stop you, even though we are not entirely sure that this is an anticompetitive merger; but if you give us a little more time, perhaps we will decide after all that the merger is not a problem or that there are some relatively easy remedies."

[38]Prior to the 1980s, such efforts to find a remedy occurred only after the agency had filed a lawsuit to try to halt the merger; since then, the efforts to find a remedy have primarily occurred before the agency reaches a final decision on challenging the merger.

areas,[39] a standard remedy is to require the merging banks to sell off sufficient branches to smaller rivals so as to decrease the HHI levels in each metropolitan area to acceptable levels.

If an acceptable remedy cannot be found, the agency will indicate its intention to challenge the merger in court. Often, this announcement will cause the parties to cancel the merger. If they choose to contest the agency's action, the agency will typically seek and quickly obtain a temporary restraining order from a Federal District Court judge. The agency then asks for a preliminary injunction (PI). Usually, within a few weeks the judge conducts a small-scale trial, lasting a week or two, that is nominally about the fairness of granting of the PI but has generally become a minitrial on the merits of the two sides' arguments. The judge's decision on the motion for the PI usually is determinative: If the agency wins, the parties cancel the merger; if the merging parties win, the agency drops the case. But, in principle, the losing side can continue its pursuit of the case. If the DOJ is the prosecuting agency, the losing side asks for a full-scale trial in a federal district court on the merits (which can involve many months of pretrial maneuvering, extensive document requests, and depositions, as well as a lengthy trial); the losing side in this trial can appeal to the relevant federal circuit court of appeals. If the FTC is the prosecuting agency, the losing side's request for a full-scale trial brings the process into the FTC, where (preceded by the months of maneuvering, etc.) the trial is adjudicated by an administrative law judge (ALJ), who then reaches a decision and writes an opinion. The ALJ's decision can be appealed to the full Commission for a final agency decision; if the merging parties are unhappy with the Commission's decision, they can appeal to a circuit court of appeals.

It should be noted that not all mergers are reviewed by the DOJ or FTC, or even subject to the *Merger Guidelines* standards. In regulated industries, primary antitrust authority often rests with the regulatory agency. The same is true for some partially or recently deregulated industries. In these cases the *Merger Guidelines* need not be followed, and even if they are, agencies often may evaluate mergers under a broader "public interest" standard of which conventional competitive concerns make up only one part.

THE CASES

The cases in this part all pertain to mergers or a joint venture in industries that could be characterized (at least by some) as concentrated. Hence, they were reviewed by the relevant enforcement agencies,[40] and economic analyses were important in the disputes (or dispute resolutions) that followed.

---

[39]For some bank services, individual metropolitan areas seem to be the relevant markets.

[40]Three of the cases involved regulated industries, in which the relevant regulatory agencies— state and federal—held the decisional authority with respect to the mergers.

In the first case, Kenneth Baseman analyzes a partial joint venture between two newspapers. In 1986 the two competing daily newspapers in Detroit ended a price war and reached an agreement for joint operations that allowed them jointly to set advertising and circulation prices while maintaining separate editorial operations. Over the objections of the Antitrust Division, this agreement was eventually approved by the Attorney General in 1988. Baseman discusses the development of this case and highlights the importance of assumptions about duopoly behavior and likely future profits in an assessment of the Attorney General's decision.

Hospital mergers pose a potential challenge to the basic market-power paradigm underlying the *Merger Guidelines*. The nonprofit status of most hospitals and the presence of third-party payers (e.g., health insurance companies, Medicare, Medicaid) for most individuals' hospital bills raise the possibility that decreased competition among hospitals might be cost and price decreasing rather than price increasing. David Eisenstadt discusses an important 1989 hospital merger case in which this question figured prominently. He also describes some of the differences in methodology and interpretation that caused the two opposing economics experts in this case to predict different market consequences from the merger.

The railroad industry has experienced a massive consolidation in the latter half of the twentieth century. In 1950 there were 127 major railroads; by 1980 their number had dwindled to 39; and by 1997 their number had shrunk to 9. John Kwoka and Lawrence White describe and analyze the 1996 merger between the Union Pacific and the Southern Pacific railroads, two large west-of-the-Mississippi lines. This merger raised some basic economic questions about the strength of intermodal and other forms of competition, the competitiveness of markets with only two sellers, the adequacy of access arrangements (trackage rights) where only one railroad has its own lines, and the likelihood of major efficiencies' being achieved.

Investor-owned electric utilities have traditionally been local in their focus, regulated (in terms of prices and profits), and vertically integrated, from electricity generation through transmission to local distribution. Federal policy in the 1990s has encouraged a reassessment and transformation of this traditional structure, whereby generation facilities could be owned separately from transmission and distribution and greater competition (and less regulation) at the "wholesale" level among competing generation units could occur. In response, electric utilities have been merging, so as to position themselves better for this forthcoming era of new competition. Paul Joskow focuses on a proposed merger between two such local utilities, Baltimore Gas and Electric (BG&E) and Potomac Electric Power (PEPCO). Since existing transmission lines may pose capacity constraints, especially at peak-demand times (and the construction of new lines is unlikely to occur rapidly), issues of the potential exercise of market power by generating units figure prominently in this discussion.

The breakup of AT&T in 1984 was a watershed event in the telecommunications industry.[41] The long-distance and equipment manufacturing portions of AT&T were separated from the local regulated service portions, in order to prevent the latter from favoring its affiliates and distort competition in long distance and equipment. The seven regional operating companies subsequently chafed at being confined to local service and pressed relentlessly to be allowed to offer long-distance service. The Telecommunications Act of 1996 tried to encourage more local competition and to specify the conditions under which the local companies could enter long-distance service. Subsequent to the Act, two mergers among the operating companies have occurred, reducing their number to five. Steven Brenner discusses the second of these mergers, between Bell Atlantic and Nynex. Issues of potential competition—was Bell Atlantic a crucial potential entrant into local service in Nynex's areas?—and whether the combined entity would have enhanced powers to discourage entry into local service or long distance featured prominently in this case.

The proposed merger between Staples and Office Depot—the two leading chains of office supply "superstores"—in 1997 attracted considerable attention in the media. "Casual empiricism" suggested that this merger might not raise competitive concerns, since thousands of other retailers sold office products and the two merging parties accounted for only a small percentage of the aggregate sales of such products. But, as Serdar Dalkir and Frederick Warren-Boulton demonstrate, extensive information on the prices charged by Staples and Office Depot indicated that office superstores were a separate market for merger analysis purposes and that the merger would significantly decrease competition in the geographic markets where the merger partners competed, with the likely consequence that prices would rise significantly. On the basis of these data, the FTC decided to challenge the merger and ultimately prevailed in court.

These six studies were written by economists who participated in these important antitrust cases. They show the useful organizational and analytical role that microeconomics plays in the antitrust process.

REFERENCES

Bain, Joe S. *Barriers to New Entry.* Cambridge, Mass.: Harvard University Press, 1956.

Chamberlin, Edward H. *The Theory of Monopolistic Competition.* Cambridge, Mass.: Harvard University Press, 1933.

Denis, Paul T. "Practical Approaches: An Insider's Look at the New Horizontal Merger Guidelines." *Antitrust* 6 (Summer 1992): 6-11.

Fellner, William J. *Competition Among the Few.* New York: Knopf, 1949.

---

[41]For a discussion of that case, see Noll and Owen (1994).

Fisher, Franklin M. "Horizontal Mergers: Triage and Treatment." *Journal of Economic Perspectives* 1 (Fall 1987): 13–22.

Fox, Eleanor M. "The New Merger Guidelines—A Blueprint for Microeconomic Analysis." *Antitrust Bulletin* 27 (Fall 1982): 519–591.

Jacquemin, Alexis, and Margaret E. Slade. "Cartels, Collusion, and Horizontal Merger." In *Handbook of Industrial Organization,* vol. 1, edited by Richard Schmalensee and Robert D. Willig, 415–473. Amsterdam: North Holland, 1989.

Kwoka, John E., Jr. "The Herfindahl Index in Theory and Practice." *Antitrust Bulletin* 30 (Winter 1985): 915–947.

Leddy, Mark. "Recent Merger Cases Reflect Revolution in Antitrust Policy." *Legal Times* (November 3, 1986): 2.

Landes, William M., and Richard A. Posner. "Market Power in Antitrust Cases." *Harvard Law Review* 94 (1981): 937–996.

Leibenstein, Harvey. "Allocative Efficiency vs. X-Efficiency." *American Economic Review* 56 (June 1966): 392–415.

Markham, Jesse W. "Summary Evidence and Findings on Mergers." In *Business Concentration and Price Policy*, 141–212. Princeton, N.J.: Princeton University Press, 1955.

Nelson, Ralph L. *Merger Movements in American Industry, 1895–1956.* Princeton, N.J.: Princeton University Press, 1959.

Noll, Roger G., and Bruce M. Owen. "The Anticompetitive Uses of Regulation: *United States* v. *AT&T* (1982)." In *The Antitrust Revolution: The Role of Economics,* 2nd ed., edited by John E. Kwoka, Jr. and Lawrence J. White, 328–375. New York: Oxford, 1994.

Posner, Richard A. "The Social Costs of Monopoly and Regulation." *Journal of Political Economy* 83 (August 1975): 807–827.

Salop, Steven C., and David T. Scheffman. "Raising Rivals' Costs." *American Economic Review* 73 (May 1983): 267–271.

Salop, Steven C., and David T. Scheffman. "Cost-Raising Strategies." *Journal of Industrial Economics* 36 (September 1987): 19–34.

Scherer, F. M. "Merger Policy in the 1970s and 1980s." In *Economics and Antitrust Policy,* edited by Robert J. Larner and James W. Meehan, Jr., 83–101. New York: Quorum, 1989.

Scherer, F. M., and David Ross. *Industrial Market Structure and Economic Performance.* 3rd ed. Boston: Houghton-Mifflin, 1990.

Schmalensee, Richard. "Horizontal Merger Policy: Problems and Changes." *Journal of Economic Perspectives* 1 (Fall 1987): 41–54.

Shapiro, Carl. "Theories of Oligopoly Behavior." In *Handbook of Industrial Organization,* vol. 1, edited by Richard Schmalensee and Robert D. Willig, 329–414. Amsterdam: North Holland, 1989.

Stigler, George J. "The Dominant Firm and the Inverted Price Umbrella." *Journal of Law & Economics* 8 (October 1965): 167–172.

Stigler, George J. "A Theory of Oligopoly." *Journal of Political Economy* 72 (February 1964): 55–69.

Werden, Gregory. "Market Delineation and the Justice Department's Merger Guidelines." *Duke Law Journal* (1983): 514–579.

White, Lawrence J. "Antitrust and Merger Policy: A Review and Critique." *Journal of Economic Perspectives* 1 (Fall 1987): 13–22.

Williamson, Oliver E. "Economies as an Antitrust Defense: The Welfare Tradeoffs." *American Economic Review* 58 (March 1968): 18–36.

Willig, Robert D. "The Role of Sunk Costs in the 1992 Guidelines' Entry Analysis." *Antitrust* 6 (Summer 1992): 23–25.

Yao, Dennis A., and Kevin J. Arquit. "Applying the 1992 Horizontal Merger Guidelines." *Antitrust* 6 (Summer 1992): 17–19.

CASE 1

Partial Consolidation: The Detroit Newspaper Joint Operating Agreement (1988)

Kenneth C. Baseman

INTRODUCTION

In 1986, the Detroit *News,* acquired that year by Gannett, and the Detroit *Free Press,* owned by Knight-Ridder, reached an agreement for joint operations. The joint operating agreement (JOA) effectively ended a price war in Detroit that had resulted in a significant period of operating losses for both papers. The JOA allows the newspapers jointly to set (monopolize) advertising and circulation prices. Editorial functions remain independently controlled by the two parties to the JOA.

While it was hardly surprising that another metropolitan area had come to be served by a monopoly newspaper organization—a strong trend since World War II—the Detroit situation was unique in that, while the *News* held leads over the *Free Press* in circulation, advertising, and profitability, those leads were diminishing, and the papers' positions were very close to equal. Certainly, there was not the kind of sharp and growing differences in size and profitability of the two papers that had characterized JOAs in other cities[1] or had characterized cities where the weaker paper simply failed. Moreover, the two papers were both very large papers, being the seventh- and eighth-largest daily papers in the United States.

Kenneth Baseman consulted for and testified on behalf of the staff of the Justice Department's Antitrust Division in the Detroit newspaper case. He gratefully acknowledges the insights and comments of Robert Reynolds. All errors are the author's responsibility.

[1]In the press release announcing the JOA, the parties stated that, "Over a period of more than a quarter century since this became a two-newspaper city, the *Free Press* and the *News* have fought to a virtual draw."

The nearly equal positions of the *Free Press* and the *News,* and the fact that both were very large papers, raised the issue of whether the losses suffered by the *Free Press* and the *News* were the unavoidable result of the underlying economics of the newspaper industry, as the JOA applicants argued, or whether the losses were the result of behavior that would change if the prospect of a JOA were removed, as the JOA opponents argued.

The antitrust review of the JOA was conducted under the terms of the Newspaper Preservation Act of 1970. This statute provides a unique procedure for the antitrust review of newspaper joint ventures. The intent of the statute is to allow preservation of two independent editorial voices in circumstances where two fully independent papers cannot remain viable under conditions of ordinary commercial competition. Applicants for a JOA are required to establish that, absent the JOA, one of the papers would probably soon fail.[2] The Attorney General is specifically required to make the final enforcement decisions, unlike other industries where the enforcement decision is usually made by the Assistant Attorney General for Antitrust. The Antitrust Division is required to review applications for joint operating agreements. After an initial review, it makes a recommendation to the Attorney General. It can recommend immediate denial, immediate approval, or a fact-finding procedure under an administrative law judge.

In Detroit, the Antitrust Division recommended, and the Attorney General approved, a hearing before an administrative law judge. At the close of the hearing, the administrative law judge recommended against the JOA, largely accepting the arguments put forth by the Antitrust Division and rejecting the arguments of the JOA applicants. Attorney General Meese disagreed, and approved the JOA. Meese's decision was upheld on appeal, and the JOA was finally implemented in November 1989, about three and one-half years after the two companies had agreed to apply for a JOA.

Background on the Newspaper Industry

Since the end of World War II, the structure of local newspaper markets in the United States has changed dramatically. At the beginning of the period, most cities were served by competing, general-interest, daily newspapers. During the period, many newspapers failed, and by the 1980s, almost all cities were served by only one daily, general readership, metropolitan newspaper.[3] By the mid-1980s, head-to-head competition between daily, general-interest newspapers remained in only about two dozen cities.

---

[2]In Detroit, the parties, apparently after some disagreement as to which paper to claim was failing, filed a JOA application listing the *Free Press* as the near failing paper.

[3]In many cities, suburban papers have emerged to provide local news coverage. But these papers do not compete very directly with metropolitan dailies. They are usually published on less than a daily basis, provide very limited coverage of national or international news, are sometimes free rather than paid circulation, and do not distribute throughout the metropolitan area. While these papers certainly compete with the metropolitan dailies, at least for some advertising and in local news coverage, the competition is far less direct than where two general-interest, daily newspapers compete head-to-head.

The decline in the number of daily newspapers is commonly attributed to a variety of factors, including economies of scale, demand-side complementarities, the growth of other media, and the growing homogenization of the American population over the period.

Economies of Scale

Economies of scale in newspaper operations are commonly thought to occur in two principal areas: first-copy costs and distribution. First-copy costs are the various editorial and news-gathering costs that must be incurred before a paper is ready to print. For a given level of quality, these fixed costs are the same regardless of the number of papers printed. Thus, if quality is held constant, this cost component will contribute to a decline in average costs with volume. Economies of scale are also thought to exist in local distribution operations. With larger volumes, delivery equipment and personnel spend less "dead time" between actual deliveries, thereby leading to lower average costs per delivery. Whether economies of scale in these two areas imply a cost disadvantage for a smaller newspaper in a particular circumstance will depend on the cost-scale relationship for other components of costs and management quality. However, it is safe to say that the overall newspaper cost function must show a strong general tendency toward economies of scale, at least over some range of output. Otherwise it is difficult to explain the sharp decline in the number of cities with more than one paper. If newspapers were a constant-cost industry over all output ranges, there would be no reason for the demand-side changes (discussed below) to result in a sharp reduction in the number of newspapers.

Changes in Demand

Given economies of scale (over some generally relevant output range), why were there so many multiple-paper cities in the first half of this century? The standard answer is that demand heterogeneity (demand for product differentiation) historically was sufficient to support a monopolistically competitive equilibrium, but that changes in the nature of newspaper demand after World War II rendered such competition financially infeasible in many cities. First, the growth of other media, in particular television, reduced the demand for newspapers. People increasingly got their news from television. Second, the demand for product differentiation fell as earlier generations of immigrants, and their children, became assimilated. Either of these factors, or both, could make monopolistic competition unsustainable.

Demand-Side Complementarities and the "Downward Spiral"

Newspapers sell to two different customer groups: advertisers and readers. The demands of these customers are interdependent. Advertisers are willing to pay more for advertisements in a paper with larger circulation, and readers are more likely to want to read and be willing to pay for a paper with more local advertising, especially classified advertising. As a newspaper begins to decline, these demand interdependencies give rise to a phenomenon referred to as the "downward spiral." A decline in circulation reduces the demand of advertisers. The reduction in advertising reduces the attractiveness of the paper to readers, which all else equal leads to a further reduction in circulation. In JOAs before the Detroit application that were approved under the Newspaper Preservation Act, applicants pointed to evidence that the failing paper was clearly in such a downward spiral.

The Advantage of the Morning Paper

In most cases where a city is served by a monopoly paper, it is the morning paper that has survived the interpaper competition to become the monopolist. There are good reasons for this. First, the emergence of alternative media has adversely affected the afternoon papers much more than the morning papers. Evening news on television has tended to displace the afternoon paper as the source of current news, because afternoon papers—which go to press in the morning—will not contain coverage of any news that occurred during the day. This is much less of a problem for morning papers—which go to press during the night—because, at least for national and regional news, very little tends to happen at night.

Second, a morning paper is cheaper to distribute than an evening paper because the deliveries of a morning paper do not have to contend with daytime traffic.

THE GREAT NEWSPAPER WAR IN DETROIT

Trends in Advertising and Circulation

The JOA in Detroit terminated over twenty-five years of competition between the *News*, the afternoon paper, and the *Free Press*, the morning paper. This head-to-head competition began in 1960 when the *News*'s parent, the Evening News Association (ENA), bought the Detroit *Times* from Hearst. This acquisition gave the *News* a substantial lead in circulation over the *Free Press*, with about 63.5 percent of combined daily circulation. Over the ensuing fifteen years, the *Free Press* continuously and steadily cut into the *News* circulation lead. By 1976, the *Free Press* attained a 49.8 percent share. From then until the JOA application in the spring of 1986, the daily circulation share of the *Free Press* fluctuated between 49 and 50 percent.[4] The *News* retained circulation leads in the

---

[4]Unless otherwise noted, the factual summary of the history of the Detroit JOA is taken from Judge Needelman's *Recommended Decision* (1987).

Detroit area,[5] and in the Sunday edition, but the *Free Press*'s trends in these circulation categories were more favorable than in total circulation. The *Free Press*'s share of circulation in the Detroit area increased steadily up to the date of the JOA application.

The *News*'s circulation lead in the Detroit area gave it a lead in advertising revenues over the *Free Press:* Locally oriented Detroit advertisers obtained greater exposure with Detroit consumers by advertising in the *News* rather than the *Free Press.* After 1960, the *Free Press* steadily gained share-of-advertising revenues from the *News,* reaching a peak share of 40.6 percent in 1983 (compared with 30.2 percent in 1960). From there, its share fell slightly to 38.5 percent in 1985 and 38.9 percent in 1986.[6]

Trends in Profitability

During the 1970s, both papers showed operating profits. During the 1980s, both papers showed losses. Table 1-1 shows operating profits (operat-

TABLE 1-1
Operating Profits for the *Free Press* and *News,* 1976–1986*

Year	Free Press	News
1976	$ 6900	$ 9648
1977	7522	12637
1978	4354	11708
1979	(1693)	12032
1980	(7364)	(28)*
1981	(10666)	(8229)
1982	(10889)	(13680)
1983	(10662)	(11508)
1984	(11793)	(8307)
1985	(12552)	(4386)
1986	(16971)	(12234)

*Figures are in thousands of dollars.

Source: *Recommended Decision* (1987), paras. 83 and 92.

---

[5]The *Free Press* had stronger outstate circulation than the *News.*

[6]Note that the *Free Press*'s share of advertising revenues fell during 1984 and 1985, even though its Detroit area circulation improved. This seems anomalous. A possible explanation is that the ENA, then the owner of the *News,* may have consciously pulled its punches in pricing advertising (i.e., discounted less aggressively) in order to "dress up" the financial statements for the *News* when the ENA was trying to sell the paper. Interestingly, the contract for the sale of the paper to Gannett required that certain minimal financial goals be met for 1985, and ENA management attributed the improved financial results in 1985 to its attempts to meet these contractual constraints.

To the extent that short-run advertising demand is relatively less elastic than long-run demand, an owner of a paper previously pricing with regard to its long-run elasticity could "create" short-run profits by increasing prices. To the extent that short-run demand is inelastic, this will result in an increase in advertising revenues.

ing revenues minus operating expenses) for the two papers from 1976 to 1986.

During the late 1970s, the *News* was more profitable than the *Free Press*, but by 1982 and 1983, the *News*'s losses exceeded those of the *Free Press*, and the papers' cumulative losses for 1981–1984 were almost identical. Between 1984 and 1986, the losses of the *Free Press* were substantially larger than those of the *News*, although, as noted in footnote 6, the *News*'s 1985 profits may have been distorted by business decisions designed to meet financial constraints in the acquisition agreement between Gannett and the ENA. The *Free Press*'s operating losses during 1984–1986 may have been overstated because of the accounting treatment of certain expenses incurred in the "Operation Tiger" programs, two business plans designed to improve the long-term competitive viability of the *Free Press*. This issue is discussed in more detail below.

The History of JOA Negotiations and the Win-Win Economics of the Great Detroit Newspaper War

Negotiations over a JOA occurred during the early 1980s between Knight-Ridder and the ENA. The Detroit economy entered recession earlier than the rest of the country, and stayed in recession longer, as the automotive industry suffered from a double hit of national recession and sharply increasing imports. Thus, during the early 1980s, both papers reported significant operating losses. It did not escape the attention of either party that such losses could provide the evidentiary basis for JOA approval. Notes from negotiation sessions indicate that both parties recognized the necessity for at least one of the papers to show a loss, and that, with a few more years of losses, the prospects for a JOA would be "ironclad."

During the negotiations between Knight-Ridder and the ENA, which occurred on and off during the first half of the 1980s, Knight-Ridder took the position that it should be the dominant partner in a JOA. It wanted more than one-half the profits and operating control of the JOA.[7] The ENA never accepted the notion that it should be the junior partner in a JOA, and it made counteroffers under which control would be shared, but the *Free Press*'s profit share would be 40 to 45 percent. Knight-Ridder rejected those offers. Because the ENA and Knight-Ridder were not able to agree on which paper was the stronger, no agreement on a JOA was reached between those parties.

Knight-Ridder may well have believed that, because it possessed greater financial resources than the ENA, it was entitled to be the dominant partner in a JOA even if the *Free Press*, on a stand-alone basis, was

---

[7]This negotiation position may have reflected Knight-Ridder's flawed assessment of the financial condition of the *News*. Knight-Ridder apparently believed that the *News*'s losses were several times worse than the losses it was taking with the *Free Press*.

the weaker paper. In Philadelphia, Knight-Ridder had in fact recently endured a newspaper war and subsequently obtained a monopoly when a larger paper owned by a financially weaker parent went out of business.

Both the ENA and Knight-Ridder made significant investments during the 1970s and early 1980s to strengthen their competitive position. The ENA's investments occurred mostly in the 1970s. Mindful of the historical trend of failure by afternoon papers, in 1976 it launched a morning edition for street sales and outstate home delivery (excluding the Detroit area). Significant expenditures on new press capacity were necessary to accommodate these plans.

Knight-Ridder also invested heavily in the 1970s, with a goal of taking the circulation lead away from the ENA. The major investment—$47 million for a new printing facility—significantly increased its postmidnight press capacity, allowing for delivery of a more timely paper, and also provided the capability for improved color and graphics.

During the 1980s, after the ENA rejected Knight-Ridder's JOA proposals, Knight-Ridder launched two investment programs, dubbed "Tiger I" and "Tiger II," which were intended to lead the *Free Press* to market dominance. This dominance could be achieved by "hurt[ing] the *News* financially [and] putting them in a position where they would have to accept an agency agreement [JOA] on our terms," or by achieving profitability through attaining market leadership in Detroit. The objective of market leadership did *not* necessarily contemplate failure by the *News*. Knight-Rider's investments were also premised on the profitability that could be realized in a two-paper market if it obtained the circulation lead.

Tiger I was planned in 1984 and phased in over the 1984–1986 period. It was budgeted at $26.8 million and included promotional and marketing activity as well as improvements in editorial quality and production. Tiger II was adopted by Knight-Ridder to build upon what it perceived to be the successes of Tiger I. The goals remained either market dominance or a JOA on favorable terms. The centerpiece of Tiger II was a $27-million expansion of the Riverfront plant. The additional press capacity would increase postmidnight production capacity, allowing greater coverage of late-breaking news and sports. Ground broke on the plant expansion in June of 1985.

The breakthrough on the JOA front occurred when Gannett acquired the ENA. Gannett sounded out Knight-Ridder on JOA prospects while it negotiated with the ENA. Gannett brought financial resources to the Detroit newspaper war that were comparable to those of Knight-Ridder and thus may have led Knight-Ridder to modify its assessment of its own chances of winning a war of attrition in Detroit. In any event, Gannett reached an agreement to purchase the ENA in August of 1985, and the acquisition was consummated in February of 1986. Simultaneously, Gannett and Knight-Ridder entered negotiations over a JOA, and the JOA agreement was announced in April 1986, a scant two months after Gannett's acquisition of the ENA.

The terms of the JOA are intriguing. The *Free Press* realized an expected profit share exceeding 49 percent. The *News* would drop its daily morning edition and become exclusively an afternoon paper. Thus, under the JOA the *Free Press* would soon become the larger paper.[8] Gannett and the *News* obtained slightly greater "control," with the right to name three of the five members of the JOA's governing board. However, since Knight-Ridder and the *Free Press* retained veto rights over virtually all decisions of economic significance, the extra "control" obtained by Gannett seems of little value. In effect, Knight-Ridder and Gannett agreed to a 50–50 JOA to end the great Detroit newspaper war.

The timing of the JOA is also interesting. The applicants were worried that if the JOA were delayed, improving economic conditions might put both papers in the black. In addition, there was political risk if the JOA were delayed, since in 1986 "the political climate [was] right for a JOA."[9]

The business decisions of all three players (the ENA, Knight-Ridder, and Gannett) were influenced by their unanimous view that the JOA approval process made the great Detroit newspaper war a "win-win" proposition. All three parties believed (correctly, as it turned out) that the JOA review process would allow both parties to a JOA to share substantially in the monopoly profits the JOA made possible. This in turn colored the business decision whether to initiate or continue the price and investment wars. Losses were good because they helped create the evidentiary basis for a JOA, and initiation or continuation of economic warfare was good because it showed determination to the potential JOA partner, thereby strengthening a claim for a larger profit share.

THE ANTITRUST ARGUMENTS OF THE JOA APPLICANTS

In all prior JOA applications, the failing paper was clearly in the "downward spiral." The antitrust review had focused on whether there were any plausible strategies under which the negative trends could be reversed. In each prior case, the allegedly failing paper was losing money, but the senior paper was earning positive operating profits.

As the previous discussion makes clear, the applicants for the JOA in Detroit could not rely on such arguments. Instead, the applicants offered a variant of the downward spiral theory. They argued that the *Free Press* had avoided the downward spiral only because of the extraordinary efforts of its deep-pocket parent to keep it afloat. Absent Knight-Ridder's willing-

---

[8]By 1994, the *Free Press* had 60% of daily circulation and the *News* had only 40%. See "Detroit Papers Pursuing Vows: for Better for Worse, for Richer for Poorer," *Chicago Tribune*, 7/10/94.

[9]The references to political climate undoubtedly referred to the two-and-one-half or so years remaining in the Reagan administration and in Attorney General Meese's tenure.

ness both to absorb operating losses and to continue major investment programs, the *Free Press* would have entered the downward spiral.

The applicants also argued that, because of its larger scale, the *News* possessed a significant cost advantage over the *Free Press*. This alleged advantage would give the News a strong leg up in the battle for dominance. They claimed, however, that this cost advantage was not reflected in the comparative financial results of the two papers because the *News* "spent" its cost advantage in extra editorial and promotional expenses as part of the battle for dominance.

The alleged cost advantage was a crucial element to the applicants' primary argument. Given economies of scale, it made sense for both parties to seek a monopoly, since, the applicants claimed, that was the only sustainable market structure. (Put differently, a two-paper equilibrium was inherently unstable because of economies of scale.) Given the *News*'s alleged cost advantage, it was certain to prevail, as long as it continued to maintain the competitive pressure. So long as the *News* refrained from increasing prices, there was no strategy available to the *Free Press* that would enable it to return to profitability. Gannett's witnesses testified that they would not increase prices if the JOA were denied, even though at higher prices both papers would be profitable. Economists for the applicants testified that this was a rational strategy for Gannett. In addition, Gannett's lawyers argued that to hope otherwise was to assume that Gannett and Knight-Ridder would violate the antitrust laws against price fixing.

THE ARGUMENTS AGAINST THE JOA

The Antitrust Division of the Justice Department recommended against approval of the JOA. The JOA's opponents had four major arguments.

First, the *Free Press* was clearly not in a downward spiral, unlike the failing paper in prior JOA applications. In fact, the *Free Press* and the *News* were evenly matched, each with some advantages and some disadvantages. In particular, the *Free Press* had the advantageous position of the morning paper, and it did not appear to suffer from any obvious or significant cost disadvantage. Thus, the opponents urged rejection of applicant's modified downward-spiral argument, which was logically based on the notion that the *Free Press*'s inherent weaknesses were being covered by subsidies from Knight-Ridder.

Second, the financial terms of the JOA were flatly inconsistent with the applicants' assertion that the *Free Press* was near failure. If Gannett believed that the *Free Press* was near failure, why would it give Knight-Ridder one-half of what were expected to be very substantial monopoly profits?

Third, the opponents argued that the behavior of the *News* and the *Free Press* would change if a JOA were denied. The papers would realize that the win-win economics supporting the price war had been broken. The papers would be less likely to engage in a price war once it became clear that one of them might actually lose it. Prices would rise above the price-war level, but would not increase to the monopoly level.

Fourth, the opponents argued that even if a JOA would ultimately be necessary in Detroit, the pending application was clearly premature. Viable competition could be expected to continue for a decade or more. In other cities, JOA's had been negotiated where the profit share of the "failing" paper was far less than in Detroit. Thus the *Free Press*'s bargaining position could deteriorate significantly, and future JOA would still be profitable for both papers, albeit with a lower profit share for the *Free Press*. Therefore there was no reason to deny consumers the benefits competition by approving the 1986 JOA application.

Modified Downward Spiral and the *News*'s Alleged Cost Advantage

The opponents strongly criticized the applicants' arguments that the *Free Press* suffered from inherent cost disadvantages or other weaknesses that doomed it to be a loser in a war of attrition. The *Free Press*'s financial performance was not worse than that of the *News* in the early 1980s—indeed the *News*'s losses exceeded the *Free Press*'s losses in 1982 and 1983, and the cumulative losses for the papers for 1981–1984 were virtually identical. Thus, the applicants' claim that the *Free Press* was in much worse shape than the *News* before the JOA rested heavily on their performances in 1985 and part of 1986, a slender reed, given that the ENA's activities apparently improved the *News*'s financial reports for 1985 (to meet constraints in its agreement with Gannett) and the *Free Press*'s operating losses on an accounting basis may have been overstated (relative to true economic losses) because of the increased expenses of the Tiger programs.[10]

The JOA opponents also strongly contested the evidence the applicants offered to support their claims that the *News* held a cost advantage over the *Free Press*. First, the econometric or statistical basis for the claimed cost advantage was weak at best. The *Free Press*, not the *News*, had lower costs per page and lower costs per copy. Applicants argued in favor of comparing costs in terms of page impressions—the total operating costs divided by pages produced times paid circulation. But even here, whether

---

[10]One of the issues identified for the administration hearing was whether the *Free Press*'s losses could be explained by accounting anomalies. In particular, many of the Tiger expenses were really investments from an economic perspective. Therefore, if these expenditures were reclassified as investments, and only the current period depreciation and amortization of those expenditures were classified as current expenses, would the *Free Press*'s losses be eliminated? The answer was clearly no, according to economic testimony filed by John Kwoka (1987) on behalf of the Antitrust Division. However, such reclassification would place the *Free Press*'s reported operating losses much closer to those reported by the *News*, especially in 1984 and 1986.

the *News* had lower unit operating costs depended on the exact proxy chosen for paid impressions.

Moreover, an intriguing question remained. If the *News* possessed (since 1960!) an inherent cost advantage related to scale, why had the trends in circulation and advertising favored the *Free Press?* One possibility, advanced by the Antitrust Division, was that the *News's* promotional and other costs of obtaining incremental customers might be higher than for the *Free Press*. This could be the case either because of diseconomies of scale in these functions, because such costs are inherently higher for afternoon newspapers, or because the *News* was simply inefficient relative to the *Free Press*. Something seemed anomalous in the applicants' argument that the News had "spent" its cost advantage on editorial and promotional costs. For one thing, editorial costs—as part of first-copy costs—were supposed to be a source of cost advantage for a larger paper, not a way to spend a cost advantage. Second, since the *News* had been outspending the *Free Press* on editorial services,[11] and given that the *New's* circulation prices were lower than the *Free Press's*, why did circulation trends favor the *Free Press?* This pattern was consistent with the *News's* need to spend more on quality to overcome its disadvantage as the afternoon paper and also consistent with the *News's* simply being less efficient than the *Free Press* in converting dollars spent into quality, but it was inconsistent with the applicants' position that the *Free Press* was doomed to failure given the *News's* advantages.

The Economic Significance of the Profit Split in the JOA

The terms of the JOA arose from a bargaining process between the stronger or more profitable paper and the weaker or less profitable one (the "senior" and "junior" papers, respectively) prior to the formation of a JOA. Consequently, the outcome (the JOA and its terms) should logically satisfy the condition that each paper fares at least as well under the JOA as it would without the JOA.[12]

The terms of a proposed JOA can therefore provide extremely useful information regarding the newspapers' assessments of the survival prospects of the junior paper. In particular, the senior paper will base its willingness to enter a JOA and its acceptance of a proposed split of JOA profits on an assessment of how long the junior paper will likely remain viable. Only if the junior paper is expected to remain in business for a

---

[11]In 1985, the editorial budgets for the *News* and *Free Press* were $16.5 million and $14.8 million, respectively.

[12]The following terminology is used throughout: the *gross* profits of a JOA are the profits prior to deducting editorial expenses (i.e., revenues less all noneditorial costs, such as printing and distribution costs). The *net* profits under a JOA are the sums of the two papers' profits remaining after the papers deduct their editorial expenses. The phrases "net profits of JOA" and "the papers' profits under the JOA" are used interchangeably. Under this terminology, the profit split in the Detroit JOA is expressed in terms of gross profits.

substantial period of time would the senior paper be willing to offer a relatively even split of the profits from collaboration, as was the case in the Detroit JOA. If the junior paper is perceived to be close to closing, the senior paper could be expected to offer a much smaller share of the profits to the junior publication. Indeed, under the profit-sharing formulas employed in new JOAs approved under the Newspaper Preservation Act prior to the Detroit application, the junior papers have received gross profit shares considerably smaller than the shares of the senior papers.

An example may help to illustrate this JOA bargaining process. Suppose that the discounted present value of a monopoly paper's profits from the inception of the monopoly is $1 billion. Also, for simplicity, assume that $1 billion would also be the discounted present value of profits (net of editorial and other expenses) for two papers operating as a monopoly under a JOA. Suppose that, absent a JOA, the senior paper earns $5 million annually until the junior paper collapses, the junior paper remains in business only one more year, and the senior paper discounts future profits at 10 percent per year. If it waits one year for the junior paper's demise, the present value of the senior paper's expected future profits would be $914 million ($5 million during the year of competition plus $909 million, the present value of the one billion dollar discounted monopoly income stream delayed one year).

Under the JOA, the present value of the senior paper's income stream is $1 billion *minus the present value of the share given to the junior paper.* Since the senior paper must do at least as well by accepting rather than refusing a JOA, this implies that the most the senior paper will offer the junior paper is $86 million ($1 billion minus $914 million) of the JOA's expected profits. Therefore, it is clear that a JOA providing a share for the junior paper exceeding 8.6 percent of the net profits ($86 million/$1 billion = 8.6%) would not be acceptable to the senior paper, since it would do better by waiting.

To convert the calculation to the junior paper's share of the gross profits, one must take account of the papers' editorial expenses. Assume that the present discounted value of the two papers' editorial costs is $300 million, split evenly between the two papers. The gross profits of the JOA are then $1.3 billion. The maximum amount from the JOA's gross profits that the senior paper would surrender to the junior paper is $236 million, equal to the junior paper's portion of the net profits calculated above ($86 million) plus the junior paper's editorial costs ($150 million). Thus, 18.2 percent is the maximum share of the JOA's gross profits the senior paper would offer to the junior paper in these circumstances ($236 million/$1.3 billion = 18.2%).

The senior paper would, of course, bargain to give a smaller share. But the maximum share it would be willing to offer is 18.2 percent of the JOA's gross profits, or 8.6 percent of the JOA's net profits.[13]

---

[13] The junior paper will make an analogous calculation. It will calculate the present value of its expected income stream without a JOA and compare that with the profits it would earn for given shares of the JOA. Although it would like a larger share of the JOA, the minimum share that it would be willing to accept under the JOA would yield profits equal to the income stream it expects

The terms of a JOA can also be combined with estimates of the expected profitability of the JOA, of a single-paper monopoly, and of two-paper competition to derive the minimum expected survival time for the junior paper consistent with the agreement by the senior paper to enter a particular JOA. The following discussion demonstrates this analysis using contemporary profit projections for the Detroit JOA from Drexel Burnham Lambert (DBL).[14]

Drexel Burnham Lambert estimated that operating margins in Detroit during the first five years of the JOA would be 5, 10, 12, 14, and 16 percent. Operating profits (in millions), after deducting editorial expenses, were projected to be $23.8, $52.5, $69.0, $88.9, and $112. To generate a present discounted value of the *Free Press*'s profits, we will assume that the profit estimates in years one through four were expressed in real terms and that operating margins and profits would remain the same in all subsequent years as they were in the fifth.[15] However, DBL noted that other big-city newspapers have operating margins of 20 percent (*New York Times*) and 21 percent (*Washington Post*). At a 10-percent discount rate, $950 million is then the estimated (net) profitability of the JOA.

The calculations below demonstrate that Gannett's decision to enter the JOA in Detroit implied a belief that the *Free Press* was viable for at least seven to ten years and, in all likelihood, considerably longer than that.

The base assumptions are as follows:

1. The JOA profits were split 50–50 between the papers.

2. The discount rate was 10 percent.[16]

3. The sum of the two papers' expected net profits under the JOA and the monopoly income stream were both $95 million per year. This annual profit stream has a present value of approximately $950 million, the amount generated by the Detroit JOA according to a conservative extrapolation of the Drexel Burnham Lambert profit projections.

4. Profits for the *News* during the period of two-paper competition would have been $5 million per year. This assumption, while it exceeds the

---

from continued operation as a second paper. Thus, the poorer the junior paper's prospects, the lower will be the minimum profit share it will require to secure its acceptance of a JOA. On the other hand, when the junior paper believes that it will return to profitability without a JOA, then it will, of course, demand a larger share of the JOA profits as a condition to entering into a JOA.

[14]Drexel Burnham Lambert, Research Abstract, April 15, 1986. Other contemporaneous sources both from outside financial analysts and from in-house assessments at Gannett and Knight-Ridder, generally provided profit estimates as high or higher than DBL's.

[15]It makes little difference to the present value calculation whether the analysts' projected stream for the first five years is assumed to be in real or nominal terms.

[16]The real cost of capital for newspaper chains in 1986 appears to be in the range of 8 to 10%, based on calculations using the capital asset pricing model. Given inflation at the time, this is equivalent to a nominal cost of capital of roughly 13 to 15%.

News's profits years immediately prior to the JOA application, is consistent with the parties' contention that the *News* was the stronger paper, and that it would have been gaining strength as the *Free Press* became weaker.

In the base case, the present value to the *News* of an immediate JOA was \$475 million (50 % of the \$95 million/0.10). If the *Free Press* was expected to survive eight years, the value of the income stream achieved by refusing the JOA would also have been very close to \$475 million. (The present value of a monopoly income stream of \$95 million in years nine and thereafter is approximately \$443 million, and the present value of \$5 million per year in the first eight years is approximately \$27 million.) If the expected survival time for the *Free Press* was less than eight years, Gannett would have lost money by entering into a 50–50 JOA, since the present value of a single-paper monopoly commencing in less than eight years would exceed \$475 million. Thus, if Gannett expected the *Free Press* to survive eight years or longer, it could conceivably have entered into a 50–50 JOA with the *Free Press*. If Gannett believed the *Free Press* would have survived less than eight years, Gannett rationally should not have entered into a 50–50 JOA.

The minimum estimated survival time for the *Free Press* is likely to understate Gannett's estimate of the *Free Press*'s likely or actual remaining survival time. In the above example, Knight-Ridder, the owner of the allegedly "failing paper," captured all of the gains from the formation of the JOA. Its 50-percent share of the JOA gives it profits of \$475 million, compared with the zero or nearly zero profits it would have achieved if no agreement on a JOA were reached. Gannett, on the other hand, would have received the same \$475 million whether or not a JOA had been reached. Thus, if Gannett expected the *Free Press* to survive about eight years, a 50–50 JOA, while perhaps satisfying a minimal rationality requirement for the owners of the *News* (Gannett was no worse off), was highly unlikely, since all gains from the JOA would likely be captured by the owners of the *Free Press*. Gannett had no bargaining ability whatsoever.

If one begins with the more plausible assumption that Gannett and Knight-Ridder possessed approximately equivalent bargaining skills, a 50–50 split of the profits from a JOA would occur only if the papers' survival prospects were roughly equal, at least over the next fifteen or twenty years. Indeed, if Gannett expected the *Free Press* to shut down in eight years, and if one assumes that the gains (higher industry profits) made feasible by a JOA were split evenly between the two firms, then the *Free Press*'s share of the JOA's net profits would have been 25 percent. The expected increase in industry profits from a JOA was \$475 million, and the *Free Press* would have received one-half of those, or \$237.5 million (237.5/950 = 25%). If discounted editorial costs over the life of the JOA were \$300 million, split evenly between the *News* and the *Free*

Press,[17] then the *Free Press*'s share of gross JOA profits would have been only 31 percent [(237.5 + 150)/1250 = 31 %].

In addition, for Knight-Ridder to have found a JOA worthwhile, the *Free Press* would have needed a minimum share that was probably only 20 percent. The *Free Press*'s editorial costs (approximately $15 million in 1985) would be covered by only 10 percent of Drexel Burnham Lambert's estimate of the JOA's annual gross profits by the JOA's fifth year. Knight-Ridder would have also required compensation for the assets it contributed to the JOA, but an additional 10 percent of the JOA's expected gross profits was likely more than adequate compensation.

Changes in the important assumptions (profitability and discount rates) fail to alter the key conclusions of this analysis. For example, using an 8 percent discount rate increases minimum expected survival to ten years. Sharply reducing the gains from monopolization—assuming JOA and single-paper monopoly profits are $50 million per year and the *News*'s profits during two-paper competition were zero—reduces the minimum expected survival time for the *Free Press*, but only to seven years.

Thus, the financial terms of the JOA agreement were inconsistent with the "story" the applicants offered in defense of their JOA. As one might expect, Gannett executives testified that the financial terms of the JOA were not the whole story. In particular, Gannett's chief executive testified that he traded off control for profits, giving Knight-Ridder a higher profit share than it was otherwise entitled to in exchange for allowing Gannett to exercise greater control within the JOA. However, Knight-Ridder maintained a veto over major issues of governance. Further, if Gannett truly valued control, and the *Free Press* was near failure, then the calculations for negotiations over control are very similar to those over money. Gannett would wait for the demise of the *Free Press* rather than yield significant issues of control if it believed that the Free Press was likely to fail soon.

Changing the Price-War Calculus

Opponents argued that the two papers had clearly engaged in a price war that they thought was a win-win situation. Each could reason that it was possible that the price war would drive out its rival. But even if that did not happen, the price war would create the accounting losses they hoped would provide an evidentiary basis for JOA approval, where each paper assumed it would get a substantial share of the profits. Thus, continuing a price war looked like a very good bet. The worst that could happen to either paper was to get half a monopoly.

---

[17]In 1985, the *News* had editorial expenses of $16.5 million, and the *Free Press* incurred editorial expenses of $14.8 million. If these expenses continued at the same rate under a JOA, then the discounted present value of those expenses at a 10% discount rate would slightly exceed $300 million.

This logic would have been severely undermined if the rules governing JOA approval did not allow the junior paper to share in the monopoly profits. In that case, since the survival prospects of the two papers were so equal, each would then reason that a strategy of continuing the price war contained real risks—the loser must absorb the losses from the price war, and get nothing from the JOA. Thus, a decision turning down the 1986 JOA application, by undoing the incentives Gannett and Knight-Ridder saw themselves facing, could well have led to an end to the Detroit price war. Increases in the prices for papers and advertising might then have allowed the two papers to earn a sustainable level of profits.[18]

A risk in turning down any JOA is that, if the junior paper continues to get weaker, the senior paper may lose interest in a JOA. However, while acknowledging the potential risk, opponents argued that the Detroit JOA was clearly premature. JOAs were successfully negotiated in other cities where the weaker paper obtained a profit share far below the nearly 50-percent share that the *Free Press* received. This strongly suggested that the *Free Press* could have become considerably weaker than it was in 1986 and still have negotiated a JOA, albeit one with a lower profit share.

THE DECISIONS

At the conclusion of the hearing, Administrative Law Judge (ALJ) Morris Needelman recommended against the JOA. He largely accepted the positions of the opponents and rejected the positions of the applicants. He found that the *Free Press* was not in a downward spiral, that it was not dominated by the *News* (did not appear necessarily to suffer from scale-related disadvantages), and that the profit split in the JOA was highly probative evidence against the JOA. He also found that there was no unilateral way for either paper to return to profitability. He placed little stock in the testimony of Knight-Ridder executives that they would recommend shutting down the *Free Press* if the JOA were denied, nor in the testimony of Gannett executives that they would not raise prices.

He ruled that applicants had failed, by a wide margin, to meet their burden of showing that the *Free Press* was in probable danger of failure. Needelman sharply and pointedly rejected the applicants' legal arguments.

[18]Applicants argued that denial of the JOA in the expectation that price increases might make both papers profitable could only be based on an expectation that collusion or price fixing would occur (see *Recommended Decision*, p. 116). This argument deserved little weight. Courts generally require much more evidence than an absence of an all-out price war to infer conspiracy. Also there is no dearth of noncollusive economic models wherein duopolists manage to avoid all-out price competition.

Indeed it was Gannett's stated intention to continue the price war if the JOA were denied that constituted a likely antitrust violation. Gannett's CEO testified that he would continue to charge low prices—even though at somewhat higher prices both papers would be profitable—because he believed that the *News* would be the surviving monopolist. Such behavior would clearly violate the Ordover-Willig (1981) test for predatory pricing. The low prices would have been profitable only if they induced the exit of the *Free Press*.

> Applicants should not be permitted to cover up their own glaring failure to prove the existence of an irreversible condition leading to a downward spiral by the expedient of a witness stand threat from the Knight-Ridder CEO that he will shut down the *Free Press* if the JOA is denied (all the pre-litigation evidence is to the contrary) or the warning by the Gannett CEO that in the face of certain losses, should he have to continue without a JOA, he will maintain current pricing practices (which requires acceptance of the odd notion that a rational and self-interested firm will persist in unprofitable behavior). As Applicants would have it, however, this testimony along with the evidence of operating losses somehow shifts the burden to the Intervenors and Antitrust Division to provide sure-fire proof that the *Free Press* and *News* will move independently to the higher prices that are . . . indispensable to profitability without a JOA. . . .

Needelman downplayed the relevance of the argument that the *Free Press* possessed no unilateral way to achieve profitability. He argued that incentives to continue money-losing economics would change if the prospects of splitting monopoly profits in a JOA were taken away from Knight-Ridder and Gannett. He noted that, "It remains to be seen whether without a JOA these interdependent firms will modify their competitive strategies in the face of the equally strong certainty that should present tactics persist the result will be continued losses for both."

On appeal, Attorney General Meese overturned the ALJ's decision and allowed the JOA. In doing so, he said that he accepted the ALJ's findings of fact, but disagreed on the implications of those facts.[19] In particular, he found that a pattern of continuing operating losses, with no prospect for unilateral reversal by the *Free Press,* qualified it as a paper in danger of financial failure.[20] Meese gave substantial credit to the testimony of Gannett executives that they would not increase prices if a JOA were denied. He noted that,

> While the Administrative Law Judge questioned the testimony of Gannett officials to this effect, it hardly reflects unsound business judgment to retain awhile longer the *News'* current depressed pricing practices with

---

[19]In fact, Meese's rendering of the facts seems inconsistent in crucial respects with both the actual facts and the ALJ's findings. Meese "found" that the *Free Press*'s losses "outstripped" the *News*'s losses in every year during the 1980s (p. 5), a gross mischaracterization that gave the impression that the *News* was a clear winner in the great newspaper war. Meese also found (p. 7) that "all seem to acknowledge . . . , the *Free Press* . . . has no realistic prospect of outlasting the *News*, given the latter's substantial advertising and persistent circulation lead. . . ." Meese's citation for this assertion is Needelman's finding (at p. 113) that there is no convincing evidence that either the *News* or the *Free Press* possessed determinative advantages. Certainly the planners and funders of Tiger II—the Knight-Ridder investment plan approved in 1985 to give the *Free Press* a circulation lead in Detroit—could not be included in the "all" people who would agree with Meese's finding that the *News* circulation lead was insurmountable.

[20]"For me, the continuing and persistent operating losses suffered by the *Free Press* over the course of nearly a decade, with no prospect of unilaterally reversing that economic condition in the foreseeable future, describes a newspaper 'in danger of financial failure.'" *Decision and Order,* 1988, pp 14–15.

so many indications that the *Free Press* and Knight-Ridder have abandoned all hope of market domination.

Attorney General Meese did not explain why, if Gannett viewed the *Free Press* as so close to failure, it gave half the JOA profits to Knight-Ridder.

AFTERMATH AND CONCLUSION

As of the early 1990s, the anticompetitive effects of the JOA were apparent. According to a survey of the papers' pre-JOA advertisers, by 1991 40 percent had reduced their advertising linage since the JOA due to higher prices, and 9 percent had stopped advertising in either paper.[21] By 1993, 29 percent of the pre-JOA advertisers had stopped advertising in either paper. However, the JOA in Detroit had not achieved nearly the profitability that the applicants originally projected. Two factors seemed responsible.[22] First, the transition to the JOA was plagued by problems that a well-run monopoly would have avoided. In particular, the timeliness of home circulation delivery was sharply degraded, leading to a subscriber backlash. In addition, advertising prices were increased sharply—prices for some advertisers were increased between twofold and threefold for the 1989 Christmas season, rather than being phased in. This sudden, sharp increase led to an advertiser backlash. Second, the Detroit economy was hit early and hard by the recession of the early 1990s. Thus, the economic foundation for the profit projections did not materialize. However, analysts' predictions generally called for profits similar to those originally projected as the Detroit economy moved out of recession. In other words, predictions of the annual profit levels to be achieved in a healthy Detroit economy had not changed. By 1995, the JOA was earning annual profits of about $50 million.[23] As noted above, even if these lower profits were the true steady state and had been correctly anticipated, the *News*'s minimum estimated survival time for the *Free Press* would have been only marginally reduced, from eight to seven years. Thus, whether one uses contemporaneous profit estimates or actual profits, Gannett's decision to enter the JOA in 1986 was inconsistent with an expectation of near-term failure by the *Free Press*.[24]

From a social welfare perspective, the appropriate outcome for the original JOA application would have been for the JOA to be denied, with an explicit acknowledgment that a JOA application where the junior paper

---

[21]See Shaver and Matthews (1995).

[22]See "15 Months in JOA, Papers Still Losing Money," *Detroit Free Press*, April 4, 1991, p. 1F.

[23]See "Deadline Pressure: Detroit Papers Face an Ugly Standoff with Striking Unions," *Wall Street Journal*, August 9, 1995.

[24]In 1995, 1996, and 1997, the JOA's profits were sharply reduced by a long and bitter labor dispute.

obtained only a share of gross profits consistent with its allegedly failing status (roughly 20%) would be quickly approved.[25] This would have allowed the two papers to reapply quickly if the *Free Press* (or the *News*) truly was near failure. Such a decision would also have allowed quick approval of a JOA application in (say) 1992, if the deterioration in the Detroit area economy rendered a two-paper equilibrium no longer sustainable.

In addition, a rule for JOA approval requiring that the junior paper realize a profit share consistent with its "failing" status—perhaps a 20-percent share in the circumstances in Detroit—would have had desirable truth-revealing features, both for a later JOA application in Detroit, if one had become necessary, and in other cities. Owners of papers would not falsely claim to be failing in order to profit from monopolization. Only truly failing papers would then agree to be listed as the "failing" paper in a JOA application.

It is now too late for Detroit, of course.[26] However, the Justice Department would appear to retain the ability to use the financial terms of future proposed JOAs as highly probative evidence.

REFERENCES

Baseman, Kenneth C. Written Direct Testimony in the Detroit JOA Administrative Proceeding, docket no. 44-03-24-8, 1987.

Decision and Order. Detroit JOA Administrative Proceeding, docket no. 44-03-24-8, 1988.

Dertouzos, James N., and William B. Trautman. "Economic Effects of Media Concentration: Estimates from a Model of the Newspaper Firm." *Journal of Industrial Economics* 39 (September 1990): 1–14.

Ferguson, James M. "Daily Newspaper Advertising Rates, Local Media Cross-Ownership, Newspaper Chains, and Media Competition." *Journal of Law and Economics* (October 1983): 635–654.

Kwoka, John E. Written Direct Testimony in the Detroit JOA Administrative Proceeding, docket no. 44-03-24-8, 1987.

Norton, Seth W., and Will Norton, Jr. "Economies of Scale and the New Technology of Daily Newspapers: A Survivor Analysis." *Quarterly Review of Economics and Business* 26 (Summer 1986): 66–83.

[25] The share of the JOA's gross profits consistent with failing status for the junior paper would be that necessary to cover expected editorial expenses and provide a reasonable, risk-adjusted return on the value of the assets the junior paper contributed to the JOA. For the *Free Press* in 1986, only approximately a 20-percent share of JOA profits would have been necessary to meet this condition.

[26] It is also too late for York, Pennsylvania, where a suspicious JOA was approved by the Justice Department shortly after Attorney General Meese's decision was upheld by the D.C. Court of Appeals. There a junior paper, which had been steadily gaining on its larger rival, and which had almost reached circulation parity, decided that it was "failing" and agreed to a JOA where it received a 42.5-percent profit share.

Ordover, Januse and Robert Willig, "An Economic Definition of Predation: Pricing and Product Innovation." *Yale Law Journal* 91 (1981): 8–53.

Owen, Bruce M. *Economics and Freedom of Expression.* Cambridge, Mass.: Ballinger, 1975.

Picard, Robert G., et al., eds. *Press Concentration and Monopoly: New Perspectives on Newspaper Ownership and Operation.* Norwood, N.J.: Ablex, 1988.

Recommended Decision, Detroit JOA Administrative Proceeding, docket no. 44-03-24-8, 1987.

Rosse, James N. "Daily Newspapers, Monopolistic Competition, and Economies of Scale." Unpublished Ph.D. dissertion, University of Minnesota, 1966.

Rosse, James N. "Daily Newspapers, Monopolistic Competition, and Economies of Scale." *American Economic Review* 57 (May 1967): 522–533.

Rosse, James N. Written Direct Testimony in the Detroit JOA Administrative Proceeding, docket no. 44-03-24-8, 1987.

Shaver, Mary A. and Martha Matthews. "Advertisers Less Satisfied as Result of Detroit JOA." *Newspaper Research Journal* 16 (1995): 114–125.

Simon, Marilyn. Written Direct Testimony in the Detroit JOA Administrative Proceeding, docket no. 44-03-24-8, 1987.

Thompson, R. Stephen. "Circulation Versus Advertiser Appeal in the Newspaper Industry: An Empirical Investigation." *Journal of Industrial Economics* 37 (March 1989): 259–271.

CASE 2

Hospital Competition and Costs: The Carilion Case (1989)

David M. Eisenstadt

INTRODUCTION

Could a merger that substantially increases concentration in a market actually cause lower prices? The special characteristics of hospital services make this an intriguing possibility. In *U.S.* v. *Carilion,*[1] the proponents of a merger between two hospitals in Roanoke, Virginia, rebuffed the Justice Department's challenge by demonstrating to the court that hospital markets function differently from those in other lines of commerce.

The basic industrial organization and antitrust law paradigm holds that increases in market concentration can adversely affect market performance and consumer welfare. Two characteristics of hospital markets, however, suggest that this paradigm could apply with less force: the prevalence of health insurance, and the dominant role that nonprofit hospitals play as providers of hospital services.

First, traditional health insurance is characterized by low co-payment provisions and deductibles and permits the insured to exercise free choice of medical provider. The effect of such policies is to reduce patients' incentives to search for low-cost suppliers and encourage the consumption of more costly, higher (perceived) quality care. As a result, hospitals are likely to compete on the basis of nonprice rather than price dimensions. The larger the number of hospitals present within a locale, the greater is the intensity of service competition. Because this form of competition drives up costs and prices, it is sometimes referred to as the "medical arms race."

David Eisenstadt testified on behalf of the merging hospitals. The author wishes to thank William Kopit, Esq., and Dr. Stephen Silberman for helpful comments.

[1]*U.S.* v. *Carilion Health System,* 707 F. Supp. 840 (Western District of Virginia, 1989).

Second, most hospitals are not-for-profit institutions. Depending on the objectives that these hospitals pursue, prices and output may not be set at the profit-maximizing level. For instance, some health experts hypothesize that nonprofit hospitals pursue charitable goals and therefore maintain lower average prices and higher outputs (Jacobs, 1974; Schlesinger et al., 1987). Others argue that some nonprofit hospitals set their prices at below profit-maximizing levels because employers, who pay insurance premiums, control their boards (Eisenstadt and Masson, 1989; Lynk 1994, 1995). In either case, increased concentration in markets dominated by nonprofit suppliers may affect market performance differently than if the hospitals were exclusively for-profit firms.

Before the 1980s, these distinguishing characteristics probably affected federal agency antitrust enforcement in this industry. However, over the past decade, changes in the nature of hospital reimbursement and innovations in hospital contracting with managed-care providers have placed increasing pressure on hospitals to engage in price competition. This appears, in turn, to have caused increased federal antitrust scrutiny of, and more frequent challenges to, hospital mergers.

In 1988, the U.S. Department of Justice (DOJ) challenged two mergers among nonprofit hospitals in the moderately sized cities of Rockford, Illinois, and Roanoke, Virginia. In both areas, hospital competition was at a crossroads. Competitive bidding among hospitals for contracts with health insurers was not significant in either area, yet prospects existed for its future growth. The situations provided a natural opportunity for judicial examination of hospital competition and the applicability of the basic industrial organization paradigm to hospital markets. When the DOJ sued to enjoin the consolidation of Roanoke Memorial Hospital (RMH) and Community Hospital of Roanoke Valley (CHRV), the debate was joined.

THE SPECIAL CHARACTERISTICS OF HOSPITAL MARKETS

As was mentioned briefly in the introduction, hospital markets have two potentially distinguishing characteristics—the prevalence of health insurance and the dominant role of nonprofit hospitals—that could dictate a different antitrust perspective than is appropriate for most other markets. This section will discuss these two characteristics at greater length.

The Importance of Health Insurance and Third-Party Payment

Health insurance is different in several respects from many other forms of indemnity insurance. First, when an insured patient suffers an illness, the insurer does not pay a fixed or predetermined amount to the patient. Instead, the insurer pays only for the specific costs incurred of treating the illness; a patient who obtains no treatment receives no payment. This provides an incentive for the insured to consume insured medical services.

Second, health insurance is unusual because those who are insured have some control over the quantity of services they receive, yet premiums are not experience rated on an individual-user basis. When an individual receives medical treatment, his or her premiums are largely unaffected because the costs of that treatment are pooled with the experience of other group members.[2] The ability to "free ride" creates an incentive for individual employees to overconsume insured services over which they exercise some discretion. If all employees covered under such a policy respond similarly, medical care expenditures and premiums for the group will rise.[3]

Through the mid-1980s, most Americans were covered under traditional indemnity insurance (frequently obtained through the employer) characterized by low coinsurance payments and freedom to choose any doctor or hospital. An employee insured under such a policy derived little advantage from choosing the lowest-price hospital because the out-of-pocket cost was a very small share of the provider's charge. Instead, the policyholder's incentive was to choose a provider that offered higher (perceived) quality. During this era, hospitals typically competed for patients by providing additional services and amenities, which increased the cost of insured care.

The Effect of Indemnity Health Insurance on Prices, Costs, and Welfare

The typical patient covered under traditional indemnity insurance values the last "units" of health care services or amenities at a fraction of their cost, creating a welfare loss from overconsumption. For example, if a patient has hospital insurance that covers 90 percent of the bill, that individual will be willing to undergo a diagnostic test that costs $1000 even if the test yields an expected benefit of only $100 for the patient. Stated differently, many patients (or doctors acting on their behalf) would not demand expensive tests or procedures if the patient paid for the test directly (or, equivalently, had the choice of receiving the cash versus opting for the test).

Resources are optimally allocated when social marginal value equals social marginal cost (and when price is equated to social marginal value).

---

[2] In contrast, when an individual has a car accident, his or her automobile insurance premiums typically increase in the following rating period.

[3] Total U.S. health care expenditures are also affected by technological change (e.g., the ability to treat an increasing number of illnesses) and by the fact that employer-paid health care premiums are a form of income on which employees pay no taxes.

Traditional indemnity health insurance produces a resource misallocation because the price paid by the patient is less than marginal resource cost.[4] Too many resources are devoted to production of insured health care, and too few resources are employed in the production of other goods and services.

Further, the size of this resource misallocation is affected by market concentration. In markets with greater numbers of hospitals, nonprice competition for patients will be more intense, and costs and prices (paid by insurers) will be higher than in markets with fewer hospitals.

Figure 2-1 helps to illustrate the adverse welfare effects and resource misallocation resulting from comprehensive health insurance. The graph depicts patient market demand and costs for hospital care under different market structures. The "coinsurance" demand curve, D^{NI}, shows the quantity of hospital care demanded as a function of the out-of-pocket price that patients pay. This demand curve represents patients' marginal valuations and is the appropriate demand curve for measuring patient surplus.[5]

FIGURE 2-1 The Consequences of Health Insurance

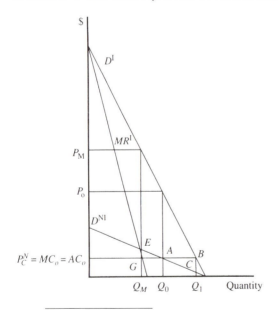

---

[4]If the patient's employer valued the test at $900, one might argue that total marginal value ($100 plus $900) equaled marginal cost. However, given some employers' frequent complaints about employee usage of medical care, and given recent efforts by most to impose greater cost sharing on employees, this seems unlikely.

Of course, physicians can limit the amount of overconsumption by refusing to recommend care that they believe is not truly cost justified. However, as the patient's agent, a doctor may often recommend a service when the perceived benefit to the patient exceeds the patient's out-of-pocket cost.

[5]Like any demand curve, the position of D^{NI} is affected by income. If patients received cash payments when they were diagnosed with particular ailments, those cash payments would increase their out-of-pocket demand for health care services.

The second demand curve, D^I, is patients' expected market demand for hospital care given the presence of insurance coverage. The D^I curve is drawn to depict employer-provided coverage that pays for 80 percent of the cost of hospital care.[6] Prices along D^I represent hospital charges per unit of care. At quantity Q_0, the difference between P_0 and P_C^N is the per unit amount covered by insurance. The ratio of P_C^N to P_0 is the patient coinsurance rate, k, which in this example equals 0.2.

Consider a hospital that sells care in a competitive, uninsured market. If D^{NI} represents patients' true valuations of hospital care, and AC_0 and MC_0 are average and marginal facility costs respectively,[7] competitive equilibrium occurs where Q_0 care is purchased and sold at price P_C^N. By way of contrast, in a competitive insured market, Q_1 units of care are consumed and total premiums equal $(P_C^N \times Q_1) \times (1-k)$. The area ABC represents the welfare loss from the excess consumption of hospital care.[8] The replacement of competition by a monopoly hospital can reduce this resource misallocation. A monopolist operating in an insured market would charge price P_M, and the associated deadweight loss from monopoly (triangle EAG) would be substantially smaller than the welfare loss from excess consumption in competively structured, insured market. Of course, the monopolist elicits a sizable wealth transfer from employers, since the difference between $[(P_M \times Q_M)(1-k)]$ and $[(P_C^N \times Q_1)(1-k)]$ represents increased premium payments, which constitute additional expected income for the monopolist.

In insured markets, the relatively low marginal value placed on additional services does not deter consumers from selecting hospitals that offer the greatest amenities. So long as marginal value to the patient exceeds the out-of-pocket cost (plus the time cost of consumption), patients will choose more expensive care, and hospitals will compete for these patients by engaging in quality or cost-increasing competition. In turn, these increases in perceived quality (even though they are valued at a fraction of their cost) shift the patient market demand up and to the right of D^I. This causes prices to rise and creates another round of cost-increasing competition. The process continues until employers resist increases in insurance premiums.

Interestingly, and not infrequently, a hospital merger that diminishes the intensity of this competition might be opposed by patients and supported by employers. Mergers that reduce the intensity of cost-increasing competition can reduce insurance premiums, which are largely paid by employers. Moreover, the expected drop in premiums could substantially

---

[6] For simplicity, the graph assumes no deductibles or other aspects of insurance coverage that would make D^I nonlinear.

[7] For simplicity in this diagram, hospitals are assumed to produce care over the relevant range of output under a constant returns-to-scale technology.

[8] This welfare loss must be compared with the consumer gain from risk spreading to compute the overall welfare loss from health insurance.

exceed the welfare loss to patients from lower quality care because the extra quality is valued at only a fraction of its cost. In sum, if the "medical arms race" paradigm is correct, hospital mergers can increase the collective welfare of patients and employers.[9]

The Advent of Managed Care

Health insurance companies and other third-party payers (e.g., the U.S. government for the Medicare program) were slow to recognize the problems just discussed. In the mid-1980s, however, the Medicare program changed the way hospitals are reimbursed when they treat elderly patients.[10] Coupled with employer frustrations over rising premiums, traditional indemnity coverage has declined in importance. Under the most prevalent, current system of Medicare reimbursement, hospitals are paid on a per-case or per-diagnosis basis regardless of the patient's length of stay. Since the level of payment is fixed, higher margins from treating Medicare patients can be earned only by reducing costs. This creates incentives for hospitals to discharge these patients earlier. It also results in excess capacity—unfilled hospital beds.

Hospitals confronted with excess bed capacity are more likely to offer discounts to private third parties or employers who promise or threaten to "steer" a large number of patients to the hospital. Collectively, third-party organizations that restrict or threaten to reduce patient choice in exchange for hospital discounts are known as managed-care plans. Today, managed care plans conduct business in almost every geographic locale within the United States. By way of contrast, managed care contracting in many communities was nascent or nonexistent in the mid-1980s.

At the time of the Carilion merger, managed-care plans had made small inroads into the Roanoke, Virginia, area. The DOJ believed that RMH recognized the growing significance of managed care and that a purpose for and effect of the merger would be to forestall entry of such plans and curtail emerging price competition.

Objectives of Nonprofit Hospitals

There is no unified theory of nonprofit firm behavior in economics. Economists have attributed varied and numerous motives to nonprofit entities,

---

[9] It is unclear what economic welfare standard the federal antitrust agencies use to evaluate a hospital merger. The DOJ and FTC *Merger Guidelines* refer to consumer welfare; however, total economic welfare is the sum of consumer plus producer welfare, known as consumer surplus plus producer surplus (profit).

[10] The elderly account for roughly 40% of all hospital admissions. Until October 1983, the federal government, which pays hospitals under the Medicare Part A program administered by the Health Care Financing Administration, reimbursed facilities on a cost-plus basis for services rendered to (Medicare) beneficiaries.

including pursuit of profit, quality, output, and market share. The simplest and most naive theory of nonprofit hospital behavior postulates that hospital administrators maximize profits or surplus and dissipate these rents through generous salaries and/or perquisites to administrative staff.

A variant of this theory presumes that profits will be spent on new programs or charity care.[11] Either way, paying patients are charged the profit-maximizing price, even though the hospital has no shareholders or owners.

A different theory of nonprofit firm behavior treats nonprofit hospitals as quasi-regulated institutions. Under this theory, hospital administrators are constrained by their boards of trustees, typically composed of community leaders and often leading employers. Board members further their own self-interests by dictating that the hospital offer affordable care. Therefore, even if a hospital administrator sought to exploit market power, the board would thwart any such efforts.

Since the economic theory of nonprofit hospitals is incomplete, one is tempted to turn to available empirical evidence on the subject for additional insight. Here too, however, the evidence is less than definitive. On the one hand, it is conventional wisdom that nonprofit hospitals "cost shift" (Dranove, 1988; Hadley and Feder, 1985), a phenomenon that is inconsistent with profit maximization. Cost shifting occurs when charges or prices to one customer group are raised in response to lower reimbursement received from another group. If a hospital starts from a break-even position, reduced reimbursement from one customer group requires price increases to other groups if the hospital is to maintain output without experiencing financial losses. Cost shifting is inconsistent with profit maximization because the latter theory presumes that prices are already set at profit-maximizing levels to each group. Hospitals that cost shift have, for whatever reasons, not fully exercised their available market power.

On the other hand, some empirical work finds few differences in performance or behavior among nonprofit hospitals and their for-profit counterparts.[12] This body of literature has been cited by the federal antitrust agencies as a basis for treating mergers among nonprofit hospitals no differently from mergers among for-profit institutions.

The presence of substantial differences in behavior among nonprofit hospitals may be one reason that theory and empirical observation provide no definitive guide. The significant variation among nonprofit hospitals

---

[11] Another theory is that nonprofit hospitals are operated for the benefit of staff doctors (Pauly and Redisch, 1973). Profits may be sought, but they are exhausted through provision of extra equipment and other practice inducements to physicians. These expenditures may show up on the hospital's books as a "cost," thereby leaving the impression that the facility earns no profit. In fact, however, the hospital could set profit-maximizing prices.

[12] See, for instance, Noether (1988). Other evidence that postdates the *Carilion* trial suggests insignificant price differences between the two types of hospitals in some areas of the country; see, for instance, Melnick et al. (1992), and Simpson and Shin (1996).

prevents generalizations and forces the parties' nonprofit status to be considered on a case-by-case basis. Of course, this approach does not ensure unanimity of opinion. In *Carilion*, the parties and the DOJ separately considered these pieces of evidence and came to fundamentally different conclusions about the role of nonprofit status and the motives of the merging institutions.

BACKGROUND ON THE CONSOLIDATION

Roanoke Memorial Hospital is a tertiary-care hospital that draws patients from a wide area of western Virginia. When the merger was announced, RMH was licensed for 677 beds and staffed with slightly over 600. Its occupancy rate based on staffed beds averaged close to 80 percent. Community Hospital of Roanoke Valley was about one-third RMH's size, staffed with about 220 beds, and had a daily patient census of about 175. During the months preceding the merger, its occupancy rate had fallen to less than 50 percent of licensed bed capacity, with projections for further declines.

The two campuses were located less than a mile apart. RMH contended that the consolidation would provide it with the physical space needed to accommodate its growing patient population. Some clinical services, notably obstetrics, were slated to be consolidated at CHRV, while others would be offered only at RMH. In the absence of the merger, RMH was committed to a capital improvements program that required expansion and refurbishment of its existing physical plant.

After the parties filed notice of the consolidation under the Hart-Scott-Rodino Antitrust Improvements Act in the fall of 1987, the matter was assigned to the DOJ for review. After a six-month investigation, the agency concluded that the proposed consolidation was likely to violate both Section 1 of the Sherman Act and Section 7 of the Clayton Act. A suit was filed in Federal District Court in western Virginia in late May 1988. From June through mid-December, the parties conducted discovery and entered pretrial motions. During this period, the court ruled that mergers among nonprofit hospitals were exempt from Section 7 of the Clayton Act, but were subject to federal jurisdiction under the Sherman Act. The court also appointed an "advisory jury" to assist in fact finding at trial; however, their verdict was not binding on the court. Trial commenced on December 12, 1988.

THE DOJ's POSITION

The DOJ believed that the merger would (1) substantially increase market concentration, (2) raise the price of inpatient acute-care hospital services, (3) permit the merged firm to engage in exclusionary conduct, and (4) convey no significant efficiencies.

Market Definition

Product Market

The DOJ contended that acute-care inpatient services provided by private, general acute-care hospitals were a relevant product market.[13] The DOJ advanced two principal arguments in favor of this product market definition. First, it is administratively convenient. While hospitals provide hundreds of different services, most of which are not demand-side substitutes for one another, only acute-care hospitals are likely to offer most of these. Therefore, even though one might define each inpatient service as a separate product market, as a practical matter it often makes little difference whether concentration is computed on a service-specific basis or by aggregating all inpatient services. This is especially true if most hospitals in an area can easily provide those inpatient services not currently offered.[14]

Second, patients admitted for a specific service often require additional services when medical complications arise. The full array of services needed is often unknown to the patient prior to admission. Hence, patients (and physicians) often prefer a hospital over an outpatient setting because only the hospital provides the complete spectrum of services that may be required.

Geographic Market

The DOJ alleged a geographic market defined as the Roanoke Valley, which included Roanoke County, the cities of Roanoke and Salem, and portions of several adjacent counties. The competitors in this alleged market were the merging hospitals and Lewis-Gale Hospital (LGH), another secondary-tertiary-care hospital (406 licensed beds, 335 staffed beds) located in Salem, about 10 miles from Roanoke. Lewis-Gale Hospital is owned by Hospital Corporation of America (HCA), one of the largest chains of for-profit hospitals in the country. According to the DOJ, the proposed consolidation would reduce the number of acute-care hospital competitors in the geographic market from three to two.

Several pieces of evidence were used by the DOJ to delineate geographic market boundaries. First, over 90 percent of Roanoke County residents used the three hospitals. The nearest acute-care facility to these institutions was located over 20 miles from Roanoke. Moreover, hospitals in the outlying rural areas were typically small and failed to provide the breadth of service or level of quality offered by LGH or the merging parties.

[13]The DOJ restricted the product market to include only private hospitals because federal facilities such as military base hospitals, Veterans Administration hospitals, and prison hospitals are not open to the general public.

[14]Further, even if some services delivered on an outpatient basis were substitutable in demand for inpatient services, a plaintiff might attempt to redefine the product market to include only those core inpatient services that do not face significant competition from outpatient providers.

Second, most Roanoke Valley physicians did not possess active admitting privileges at outlying hospitals. Therefore, even if these institutions provided comparable services to RMH, CHRV, and LGH, Roanoke Valley residents would have to switch doctors to obtain admission there.

Third, patients from outlying areas who traveled to hospitals in the Roanoke Valley often needed services not provided at the smaller hospitals closer to their residences. For these services, the outlying hospitals were not in competition with RMH, LGH, or CHRV, even for the local population residing in these areas.

Fourth, key purchasers of inpatient hospital care, notably Virginia Blue Cross and Blue Shield (VABCBS), believed that contracts with at least one of these three hospitals were required for Blue Cross to offer a saleable insurance product to Roanoke Valley employers.

Barriers to Entry

Virginia Certificate of Public Need (COPN) laws regulate expansion and entry of new hospitals. The statute requires hospitals to obtain state government approval for any sizable capital expenditure. Gaining approval typically requires a demonstration that the proposed service or additional capacity is "needed" by residents of the affected area. A hospital that circumvents the COPN process risks losing reimbursement for its Medicare patients. Regulators employed by the Virginia Department of Health and Human Resources considered the Roanoke Valley to be an "overbedded" area, partly based on CHRV's substantial excess bed capacity. The DOJ contended that obtaining a COPN for new beds would therefore have been extremely difficult.

Market Concentration

In the DOJ's alleged market, consolidation of CHRV and RMH would increase RMH's market share (based on admissions) from 49 percent to approximately 73 percent and increase the Herfindahl-Hirschman Index (HHI) from approximately 3700 to 6050.[15]

Likely Competitive Effects

The DOJ alleged that the consolidation would substantially reduce price competition. It relied on several pieces of evidence to support its position of adverse competitive effects. First, several purchasers of hospital care opposed the merger. The CEO of VABCBS testified that the consolidation

---

[15]Government exhibit 145. Calculation of market concentration statistics using setup and staffed beds and licensed beds showed similar levels of premerger and postmerger concentration.

might decrease discounts offered by the party hospitals,[16] and smaller purchasers of hospital care expressed similar concerns.

Second, the DOJ's economic expert prepared an original econometric study examining the relationship between VABCBS' per-diem hospital reimbursement rates (and, alternatively, discounts) and hospital market concentration. One exhibit entered into evidence depicted a 14-percent per-diem rate increase by RMH (to VABCBS) after the merger.[17]

Third, the same expert testified that several published studies, as well as some unpublished research, showed a positive correlation between market concentration and hospital prices.

Fourth, the DOJ alleged that documents obtained during discovery revealed RMH's resentment toward managed care. According to the DOJ, an effect of the merger would be less price competition for managed care contracts.

Fifth, LGH opposed the consolidation. Its administrator testified that the merger would give RMH market dominance and create the potential for predatory conduct: presumably prices below RMH's costs.

Sixth, the DOJ rejected the nonprofit status of the merging parties as a mitigating factor. The DOJ asserted that the hospitals' boards generally do not micromanage the activities of the respective administrations. While boards may approve overall budgets, they do not supervise individual contract negotiations with payors. Therefore, the merger would create opportunities for the exercise of market power.

Seventh, the DOJ discounted estimates of merger-related savings claimed by the parties. Roanoke Memorial Hospital believed that the merger created substantial capital avoidance because it gained access to vacant space at CHRV. The DOJ's economic expert criticized the estimates of capital saved because unused space at CHRV was valued at zero dollars. Another DOJ expert was sharply critical of the parties' line-item estimates of administrative and clinical operating savings. Estimated savings either were not merger related or failed to reflect true costs of departmental consolidations.

From these various pieces of evidence and testimony, the DOJ's expert was confident that "negotiated" prices would rise in the Roanoke Valley by at least 5 percent after the merger.

---

[16]Virginia Blue Cross and Blue Shield did not operate a managed care plan in the Roanoke Valley. It did, however, negotiate contract rates separately with each hospital for its traditional indemnity business. The threat of being excluded from VABCBS participation created the semblance of selective contracting and provided the area hospitals with a rationale for extending discounts.

[17]Government exhibit 249. Contract rates were predicted to rise from $715 to $818. That price increase was derived from the results of a regression equation attached to the exhibit. A separate discount regression predicted that the merger would drop RMH's discount to VABCBS by about 3 percent. Thus, 11 percent of the predicted 14-percent price increase imposed by RMH to VABCBS was arguably attributable to the predicted increase in list prices.

THE DEFENDANTS' POSITION

The defendants did not offer expert testimony to challenge the DOJ's assertions about relevant product or geographic market. The cornerstones of their defense were the lack of any likely anticompetitive effect and the presence of significant cost savings.

Likely Competitive Effects

The defendant hospitals argued that there was a lack of evidence supporting the DOJ's position that the merger would raise prices. The parties based this contention on four factors: (1) LGH's opposition to the merger; (2) research conducted by the defendants' economist; (3) a critique of the research relied on by the DOJ's economic expert; and (4) the substantial support for the merger among local employers and Virginia regulators.

LGH Opposition

The hospitals argued that LGH's opposition to the merger reflected its fear that the merged entity would become more efficient. In merger analysis, the existence of a complaining competitor is often a signal that the proposed transaction is procompetitive. After all, why would a (horizontal) competitor truthfully oppose a consolidation unless it feared the merged firm would gain a cost advantage? Moreover, a competitor who believes that marketwide prices would increase after the merger should support the transaction, or perhaps profess "neutrality."[18]

In addition, LGH's purported fear of below-cost pricing was less than convincing for several reasons. First, if LGH was concerned about "classic" predatory pricing—that is, pricing below one's own marginal cost—the strategy is plausible only if the defendant lacks a cost advantage over

---

[18]Competitors could behave strategically when polled about their views of a transaction. Those who believe that a merger will cause price increases could voice opposition, hoping that antitrust authorities will conclude the merger is procompetitive. Alternatively, those wishing to stop a merger could pledge their support.

To be sure, there are theories of exclusionary conduct that would predict harm both to competitors and to competition (consumers) from a merger. Suppose, for example, that in a three-hospital market employers wish to offer a managed-care plan composed of any two of the three hospitals. When all three hospitals are independent, each has a two-thirds likelihood of getting selected by managed care plans. If, however, two of the hospitals merge and keep both sites open, the combined entity could insist that the employer contract with both sites. A way to enforce this demand is for the merged firm to refuse to contract with any payer who contracts with the nonparty hospital. Since buyers have a preference for a network that contains two of the three available facilities, they have no choice but to contract with the merged hospital. Postmerger, the likelihood that the merged firm will be selected by managed care plans is "one." And, the nonparty hospital in necessarily excluded from the buyer's network. This is an example of full-line forcing that produces both harm to competition (higher prices) and harm to competitors (exclusion). Second, a nonparty hospital might fear that the merged entity will gain greater control over local physician admissions, thereby foreclosing it from access to doctors.

the victim. A predator with a lower cost structure than the target could take sales away simply by pricing above its own costs and below the intended victim's costs. Since LGH's documents reflected a genuine concern that the merged entity would achieve a cost advantage, apprehension about classic predatory pricing seemed misplaced.[19]

Second, texbook examples of classic predatory pricing assume that the predator has a deep pocket and can sustain short-run losses for a longer period than the victim. While the combined RMH-CHRV hospital was a larger facility than LGH, the latter probably had greater financial resources because it was owned by HCA, a large hospital chain that dwarfed the Carilion Health System.[20]

Statistical Evidence Concerning Market Concentration and Hospital Prices

The defendants' case included several studies that correlated hospital prices and market concentration. The first was an event study, which analyzed postmerger price increases in other areas of the country where consolidations among nonprofit hospitals occurred.[21] The list prices of hospitals located in the markets where mergers occurred did not increase at a statistically different rate from the list prices in control markets.

A second analysis examined the relationship between hospital prices and market concentration in Virginia during the period 1986–1988. Several alternative price measures were used in the statistical work, including list price per day, average price per day net of contractual allowances and discounts, and per-diem reimbursement by VABCBS to individual hospitals.[22]

---

[19] This of course does not mean that Lewis-Gale would have been unaffected by the merger. Unless it could obtain similar efficiencies, its postmerger market share would fall because it would be a less efficient institution. Such harm to competitors, however, does not equate with harm to competition.

[20] Additionally, predatory pricing is a more plausible strategy when used against a firm that competes with the predator in multiple markets. In effect, profits sacrificed because of below-cost pricing in one market send a signal to the victim that aggressive price competition will not be tolerated in other markets. For example, suppose the merged firm announces its intention to raise prices unilaterally in Roanoke, and LGH responds by lowering its prices. The merged hospital could discipline LGH by pricing below cost until LGH relented and agreed to raise prices to more "desirable" levels. If the merged institution and LGH competed head-to-head in other markets, the experience might deter LGH from unilateral price cutting in those areas. In effect, the profit sacrifice made in one market is amortized over the expected price increases in other markets. However, since Carilion and HCA-majority-owned hospitals did not compete in locales outside the Roanoke Valley, no such benefit would have accrued.

[21] Six of the consolidations examined were mergers to "monopoly," one was a merger to "duopoly," and the last was a merger to "triopoly." Each market in which a merger occurred was paired with a group of control markets to assess whether the rates of price increase in the former were significantly different from those in control markets. All control markets were as or more competitively structured than were each of the merger markets before their consolidation.

[22] Multiple regression equations were estimated for each year using the same underlying Blue Cross price data relied on by the government's expert. The regressions controlled for numerous factors besides market concentration, including costs, demand, and hospital organizational structure.

None of the regressions showed a positive correlation between increased market concentration among nonprofit hospitals and higher prices. The coefficient on the HHI was typically negative, indicating that higher concentration tended to be associated with lower prices. However, the negative coefficients were not usually statistically significant.[23]

The results suggested that the nonprofit form of organization and/or the system of voluntary hospital rate regulation in Virginia[24] prevented the exercise of market power. With respect to the former theory, Blue Cross's daily reimbursement rates to for-profit hospitals classified as monopolies were, all else equal, over $100 a day higher than per diem rates paid to sole community provider nonprofit hospitals.

Rebuttal to the DOJ's Evidence

The hospitals claimed that other research relied on by the DOJ actually supported the position that the merger would not harm competition. For instance, one published study showed a statistically significant and positive association between Blue Cross preferred provider organization (PPO) contract rates and hospital market concentration in one midwestern state (Staten et al., 1988). The parties retained one of the authors of that study to analyze further the underlying sample data. Additional work indicated weaker findings than those published.[25,26]

Probably the greatest point of controversy pertained to original research presented by economists for both sides. Both economists relied on the same underlying VABCBS price data and, for the most part, the same market concentration data when correlating prices and concentration among Virginia hospitals. The government's economic expert testified to a

---

[23]These results cast doubt on the importance of the "medical arms race" theory of hospital competition among Virginia hospitals during this period. If competition among sample hospitals had been primarily cost increasing, more competitively structured markets should have experienced higher costs and prices.

[24]All hospitals in Virginia are required to submit proposed budgets and list prices to the Virginia Health Services Cost Review Commission for review. The Commission screens the proposed charges for reasonableness, and the names of facilities that do not adhere to the Commission's recommendations may be published.

[25] For instance, there was no statistical difference between bid prices submitted by hospitals that were located in three-hospital and two-hospital markets. Therefore, over the "range" of market concentration allegedly affected by the Carilion merger, there was no evidence (from this sample) that prices to managed-care plans would rise. Additionally, there was no statistically significant relationship between bids selected by hospitals chosen by the PPO and hospital market concentration. The coauthor, Dr. Michael Staten, submitted affidavit testimony at trial.

[26]The DOJ also relied on another published study (Robinson and Luft, 1988) that compared the rates of cost increase from 1983 through 1986 in California and in markets across the country. Competitively structured markets (those with more than twelve hospitals) experienced lower rates of cost increase than the least competitive markets (those with one hospital). However, there was no significant difference between the rates of cost increase in markets with three to five hospitals versus those with two or fewer institutions. Again, over the range of market concentration allegedly affected by the Carilion merger, the evidence failed to suggest any adverse effect of the merger on price competition.

positive association between price and market concentration and a significant likely postmerger price increase. The economist testifying on behalf of the parties found no statistically significant relationship, and could find no statistical evidence supporting predictions of a price increase. A major reason for the different predictions was disagreement over the magnitude of, level of statistical significance of, and computational methodology used to compute expected price effects.

Efficiencies

One could argue that the merger should have been struck down because the potential existed for a large price increase, even though the statistical evidence presented by the parties indicated that likelihood was low. Hence, evidence demonstrating that the merger produced substantial cost savings was important to the parties' case.[27]

Because RMH needed space to expand, and because CHRV was half empty, RMH asserted that the consolidation provided access to an unused hospital. A hospital facilities planner testified that the merger created substantial capital avoidance because construction of needed space at RMH would cost $15 to $30 million. In addition, the hospitals claimed that operating cost savings in administrative and certain clinical areas would total another $20 million over five years.

OUTCOME

The court asked an advisory jury to make findings on three questions of fact: (1) the correctness of the DOJ's alleged geographic market; (2) the DOJ's assertion that the relevant product market consisted of only inpatient hospital care; and (3) the consolidation's likely effect on competition.

The jury concluded that the DOJ's alleged geographic market was correct. But it concluded both that the product market included some outpatient care and that the consolidation would not have an anticompetitive effect.

The District Court endorsed the jury's findings on the second and third issues and reversed its findings on geographic market. The court concluded that the relevant geographic market consisted of a broader area than the Roanoke Valley. In so doing, the court defined separate geographic markets for primary-secondary care and for tertiary hospital services. For primary-secondary services, it found that Roanoke area hospitals were in direct competition with smaller facilities in outlying areas. Further, the court rejected the argument that Roanoke Valley residents were dissuaded from using facilities other than RMH, LGH, and CHRV

---

[27]If the exercise of market power was unlikely, then the merger should have been motivated by a desire to achieve efficiencies.

because of a need to switch physicians. It referenced the testimony of one physician who indicated that such referrals and admissions could be accomplished with little difficulty. Ultimately, the court determined that the relevant geographic market included all counties and cities from which RMH drew at least 100 patients a year. This area is composed of twenty hospitals located in sixteen counties in Virginia and three in West Virginia. Because of the large number of hospitals in this area, the court concluded that RMH's premerger and postmerger market share was well below the levels alleged by the DOJ.[28,29]

The court concluded that the defendants' nonprofit status was a mitigating factor in favor of the combination. The boards of both hospitals included business leaders who would insist that cost savings be used to lower hospital charges. The court also determined that nonprofit hospitals tend to charge lower rates than for-profit hospitals. Further, the system of voluntary hospital rate regulation in Virginia provided an additional deterrent to the exercise of postmerger market power. Last, the court rejected testimony by the DOJ's expert regarding the predicted rise in contract rates to VABCBS.

With respect to reasons why the merger was procompetitive, the court noted that announcement of the merger caused LGH to behave as a more aggressive (procompetitive) competitor in that it rolled back charges and contemplated an affiliation with a medical school in North Carolina. It also credited the parties' estimates of efficiencies. It recognized RMH's need for space and CHRV's excess capacity as providing a legitimate business rationale for the transaction. The merger created substantial capital avoidance and ongoing operating savings totaling $40 million over the first five years of the affiliation.

After an appeal by the DOJ, the Fourth Circuit Court of Appeals upheld the lower court's ruling by finding that the district court's opinion was not "clearly erroneous."[30] In reaching this determination the appellate court noted that the district court had latitude in the interpretation of evidence and evaluation of witness testimony.

---

[28]With respect to the geographic market for tertiary care, the court conceded that the three Roanoke Valley hospitals do not face competition from small hospitals in surrounding counties but do compete with large institutions in other parts of Virginia and North Carolina, notably Charlottesville, Winston-Salem, and Durham. These competing tertiary-care hospitals should be properly included within the relevant geographic market.

[29]In accepting the advisory jury's opinion on relevant product market, the court found that a significant number of medical problems could be treated on either an inpatient or an outpatient basis. Moreover, insurance carriers have restructured their reimbursement policies to encourage the substitution of outpatient for inpatient care. Therefore, outpatient providers in the nineteen-county area should have been included as competitors to the merging hospitals.

[30] *U.S.* v. *Carilion Health System*, unpublished opinion, 1989–1992 Trade Cas. (CCH) 68,859 (4th Circuit 1989).

CONCLUSION

In this case, the key issues litigated were the likely effect on competition and the presence of efficiencies. The outcome indicates that the court believed that the DOJ failed to meet its burden in demonstrating adverse competitive effects, and that the parties more than met theirs in establishing merger-related cost savings.

Because econometric evidence played a central role in the proceeding, it is useful to consider its use in a merger case. Regression results depict the average relationship between two variables of interest—for example, between price and market concentration. Statistically insignificant results do not prove that the two specific merging firms will refrain from a price increase. Hence, it is important to consider the underlying motives of the parties when assessing the applicability of regression results to an individual transaction.

Several pieces of independent market evidence suggested the absence of a strong anticompetitive motive in this case. First, RMH was space constrained, and CHRV was not; in the absence of the consolidation RMH would have been forced to embark on an aggressive building program. Second, the concerns expressed by LGH suggested that the affiliation offered prospects for cost savings. Third, CHRV was consistently ranked in consumer surveys (conducted before the merger) as the least desirable of the three area hospitals and RMH was the most preferred. It is questionable whether managed-care plans could have used it as effective leverage against RMH in price negotiations. If RMH sought a merger to preempt an outbreak of discounting, LGH would have been a better merger partner. Fourth, regressions (relating price to market concentration across different Virginia hospital markets) presented by the parties showed that RMH's predicted prices were typically within 2 standard deviations of its actual prices. This is important because the government's case emanated from a concern that RMH was controlled by an opportunistic administrator who would exploit the hospital's postmerger market position. But, if RMH were oriented toward especially high prices, its actual current prices should have greatly exceeded those predicted from the regressions. That this result was not found suggests that it was no more aggressive than the average nonprofit hospital in the sample.

The outcome in *U.S.* v. *Carilion* did not resolve policy issues concerning the efficacy of hospital competition. The court neither endorsed nor rejected the basic antitrust paradigm. For instance, it found that prices were generally lower in areas with fewer hospitals—an apparent rejection of the basic industrial organization tenet. However, it also held that the merger would not create significant market power because RMH had a small market share and LGH was a formidable competitor. These findings constitute implicit acceptance of the basic industrial organization paradigm that increased concentration warrants concern. It is conceivable that the court believed that the competitive model was not particularly relevant to the industry, but that this merger would not lessen competition even if it applied. However, this logic was not clearly spelled out in the opinion.

Since the *Carilion* decision, federal court opinions have been issued in at least six hospital merger cases. In all but two, the merging hospitals ultimately prevailed. From a policy perspective, counting wins and losses provides little probative information because the published opinions are so varied and emphasize different evidence. In several of the cases, the government lost either because it failed to prove a relevant geographic market or because the parties demonstrated a "large" geographic market in which the increase in market concentration (caused by the merger) was minimal. In some of these same cases, the district and/or appellate court rejected nonprofit status and claimed efficiencies as relevant issues or mitigating factors. In another case, a district court's decision to allow a merger on grounds that nonprofit status and wasteful competition were relevant to the antitrust analysis was overturned by the reviewing federal appellate court. In yet another transaction, the government prevailed on market definition yet lost the overall challenge because the district court found that nonprofit status, significant efficiencies, and the lack of any demonstrable anticompetitive effects (as reflected in econometric work similar in basic construct to that offered in *Carilion*) were more salient evidence. This merger was affirmed by the appropriate appellate court, also on grounds that it was not clearly erroneous.

Probably the best explanation for the different findings on those issues that are repeatedly litigated is that hospital merger litigation, like all antitrust work, is a fact driven process. Although the number of litigated issues is both finite and quite similar across the different merger cases, the evidence presented in support or rejection of the different arguments varies sharply from case to case. Hence, one court rejects claims that another trier-of-fact credits.

Carilion was one of the first litigated merger cases where evidence on likely competitive effects of a transaction was deemed to be more relevant (by the defendants) than evidence on market definition. Making measurement of likely competitive effects the predominant focus in antitrust merger litigation has gained acceptance among economists within the last decade. Indeed, many antitrust economists contend that market definition is an imperfect and often abused process and that direct measurement of a merger's likely impact on consumers is the preferred inquiry. While the industrial organization paradigm holds that performance can be inferred from structure, the *Carilion* decision and some subsequent cases imply that clear and convincing evidence on both prongs is required before mergers in the hospital industry will be deemed unlawful.

REFERENCES

Dranove, David. "Pricing by Non-Profit Institutions: The Case of Hospital Cost-Shifting." *Journal of Health Economics* 7 (1988): 47–57.

Eisenstadt, David M., and Robert T. Masson. "Price Effects from Recent Non-Profit Hospital Mergers." Presented at American Public Health Association Meeting (October 23, 1989), Chicago.

Hadley, J., and J. Feder. "Hospital Cost-shifting and Care for the Uninsured." *Health Affairs* 4 (1985): 67–80.

Jacobs, Philip. "A Survey of Economic Models of Hospitals." *Inquiry* 11 (June 1974): 83–97.

Lynk, William. "Property Rights and the Presumptions of Merger Analysis." *Antitrust Bulletin* 39 (1994): 363–383.

Lynk, William. "Nonprofit Hospital Mergers and the Exercise of Market Power." *Journal of Law and Economics* 38 (1995): 437–461.

Melnick, Glen, Jack Zwanziger, Anel Bamezai, and Robert Pattison. "The Effects of Market Share and Bargaining Position on Hospital Prices." *Journal of Health Economics* (October 11, 1992): 217–234.

Noether, Monica. "Competition Among Hospitals." *Journal of Health Economics* 7 (1988): 259–284.

Pauly, Mark. "Nonprofit Firms in Medical Markets." *American Economic Review* 77, no. 2 (May 1987): 257–262.

Pauly, Mark, and Michael Redisch. "The Not-For-Profit Hospital as a Physicians' Co-operative." *The American Economic Review* 63, no. 1 (March 1973): 87–99.

Robinson, James, and Harold Luft. "Competition, Regulation, and Hospitals' Costs, 1982 to 1986." *Journal of the American Medical Association* 260, no. 18 (November 11, 1988): 2676–2681.

Schlesinger, Mark, Theodore R. Marmor, and Richard Smithey. "Nonprofit and For-Profit Medical Care: Shifting Roles and Implications for Health Policy." *Journal of Health, Policy and Law* 12, no. 3 (Fall 1987): 427–457.

Simpson, John, and Richard Shin, "Do Nonprofit Hospitals Exercise Market Power?" Federal Trade Commission, Bureau of Economics Working Paper 214, December 1996.

Staten, Michael, John Umbeck, and William Dunkelberg. "Market Share/Market Power Revisited." *Journal of Health Economics* 7 (1988): 73–83.

CASE 3

Manifest Destiny?
The Union Pacific and Southern
Pacific Railroad Merger (1996)

John E. Kwoka, Jr. and
Lawrence J. White

INTRODUCTION

The Union Pacific (UP) and the Southern Pacific (SP) railroads have had long and intertwined histories. The UP and the Central Pacific (a predecessor to the SP) were the two railroads commissioned by President Abraham Lincoln in 1862 to construct a transcontinental rail system. The UP laid rail westward from Kansas while the CP began construction in Sacramento. The driving of the Golden Spike into the rail that joined the two at Promontory, Utah, in 1869 helped realize the country's "manifest destiny" of integrating from coast to coast.

Over the next century the UP and the SP (in various corporate guises) provided rail transportation services throughout the western United States. They expanded and in the early 1900s even sought to combine, though they were rebuffed by the courts.[1] In 1995 they tried again, this time successfully. In August of that year the managements of the UP and SP announced their intentions to merge into a single integrated railroad. The

The authors filed comments in this case on behalf of the Dow Chemical Company and the Kansas City Southern Railway Company, respectively. The authors wish to thank Nicholas DiMichael, Gregory Bereskin, William Mullins, and John Spychelski for helpful comments on an earlier draft, which was presented at the Transportation and Public Utilities Group session at the American Economic Association meetings, January 4, 1998.

[1]In 1901 the UP purchased 38% of the SP's stock and gained effective control of the company, but in 1913 the UP was ordered by the courts on antitrust grounds to relinquish its ownership interest and control.

proposed combination immediately sparked controversy, which persisted well after its approval and implementation.

Though U.S. railroads were deregulated extensively in 1980, vestiges of regulation have remained, including a special regime for dealing with mergers. Instead of being subject to the Department of Justice's or Federal Trade Commission's merger review and enforcement procedures that apply to most other companies, railroad mergers were reviewed by the Interstate Commerce Commission (ICC) until the end of 1995 and since then by the ICC's successor, the Surface Transportation Board (STB).

The ICC/STB's legislative mandate in assessing mergers is broader than that of Section 7 of the Clayton Act. Rather than focusing just on the competition and efficiency issues and the trade-offs (if any) between them, the ICC/STB is instructed by legislation also to consider a railroad merger's effects on "the adequacy of transportation to the public" and "the interest of carrier employees," among other things. But a major focus of the agency has been on the same antitrust issues—market power versus efficiencies—that have held the attention of traditional antitrust merger enforcement.

On the other hand, while the issues are in principle the same, the ICC/STB has been more accommodating toward railroad mergers. This posture is evident in two ways. First, the agency has tended to accept claims of efficiencies by merger advocates without substantial proof[2] and without inquiring whether the efficiencies are uniquely attributable to the merger. Second, where there are competitive concerns with a merger, the ICC/STB has usually sought to remedy them with modest requirements, such as trackage rights for other railroads.[3] The result has been a strong presumption in favor of railroad mergers.[4]

After the UP-SP merger proposal was formally filed with the ICC, dozens of interested and affected parties—eleven other railroads; thirty-eight individual shippers and nineteen trade associations representing shippers (the largest of which represented 1400 individual shippers); five federal agencies; twelve state governments (as well as many individual communities within those states); and five labor unions—offered comments to the ICC/STB on the proposed merger.

In July 1996, eleven months after the initial announcement of the proposed merger, the STB announced its decision: approval of the merger largely as proposed by the UP and SP. The combined UPSP became the

---

[2]By contrast, the antitrust agencies have traditionally been more skeptical with respect to efficiency claims.

[3]As discussed below, trackage rights permit a second railroad access to otherwise captive shippers over the first railroad's tracks. The adequacy of such remedial conditions is a matter of continuing controversy.

[4]Railroad managements understood this presumption quite well. When the ICC was abolished, they lobbied strenuously and successfully to transfer antitrust authority to the STB rather than allow it to go to the Justice Department's Antitrust Division. The chief proponent of the STB plan was the CEO of the UP (Machalaba and Nomani, 1996; Wilner, 1997, p. 306).

largest railroad in the United States in terms of trackage, freight haulage, and revenues. Whether it thereby gained efficiency and/or achieved market power were the hotly disputed questions before the STB.

BACKGROUND

Rail Transportation in the Twentieth Century

For much of the twentieth century railroads have fought a losing competitive battle against the other surface modes of freight transportation: trucking, pipelines, and water (ship and barge) transport. Though railroads continue to play a major role in U.S. intercity freight transportation, the industry's share—41 percent in 1995—is substantially lower than was the case in the early decades of the century. To some extent rail's defeats have been the natural consequences of the technological gains of the other modes, especially trucks. But rail's competitive position was clearly impeded by the ICC's all-encompassing rate and service regulatory structure, in which the industry had been enmeshed since 1887.[5] Even the inclusion of interstate trucking into the ICC's regulatory regime in 1935 failed to stem the tide.

This losing competitive battle was first reflected by rail's declining share of intercity freight hauled and then by widespread financial losses and bankruptcies. At least partly in response to the railroads' competitive and financial losses, the industry engaged in a long series of mergers, which reduced the number of Class I railroads[6] from 186 in 1920 to 39 by 1980. The mergers enlarged railroads' traditional regional scope, but no railroad gained direct national, or even coast-to-coast, coverage.[7]

The Congress in 1980 passed the Staggers Act, which substantially deregulated the industry and gave railroads wide discretion for pricing flexibility, up as well as down. The industry quickly made use of its newly acquired flexibility. Prices (freight rates) adjusted to new levels, reflecting in some instances competitive influences and in others railroads' exercise of market power. With greater flexibility generally, the railroad industry's share of freight haulage stabilized and actually increased by a few percentage points.

And mergers proceeded apace. The thirty-nine Class I railroads of 1980 had diminished to only eleven by early 1995. As shown in Table 3-1,

[5]Standard critiques of the ICC's general discouragement of competition and creation of inefficiencies can be found in Meyer et al. (1959), Friedlaender (1969), Friedlaender and Spady (1981), and Keeler (1983). Some specifics can be found in MacAvoy and Sloss (1967).

[6]Class I railroads refer to those above a specific size criterion set by the ICC. As of 1950, a Class I railroad had to have at least $1 million in revenues; as of 1996, the minimum size was $255 million.

[7]Because of interchange arrangements, all railroads are connected to each other (their freight cars run on each others' tracks), and freight shippers that are at or close to a rail terminal can reach any other place that is close to a rail terminal.

TABLE 3-1
Class I Railroads in the Western U.S.

	Route Structures (mi)	Revenues ($ million)	Employees
Burlington Northern (BN)	22,189	4,995	30,711
Union Pacific (UP)	18,759	5,167	29,946
Southern Pacific (SP)	17,499	2,942	18,251
Santa Fe (SF)	8,352	2,681	15,020

Source: *Railroad Fact Book 1995.*

only four major railroads remained in the western United States. The Union Pacific and the Burlington Northern (BN) were roughly comparable in route structure, revenues, and employees, followed by the Southern Pacific and the Santa Fe (SF). Within a span of just twelve months in 1995–1996, the BN and the UP each had merged with one of the other two large railroads, leaving western railroading in the hands of just two carriers.

The first of these huge mergers was Burlington Northern's acquisition of the Santa Fe, proposed in August 1994. That combination had 33,000 miles of track and $7.1 billion in revenue and became, by a substantial margin, the largest railroad. The parties promised cost reductions and improved service, such as new single-line service to the Pacific Northwest to SF customers and access to California markets for Burlington shippers. Concerns over reduction in competition were addressed by providing other railroads (including the UP and the SP) with trackage rights in key areas. This merger was approved by the ICC in August 1995.[8]

The Proposed Merger

Two weeks before the BN-SF merger secured final approval, the UP announced its intention to acquire the SP. This would create a railroad with 35,000 miles of track and $9.5 billion in revenue, vaulting it into first place. The companies claimed that the combination would be able to offer new and improved services to shippers, to relieve capacity constraints that the UP and SP faced on certain routes, and to save $500 million in annual expenses, an estimate that was later increased to $750 million.

[8]A key opponent of this merger before the ICC was the UP itself. When later the UP unexpectedly withdrew its opposition, some speculated that this represented an implied agreement between UP and BN not to oppose each others' mergers (Gruley and Machalaba, 1996). No evidence to this effect was found. The UP also entered its own bid for the SF, driving up the BN purchase price from $2.7 billion to $4 billion.

As shown in Figure 3-1, the UP's route structure connected three West Coast areas—the Pacific Northwest, northern California, and southern California—with Utah, from which its high-capacity double track extended east to Iowa and Kansas through what is known as the "central corridor." Previous acquisitions plus trackage rights with other railroads gave the UP access to Chicago, Milwaukee, and points in Minnesota to the north, as well as to Memphis, New Orleans, and the Texas Gulf Coast to the south. The UP enjoyed a reputation for strong management, attention to service, and cost efficiency.[9]

The SP and its related companies had major lines from Portland to Los Angeles—the so-called "I-5 corridor"—and then to San Antonio, Houston, and New Orleans, together with important gateways to Mexico. Its central corridor route ran from northern California to Utah and Kansas and then to St. Louis. From there, SP lines branched south to Louisiana and Texas and north to Chicago. Despite a strong route structure, the SP was widely perceived as having inadequate terminals and outdated locomotives and providing poor service.

FIGURE 3-1 The Merging Railroads.

---

[9] The UP had been encountering some difficulties, however, as a result of its recent acquisition of the Chicago & Northwestern Railroad.

Even a quick review of the UP and SP routes highlighted certain competitive problems with this merger. The combined UPSP would reduce to two or sometimes one the number of railroads serving hundreds, perhaps thousands, of shippers throughout the west. In addition, it would dominate all the major gateways to Mexico and control access to the huge petrochemical shippers along the Texas Gulf Coast.

The principal substantive response by the UP and SP to these concerns was to allow their major competitor, the newly formed BNSF, to run its trains over some of their tracks. Nearly 4000 miles of the combined UPSP track would be subject to track-use agreements, by far the largest reliance on this technique ever attempted. By contrast, UPSP would divest only a minimal 335 miles of routes, also to BNSF, for about $150 million. Though these remedies left many shippers with fewer alternatives, the applicants appealed to the prospect of stronger competition and cost efficiencies as a solution. The adequacy of this response was a central issue in the competitive analysis.

Analyzing Railroad Competition

Railroad competition has some unique properties that bear examination. To begin, the basic output or service provided by railroads is the transportation of commodities from suppliers (shippers) to their customers. Since the locations of both the shipper and its customer are fixed (at least in the short run), rail service must connect the point of origin with the destination in an efficient manner. But the technology and costs of rail service drastically limit the number of viable connections; any rail connection involves huge fixed and (literally) sunk costs in the form of rights-of-way, bridges, tunnels, the track itself, and the maintenance of all of these facilities. Such a cost structure implies that a substantial range of declining long-run unit costs is likely and that relatively high volumes of freight are necessary for break-even operation.

Direct "door-to-door" service is feasible for some large-volume shippers and recipients—for example, large-volume shipments of coal in lengthy "unit trains" from mines to electric utilities. But much more typically, the commodities (in freight cars) of many shippers are collected and assembled at a marshalling yard into a larger-volume, multiple-car train in order to achieve economies. At the terminating rail center, the trains must be disassembled and the freight cars sent to their respective customers.

In such a network competitive restraints on freight rates can occur in a number of ways, including intramodal and intermodal competition, source competition, and destination competition.

Intramodal Competition

Despite the cost structure described above, major city-pair connections that generate sufficient freight shipments often have more than one railroad providing freight service.[10] Where such direct competition exists, shippers might expect the most vigorous rivalry and most favorable rates. Yet even in these circumstances, there may be limits on competition. One rail carrier may have a cost advantage because of superior equipment, superior management, or a superior route. Or oligopolistic interactions may arise between the railroads, resulting in higher freight rates anyway. Also, if the same railroads provide rail service over many routes, these multi-market contacts serve to convey signals and implicit reassurances that can provide the basis for oligopolistic coordination.

Oligopoly coordination may be restrained by other transport modes, but it is unlikely to be deterred by the threat of entry, since the cost structure of railroads makes entry prohibitively expensive.[11] A different possible constraint takes the form of a threat of potential entry. Even where a shipper/recipient is served by only a single railroad, a second railroad may be close enough that it can realistically threaten to build a short spur line to connect to the shipper.[12]

One other special form of intramodal competition is important to note: Sometimes a railroad will extend "trackage rights" to a second railroad, so that the latter can run its trains over the former's track (typically for a relatively short distance) and thereby connect shippers/recipients to the second railroad's track network. In principle this can result in competition between the two carriers despite the single track. However, the relationship between the two railroads is that of landlord and renter, and there are many ways that the landlord can use its position to mute the competitive threat from the tenant. For example, the fee for use of the tracks may be set so high that the second railroad has to price its service noncompetitively. In addition, the landlord railroad can use its train scheduling ("dispatching") prerogatives, track maintenance routines, and longer-run investments affecting the route to favor itself and raise its rival's costs or degrade the latter's service. And the extensive and close contact between the two railroads, especially on routes where they are the only providers of rail service, may provide the basis for oligopolistic coordination.

Intermodal Competition

Some types of rail freight, for some distances, and at some locations can be economically hauled by alternative modes: truck, barge, or pipeline. Truck is most competitive for shipments over shorter distances (usually less than 500 miles), for shipments that are not in large volumes, and

---

[10]At least part of the reason for the multiple-line service is the legacy of railroad construction in the nineteenth century, when the fixed costs loomed relatively less large.

[11]Even the construction of extensive new branch or feeder lines by incumbent railroads is a rare event.

[12]This is usually described as a "build in"; if the shipper pays for the spur line, it is called a "build out."

for "high-value" goods (i.e., goods that have a high sales value per weight or cubic measure).[13] Barge is best suited for "low-value" commodities and is relevant only where the shipper and recipient are both on or near navigable waterways.[14] Pipeline is limited to a few commodities (primarily petroleum, petroleum products, and natural gas) and to shippers and recipients that are at or near pipeline connections.

Source Competition

A shipper often must compete for customers at a particular destination with other suppliers located at different points of origin. If the other origin points connect to the recipient's location via *other* railroads, then the railroad serving the first shipper is in indirect competition with the other railroads.[15] The extent to which this indirect competition among railroads is effective depends on whether the competing shippers themselves have similar costs and the rail distances are not too dissimilar.

Destination Competition

In some cases a shipper may have alternative destinations, with direct connections via different railroads, to which it might ship its goods. One example is the inland shipper that is sending goods overseas and could use any of a number of seaports, served by different railroads, as its point of export.[16] Again, the railroads are in indirect competition with each other, and the effectiveness of this competition will depend on ocean shipping charges from the various ports, the ports' charges themselves, and the rail distances from the shipper to the ports.

The UP-SP's Case for the Merger

The Union Pacific and Southern Pacific filed extensive documentation with the ICC/STB in support of their proposed merger. They claimed that the combined UP and SP would strengthen competition throughout the western United States in several specific ways. They expected to achieve substantial cost reductions and significant improvements in the quality of

---

[13]Truck transport is often faster than rail, which usually involves delays because of the assembling/disassembling process described in the text. The inventory-holding costs for high-value goods are greater, and truck's speed thus gives it an important advantage vis-à-vis rail.

[14]Barge tends to be slower than rail or truck, so high-value goods are not suitable for this mode.

[15]This point is clearest in the instance where the shipper has a second branch location, served by a second railroad, from which it can serve the recipient. Equivalently, an overseas shipper that is sending goods to a U.S. recipient at an inland location is likely to have a choice of ports and possibly of railroads that connect to the recipient.

[16]It can also arise when the shipper can send its goods to alternative domestic customers; e.g., a coal mine may have a choice of electric utilities, to which it is connected by different railroads, to which it might ship its coal.

rail service. Service improvements for SP customers would be especially noticeable given the recent inadequacies in the SP's operations. In addition, the merged system would become a more effective rival to the larger, just-formed BNSF. And finally, to address possible competitive concerns, the UP and SP had prearranged an extensive trackage rights agreement with the BNSF. Overall, therefore, the merger would result in "a pervasive, dramatic intensification of transportation competition throughout the West" (Peterson, 1995, p. 6).

Efficiencies

The UP and SP provided detailed projections of the various types of competitive benefits that would occur. Several of these involved direct operational matters, such as route length, single-line versus joint-line service, and alleviation of capacity constraints. Since costs—both explicit transport costs and implicit time costs to shippers—are a direct function of route length, the UP and SP documented the mileage reductions that the integration of their track networks would make possible along major routes. For example, the shortest mileage between Oakland and Chicago would decrease by 189 miles for shippers who previously were served only on UP track, and by 388 miles for SP's customers. Between Portland and Houston there would be savings of 262 miles for SP customers and 249 for the UP's. Numerous other instances of significant mileage savings were noted. In most cases the UP and SP focused on how their integrated route mileage would compare with that of the merged BNSF, underscoring their belief that they needed to shorten traffic distances to remain competitive.

A companion benefit of the merger would be far more extensive single-line service. In contrast to joint-line service in which shippers' products are handled by two railroads along a continuous route, single-line service eliminates delays, reduces loss and damage, simplifies rate determination, and avoids incompatibilities in operating procedures and priorities between carriers.[17] One important example concerned the I-5 corridor from the Pacific Northwest to Los Angeles and continuing to points in the southwest, which previously lacked single-line service and lost much traffic to truck or water transport. The applicants anticipated gaining substantial portions of that traffic once they offered single-line service. Numerous other examples were provided.

The applicants also noted that capacity constraints impinging on the UP and even more seriously on the SP would be alleviated by the merger. On many single-line routes, growing traffic had caused substantial increases in congestion costs. With more trains operating at different speeds

---

[17]In essence, the replacement of joint-line with single-line service is a form of vertical integration, since a supplier-customer transaction between two carriers (the freight hand-off in a joint-line movement) is being replaced by single ownership.

or needing to move in both directions, rail system efficiency declined. Integrated management of alternative or parallel routes would permit flexibility in asset utilization, concentration of trains by speed or direction on single lines, and ultimately lower costs. Similar considerations were raised in the case of yards and other facilities.

All of these improvements in operations would result in faster, more frequent, more reliable, and cheaper service to shippers throughout the western United States. Other benefits involved improved access to terminal facilities together with improvements to those facilities.[18] Combining the best of the UP and SP terminal facilities would strengthen the merged entity's ability to provide shippers with such services. In addition, the applicants promised to upgrade some facilities, build one new intermodal facility in Colton, California, and improve coordination among others in the merged system.

Further benefits would accrue from improved deployment and utilization of equipment. Freight cars could be used more frequently, especially specialized equipment such as refrigeration cars. These savings alone were estimated to produce the equivalent of 3000 additional rail cars' becoming available. Equipment could be positioned to minimize downtime and empty backhauls. For example, the UP's routes west of Utah spread like three fingers to the Pacific Northwest, the Bay area, and the Los Angeles basin, but lacked connections up and down the West Coast. That meant that UP equipment in, say, Seattle could not assist in relieving a bottleneck in Oakland without repositioning through an out-of-the-way third point. The addition of the SP's I-5 corridor lines would enable the UP to move equipment directly from Seattle to Oakland. In addition, this route structure would permit "triangulation" of traffic movements; for example, refrigeration cars with citrus from Florida to Los Angeles could next go to Idaho and return with potatoes to Florida. These movements would have required added cars or costly repositioning in the absence of an I-5 corridor link. All of these factors would provide shippers with better and cheaper service.

Lastly, the applicants listed other ways in which they could achieve efficiencies, including the reduction of corporate overhead, consolidation of computer systems, and more economical purchasing. Planned layoffs totaled 4900 out of a combined work force of 53,000.

The applicants sought to quantify the annual cost savings that they anticipated from the merger. From voluminous materials about individual routes, facilities, equipment, and operations, the parties stated that the savings would amount to $290 million in the first year of the merger and grow to a total of $750 million per year at the point in time when the process

---

[18]Terminals include intermodal facilities for truck-rail or barge-rail transport, auto ramps for off-loading automobiles, storage-in-transit yards in which customers use their own rail cars for temporary storage, transloading facilities for shippers that truck their product to the terminal, etc.

was completed. As shown in Table 3-2, more than one-third of the total would come in the form of labor savings, and roughly an additional one-fifth each would come from operations and from general and administrative. Although the one-time costs of integration would total nearly $1.5 billion, these costs would cease after four years whereas the annual savings would persist indefinitely.

Other Motivations: Weakness of the SP; the BN-SF Merger

Apart from these claims concerning cost savings, the applicants made two other significant arguments for the merger. First, the Southern Pacific was very much an ailing firm with diminishing competitive vigor. It needed new equipment, upgrading of yards, improvements in rights of way, and installation of advanced operating systems for planning, routing, tracing, and billing purposes. The BN-SF merger had heightened competitive pressure on the SP and cast doubt on the latter's future capabilities. In its SEC filing for the third quarter of 1995, the SP declared that without the proposed merger it lacked the resources to compete with the BNSF and with an independent UP and suggested that it would have to reduce its service.

As a consequence the UP and SP argued, "The only certain solution for SP is a merger with UP" (Peterson, 1995, p. 83). Part of the merger proposal, in fact, was a promise to invest $1.3 billion within four years in

TABLE 3-2
Summary of Benefits ($ thousands)

| | YEAR 1 | | YEAR 5 | |
	Annual	One-Time	Annual	One-Time
Net revenue gains	22,814		76,045	
Operating benefits				
Labor savings	90,585		261,150	
Nonlabor savings				
Car utilization	3,803		12,677	
Communications/computers	(11,861)	(82,479)	14,214	
Operations	46,501	(529,947)	157,756	9,905
General/administrative	110,797	139,805	137,970	_____
Total operating benefits	239,825	(472,621)	583,767	9,905
Employee relocation		(26,594)		
Labor protection/ separation		(107,411)		
Shipper logistics savings	27,251		90,836	
Total benefits	289,890	(606,626)	750,648	9,905

Sources: UP and SP, *Railway Merger Application*, vol. 1, p. 93.

upgrading some SP facilities, building additional terminals, and so forth. The greatest beneficiaries of the merger would be the SP's customers, who would no longer experience the service problems that had been plaguing its operations. A considerable number of SP shippers submitted comments favoring the merger.

The applicants' final reason for their merger was the BN-SF merger itself. Throughout their filing, they repeatedly stated that the BN-SF merger precipitated—indeed, necessitated—their own combination, although the logical connection was often not made explicit. The BNSF was said to be "far larger" than the UP or the SP, whether measured by mileage, employees, tons of freight hauled, freight revenues, or operating income. In addition, the BNSF was described as leading in various technologies and moving rapidly to consolidate its gains from the BN-SF merger.

Thus, the applicants claimed, a UP-SP merger was required in order to create an entity capable of competing on even terms with the BNSF. Leaving the UP and the SP separate, by contrast, would handicap the UP and actually imperil the SP, with significant adverse effects on shippers. For competitive reasons, too, the UP and SP concluded, they must be allowed to merge.

Dealing with Competitive Concerns

An important element in their case for the merger was the applicants' concession that on some routes competitive questions needed to be addressed. For numerous shippers, the UP and the SP represented the only two railroads to which the shippers had access. The merger would, of course, reduce this number to just one. Many more shippers had the UP, SP, and a third railroad—typically, the BNSF—as alternatives. They, too, would face a reduction in their choices. These so-called "2-to-1" and "3-to-2" shippers were the focus of much attention from the outset.

Trackage Rights

The merger applicants sought to preempt competitive concerns over 2-to-1 shippers through a trackage rights agreement with BNSF. The guiding principle of this agreement was that the BNSF—the strongest possible alternative railroad, but also the primary, even sole, competitor on most routes—would be granted access to all 2-to-1 shippers on the merged UPSP lines.[19] Every such shipper was identified, and trackage rights were granted in a manner designed to preserve their competitive options. This was done even where shippers previously made little use of one of their rail alternatives, where other railroads existed but with somewhat circuitous routes, and where the BNSF already had a good competitive route.

---

[19]In return for trackage rights, BNSF agreed not to oppose the UP-SP merger.

The result of the trackage agreement would be that all 2-to-1 shippers would have as many railroad alternatives as before. Moreover, since the alternatives would be more efficient than previously, shippers would in fact be better off. The merger application cited a number of shippers that approved of these trackage rights agreements.

The applicants calculated that the traffic covered by trackage rights totaled over $900 million for 2-to-1 shippers. Even more striking was the extent of the track miles subject to this agreement—about 4000 track miles, or about 11 percent of the entire UP-SP system. Whereas trackage rights had previously been used selectively to address competitive problems, the UP-SP proposal made such rights a centerpiece of their merger proposal.

Vigorous Competition

Another key consideration involved 3-to-2 shippers. The applicants contended that all such shippers would be better off as a result of the merger, since they would have access to two financially sound railroads with comprehensive networks throughout the west. This would be better than their existing alternatives, namely, the "powerful BNSF, a smaller UP, and a weak SP that will become even weaker."[20]

The applicants went on to assert that, despite the presence of only two railroads, the UPSP and BNSF would compete vigorously. As proof, they cited current examples: duopoly competition for coal traffic in the Powder River Basin in Wyoming and for Seattle-Chicago intermodal traffic. They also noted that rail rates had decreased on routes in Texas, Oklahoma, and Kansas after the UP had acquired the Missouri-Kansas-Texas line in 1988.

Furthermore, the applicants argued that there was "no valid economic empirical evidence . . . showing that a 3-to-2 merger of rail carriers would lead to price increases" (Willig, 1995, p. 550). Existing studies were said to suffer from data inadequacies, incorrect specifications, statistical biases, and other problems that made them unreliable and irrelevant to the present merger. More relevant, in this analysis, was a number of factors that made competition between UPSP and BNSF overwhelmingly likely. The applicants argued that monitoring and policing among even two sellers in rail markets would be difficult, since the railroads' service offerings could be extensively differentiated (in terms of speed of delivery, extent of damage to shipments, information provided to customers, billing systems, etc.) and this differentiation could easily mask secret price cutting.

Also, many freight shippers were large and capable entities who could shop around and play the rail carriers off against each other. The op-

---

[20]UP and SP Railroad Merger Application, vol. 1, p. 19.

portunity to obtain the freight business of a large shipper (through a price cut) would be tempting enough to cause the carriers to engage in secret price cutting and thus undermine any "cooperative" or "noncooperative" price discipline. In essence, a large shipper could hold an "auction" for the right to carry its freight, and this auction environment would yield competitive outcomes. In sum, the "Bertrand" model of unfettered price competition among sellers was a reasonable approximation to rail markets with even as few as two carriers.

For all these reasons, the applicants contended that no remedial action was required to protect 3-to-2 shippers. In taking this position they knew that they were "preaching to the choir": Past ICC rulings had specifically found that going from three to two railroads would increase competition, so long as the merger entailed superior "character of competition," "more competitive routes," "more diverse geographic competition," and stabilizing a weak competitor.[21] The UP-SP anticipated a similar judgment in this case.

THE ARGUMENTS AGAINST THE MERGER

The opponents[22] of the merger offered three basic arguments: (1) The merged entity would be able to exercise market power, individually or in concert with one or more other railroads, on a large number of routes involving billions of dollars of shipments; (2) The UP-SP's proposed solution to part of the market power problem—the offering of trackage rights to the BNSF—was wholly inadequate; and (3) the promised efficiencies were highly speculative, especially given the difficulties that the UP had recently experienced in absorbing the Chicago & North Western Railroad (CNW). The opponents recommended that the ICC/STB either reject the merger outright or condition its approval on the UP-SP's divesting (that is, selling) substantial amounts of its postmerger duplicative track to rival railroads where the merger threatened to create market power.

The Exercise of Market Power

The UP-SP merger, by the applicants' own admission, would reduce the number of rail carriers in hundreds of (city-pair) rail markets for thousands of categories of goods. But the applicants had substantially underestimated the extent of the problem.

---

[21]*Norfolk Southern Corp.—Norfolk & Western Ry. and Southern Ry.,* 366 ICC 171, 223 (1982). *Guilford Transportation Industries—Delaware & Hudson Ry.,* 366 ICC 396, 411 (1982).

[22]The opponents included many (but not all) shippers, other railroads (but not the BNSF), and the U.S. Departments of Justice, Transportation, and Agriculture.

2-to-1 Markets

The instances where the merger would create effective monopolies—reducing the number of rail carriers from two (the UP and the SP) to one (the new, combined railroad)—were numerous. They accounted for as much as $2 billion of rail freight revenues out of about $18 billion in total western freight revenues in 1994. This was substantially above the applicants' estimate of $900 million. The difference was largely due to the applicants' counting as "2-to-1" only those instances where both the shipper and the recipient were directly connected to the UP and the SP (and only the UP and SP). This neglected instances where either the UP or the SP might be close enough to the shipper or the recipient (or both) so that the threat or actuality of using truck or barge for short trans-shipments or the possibilities of build-ins/build-outs effectively kept the two lines in competition with each other.[23] The applicants counted such instances as pre-merger monopoly that would not experience any reduction in competition.

The applicants also ignored instances where the UP or SP might have a monopoly at one end of the shipment but the other carrier was one of two different carriers that were competing at the other end and thus interline shipments were currently necessary[24]; the merger would effectively create a single-line service monopoly. And finally they overlooked instances of source competition and destination competition where the UP was the sole carrier on the one route and the SP was the sole carrier on the other.

In short, even if the granting of trackage rights to BNSF was an adequate solution where it was proposed, it did not address the creation of effective monopolies in markets that were about as quantitatively important. Freight-rate increases of about 20 percent were estimated[25] to be the likely result of the reduction in the number of carriers from two to one.

3-to-2 Markets

In hundreds of markets the merger would reduce the number of effective rail carriers from three to two and thus create or exacerbate problems of oligopolistic behavior among the remaining two carriers.[26] These

---

[23]One of the largest shippers affected by the merger, Dow Chemical, was in this situation. Its huge petrochemical complex in Freeport, Texas, was exclusively served by the UP, but both the SP and the BNSF operated lines that passed within about 35 miles. For various reasons the BNSF was not interested in building in, but the SP had engaged in extensive discussions with Dow about such a possibility. The UP-SP merger would eliminate this competitive threat, and Dow anticipated price increases.

[24]Recent research (Winston et al., 1990; Grimm et al., 1992) has shown that in such instances the monopoly carrier did not capture all of the potential rents.

[25]On the basis of cross-section regression models that compared rates on routes with one, two, three, etc., rail carriers, holding constant the other important features of the routes (e.g., distance, type of goods being shipped, etc.). See Majure (1996) and Grimm (1996).

[26]Similar concerns were raised, though with less potency, with respect to the $265 million in markets where the merger would cause the number of rail carriers to be reduced from four to three.

instances were estimated to involve about $5 billion in rail freight revenues. Further, in a large fraction of these markets the second carrier would be the BNSF, so the merged UPSP and the BNSF would experience a multitude of multimarket contacts, threatening to exacerbate the potential oligopoly problems. The applicants' claims that competition would remain vigorous in these markets was supported neither by theory nor by the evidence.

Most strands of oligopoly theory indicate that a market with only two sellers and high barriers to entry would be likely to result in a noncompetitive outcome: a higher price and lower output than would be true if complete price competition were to prevail. Theories of "cooperative" behavior would predict that the two would be aware of each other's presence and of the consequences of aggressive actions and would mutually try to monitor and police each other's actions, resulting in a non-competitive outcome. The "Cournot" theory of "noncooperative" behavior—each seller uses quantity as its strategic tool and assumes that its rival will not change its quantity in response to any strategic move—would predict a noncompetitive outcome. A "dominant firm" model, where one firm dominates a market (in terms of market share) and has a cost or product differentiation advantage over its rivals, would predict a noncompetitive outcome.[27] Only the "Bertrand" theory of noncooperative behavior—that each seller uses its price as its strategic instrument and assumes that its rival will hold its price unchanged in the face of price reductions—would lead to the prediction of a competitive outcome in a market with only two firms.

The applicants had claimed that coordinated or cooperative behavior, even among as few as two railroads, would be difficult because of the differentiated nature of rail service and the opportunities for secret price cutting that thereby were present and that the Bertrand model was the best approximation for rail service. But, the critics replied, with only two carriers and a service (freight haulage) that is readily observed, monitoring and policing would still be feasible and would be strengthened by the multitude of markets in which the UPSP and the BNSF would repeatedly be in contact with each other. Also, the applicants' reliance on the differentiated nature of rail markets and on the Bertrand model to support their claims concerning the competitiveness of rail markets implied a logical inconsistency: The Bertrand model's prediction of a competitive outcome applies only for sellers with uniform products. Extensions of the Bertrand theory to sellers with differentiated products (the existence of which appeared to be crucial to the applicants' claim that monitoring and policing of each other's behavior would be difficult) indicate that the product differentiation "softens" competition between them, leading to a noncompetitive outcome. In addition, though the applicants had likened rail competition for

---

[27]On $2 billion of the 3-to-2 routes, the combined UPSP would have market shares of 70% or greater.

large customers to auctions, standard auction theory (McAfee and McMillan, 1987) predicts that the fewer are the bidders in a sealed-bid (secret) auction, the less favorable will be the prices from the perspective of the auctioneer.

Equally important, a huge body of empirical literature supported the application of oligopoly theory predictions to real-world markets. Higher seller concentration (a reduction from three sellers to two sellers in a market would represent a sharp increase in seller concentration) is generally associated with higher prices and higher profits (Bresnahan, 1989; Schmalensee, 1989; Weiss, 1989). Especially relevant was research (Kwoka, 1979) indicating that the shares of the leading two firms are crucial in this relationship and that the presence of a sizable third firm could cause price-cost margins to decline. Further, recent empirical research on railroad freight markets, as well as specific econometric studies conducted by the critics to buttress their arguments, showed that the number of carriers on a route influenced freight rates in the expected ways.[28] A reduction from three carriers on a route to two would be expected to cause freight rates to rise by about 10 percent. And research on airline markets (Evans and Kessides, 1994) showed that increases in multimarket contacts led to higher prices. Also, empirical research on auction markets showed that the theoretical predictions as to the consequences of numbers of bidders were borne out in real-world auction markets. And an analysis of the bids that the Department of Defense (DOD) received for rail freight movements of military equipment showed that the number of bidders mattered (Ploth, 1996).

The SP as a Weak Carrier

Though, as the applicants claimed, the SP was a financially weak carrier, it was not in danger of failing; it had successfully raised capital in recent years, and its recent operations had shown some improvements. Further, its presence in many rail markets clearly made a difference in terms of the competitive vigor of those markets. Empirical analysis using regression techniques showed this to be the case; an analysis of the DOD bid results showed that the presence of the SP as a bidder caused the winning bids to be lower (i.e., more favorable to the DOD as customer) (Ploth, 1996).

The Trackage Rights Agreement

The UP-SP's trackage rights agreement, critics argued, was wholly inadequate as a remedy for the likely competitive problems that would be created by the merger. First, the agreement did not cover half (about $900

---

[28]See Grimm (1985, 1996); MacDonald (1987, 1989a, 1989b); Winston et al. (1990); Grimm et al. (1992); Burton (1993); Wilson (1994); and Majure (1996).

million) of the markets where 2-to-1 problems would effectively arise and was not applicable to any of the 3-to-2 markets (about $5 billion).

Second, the agreement raised all of the landlord-tenant problems discussed above: The UP-SP had structured the arrangement so as to disadvantage the BNSF and mute the vigor of the latter's competition. The pricing arrangement converted the UP-SP's *fixed* costs of track ownership and maintenance into *variable* (per-ton-mile) charges on the BNSF's traffic, clearly pushing BNSF's prices upward. In addition, numerous instances were cited of the BNSF's being given inferior track routings or inadequate access to complementary facilities.

Third, the fact that it was the BNSF that was the "tenant" in virtually all of the trackage rights agreements meant that the number of multimarket contacts, with their risks of heightened oligopolistic coordination, was increased substantially.

The Promised Efficiencies Were Highly Speculative

The primary justification for the merger was the very large efficiency improvements that the merged entity would achieve. But, the critics argued, these projected gains greatly overstated the likely actual gains that could be attributed to the merger:

First, the merger would mean a larger organization, which would be harder to manage. And the melding of the two corporations could yield the same problems of *inefficiencies* that the UP had recently experienced in its absorption of the CNW.[29]

Second, some of the applicants' estimates of cost savings involved the inclusion of trends in productivity improvements that would likely occur anyway, even in the absence of the merger.

Third, some of the cost savings involved transfers from other parties, which meant no real social gains.

Fourth, some of the single-line integration efficiencies could instead be achieved by better coordination between the independent UP and SP. For example, as a means of providing better service to each carrier's customers, each line might grant trackage rights to the other for through service on a cooperative basis.[30] Indeed, many railroads already engaged in mutually advantageous trackage rights or reciprocal switching arrangements whereby, on a mutual basis, one carrier would locally transfer rail

---

[29]The *Wall Street Journal* began a news report on that experience as follows: "Union Pacific Corp., plagued by widespread delays and service disruptions, is rushing to correct the problems caused by surging grain traffic, locomotive and crew shortages and troubles digesting its takeover of Chicago & North Western Transportation Co. earlier this year" (Machalaba, 1995).

[30]Such cooperative granting of trackage rights would introduce new and improved service where there had been less attractive (joint-line) service and would be less likely to encounter the problems enumerated for the BNSF trackage rights arrangement.

cars from a shipper's siding to another carrier's tracks or deliver the cars from another carrier's tracks to a recipient's siding.[31]

One especially skeptical critic estimated that, after all of these adjustments were made, the applicants' claimed cost savings of $750 million per year might actually be as little as $73 million annually (Christensen, 1996).

A Summing Up

The merger's opponents argued that the risks of new or enhanced market power in hundreds of rail freight markets were quite high, that the trackage agreement with BNSF was woefully inadequate as a remedy, and that the promised efficiencies were speculative at best. They urged outright rejection of the merger or alternatively conditioning its approval on the divestiture of duplicative tracks. In the hands of rival carriers, trackage would be less likely to create oligopolistic problems.

THE STB'S DECISION

The UP and SP filed their merger application with the ICC in November 1995. Over the next several months the ICC and then the STB reviewed a voluminous record and conducted public hearings on the major issues. In arriving at its decision, the STB heard both protests against the merger and testimony urging its approval, generally conditional on the BNSF trackage agreement. The BNSF itself took no position. Rather, it emphasized that it was the sole railroad that would be able to provide strong competition to the now-larger UPSP and could do so if and only if the trackage agreement were fully implemented.

On July 3, 1996, the STB announced its decision to approve the merger subject to a slightly modified BNSF trackage agreement together with other requirements affecting individual routes and shippers. Overall, its decision reflected the UP-SP position on all the major issues. The Board concluded that the merger would result in superior service, substantial cost savings, enhanced competition, and by virtue of the trackage rights agreement full protection to captive shippers.

With respect to cost savings, the STB endorsed the UP-SP list of "non-quantifiable benefits" such as shorter routes and more reliable service. It assessed the quantifiable annual benefits from the merger at $627 million, excluding only two items from the list advanced by the applicants. These were $76 million in revenues from diverted traffic (since this was not a cost

---

[31]But, a critic of the critics might ask, if the coordination was so easy to do, why hadn't the UP and SP already done it? One response might be that the BN-SF merger had awakened them to new possibilities—like the merger itself—that had not seemed relevant before.

savings to the UP-SP), and about $48 million in trackage rights proceeds from BNSF (which were transfers rather than real resource savings).

The far more conservative evaluation of cost savings advocated by the critics was characterized as "largely theoretical concerns" (Surface Transportation Board, 1996, p. 110) and essentially rejected. The argument that the parties could achieve major efficiencies by greater interfirm coordination was dismissed as unrealistic and inconsistent with the companies' past behavior, which after all did not do so. Moreover, the critics' belief that considerable productivity gains would occur anyway did not undermine the validity of the efficiencies identified as specifically flowing from this merger. Only with respect to the two relatively minor cost items noted above did the Board concur with the critics' position.

The Board went on to address the many competitive concerns that had been raised. The critics' claim that the merger would cause 2-to-1 shippers substantial harm was rejected on the grounds that it was based on the premise that BNSF, through its trackage rights agreement, would have no effect on rates. The Board asserted that the latter "will effectively replace the competition that would otherwise be lost" so that competitive harm, if any, would be "negligible" (Surface Transportation Board, 1996, p. 103).

While the circumstance of 3-to-2 shippers was not addressed in the merger agreement, the Board was adamant that the evidence did not support the view that they would be significantly harmed. Shipper statements favoring the merger were cited; empirical studies based on particular commodities were declared unrepresentative; studies of nonrailroad markets were dismissed; the applicants' criticisms of these studies were cited without qualification. On the basis of such reasoning, the Board concluded what it had concluded in earlier merger applications: that two railroads were sufficient to bring about competition. And if there was any possibility of competitive harm, it would be outweighed by the very large efficiency benefits of the merger (Surface Transportation Board, 1996, p. 121).

The STB cited approvingly the prearranged trackage rights agreement with the BNSF. It modified the agreement slightly to provide more extensive coverage to the BNSF and greater protection to certain shippers. In particular, for those shippers that were currently captive to (say) the UP but had opportunities for build-ins/build-outs or transloading to the SP, the Board extended BNSF's trackage rights to points that preserved those build-in/build-out and transloading possibilities.

Concerns that the trackage agreement might not result in effective competition because of the rates charged by the UPSP or because of the terms under which the BNSF would operate were rejected. The Board's response was to assert that the full mileage charge inclusive of fixed costs was consistent with past practice and "well within a reasonable level" (Surface Transportation Board, 1996, p. 140). It stated that any concerns over discrimination in dispatch and other constraints on the BNSF's operations were addressed by the detailed trackage rights protocol that the UP-SP had entered into with BNSF. The Board rejected arguments in favor of more divestiture, asserting that this would be more burdensome than monitoring the trackage agreement.

Finally, the STB addressed the allegation that the merger would result in an overall western railroad duopoly that would likely collude rather than compete. It cited its experience with other mergers and the lack of a specific example of two-railroad collusion as a basis for summary rejection of such concerns.

Having thus disposed of all contrary arguments, the Board concluded,

> [T]he merger as conditioned [by the trackage rights agreement] clearly will be pro-competitive in the sense that it will stimulate price and service competition in markets served by the merged carriers. The merger will create a more efficient and competitive UP/SP system competing head-to-head throughout the West with BNSF. UP/SP customers will benefit from tremendous service improvements brought about by reductions in route mileage, extended single-line service, enhanced equipment supply, better service reliability, and new operating efficiencies [Surface Transportation Board, 1996, p. 108].

LOSING TRACK: THE AFTERMATH

> "We learned a lot [about] how to do it right next time. . . . I guarantee there won't be a repeat of service problems in the future with or without the Southern Pacific."
>
> RONALD J. BURNS,
> President and CEO, Union Pacific Railroad (Machalaba, 1995)

The railroad industry has continued its process of consolidation. Three months after the STB's approval of the UP-SP merger, the managements of the CSX Railroad (one of the two major railroads in the southeast) and of Conrail (the sole major railroad in the northeast) announced an agreement to merge Conrail into CSX. A week later the other major southeastern railroad, the Norfolk Southern (NS), made a higher offer for Conrail. After a few months of further offers and counteroffers and legal wrangling, the three parties agreed that CSX and the NS would jointly buy Conrail and divide its route structure and accompanying equipment between them. This transaction was approved by the STB in June 1998.

With the dismemberment and absorption of Conrail, the number of Class I railroads in the United States will be down to eight, with only two large carriers in the west (the UPSP and the BNSF) and two in the east (CSX and the NS). It seems only a matter of time until the managements of these four railroads will begin exploring the possibilities of the "inevitable" east-west pairings that will create the nation's first true transcontinental railroads, with their attendant promises of seamless coast-to-coast single-line service. The manifest destiny symbolized by the Golden Spike may finally be achieved.

And what of the UP-SP merger itself? The first year or so is too soon to tell which set of predictions about the *long-run* consequences of the merger—the greater efficiencies and more vigorous competition predicted by its proponents, or the reductions in competition and modest (at best) efficiencies predicted by its opponents—will prove to be accurate. For the *short run,* however, the picture is painfully clear. The warnings of the critics as to the difficulties of merging the two organizations and managing a larger railroad have been disastrously prescient. The UP executive's assurances (quoted above)—that the railroad had learned from its problems in absorbing the CNW—have proved ill founded.

The merger was implemented in September 1996, and the UP began its integration efforts. By the summer of 1997, however, these efforts were unraveling. One harbinger was a deterioration in safety. The UP experienced three major train crashes that resulted in seven deaths. The Federal Railway Administration, which is responsible for enforcing safety standards, launched an unprecedented investigation of the UP's entire network.

Simultaneously, the UP began experiencing congestion and service problems, as trains and shipments began slowing down and backing up and shippers and recipients began complaining about lost shipments and long delays. Despite the UP management's assurances in August 1997 that the problems were being solved, the carrier's service worsened. Newspaper articles described the UP's rail system as "near gridlock" in many places and recounted many instances of losses and delays.[32] Shippers were not only complaining to the UP but also were beginning to present claims for reimbursement for their losses.

Press accounts also described the managerial and logistics problems that the railroad had experienced in implementing the merger. For example, the UP and SP had different computer systems and dispatching methods, and workers from the one system were unable to adapt readily to the other's computers and operations. Cutbacks in management, crews, and equipment—part of the projected efficiencies of the merger—made the problems worse.

In September 1997, the UP proposed measures that were both extreme and embarrassing to a major railroad, but necessary given the extent of its problems. First it announced a plan to charter a large container ship on the West Coast, load it with the backed-up containers stored in its western rail yards, and send it through the Panama Canal for delivery at the Texas Gulf Coast. That plan was scrapped within a few days in favor of a proposal to

---

[32] See Machalaba (1997b) and Mathews and Machalaba (1997). The stories include one bizarre episode in which a rail car full of liquid argon departed Houston for a customer in southern California. Delays in shipment resulted in 90 percent of the contents' escaping prior to delivery.

send its freight on competing truck and rail carriers, including the BNSF. That plan proved to be of limited help. Long after the merger and despite repeated assurances of service improvement, the UP-SP continued to experience enormous problems, especially in the Gulf Coast area. Some shippers even called for reversing the merger. In 1998 the UP-SP reported substantial operating losses and agreed to share track ownership and train dispatching in some areas with the BSNF. Meanwhile, congressional hearings gave a forum for critics of STB policy and this merger in particular.

The UP will eventually solve its logistics problems, and its predictions about the long-run consequences of the merger may even prove true. But the short- and even medium-run costs of the UP-SP merger have clearly been substantial,[33] and the experience provides an important cautionary counterweight to facile acceptance of supposed efficiencies and to the dismissal of concerns about market concentration.

REFERENCES

Bresnahan, Timothy F. "Empirical Studies of Industries with Market Power." In *Handbook of Industrial Organization,* vol. 2, edited by Richard Schmalensee and Robert Willig, 1011–1057. Amsterdam: North-Holland, 1989.

Burton, Mark L. "Railroad Deregulation, Carrier Behavior, and Shipper Response: A Disaggregated Analysis." *Journal of Regulatory Economics* 5 (December 1993): 417–434.

Christensen, Laurits R. "Verified Statement," on behalf of the U.S. Department of Justice, April 9, 1996.

Evans, William N., and Ioannis N. Kessides. "Living by the 'Golden Rule': Multi-Market Contact in the U.S. Airline Industry." *Quarterly Journal of Economics* 109 (May 1994): 341–366.

Friedlaender, Ann F. *The Dilemma of Freight Transport Regulation.* Washington, D.C.: Brookings Institution, 1969.

Friedlaender, Ann F., and Richard H. Spady. *Freight Transport Regulation: Equity, Efficiency, and Competition in the Rail and Trucking Industries.* Cambridge, Mass.: MIT Press, 1981.

Grimm, Curtis M. "Horizontal Competitive Effects in Railroad Mergers." *Research in Transportation Economics* 2 (1985).

Grimm, Curtis M. "Verified Statement," on behalf of the Kansas City Southern Railroad, March 26, 1996.

Grimm, Curtis M., Clifford Winston, and Carol A. Evans. "Foreclosure of Railroad Markets: A Test of Chicago Leverage Theory." *Journal of Law & Economics* 35 (October 1992): 295–310.

---

[33]One newspaper account (Machalaba 1997c) estimated the costs (as of October 1997) at over $1 billion. Also, an account of the BNSF's short-run experience with its merger has indicated problems (Machalaba, 1997a).

Gruley, Bryan, and Daniel Machalaba. "Proposed Big Railway Merger Draws Criticism from the Justice Department." *Wall Street Journal,* April 15, 1996, p. A6.

Keeler, Theodore E. *Railroads, Freight, and Public Policy.* Washington, D.C.: Brookings, 1983.

Kwoka, John E., Jr. "The Effect of Market Share and Share Distribution on Industry Performance." *Review of Economics and Statistics* 41 (February 1979): 101.

Kwoka, John E., Jr. "Does the Choice of Concentration Measure Really Matter?" *Review of Industrial Organization* 39 (June 1981): 445–453.

MacAvoy, Paul W., and James Sloss. *Regulation of Transport Innovation: The ICC and Unit Coal Trains to the East Coast.* New York: Random House, 1967.

MacDonald, James M. "Competition and Rail Rates for the Shipment of Corn, Soybeans, and Wheat." *Rand Journal of Economics* 18 (Spring 1987): 151–163.

MacDonald, James M. "Railroad Deregulation, Innovation, and Competitive Effects of the Staggers Act on Grain Transportation." *Journal of Law & Economics* 32 (April 1989a): 63–96.

MacDonald, James M. "Concentration and Railroad Pricing." In *Concentration and Price,* edited by Leonard W. Weiss, 205–212. Cambridge, Mass.: MIT Press, 1989b.

Machalaba, Daniel. "Union Pacific Struggles to Clear Up Delayed Shipments." *Wall Street Journal,* November 30, 1995, p. B4.

Machalaba, Daniel. "Burlington Northern Struggles to Get Merger on Track." *Wall Street Journal,* April 22, 1997a, p. B4.

Machalaba, Daniel. "A Big Railroad Merger Goes Terribly Awry in a Very Short Time." *Wall Street Journal,* October 2, 1997b, p. A1.

Machalaba, Daniel. "Union Pacific Faces Increasing Prospect of Federal Intervention in Rail Tie-Up." *Wall Street Journal,* October 27, 1997c, p. A4.

Machalaba, Daniel, and Asra Q. Nomani. "More Rail Deals May Be Down the Track." *Wall Street Journal,* July 5, 1996, p. A2.

Majure, W. Robert. "Verified Statement," on behalf of the U.S. Department of Justice, April 11, 1996.

Mathews, Anne W., and Daniel Machalaba. "An Unsolved Mystery: Where Are Shippers' Rail Cars?" *Wall Street Journal,* October 13, 1997, p. B1.

McAfee, R. Preston, and John McMillan. "Auctions and Bidding." *Journal of Economic Literature,* 25 (June 1987): 699–738.

Meyer, John R., Merton J. Peck, John Stenason, and Charles Zwick. *The Economics of Competition in the Transportation Industries.* Cambridge, Mass.: Harvard University Press, 1959.

Peterson, Richard B. "Verified Statement," on behalf of the Union Pacific and Southern Pacific Railroads, November 17, 1995.

Ploth, I. William. "Verified Statement," on behalf of the Kansas City Southern Railroad, March 25, 1996.

Schmalensee, Richard. "Inter-industry Studies of Structure and Performance." In *Handbook of Industrial Organization,* vol. 2, edited by Richard Schmalensee and Robert Willig, 951–1009. Amsterdam: North-Holland, 1989.

Surface Transportation Board. "Decision No. 44, Finance Docket No. 32760," concerning the Union Pacific and Southern Pacific Railroads, August 6, 1996.

Weiss, Leonard W. *Concentration and Price.* Cambridge, Mass.: MIT Press, 1989.

Willig, Robert. "Verified Statement," on behalf of the Union Pacific and Southern Pacific Railroads, November 20, 1995.

Wilner, Frank N. *Railroad Mergers: History, Analysis, Insight.* Omaha, Neb.: Simmons-Boardman, 1997.

Wilson, Wesley W. "Market-specific Effects of Rail Deregulation." *Journal of Industrial Economics* 42 (March 1994): 1–22.

Winston, Clifford, Thomas M. Corsi, Curtis M. Grimm, and Carol A. Evans. *The Economic Effects of Surface Freight Deregulation.* Washington, D.C.: Brookings, 1990.

CASE 4

Restructuring Electric Utilities: BG&E and PEPCO Propose to Merge (1997)

Paul L. Joskow

INTRODUCTION

Baltimore Gas and Electric Company (BG&E) is an electric and gas utility serving the City of Baltimore and ten central Maryland counties. Potomac Electric Power Company (PEPCO) is an electric utility serving Washington, D.C., and the surrounding suburbs of Montgomery and Prince George's counties in Maryland. In late 1995, the companies announced that they planned to merge to create a new company called Constellation Energy Corporation ("Constellation").

This merger is one of many electric utility mergers that have recently been reviewed by regulatory authorities or are in the process of being reviewed as this is written. Changes taking place in the electric power sector aimed at expanding competition in wholesale and retail markets and reforming the regulation of residual monopoly services (Joskow, 1997) make it likely that merger activity will increase significantly in the next few years and that issues associated with the effects of electric power company mergers on competition will become more important as well.

Mergers of electric and gas utilities are subject to the same premerger notification requirements of the Hart-Scott-Rodino Act (HSR) that apply to mergers of firms in most other industries. However, mergers of electric utilities are also subject to review by their respective state (or in this case, District of Columbia) regulatory commissions and by the Federal Energy Regulatory Commission (FERC). The U.S. Department of Justice re-

The author was an expert witness for the merging companies in this case.

viewed the Constellation merger under the HSR, but did not choose to challenge it. However, the merger was closely scrutinized by both FERC and the respective state regulatory agencies. This essay focuses on the review of the proposed merger at FERC.

In January 1996, the companies filed an application with FERC under Section 203 of the Federal Power Act to merge their electric facilities. On July 31, 1996, FERC decided to set the merger application for trial-type hearings on the issue of its effects on competition. During the subsequent hearings, the FERC trial staff opposed the merger as proposed, arguing that it would significantly reduce competition in the supply of electricity in certain wholesale and retail markets. The FERC trial staff proposed that the merger be conditioned on divestiture of a significant amount of Constellation's generating assets and/or expansion of the transmission capacity available to competing suppliers in order to mitigate the anticompetitive effects of the merger.

Following evidentiary hearings, FERC issued an order on April 16, 1997, approving the merger. It rejected the trial staff's arguments that the merger would adversely affect competition in wholesale markets. It also concluded that it would consider the effects of mergers in retail markets only when state regulatory authorities did not have independent authority to do so. The Maryland Commission and the D.C. Commission subsequently approved the merger subject to several conditions that would have required the company to make price reductions after the merger was completed. However, on December 22, 1997, BG&E and PEPCO announced that they were calling off their merger. The companies concluded that the required price reductions would have been detrimental to their shareholders.

THE U.S. ELECTRIC POWER SECTOR[1]

Electricity is supplied to consumers in the United States by regulated investor-owned utilities (IOUs), publicly owned (municipal, state, and federal) utilities, and rural electric cooperatives that have de facto exclusive franchises to sell electricity to retail customers in specific geographic areas. The discussion here focuses on the IOU segment of the industry, which accounts for over 75 percent of U.S. retail electricity sales and is the major focus of competition policy in electricity.

Today, retail consumers must buy their electricity from the regulated monopoly supplier that has the legal right to distribute electricity at their locations. These franchised monopolies have a legal obligation to supply and plan for the needs of all retail customers within their franchise areas and to make electricity available to them at prices that are regulated by state public utility commission. Most IOUs have historically met their obligations to

[1] The discussion in this section is taken from Joskow (1996, 1997).

supply by owning and operating all of the facilities required to supply a complete "bundled" electricity product to retail customers. That is, the typical utility is vertically integrated into four primary electricity supply functions: generation, transmission, distribution, and retailing.

The *generation* of electricity involves the creation of electric energy using falling water; internal combustion engines; turbines powered with steam produced with fossil fuels, nuclear fuel, and various renewable fuels; wind driven turbines; and solar energy technologies. The demand for electricity varies widely from hour to hour, day to day, and season to season. In addition, electricity generally cannot be stored economically, so that demand at any point in time must be served by the generation of electricity at the same point in time.

The *distribution* of electricity to residences and businesses at relatively low voltages relies on wires and transformers along and under streets and other rights of way.

The *transmission* of electricity involves the use of wires, transformers, and substation facilities to make possible the high-voltage "transportation" of electricity between generating sites and distribution centers, the interconnection and integration of geographically dispersed generating facilities into a stable synchronized alternating current (AC), the scheduling and dispatching of geographically dispersed generating facilities that are connected to the transmission network to balance economically the demand and supplies of electricity in real time, and the management of equipment failures, network constraints, and relationships with other interconnected electricity networks.

Electricity is sold at both "wholesale" and "retail" levels. Wholesale transactions refer to purchases and sales of energy by utilities, which then resell the electricity they generate from their own facilities or purchase in wholesale markets to "retail" consumers that they serve exclusively in defined geographic areas. The prices paid by retail consumers for electricity are regulated by state public utility commissions and reflect the aggregate capital and operating costs of these facilities.

While the IOUs in the United States are typically vertically integrated into generation, transmission, and distribution, there are over 100 of them serving specific geographic areas on an exclusive basis, and they vary widely in size, reflecting the geographic expanse and customer composition of their franchise areas. In addition, there exist thousands of relatively small unintegrated public and cooperative distribution entities that buy power from unaffiliated generating and transmission entities. From a physical perspective, the U.S. sector (combined with portions of Canada and northern Mexico) is composed of three large synchronized AC networks: the Eastern Interconnection, the Western Interconnection, and the Texas Interconnection. However, there are over 140 separate "control areas" superimposed on the three networks, where individual vertically integrated utilities or groups of utilities operating through power-pooling arrangements are responsible for generator dispatch, network operations, and maintenance of reliability on specific portions of each of the three physical networks. BG&E and PEPCO are both members of a tight power pool called the PJM Interconnection, which operates as a single control area covering Pennsylvania, New Jersey, Maryland, Delaware, and the District of Columbia.

The decentralized structure of the U.S. electricity sector has also led to the development of competitive wholesale markets through which utilities buy and sell electricity among one another to reduce the costs of supplying their franchise customers. Municipal and cooperative distribution companies have also traditionally relied on full or partial wholesale requirements contracts with proximate vertically integrated utilities to supply their generation service needs. Wholesale power transactions and supporting transmission or "wheeling" arrangements are regulated by FERC. However, historically most of FERC's rate regulatory activity focused on the terms and conditions of sale of power and transmission service to unintegrated municipal and cooperative distribution utilities. Wholesale transactions of energy and capacity involving vertically integrated utilities have been subject to little regulation, relying instead primarily on bilateral trading in wholesale electricity markets. Until the passage of the Energy Policy Act of 1992, FERC had only limited authority to order vertically integrated utilities to provide transmission service to other utilities. However, the Energy Policy Act of 1992 and subsequent FERC rules governing transmission access and pricing[2] require utilities to provide transmission service to other utilities to support wholesale transactions based on nondiscriminatory terms and conditions specified in FERC-regulated tariffs.

Wholesale trade in electric energy expanded rapidly in the 1970s, initially in response to large differences in the short-run marginal cost of hydroelectric coal, oil, and natural gas generating units as well as variations in demand and capacity availability among utilities in the same region. Long-term contracts between vertically integrated utilities and certain types of independent generating companies (called Qualifying Facilities or QFs) were spurred significantly by the Public Utility Regulatory Policy Act of 1978 (PURPA), which required utilities to buy power from cogenerators and small power producers using renewable fuels (Joskow, 1989). Opportunities for independent power producers to sell wholesale electricity to utilities for resale were further expanded by the Energy Policy Act of 1992 and state programs requiring utilities to meet additional generation needs through competitive bidding.

As a consequence of de facto retail franchise exclusivity, there is not very much meaningful competition at the *retail* level as the industry is

---

[2] FERC Order 888 issued May 10, 1996.

now structured.[3] Until very recently, the general direction of competition policy in the U.S. electric power sector has been to extend and accelerate the spread of "wholesale competition," expanding opportunities for electricity trade between vertically integrated utilities but, more important, increasing opportunities for nonutility independent generating facilities to enter the market to sell electricity *to utilities* for resale to retail customers, thus building on the reforms embodied in PURPA and the Energy Policy Act of 1992. This wholesale competition "model" envisioned the local distribution utility as retaining its traditional obligation to supply customers within de facto exclusive franchise areas with bundled retail electricity service. However, in this model, the distributor relies on competitive procurement mechanisms to buy electricity from the lowest cost generators in competitive wholesale markets rather than building new generating facilities themselves to serve growing electricity demand in its franchise area. The price for the electricity received by retail consumers continues to be regulated by state commissions, since the consumers must buy their electricity from the local monopoly distributor. But the regulation of the generation cost component of the retail price would presumably be based on wholesale market price indicia, rather than (as in the traditional method) trying to track the underlying accounting costs and performance of generating plants owned by the distributor (Joskow, 1989).

A more radical model for expanding competition in electricity is the "customer choice" or "retail wheeling" model. In this model, retail customers are no longer required to purchase their generation supplies from their local distribution utility. Instead, they would be allowed to buy generation services directly in the wholesale market by purchasing "unbundled" distribution and transmission services from their local utility. Individual consumers then take on the obligation to arrange for their own generation service supplies with independent competing electricity suppliers. The electricity suppliers can either be companies with physical generating assets or retail marketers that provide a bundled product of generation service procurement and risk management services to retail consumers. In this retail wheeling model, generators can sell energy in a competitive wholesale spot market, as well as arrange for longer-term financial contracts with electricity supply intermediaries or directly with retail consumers. The role of local distributors is to provide "wires services" to retail customers for "access" to the generation market. A network operator of some kind is responsible for operating (or owning and operating) the transmission network so that reliability is maintained and competition to supply energy from competing generators can proceed efficiently. The

---

[3] The literature contains discussions of forms of retail competition other than head-to-head competition. These include interfuel competition, industrial location competition, fringe area competition, and franchise competition. See Joskow and Schmalensee (1983) for a critical discussion of the significance of these forms of retail competition in the recent past.

prices for these distribution and transmission services would still be subject to (better) regulation since they continue to be monopoly services.[4] The restructuring initiative that began in California in 1994 has stimulated much more interest in the "customer choice model" in the United States. This customer choice or retail wheeling model is now guiding the electricity restructuring and regulatory reform initiatives in New England, New York, Pennsylvania, New Jersey, Michigan, and other states and is the focus of legislation that has recently been introduced in the U.S. Congress. However, at the time that the Constellation merger was under consideration at FERC, neither the Maryland nor District of Columbia commissions were at the forefront of changes promoting a retail wheeling or customer choice model, and the first major implementation of retail wheeling in the United States was not anticipated until 1998 in California and a few other states.

BG&E, PEPCO, AND THE PJM POOL

BG&E and PEPCO are fairly typical vertically integrated IOUs and are of approximately equal size. BG&E serves retail customers in de facto exclusive geographic areas encompassing Baltimore and its surrounding suburbs. Its retail rates are regulated by the Maryland Public Service Commission. BG&E also provides wholesale generation and transmission service to one cooperative distribution company under a long-term contract with a nine-year notice provision that is regulated by FERC. PEPCO serves retail customers exclusively in the District of Columbia and the Maryland suburbs adjacent to the District. Its retail prices are regulated by the District of Columbia Public Utilities Commission and by the Maryland Public Service Commission. It has no municipal or cooperative distribution entities to which it provides service under firm long-term contracts. The retail service areas of the two companies are contiguous, sharing a border of about 75 miles.

Both BG&E and PEPCO are vertically integrated into generation, transmission, and distribution. BG&E has about 6800 megawatts (Mw) of generating resources, some of which it owns and operates, some of which it owns jointly but is operated by other utilities, and some of which it neither owns nor operates but to which it is entitled to receive generation service under long-term contracts. PEPCO also has about 6800 Mw of generating capacity resources composed of stations it owns and operates, stations it owns jointly with other utilities, and generation supplied to it under long-term contract. Table 4-1 displays BE&E's and PEPCO's generation resource portfolio. The generation resource portfolios of both utilities include facilities located in or near their retail service areas as well

TABLE 4-1
Generating Capacity Portfolios for BG&E and PEPCO
1996

	BG&E	PEPCO
Utility-owned Capacity		
Nuclear	1675 Mw	0 Mw
Coal	2667	3040
Oil	861	1116
Gas	735	1886
Hydro	277	0
Nonutility	227	238
Utility Purchases	347	534
Total:	6789 Mw	6814 Mw

Source: BG&E/PEPCO FERC Application, January 1996.

as remotely located generating facilities situated as far away as western Pennsylvania. Both companies rely on a 500-kilovolt (Kv) transmission network that they own jointly with other members of the PJM Interconnection to deliver the energy from these remote resources to the two utilities' retail service areas.

The primary differences between the generation resource portfolios of the two companies is that BG&E has relatively more nuclear and coal capacity with relatively low marginal operating costs and PEPCO has relatively more conventional oil and gas generating capacity with relatively high marginal operating costs. As a result, BG&E is more likely than is PEPCO to have economical capacity available beyond what it requires to meet its obligations to its retail customers, which it has available to make sales of energy to other utilities in the wholesale market. Indeed, BG&E made five times more energy sales into the wholesale market during the period before the merger than did PEPCO. PEPCO's sales were at much higher prices than BG&E's, reflecting the fact that PEPCO had economical energy to supply to the wholesale market only during periods when market clearing prices were high, while BG&E had economical energy available to sell even during periods when wholesale prices were relatively low. These facts played an important role in FERC's evaluation of the effects of the merger on competition in wholesale markets and are discussed in more detail presently.

The PJM Interconnection is a centrally dispatched "tight" power pool that encompasses most of the vertically integrated utilities in New Jersey, Maryland, Pennsylvania, Delaware, and the District of Columbia.[5] PJM

---

[5] Subsequent to the announcement of the merger of BG&E and PEPCO, the two smallest members of the PJM Interconnection—Delmarva and Atlantic City Electric—also proposed to merge. FERC approved this merger in July 1997.

performs a real-time least-cost integrated dispatch of the generating facilities owned by all the members of PJM, without regard to ownership, effectively allowing utilities with generating resources with low marginal operating costs to sell any energy they may have available in excess of the needs of their own retail customers to displace higher-operating-cost generating resources owned by other utilities. PJM also facilitates energy transactions with neighboring electric utilities to the west, south, and north of PJM with which it has transmission interconnections. Substantial amounts of energy are routinely imported into PJM from coal-fired facilities to the west and from the north. The incremental costs of transmission to effect these energy transactions is effectively zero (except for transmission losses), since the PJM members rely on the transmission facilities they own and whose costs are primarily fixed costs in the short run. From a real-time operating perspective, PJM operates as a single, integrated generation and transmission network, although the owners of generating facilities retain discretion to self-dispatch their own generating facilities should they choose to do so.[6]

Although PJM operates a free-flowing transmission network incorporating the transmission facilities of several utilities in four states and the District of Columbia, congestion does arise on the network from time to time. The predominant flow of energy on the PJM network is typically from west to east. Under certain conditions, there may be more low-marginal-cost energy available to flow across the network than the network has the capacity to carry. Import constraints into PJM are sometimes reached at points of interconnection with generators to the west and south of PJM. In addition, transfer limits are sometimes reached at three network interfaces inside PJM that run roughly north to south across PJM: the western, central, and eastern reactive interfaces. Transfer limits on the first two internal interfaces are reached only a few hours each year, while the transfer limits on the eastern interface are reached less than 5 percent of the hours during a typical year. BG&E and PEPCO's service areas and generating facilities are all located to the west of the eastern interface.

COMPETITION ISSUES IN ELECTRIC UTILITY MERGERS

The basic competition issues that arise in electric utility mergers are no different from those for mergers in other industries. Will the merger create or enhance market power associated with the sale of products that the merging firms compete to supply premerger? This question must be answered in the context of the economic and institutional attributes that char-

---

[6] PJM has sought to comply with FERC Order 888 by transforming itself into an independent system operator (ISO), filing a PJM-wide open-access transmission tariff available to wholesale buyers and sellers on a nondiscriminatory basis, and transforming the cost-based central dispatch mechanism into a bid-based market clearing price mechanism.

acterize the electric power sector in the United States. The previous discussion of these attributes leads to the following conclusions regarding the factors that should be examined to evaluate the effects of a merger of utilities on competition:

1. Under prevailing institutional arrangements (i.e., retail franchise exclusivity and regulation of retail prices and utility service obligations), the focus of the review of the effects of a utility merger on competition should be on whether it creates or enhances market power in the supply of one or more *wholesale generation services.* This was the merging companies' position. The FERC staff's analysis focused on wholesale market competition, but also examined retail market competition in an assumed retail wheeling regime.

2. Competition to supply generation services at either the wholesale or retail levels is critically affected by access to, pricing of, and congestion on the high-voltage transmission network. Both buyers and sellers need transmission service to trade in the market. The availability and prices of transmission service therefore affect the geographic expanse of the market and the number and size distribution of incumbent suppliers in the market. For the last decade FERC has required utilities proposing to merge to file "open-access" transmission tariffs as a condition for merger approval. These tariffs make transmission service available to all wholesale customers who request it at cost-based prices subject to FERC regulation. FERC's authority to order utilities to provide transmission service was expanded by the Energy Policy Act of 1992. FERC Order 888 issued in May 1996 requires all utilities subject to FERC's jurisdiction to file open-access transmission tariffs meeting very strict access and pricing requirements. These regulations ensure access to the transmission network at cost-based prices and are assumed by FERC to mitigate market power (vertical and horizontal) associated with ownership of transmission assets. However, the prices charged for these transactions and limits on transmission capacity at certain locations and at certain times have implications for the geographic expanse of the market. Accordingly, the availability and prices of transmission service must be examined to specify the expanse of the relevant geographic market and to determine the number and size distribution of competitors that can supply generation service to wholesale customers that the merging firms compete to supply premerger. In the end, the position of the merging companies and the FERC staff did not differ very much on the effects of transmission prices and congestion on the definition of the relevant geographic markets.

3. The number and size distribution of incumbent generation service suppliers competing to supply the products traded in the wholesale market must be evaluated to assess competition in short-term energy markets. As in other industries, the measurement of the competitive significance of

competing suppliers should take account of the ownership patterns of the supply resources that can compete in the relevant markets and the economic attributes of these resources. Here, the appropriate identification of resources available to compete in wholesale markets, after accounting for regulated retail and long-term contract supply obligations, under different time-related supply and demand conditions, is especially important because of time-varying demand and the limited opportunities to store electricity. The evaluation of any resulting market share and seller concentration measures should take account of the fact that the buyers are typically vertically integrated utilities that can self-supply generation services or, in the case of unintegrated municipal utilities, can have service supplied to meet the needs of their retail customers at prices regulated by FERC. The merging companies and the FERC staff's analysis diverged most significantly over how to measure and interpret generation market shares and concentration ratios.

4. The conditions of entry must be taken into account with regard to the supply of each of the relevant generation service products and the competitive conditions applicable to each. For example, the role of entry is likely to be different for short-term energy and capacity transactions than it is for longer-term energy and capacity transactions. Entry conditions, however, did not play much of a role in the evaluation of this merger, which focused primarily on incumbent shares of generating resources and associated HHIs to assess the effects on the merger on competition in short-term energy markets.

5. Where retail wheeling models are being introduced, the effects of mergers on competition may be very different from what they would be under prevailing institutional arrangements. To understand whether and how they are different the details of the retail wheeling program, transition arrangements for introducing it, and residual regulatory constraints on prices and service obligations must be taken into account. The merging companies and the FERC staff had significant differences about whether and how the uncertain introduction of retail wheeling in the future should be reflected in the evaluation of the effects of the merger on competition at the retail level.

FERC MERGER REVIEW PROCEDURES

FERC's authority to review and approve mergers for electric utilities is specified by Section 203 of the Federal Power Act (FPA). Section 203 of the FPA is not an antitrust statute and specifies only a general "public interest" standard for reviewing mergers. FERC and the federal courts have interpreted this public interest standard as including an examination of the effects of proposed mergers on competition. While the DOJ and FTC also

have the legal authority to review utility mergers under the federal antitrust laws, neither agency has played an important role in the review
of electric utility mergers or in the development of FERC's methods for
evaluating the effects of mergers on competition.

FERC's administrative procedures for reviewing mergers are as follows: The utilities desiring to merge file an application with FERC. The
application typically includes analyses of the effects of the merger on
competition and on costs and prices subject to regulation, and discusses issues associated with cost accounting and postmerger regulation. Interested
parties are then given time to file responses to the application with FERC.
FERC's staff reviews the application and the comments on the application,
and then makes recommendations to the Commission. The Commission
determines whether the merger will be (a) approved as filed, (b) approved
subject to conditions, or (c) set for trial-type hearings before an administrative law judge (ALJ) to examine issues that the Commission determines
require further scrutiny. Such hearings typically lead to an opinion by the
ALJ, which is forwarded to the Commission for final disposition.

When mergers are set for hearing, the effects of the merger on competition is typically the major issue about which the Commission seeks further
evidence. Despite the fact that FERC's review of competition issues nominally has included both wholesale and retail competition, and there is a long
tradition of rhetoric about various types of retail competition despite the
presence of exclusive retail franchises, in recent merger cases FERC's focus
has been on wholesale competition. However, FERC's detailed standards
for reviewing mergers were in a state of "evolution" during the entire period
of its review of the Constellation merger application, reflecting in part the
rapid changes that were and are taking place in the role of competition in the
electric power industry. In early 1996 FERC issued a Notice of Inquiry into
its procedures for evaluating mergers, stimulated largely by the growing
number of merger applications that it was receiving and criticisms of its
existing procedures and evaluation methods. FERC issued a new Merger
Policy Statement in December 1996. In its new Merger Policy Statement
FERC announced that it would apply the general analytical framework contained in the DOJ/FTC *Horizontal Merger Guidelines* (*"Merger Guidelines"*) to mergers of electric utilities.

THE MERGING COMPANIES' INITIAL
COMPETITION ANALYSIS

The merger application filed with FERC included an economic analysis of
the effects of the merger on competition that followed FERC's then prevailing evaluation procedures. The study examined markets for three
wholesale generation services: short-term energy, uncommitted (or short-
term) capacity, and long-term capacity. The evaluation of generation mar-

ket power for the first two products focused on incumbent suppliers, while the analysis of the third focused on the conditions of entry. To define the relevant geographic market, the study examined transmission pricing and transmission constraints in the PJM area where the merging companies made virtually all of their wholesale transactions. The study found no significant transmission constraints internal to the PJM network and also found that the effective price of transmission service for short-term sales of energy to and among PJM members from inside PJM and from utilities with direct interconnections to PJM was close to zero. This analysis led to the conclusion that all of the utilities inside the PJM network could be considered to be a single integrated geographic "destination" market. The suppliers in this market included all of the PJM members as well as utilities with direct transmission interconnections to PJM.

In previous evaluations of generation market power, FERC had generally found that market power was not an important issue in *long-term generating capacity markets* unless the merging parties or the applicant for market-based pricing authority was in a position to erect entry barriers to new generation suppliers. This view reflected the fact that modern gas-fired combined-cycle generating capacity could be built relatively quickly, at relatively small scale, and was the lowest-cost generating technology in most areas of the United States. Accordingly, the merging companies' study proceeded to examine whether the merger created barriers to entry associated with the construction of new generating capacity. It concluded that the merger would not affect competition in long-term capacity markets as a consequence of ease of entry of new gas-fired generating technology relative to the multiyear planning horizons that utilities typically utilize to make long-term capacity commitments, abundant sites for new plants of efficient scale, and transmission access and pricing provisions of the open-access transmission tariffs that the companies had agreed would accompany the merger. (Order 888 had not yet been issued when this testimony was prepared, although much of its substance had been included in a Notice of Proposed Rulemaking.)

The merging companies' study then proceeded to measure market shares, concentration, and changes in concentration to screen for the effects of the merger on competition in short-term energy and short-term capacity markets. Since BG&E had essentially no uncommitted generating capacity and PEPCO had only a small amount, which declined to zero after the year 2000, the analysis concluded that the merger had essentially no significant effect on the concentration of ownership of uncommitted or short-term generating capacity in any geographic destination market.

Regarding the markets for short-term energy, the study examined shares of total generating capacity from the perspective of several groups of wholesale purchasers that purchased short-term energy from the companies as well as historical patterns of actual wholesale energy sales to these purchasers. Following FERC's then prevailing procedures for defining relevant geographic markets and calculating market shares, all of the generating capacity of PJM utilities and interconnected utilities was included in the computations of market shares and HHIs. These calculations ignored transmission limitations between the PJM area and areas to the west, south, and north. Constellation's postmerger market share using this approach was about 10 percent, and the postmerger HHI was about 1000 with an increase of less than 100 for each of the destination markets. Table 4-2 displays these calculations.

As discussed earlier, shares of total installed generating capacity are not likely to provide meaningful measures of competition in *wholesale* energy markets under prevailing institutional arrangements where there are vertically integrated utilities that can sell in the wholesale market only from capacity that is not required to meet their regulated retail service obligations. As a result, the companies' analysis did not rely heavily on the favorable results obtained from the analysis of total installed generating capacity. Instead their study emphasized the actual patterns of historical short-term wholesale energy sales and purchases, including sales by utilities located outside of PJM into the PJM area, as a better way to

TABLE 4-2
Merging Companies' Initial Analysis of Market Shares in PJM Market Using FERC's Premerger Policy Statement Methodology (1993–1995)

Suppliers	Total Generating Capacity (Mw)	Share (%)
BG&E	6,215	6.9
PEPCO	6,042	6.7
Other PJM Utilities		
ACE	1,745	1.9
GPU	7,393	8.2
DPL	2,741	3.0
PECO	8,795	9.8
PP&L	8,290	9.2
PSE&G	11,479	13.5
Direct Interconnects		
Con Ed	8,670	9.6
APS	8,527	9.5
VEPCO	12,205	13.5
Merged firm's market share:	13.6%	
Postmerger HHI:	980	
Change in HHI:	92	

Source: Prepared direct testimony of Joe D. Pace.

characterize the size distribution of suppliers in wholesale energy markets (see Table 4-3). The analysis of market shares, HHIs, and changes in HHIs using the short-term energy sales measures in the PJM geographic market indicated that the merged firm had about a 12-percent market share, with a postmerger HHI of 1435 and an increase in the HHI of less than 50. The largest seller of energy into the PJM destination market in the previous few years had been a utility (APS) located to the west of PJM. The merging companies' study concluded that the merger would not have an adverse effect on competition in any of the wholesale energy markets examined on the basis of postmerger market shares, HHIs, and changes in HHIs that it identified.

The study also included a short discussion of four types of retail competition: interfuel competition, fringe-area competition, industrial location competition, and yardstick competition. It concluded that none of these forms of retail competition was of any importance and that to the extent

TABLE 4-3
Merging Companies' Analysis of Wholesale Energy Sales in PJM Market (1993–1995)

Suppliers	Generating Capacity (Mwh)	Share (%)
BG&E	9,728,091	10.26
PEPCO	2,058,522	2.17
Other PJM Utilities		
ACE	3,735,878	3.94
GPU	6,304,509	6.65
DPL	6,259,935	6.60
PECO	17,796,750	18.76
PP&L	10,520,403	11.09
PSE&G	3,244,880	3.4
Direct Interconnects		
Con Ed	756,240	0.8
APS	24,801,260	26.15
VEPCO	2,274,906	2.40
NYSEG	3,599,144	3.79
NIMO	841,013	0.89
Orange & Rockland	24,195	0.03
Cleveland Electric	2,914,977	3.07
Merged firm's market share:	12.43%	
Postmerger HHI:	1435	
Change in HHI:	45	

Source: Prepared rebuttal testimony of Joe D. Pace.

that they existed at all, the merger would not adversely affect the intensity of such competition.[7] The testimony contained no discussion of the potential introduction of customer choice or retail wheeling models that would give retail customers direct access to generation markets by unbundling distribution and transmission service from the sale of generation services. Neither Maryland nor the District of Columbia had indicated that it would introduce a customer choice program at that time.

The five FERC Commissioners were divided on their assessment of the merging companies' study. Two Commissioners argued that the study met the applicants' burden of proof that the merger would not have a significant effect on competition. As a result, these two Commissioners argued that the merger should be approved without further administrative hearings. However, three Commissioners felt that the study had not adequately examined the impact of transmission constraints and cumulative transmission charges within PJM on the proper boundaries of the relevant geographic markets. They suggested that a more careful examination of transmission congestion inside the PJM network might imply smaller geographic markets and that the merger would have a larger impact on concentration in these narrower markets than the study indicated.

In a 3-to-2 vote the Commission set the merger for expedited hearings on the issue of its effects on competition. In an unusual procedure, the Commission asked the ALJ to conduct a hearing, but to certify the record directly to the Commission without first writing an ALJ opinion. They did so to expedite the process, reflecting both the split views of the Commissioners on this merger and growing public criticism that FERC had become a "black hole" for merger applications with many going in, but nothing coming out for years.

FERC TRIAL STAFF'S COMPETITION ANALYSIS[8]

Once the merger was set for hearings, the FERC staff presented its own study of the effects of the merger on competition in wholesale and retail markets. The staff analysis effectively abandoned the analytical methods that the Commission had previously used to analyze market power and that the merging companies' initial competition analysis had applied.

---

[7] This conclusion is consistent with Joskow and Schmalensee's (1983) discussion of these types of retail competition.

[8] Testimony prepared by economists was also filed by the District of Columbia's Office of People's Counsel and the Maryland People's Counsel. Neither analysis was as comprehensive as that performed by the FERC staff and was apparently given no weight in the Commission's decision. The Maryland People's Counsel did not actually perform an analysis of the merger, but simply raised a number of issues that he felt required further or different analysis from what was performed by the applicants. Accordingly, the focus here is on the FERC staff's testimony, and any significant differences with testimony supported by the District of Columbia People's Counsel will be noted.

Instead, the FERC staff analysis represented an effort to apply its interpretation of the DOJ/FTC *Merger Guidelines* to electric utility mergers. In retrospect, the staff's analytical framework reflected much of what subsequently was included in FERC's Merger Policy Statement, at least with regard to the effects of mergers of proximate utilities on competition in *wholesale* markets.

The staff's analysis of competition at the wholesale level focused on essentially the same issues as did the companies' study. The staff concluded, contrary to the Commission's concerns that led to the hearing, that transmission constraints internal to PJM and cumulative transmission prices were *not* significant. The staff's analysis focused on short-term energy markets, but relied on new measures of generating capacity to evaluate market power in this product market. The staff defined the relevant geographic or destination market as including generators within the PJM area and suppliers from outside PJM that could compete to sell to buyers inside PJM. This is essentially the same geographic market definition relied on by the merging companies' study. However, the staff treated imports from outside PJM quite differently from FERC's then-prevailing approach, which the companies' study of competition had relied on. Rather than counting all of the generating capacity by utilities with direct transmission interconnections to PJM as being in the market, the staff's study argued that external capacity included in the market had to be "scaled down" so that it did not exceed the import limitations of the transmission lines into the PJM area.

The FERC staff's study also argued that market shares and concentration indices should be based on various measures of installed generating capacity and rejected taking actual wholesale energy sales patterns into account at all in the analysis of the competitive effects of the merger. Indeed, the staff analysis utilized no information drawn from the behavior observed in the wholesale markets for which the analysis of the competitive effects of the merger was focused. Instead, the staff study relied on three alternative measures of installed generating capacity to measure market shares and concentration: total installed capacity, "economic" capacity, and "marginal" capacity.[9] It defined "economic" capacity as generating capacity with marginal generation costs of less than $25/Mwh. The $25/Mwh cutoff was chosen because the effective market clearing price for wholesale energy within PJM was less than or equal to $25/Mwh roughly 80 percent of the time during the year. During these hours, higher running-cost capacity was not economical and would not represent a competitive constraint on market prices. The staff's study defined "marginal" capacity as generating capacity with marginal generation costs in the $15/Mwh to $25/Mwh range. Their argument was that capacity in this range defined the market clearing

9 The District of Columbia People's Counsel argued that market shares based on total installed generating capacity provided the best structural measure of competitive conditions.

price 65 percent of the time and that competitive conditions for the kinds of flexible capacity that cleared the market could be as important or more important than competitive conditions for base-load generating capacity that would run whenever it was available and was costly to cycle up or down to influence the supplies of energy placed on the market.

Using these measures and taking limitations on transmission capacity into PJM into account, the FERC staff found that the postmerger HHIs were generally well into the moderately concentrated range defined by the *Merger Guidelines* (about 1400 to 1900), with increases between about 250 and 580 points depending on the capacity measures and transmission assumption utilized. In addition, Constellation itself would have a market share of 22 to 34 percent. Table 4-4 displays representative calculations presented by the FERC staff. These results led the staff to conclude that the merger raised serious competitive concerns at the wholesale level. The FERC staff study went on to state that other factors such as entry would not mitigate these concerns.

TABLE 4-4
Examples of FERC Staff's Analysis of Market Shares and HHIs for PJM Market
(Import Capability = 1975 Mw)

Supplier	Total Capacity Share (%)	Economic Capacity Share (%)	Marginal Capacity Share (%)
BG&E	11.2	11.9	13.3
PEPCO	11.2	10.4	17.9
Other PJM Utilities			
ACE	4.3	4.2	6.7
GPU	16.7	17.3	16.2
DPL	5.4	5.7	9.6
PECO	13.9	16.7	6.8
PP&L	12.9	11.3	3.6
PSE&G	18.3	14.4	12.3
Interconnects			
APS	1.8	2.3	4.7
Cleveland	0.6	0.7	1.5
VEPCO	0.3	0.5	0.9
NYSEG	1.9	2.5	5.0
Others	1.3	1.6	0.7
Constellation share:	22.4%	22.4%	31.2%
Postmerger HHI:	1527	1470	1607
Change in HHI:	252	249	467

Source: Prepared direct testimony of Mr. David B. Patton for the Commission staff.

The FERC staff also argued that the Commission should consider the effects of the merger on retail competition, under the assumption that retail wheeling would be made available to all retail customers in the service areas of the merging firms and that sales of generation services to them would be made at unregulated market-based rates. Thus, the FERC staff focused on a new form of retail competition that it argued could arise in the future but did not yet exist in Maryland or the District of Columbia or anywhere else in the United States.[10] The staff study did not provide any detailed specification of how the retail access regime it envisioned emerging in the future would be introduced, when it would be introduced, or what institutional arrangements would govern its operation. It appears, however, that the staff envisioned a retail access regime in which all retail customers would buy generation service directly in unregulated generation service markets, rather than relying on their local utility to serve their needs at regulated cost-based prices. For example, the staff apparently envisioned that a retail customer in the District of Columbia would gain access to the wholesale market over PEPCO's distribution and transmission system and then would buy all of its electricity at unregulated prices from competing generation suppliers. Rather than PEPCO's buying and selling energy in the wholesale market to manage the costs of supplying retail customers at regulated rates, retail customers would be shopping directly (and through intermediaries) in a market in which all generating capacity was deregulated, *including* the generating capacity owned by PEPCO and BG&E that was presently dedicated to retail customers at regulated prices.

The FERC staff argued that to evaluate the effects of the merger on this type of retail competition, the BG&E and PEPCO retail service areas had to be examined as a separate geographic market. In this case, transmission constraints into these local areas had to be taken into account. The staff's analysis indicated that during a significant fraction of the hours during the year the retail demand within the BG&E/PEPCO service area far exceeded the transmission import capability into these areas. Accordingly, during high-demand periods, the market would have to clear with either BG&E or PEPCO generating capacity. During these time periods, BG&E and PEPCO would (roughly) have a duopoly premerger over marginal capacity while they would (roughly) have a monopoly postmerger over marginal capacity in the unregulated retail market. Thus, the staff argued that this was a merger to monopoly in the hypothetical retail access regime that they hypothesized would exist in the future; as a result, they argued, the merger raised serious competitive concerns.

The FERC staff's overall conclusion was that the Constellation merger raised serious competitive concerns at both the wholesale and retail levels and that the merger should either be rejected by the Commission or the Commission should require the merging companies to mitigate the competitive problems by divesting generating capacity and/or expand the transmission capacity available to competing suppliers into the relevant geographic markets.

FURTHER ANALYSIS BY THE COMPANIES AND FERC STAFF

The merging companies were permitted to respond to the FERC staff's study by filing rebuttal testimony as part of the hearing process.[11] The rebuttal testimony argued that the market shares based on total capacity, economic capacity, and marginal capacity relied on by the FERC staff did not provide meaningful measures of the size distribution of suppliers in the relevant wholesale energy markets. This is the case because these measures fail to recognize that under prevailing institutional arrangements, the wholesale market is a *net energy* market in which utilities make sales of energy from capacity that is not needed to meet their regulated retail and long-term contractual supply obligations. The importance of focusing on generating capacity *available* to compete in the wholesale market rather than total generating capacity is apparent from a comparison of the size distribution of actual historical sales of wholesale energy within the PJM area with the staff's capacity-based "market shares." The wholesale energy sales data represent the sales of energy from generating capacity that is available to make economical sales into the wholesale market *after* serving retail customer demands at regulated prices, which is what the evaluation should focus on.

As shown in Table 4-5, for example, PSE&G, the largest utility in PJM, accounts for about 18 percent of total generating capacity and 14 percent of economic capacity in the FERC staff's study. However, PSE&G accounted for only 3 percent of sales of wholesale energy in PJM because it tends to be a buyer rather than a seller of energy in the wholesale market. Similarly, BG&E and PEPCO are portrayed as having a combined market share of 22 percent of total capacity and economic capacity. However, their aggregate sales of wholesale energy were about 12 percent and PEPCO's share alone was only about 2 percent. APS, an interconnected utility located outside of PJM, is depicted as having less than a 5-percent share of total capacity, economic capacity, and marginal capacity but it is the largest seller of wholesale energy to PJM, with a share of economy energy transactions of over 25 percent.

The merging companies' rebuttal study concluded that data on actual market transactions provided a better, though not necessarily perfect, measure of the competitive significance of various suppliers and the overall

---

[11] The author was one of the rebuttal witnesses.

TABLE 4-5
**Comparisons Between FERC Staff's Capacity-based Market Shares and
Actual Wholesale Energy Sales in PJM**

| | Summary of FERC Staff Analysis | | | |
Selected Suppliers	Total Capacity Share (%)	Economic Capacity Share (%)	Marginal Capacity Share (%)	Actual Wholesale Energy Sales Share (%) (1993–95)
BG&E	11.2	11.9	13.3	10.3
PEPCO	11.2	10.4	17.9	2.2
PSE&G	18.3	14.4	12.3	3.4
PECO	13.9	16.7	6.8	18.8
APS	1.8	2.3	4.7	26.2
Constellation share:	22.4%	22.4%	31.2%	12.4%
Postmerger HHI:	1527	1470	1607	1435
Change in HHI:	252	249	467	45

Source: Tables 4-3 and 4-4.

structure of the wholesale energy market under prevailing institutional arrangements than did the FERC staff's capacity-based measures of market shares. The postmerger market shares, HHIs, and changes in HHIs based on energy sales data were well within the *Merger Guideline*'s screening criteria. The study also concluded that a closer analysis of actual sales data indicated that BG&E and PEPCO were even less significant competitors than the aggregate annual energy sales data indicated. This is the case because the merging companies tended to be sellers under different supply and demand conditions. PEPCO was primarily a net buyer of energy and was a seller only when wholesale market prices were relatively high. BG&E was a net seller in the wholesale market during a much larger fraction of the hours of the year and had economical capacity to sell even when prices got relatively low. Accordingly, the average price of BG&E's sales of energy in 1995 was $17/Mwh, while PEPCO's average sales price was $44/Mwh. Similar price disparities existed in 1993 and 1994 as well. These large differences in sales prices implied that the two companies were selling energy at different time periods.

The rebuttal response to the FERC staff's analysis also uncovered several numerical errors which, when corrected, reduced significantly Constellation's postmerger market share and the effects of the merger on concentration *using the capacity-based measures favored by the FERC staff*. The primary errors resulted from the use by the FERC staff of cost information at the generating plant rather than the generating unit level. Generating plants typically have more than one generating unit, and these generating units are dispatched independently of one another and may have very different marginal generating costs. The FERC staff's study classified generating plants for purposes of developing its economic and marginal capacity measures using the *average* generation cost of all of the units at a plant site. For example, if a two-unit plant had one generating unit with a marginal generation cost of $12/Mwh and another unit with a marginal cost of $28/Mwh, all of the plant's capacity was classified as if it had a marginal generating cost of $20/Mwh—a clear error. The rebuttal analysis disaggregated the data to the generating unit level and grouped the generating units based on their individual unit operating costs and then recomputed the economic capacity and marginal capacity measures used in the FERC staff study. This correction showed that the postmerger increases in concentration claimed by the FERC staff were overstated significantly *and* that they were very sensitive to small changes in precisely what costs were included as variable generation costs for classification purposes and precisely where the cutoff was defined for marginal capacity.

The rebuttal response also argued that the staff was applying the *Merger Guidelines* in a mechanical fashion that was not compatible with the way the *Guidelines* are applied by the enforcement agencies. A merger with a postmerger HHI (after correcting the staff's numerical errors) at the low end of the moderately concentrated range defined in the *Guidelines* and with an HHI increase ranging between zero and 200 points would not, on the basis of historical practice, lead the antitrust enforcement agencies to challenge such a merger, especially in light of the evidence that the two companies tended to be in the market as sellers at different times. In contrast, the FERC staff assumed that an HHI increase of greater than 100 points (or 50 points for a merger with a postmerger HHI of more than 1800 points) represented a de facto bright line for rejecting a merger.

Finally, the rebuttal response argued that the staff's analysis of the competitive effects of the merger in a retail access regime was superficial and speculative. Neither Maryland nor the District of Columbia had undertaken to implement a specific retail access program at the time the merger was being considered. Whether and how the merging companies might exercise market power premerger or postmerger depended on the institutional arrangements governing the retail access regime chosen. For example, it is generally agreed that the four-year retail rate freeze and associated sunk cost recovery mechanisms that are part of California's restructuring for retail competition program completely mitigate any incentives the utilities in California have to exercise market power by increasing market prices for energy above competitive levels.[12] This is the case when the utilities are net buyers of energy in the wholesale market,

---

[12] See Initial Comments of the Public Utilities Commission of the State of California on the March 31, 1997, Phase II Filings in Docket nos. EC96-19003 and ER96-1663-003 at the Federal Energy Regulatory Commission, June 5, 1997.

because an increase in the wholesale price of energy reduces the "head room" under the rate freeze available for sunk cost recovery more than it increases the net revenues earned by the utility's own generating plants. Moreover, if and when Maryland and the District of Columbia initiate a retail wheeling program, they could incorporate a market power mitigation program into it as has been done in California. Indeed, if the FERC staff's analysis of the companies' market power in retail markets in a retail wheeling regime were correct, such a mitigation program would be necessary whether or not there were a merger.

During the hearings, the ALJ allowed the FERC staff to introduce additional analysis that responded to the companies' argument that the staff's capacity-based market share measures were meaningless because they did not net out obligations to supply retail demand with the lowest operating-cost generation first before sales could be made to the wholesale market. The staff presented new calculations for a measure defined as "Economic Capacity" less "average retail load." These calculations indicated that even with this adjustment, the merger led to increases in HHIs of between 200 and 330 points and postmerger HHIs in the middle or upper end of the moderately concentrated range (see the first set of columns in Table 4-6).

The ALJ then gave the merging companies the opportunity to respond to this new staff analysis. This second rebuttal analysis demonstrated that the FERC staff's revised analysis contained two serious errors. First, it failed to correct the errors associated with aggregation of generating units discussed earlier. When this correction was made, the market shares of the merging firms fell and the increase in the HHI was less than 100 (see Table 4-6). The merging companies' supplemental analysis

TABLE 4-6
Merging Companies' Corrections to FERC Staff's Adjustments for Retail Load Obligation
(Economic Capacity less Average Retail Load)

Selected Suppliers (Import limits)	FERC Staff Share Calculations (%) (1975 Mw)	FERC Staff Share Calculations (%) (4150 Mw)	Companies' Corrected Share Calculations (%) (1975 Mw)	Companies' Corrected Share Calculations (%) (4150 Mw)
BG&E	12.0	10.7	11.1	9.7
PEPCO	10.5	9.3	4.0	3.5
PSE&G	10.0	8.9	11.5	10.0
APS	6.2	11.6	7.2	13.2
Constellation share:	22.5%	20.0%	15.1%	10.0%
Postmerger HHI:	1393	1224	N/A	N/A
Change in HHI:	252	199	89	68

Source: Hearing Exhibit 90 prepared by David Patton and Hearing Exhibit 95 prepared by Joe D. Pace.

also argued that taking "economic capacity" and subtracting "average" retail load yielded a variable that is not meaningful because demand varies widely from hour to hour as does the market clearing price for wholesale energy and the associated equilibrium marginal cost. The merging companies performed a new study using a simulation model for PJM that simulated the capacity, net of retail demand obligations, that each utility would have available to sell into the wholesale market when the market clearing price was at different levels. These simulations excluded imports from outside PJM, which represent a significant fraction of the wholesale energy market, yielding an upper bound for the market shares of BG&E, PEPCO, and the other PJM utilities. These simulations showed that BG&E and PEPCO had a combined share of "available economic capacity" for sale in the wholesale market that was significantly lower than the FERC staff's market share numbers and was very consistent with the historical data on energy sales in the wholesale market (see Table 4-7).

FERC'S DECISION

In December 1996, after the ALJ's hearings on this merger were completed, FERC issued its new Merger Policy Statement in which it adopted

TABLE 4-7
Merging Companies' Simulations of Capacity Available to Wholesale Market at Various Market Prices (January to September 1996)

Marginal Dispatch Price ($ / Mwh)	Hours in Range	BGE Share (%)	PEPCO Share (%)	Change in HHI Share
0–14	1247	1.1	0.0	0
14–15	485	4.1	0.0	0
15–16	648	28.5	0.0	0
16–17	740	23.0	0.1	5
17–18	632	25.4	0.1	5
18–19	369	24.9	0.4	20
19–20	225	22.6	2.4	108
20–21	160	20.9	3.1	130
21–22	153	19.1	3.4	130
22–23	130	17.7	2.5	89
23–24	97	16.6	2.6	86
24–25	119	14.9	2.3	69
Weighted average in staff's economic capacity range (<$25 / Mwh):		16.2	0.5	17

Does not include imports from outside PJM.

Source: Hearing Exhibit 96 prepared by Joe D. Pace.

the framework of the DOJ/FTC *Merger Guidelines* for evaluating electric utility mergers and provided guidance for how the *Merger Guidelines* should be applied to electric utility mergers. In April 1997 the Commission issued its decision on the Constellation merger and effectively applied the Merger Policy Statement's principles to it, despite the fact that it was litigated before the Merger Policy Statement was issued. The Commission approved the merger as proposed and rejected its trial staff's position that the merger would have a significant adverse impact on competition in wholesale energy markets.[13] The Commission also concluded, consistent with the Merger Policy Statement, that it would leave retail competition issues to the state commissions to review unless they requested FERC to address retail competition issues because they lacked authority to do so. Both the Maryland and District of Columbia Commissions had indicated that they had the authority to review retail competition issues and to mitigate any market power problems that arose. Indeed, the Maryland Commission objected to FERC's addressing retail competition issues or mandating mitigation measures such as divestiture of generating capacity. Accordingly, the Commission rejected its trial staff's argument that the merger should be rejected or conditioned on generation divestiture because of its adverse impacts on future retail competition that might arise if a retail access regime were to be introduced in the future in Maryland and the District of Columbia.

With regard to competition in wholesale energy markets, the primary difference between the FERC staff and the merging companies was how to measure and interpret market shares and concentration measures. The Commission stated that its preferred approach was to use "available economic capacity" that could be sold in the wholesale market as defined in the Merger Policy Statement to measure market shares and concentration. Available economic capacity is defined as economic capacity evaluated at different price levels *less* the retail demand that must be met by the utility when wholesale prices are at those levels. This is the measure presented by the merging companies and displayed in Table 4-7. The Commission did not place much weight on the historical energy sales information relied on by the merging companies, despite the fact that it is directly related to its concept of available economic capacity. However, the Commission placed considerable weight on the merging companies' arguments that the staff had failed properly to net out retail load obligations in calculating available economic capacity and to disaggregate generating units when assigning them to different cost categories. The Commission also found that the staff improperly relied on studies that underestimated transmission capacity available to external suppliers when

---

[13]FERC also approved the merger between two other PJM members, Delmarva and Atlantic City Electric, in July 1997 but rejected the proposed merger between Northern States Power and Wisconsin Electric Power a month earlier because of wholesale market power concerns.

the merging companies were likely to be sellers rather than buyers of wholesale energy. On the basis of corrections and adjustments that the merging companies made to the staff's "available economic capacity" calculations, and the associated postmerger HHIs and increases in HHIs resulting from the merger, the Commission found that the merger fell within the "safe harbor" structural screening criteria specified in the Merger Policy Statement and the *Merger Guidelines*. The evidence in Tables 4-6 and 4-7 above played a critical role in FERC's decision.

DISCUSSION

The economic evaluation of the effects of this proposed merger on competition had to confront a number of challenges. First, the way that FERC evaluated the effects of a merger on competition was a moving target during the entire process. Second, the electric utility industry is in the process of change, and as the merger review process proceeded, the pace of these changes, especially regarding retail wheeling, increased significantly. However, the speed and direction of these changes remain quite uncertain. Should an electric utility merger be evaluated in the context of prevailing institutional arrangements that are likely to persist for an uncertain period of time into the future? Or should the evaluation be based on assumptions about future and uncertain changes in the structure, regulation, and institutional arrangements for the industry? Merger analysis should be forward looking but not completely speculative.

At the very least, the proposed merger had to pass muster under prevailing institutional arrangements. The wholesale energy market today is a "net energy" market. For that reason, data on actual sales of energy in the wholesale market are very informative about the competitive significance of the suppliers, and this is why when "available economic capacity" is properly calculated, both measures yield similar results. In particular, the merging utilities were not likely to be significant competitors with one another absent the merger in the sale of wholesale energy, given the economic attributes of their generation capacity portfolios and their regulated retail demand obligations. A sound economic approach would rely on both actual sales data and proper calculations of available economic capacity; when these measured lead to very different results, an effort should be made to understand why and what the implications are for competition.

The Commission's views on this matter raise a deeper issue with its efforts to apply the DOJ/FTC *Merger Guidelines*. While the Merger Policy Statement defines a superior framework for evaluating mergers than FERC's earlier approach, it appears to view the DOJ/FTC *Merger Guidelines* as a kind of cookbook that should be applied mechanically. But in the enforcement process the lyrics of the *Guidelines* and the music of actual enforcement are quite different. The agencies do not pay as much attention to the HHI screens that are written in the *Guidelines* nor treat them as bright lines in the ways that FERC appears to believe. Perhaps because of inexperience with the process, FERC merger and market power policy focuses excessively on these structural market-share and HHI screens and pays inadequate attention to actual behavioral information. It also places too little emphasis on the powerful role of entry of new generating capacity *given* the planning lead times on which utilities rely under prevailing institutional arrangements, the attributes of modern combined-cycle generating capacity, and the effects of transition regulatory arrangements that are accompanying state implementations of retail access on the incentive and ability to exercise market power.

FERC was correct to leave the issues of the effects of the proposed merger on retail competition to the states. Whether and how market power could be a problem in a retail access regime depends critically on how and how fast retail access is introduced and the nature of the transition and residual regulatory arrangements affecting retail prices and service. The institutional details associated with the introduction of retail wheeling do matter, and trying to evaluate market power issues without considering them is not likely to be useful. Moreover, to the extent that the states eventually find that there is a retail-market power problem and that divestiture of generating capacity is the appropriate mitigation strategy, utility mergers do not create the classical "scrambled eggs" problem that in other contexts would make postmerger divestiture difficult. This is the case because the focus of any divestiture remedy would be on generating plants, which are distinct physical assets whose independent identities are largely unaffected by a merger.

Since FERC's decision in the Constellation merger, it has approved another merger of two smaller electric utilities in PJM, approved a merger of three small electric utilities in the midwest, rejected a merger of two larger electric utilities in the midwest, and raised serious questions about another merger involving electric utilities in Ohio. In the process FERC continues to refine the mechanics of its Merger Policy Statement. Thus far, however, mergers between electric utilities in the same region are being very closely scrutinized by FERC using the HHI screens in the *Merger Guidelines* as bright-line tests rather than as screening criteria. As an ironic ending to this proceeding, on December 22, 1997, BG&E and PEPCO announced that they were calling off their merger. Their proposal had been approved by FERC and the companies' respective state regulatory commissions. However, the state commissions had imposed conditions that would have required the merged company to make price reductions after the merger was completed. The companies concluded that the required price reductions would have been detrimental to their shareholders, and they abandoned the proposed merger.

REFERENCES

Joskow, Paul L. "Regulatory Failure, Regulatory Reform and Structural Change in the Electric Power Industry." In *Brookings Papers on Economic Activity: Microeconomics*, 1989, pp. 125–199.

Joskow, Paul L. "Introducing Competition into Network Industries: From Hierarchies to Markets in Electricity." *Industrial and Corporate Change,* 5, no. 2 (1996): 341–382.

Joskow, Paul L. "Restructuring, Competition and Regulatory Reform in the U.S. Electricity Sector." *Journal of Economic Perspectives.* 11, no. 3 (Summer 1997): 119–138.

Joskow, Paul L., and Richard Schmalensee. *Markets for Power.* Cambridge, Mass.: MIT Press, 1983.

CASE 5

Potential Competition in Local Telephone Service: Bell Atlantic-NYNEX (1997)

Steven R. Brenner

INTRODUCTION

On April 21, 1996, Bell Atlantic Corporation and NYNEX Corporation announced that they had reached an agreement to merge. Nearly sixteen months later, after the Department of Justice, the Federal Communications Commission, and many state public utility commissions finally cleared the transaction, the two companies completed their merger, one of the largest in U.S. history. Bell Atlantic was the local telephone company for most customers in six eastern states from Virginia through New Jersey, and NYNEX provided local telephone service for most customers in seven states from New York to Maine. Together, the two companies had assets of $51.3 billion and operating revenues of $27.8 billion.[1] Public attention focused on the size of the merging companies, but the combination also raised serious competitive issues.

Authorities reviewing the merger were most concerned with the merger's effects on potential competition. The two firms were not head-to-head competitors in any relevant antitrust market when they announced their merger. Although each supplied essentially the same range of telecommunications services, they did so to different consumers in adjacent east

Steven R. Brenner consulted with and filed testimony for MCI Telecommunications Corporation with the New York Public Service Commission analyzing this merger. The author would like to acknowledge the contributions of Professor Franklin M. Fisher of M.I.T. to the analysis of this merger for MCI, but the author alone is responsible for the views expressed here.

[1] These data, which are as of December 31, 1995, are reported in New York Telephone, et al. (1996, p. 33).

coast regions. The Telecommunications Act of 1996, signed into law only months before the merger was announced, was intended to open the way for competition in markets for local telephone service. Local telephone providers, such as Bell Atlantic and NYNEX, were expected to face entry and competition from new suppliers. A key question was: If the two did not merge, would one or both of the companies enter and compete with its neighbor? If so, would elimination of that entry harm competition?

A second competitive concern was predicated on the vertical integration likely to result from the merger. The 1996 Telecommunications Act established conditions under which the individual Bell companies, including Bell Atlantic and NYNEX, could be allowed to begin supplying interregional and interstate long-distance service.[2] If this occurred, the merged firm would supply access services to its own long-distance service that, in the absence of the merger, each firm would have purchased from the other to originate or terminate calls in the other's territory. The competitive concern was whether the vertical combination would create or increase incentives for the merged firm to disadvantage rival long-distance carriers that had little option but to purchase access from the merged firm.

Analysis of both competitive issues depended on predicting behavior in future market conditions, and, more than in most merger analyses, future market conditions were likely to differ substantially from current conditions. Analysis of potential competition had to consider the effects not only of possible entry by one of the merging firms, but also of entry by other firms as a result of the 1996 Telecommunications Act. If enough other firms were going to be successful entrants, eliminating entry by one of the merging firms would have little effect on competition. Analysis of the merger's vertical effects had to project not only the consequences of increased vertical integration, but also whether the merging firms would or could try to discriminate in supplying access services after they were allowed to provide long-distance service. The difficulty of projecting such future market conditions made it harder than usual to find clear evidence to establish the presence or absence of anticompetitive effects.

At the same time, it was difficult to be comfortable with the simple argument that, if one could not see into the future clearly enough to be certain that competition would be harmed, then the merger should be approved. At stake might be whether and how fast competition would develop for local telecommunications services for which incumbent suppliers, like Bell Atlantic and NYNEX, were until recently nearly the only providers. The Telecommunications Act of 1996, together with other regulatory initiatives, intended to open those markets to competition. Such changes in the regulatory environment, together with ongoing changes in

---

[2]The Bell companies had been restricted from providing so-called interLATA service by the Modification of Final Judgment (MFJ), the 1982 agreement settling the government's antitrust case against AT&T; see the discussion below.

technology, could be expected to result in structural changes as firms re-configured themselves to deal with new market conditions. (Indeed, the Bell Atlantic-NYNEX merger was but one of several large telecommunications mergers and acquisitions in this period, including the nearly simultaneous merger of two other Bell holding companies—SBC Corporation and Pacific Telesis—and connections between British Telecom and MCI Telecommunications, and among Sprint Corporation, France Telecom, and Deutsche Telekom.) The question was: Were the two firms merging so that they could supply services more efficiently in the new market environment, or because they hoped to shore up their old, dominant positions when regulatory barriers that had protected them were lowered?

BACKGROUND

Regulatory Changes

From the early decades of the twentieth century into the 1960s, telecommunications service essentially was supplied as a regulated monopoly.[3] Local telephone service was provided by *the* local telephone company, and that single company alone was authorized by regulatory authorities to provide service; regulation enforced absolute barriers to entry. For most areas and customers, the local telephone company was part of the AT&T Bell System, known familiarly as Ma Bell.[4] AT&T's Long Lines Division also provided the great bulk of long-distance services throughout the country—both the switched service for normal long-distance calls and the circuits that businesses use between two fixed locations.

Cracks began to appear in this edifice of regulated monopoly beginning in the 1950s. MCI helped to drive a competitive wedge into this structure when, in the late 1960s and early 1970s, it sought authorization for, first, a competing private line service to business, and then a competing switched long-distance service. In both cases, the company wanted to interconnect and use facilities of the local telephone company to give its customers access to MCI's facilities.

AT&T balked at providing its competitor with these complementary inputs. The result was a protracted dispute involving both the FCC and the courts over which access services AT&T had to provide at what prices. MCI ultimately won the right to interconnect to the Bell System, but AT&T's actions became an important part of the antitrust case that the

---

[3] The discussion in the next few paragraphs reviews only selected developments in the movement from regulated monopoly toward competition. For more complete summaries, the reader can turn to Brock (1981) and Temin (1987).

[4] Companies other than AT&T supplied telephone service to some areas, but each company served only its own territory and customers.

government filed against AT&T in 1974. AT&T, the government charged, had violated the antitrust laws by using its control over interconnection and access service to block the development of competition and retain its monopoly.[5] The case went to trial in January 1981, and one year later, after its motion for summary judgment in its favor was denied, AT&T agreed to settle the case with the government.

This settlement was known as the *Modification of Final Judgment,* or MFJ.[6] AT&T agreed to divest itself of its local operating companies, while retaining its long-distance and equipment manufacturing operations. The divested local operations were turned over to seven newly created holding companies, each of which was to provide local service in a different region of the country. These new offspring of Ma Bell quickly became known as Baby Bells, or RBOCs (for "regional Bell operating companies"). Bell Atlantic and NYNEX were two of the new RBOCs.

The basic idea of the MFJ was simple: splitting AT&T along vertical lines would eliminate, or at least sharply reduce, the incentive of the divested local telephone companies to behave anticompetitively in providing interconnection and access. The new RBOCs would provide interconnection and access services to long-distance companies—such as MCI, Sprint, and a newly separate AT&T—but would not compete with those companies. The MFJ prohibited RBOCs from providing any services that crossed the boundaries of newly created regions called LATAs.[7]

The MFJ framework was designed to encourage competition for services that crossed LATA boundaries, but made little direct provision for competition within LATAs. As time passed, however, firms began to be interested in providing local services that competed with those of the RBOC and non-RBOC local exchange companies. Firms that became known as competitive access providers, or "CAPs," began to install fiber optic cable in large metropolitan areas to provide businesses with a competing source of supply for dedicated-circuit, point-to-point service within local or regional areas. Throughout the latter part of the 1980s and into the 1990s, state commissions and the FCC grappled with questions about which local

---

[5] The government case also considered AT&T's actions involving other forms of interconnection. In particular, it covered AT&T's attempts to limit the connection to its phone system of so-called "customer premises equipment" supplied by competitors—the phone instrument itself and switching equipment used by businesses. The discussion here summarizes selected issues of the case and its settlement; for a more complete review see Noll and Owen (1994).

[6] The MFJ was so named because formally it modified a 1956 consent decree that settled an earlier antitrust case the government had brought against AT&T.

[7] "LATA" is an acronym for "local access and transport area." Individual LATAs varied in size from a few counties in more populous areas to entire states with lower population densities. The MFJ also required the RBOCs to provide "equal access" to all long-distance companies, so that customers could use the same 1+ dialing sequence to place long-distance calls with any long-distance company they might choose. Previously, a customer who used a long-distance service other than AT&T first dialed a local number to reach the other carrier, and then dialed the long-distance number being called and a personal identification number.

services competing firms should be allowed to supply and what kinds of interconnection the established carrier should provide.

These developments put pressure on the MFJ framework. Proponents of local telephone competition pushed to sweep away the remaining regulatory barriers that limited the ability of competing firms to enter and provide local services. Meanwhile, the RBOCs argued that they should not continue to be restricted from providing interLATA service at the same time they were facing increased competition for local service. These and other pressures for change culminated in the Telecommunications Act of 1996.

The 1996 Act prohibited laws or regulations that directly or indirectly prevented competing firms from providing any local telecommunications service. Local companies were required to interconnect with each other at cost-based rates so that customers of different companies could call each other. Incumbent local telephone companies were required to sell or rent so-called "unbundled network elements" at cost-based rates. For example, the incumbent telephone company had to allow new local carriers to rent the use of elements such as the "local loop," or common line, that connects each customer to the local network and an incumbent's local switches. All local telephone companies also were required to allow other firms to purchase their local service at a wholesale rate and then rebrand and resell that service. These provisions were intended to reduce the sunk costs a competing firm would have to commit to begin service; purchased network elements offered an alternative to capital expenditures on network facilities, and resold services allowed a new carrier to market its service to customers without building facilities to serve them. Resale also allowed firms to market a bundle of services—for example, long-distance and local service—with committing to substantial investments in both local and long-distance network facilities.

The 1996 Act also set conditions under which the RBOCs could be released from the MFJ restriction on offering interLATA service. Once they satisfied a checklist of conditions related to opening up local markets to competition, RBOCs could apply to the FCC for authority to offer interLATA service.

The 1996 Act, therefore, presaged significant changes in the market conditions faced by Bell Atlantic and NYNEX, with or without their merger: competition from other companies for the local services they provided and the prospect that each could begin providing interLATA long-distance services in competition with AT&T, MCI, Sprint, and other firms, to which they also would be selling access services.

The Merging Companies

Bell Atlantic and NYNEX each offered a wide range of local and regional telephone services to a wide range of customers. Understanding both the range of services and the range of customers is important for defining antitrust markets and analyzing competitive conditions in those markets.

The basic and largest local service is plain old telephone service, or "POTS" as it sometimes is called in the industry. POTS is the service that allows a customer to pick up a phone and dial a call to any other telephone line in a local area, and to receive calls from any other local customer. Bell Atlantic provided POTS to about 18 million people via 17.7 million access lines in six states—Maryland, Pennsylvania, Virginia, New Jersey, West Virginia, and Delaware—as well as the District of Columbia. NYNEX provided local service to about 20 million people via 20.6 million access lines in New York, parts of Connecticut, and the five New England states (Federal Communications Commission, 1997, paras. 17–18).

Providing switched local service is very capital intensive. First, the telephone company must run a local loop to each customer to provide a connection to the first or end office switch of the telephone network. Multiple, sophisticated, electronic switches are needed to route calls to the local loop of the person being called over circuits or trunks that carry traffic between the switches. Sophisticated signaling networks and computers help direct the call flows, monitor information for billing, and signal network conditions (such as a "busy signal").

Bell Atlantic and NYNEX, like other local telephone companies, also supply local switched-access service. When a customer picks up the telephone and dials "1+ area code," the telephone company switch identifies this as a long-distance call, determines if the call is going outside the customer's LATA, and if it is, looks up the customer's designated long-distance company and routes it to that company. The call may then be routed to a dedicated circuit that transports the call to the long-distance company. This transport function, effectively a separate service, may be provided by the local telephone company or by a competing firm. Essentially the same access services are provided on the terminating end of a long-distance call: the long-distance carrier hands off the call for transport to the called party. Bell Atlantic and NYNEX also supply long-distance calling, including 800 service, for calls that stay within a single LATA.

Local telephone companies like Bell Atlantic and NYNEX further provide a wide range of unswitched, dedicated-circuit services. A business with its main office in downtown Philadelphia and a branch in a Philadelphia suburb can lease from Bell Atlantic a dedicated circuit between those two locations to carry voice or data traffic, or both. Circuits can be purchased in a range of capacities; the greater the volume of traffic to be carried, the larger the "pipe" a customer will want. If the business wants a circuit from its Philadelphia office to a branch in Washington, D.C., it must purchase the interLATA circuit from a long-distance carrier. It likely will still need a dedicated, unswitched circuit in each city to connect its premises to the premises of the carrier providing the interLATA circuit, and Bell Atlantic can supply these dedicated or special-access services.

Businesses also use unswitched, special-access connections from their locations to the interLATA carrier to carry switched long-distance traffic. In that case, the business's own internal switch, or PBX, directs its long-distance traffic to the special-access circuit, which then routes it to the long-distance carrier.

Local telephone companies also supply other specialized business services. Centrex and similar services allow a business to use the local telephone company's switches, rather than the business's own PBX switch, to handle calls between extentions within a business. Switched data services route and carry data among multiple locations. So long as such locations are within a single LATA, Bell Atlantic and NYNEX can provide the service.

Before their merger, Bell Atlantic and NYNEX each supplied this range of services throughout their separate service areas. They also supplied wireless mobile, or cellular, telephone services. Bell Atlantic and NYNEX in fact had already formed a joint venture—Bell Atlantic-NYNEX Mobile—to supply cellular service to areas both in their combined local telephone service areas and elsewhere in the country. Each firm also had assets in international operations. Neither the cellular nor the international operations of either firm, however, figured importantly in the merger review.

Review by Authorities

The Department of Justice carried out the required Hart-Scott-Rodino (HSR) review of this proposed merger. The DOJ issued a "second request" for extensive additional documents and information, with which the companies complied by July 1996. In April 1997, the DOJ announced that it had completed its review and concluded that the proposed transaction did not violate the antitrust laws. The Department did not seek modification of the proposed transactions or commitments from the merging parties in a consent decree. As is usual in such cases, the Department provided no further information on the analysis by which it reached its conclusions or on the evidence on which it relied. The wide range of information and documents collected by the Department is not publicly available.

The transaction also was reviewed and cleared by thirteen state commissions. (Only three of these, however, presented their own discussion of the effects of the merger on competition.)

The FCC also reviewed the transaction. The Commission had authority under the 1934 Communications Act to determine if the transfer of certificates, licenses, and authorizations involved in the merger was in the public interest. The FCC also has concurrent jurisdiction with the Department of Justice and Federal Trade Commission under Sections 7 and 11 of the Clayton Act to determine if acquisitions of communications common carriers would have the effect "substantially to lessen competition, or to tend to create a monopoly" (Federal Communications Commission, 1997, paras. 29–33). In this case, however, the FCC chose not to exercise its Clayton Act authority. The Commission instead examined whether the merger met the broader public interest standard of the Communications Act. Under the Act's public interest standard, the burden of proof is on the applicants, not the Commission. Nonetheless, the Commission used the framework of the 1992 Department of Justice and Federal Trade Commission *Horizontal Merger Guidelines* for its competitive analysis (para. 37). Furthermore, the Commission was concerned with the effects of the merger on competition, notwithstanding the fact that many of the services involved were regulated. Market competition remained important both because moving to a deregulated market required the development of competition and because, in any event, regulation could not completely or costlessly constrain market power (para. 45).

The Commission concluded that the applicants had failed to carry their burden of demonstrating that the transaction was in the public interest without any modifications. The FCC approved the merger, but only after Bell Atlantic and NYNEX made a series of enforceable commitments that the Commission believed would promote competitive entry and provide procompetitive benefits sufficient to offset the otherwise negative effects of the merger. The Commission approved the merger on August 14, 1997. Later the same day, Bell Atlantic and NYNEX consummated their merger.

POTENTIAL COMPETITION ISSUES

The merging firms were not current competitors, but they might have become competitors in the future if they had not merged. This was the competition issue that most concerned the authorities—at least so far as one can tell from the public record. This section reviews potential competition issues. The next section discusses other possible effects of the merger on competition.

The Potential Competition Doctrine

Economic theory suggests two circumstances in which a merger could reduce competition by eliminating a firm that is a potential entrant into a market served by the merger partner. First, competition could be reduced if, but for the merger, one of the merging firms would actually have entered a market supplied by the other, and that entry would have decreased concentration and increased competition. Second, competition could be reduced if one of the merging firms is perceived as a potential entrant into a concentrated market supplied by the other, and this perceived possibility of entry disciplines suppliers in that market. Courts have recognized each as a theory under which elimination by merger of a potential competitor may violate Section 7 of the Clayton Act (ABA Antitrust Section, 1992, pp. 322–329). The first is called the "actual potential entrant" theory, and the second the "perceived potential entrant" theory.

The second of these, the perceived potential entrant theory, was not particularly important for analysis of the Bell Atlantic-NYNEX merger. Entering and capturing a significant market share as a producer of most telecommunications services both takes time and requires a firm to commit subsantial sunk investments. The perceived possibility that a firm might enter, without actual entry, was unlikely to discipline pricing in markets supplies by Bell Atlantic or NYNEX.

The serious competitive question was: Would the merger harm competition by removing Bell Atlantic or NYNEX as a future, actual entrant into one or more markets served by the other? More specifically, attention focused on whether Bell Atlantic would have competed with NYNEX by supplying local telephone service in the New York metropolitan area, which was adjacent to Bell Atlantic territory in New Jersey, or in other parts of NYNEX territory.

Arguments of Bell Atlantic and NYNEX

The position of Bell Atlantic and NYNEX was straightforward. In the first place, Bell Atlantic was not an actual potential competitor of NYNEX. In any event, the merger would have little effect on the structure of the market or on prices and service quality, even if it did eliminate Bell Atlantic as an entrant, because many other firms were equally or better able to enter and compete effectively (New York Telephone et al., 1996, especially pp. 62–63). The merging parties presented the following evidence and arguments to support these positions.

First, Bell Atlantic had no plans to compete with NYNEX. Bell Atlantic's vice chairman, James G. Cullen, filed an affidavit with the FCC in which he stated that "Bell Atlantic has not at any time had plans to enter NYNEX's local service markets" (Federal Communications Commission, 1997, para. 239). NYNEX claimed that it had not perceived Bell Atlantic as a potential competitor in any New York local exchange or access market (New York Telephone et al., 1996, p. 64). Therefore, the merging parties argued, Bell Atlantic could not be considered an actual potential competitor.

Second, Bell Atlantic had no special advantages, compared with other potential competitors, that would make it a more likely entrant into markets served by NYNEX. Specifically, Bell Atlantic (in filings made jointly with NYNEX) claimed it had "no network facilities in New York from which to supply services, no existing customer base and no marketing presence or brand recognition of any significance" (New York Telephone et al., 1996, p. 64). The merging parties claimed that many other firms had advantages greater than those of Bell Atlantic, which made them more likely entrants than Bell Atlantic. For example, interexchange carriers such as AT&T and MCI, competitive access providers such as MFS and Teleport, cable television companies such as Time Warner, and wireless providers such as Sprint Telecommunications Venture were more likely entrants because they could make use of their current network equipment, marketing and brand name recognition, or existing customer base (New York Telephone et al., 1996, pp. 65–66). Bell Atlantic and NYNEX pointed out that the 1984 *Merger Guidelines* stated that the Department of Justice was unlikely to challenge a merger unless the merging firm was considered an actual potential entrant that had a specific advantage possessed by fewer than three other firms.[8]

Third, NYNEX already faced competition from many other suppliers. Over fifty competitive local exchange carriers were certified by the New York Public Service Commission to provide local service, with more applications for certification pending.[9] Competing firms already had deployed twenty-seven switches in New York City and been assigned eighty-two NXX codes, seventy-one of which also were in New York City; eighty-two NXX codes would provide telephone numbers for up to 820,000 customers.[10] The merging companies said NYNEX already had lost customers to these competitors, claiming that 50 percent of high-capacity dedicated lines in Manhattan for special access to interexchange carrier locations and between the local points of presence (or POPs) of interexchange carriers were supplied by CAPs. Nationwide, CAPs were said to have captured 10 to 15 percent of the "national carrier access market."

Bell Atlantic and NYNEX went on to describe the activities of firms they saw as more likely entrants. Fiber deployment by MFS, a CAP, reached 638 buildings in New York City. Teleport, another CAP, had three switches and 600 New York area customers. Interexchange carriers were acting on plans to offer local dial tone service. AT&T had switches and other facilities under construction in Manhattan, and its recent purchase of McCaw Cellular gave it access to local networks. The merging firms quoted statements of AT&T's chairman that AT&T looked forward to the opening up of the local market and believed it could win one-third of that market over the next five to ten years. The two firms described plans of MCI to install fiber optic cable in Western Union conduit in various cities that would run through high-traffic corporate corridors accounting for a high proportion of long-distance traffic. An MCI subsidiary, MCImetro, had a switch and other facilities in the NYNEX region, and had installed

---

[8] New York Telephone et al. (1996, p. 63). The language of the text paraphrases the Bell Atlantic-NYNEX restatement of the DOJ position. The 1984 *Merger Guidelines* themselves phrase the standard in terms of whether other potential entrants possess "comparable importance." While the 1984 *Guidelines* largely have been superseded by later revisions, the revisions have not specifically addressed the treatment of potential competition issues.

[9] This and the other evidence described here and in the next paragraph were presented in New York Telephone et al. (1996, pp. 66–80).

[10] "NXX" refers to the first three digits of a seven-digit local telephone number. For traditional local telephone companies, the NXX identifies the exchange, or local switch, to which a customer's line is connected.

an advanced SONEX fiber ring to carry traffic in New York City and parts of Westchester County. MCI had recently begun advertising local telephone service to businesses in large cities, including New York City.

Fourth, the 1996 Telecommunications Act promised to accelerate competition by lowering regulatory and technological barriers to entry into local exchange markets. The resale provisions in the Act made it possible for an interexchange carrier or cable television company to enter the local telephone market "with minimal investment and minimal risk" (New York Telephone et al., 1996, p. 84). While full facilities-based entry required investment in sunk network costs, Bell Atlantic-NYNEX argued that the Act encouraged the development of facilities-based competition by requiring that incumbent carriers supply unbundled network components. In sum, they concluded, the 1996 Act "sharply reduced barriers to entry" (New York Telephone et al., 1996, pp. 84–85).

Finally, Bell Atlantic and NYNEX claimed that the merger offered various efficiencies and other public interest benefits (although they denied that there would be any adverse effects of the merger for these efficiencies to offset). First, the increased size of the new firm would allow it to take advantage of economies of scope and scale. The merging parties told the New York Public Service Commission that, "Without these economies of scale and scope (and concomitant efficiencies), New York Telephone would be far less able to compete in that it would not have an ability comparable to that of the large telecommunications companies to provide high quality service at competitive rates and to introduce new and innovative products and services" (New York Telephone et al., 1996, p. 13). Other claimed efficiencies or benefits included: (1) saved research and development costs from the spreading of fixed R&D costs; (2) reduced unit costs from such sources as reduced corporate staff, and reduced costs for procurement, advertising, and information system development; (3) improved service quality from the application of each company's best practices; and (4) increased ability to enter and compete as a long-distance provider (New York Telephone et al., 1996, pp. 43–59).[11]

Points of Contention

The Bell Atlantic-NYNEX arguments identified the major points for evaluating whether their merger would reduce competition by removing a potential entrant.

1. Did corporate plans and the firms' economic position provide evidence that Bell Atlantic (or NYNEX) was a potential entrant into markets served by the merger partner?

---

[11] Also see Federal Communications Commission (1997, paras. 160–167).

2. Was the number of other firms that could and likely would enter in place of the merging firm sufficiently great that structural conditions in the relevant markets were unlikely to be affected by the merger?

3. Was the merger's elimination of an entrant unlikely to affect competition, either because markets already were unconcentrated and competitive, or because entry barriers were sufficiently low that entry could prevent the exercise of market power in the future?

The Bell Atlantic-NYNEX arguments, and the points they identified, closely followed tests that the courts have established for determining whether a merger violates the antitrust laws by eliminating a potential competitor.[12]

Not surprisingly, these three points also became points of contention between the merging companies and those who argued that the merger did threaten competition. Each is discussed below, but first it will be useful to explain the underlying questions of market definition.

Market Definition

Analysis of the competitive effect of a merger usually begins by identifying the relevant antitrust markets supplied by the merging companies. In this case, however, the various parties did not explicitly identify relevant antitrust markets, at least in the public record (Federal Communications Commission, 1997, para. 49). Precise delineation of the antitrust markets in which telecommunications services are supplied is difficult, but important issues in this case turn on whether various groups of telecommunications services are supplied in the same or different product markets. Boundaries could exist between the product markets in which services are supplied because (a) the services are not good substitutes, (b) they are offered to different customer groups, or (c) one is a retail and the other a wholesale service.

At its most basic, the demand for a telecommunications service is the demand to transport information between point A and one or many points B. It does not follow, however, that all the different ways of conveying information between points A and B are close substitutes for all consumers.

---

[12] The courts have established several prerequisites for showing that a merger violates the Clayton Act under the actual potential competition doctrine:

1. The market that one of the merging firms otherwise would have entered is concentrated.

2. Few other potential entrants are equally able to enter.

3. In the absence of the transaction, one of the merging firms in fact was likely to enter the market served by the other. More specifically, the firm had a means of entry other than the proposed merger, and that alternative means offered a substantial likelihood of promoting competition by deconcentrating the market or otherwise promoting competitive behavior.

See ABA (1992 pp. 322–329).

Those alternatives are likely to differ in cost and perhaps in other characteristics, and which alternatives are sufficiently close in cost and other attributes to be good substitutes often depends on the nature of a customer's demand (such as the volume and frequency of use).

One prominent candidate for a boundary that separates product markets is the distinction between switched service and dedicated-circuit services. With dedicated-circuit service, the customer pays for a circuit or "pipe" of given capacity connecting two specific points, regardless of how much or little traffic is transported over the circuit while it is being rented. In contrast, switched service gives the customer the ability to communicate with many different locations, and the amount paid often varies with the number and duration of calls. Switched and dedicated service can be close substitutes for some customers and applications, but not for others. For example, dedicated circuits may be substantially more costly than switched service for customers sending limited traffic over particular routes, but less costly than switched service for customers that can spread the cost of a dedicated circuit over substantial volumes of traffic. Dedicated and switched services will be close in cost only for customers whose traffic falls in the intermediate range. As a result, switched service is a poor substitute for dedicated service for a business customer needing an access connection to a long-distance carrier for an interstate private line or large volumes of switched long-distance traffic, or for a long-distance carrier connecting two of its switches or POPs in the same local area. On the other hand, for a residential customer placing local or long-distance calls, dedicated circuit service is a very poor substitute for switched service. Each type of service is used by enough customers for whom the other is not a good substitute that it is unlikely that most switched local and long-distance services are supplied in the same product market as most dedicated-circuit services—even though it may be difficult to locate the precise product market boundaries.

There also are product market divisions based on the geographic dimension of service. (This is an issue of product market definition, although this geographic dimension to consumer demand can create confusion in distinguishing between product and geographic market definitions.) Few consumers would consider calling between, say, New York City and Albany to be a good substitute for calling between New York and Boston. Identifying separate, route-specific product markets usually serves little analytical purpose, however, when the same set of carriers serves a group of routes.[13] At present, however, at least three categories of routes are not all supplied by the same set of carriers: local calling (which is only rarely supplied by interexchange carriers), interLATA calling (supplied by interexchange carriers but not by RBOCs), and intraLATA calling (usually supplied by both interexchange carriers and local carriers).[14] Discussions of this merger did recog-

---

[13] Furthermore, the very nature of switched service is to provide calling to a collection of routes.

[14] There also are differences in the firms that supply dedicated-circuit services within metropolitan or regional areas and over national (or international) routes.

nize these product market divisions, at least implicitly. Virtually all of the attention in this merger focused on product markets for local calling service.

Product market divisions also may exist between services sold to different customer groups. An important issue in this case was whether there are divisions between the product markets in which local (switched) services are supplied to residential customers, small businesses, and larger businesses. These services could be supplied in different product markets if it is possible to price discriminate among the services sold to different customer groups. Traditionally, different rates have been charged for local service to business and residential customers. In addition, as the FCC noted, residential and business customers also may demand somewhat different bundles of service characteristics.[15]

Finally, market boundaries can be drawn on the basis of what actually is being supplied. The 1996 Telecommunications Act requires local carriers, including Bell Atlantic and NYNEX, to allow their local service to be rebranded and resold by others. In the future, carriers may not use facilities that they own or control to produce all the local service they sell to customers. Instead, they may purchase service at wholesale from the producing carrier and act as a retailer by reselling it. In this situation, competitive analysis should distinguish separate product markets for the production and the retailing of local telephone services.

Bell Atlantic's Plans to Enter NYNEX Markets

Bell Atlantic's assertions that it had no company plans to compete with NYNEX relied on a careful definition of what constitutes "company plans": plans approved by governing levels of corporate management and supported by financial commitments. Bell Atlantic acknowledged that its staff had studied the possibility of entering New York markets, but it said that these had never matured into company-approved plans and, therefore, Bell Atlantic could not be considered an actual potential entrant.[16]

Bell Atlantic could hardly have denied that it had studied entering New York markets. In 1993 Bell Atlantic and TeleCommunications, Inc. (TCI) announced plans to merge, and said that the merged firm would build on TCI's cable TV facilities to provide telephone service. An affidavit of a Bell Atlantic official stated:

> Outside Bell Atlantic's service area, BA/TCI will provide telephone service in direct competition against the incumbent providers of such services. Within approximately two and a half years of closing, I expect to be operating full service networks in competition with incumbent telcos

---

[15] The FCC gave the example that residential customers may demand Call Waiting services that are of little value to a business with multiple lines and a PBX system with voice mail, while large businesses may want ISDN digital service options or carrier-provided voice mail (Federal Communications Commission, 1997, para. 53).

[16] Federal Communications Commission (1997, paras. 240–241), citing Bell Atlantic statements.

in approximately 30 cities outside Bell Atlantic's current region. If the merger is completed on schedule, we expect BA/TCI to be providing competing local telephone services in geographic areas totaling more than 40 million people outside Bell Atlantic's current service area by the end of the 1990s. (Oliver, 1994, paras. 8–9)[17]

At the time, NYNEX staff apparently thought that Bell Atlantic's entry plans probably included New York.[18]

Bell Atlantic and TCI abandoned their merger, and Bell Atlantic later said it had decided not to pursue any of the entry strategies it had studied. Bell Atlantic's internal strategic plans and studies were important evidence, but they are not part of the public record. They were provided to the Department of Justice and the FCC, however, and no doubt formed an important part of those agencies' review of the merger. The Department said nothing of its review, but the FCC did describe what it found.

> Bell Atlantic's internal documents establish that Bell Atlantic was, until merger discussions were well underway, engaged in planning out-of-region entry into local exchange, exchange access, and long distance services in a number of locations in the NYNEX region, most notably LATA 132. The extent of planning reflected in the documents persuades us that Bell Atlantic would likely have entered LATA 132. The documents also show Bell Atlantic would have been most likely to target mass market, not business customers.[19]

The FCC rejected Bell Atlantic's claim that these documents represented only the activities of middle management and did not constitute evidence that Bell Atlantic was an actual potential entrant, because senior management had not formally approved and committed resources for entry. Formal approval of entry by the Bell Atlantic board of directors would have been conclusive evidence of intent to enter, said the FCC, but the planning revealed by the Bell Atlantic documents, under the continued oversight of senior management, was evidence supporting a finding that Bell Atlantic likely would have entered NYNEX markets but for the merger (Federal Communications Commission, 1997, para. 75).

Relative Advantages of Potential Entrants

Bell Atlantic and NYNEX claimed that other firms had greater advantages as entering suppliers of local telephone service than did Bell Atlantic, a

---

[17] The affidavit was filed in connection with a request for waivers from the MFJ that would have been required to complete this merger.

[18] A NYNEX staff review at that time noted that TCI had substantial cable operations in the New York area (LATA 132) and stated that Bell Atlantic might well enter the New York City market at some point. See the Affidavit of Jeffrey A. Bowden, submitted to the FCC, July 2, 1996, p. 4.

[19] Federal Communications Commission (1997, para. 73). LATA 132 covers essentially the same territory as NYNEX's New York Metropolitan Calling Area.

claim that was disputed. Evidence on the relative advantages that Bell Atlantic and others possess as entrants bears both on whether Bell Atlantic was a potential entrant and on whether elimination of this entry by merger would affect competition. If Bell Atlantic had fewer advantages than other firms as an entrant, the profitability of its entry, and therefore the likelihood of its entry, could be questioned. Furthermore, if many other firms were as well positioned as Bell Atlantic to become viable, successful entrants, loss of Bell Atlantic as an entrant would be less likely to result in increased market concentration and reduced competition.

Bell Atlantic and NYNEX emphasized that Bell Atlantic would have the advantages of neither network facilities nor an established customer base as an entrant into NYNEX markets. Others pointed out, however, that Bell Atlantic was not without other assets it would find valuable as an entrant. Bell Atlantic had in-place operational support systems developed for local service, overseeing such functions as the monitoring and measuring of usage, billing, service order and provisioning, network management, and customer service. Such systems are complicated, costly to develop, and crucial for providing high-quality local service (Mosca, 1996, pp. 2–4). As an entering local service supplier, Bell Atlantic could have avoided not only the substantial cost of developing operational support software and procedures for local service, but also the inevitable glitches in service that occur as such systems are being debugged. Bell Atlantic also had corporate experience and know-how as a local service provider. It employed seasoned personnel with expertise in engineering and planning, as well as in operating local networks and in marketing local services. Bell Atlantic had been in business long enough to understand customer demands for service and support, to design and market services responsive to those demands, and to implement management structures facilitating the efficient delivery of such services.

Bell Atlantic's experience and expertise also would have been valuable in negotiating interconnection agreements with NYNEX as the incumbent local carrier, and in presenting information to regulators about how NYNEX should fulfill its obligations as an incumbent local carrier.[20] Under the Telecommunications Act of 1996, entering local carriers have the right to interconnect with the incumbent local carrier to exchange calls between the networks, and to purchase unbundled network elements and wholesale local service. The economic success of an entering carrier, however, will be heavily dependent upon the prices, terms, and conditions under which it can purchase these services.

The merging companies also argued that Bell Atlantic possessed no marketing presence or brand recognition of any consequence that would aid

---

[20] The FCC made a related point, that Bell Atlantic's experience would have allowed it to make significant procompetitive contributions to efforts of regulators to implement procompetitive policies and rules (Federal Communications Commission, 1997, para. 127).

entry into NYNEX markets. The FCC, however, pointed out that Bell Atlantic regularly advertises to its northern New Jersey customers via New York metropolitan area broadcast and print media that reach customers in New York. The FCC also reported that marketing information in Bell Atlantic and NYNEX documents showed that Bell Atlantic had greater brand recognition or acceptance as a potential local service provider among customers in New York markets than the smaller interexchange carriers, cable television providers, or CAPs. The FCC concluded that Bell Atlantic's brand recognition and reputation gave it an advantage in supplying local service to residential and small business customers in New York that, among possible entrants, was matched only by the three largest interexchange carriers, AT&T, MCI, and Sprint.[21]

What of the remaining advantages that the merging firms claimed other firms possessed? The significance of these advantages also was disputed. The merging firms pointed to the network facilities that cable TV firms, CAPs, and interexchange carriers had in NYNEX territory. Much existing cable TV infrastructure, however, was poorly suited to the provision of telephony. Cable firms are investing in new plant better able to support telephony. The FCC pointed out, however, that questions about the technological and financial constraints faced by these firms cast doubt on how soon they could become effective, competing suppliers of telephone service (Federal Communications Commission, 1997, para. 86). CAPs have installed their facilities only in certain metropolitan areas, and typically have chosen locations within those areas that are best suited for providing service to concentrations of business customers. Interexchange carriers historically have designed and installed their network infrastructure to provide long-distance service, which limits its adaptability to local service. For example, interexchange carriers do not plan to use their existing switches to provide local service; they install new switches where they plan to provide their own local switching capacity. Similarly, the great bulk of the installed infrastructure of wireless carriers is designed to provide mobile service; as such, it is less suited to providing service fully equal in quality to wireline local exchange service. Furthermore, rates for mobile service, and apparently the costs of supply, remain well above the rates charged for traditional local telephone service (Federal Communications Commission, 1997, para. 90).

Finally, the arguments of the merging parties did not address the possibility that Bell Atlantic need not enter de novo to deconcentrate markets. Bell Atlantic also might enter by combining with another firm that possessed an asset valuable for supplying local telephone service in New York that Bell Atlantic lacked. Bell Atlantic entry by this route could still be

---

[21] Federal Communication Commission (1997, paras. 78–79, 82, 84, 86, 88). In support, the FCC reported findings from Bell Atlantic's own market research on its brand reputation among residential and small business customers in the New York metropolitan area.

deconcentrating, so long as the other firm would not have entered on its own or could not by itself have commanded as great a market share and competitive significance as it could by merging with Bell Atlantic. This possibility is significant because the assets or advantages of Bell Atlantic and some other types of firms apparently were complementary. Bell Atlantic possessed experience, reputation, and operational support systems for local switched telephony, but no network facilities in NYNEX areas; cable television firms and CAPs possessed network facilities but lacked local switched telephony experience, reputation, and operational support systems.

Earlier, Bell Atlantic itself had recognized this complementarity of assets when it argued that a merged Bell Atlantic and TCI would promote local telephone competition. At that time, Bell Atlantic suggested that cable systems were not strong potential suppliers of local telephone service because they lacked operational support systems, sophisticated billing systems, and technical experience important for providing local telephone service. In contrast, a combined Bell Atlantic/TCI would be a strong entrant because, "As a current provider . . . Bell Atlantic possesses exactly those areas of expertise and capabilities needed to provide telephone service that TCI and Liberty lack" (Oliver, 1994, paras. 9–10).[22]

In sum, Bell Atlantic probably was not uniquely well positioned to enter New York local service markets, but a good case could be made that it was one of a limited number of potential entrants with comparable advantages for supplying local telephone service to residential and small business consumers. The FCC identified four firms as the most likely future, new suppliers to markets for local telephone service to residences and small businesses in the New York metropolitan area: Bell Atlantic, AT&T, MCI, and Sprint. The question was: How small must be the number of potential entrants for the merger to pose a threat to competition? The 1984 *Merger Guidelines,* as Bell Atlantic and NYNEX pointed out, say that the Department is unlikely to challenge a merger—all else equal—if three or more other firms possess advantages comparable to those of the merging firm. On a mechanical application of this standard to the FCC findings, the Bell Atlantic-NYNEX merger would not be challenged: the FCC identified exactly three other entrants with comparable advantages.

As is so often the case, however, it is important to keep sight of the economic analysis underlying the *Guidelines,* and not to treat these criteria as cookbook rules. The analytical issue is: Will the merger, by removing one of the entering firms as an entrant, result in a market that is more concentrated and less competitive in the future than it would be in the future if the merger did not take place? In a relatively stable but concentrated market, three other firms with comparable advantages that are not current suppliers could promise sufficient entry that the merger would not reduce

---

[22] Liberty was part of the TCI corporate family with which Bell Atlantic was planning to merge.

competition in the future. To give some simple, heuristic examples, the evidence might indicate that entry by no more than one of the firms likely would be profitable and viable. With three firms left to take the place of the merging firm as the single viable entrant, the likelihood would be strong that the extent of entry and future concentration would be approximately the same with or without the merger. Alternatively, analysis might indicate that entry could be profitable for all four well-placed entrants, but entry by two or three firms would deconcentrate the industry sufficiently that it would perform competitively. In that case the merger still would not reduce competition in the future because it would perform competitively even if that meant three rather than four firms entered.

It was far from clear that local telephone service markets fit either situation, and the merging firms did not explain why the *Guidelines* standard should be sufficient in the particular, and rather unusual, circumstances of these markets. NYNEX now has a monopoly or near-monopoly in supplying local switched telephone service to residences and small businesses in its local exchanges. Would entry by three firms sufficiently deconcentrate these markets that a fourth entrant would not improve competitive performance? Alternatively, is it clear that only a subset of the four firms could become viable entrants, with or without the merger, and that therefore eliminating Bell Atlantic as an entrant would not affect the number of entrants or the equilibrium level of concentration?[23]

Competition Now and in the Future

Bell Atlantic and NYNEX also argued that NYNEX already faced competition from a large number of other firms, and that this competition would increase because the 1996 Act had substantially lowered entry barriers. The merging firms, however, often did not clearly identify the markets supplied by these present and anticipated competitors. It thus was not clear that these firms were evidence that NYNEX already faced competition in the same markets that Bell Atlantic might have entered to supply local switched telephone service to residential and smaller business customers in NYNEX territory.

Bell Atlantic and NYNEX pointed to the growth of CAPs and their success in selling high-capacity circuits for special access, for traffic that long-distance carriers moved between their locations or POPs within a metropolitan area, and in a "national carrier access market." These, however, are all dedicated-circuit services sold to business customers. The merging parties did not demonstrate that the product market should be defined broadly enough that these dedicated services are in the same product market as local switched services supplied to residences and small businesses.

---

[23]The second alternative seems inconsistent with the tenor of Bell Atlantic-NYNEX arguments that the 1996 Telecommunications Act has resulted in low entry barriers.

Some CAPs are beginning to supply local switched services (at least to business customers), but the merging parties also did not explain why the CAPs' success as suppliers of dedicated-circuit service would predict their future market shares or significance in markets for local switched services.

Bell Atlantic and NYNEX pointed to the number of firms authorized (or seeking authorization) as competitive local exchange carriers (CLECs) by the New York Public Service Commission as another index of competition. The FCC gave little weight to this evidence. Authorization did not establish that a firm had the ability to become a substantial competitive presence and did not identify the market to be supplied. Many of these firms, according to the FCC, target large business customers with specialized service offerings (Federal Communications Commission, 1997, para. 81).

There also was a tension between the competitive role that Bell Atlantic and NYNEX implied many smaller firms could play in the future and some of the efficiency claims they made for their own merger. The merging companies claimed they would find it more difficult to offer competitive rates and innovative services as separate companies than as a merged firm, because as separate firms they could take less advantage of economies of scale and scope. If, however, Bell Atlantic and NYNEX individually would be disadvantaged competitively by an inability to realize scale and scope economies, did this not imply that considerably smaller CAPs, newly certificated local carriers, and other smaller firms also would face scale and scope diseconomies that would make it difficult for them to put competitive pressure on a much larger NYNEX?

The Bell Atlantic-NYNEX arguments emphasized how resale and the availability of unbundled network elements could support entry, but paid little attention to how reliance on such inputs would affect the competitive significance of such entrants. On the one hand, an entering producer of local telephone service can reduce the sunk investment it must put at risk in the early stages of its entry by purchasing unbundled network elements or service at wholesale. This should encourage the eventual development of competing sources of supply. On the other hand, an entrant's ability to constrain the exercise of market power by the incumbent remains limited so long as its ability to provide service continues to depend on purchasing wholesale services or unbundled network elements from the incumbent local telephone company. By controlling the price that an entrant pays for these inputs, the incumbent can directly affect the entrant's costs and the price that the entrant can charge in downstream markets for telephone services sold to consumers, where it was trying to compete with the incumbent.[24]

Bell Atlantic and NYNEX paid little attention to these issues in identifying competing suppliers of local service and projecting their market

---

[24] The prices charged by the incumbent local telephone company for wholesale service and unbundled network elements are subject to some statutory restrictions in the 1996 Telecommunications Act, and could be regulated. In that case, however, competitive performance in the downstream market would depend in part on regulatory constraints rather than on competitive forces.

success. They did not identify how many announced sellers of local service in New York were planning only to resell NYNEX service. Nor did the merging parties distinguish between produced and resold service in the plans of firms that planned to market both. For example, they cited the optimistic prediction of AT&T's chairman that his company would sell one-third of local telephone service in the future, but did not discuss the likelihood that any such success, if at all possible, would involve a heavy component of resold service. Similarly, the merging parties presented no analysis of the extent to which competing suppliers would have to rely on unbundled network elements supplied by NYNEX in order to supply significant proportions of local service.

Finally, there was the general question of whether the new regulatory regime created by the 1996 Telecommunications Act made general entry conditions sufficiently easy to prevent the exercise of market power. Bell Atlantic-NYNEX claimed that the Act did sharply reduce barriers to entry for a wide range of firms. The *Merger Guidelines* distinguish between uncommitted and committed entry. Uncommitted entry is unlikely to play a large role in local telephone markets, as the FCC observed (Federal Communications Commission, 1997, para. 131). An entrant might reduce its sunk costs by relying on resale and unbundled network elements, but it would still face sunk costs for marketing and for nonrecurring charges for unbundled network elements. Reliance on resale and unbundled network elements also would limit competitive significance. Committed entry, the FCC argued, was not sufficiently easy to allay market power concerns: all but a small number of firms still faced substantial obstacles as entering suppliers of local service to residences and small businesses. Entry, and expansion of sales to large numbers of customers, would require very significant sunk costs, for both building network facilities and establishing brand reputations. Entry by firms other than those few with market advantages could not be relied on as likely, timely, and sufficient to prevent the exercise of market power in markets for local switched service (Federal Communications Commission, 1997, paras. 132–134).

OTHER COMPETITIVE ISSUES

While the question of potential competition was the primary focus of those evaluating the Bell Atlantic-NYNEX merger, at least two other competitive concerns were raised.

Incentives for Nonprice Discrimination Against Rival Long-distance Carriers

Divestiture and the MFJ's prohibitions against interLATA service by the RBOCs were intended to eliminate most of the incentives of local Bell companies to discriminate against or among long-distance carriers in providing access services. Local Bell operating companies could no longer benefit by diverting customers to their own interLATA, long-distance services. The 1996 Telecommunications Act established procedures and conditions for allowing the Bell operating companies to again begin supplying interLATA long-distance service. This raised two questions in the context of the announced merger. First, was there a substantial risk that the reentry of Bell Atlantic or NYNEX, or both, into full long-distance service would result in discrimination against rival long-distance carriers that would harm competition? Second, if so, would the risk or extent of discrimination and harm be increased by the announced merger?

Bell Atlantic and NYNEX, to the limited extent that they addressed these issues, insisted that there was no risk that they would discriminate in supplying access services; regulatory safeguards and the competitive conditions under which they would be allowed to supply interLATA service made discrimination impossible. In any case, they argued, this was not a merger issue; issues of discrimination were unrelated to and unaffected by the merger. The FCC basically agreed in its brief discussion of this issue (Federal Communications Commission, 1997, paras. 119–129).

Analysis presented by other parties, however, showed that the merger might increase discrimination, if regulation did not completely prevent all discrimination (Brenner, 1996, pp. 46–61). If regulation can constrain some nonprice discrimination, but is unable to detect and deter all discrimination, the possibility of detection and enforcement becomes a cost that the local carrier must weigh against benefits when deciding whether and how much to discriminate. Increasing the level of discrimination increases the expected cost because the risk of detection and penalty rises, but it also increases the expected payoff because it increases the disadvantages faced by long-distance rivals. Increasing the payoffs that Bell Atlantic or NYNEX would receive from any given level of discrimination changes the balance of benefits and costs, and could increase the "optimal" or profit-maximizing level of discrimination for the company.

The merger between Bell Atlantic and NYNEX could increase the payoffs each would receive from nonprice discrimination against long-distance rivals. Nonprice discrimination would degrade the quality of the access connections that long-distance carriers purchase from Bell Atlantic or NYNEX to originate or terminate long distance calls.[25] The local carrier might be able to target discrimination to degrade the quality of service received by a particular long-distance company, but probably could not

---

[25] Nonprice discrimination might take a variety of forms, including: (1) poorer maintenance that resulted in increased circuit outages, (2) provisions of new features in forms better suited to the carrier's own service rather than that of rivals, (3) delays in notifying rivals of new features that slowed their ability to offer improved service to customers, and (4) errors in billing for access that required the purchasing long-distance carrier to increase the staff devoted to detecting and resolving billing disputes.

target the discrimination so it affected only particular calls. In that case, nonprice discrimination by NYNEX would affect the access that NYNEX provided for all calls originated or terminated in NYNEX territory by, say, an AT&T or MCI regardless of whether the calls were between two locations in NYNEX territory, or between locations in NYNEX and Bell Atlantic territory. NYNEX discrimination on access provided in New York would have the same effect on calls that AT&T was completing between New York and Boston and between New York and Philadelphia.

Because discrimination could not be precisely targeted, the discriminating carrier might not benefit from all of its effects on rival long-distance carriers. For example, the premerger NYNEX would realize no benefits from making AT&T or MCI service less attractive to customers in Philadelphia who call New York if NYNEX did not offer long-distance service to customers in Bell Atlantic territory. (A Bell Atlantic long-distance service might benefit from NYNEX's discrimination, but the premerger NYNEX would not care.) The premerger NYNEX also would not benefit if it marketed a long-distance service to a Philadelphia customer that resold the service of a carrier against whom it discriminated in New York (since NYNEX discrimination also would affect calls to New York over the service NYNEX was marketing to Philadelphia customers). Merger with Bell Atlantic would eliminate these limitations. The merged Bell Atlantic-NYNEX could offer a competing long-distance service over its own combined network facilities to which Philadelphia customers could turn to avoid the degraded service on calls from Philadelphia to New York offered by rival carriers.

The merger also could increase the companies' benefits from discriminating if, but for the merger, NYNEX and Bell Atlantic each would have built facilities to supply long-distance service to customers in the other's region. In this case, absent the merger, Bell Atlantic and NYNEX each would have an incentive to discriminate against the other's long-distance service, so each could face discrimination from the other on one end of calls between the two territories. Each would have an advantage over other long-distance carriers that faced discrimination on both ends of these calls, but the benefits they realized from this advantage would be limited. The profits each could realize would be limited by competition from the other, which would be similarly situated, and by the discrimination each faced from the other. The merger would eliminate both this competition and the discrimination against each other.

These effects of the merger on payoffs to discrimination would be of little concern if rival long-distance carriers could avoid NYNEX or Bell Atlantic discrimination easily by buying local switched access from another carrier. If an AT&T or MCI could produce and sell local service as well as long-distance service to a customer, it would not have to rely on NYNEX or Bell Atlantic switched access to reach that customer.[26] This

---

[26] The long-distance company need not supply the local service itself. The local service also could be supplied by an independent "partner."

possibility, however, does not guarantee that long-distance companies could avoid the effects of NYNEX or Bell Atlantic discrimination. First, a long-distance carrier gets an alternative supply of switched access only if it or another competing local carrier succeeds in supplying and selling local service to customers. It may be some time before most custormers can be offered this option.[27] Second, by inducing a customer to switch to a different local carrier, the long-distance carrier could avoid NYNEX-Bell Atlantic switched access on the originating end of the customer's calls, but not on the terminating end of calls within the merged firm's territory. The long-distance company still must use switched access supplied by the local carrier serving those called customers. So long as most customers in their territories continue to choose local service from a merged Bell Atlantic-NYNEX, long-distance companies will have to buy switched access from Bell Atlantic-NYNEX to terminate calls to these customers. Furthermore, it is the payoffs to discrimination in the supply of terminating access that are increased by merger. The merged company benefits from the effects that discrimination in New York has on calls that Philadelphia customers place to New York.

Thus, the merger could increase the threat that the historic problems surrounding the supply of access services might re-emerge. The MFJ reduced incentives for nonprice discrimination in the supply of access not only by mandating divestiture and prohibiting interLATA service by local companies, but also by dividing the old Bell operating companies into seven, separate holding companies. This last provision made little difference so long as the restrictions on interLATA calling remained in place. If that restriction is dropped, the division into multiple local companies could matter, and it is that division that would be affected by the merger. Further analysis would be needed to determine the magnitude and seriousness of the threat to competition, but this issue received little attention—at least so far as is evident from the public record.

Regulatory Benchmarking

The FCC pointed to another effect of reducing by merger the number of separate Bell companies. The merger reduced the number of independent companies that regulators could use to "benchmark" the conduct of other carriers or of the industry. Regulators find such comparisons valuable for a variety of purposes, including comparing service quality to detect nonprice discrimination, comparing prices to determine whether proposed tariffs are reasonable, establishing the level of productivity factors for price-cap regulation, and revealing better ways to implement the provisions of the 1996 Telecommunications Act as multiple local companies each make their own proposals. The FCC expressed concern about these effects, but

---

[27] Resale is not sufficient because the local access service is still supplied by the underlying wholesale supplier of the local connection.

concluded that reducing the number of Bell companies from six to five would not have a sufficiently large effect to establish that the merger was not in the public interest—although it warned that further mergers might present serious concerns (Federal Communications Commission, 1997, paras. 147–156).[28]

DISPOSITION OF THE MATTER

As noted above, the Department of Justice cleared the merger with only a short statement stating that it had found that the combination did not violate the antitrust laws. State commissions in the NYNEX and Bell Atlantic territories also approved the merger. Some, notably the New York Public Service Commission, did impose conditions, but these bore more on issues of service quality and state regulatory control than on competition issues.[29]

The most complete public review of the merger's competitive effects was that of the FCC. The FCC found that the applicants had not carried their burden of showing that the merger satisfied the public interest standard of the Communications Act (Federal Communications Commission, 1997, paras. 8–12). The FCC found that the merger eliminated Bell Atlantic as a likely, significant competitor in markets to supply local exchange and exchange access service to residential and smaller business customers in the New York metropolitan area. But for the merger, the FCC concluded, Bell Atlantic had planned to enter. The FCC further concluded that eliminating Bell Atlantic by merger increased the risk that NYNEX would find it profitable to exercise unilateral market power. Bell Atlantic not only would have been a significant competitor in general, but was likely to have been the "second choice," or closest substitute to NYNEX service, for many consumers in the relevant markets (paras. 101–108). The FCC concluded that elimination of Bell Atlantic, as one of only five likely significant market participants—four likely entrants plus NYNEX—also substantially increased the risk of coordinated interaction in these markets (paras. 121–124). The FCC maintained that the applicants had failed to show that such harms to competition would be mitigated either because of easy entry conditions or by efficiencies generated by the merger. Therefore, the merger, as proposed, was not in the public interest.

Nonetheless, the Commission did approve the merger. The FCC found that the transaction was in the public interest when supplemented by

---

[28] The previously approved merger of SBC Corporation and Pacific Telesis had reduced the number of Bell companies from seven to six.

[29] See "New York PSC Conditionally Approves Merger of Bell Atlantic, NYNEX" in *Telecommunications Reports*, March 24, 1997, p. 5.

commitments that Bell Atlantic and NYNEX made regarding how they would implement provisions of the 1996 Telecommunications Act (paras. 13–14). Among these commitments were the following: (1) to develop operations support systems and interfaces that would make it easier for other firms to order unbundled network elements and services to be resold; (2) to provide detailed performance-monitoring reports to competing carriers that could help detect poor performance or discrimination in the supply of unbundled network elements or resold services; and (3) to set rates for interconnection and unbundled network elements based on forward-looking economic cost. Many of these commitments addressed disputed issues between the merging firms and the competing companies with which they were negotiating interconnection agreements.

The Commission argued that these commitments would help other firms to enter or expand and thereby become more significant competitors. In this way, the commitments mitigated the competitive harms of eliminating Bell Atlantic as a likely competitor.

CONCLUSION

There has been relatively little government enforcement activity under the potential competition doctrines recently, perhaps because of the difficult evidentiary burdens that they involve (ABA, 1992, p. 324). To demonstrate that a merger violates the antitrust laws under the actual potential competition doctrine requires showing (among other things) that one of the merging firms would have entered but for the merger, and that the market in the future will be more concentrated and less competitive for the loss of this entry.

In this case, there was relatively strong evidence that Bell Atlantic would have entered and competed with NYNEX in at least some relevant markets but for the merger. There were the facts of Bell Atlantic's experience as a local carrier, location as a geographically adjacent carrier, and past public statements about an interest in entering local service markets outside its home territory. According to the FCC, internal documents of Bell Atlantic provided strong evidence of plans to compete with NYNEX.

The more difficult part of the case to prove might have been to show that loss of Bell Atlantic as an entrant would make markets more concentrated and less competitive. This would have required projecting future conditions for markets where past conditions were much less a guide to future conditions than would usually be the case. The 1996 Telecommunications Act made entry by competing suppliers of local services easier, but how much easier? What types of firms would prove to have the advantages necessary to make them successful entrants, and how much market share could they capture how quickly? How many firms would enter and supply which services to which customers? All were relevant questions for determining the effect of eliminating Bell Atlantic as an entrant on market competition in the future.

Past market experience provided only limited evidence on the correct answers to these questions. The significance of what current competition did exist would be surrounded by disputes over the appropriate definitions of product and geographic markets—where again the lack of experience with functioning, competitive markets would limit the evidence available to resolve disputes. The simple evidence presented by Bell Atlantic and NYNEX about the present and anticipated competition faced by NYNEX could be questioned, but establishing an alternative scenario of how market conditions would evolve also would be difficult. From this perspective, it is not surprising that authorities examined the merger closely and expressed concern, but in the end did not challenge it.

REFERENCES

ABA Antitrust Section. *Antitrust Law Developments,* 3rd ed., 1992.

Brenner, S. R. "Direct Testimony," submitted to New York Public Service Commission in Case nos. 96-C-0599 and 96-C-0603, November 25, 1996.

Brock, G. *The Telecommunications Industry: The Dynamics of Market Structure.* Cambridge, Mass.: Harvard University Press, 1981.

Federal Communications Commission. *Memorandum Opinion and Order.* File No. NSD-L-96-10, In the Application of NYNEX Corporation and Bell Atlantic Corporation For Consent to Transfer Control of NYNEX Corporation and Its Subsidiaries, August 14, 1997.

Mosca, W. K. Jr. "Affidavit," attached to Petition of AT&T Corporation to Deny or, in the Alternative, to Defer Pending Further Investigation and Briefing, FCC Report No. 960205, September 23, 1996.

New York Telephone, et al. "Initial Panel Testimony of New York Telephone, NYNEX Corporation, and Bell Atlantic Corporation." Submitted to New York Public Service Commission in Case nos. 96-C-0599 and 96-C-0603, November 25, 1996.

Noll, R. G., and B. M. Owen. "The Anticompetitive Uses of Regulation: *United States v. AT&T* (1982)." In *The Antitrust Revolution,* edited by J. E. Kwoka, Jr., and L. J. White. New York: Oxford University Press, 1994.

Oliver, B. D. "Affidavit," submitted to the U.S. District Court for the District of Columbia, *U.S. v. Western Electric Company, Inc. and AT&T.* January 1994.

Temin, P., with L. Galambos. *The Fall of the Bell System.* Cambridge: Cambridge University Press, 1987.

CASE 6

Prices, Market Definition, and the Effects of Merger: Staples-Office Depot (1997)

Serdar Dalkir and
Frederick R. Warren-Boulton

INTRODUCTION

On September 4, 1996, the two largest office superstore chains in the United States, Office Depot and Staples, announced their agreement to merge. Seven months later, the Federal Trade Commission voted 4 to 1 to oppose the merger on the grounds that it was likely to harm competition and lead to higher prices in "the market for the sale of consumable office supplies sold through office superstores." The merging parties chose to contest the FTC's actions in court. On June 30, 1997, after a seven-day trial, Judge Thomas F. Hogan of the U.S. District Court for the District of Columbia agreed with the FTC and granted a preliminary injunction, effectively dooming the merger.

Staples broke new ground in terms of both the economic theory and the type of evidence presented at trial in an antitrust case. The antitrust enforcement agencies had traditionally focused on the increased probability of collusion following a merger as the primary theoretical underpinning for merger policy. In contrast, *Staples* spotlighted the potential for a merger to have "unilateral effects," a shift in focus first signaled by the 1992 revision of the Department of Justice and FTC *Merger Guidlines.*

Frederick R. Warren-Boulton served as an expert witness for the FTC in this case. Serdar Dalkir contributed to the preparation of the expert testimony, and contributed substantially to the event-probability study. Thanks are also due to Stephen Silberman, Robert Levinson, Melvin Orlans, and James Fishlein for helpful comments on earlier drafts.

Focusing on the characteristics of individual suppliers, the FTC argued that Staples, Office Depot, and OfficeMax were sufficiently different from other suppliers of office products, and sufficiently close competitors to each other, that the "sale of office supplies through office superstores" could be defined as a market separate from the sale of office supplies in general. In another departure, for evidence of the likely anticompetitive effect of the merger, the FTC relied primarily on direct estimates of the merger's effect on prices, rather than just predicting that an increase in seller concentration would cause significant (but vaguely specified) price increases. In addition to internal documents describing pricing policies and simple (but powerful) price comparisions between cities where Office Depot and Staples currently competed and those where they did not, the FTC's evidence on price effects included a large-scale econometric model that predicted the effect of the merger on prices. It also included an "event study" that used stock market data to calculate both the effect of the merger on shareholders and the financial market's implicit estimate of the effect of the merger on the prices charged by office superstores.

BACKGROUND

Office Depot and Staples are, respectively, the first- and the second-largest office superstore (OSS) chains in the United States. Staples pioneered the office superstore concept in 1986. In 1997, Staples operated approximately 550 stores in twenty-eight states. It had 1996 revenues of some $4 billion and a stock market valuation of approximately $3 billion at the end of 1996. Office Depot, which adopted the concept of superstores within months after Staples invented it, operated more than 500 stores in thirty-eight states, had 1996 sales of approximately $6.1 billion, and had a stock market value of about $2.2 billion at the end of 1996. The rationale for the superstore concept was simple: While large businesses were able to purchase office supplies through high-volume contract stationers, small businesses and individuals had no comparably convenient, low-cost source of office supplies and other business-related products. The office superstore was to do for office supplies what the supermarket had done for home groceries.

The typical superstore is approximately 23,000 to 30,000 square feet in area, stocks 5000 to 6000 items, is located in an urban business area, and looks like a warehouse. Approximately half of Staples' and Office Depot's revenues are derived from sales of office supplies, with the rest coming from the sale of computers, office furniture, and other business-related items. Both chains purchase virtually all of their inventory directly from manufacturers in large quantities, enabling them to receive volume discounts that are unavailable to small and medium-sized retailers. These lower costs have led to dramatically lower prices: office supplies are typically sold by superstores at discounts of 30 to 70 percent below manufacturer-suggested retail prices.

At one time, twenty-three competing OSS chains slugged it out in the market. By the time of the proposed merger, however, OfficeMax was the only remaining close rival to Staples and Office Depot. Spun off from K-Mart in 1994, OfficeMax operated 575 superstores and seventeen delivery centers in over 220 areas in forty-eight states. Like Staples and Office Depot, each OfficeMax superstore offered an extensive selection of over 7000 items at discount prices, selling primarily to small and medium-sized businesses, home office customers, and individuals. OfficeMax's total revenues for fiscal year 1997 were $3.2 billion, with office supplies making up about 40 percent of total revenues.

The success of the OSS concept had redefined the retailing of office supplies in the United States, driving thousands of independent stationers out of business, just as the growth of supermarkets had driven out thousands of small "Mom and Pop" grocery stores. The competitive rivalry between the superstores had, however, benefited consumers substantially. Each OSS chain slashed prices; drove down costs; developed innovative approaches to marketing, distribution, and store layout; and expanded rapidly, bringing to increasing numbers of consumers the convenience of one-stop shopping at low prices. Office Depot had, at least in recent years, been the most aggressive and lowest-price competitor.

On September 4, 1996, Staples and Office Depot announced an agreement under which Staples would acquire Office Depot by exchanging 1.14 Staples shares for each outstanding Office Depot share, a roughly $4 billion deal. After a seven-month investigation, the FTC decided to challenge the merger.[1]

THE FTC'S CASE

The FTC argued that this merger could be expected to lead to a significant decrease in competition in the market for consumable office supplies sold through office superstores, and that the resulting price increases could be expected to be substantial. To prove its case, the FTC used a number of sources of data and analytical approaches to predict the price effects of the proposed merger. It argued that all of the evidence indicated that there would be large and long-lasting price increases, and therefore considerable harm to consumers.

The FTC was careful to compare the expected merger-related changes

---

[1]After the Commission's initial vote, the FTC staff negotiated a tentative agreement (subject to the Commission's approval) with Staples and Office Depot that would have authorized the merger to proceed unchallenged if the two companies agreed to divest a sufficient number of stores to OfficeMax to preserve two competitors in cities where Office Depot and Staples were currently the only two superstores. On March 26, 1997, OfficeMax signed an agreement to buy sixty-three Staples and Office Depot stores for the fire-sale price of $108.75 million, subject to the consent of the FTC. But on April 4, 1997, the Commission voted to reject the proposed settlement and thus to challenge the merger.

in prices and costs with the prices and costs that would have prevailed in the absence of the merger. Specifically, the FTC recognized that OSS prices might continue to fall after the merger, but argued that because prices would fall significantly further without the merger, the merger would still harm competition. Likewise, the FTC stressed that the efficiencies claimed by the defendants must be merger specific.

Concentration and the Competitive Effects of a Merger

The underlying theme of merger policy is that mergers or acquisitions should not be permitted to create, enhance, or facilitate the exercise of market power, defined as the ability profitably to maintain prices above competitive levels for a significant period of time. The *Merger Guidelines* emphasize two ways in which mergers can lead to higher prices: coordinated interaction and unilateral effects.

When only a few firms account for most of the sales of a product, those firms can sometimes exercise market power by either explicitly or implicitly coordinating their actions. Coordinated interaction is of particular concern in homogeneous product markets, where all firms must charge very similar prices. Circumstances may also permit a single firm, not a monopolist, to exercise market power through unilateral or noncoordinated conduct, that is, without the concurrence of other firms in the market or in the absence of coordinated responses by those firms. Unilateral price effects are of particular concern if the products or services are differentiated, but those supplied by the merging firms are much closer substitutes for each other than for those of other suppliers. In any case, the exercise of market power causes a transfer of wealth from buyers to sellers and a misallocation of resources.

Defining the Relevant Market: "Consumable Office Supplies Sold Through Office Superstores"

The FTC argued that the relevant product market was "the sale of consumable office supplies through office superstores." The FTC supported its market its market definition, in part, by introducing evidence showing that: (1) OSSs offer a distinct set of products and services; (2) OSSs regard each other as their primary competitors; (3) non-OSS retailers do not tightly constrain OSS pricing; and (4) a hypothetical merger to monopoly among all three OSSs could be expected to result in a significant increase in their prices for consumable office supplies—an outcome that would not occur if OSSs and other stores selling office supplies were in the same product market.

1. *Office superstores offer a distinct set of products and services.* The FTC argued that OSS firms were different from other vendors of office

products because they carried a broad range of consumables and maintained large amounts of stock on hand. These attributes of office superstores created a one-stop-shopping opportunity for consumers that was not provided by other retailers or mail-order suppliers of office products.

Like customers of supermarkets and department stores, customers of office supply superstores benefit from being able to buy a large number and variety of products on a single visit. The full "price" to an office superstore customer of acquiring these products is the amount paid to the store, plus the customer's noncash costs of shopping. These noncash costs include the value of the time required to visit the store, gather information about products and prices, and shop. Since each visit to a store involves a fixed cost, customers prefer to purchase a bundle of items on each visit, especially low-cost "consumable" items that need to be purchased regularly.

Customers who purchase a bundle or basket of items need to decide: (1) which store to go to and (2) what products to buy on each visit. The first decision is relevant if one is analyzing a merger among a particular class of retailers (e.g., office superstores, department stores, or supermarkets) and needs to define a market for a particular type of retailing service. The second decision is relevant if one is analyzing a merger among manufacturers of particular products sold by those retailers (*e.g.*, binders, women's dresses, or canned tuna).

OSSs devote significant shelf space to consumable office products and maintain a large inventory to ensure the convenience of one-stop shopping for customers. Superstores carry up to 7500 items of consumable office supplies, computers and computer-related products, and office furniture. While certain non-OSS retailers (mass merchandisers, warehouse club stores, computer stores, and consumer electronics outlets) sell a number of the same products that OSSs sell, they typically stock far fewer office supply items[2] and/or carry a very limited assortment of consumable office supplies.

In court, both sides presented witnesses, exhibits, and affidavits that addressed the extent to which OSS retailers differ from non-OSS retailers of office supplies. Faced with a mass of conflicting evidence, the FTC strongly recommended that the judge visit several sellers of office supplies to see for himself how superstores differ from other office supply retailers. As one FTC expert witness put it, "One visit would be worth a thousand affidavits."

2. *OSSs regard each other as their primary competitors.* The parties' internal documents (at least those predating the merger announcement) showed that each was concerned primarily or exclusively with competition from other office superstores. Indeed, Staples defined "competitive"

---

[2]Estimates of office supply items carried by the warehouse club stores range from 100 to 289. Mass merchandisers like K-Mart and Target typically carry fewer than 570 office supply items. Even Wal-Mart, which carries a relatively broad range of office supply items (between 1067 and 2400), nonetheless did not appear to be a significant competitor of the OSS firms.

and "noncompetitive" markets solely in terms of the presence or absence of OSS competitors,[3] and referred to its participation in an "office super-store industry."[4] Office Depot's documents similarly focused primarily on other OSS firms as competitors. The FTC argued that such evidence demonstrated that Staples and Office Depot recognized that other OSS firms were their main competitors.

3. *Non-OSS retailers have little effect on OSSs' price changes.* The FTC argued that the presence of non-OSS retailers could be expected to have little effect on the prices charged by OSS, especially in markets where more than one OSS was present. This implied that the presence of non-OSS retailers in an area would not prevent the merged office super-store from raising prices and that such non-OSS retailers should not thus be included in the relevant market.

The FTC did not dispute the fact that, in markets defined by Staples as "noncompetitive markets" (i.e., in markets where only one OSS was present), retailers like warehouse clubs and computer stores would be the closest competitors of the OSS. But the FTC argued that one could not infer from this that non-OSS retailers would provide effective competition for OSS firms in "competitive" markets, those where two or more OSSs already were present. A monopolist maintains a price so high that any further increase would cause a sufficient loss of customers to be unprofitable. Thus, a monopolist is distinguished not by the fact that it faces no competition, but by the fact that its closest competitors are too distant to prevent it from maintaining its price at a level significantly above cost. Ultimately, however, every monopolist "creates" its own "competitors" by maintaining its own price sufficiently high.

Thus, in a market with two OSS firms, each OSS could overwhelmingly be the other's primary "competition" and provide the only effective force holding the other OSSs pricing at present levels. If these two OSSs merged, the new firm would find it profitable to raise its prices until competition from non-OSS retailers eventually made further price increases unprofitable. The post-merger OSS monopoly would then be constrained by the prices charged by these new, non-OSS "competitors." In short, even though warehouse price clubs or Wal-Mart might be important competi-

---

[3]For example, Staples' FY95 Marketing Plan defined competitive markets as markets with another office superstore (i.e., Office Depot or OfficeMax or both), and noncompetitive markets as those with only local stationers or warehouse clubs.

[4]Staples's internal documents further established that it viewed OSS firms to be its primary competitive constraint. A March 1996 memorandum discussing possible price increases if Staples bought OfficeMax specifically referenced only one competitor, Office Depot, as a possible price-constraining influence. In a document analyzing new store openings, under the heading "Competitive Store Additions in Staples Markets," only Office Depot and OfficeMax store openings were listed. No other entity was listed as a competitor. In a similar vein, it is clear that Staples did not view mail-order firms, independent stationers, or other nonsuperstore-format vendors of office supplies as price-constraining influences.

tors to Staples in geographic markets that have no other OSS rivals, such non-OSS suppliers are not significant competitors to Staples in geographic markets where Staples faces other OSS competitors, that is, in the markets that the FTC thought were relevant to analyzing this merger.

The FTC's econometric analysis supported the conclusion that non-OSS competitors do not constrain OSS pricing in geographic markets where two or three OSS chains are present. Indeed, simulations of the effects of eliminating individual non-OSS retailers from such markets showed that none of those retailers (except Best Buy, which had tried and failed to implement an OSS-type format, and had effectively exited by the time of the merger) had any statistically significant effect on Staples' prices.

Further evidence of differences between OSS firms and other office supplies retailers involved price differences. In general, suppliers that compete in the same market have similar prices for the same products. If consumers can easily switch among suppliers, higher prices, adjusted for quality, will not be sustainable.[5] The FTC presented evidence that office superstores in the same geographic market tend to price office products at the same level, just as warehouse clubs in the same geographic market tend to price office products at the same level. However, prices for office products in the same geographic market often differ significantly between OSS firms as a group and warehouse clubs as a group.[6]

4. *Econometric evidence supported an OSS product market.* Under the *Merger Guidelines,* the relevant product market in this case turned on the following question: Would a merger to monopoly among the OSS chains in a city allow the merged entity to raise the prices of consumable office supplies by 5 percent or more? If the answer is yes, then "office supplies sold through office superstores" is a relevant market under the *Guidelines.*

The FTC addressed this question by constructing a large-scale econometric model of prices for office supplies. The analysis was designed to determine how Staples' prices varied from one store to another as a function of the number of nearby Office Depot or OfficeMax stores, the number and identity of potential nonsuperstore rivals such as discount mass merchandisers or warehouse club stores, and differences in costs and demand conditions across local markets. The FTC had weekly data from the parties, for over eighteen months, covering more than 400 Staples stores in

---

[5]When consumers are deciding among stores where they can purchase a group or bundle of products, competing stores in the same market would be expected to show a very similar price index for a representative basket of products, without necessarily showing very similar prices on individual items.

[6]A Prudential Securities survey reported that in Detroit all three OSS firms had virtually identical prices for the basket of office supplies sampled (total prices differed by from 0.4% to 2.0%). In contrast, the price of a basket of items common to any of the three OSS firms and to Best Buy was 18% to 19% higher at Best Buy (Prudential Securities, 1995, pp. 64, 67).

more than forty cities. The data included prices for a large number of individual stock-keeping units (SKUs) as well as a price index for consumable office supplies.

The FTC's analysis predicted that a merger to monopoly in markets where all three OSS firms were present would raise the price for office supplies sold through OSSs in those markets by 8.49 percent. Such an increase would not be possible if OSS firms were constrained by other retailers. These results confirmed that "consumable office supplies sold through office superstores" was a relevant market under the *Guidelines* criteria.

The Merger's Likely Anticompetitive Consequences

The FTC argued that voluminous evidence—structural, documentary, and statistical—all supported the conclusion that the combined Staples/Office Depot entity would raise prices for office supplies. As to the structural evidence, a merger between the OSS firms in a hypothetical market with many OSS chains would not necessarily have any anticompetitive effect, because the merged firm would still have many close competitors. As we have seen, however, only three OSS chains compete anywhere in the United States. Therefore, OSS market concentration would increase significantly in all local markets in which both Staples and Office Depot were present as the number of OSS competitors fell from either three to two or from two to one. The companies' own documents indicated that Office Depot was the main constraint on Staples' prices[7] and that, but for the merger, Staples planned to cut prices significantly over the next few years in response to current and future competitive pressures from Office Depot. The proposed merger would eliminate these pressures.[8] Finally, statistical analyses of the potential effects of this transaction predicted that, absent efficiencies, the merger could be expected to lead to large price increases. In addition, data from financial markets indicated that investors implicitly believed the merger would lead to significantly higher prices even after allowing for the effects of any efficiencies.

Structural Evidence: The Change in Concentration and Market Power

The structural effect of the proposed merger would have been to reduce from three to two the number of suppliers in markets where all three OSS firms would otherwise have competed and to create a monopoly in markets where only Staples and Office Depot currently competed, at least until entry by OfficeMax could reasonably be expected.

---

[7] The CEO of Staples, Tom Stemberg, testified to this point by arguing that, "Office Depot is our best competitor" and "our biggest competitor." Stemberg described that this "best" and "biggest" competitor posed a more severe pricing constraint upon Staples than did the third office supply superstore chain, OfficeMax.

[8] In fact, in anticipation of the merger, Staples canceled a 3% price cut on nonpaper supply items.

Table 6-1 shows Staples management's estimate for the percentage of Staples stores located in "Staples-only," "Staples and Office Depot," and "Staples, Office Depot, and OfficeMax" markets in 1995 and their projection for the year 2000. Absent the merger, Staples management anticipated a significant increase in competition from Office Depot and OfficeMax, as indicated by its projection that by 2000 markets with all three chains would account for 69 percent of Staples stores, up from 17 percent in 1995.

Therefore, the eventual effect of the merger would be to reduce the number of competitors from three to two in most geographic markets and from two to one in all but a few of the remaining geographic markets. (A small number of markets still would have only one OSS by 2000 even in the absence of the merger.)

Empirical Evidence Pointing to Likely Price Increases

In almost all merger cases before *Staples,* the DOJ or FTC relied primarily, if not exclusively, on indirect structural evidence of the kind presented above to infer that a significant price increase could be expected from that merger. *Staples* is unique, however, in terms of the large number of independent sources of strong, consistent, and direct evidence that were introduced at trial to show that prices would likely increase as a result of their merger. Five of these sources are discussed below.

Predictions of Staples' Management: Staples' own documents showed that, absent this merger, Staples' management expected that wider competition would force it to lower prices and/or raise quality. Its *1996 Strategy Update,* part of the FTC's trial evidence, forecasted that the percentage of three-player markets would increase to nearly 70 percent by the year 2000. It went on to predict that this could intensify the pressure on Staples' prices and also lead to greater operating expenses as a result of a higher service quality and higher marketing expenditures.

TABLE 6-1
Percentage of Staples Stores in Staples-Only Markets, Two-OSS Markets, and Three-OSS Markets

Year	Staples Only	Staples & Office Depot	Staples & OfficeMax	All Three	Total
1995	17%	29%	37%	17%	100%
2000	12%	7%	12%	69%	100%

Source: Plaintiff's Exhibit 15, p. 32.

Staples also predicted that, absent the merger, its retail margins, averaged over its entire sales (i.e., arranged not just over consumable office supplies and not just over markets where it faced competition from Office Depot) would decline by 150 basis points ("bps"), or 1.50 percentage points, by the year 2000 as a result of increased competitive pressure (ibid., p. 66). Of that margin fall, 60 bps would come from markets where Staples competed only with Office Depot and reflected Staples goal (absent the merger) to eliminate the price differences on nonpaper supply items between Staples and Office Depot.

Internal Comparisons of Prices Across Local Markets: Statistical data generated during the ordinary course of business by the companies showed that, on average, both Staples and Office Depot priced significantly lower when they confronted each other in local markets. As shown in Table 6-2, Staples' office supplies prices were 11.6 percent lower in markets occupied by Staples and Office Depot than in Staples-only markets; they were 4.9 percent lower in markets with all three OSSs than in markets where Staples faced only OfficeMax. Competition between Staples and Office Depot also had a significant restraining effect on Office Depot prices.These data could be used to infer the likely increases in prices after the merger (on the assumption that Staples' price patterns would dominate): +11.6 percent for the markets where premerger there was a Staples-Office Depot duopoly (accounting for 29% of Staples' stores); and +4.9 percent for the markets where premerger all three OSSs were present (accounting for 17% of Staples' stores).

Estimates from Econometric Analysis: The FTC performed an econometric analysis using store-level price data to estimate how prices differed across markets depending on the number and identity of firms in a

TABLE 6-2
Average Price Differentials for Office Superstore Products, Differing Market Structures

Benchmark OSS Market Structure	Comparison OSS Market Structure	Price Reduction
Staples only	Staples + Office Depot	11.6%
Staples + Office Max	Staples + Office Max + Office Depot	4.9%
Office Depot only	Office Depot + Staples	8.6%
Office Depot + Office Max	Office Depot + Office Max + Staples	2.5%

market.[9] In essence, this econometric analysis was a more formal and complete analysis of the kind of data just discussed. Using these estimates, the FTC calculated the overall price effects of the proposed merger: an average of 7.3 percent for the two- and three-firm markets where the merger partners were both present.

Estimates from the Prudential Study: A Prudential Securities (1996) study reported the results of a pricing survey that compared prices for office supplies at office superstores in Totowa, New Jersey, a three-player market, and in Paramus, New Jersey, a nearby (25-minute drive) two-player market (Staples and OfficeMax). The survey showed that prices, especially on visible general office supply products, were more competitive in three-player markets than in two-player markets. In particular, the survey found that Staples' prices on a basket of general office supplies that included the most visible items on which the office supply superstores typically offer attractive prices were 5.8 percent lower in three-player Totowa than in two-player Paramus.

Estimates from a Stock-Market Event-Probability Study: Financial market investors vote with their dollars (or bet) on whether a merger will raise or lower prices. A merger that raises market prices will benefit both the merging parties and their rivals and thus raise the prices for all their shares. Conversely, suppose the financial community expects the efficiencies from a merger to be so large that the merged firm will drive down market prices. In this case, the share values of the merging firms' rivals would fall when the probability of the merger goes up. Thus, evidence from financial markets can be used to predict market price effects when significant merger-related efficiencies are alleged.[10]

An FTC expert analyzed the effect of the proposed merger on the share price of OfficeMax and concluded that, if consummated, the merger would raise the value of OfficeMax's shares by 12 percent. This estimate was not only statistically highly significant and quantitatively large, but also well within the range (9–15%) of the effect that the merger was estimated to have on the combined values of Staples and Office Depot. Thus, the financial community was betting that the proposed merger would raise

---

[9]The statistical analysis was based on a large sample of store-level price data, drawn from 428 Staples stores in the United States over the twenty-three-month period from February 1995 to December 1996. The model examined statistically how Staples' prices varied with the extent of OSS competition, the presence of non-OSS firms (such as Wal-Mart, K-Mart, Target, and Best Buy), and potentially location-specific cost and demographic variables. See Baker (1997) for an extensive discussion of the econometric studies that examined the extent of localized competition between the merging firms.

[10]For a survey of the event study literature that includes definitions of the terms used in event studies and a discussion of the common methodologies, see MacKinlay (1997).

the prices charged by all superstores and would not reduce the merged firms' costs relative to OfficeMax's costs.

The FTC expert used two different approaches for the event-probability study. The first approach (described more fully in McGuckin, Warren Boulton, and Waldstein, 1992) involved an analysis of abnormal stock returns during the entire ten-month period following the announcement of the merger. The second approach involved an analysis of abnormal stock price changes during separate, shorter time periods ("event windows") when merger-related events are known to have occurred.[11] The estimated effects of each event on each firm's stock price (and for Staples and Office Depot combined) were then averaged over all six events, with each event weighted by its effect on the expected probability of the merger actually occurring.[12]

The results of the two approaches were quite similar: The investment community perceived that the merger would harm Staples' shareholders (who suffered a critical loss of about 7–9%), would benefit Office Depot's shareholders (who received a gain of 33–40%), and would increase the combined market value of Staples and Office Depot assets by 9–15 percent. Most important, the $200-million estimated increase in the value of Office-Max was consistent with the increase in OfficeMax profits that a 6.7 percent price increase for office supplies would generate in markets where Office-Max competed with both Staples and Office Depot. This price increase was close to, or consistent with, the merger-related price increase predicted from price comparisons across markets.

Finally, the merger was found to have little or no effect on the share values of other retailers of office supplies. This indicates that investors regarded these firms as competing less closely than OfficeMax with Staples and Office Depot.

Entry

Potential Entry of Other OSS Firms Did not Constrain the Incumbents

The FTC argued that the threat of entry by a new OSS supplier would not prevent the merger from raising prices until such entry actually occurred. A potential entrant would assess the profitability of entry on the

---

[11] The events were: the merger announcement plus a two-week window; the expiration of the FTC second request period; the end of the waiting period for the FTC second request; the decision by the Commission to oppose the merger, closely followed by an announcement that the parties had reached an agreement with OfficeMax that they believed would satisfy the Commission's concerns (which involved the sale of a substantial number of stores to OfficeMax); the FTC's decision to reject the proposed fix and proceed with its challenge of the merger; and the District Court's decision.

[12] For the methodology for estimating the merger probability, see McGuckin, Warren-Boulton, and Waldstein (1992).

basis of what it expected prices to be after its entry, not before. Therefore, as long as incumbents could adjust their prices rapidly in response to entry, pre-entry prices would be irrelevant to the entry decision. And, since incumbents could not deter entry by keeping prices below the pre-entry profit-maximizing level, the best pricing strategy would be to "make hay while the sun shines." In other words, "investing" in entry deterrence by maintaining low prices was not a profitable strategy for incumbents.

Under certain conditions, however, potential competition can affect the prices of the incumbents. Usually, this requires both low sunk costs of entry and an inability on the part of incumbents to reduce their prices rapidly in response to entry.[13] These conditions, however, were not present in the OSS industry. To the contrary, a significant share of entry costs into a local area was sunk costs, and incumbents could adjust their prices quite rapidly in response to entry. Therefore, prices of office superstore products could not be affected by potential entry.

This conclusion was supported by evidence in the documents. (For example, according to Thomas Stemberg, the CEO of Staples, Staples had not changed its prices in anticipation of entry by rivals.) The documents also showed that, when Staples considered entering a local market, it did not look at the prices in that market, but rather at the number of competitors.

Significant Barriers to Entry

While an individual office superstore could take advantage of store-level economies of scale and scope, a chain of superstores could also take advantage of economies of multistore operation. The latter economies appeared at different levels for different functions. Economies of scale in advertising, for example, clearly appeared at the local and regional levels. Thus, Staples' strategy for entry into a large urban market consisted of first establishing a number of stores in the periphery and advertising only in local suburban papers until a critical mass was reached sufficient to make advertising in the large metropolitan newspaper or on television economical. For major markets, this implied a critical, minimum efficient scale of operation (a minimum number of stores) at the local level, with economies of scale or multistore operation that could extend into the regional level. The effect of such economies of scale on entry was described by Stemberg (1996, p. 59):

> By building these networks [of stores] in these big markets like New York and Boston, we have kept competitors out for a very, very long period of time. Office Depot only came to metro New York in late 1995. They're

---

[13]If sunk costs are low (or firms are able to enter into long-term contracts with customers before actually entering) and incumbent suppliers are not able to change their prices quickly in response to entry, then the incumbents may not wish to encourage entry or to risk a significant loss of market share if entry occurs by maintaining high pre-entry prices.

not in New York with any meaningful presence, they're not in Boston, and they're not in Philadelphia or anywhere in between. One of the reasons is that we have a very, very good network and it's really tough to steal the customer from a direct competitor when you don't have the economies of advertising leverage.

Stemberg's description of Staples' strategy to deter entry in its home base was similar: "Staples was trying to build a critical mass of stores in the Northeast to shut out competitors and make it cost-effective to advertise in the region's high-cost media" (p. 61).

Some economies of scale in advertising even extend to the national level, perhaps due to a better ability to use network television advertising. Such economies give Staples a stronger incentive to enter markets where Office Depot and OfficeMax are already present, since this reduces advertising costs per dollar of revenues for Staples by increasing the total number of stores and the sales over which such costs can be spread.

All three OSS chains assess prospective new markets in terms of the existing numbers of OSS firms and the demand for additional OSS locations. Markets that have little or no "room" for additional stores are said to be "saturated."[14] Because multiple-store entry is typically necessary to enter a given metropolitan market, markets that are already saturated or nearly saturated are difficult to enter. An Office Depot document listed every market (as defined by Office Depot) in the United States and gave the total number of existing Office Depot, Staples, and OfficeMax stores, as well as estimates of the total number of OSS locations each area could support. The Office Depot estimates implied that, in many major markets in the United States today, there is insufficient demand for new office supply superstores to allow an entrant to achieve competitive-scale economies. In short, the time has passed for a new chain to enter by building a significant number of stores in a new market without creating a glut of superstore capacity or locations. Thus, a firm currently attempting to enter cannot do so under the profitable conditions that the three incumbents faced in the past.

Efficiencies Were Not Sufficient to Offset Price Increases

The FTC argued that the efficiency claims made by the merger parties were exaggerated for several reasons. First, only efficiencies that are merger specific should be credited; that is, efficiencies likely to be achieved absent a proposed merger are irrelevant to the analysis of that merger. In this case, much of the anticipated efficiency gains were the result of the merged firm's increased scale. This in turn raised several questions: (1) Given the rate at

[14] The parties defined "store potential" as the maximum number of OSS firms that can be supported in a given market, given existing market conditions, and defined the ratio of the number of OSS firms in a market to store potential as the degree of "market saturation."

which the parties were growing independently, many scale-related efficiencies could be expected in a short time through internal growth. (2) Achieving economies of scale in procurement does not require the expansion in retail operations that a merger would bring. Procurement cost reductions can be achieved by expanding sales through mail order or contract stationer operations, and both Office Depot and Staples had expanded such operations before their merger announcement. Thus, even if the parties had presented evidence to show that past expansions had lowered procurement costs, this would not have established that the claimed efficiencies were merger-specific. (3) Scale economies seldom continue indefinitely. Thus, particularly in the case of procurement costs, Staples and Office Depot may already be large enough to achieve the maximum sustainable price discounts that their suppliers can offer.

The second reason for the FTC's skepticism as to the parties' efficiency claims was the lack of support by reliable evidence. In particular, the efficiency claims made by the parties increased dramatically between the time that the deal was first approved by the Staples' board and the time that the parties submitted an efficiencies analysis to the FTC. Because it was not clear what new information or insights the parties gained in that time period, there was a strong presumption that the substantially lower cost-saving estimates first presented to the Staples board were more reliable.

Third, under the *Guidelines,* efficiency gains are relevant only insofar as they result in a lower price to consumers. The share of any cost reductions that is passed on by a profit-maximizing firm increases with the proportion of those cost reductions that is attributable to variable (rather than fixed) costs; with the competitiveness of the industry; and with the share of firms in the market to which the cost reductions apply. In this case, the proposed merger would have substantially reduced competition. Further, any cost savings would have been limited to the merged firm. Therefore, historical estimates of the share of cost savings that the parties had passed on to consumers would significantly overstate the share of any merger-specific cost savings that would be passed on.

Specifically, the FTC's analysis showed that the merger would bring true efficiencies that were the equivalent of only 1.4 percent of sales and that only a seventh of these cost savings would be passed through to consumers. Thus, the net price effect of the merger would be substantial: the 7.3-percent price increase predicted by the FTC's econometric model of pricing, less an efficiency pass-through of 0.2 percent (= 1.4% x 0.15), for a net increase of 7.1 percent.

THE DEFENDANTS' ARGUMENTS

Staples and Office Depot argued that the merger would not have anti-competitive consequences. Their defense focused on two main arguments:

(1) the FTC's product market definition was erroneous; and (2) regardless of the market definition, the efficiencies from the merger, ease of entry into OSS retailing, and the defendants' track record of lowering prices after their past acquisitions of other OSS firms all indicated that the merger would not raise prices.[15] Either of these two arguments, if accepted, would have disproved the FTC's argument that the proposed merger would lead to a substantial lessening of competition in the relevant antitrust market.

Market Definition

The defense vigorously challenged the FTC's claim that OSS firms constituted a relevant market for antitrust purposes. Staples and Office Depot argued that the FTC's market definition was based exclusively on the *identity* of the seller and not on the *characteristics* of the product or service supplied by sellers. The respondents claimed that OSS firms were part of a broad market for retailing office supplies in which they held a low share. An OSS firm was constrained in its pricing not just by other OSS firms, but by all office product retailers.

The defendants argued that a retail product market is defined by the nature of the product being retailed; since office supplies sold by an OSS are not different from those sold by other retailers, both types of retailers are in the same market. The fact that OSS chains use different retail formats implies that they have found a particularly good way of competing with other retailers and does not imply that other retailers are in a different market. Thus, the defendants rejected the notion that office superstores supply a distinct bundle of goods and retail services that would enable a monopoly OSS to raise OSS prices.

The defendants also rejected the FTC's argument that Staples' and Office Depot's own documents define OSS firms as "the competition" and "the market." Citing a previous court decision, they argued that the term "market" does not necessarily mean the same thing to a company and to an antitrust agency. Further, they contested the FTC's use of selected passages in Staples and Office Depot documents as evidence in this regard: they claimed that other passages in the same documents used the term "market" also to include non-OSS firms. The defendants submitted exhibits showing that each regularly checked the prices of non-OSS firms, such as Wal-Mart, Viking, Best Buy, and Comp USA, along with the prices of other OSS firms. According to the defense, this illustrated the intense competition between OSS and non-OSS firms. As another illustration, the defense submitted a study that showed that the sales of a Staples

[15]The defense cited two past acquisitions as examples of the two companies' record of lowering their prices after a merger. According to the defense, the price of office supplies had fallen in each of the respective areas after Office Depot's acquisition of Office Club in Dallas, Texas, and Staples' acquisition of HQ Office Supplies Warehouse in Los Angeles, California (both in 1991).

store would fall by 1.4 percent with the opening of a new computer super-store, 2.4 percent with a new Wal-Mart, 3.7 percent with a new warehouse club, and 7.2 percent with a new Best Buy.

Efficiencies and the Net Price Effect

The defense claimed that OSS firms were founded on the principle of providing low prices through large sales volume. Thus, the defendants argued, the merger would increase the total volume of their (combined) purchases and lower the prices that they paid to manufacturers of office supplies. They also claimed that the merger would lower administrative, marketing, advertising, and distribution costs. Under the defense's assumption that the merged entity would pass on to consumers two-thirds of the cost reductions, Staples and Office Depot would be able to cut prices significantly after the merger.

The defendants disputed the FTC's argument that much of their claimed efficiencies could be achieved absent the merger. Moreover, they argued, even if some of those efficiencies could eventually be achieved through internal expansion, a merger would allow those efficiencies to be achieved much faster.

The defendants submitted an econometric study that suggested that Office Depot had a relatively small effect on Staples' pricing and that a merger between the two would (absent efficiencies) increase prices for consumable office supplies by only 2.4 percent (compared with the FTC's estimate of 7.3%) at Staples stores in markets with both Staples and Office Depot present, by 1.3 percent when averaged over office supplies at all Staples stores, or by 0.8 percent when averaged over all products and all Staples stores. The defendants also argued that, based on their estimate of cost savings and of the proportion that would be passed through to consumers (0.67% versus the FTC's estimate of 0.15%), the efficiency gains alone would cause prices to be lower by 3 percent over all Staples' products and stores. Thus, the net effect of the merger would be to *reduce* the prices faced by the average Staples customer by 2.2 percent (0.8–3.0% = –2.2%).

No Barriers to Entry and Ease of Expansion

The defendants argued that entry into the office supplies business was easy. Stores could be constructed within months, and sunk costs were low because the product did not decay and there were no fashion crazes.[16] In addition, OfficeMax had increased its planned new store openings in 1997, demonstrating ease of expansion by existing competitors. Finally, entry or

---

[16]Two examples offered to demonstrate the ease of entry were U.S. Office Products Co. and Corporate Express. Office Products had been founded recently (in 1994); both firms had expanded rapidly by acquiring small local dealers; their sales had also increased fast within the past few years.

expansion did not necessarily entail costly new store openings: existing multiproduct retailers could enter, or expand into, the office supplies business by increasing the share of the shelf space they allocated to office supply items.[17]

Public and Private Equities

The defense argued that blocking the merger would impose losses on both consumers and shareholders. The main consumer benefits from the merger that would be lost were the claimed efficiencies and lower prices discussed above; in addition, the combined company would be able to expand faster than either could individually, creating value for customers and for the U.S. economy. Any cost savings not passed on to consumers would benefit the shareholders of Staples and Office Depot. Finally, the defense argued that there was no need for a temporary restraining order or a preliminary injunction to stop the merger because the merger was reversible. If post-merger evidence demonstrated an anticompetitive effect, the merged entity could always be split back into two separate companies.

JUDGE HOGAN'S DECISION

The court agreed with the FTC and granted a preliminary injunction. Judge Thomas F. Hogan first noted that the law required the FTC to show only a reasonable probability of harm to competition to obtain a preliminary injunction. In his decision, Judge Hogan defined the relevant product market as the OSS submarket and found that Staples and Office Depot would have a "dominant market share" (between 45 percent and 100 percent) in many geographic markets after the merger. He also concluded that FTC's pricing evidence demonstrated a reasonable likelihood of anticompetitive effects.

The judge noted that neither the public nor the private equities claimed by the defendants were sufficient to offset the likely anticompetitive effects.[18]

The Product Market

The court found that the sale of consumable office supplies by office superstores was a submarket within a larger market of all office supply re-

---

tailers.[19] Baker (1997) discusses the judge's opinion on the product market in light of the April 8, 1997, revised *Merger Guidelines* and concludes that the court's "hidden opinion" treats the submarket argument as "a legal hook for reaching unilateral competitive effects from a merger among the sellers of close substitutes."

Judge Hogan recognized that it was difficult to overcome the "initial gut reaction" to the definition of the product market as the sale of consumable office supplies through office superstores. Since the products sold by OSS firms are the same as the products sold by non-OSS retailers, "it is logical" to conclude that all these retailers compete. However, he noted, a firm could be a competitor in the "overall marketplace" without also being included in the relevant antitrust market.[20] He found plausible the FTC's argument that a small but significant increase in one superstore's prices would not cause a large number of its customers to switch to non-OSS retailers; instead, those customers would turn primarily to another OSS.[21]

The judge observed that office superstores were very different from other office supply retailers in terms of appearance, size, format, the number and variety of items offered, and the type of customers targeted. While it was "difficult fully to articulate and explain all of the ways in which superstores are unique," he found that: "No one entering a Wal-Mart would mistake it for an office superstore. No one entering Staples or Office Depot would mistakenly think he or she was in Best Buy or CompUSA. You certainly know an office superstore when you see one."[22] He argued that this is one practical indication for the OSS firms' constituting a submarket within a larger market.

Another practical indication for determining the presence of a submarket was "the industry or public recognition of the submarket as a

---

[19]In reference to submarkets within a market, the court decision cited the Supreme Court in *Brown Shoe*: Well-defined submarkets may exist that, in themselves, constitute product markets for antitrust purposes, and it is necessary to examine the effects of a merger in each such economically significant submarket to determine if there is a reasonable probability that the merger will substantially lessen competition. *Brown Shoe* defined several practical indicia to determine the presence of a submarket within a broader market, which Judge Hogan used to determine whether OSS chains constitute a submarket. See *Brown Shoe* v. *United States,* 370 U.S. 294 (1962).

[20]The court cited the notion of functional interchangeability in *Du Pont* (referring to interchangeability between cellophane and other wrapping materials) and *Archer-Daniels-Midland* (referring to interchangeability between sugar and corn syrup) cases. Noting that the *Staples* case is an example of perfect functional interchangeability in the sense that a legal pad sold by Staples or Office Depot is functionally interchangeable with a legal pad sold by Wal-Mart, it recognized that the analysis should go further and look at the cross-elasticity of demand between products, again citing the *Du Pont* case. See *U.S.* v. *E. I. Du Pont de Nemours and Co.,* 351 U.S., 377 (1956); and *U.S.* v. *Archer-Daniels-Midland Co.,* 866 F.2d 242 (1988).

[21]The court did note some limitations of the data underlying the FTC's individual analyses, and it further noted that the FTC could be criticized for looking at only brief snapshots in time or for considering only a limited number of items, but it concluded that taken together, there was sufficient evidence for a low cross-elasticity of demand between the consumable office supplies sold by the superstores and those sold by other retailers.

[22]*Federal Trade Commission* v. *Staples, Inc.,* No. 97-701 (1997).

separate economic entity." The judge found that the FTC had offered "abundant evidence" from the merging companies' internal documents that they evaluated their competition as other OSS firms and interacted with other OSS firms in making long-term plans. While Staples and Office Depot did not completely ignore non-OSS retailers, there was sufficient evidence that showed that Staples and Office Depot consider other OSS firms as their main competition.

Likely Effect on Competition

The judge was convinced that the proposed merger would likely have anti-competitive effects. He reached this conclusion from two pieces of evidence. First, having accepted the FTC's product market definition, he found the concentration statistics to be a source of serious concern.[23] After the merger, a combined Staples-Office Depot entity would have a dominant market share in many local geographic markets.[24]

Second, the pricing evidence showed that an OSS was likely to raise its prices when it faced less competition from other OSS firms. Furthermore, without the merger, Staples and Office Depot would probably enter into each other's markets and reduce prices. The merger would mean that these future benefits from increased competition would never be realized.

Entry

In a market defined as office supplies sold through superstores, the court focused on the entry of new OSS firms, not just any office products retailer. To achieve economies of scale and be profitable, a new OSS would have to open many stores and incur high sunk costs. Further, an entrant could not easily achieve economies of scale at the local level because many of the OSS markets were already saturated by existing OSS firms. The judge found it extremely unlikely that a new OSS would enter the market and counterbalance the anticompetitive effects of the merger.[25]

---

[23]The pre-merger Herfindahl-Hirschman Index for the least concentrated market, Grand Rapids-Muskegon-Holland, Michigan, was close to 3600, whereas for the most concentrated market, Washington, D.C., the pre-merger HHI was about 7000.

[24]The combined market share would be 100% in fifteen metropolitan areas. In addition, in twenty-seven other metropolitan areas where the number of OSS firms would drop from three to two, the combined Staples-Office Depot market share would be above 45%. The HHI would rise on average by 2715 points because of the merger.

[25]As for the expansion of non-OSS suppliers into the OSS markets, the judge noted that it was unlikely that they would undo the merger's anticompetitive effects. Specifically, the expansions by U.S. Office Products and Wal-Mart would be unlikely to constrain a potential increase in the prices of the merged entity. In relation to the defense's argument that existing retailers could simply expand into the office products business by reallocating shelf space, the judge reasoned that while these retailers certainly had the power to do so, there was no evidence that they in fact would, following a 5% (small but significant) increase in the prices of the merged entity.

Efficiencies

The judge noted that under the law it is unclear whether efficiencies constitute a viable defense. He stated that even if efficiencies can provide a legal defense in principle, in this case the defendants had not shown efficiencies sufficient to refute the FTC's presumption of anticompetitive effects from the merger. He found that the defense's estimates of the efficiencies were unreliable, unverified, and unrealistic. Among other problems, the defendants did not distinguish between merger-specific and other kinds of efficiencies, and given Staples' historical pass-through rates their assumption that two-thirds of the cost savings would be passed through to the customers was unrealistic.[26]

CONCLUSION

The FTC's victory in *Staples* came as a surprise to many observers. The casual empirical facts—there were many retailers of office supplies, and Staples and Office Depot together accounted for only a small percentage of the aggregate sales of such products—seemed determinative.

But the FTC's careful marshalling of the data—especially, its use of the price data to show that the office superstores were a separate market—proved important in convincing the Commission itself and then Judge Hogan that the merger would be anticompetitive. It seems likely that these kinds of data, which have become readily available from the scanner technology that has become common in retailing, will become increasingly important in the legal judgments related to mergers involving retailers or manufacturers of goods that are sold primarily at retail.

REFERENCES

Baker, Jonathan B. "Econometric Analysis in *FTC* v. *Staples.*" Prepared remarks before American Bar Association's Antitrust Section, Economics Committee, July 18, 1997.

Federal Trade Commission v. *Staples, Inc.,* No. 97-701 (1997).

MacKinlay, A. Craig. "Event Studies in Economics and Finance." *Journal of Economic Literature* 35 (March 1997): 13–39.

McGuckin, Robert H., Frederick R. Warren Boulton, and Peter Waldstein. "The Use of Stock Market Returns in Antitrust Analysis of Mergers." *Review of Industrial Organization* 7 (1992): 1–11.

---

[26]Historically, Staples passed through 15–17% of its cost savings to customers, as estimated by the FTC's econometric analysis. For a discussion of the FTC's estimation of the extent to which the merged firm would pass on cost savings from the acquisition to buyers, see Baker (1997).

Prudential Securities. *Office Supply Superstores: Industry Update,* October 3, 1995.

Prudential Securities. *Office Supply Superstores: Industry Update,* March 28, 1996.

Stemberg, Thomas G., ed. *Staples for Success: From Business Plan to Billion-Dollar Business in Just a Decade.* Santa Monica, Calif.: Knowledge Exchange, 1996.

U.S. Department of Justice and the Federal Trade Commission. *Horizontal Merger Guidelines,* 1992.

PART 2

Horizontal
Practices

The Economic and
Legal Context

Anticompetitive horizontal practices may occur in any market setting, from atomistic firms to oligopolies and dominant firms. Although atomistic firms are likely to achieve low costs and prices, such firms may engage in explicit price fixing or some form of implicit coordination of behavior to enhance their profitability. Oligopolists and dominant firms have an even wider range of possible behavior from which they may choose. They, too, may cooperate or collude with their rivals, but they may also undertake deliberately aggressive actions against actual or potential rivals to enhance their market power.

The antitrust laws address this spectrum of anticompetitive conduct. Section 1 of the Sherman Act forbids any "contract, combination, . . . or conspiracy in restraint of trade . . . ," language intended to prevent collusion among firms. Section 2 of that act prohibits actions that would "monopolize, or attempt to monopolize . . ." a market. This is directed at deliberately hostile acts designed unfairly to achieve or maintain market dominance. Section 5 of the Federal Trade Commission Act encompasses all of this in its ban on "unfair methods of competition."

Issues of horizontal practice differ from the problems addressed in Part 1 of this book. There, market structure changed as firms merged or formed joint ventures, and in the process the nature of competition in the industry may have been altered. The practices discussed in this section are not the result of any structural change in an industry. Rather, they represent behavior patterns that arise within a given industrial structure, as firms seek to increase their profitability either through closer cooperation with horizontal competitors or through excessive aggression against one or more of them.

Ten cases in this book illustrate the wide variety of such practices. Four cases in this part involve allegations of cooperative action among firms; two cases focus on allegations of aggressive conduct—either predatory or exclusionary—by a single entity to achieve or defend an advantageous market position; one case involves both collusion and predation. Three additional cases in Part 3 are concerned with anticompetitive conduct by dominant firms or oligopolists where the suspect conduct primarily involves vertical or complementary products. To understand all of these more fully, we begin with some background on the practices themselves.

COLLUSION AND COOPERATION

Economic Theory

A simple demonstration in microeconomic theory shows how a cartel of firms can achieve the monopoly price level by means of collusion. Where this occurs, the usual deadweight loss arises, and, in addition, firms may fail to minimize their costs. But in one important respect, the adverse efficiency consequences of a cartel may be even worse than under pure monopoly. Colluding firms are far less likely to be able to achieve any actual cost savings from scale economies, for example, since they remain separate firms with distinct production facilities. By contrast, as discussed in the previous section, merging firms may be able to conserve on fixed costs or achieve other cost savings that allow them to claim an offset to any adverse price effects.

Also as noted above, success in efforts to collude is by no means certain. Cartels and cooperating firms generally must be able to resolve two issues: reaching an agreement, and maintaining the agreement by detecting and deterring cheating. Without both, any effort at collusion will soon fail. Firms' probability of success is a function of numerous underlying conditions related to demand, the product, and the market. These include at least the following specific factors: the number of firms, their size distribution, entry conditions, cost similarity or differences among firms, product differentiation, order pattern (small and frequent vs. large and infrequent), knowledge of rivals' prices, demand stability, and cost structure (fixed vs. variable costs).[1]

Where conditions are especially favorable, firms may succeed in "tacit coordination"—that is, spontaneous cooperation resulting from strongly perceived interdependence. But in most circumstances, one or more factors may represent serious impediments to purely tacit cooperation. In these instances, firms are confronted with the choice of accepting merely competitive profit levels or undertaking some stronger cooperative action. In the most unfavorable circumstances, firms' only alternative to more competitive profitability may be outright collusion. For example, if firm numbers are large, perceived interdependence is likely to be weak and nothing short of

---

[1]For discussion of these factors, see, for example, Scherer and Ross (1990).

explicit agreement will suffice (and indeed, even that may fail). Thus, economic theory would predict that cases of explicit conspiracy are likely to arise where conditions are distinctly unfavorable and looser forms of cooperation will not suffice. The evidence in fact supports that prediction (Hay and Kelley, 1974).

In some circumstances, although spontaneous cooperation may not succeed, explicit conspiracy may not be necessary either. Where feasible, firms can be expected to adopt or develop some mechanism to help them sustain a measure of cooperation—a so-called "facilitating practice" or device. For example, "most favored customer" clauses may play this role by reducing each seller's incentive to cut prices. Long-term customer contracts and exit fees from contracts may insulate existing sellers from new competitors and prevent existing firms from bidding away each other's customers. Advance announcements of price changes or rapid ex post dissemination of information about such changes may assist oligopolists' efforts to come to an agreement on and to maintain prices.[2]

Each of these mechanisms may facilitate anticompetitive outcomes in the market. From a policy perspective these have the advantage of being easier to address with remedial action than are, say, the underlying conditions that give rise to purely tacit coordination. The dilemma for policy in this area is that most of these facilitating practices also have benign or pro-competitive explanations and therefore cannot simply be prohibited. Disentangling these two possibilities remains a major challenge for economics and policy.

Although perfect collusion may be extremely difficult to achieve, it should be stressed that perfection is not necessary for a cartel's "success." Sellers in an industry may be considerably better off simply by moderating the rivalry among themselves, even if full monopoly cooperation is not achieved. Moreover, in the case of a dominant firm and for some other market structures as well, cooperation among all firms is unnecessary for above-competitive pricing. A single leading firm or core of cooperating firms may be able to raise price by reducing their own output. That will be possible if the supply elasticity of the fringe of nonparticipating firms is low enough (or product differentiation strong enough) and longer-run expansion and entry slow enough so that price may rise without inducing very large output increases.[3] Although the dominant firm or core would surely prefer fringe firms' cooperation in order to spread the burden of output contraction, the leading firm or core of firms may nonetheless find unilateral action advantageous.

Economic literature does predict that pursuit of higher prices is likely

[2]Discussion of some of these practices can be found in Salop (1986).

[3]This model of the declining dominant firm was first set out by Worcester (1957). The modern version is due to Gaskins (1971), from which has followed a substantial literature. For a survey, see Encaoua, Geroski, and Jacquemin (1986).

to result in the erosion of the market share and profitability of a dominant firm, as new entry and expansion lead over time to the decline of its position. That outcome, of course, does not indicate failure of the dominant firm's strategy, since the alternative may be merely competitive profits. In addition, it does not imply that the erosion will be sufficiently fast to make policy action moot. It does illustrate, however, the temporal limits to market power.

Antitrust

The longest-standing precedent in all of U.S. antitrust policy may be the per se prohibition on explicit price fixing among competitors. A per se approach requires showing only that the actions or events occurred; the accused firms cannot offer any justification for the actions and so must dispute what actually occurred. Beginning with the *Trans-Missouri Freight Association* case[4] and strongly affirmed in the *Trenton Potteries* decision,[5] the Supreme Court has ruled that horizontal price fixing constitutes this type of automatic violation of the Sherman Act's ban on "contracts, combinations and conspiracies in restraint of trade." This approach stems from a literal reading of Section 1 of the Act, but it is also an efficient rule for certain types of conduct.

Per se prohibition is an appropriate policy stance in any of three circumstances: where the action *always* has adverse consequences; where it always has either adverse *or* at best neutral consequences; or where it *almost* always has adverse or neutral consequences and its positive outcomes are both infrequent and difficult to distinguish. Each of the first two cases represents fairly clear grounds for a per se rule, since neither prohibits beneficial actions.[6] The third case is more problematic in that it concedes the possibility of occasional policy error—attacking beneficial actions. The justification is that these outcomes are relatively few and very costly to identify. A "perfect" rule in these circumstances would be very costly to administer (all possible cases would have to be fully examined), and the result might not be correct categorization in any event.

Given the earlier economic discussion, the court's per se approach to horizontal price fixing would seem entirely appropriate. To be sure, the courts have muddied the waters a bit by some minor inconsistencies in their treatment of price fixing, notably in the Depression-era *Appalachian Coals* decision.[7] Yet over its long history this branch of antitrust policy has been largely free of ambiguity.

---

[4]*United States* v. *Trans-Missouri Freight Association,* 166 U.S. 290 (1897).

[5]*United States* v. *Trenton Potteries Co. et al.,* 273 U.S. 392 (1927).

[6] The second may not be entirely free of controversy insofar as it occasionally attacks actions that have no anticompetitive effects.

[7]*Appalachian Coals Inc.* v. *U.S.,* 288 U.S. 344 (1933).

More recently, the courts have been presented with substantial arguments on the benefits—indeed, the necessity—of allowing direct competitors in certain circumstances to coordinate prices or other matters. Generally, those circumstances arise when a product would otherwise not be offered at all. For example, transactions costs or some other impediment causes a market failure that can be remedied only by interfirm coordination. Beginning with the *ASCAP* case,[8] the Supreme Court has accepted this logical possibility and in those cases in fact has allowed price coordination.

One logical consequence of this exception to the per se ban is that companies being investigated for price coordination may now argue that they fall within the exception. Such was the case in the *NCAA* case and to some extent in the MIT financial aid case in this part.[9] In principle this approach might require the enforcement agencies and courts first to decide whether the exception applies before applying the per se rule in any matter, thus threatening to undermine the per se approach altogether. In an effort to prevent this and to preserve the administrative ease of the per se rule, the agencies have developed a so-called "modified per se" approach toward such practices. The latter asks a series of questions designed to screen out— quickly, cheaply, and accurately—all those practices that lack any such justification, treating them under the standard per se rule and leaving only a small fraction of cases for a more comprehensive analysis.[10]

No similarly tidy approach has been found for exchanges of information that may set the stage for a tacit agreement among firms. Since neutral and even beneficial effects are possible—for example, sharing information about future demand can help correct errors by individual firms—no per se prohibition seems appropriate. Yet many such exchanges clearly can aid in the process of coordinating price, output, and capacity decisions to the detriment of consumers. Here the courts have tried to fashion rules from the particulars of each case brought before them. In the *Container Corporation* case,[11] for example, the Supreme Court struck down exchanges of price information among direct competitors when they involved customer-specific information (which is the most helpful for colluders in detecting cheating among themselves) and when industry characteristics suggested that an agreement was likely to have an adverse market effect.[12]

---

[8]*American Society of Composers, Authors, and Publishers et al. Inc. v. Columbia Broadcasting System Inc.,* 441 U.S. 1 (1979).

[9]*National Collegiate Athletic Association v. Board of Regents of the University of Oklahoma and University of Georgia Athletic Association,* 468 U.S. 85 (1984). The MIT case was part of *U.S. v. Brown University et al.,* 805 F.Supp. 288 (E.D.Pa. 1992).

[10]The first question asked is whether the practice is "inherently suspect," that is, whether absent an efficiency justification, it is automatically anticompetitive. If not, a rule of reason must be applied right away. Next asked is whether there is a plausible efficiency justification. If not, the practice is subject to per se prohibition. If there is a plausible justification, a full inquiry is required. This approach was first adopted in the FTC case, *Massachusetts Board of Registration in Optometry* (1988).

[11]*United States v. Container Corp. of America et al.,* 393 U.S. 333 (1969).

[12]Paradoxically, the Court accepted very ambiguous evidence on the likelihood of success in this case.

If the effects of a particular practice depend on the facts of each case, a so-called "rule-of-reason" must be used instead of per se. The rule of reason is appropriate when a practice may have either adverse or beneficial effects, both in significant proportion, and when it is feasible to distinguish these alternative outcomes in practice. While information exchanges fall into this category, a brief review of the courts' attempts to draw relevant distinctions illustrates the difficulties. For example, trade associations cannot take any action intended to force compliance by its members with published prices, but they are permitted to collect and disseminate considerable price information, some of it clearly helpful in efforts at coordination. Moreover, the courts have been even more reluctant to prohibit exchanges of information about nonprice matters, apparently in the belief that these are less important than price and carry less risk of coordination.

Further problems have accompanied the courts' recent efforts to judge facilitating practices—those institutional arrangements and mechanisms that promote coordination among companies without explicit agreements. These cases have involved such practices as adherence to common pricing books that reduce the complexity of pricing heterogeneous products (as in the *GE-Westinghouse* case[13]), the use of most-favored-customer clauses as incentive-altering devices (as in the *Ethyl* case[14]), and reliance on central data bases to disseminate, virtually instantaneously, information about competitors' prices (as in the *Airline Tarriff Publishing* case[15]. The courts have been willing to consider some of these as undue intrusions on the market process, but a common theme has been their insistence on guidance regarding circumstances in which these represent anticompetitive behavior as opposed to normal business practice. They have often found such guidance lacking.

From the enforcement agencies' perspective, the advantage of the facilitating practices doctrine is that it allows antitrust action against at least those instances of tacit collusion that appear to be aided by such practices. By contrast, the courts have been extremely reluctant to convict companies for purely tacit collusion, since that comes close to prohibiting conduct that seems virtually inevitable in an oligopoly setting, for example, following a rival's price change. Moreover, prohibition of purely tacit collusion may not be as straightforward as it seems, since it may not be clear, for example, whether any or all matching price responses are to be proscribed. For this reason, such cooperation has been largely outside the reach of the antitrust laws and is likely to remain so unless facilitating practices can be identified in particular cases and the courts convinced of the practicality of that approach.

---

[13]*United States* v. *General Electric Co. et al.,* C.A. No. 28,228 (E.D.Pa.), Dec. 1976.

[14]*In re Ethyl Corp. et al.,* FTC Docket no. 9128, 1975. See Case 7 in this part.

[15]*United States* v. *Airline Tariff Publishing et al.,* CA No. 92-2584 (D.D.C.), August 1994. See Case 13.

MONOPOLIZATION: PREDATION AND EXCLUSION

Economic Theory

Oligopolists and dominant firms do not always seek to "soften" competition by cooperation with their rivals. Competition may be attenuated and profits increased by any one of several aggressive actions. A firm may attempt to exclude potential entrants from its market or to drive out one or more of its rivals. Alternatively, it may seek to discipline its rivals so that while they remain in the market, their behavior will be less competitive and less constraining to the dominant firm. Various practices, going under such names as predation, selective price discrimination, exclusion, and foreclosure, may serve these objectives. Although some practices involve short-term costs, the strategies may ultimately result in enhanced market power and profitability to the dominant firm.

Of all these practices, perhaps the most extensive body of antitrust law and economic analysis concerns predatory pricing. In the classic predation story, a leading or dominant firm would lower its price (presumably by increasing output) sufficiently to impose losses on rivals. Those rivals would then exit, leaving the predator firm with unconstrained (or at least less constrained) market power and resulting in yet higher market price and additional consumer harm.

The prototypical case of such predation, together with other alleged anticompetitive practices, involved the rise of Standard Oil to dominance of petroleum markets in the late nineteenth century. There is little dispute that Standard Oil was a harsh competitor, that many rivals exited the market, and that Standard came to possess substantial market power. But much controversy has arisen as to whether the facts confirm that it did engage, or even could have engaged, in predatory pricing.[16] Many have argued that Standard was simply a tough, efficient competitor, inevitably displacing smaller and less capable companies.

Chicago School critics of the classic predation story have argued that the circumstances under which predation can succeed are very limited, that rational firms will therefore rarely attempt it, and hence that predation is not a significant policy problem. More specifically, they note that the dominant firm's larger size implies that it will incur losses proportionally greater than those of the target firm or firms, the proportion being its share relative to that of its rivals. Thus, the would-be predator is likely to injure itself more than it damages its rival. Moreover, even if successful in driving rivals out, the dominant firm will benefit from this strategy only if it has the protection of entry barriers in the postpredation period. Without such barriers, any effort by the firm to raise price will simply induce entry,

---

[16]The Supreme Court did conclude, however, that Standard Oil did engage in predation. *U.S. v. Standard Oil*, 221 U.S. 1 (1911).

and it will never earn back profits sufficient to justify the losses that it initially incurred. All of these considerations, it has been argued, make predation rarely rational (McGee, 1958).

Together with a close reexamination of past predation cases, this argument led many economists and antitrust analysts to conclude that instances of true predation are sufficiently infrequent that "true predation" can be safely ignored. While that conclusion is now understood to be too sweeping, there is widespread agreement that true predation is far less common than alleged. Most instances of alleged predation consist of rivals confronted by hard competition, often by more efficient larger firms, with adverse consequences for their own market share and profitability. But these adverse consequences for a competitor do not imply adverse consequences for competition. Thus, in a great many instances, the Chicago School's skepticism with respect to predation is fully justified.

However, recent economic analysis has demonstrated the existence of circumstances where predation may indeed be rational. Models of rational predation now include the following scenarios[17]: A dominant firm may predate in one market or against one competitor to deter competitors in other markets (if it operates in numerous markets) or in the future against competitors in the same market. Even if "irrational" when considered in isolation, such conduct may create a reputation for aggressive response that discourages any other competitors from initiating action. Another possible mechanism arises if the dominant firm has a "deeper pocket"—that is, access to greater financial resources with which to battle its rival—due to differential access to capital markets. Small firms may have to pay a premium to borrow funds, to the degree that lenders favor the prospects of the leading firm, and also to the extent that the leading firm deliberately disrupts the business prospects of smaller rivals. Most recently, some economic models have shown that a dominant firm may use pricing in an effort to convince ("signal") actual and potential rivals that it has lower costs. Even if this is not the case, rivals may decide that they would be better off tempering their actions or simply operating in some other market.

Other economists have reexamined the premises of the classic predation scenario. Whereas that story almost always has a large firm lowering its price (thereby penalizing itself greatly), the crucial elements in fact are simply (a) the ability of the would-be predator to expand output readily in order to lower price and (b) the inability of the target firm to decrease output easily and thus avoid having to produce at a loss. But those conditions can sometimes be met by a nondominant firm that may therefore be well positioned to exercise predation against a larger firm.[18]

Furthermore, the classic predation story presumes that the dominant firm simply lowers price indiscriminately in the market. This results in harm

---

[17]For extended discussion, see Ordover and Saloner (1989).

[18]For discussion of such a scenario, see Burnett's presentation of Case 10 in this part.

to the aggressor firm, and to that extent the strategy is self-deterring. By contrast, more selective price reductions targeted against particular rivals will be relatively more costly to those rivals. Such "strategic price discrimination" seeks to win sales away from one particular rival in order to blunt its encroachment in a market, to send a signal to an especially aggressive "maverick" firm, or to offer a demonstration to other rivals.[19]

In addition, price is only one of a large number of strategic variables available to an aggressive firm, and its relatively indiscriminate nature may well make it an inferior choice. This recognition has led to analyses of alternative strategies against existing rivals or against those contemplating entry. These include strategic use of advertising (Hilke and Nelson, 1984), product innovation (Ordover and Willig, 1981), product proliferation (Schmalensee, 1978), product replacement (Menge, 1962), and cost manipulation (Salop and Scheffman, 1983). Which of these might be employed depends on the circumstances—in particular, the aggressor firm's perception of the most readily exploitable weaknesses of its rivals.

Finally, the classic focus on actually forcing rivals from the market may not be the most likely scenario. A dominant firm may benefit substantially simply by convincing its rivals to act in a less competitive manner—that is, by "disciplining" them. Successful discipline consists of using any of the above strategies to modify the response function of rivals rather than necessarily forcing them from the market or requiring complete cooperation. The objective is to secure enough behavioral restraint so that the dominant firm's output contraction is no longer offset by its rivals' expansionary responses.

Closely related to the strategy of attacking present rivals are actions by a dominant firm or monopoly to exclude or foreclose potential entrants from the market. Indeed, many of the above-noted predation strategies can be applied with minor modification to firms that are contemplating entry into its market. That includes, for example, selective price discounting in niches or to customers most likely to be subject to entry, new product introduction and placement that make entry less attractive, long-term contracts with present customers to deny demand opportunities to entrants, advertising directed at specific niches and potential entrants, and so forth.

But exclusion may take somewhat different forms as well. Beginning with Spence (1977) and Dixit (1980), economists have developed a series of models demonstrating that capacity expansion may rationally be used to preempt entry opportunities. Generally, the incumbent firm uses its "first move" advantage, taking an action prior to the potential entrant's decision in an effort to affect the latter firm's decision. Early models showed how the incumbent may select capacity—therefore committing to a postentry output strategy[20]—in an amount that may leave little opportunity for

---

[19]For a possible example of this strategy, see Pittman (1984).

[20]Precisely what makes the commitment credible is an important distinguishing feature of these models.

viable entry. The result may be either no entry at all, or at worst entry at a smaller and less competitive scale. Numerous such models have now been developed, examining various assumptions and parameters giving rise to credible entry deterrence.[21]

Other exclusionary practices arise under special circumstances. An extreme case is represented by so-called "essential facilities," those for which access is necessary for effective operation in a market. A classic case is that of a single railroad terminal—a high-scale, high-cost facility for aggregating and loading or off-loading shipments on a railroad. In many locales a single such terminal represents the only efficient number, but if it is owned by the incumbent carrier, a new railroad can be denied access and therefore prevented from entering.[22] A related scenario concerns denial of membership to some organizational entity in a market where that entity is important to the provision of low-cost or high-quality service. These can range from quality certification programs to joint ventures such as real estate listing services or credit card networks.

Finally, it should be noted that exclusionary practices may arise in the context of markets that are vertically related or related with complementary products. For example, companies whose products dominate one market may seek to link purchase of that product to another where they have no such dominance but are interested in establishing a presence. Such "leveraging" of market power from one market to another may displace rivals in the second, "competitive" market and raise barriers to subsequent entry. The conditions under which this is a rational, profit-maximizing strategy for the incumbent firm have only recently begun to be understood.

In sum, there is clearly an enormous variety of practices that dominant firms may employ to handicap both small rivals and entrants. Many of these—increasing capacity, choosing to deny a competitor admission to some organization, operating in related markets, and so forth—may also have innocent purposes and raise no competitive concerns. It is an ongoing challenge for economics to determine the circumstances that distinguish procompetitive versus anticompetitive consequences.

Antitrust

Antitrust law has not been able to await resolution of these conceptual and practical difficulties before having to deal with allegations of predatory and exclusionary behavior. Clearly, the difficulties of distinguishing predation from hard, but honest and procompetitive, conduct by large firms may result in policy errors. Treating dominant firm actions too harshly is likely to stifle the competition that antitrust was designed to foster. A policy that

---

[21]For extended discussion, see Shapiro (1989) and Martin (1993).

[22]The actual case that raised these issues was *United States* v. *Terminal Railroad Association of St. Louis,* 224 U.S. 383 (1912).

is too lenient, on the other hand, risks harm to competitors and consumers alike. At various times the enforcement agencies and courts may have made mistakes of both types.

Early cases against monopolies and dominant firms revealed the courts' willingness to interpret adverse effects on competitors as evidence of predation. In the previously mentioned Standard Oil case, the dominant firm was alleged to have engaged in nasty practices toward rivals. Whether or not this was true, it was primarily on that basis that the Supreme Court found that Standard Oil "monopolized" its market. The logic of this position would imply the opposite verdict if a firm's dominant position was achieved without victimized rivals. And in fact, market dominance by U.S. Steel[23] that resulted in *higher* prices was found not to violate the antitrust laws since there was no evidence of "brutalities and tyrannies" against smaller rivals.[24] Indeed, its higher prices drew favorable reviews from its competitors.

Judicial focus on and hostility toward the conduct of large firms may have reached its peak during the 1960s. Cases involving mergers, price discrimination, and monopolization routinely included allegations of predatory conduct by some large firm in the market. In the *Utah Pie* case,[25] for example, large food manufacturing firms were convicted of predatory price discrimination against a local firm despite the fact that the latter remained the market leader and was profitable throughout. Such decisions raised questions as to whether price competition itself was being sacrificed to protect smaller firms.

In an effort to advance the debate concerning predatory conduct, in 1975 two leading antitrust scholars published an analysis seeking to establish enforceable rules for predation. In their analysis, Areeda and Turner (1975) sought to limit judicial prohibitions on low prices to those cases that they believed were demonstrably anticompetitive by contemporary economic standards. Their survey of various possible price and cost patterns led them to conclude that anticompetitive effects were likely only if the leading firm priced below its own marginal cost, and they proposed using average variable cost as a surrogate for marginal cost.

This Areeda-Turner rule now has many critics, but the criticism in no way detracts from the importance of its contribution. For one thing, in the confusion that had pervaded judicial opinions with respect to predation, the concreteness of the Areeda-Turner rule had an immediate attraction, and many (but not all) courts seized upon it for their own use. Moreover, that original rule caused an explosive growth in research attempting to clarify the economics of predation and to develop an operational rule to identify it (Hay, 1981). It did not, however, resolve the issues. Advances

---

[23]*U.S. v. United States Steel Corp.*, 251 U.S. 417 (1920).

[24]The language is taken from *Standard Oil*.

[25]*Utah Pie Co. v. Continental Baking Co.*, 386 U.S. 685 (1967).

have been made in economic analysis of rational predation, but these have made virtually no impression on the courts thus far (Klevorick, 1993). With respect to the development of rules, there have been, if anything, too many such rules proposed, each capturing somewhat different conduct as predatory.

Analogous difficulties have arisen with policy toward exclusionary behavior by dominant firms. Distinguishing legitimate conduct—even hard competition—by a dominant firm from anticompetitive exclusion of potential competitors is as formidable a policy task as determining true predatory conduct. Examples of alleged exclusion include cases brought against such familiar dominant firms as Kodak, IBM, Kellogg/General Mills/General Foods, and DuPont. In *Berkey* v. *Kodak,*[26] the plaintiff alleged that Kodak sought to monopolize film and photofinishing by its introduction of a new camera/film system without predisclosure to its rivals in film and processing. A whole series of cases brought by peripheral equipment manufacturers[27] and later by the Justice Department against IBM alleged selective price discounting, strategic equipment modification, and other harmful practices designed to exclude potential entrants. In the breakfast cereal case,[28] the Federal Trade Commission developed a novel economic argument that the three major manufacturers shared a monopoly and collectively "packed product space" with new cereals so as to leave inadequate opportunity for new entrants. The FTC also pursued monopolization allegations against DuPont for using its cost advantage in the market for the paint whitener titanium dioxide to preclude expansion by rivals.[29]

With minor exceptions all of the defendant firms in these cases prevailed. The court ruled that Kodak had no obligation to predisclose product innovations for the benefit of rivals. IBM won most of the myriad private suits it faced, and the Justice Department ultimately withdrew its suit. The FTC acquitted the three breakfast cereal manufacturers, in part balking at the proposition that more products could be anticompetitive. In the DuPont case, the FTC concluded explicitly that a dominant firm is under no obligation to avoid hard competition against smaller or newer rivals, regardless of the fate that might befall the latter.

The view that a dominant firm should have much the same degree of discretion in its behavior as a competitive firm grants considerable license to the dominant firm. It certainly had a chilling effect on companies inclined to bring suits against large rivals, and the number of such cases dwindled during the 1980s. More recently, however, the enforcement agencies and courts have on occasion been persuaded of instances in which dominant

---

[26]*Berkey Photo* v. *Eastman Kodak Co.,* 603 F.2d 263 (2d Cir. 1979).

[27]See Brock's discussion of several cases brought by peripheral equipment manufacturers against IBM (Brock, 1989).

[28]*In re Kellogg et al.,* FTC Docket No. 8883 (1981).

[29]For an extended analysis of this case, see Dobson et al. (1994).

firms' actions have crossed the line. This appears to be the case in both the recent *Kodak* (Case 16) and *Microsoft* (Case 17) proceedings discussed in Part 3 of this volume. These and certain other cases may simply represent anomalies, but it is also possible that they presage an enforcement and judicial process more receptive to claims of anticompetitive actions and to proof based on the focused application of economic theory and evidence.

THE CASES

The cases in this part illustrate the wide variety of possibly anticompetitive horizontal practices that firms may engage in. These range from attempts at cooperative pricing to predation against rivals, with exclusionary practices in between.

The belief that most price cooperation is not self-sustaining has led to a focus on facilitating practices. In the first case George Hay explains the fine line that distinguishes suspect pricing from normal business behavior and the key role that may be played by facilitating practices in sustaining cooperation. In the *Ethyl* case there were four such practices at issue—price preannouncements, use of press notices, uniform delivered pricing, and most-favored-customer clauses. This case represented an initial effort by the Federal Trade Commission to convince the courts of the relevant theory. While the argument ultimately failed in this particular matter, the court's opinion left open the possibility that more carefully constructed economic and legal arguments for facilitating practices might succeed.

Direct communication and agreements on price by horizontal competitors have essentially always been per se illegal. But in very narrow instances the parties may be permitted to engage in such conduct. Such was the issue in the case involving the colleges and universities that made up the National Collegiate Athletic Association, which jointly marketed football games to the television networks. Ira Horowitz explains how the Supreme Court, in a landmark antitrust ruling, distinguished the NCAA's conduct from an earlier case in which similar practices were found to be legal. The key distinction proved to be the issue of whether cooperation on pricing and marketing was necessary for the product to be produced and offered for sale at all. Finding no such rationale here, the Court concluded that the NCAA's behavior did not fall within the narrow exception previously carved out.

Antitrust law with respect to predatory pricing has been defined by two major cases in recent years. The first of these—the *Matsushita* case—is described by Kenneth Elzinga. The plaintiffs were a group of domestic television manufacturers who alleged that a group of Japanese electronics companies were conspiring to depress U.S. prices in order eventually to seize control of the market. The claim therefore included both collusion and predation, and as Elzinga recounts, for these simultaneously to be true would require some specific facts to hold. Presented with convincing evidence that the defendants could never recoup their initial losses from alleged predation, the Supreme Court concluded that the claim "made no economic sense" and granted summary judgment in their favor.

The *Liggett* case differs in several respects. The alleged predator, Brown & Williamson, was not the dominant firm but it was the firm most adversely affected by Liggett's strategy with respect to low-priced generic cigarettes. In addition, the pricing strategy appeared designed to take advantage of certain unique distributional and marketing practices in the industry. Also, success for Brown & Williamson did not require Liggett's demise, but simply its abandonment of low prices. William Burnett describes this unusual setting, the nature of economic and documentary evidence at trial, and the extremely unusual path taken by this case from jury trial to Supreme Court.

As in *NCAA* before, the government alleged that the agreement among the Ivy League schools plus MIT regarding financial aid awards to common applicants represented simple price fixing. Gustavo Bamberger and Dennis Carlton describe the schools' various responses to these allegations, among them that they were nonprofit entities and therefore not subject to the same antitrust standards and that their agreement served the larger purpose of spreading financial aid more widely and thereby ensuring access to the universities on the part of the truly needy. All of the Ivys settled this matter by accepting various restraints on their conduct, but MIT chose to pursue it to trial. The District Court adopted a modified per se approach, but then found MIT guilty of price fixing. On appeal, the Circuit Court overturned that ruling and instructed the lower court to conduct a full rule of reason evaluation of the "social purposes" of the agreement, at which point the Justice Department also settled with MIT but on terms that allowed much of the previously challenged conduct.

Exclusion from membership in a joint venture may be harmful to competition under certain circumstances. David Evans and Richard Schmalensee describe a proceeding in which Dean Witter (which had launched the Discover Card in 1986) sought in various ways to become a member of the Visa network and thereby also issue Visa cards. Visa refused, and Dean Witter claimed that the refusal represented an illegal restraint of trade. The threshold argument in the case involved market power: Did Visa have market power because its members had a large share of general-purpose credit cards, or was there essentially atomistic competition among countless potential issuers of Visa cards, so that exclusion of one—Dean Witter—would be inconsequential?

The final case returns discussion to allegations of price coordination. Economic theory stresses that what deters price increases is the fear that rivals will not follow and that the initiator of a price increase will suffer a loss of business until it can retract the increase. But what if the parties can announce future price increases, reconcile differences, and move in unison to a new price level? Alternatively, is it much different when the parties cannot pre-announce price increases, but they can respond virtually instantaneously to each others' initiatives and thereby avoid putting much business at risk? As Severin Borenstein describes, electronic data bases allow airlines to engage in these very practices. The Justice Department challenged certain uses of these data bases as devices whose effect was to faciliate price coordination and secured an important restraint on their use.

REFERENCES

Areeda, Philip, and Donald Turner. "Predatory Pricing and Related Practices Under Section 2 of the Sherman Act." *Harvard Law Review* 88 (February 1975): 697–733.

Brock, Gerald W. "Dominant Firm Response to Competitive Challenge: Peripheral Manufacturers' Suits Against IBM (1979–1983)." In *The Antitrust Revolution,* edited by John E. Kwoka, Jr. and Lawrence J. White, 160–182. New York: HarperCollins, 1989.

Dixit, Avinash. "The Role of Investment in Entry Deterrence." *Economic Journal* 90 (March 1980): 95–106.

Dobson, Douglas C., William G. Shepherd, and Robert D. Stoner. "Strategic Capacity Preemption: *DuPont.*" In *The Antitrust Revolution: The Role of Economics,* edited by John E. Kwoka, Jr. and Lawrence J. White, 157–188. New York: Oxford University Press, 1994.

Encaoua, David, Paul Geroski, and Alexis Jacquemin. "Strategic Competition and the Persistence of Dominant Firms: A Survey." In *New Developments in the Analysis of Market Structure,* edited by J. Stiglitz and G. F. Mathewson, 55–86. Cambridge: MIT Press, 1986.

Gaskins, Darius. "Dynamic Limit Pricing: Optimal Pricing Under Threat of Entry." *Journal of Economic Theory* 3 (September 1971): 306–322.

Hay, George. "A Confused Lawyer's Guide to the Predatory Pricing Literature." In *Strategic Predation and Antitrust Analysis,* edited by Steven Salop, 155–202. Washington, D.C.: Federal Trade Commission, 1981.

Hay, George, and Daniel Kelly. "An Empirical Survey of Price-Fixing Conspiracies." *Journal of Law & Economics* 17 (April 1974): 13–38.

Hilke, John, and Philip Nelson. "Noisy Advertising and the Predation Rule in Antitrust." *American Economic Review* 74 (May 1984): 367–371.

Klevorick, Alvin. "The Current State of the Law and Economics of Predatory Pricing." *American Economic Review* 83 (1993): 162–167.

Martin, Stephen. *Advanced Industrial Economics.* Cambridge, Mass: Blackwell, 1993.

McGee, John. "Predatory Price Cutting: The Standard Oil (N.J.) Case." *Journal of Law & Economics* 1 (October 1958): 137–169.

Menge, John. "Style Change Costs as a Market Weapon." *Quarterly Journal of Economics* 76 (November 1962): 632–647.

Ordover, Janusz, and Garth Saloner. "Predation, Monopolization, and Antitrust." In *Handbook of Industrial Organization,* edited by R. Schmalensee and R. Willig. Amsterdam: North-Holland, 1989.

Ordover, Janusz, and Robert Willig. "An Economic Theory of Predation." *Yale Law Journal* 91 (November 1981): 8–53.

Pittman, Russell. "Predatory Investment: *U.S. v. IBM." International Journal of Industrial Organization* 2 (December 1984): 341–365.

Salop, Steven. "Practices That (Credibly) Facilitate Oligopoly Coordination." In *New Developments in the Analysis of Market Structure,* edited by J. Stiglitz and F. G. Mathewson. Cambridge, Mass.: MIT Press, 1986.

Salop, Steven, and David Scheffman. "Raising Rivals' Costs." *American Economic Review* 73 (May 1983): 267–271.

Scherer, F. M. and David Ross. *Industrial Market Structure and Economic Performance.* 3d ed. Boston: Houghton Mifflin, 1990.

Schmalensee, Richard. "Entry Deterrence in the Ready-to-Eat Breakfast Cereal Industry." *Bell Journal of Economics* 9 (Autumn 1978): 305–327.

Shapiro, Carl. "Theories of Oligopoly Behavior." In *Handbook of Industrial Organization,* edited by R. Schmalensee and R. Willig. Amsterdam: North-Holland, 1989.

Spence, Michael. "Entry, Capacity Investment, and Oligopolistic Pricing." *Bell Journal of Economics* 8 (Autumn 1977): 534–544.

Worcester, Dean. "Why Dominant Firms Decline." *Journal of Political Economy* (August 1957): 338–347.

CASE 7

Facilitating Practices:
The Ethyl Case (1984)

George A. Hay

INTRODUCTION

Section 1 of the Sherman Act makes "every contract, combination . . . or conspiracy in restraint of trade" illegal. The most obvious application of Section 1 is to price-fixing agreements, and through its prohibition of price-fixing agreements Section 1 seeks to protect consumers against supracompetitive prices. However, the economic theory of oligopoly teaches us that there are circumstances in which a group of firms can achieve supracompetitive prices without the need for any formal agreement.

This case study is about this "oligopoly problem" and the efforts of the antitrust authorities to deal with it. It involves an antitrust case brought by the Federal Trade Commission (FTC) against the four manufacturers of lead-based antiknock gasoline additives, who were alleged to have succeeded in substantially eliminating price competition among themselves without entering into any formal price-fixing agreement.

Lead-based antiknock compounds have been used in the refining of gasoline since the 1920s to prevent engine "knock," the premature detonation of gasoline in the engine's cylinders. From the 1920s until 1948, the Ethyl Corporation was the sole domestic producer of lead-based antiknock compounds. Demand for the compounds increased with the increase in gasoline use, however, and in 1948 DuPont entered the industry and cap-

---

George A. Hay consulted with and testified for the Federal Trade Commission in connection with this case.

tured a substantial market share. In 1961, PPG Industries began to manufacture and sell the compounds, followed by the Nalco Chemical Company in 1964. From 1974 to 1979 (the relevant period for the case), these were the only four domestic producers of lead antiknock compounds. DuPont had 38.4 percent of the market; Ethyl, 33.5 percent; PPG, 16.2 percent; and Nalco, 11.8 percent. There were no significant imports into the United States.

In 1973, the Environmental Protection Agency (EPA) required that all automobiles manufactured in the United States beginning in 1975 be equipped with catalytic converters. Since the lead in antiknock compounds fouls such converters, almost all new cars sold in the United States since 1975 have required unleaded gasoline. As a result of this and other measures, the use of lead antiknock compounds declined from more than 1 billion pounds in 1974 to approximately 400 million pounds in 1980.

The drop in demand resulted in substantial excess capacity, a situation that economists would normally expect to lead to intensified price competition. Nevertheless, the FTC claimed that during the 1974 to 1979 period the companies substantially eliminated price competition among themselves and charged uniform supracompetitive prices. The FTC did not claim that this was the result of an agreement among the firms. Rather the absence of effective price competition could be traced to several specific practices that some or all of the firms employed, within the framework of a highly oligopolistic market structure. The FTC asserted that these practices "facilitated" the elimination of horizontal competition and ought to be prohibited.

ANTITRUST AND OLIGOPOLY: THE POLICY DILEMMA

A traditional horizontal price-fixing agreement is an effort by a group of firms explicitly to coordinate their activities so as to eliminate competition among themselves and thereby achieve noncompetitive prices and supranormal profits. These kinds of price-fixing agreements have long been regarded as unlawful.

The classic economic theories of oligopoly, on the other hand, do not focus on explicit efforts to coordinate conduct but instead on the profit-maximizing behavior of individual firms in an interdependent environment. The typical oligopoly model posits a number of firms, each deciding what level of a homogeneous output to produce. Since the market price depends on the sum of all firms' output, each firm must make certain assumptions about the combined output of its competitors and how that output will change in response to its own decision. On the basis of these assumptions, the firm chooses its own profit-maximizing course of action.

The collective result of all such individual decisions can be a price above the competitive level.[1]

The emphasis of oligopoly theory on individual profit maximization, as opposed to explicit coordination, is highly significant for antitrust policy. Since the applicability of the Sherman Act seems to turn on the existence of an agreement, and since by assumption there is no explicit agreement in a classic oligopoly situation, it would appear that firms can enjoy the supracompetitive prices and profits that are associated with price fixing without violating the Sherman Act. If so, there is a potentially troublesome gap in the coverage of the antitrust laws. One could argue that oligopolistic behavior leading to supracompetitive prices could be brought within the scope of the Sherman Act by characterizing the end result of oligopolistic interdependence as "tacit" or "implicit" agreement. Unfortunately, the semantic simplicity of such a solution masks a very serious underlying difficulty.

The problem can be illustrated with a simple example. Consider two essentially identical gas stations selling private-brand gasoline directly across the road from one another on a long, isolated highway with no rivals for miles around and no likelihood of new entry. Prior to today, both stations have been charging $1 a gallon, which we assume to be the competitive price. Since the two stations are regarded by consumers as offering virtually identical products, we assume that, at the $1 price, each enjoyed 50 percent of the total gasoline sales.

One station (station A) is contemplating raising the price to $1.25, which its resident economist has computed to be the profit-maximizing monopoly price: the price that would maximize total profits if both stations were to charge the identical price. The scheme will be profitable for A only if station B matches the $1.25 price, since if A raises the price and B does not follow, all of A's customers will switch to B.

---

[1]The basic Cournot (1963) model is typical of the methodology and the results of the early models. Under the simple (and probably unrealistic) assumption that rivals' output will not be influenced by changes in the output level of the individual firm, Cournot established that the collective result of each firm's individual profit-maximizing output decision would be an industry output level that deviated sharply from the competitive level as the number of firms became smaller. Thus, for example, a two-firm industry—that is, a duopoly—would yield a price that was much closer to the single-firm monopoly price than to the competitive price without the firms' having had any explicit communication or agreement. Other early models employed different reaction functions but generated similar results. Chamberlin (1933), for example, showed that if each firm expected its rivals to follow perfectly its own behavior, then the collective result of each firm's individual profit-maximizing behavior would be the monopoly price, even with a large number of firms.

The more recent oligopoly literature has criticized these simple reaction functions. Stigler (1964), for example, emphasized the links between industry concentration and the likelihood that rivals will follow a price increase. Others (see Scherer and Ross [1990, ch. 6] for a brief survey) have emphasized the dynamic aspects of oligopolistic interdependence and have argued, among other things, that where firms confront one another frequently over time, they will learn something about the way their rivals will react. The model presented in this case study, if interpreted within the context of the traditional oligopoly literature, emphasizes how firms can behave so as to influence their rival's reaction functions in an effort to produce Chamberlin-type conduct.

At first glance, it appears risky for A to go ahead with the price increase without prior assurance (i.e., agreement) that B will follow, since a
possible strategy for B is not to match A's price increase and to capture all
the business. However, if A raises the price to $1.25, it will learn very
quickly whether B has followed, since the same signs that communicate
B's price to potential customers can be seen by A.[2] If B has not followed
the increase, A can promptly restore its $1 price. In the interim, A will
have lost some sales, but as long as it is able to detect B's price cutting and
responds immediately, the losses will not be too great.

Station A's ability to detect and respond quickly to B's failure to
match A's price affects B's optimal strategy. By keeping the price at $1, B
would enjoy a brief period when it would capture nearly 100 percent of the
business. However, once A retracted its increase, the firms would go back
to sharing the market at $1. If instead B were to match A's increase (which
it can do easily by observing A's prices directly), it forgoes the brief period
of extra business in return for a possible long-term equilibrium in which it
shares the market with A at $1.25. Hence, B has an incentive to go along
with an increase by A, and A, knowing that B's best strategy is to follow,
can initiate the price increase with minimal risk.

If the scene unfolds as described, the firms jointly achieve monopoly
profits without the need for any formal agreement of the kind usually
involved in a Section 1 price-fixing case. What we want to consider is
whether it is feasible to bring the situation within the reach of the Sherman
Act by labeling it a tacit or implicit agreement and arguing that the antitrust laws ought to extend to such agreements.

To see the difficulty of applying the Sherman Act to such conduct,
consider how one would explain to a judge or jury precisely what A did
that is objectionable, or how one would fashion an effective remedy. It
seems foolish to argue that A should have ignored the fact that B would
likely follow an increase by A. This is essentially requiring A to pretend
that it is in perfect competition rather than in a situation of duopoly. What
the argument comes down to, then, is that A should have kept its price at
$1 even though it knew that $1.25 would be more profitable.

But if that is the argument, what is the criterion for determining when
A has acted illegally? Is it simply the fact that B followed A's price increase? Surely not, since that would essentially make any price increase
that is not subsequently rescinded (because rivals failed to follow) illegal.
Can A never initiate a price increase without risking a violation of the antitrust laws in the event its rivals follow? (Of course if rivals do not follow,
the price increase is useless to A.) Would we interpret the law to mean that
A can increase prices only when and to the extent that costs go up?

Similarly, it is difficult to argue that B committed an antitrust violation

---

[2]Even if A could not observe B's price directly, the immediate and large shift in business from A
to B would be an almost certain indication that B was keeping its price low.

when it matched A's increase, knowing that if it failed to match, A would simply retract the increase. Can B ever follow an increase by A without itself violating the antitrust laws? Can it follow A's increase only if it is cost justified? (Is the cost justification based on A's costs or B's? Or B's estimate of A's cost?) Finally, if the relationship between price and costs is to be determinative, are the federal courts equipped to carry out this regulatory function? These questions suggest the great difficulty of attempting to apply the antitrust laws to classic oligopolistic behavior.[3]

THE DIFFICULTY OF OLIGOPOLISTIC COORDINATION IN COMPLEX MARKETS

Although the policy dilemma posed by the classic oligopoly model as described in the preceding section is analytically troublesome, the dilemma may be more theoretical than real. In this section we focus on the difficulties faced by an industry seeking to achieve supracompetitive prices and profits under more realistic conditions and assess how likely the industry is to achieve those prices and profits without some kind of explicit effort at coordination. We then seek to describe an antitrust approach that "picks up" most such efforts, even those that cannot be described as "agreements."

Complicating Factors

To focus the discussion, it will be helpful to revisit the gas station example. The key to eventual success for the gas stations was that station A was willing to initiate a price increase without any formal agreement from station B to follow. Nevertheless, A was quite confident that B would follow and that there would be little risk associated with initiating the price increase. (Station A also knew that, even if B did not follow, A could retract the price increase without having suffered any serious financial consequences.)

The confidence of A that B would follow the price increase was based on two factors: (1) Since B could readily observe A's price, it would not be difficult for B to follow A's increase exactly, if B wanted to, (2) Since A would promptly withdraw the price increase if B failed to follow (so that B would enjoy only the most temporary gain in sales), it was in B's interest to follow A's increase, if B could do so. The two factors, ability and incentive, are equally important. If B is unable to follow A (because it does not know what A has done), it does not matter that B would like to follow. And, if it is not in B's interest to follow, it doesn't matter that B is able to.

However, B's ability to follow A's increase depends critically on the facts that B can easily observe A's prices and that A's prices are unambiguous in their meaning. The same mechanism that informs consumers about A's price increase (the large signs facing the highway) promptly informs B as well. Moreover, there is little chance of any confusion on B's part as to what the signs mean. In our simple model, A sells only a single variety of gasoline (e.g., regular unleaded), and there is no ambiguity about what the customer gets for the posted price (one gallon of the gasoline). Finally, the products sold by A and B are regarded by consumers as perfect substitutes, so that if B does increase its price by the same dollar amount there should be no shift in the distribution of business.

Likewise, B's incentive to follow A depends critically on the fact that B's failure to follow would be detected by A, who could retract the price increase promptly. Even if A could not observe B's prices directly, the fact that there are only two firms means that any increase in B's business would result in a corresponding drop in A's business. Hence, station A would immediately feel the impact of B's increase in business and is very likely to conclude that the reason for the shift in business is B's lower price. Moreover, the impact on A would be substantial enough that A's only realistic strategy, once it has suspected that B has not followed the price increase, is to withdraw it; and B knows that.

Real markets, however, are frequently more complicated, so that a firm that seeks to initiate a price increase to noncompetitive levels cannot always be confident that the move will result in increased profits, either because its rivals will be unable to raise their own prices in the exact amount necessary to preserve the preexisting distribution of business or because they will not want to do so (or both). The following is an illustrative (not exhaustive) list of the factors that are likely to complicate oligopolistic coordination.[4]

Nonpublic Prices

An obvious and important characteristic of the gas station example was that B had no trouble following A's price because it always knew precisely what A's price was. The same mechanism used to inform A's customers (signs) promptly and accurately informed B. Similarly, A had no trouble determining promptly whether B had in fact followed. While this might be characteristic of most goods sold off the shelf in retail outlets, there are many marketing contexts (e.g., sales to industrial buyers) in which the process of informing actual or potential customers of prices (and price changes) does not necessarily inform rivals. This is not to say that rivals can never find out about a price increase, but the time delay and potential for inaccurate information increase the risk to the initiator of a price increase that a rival will not follow. The same phenomenon also affects rivals' incentives to follow a price increase as well as their ability to do so. If A will not learn promptly whether B has matched the increase, the

---

[4]For a more extensive treatment, see Hay (1982).

profits that B can make in the interim are higher, thereby increasing B's incentive not to follow and increasing A's risk in initiating the increase.

Lumpy Sales

In the gas station example, A did not lose much business in the brief period during which its prices were higher than B's. This is because any station's total gasoline sales are made to a large number of separate buyers in relatively small amounts spread throughout the day or month or year. In some contexts, however, sales occur in large, discrete batches. An example is the process whereby the major auto manufacturers bid once or twice a year on a contract to supply the major rental car companies with new cars. Suppose Ford became aware that GM intended to raise prices during the next round of bids. If Ford were to refuse to follow GM, GM would almost certainly find out, but probably not until Ford had won a major contract for the coming year. This big chunk of sales may give Ford an incentive not to follow GM even though the result may be for GM to rescind its increase during the next round of bidding. More generally, the lumpiness of sales increases the incentive not to follow a leader's increase and thereby increases the risks in initiating one.[5]

Complex and Nonfungible Products

Where the product in question is simple and fungible across sellers, it is easier for rivals to follow a price increase in such a way as to maintain the preexisting distribution of sales. Where there is not a single product but an entire product line, there are more prices to coordinate. The broader the array of products, the more complicated the problem. In addition, when the products are not fungible across sellers, coordination is difficult because if A charges a particular price, it is not obvious that market shares will be stable just because B matches that price.

One important dimension of fungibility is associated with location. For a steel customer in Detroit, the steel from a manufacturer in Gary, Indiana, and the steel from a manufacturer in Birmingham, Alabama, are not perfect substitutes if the buyer has to pay the freight from the manufacturer's plant. Hence, the fact that FOB prices are the same from both manufacturers (or are increased by the same dollar amount) does not mean that buyers will be indifferent as to their source and that market shares will not shift after a price change. Alternatively, if freight rates change frequently, market shares may shift even if FOB prices remain unchanged,

---

[5]While lumpiness often occurs "naturally" (e.g., for business reasons on the part of the buyer or seller that have nothing to do with oligopolistic behavior), buyers sometimes have the ability to lump their purchases into big batches precisely to provide an inducement for sellers to cut prices. This can be done either by actually purchasing and storing large quantities at one time, or by entering into a long-term contract calling for delivery over the life of the contract. It is also worth noting that frequently both lumpiness and secrecy are present, and the effect is, of course, cumulative.

and compensating changes in FOB prices will have to be coordinated to restore the preexisting distribution of sales.

Market Concentration

A basic tenet of oligopoly theory is that the less concentrated is the market, the more likely are individual firms to find it in their own self-interest to undercut a noncompetitive price.[6] The reasons have to do with the potential for a small rival to increase profits significantly above its share of the "cooperative equilibrium" if it lowers prices while rivals' prices remain unchanged. In an industry of many firms, rivals may not notice when one firm increases sales by taking a little from each of them, and even if they notice, retaliation may not be worthwhile. Hence, the more unconcentrated the market, the harder it will be to maintain an equilibrium at supracompetitive prices.

Facilitating Practices

Once we move beyond the simple oligopoly models, or uncomplicated but unrealistic examples such as the gas station case, complicating factors such as those just described are likely to be present in many markets to a degree that firms in those markets are unlikely to be able to approximate the monopoly level of prices and profits solely as the result of perceived interdependence; something more will be needed. In many cases, what is required is explicit agreement—the usual stuff of a Sherman Act Section 1 price-fixing case—and nothing less will suffice.[7] However, this is not the only possibility. In this chapter we want to consider a situation in which some explicit behavior that falls short of a traditional agreement will serve to *facilitate* a noncompetitive equilibrium. This is behavior that, either by design or happenstance, helps the firms in the market overcome the complicating factors that make pure oligopolistic interdependence infeasible or insufficient to yield monopoly profits.

A focus on the specific practices used to facilitate the noncompetitive result circumvents the major policy problem of dealing with oligopolistic interdependence—the absence of culpable conduct. The treatment of facilitating practices need not differ fundamentally from the treatment of agreement under Section 1, where firms are guilty not merely because they have achieved noncompetitive prices, but because they have done so by entering an agreement. Under a "facilitating practices" approach, it would be unlawful to achieve noncompetitive prices via the use of one or more facilitating practices.

While such an approach to dealing with oligopolistic behavior seems

---

[6]The classic derivation of this theorem is from Stigler (1964).

[7]Market structure will sometimes be sufficiently unfavorable that even explicit agreement will be inadequate to produce supracompetitive prices and profits for any significant period of time.

attractive, we need to determine if it can be implemented under the antitrust laws. Several possibilities exist. First, it will sometimes be the case that, although there is no agreement to fix prices, there is an agreement on the part of several firms to implement the facilitating practices, such as an agreement to exchange current prices when each firm's prices would not normally be observable by its rivals. If so, there is no special legal issue. Section 1 applies to any agreement in restraint of trade, and it need be proved only that the agreement, here the agreement to exchange prices, does in fact result in a diminution of competition.[8] Moreover, the agreement need not be contained in a formal written or oral agreement.

Second, in the case in which a noncompetitive outcome is achieved through the use by one or more firms of certain facilitating practices, without any explicit agreement on price or any agreement to use the facilitating practice, one could simply define the noncompetitive outcome (the "meeting of the minds") that is achieved through the use of facilitating practices to be an illegal tacit or implicit agreement. The major policy objection to using the tacit-agreement approach to pure oligopolistic interdependence—the absence of identifiable culpable conduct and the lack of effective remedy—is not present in the facilitating practices approach.[9]

Finally, it may be possible to avoid the Sherman Act altogether. Section 5 of the Federal Trade Commission Act prohibits "unfair methods of competition." Traditionally, the FTC has interpreted Section 5 to cover more or less the same conduct as that which is covered by the Sherman Act. Specifically, in oligopolistic situations the FTC has traditionally alleged at least a tacit, if not an explicit, agreement. But neither the statutory language nor the legislative history would appear to limit the FTC to situations involving agreement, and facilitating practices could arguably be condemned as "unfair methods of competition."[10]

Our case study involves the last approach. It involves an action brought by the FTC under Section 5, in which the FTC declined to characterize the conduct as constituting an agreement. The action was a deliberate effort to test the limits of Section 5 in relation to oligopolistic behavior.

THE LEAD-BASED ANTIKNOCK INDUSTRY AND THE FTC COMPLAINT

The lead antiknock compound market had several of the characteristics generally viewed by economists as being conducive to noncompetitive

---

[8]There have been several major antitrust cases along these lines, including *United States v. Container Corp.*, 393 U.S. 333 (1969).

[9]For an example of this approach, see the Justice Department's memorandum on the degree of modification governing General Electric and Westinghouse in their marketing of turbine generators, *United States v. GE Co.* (1977-1) Trade Cas. (CCH) 712.

[10]These aspects of the FTC Act are discussed in some detail in the various opinions in the *Ethyl* case. Two major consequences of relying on the FTC Act are that there is no right of private

outcomes. There were only four domestic sellers, with two firms (DuPont and Ethyl) dominating the industry. The two larger firms apparently had similar costs of production. The product was relatively simple. There were two basic lead antiknock products—tetraethyl lead (TEL) and tetramethyl lead (TML)—that were usually combined in various proportions. Individual antiknock compounds of a given type produced or sold by one of the firms were substantially similar to those of the same type sold by the others—that is, the product was essentially fungible. The product had no reasonably close substitutes and constituted such a small percentage of the cost of refining a gallon of gasoline that the overall industry demand faced by the sellers was highly inelastic: increases in the industry price would result in relatively small reductions in consumption.

Moreover, it seemed unlikely that high prices would be deterred or undercut by new entry. After 1964 (when Nalco, the last of the four current producers, entered the industry) there were no new entrants into the industry. Given the overcapacity that characterized the industry in 1974 and the forecasts for further substantial drops in demand due to the government regulations, there was little likelihood of new entry even if existing firms were earning "monopoly" profits.[11]

However, other industry characteristics reduced the likelihood that supracompetitive prices could result merely from oligopolistic interdependence. These are the "compelling factors" referred to earlier; they can be enumerated as follows:

1. Sales of antiknock compound were not made to the general public but to the major oil refiners in essentially private transactions. Hence, it was not inevitable that one firm's price changes would immediately be observed by its rivals. This absence of transparency complicated the task of coordinating price changes so that there would be no shift in the distribution of sales and provided an incentive for secret discounts (since such discounts would not necessarily be detected quickly).

2. The major oil companies were sophisticated customers buying large quantities each year. There was ample incentive to bargain hard for discounts and to offer to shift significant business in return for discounts. Moreover, the huge excess capacity provided a strong incentive for one seller to offer a discount if it would result in significant additional sales.[12]

---

action under the FTC Act and there are no sanctions imposed on firms that have been found to have engaged in unfair methods of competition; they are merely given an order to "cease and desist" from using the practices.

[11] The fixed costs of a plant of minimal optimal scale were large enough that new entry would substantially depress prices. Since many of the fixed costs would also be sunk costs, this would result in losses for the entrant. Although there was widespread agreement on the low likelihood of independent entry, the possibility of backward vertical integration by one or more of the major oil companies was perceived by the Court of Appeals to be a significant factor.

[12] The excess capacity meant that the marginal costs of additional output were relatively low and that the incremental profits on additional sales would be substantial.

3. The four producers had a total of six plants: one in California; one in New Jersey; one at Baton Rouge, Louisiana; and three in Texas. The customers' plants were dispersed throughout the country. While, on average, transportation costs were not large as a percentage of the price of the product (about 2%), the transportation costs to any given customer from each of the four producers could differ significantly. Hence, even if FOB prices were equal for all four producers, the effective delivered price from one producer to a given customer could be substantially different from the effective delivered price from another producer to that customer. Since the product was otherwise fungible, the lowest effective delivered price would in all likelihood get the business, with no guarantee that, after all the business was allocated on this basis, the market shares would be distributed in a way that would be "satisfactory" to all producers. Moreover, nonproportional changes in freight costs to different locations could cause market shares to shift unpredictably.

In light of these complicating factors, the FTC did not believe that pure oligopolistic interdependence could be entirely responsible for the lack of effective price competition. Rather, the FTC identified four practices that contributed materially to the noncompetitive outcome.

Advance Notice of Price Changes

All four firms gave notice to their customers of price increases at least thirty days in advance of the effective date of the price increase. For example, if Ethyl were attempting to initiate a price increase to be effective on July 1 of a given year, it would notify customers of the increase no later than June 1 and typically a few days earlier. The FTC argued that such advance notice gave rivals an opportunity to respond so that uncertainty about whether rivals would follow would be eliminated *before* the price increase actually went into effect, thereby permitting modification or rollback of the price increase prior to its effective date if rivals did not follow precisely. For example, Ethyl might actually announce the increase on May 28. The other firms would then have three days to make matching announcements, which would ensure that, when the price increases actually went into effect, all firms would have identical prices. Even if one or more of the rivals did not make an announcement until, say, June 3, Ethyl would at least be sure that rivals would be matching the increase no later than July 3, and if necessary, could defer the effective date of its own price increase until then.

Ensuring that the initiator will not be alone in the market with a higher effective price prevents a possible shift of short-term business to lower-priced competitors and, as a result, reduces risk associated with the price move. It also permits time for "adjustment" if one or more of the competitors should favor a price increase of a different amount. The actual record of price increases showed that during the period 1974 to 1979, there were twenty-four price increases. In twenty instances, all the firms had an identical list price that was effective on the same date. In the other four instances, there was an identical price list and a difference of only a day or two in the effective dates of the increase.

Press Notices

Until about mid-1977 (when the practice was stopped on advice of counsel), all the firms issued press notices concerning price increases. While the producers had other sources of information (customers voluntarily notified the other firms of one firm's announced price increase, so as to learn promptly if the others would follow), the FTC claimed that these other sources of information were not always timely and were sometimes inaccurate. The fact that information may be unreliable may make it difficult for a price leader to "communicate" its move or to learn whether rivals have followed. Either consequence increases the risk of initiating a price increase, and the press releases helped ease this uncertainty by providing early and accurate information of price moves.

Uniform Delivered Pricing

All the firms quoted antiknock prices only on the basis of a delivered price inclusive of transportation and quoted the same delivered price regardless of the customer's location. The effective list price for any one firm was therefore identical throughout the United States. A delivered pricing formula removes transportation cost variables from the pricing structure, thus simplifying each producer's price format. A producer seeking to match a competitor's price under this system need not deal with complications engendered by freight tariffs or speculate on its competitors' transportation cost variables. Rather, a producer seeking to have the identical effective price as its rival to each of its 150 actual or potential customers need only be concerned with matching the single uniform delivered price.[13]

The courts had recognized for years that an agreement to use a delivered pricing formula such as uniform delivered prices has sufficient potential for eliminating price competition. Such agreements have routinely been held illegal. The FTC argued here that the same anticompetitive

---

[13]Scherer (1980, p. 329) has commented on the role that delivered pricing plays in facilitating and maintaining uniform prices: If each producer independently and unsystematically quoted prices to the thousands of destinations it might serve, it would almost surely undercut rivals on some orders, touching off retaliatory price cuts. But common adherence to basing point formulas in effect eliminates discretion and uncertainty, and if each firm plays the game and sticks to the formulas, price competition is avoided. Identical prices are quoted to a given customer by every producer, leaving the division of orders to chance or nonprice variables (such as delivery times, special service, the dryness of martinis provided by salesmen at business luncheons, etc.—bases on which oligopolists often prefer to compete).

consequences follow even where the common use of the pricing formula is not the result of agreement.

"Most-Favored-Customer" Clauses

A "most-favored-customer" clause in a sales contract is a promise by a seller to offer its customer the benefit of any lower price the seller gives another customer. While the precise terms of a most-favored-customer clause can vary from contract to contract, the essence of the clause in the present context was that any discount off the uniform delivered list price granted to a single customer would have to be extended to all customers of that seller. Ethyl and DuPont were the primary users of most-favored-customer clauses during the 1974 to 1979 period, although the other two firms did employ them in various ways.

As discussed earlier, one of the problems confronting any oligopoly seeking to maintain a supracompetitive price is the incentive that exists for any one firm to shade the price slightly in an effort to pick up additional sales by "stealing" them from its rivals. The incentive is particularly strong where the discount need be extended only to the incremental customer, that is, where the firm can continue to charge the prevailing industry price to its existing customers and to provide the discount only to those customers who would otherwise buy elsewhere. In many contexts, especially in sales to consumers in traditional retail establishments (such as gas stations or supermarkets), such discrimination is often impractical.

In the case of antiknock compounds, however, where sales are made privately to each of many industrial customers (the oil refiners), discrimination in the form of secret discounts is feasible and, given the difficulty of detection and effective retaliation (because sales are secret and at least potentially lumpy), probably attractive. Most-favored-customer clauses effectively prohibit discrimination. This has the effect of discouraging discounting from list prices, since cutting prices "across the board" to all customers would be less likely to be profitable than would selective cuts to targeted customers (to keep them loyal or to woo them away from rivals). In addition, where the discount is offered widely, it is much more likely to be detected by rivals.

Most-favored-customer clauses not only create disincentives to discount, they also reduce uncertainty about rivals' prices and pricing actions in significant ways. Since such contractual provisions discourage discounting, a firm's knowledge that its rivals employ them provides assurance that the latters' discounting will be restrained. As a result of this reduction in uncertainty about rivals' transaction prices, most-favored-customer clauses facilitate noncompetitive price increases by improving confidence that information regarding a competitor's prices, gathered from only one or two sources, is applicable to all customers. Therefore, if a firm that has initiated a price increase learns from a few customers that a rival has matched the increase for sales to those customers, it can be reasonably confident that the rival's matching increase applies to all customers.

ISSUES FOR THE COURT

As structured by the FTC, the case presented two main economic questions: (1) Was the industry performing noncompetitively? (2) If so, was the poor performance attributable to the challenged practices? The case also presented the legal and policy issue of whether Section 5 of the FTC Act is applicable to noncollusive horizontal conduct, and if so, what are the general guidelines for when noncollusive horizontal conduct violates Section 5?[14]

Economic Issues

Industry Performance

The FTC made the following arguments about the antiknock compound industry's performance:

1. The overall level of prices was high, as evidenced by profit levels and industry statements about the profitability of the industry and the possibility of much lower prices if competition "broke out." The FTC compared the profit level in this business for the 1974 to 1979 period with the average return on net assets for all manufacturing and for the chemicals industry generally and found, for example, that Ethyl's and DuPont's rates of return exceeded 150 percent of any benchmark comparison in every year during the period. The FTC also made much of a document in which an Ethyl executive characterized the business as a "golden goose," and there were similar (albeit less colorful) characterizations from some of the other firms as well.

2. The structure of prices geographically was not compatible with assertions that the industry was performing perfectly competitively. Since

---

[14]The judicial process in an FTC matter works as follows: First, on the basis of a staff recommendation, the Commission (five members, each appointed by the President for a term of seven years) votes whether to issue a complaint; if a complaint is issued, the matter is heard by an FTC administrative law judge, who issues what is called an "initial decision." The matter then returns to the Commission itself which, based on the record compiled at the hearing, along with subsequent argument by the Commission staff and the defendants, either issues an opinion and an order (normally a prohibition on certain conduct in the future) or dismisses the complaint. If the Commission's decision is adverse to the defendants, they may appeal to a U.S. Circuit Court of Appeals. Either party may seek to appeal a decision of the Court of Appeals to the U.S. Supreme Court. However, the Supreme Court accepts only a small percentage of the petitions it receives. In this case, both the initial decision and the Commission's opinion were adverse to defendants. The Second Circuit Court of Appeals, however, reversed the Commission and ordered the complaint dismissed; see *E. I. DuPont de Nemours & Co.* v. *FTC,* 729 F.2d 128 (1984). The matter was not appealed to the Supreme Court. In the text that follows, I refer to the three layers collectively (i.e., the administrative law judge, the Commission, and the Court of Appeals) as "the court."

delivered prices were uniform even though transportation costs differed depending on the seller's and the buyer's location, even if prices to some buyers were at the competitive level (i.e., buyers for whom transport costs were relatively high), it must be the case that prices to other buyers (those for whom transport costs were relatively low) were above the relevant marginal costs. Put simply, in a competitively functioning industry, buyers who are close to the plants of two or more sellers should pay less for delivered compound than buyers located at greater distances.

3. While it is true that, in a "perfect" market, prices for identical products tend toward equality, there is generally enough friction in the system that the process does not work instantly or produce perfect equality. Hence, the FTC argued that it was simply unrealistic to attribute the identical prices to an abundance of competition. Especially given the presence of big, sophisticated buyers and the considerable excess capacity, one should have observed more variation in the system.

The defendants challenged the FTC's assertions about performance in two important respects. First, they established that prices were not perfectly uniform. While Ethyl and DuPont consistently sold at list price, a substantial portion of Nalco's and PPG's sales were made at a discount. Overall, approximately 15 to 20 percent of industry sales during the period were at a discount from list prices. The FTC argued that these discounts could be explained by special factors (for example, Nalco continued to give discounts to the refiners who first gave Nalco some business when it entered the industry) and were not enough to rebut the overall characterization of the industry performance as noncompetitive.

Second, there was substantial evidence of nonprice competition in the form of various free services. Most were directly related to provision of the antiknock compounds (such as safety services and product equipment and inspection services) that arguably would be provided even in a competitive environment, but others were clearly disguised discounts. Examples included installing lead tanks for refiners, paying architectural fees incurred by a refiner in building an employee cafeteria, and building a railroad spur to facilitate antiknock compound delivery. The parties disputed the significance of this nonprice competition. The FTC argued that customers would have preferred a straight price cut and that the nonprice concessions were actually a symptom of the elimination of direct price competition. Defendants, anticipating their main defense (discussed below), argued that the nonprice competition was in many cases the practical equivalent of a price cut and, in any event, the best that could be expected in an oligopolistic industry, where direct price cuts would be quickly observed and matched, thereby rendering them unprofitable.

Causation

Using the documentary evidence and the opinion of its economic expert, the FTC argued that the noncompetitive performance was attributable, at least in part, to the identified facilitating practices and that, but for the practices, industry performance would have been measurably improved. The FTC acknowledged that structure was important but claimed that, because of the complicating factors, structure alone could not account for the poor performance. Defendants took the position that, to the extent that the industry performed unsatisfactorily, it was the natural result of the oligopolistic structure of the industry.

Defendants also took specific exception to some of the FTC's claims about the importance of the practices.

1. As to the press announcements, defendants argued that information about price changes initiated by one firm would spread quickly to the firm's rivals as customers sought to inquire whether the other firms intended to go along with the increase.

2. The practice of uniform delivered prices was not significant in light of the relatively low transportation costs as a percent of the total price. Since the product was fungible, competitive forces would lead to freight absorption by more distant sellers in an effort to compete against more favorably situated sellers for a customer's business. Since freight rates between any two points could easily be determined, firms would have no trouble matching one another's effective delivered price even if prices were quoted on an FOB basis.

3. The most-favored-customer clauses simply put into contractual language what the firms regarded as the sensible policy from a customer relations standpoint of not discriminating among customers by giving discounts that other customers would learn about anyway. Testimony indicated that customers on an individual basis desired contractual protection against discrimination.[15]

These arguments on causation presented an interesting dilemma for the court. Given the FTC's admission that some oligopolistic interdependence was at work and that, even without the facilitating practices, it was unlikely that the industry would behave perfectly competitively, how should the court assess how much worse the performance was as a result of the facilitating practices? There is no obvious way to measure this factor, and the courts were left to some extent with the conflicting judgments of the parties' expert economic witnesses.[16] The FTC's expert claimed that in his opinion the industry would have performed significantly better in the absence of the facilitating practices, although he acknowledged that there was no scientific way to determine precisely how much. The experts for the defendants took the position that the practices really didn't matter much at all, but neither did they offer any "scientific" proof.

---

[15]It can be entirely rational for each individual customer to demand such protection even if it would be in the collective interest of customers to have the practice prohibited.

[16]The court also had available, from documents and from the testimony of live witnesses, perceptions from those in the industry as to whether the practices played any role in the decision-making process. This evidence was still of limited utility, however, in assessing precisely how much of a difference they made.

Both the administrative law judge and the Commission (with a dissent by Chairman Miller) determined that the practices contributed significantly to the poor performance. However, the defendants appealed to the Second Circuit Court of Appeals, and that court's decision in early 1984 determined that the Commission had not carried the burden of showing that there had been a significant lessening of competition due to the challenged practices. The Court of Appeals argued that the degree of price uniformity was not as great as the FTC had characterized it and that the extensive nonprice competition, combined with the frequent discounts, presented a picture of a workably competitive market in which large, sophisticated, and aggressive buyers were making demands on the sellers and were satisfied with the results. Even if the industry performance was less than fully satisfactory, the Court of Appeals was prepared to attribute that result to the underlying structure rather than to the practices.

Legal and Policy Issues

While the economic issues just discussed were important to the outcome of the case, in many ways the most important questions that had to be addressed were whether Section 5 could be used at all in a horizontal context in the absence of agreement (if not an explicit agreement, then at least a tacit agreement) and, if so, under what circumstances it was appropriate for the FTC to challenge behavior that firms individually engaged in, without any prior agreement to do so. Defendants observed that each of the challenged practices was initiated by Ethyl during the period prior to 1948, when it was the sole producer in the industry. For example, Ethyl began quoting prices on a delivered price basis in 1937 in response to customer demand. Each of the three subsequent manufacturers, on entry into the market, followed that practice. Customers demanded a delivered price because it would require the manufacturers to retain title to and responsibility for the dangerously volatile compounds during transit to the refiner's plant.

Similarly, Ethyl adopted the most-favored-customer clause when it was the sole producer, as its guarantee not to price discriminate among its own customers who competed against each other in the sale of gasoline. The clause assured the smaller refiners that they would not be placed at a competitive disadvantage on account of price discounts to giants such as Standard Oil, Texaco, and Gulf. For the same reason, DuPont adopted the same contractual clause when it later entered the industry. Finally, the issuance of advance notice of price increases to both buyers and the press, a common practice in the chemicals industry, was initiated by Ethyl well before the entry of DuPont or the other two producers, as a means of aiding buyers in planning their purchase decisions.

The Court of Appeals agreed with defendants' argument that, since the practices were adopted when there was no competition, it could not be that their *purpose* was to reduce competition. Furthermore, in the opinion of the court, the conduct was not inherently collusive, coercive, predatory, restrictive, or deceitful. Thus, the essence of the FTC challenge was that at some point the practices resulted in a substantial lessening of competition. The Court of Appeals expressed great concern that a test based solely on the fact of an impact on competition would be so vague "as to permit arbitrary or undue government interference with the reasonable freedom of action that has marked our country's competitive system." The court asserted that before business conduct in an oligopolistic industry may be labeled "unfair" within the meaning of Section 5 (in the absence of a tacit agreement), there must be a showing of either evidence of anticompetitive intent or the absence of an independent legitimate business reason for the conduct. In a case such as *Ethyl,* in which the conduct was implemented when the original firm did not confront any competition, the absence of an independent business meaning cannot be presumed.

CONCLUSION

The "facilitating practices" theory was enthusiastically endorsed both by the administrative law judge who conducted the hearing and by the Commission itself in its role as a review panel. In principle, the Court of Appeals did not reject the basic approach, but its reversal of the Commission's application of the theory to the antiknock industry at least raises a question about how frequently the evidence would be strong enough to satisfy the court's criteria, except in those situations where there is enough interaction among the firms that the plaintiff can follow the traditional approach of asserting the existence of an agreement.

Subsequently, the combination of the unfavorable decision from the Court of Appeals and the generally more conservative attitude of the Reagan administration toward antitrust enforcement resulted in the "facilitating practices" approach not being used during the decade of the 1980s. However, in recent years there have been several cases that seem to fit that category.

In a private case involving oil refining and marketing, plaintiffs argued that defendant oil companies conspired to raise or stabilize prices for refined oil products, including gasoline. One of the allegations was that defendants disseminated information concerning their wholesale and retail prices for the purpose of quickly informing competitors of a price change in the hope that these competitors would follow the move. Key to the court's analysis was that, for some of the information disseminated, there was no other business purpose than to facilitate interdependent or collusive interaction.[17]

---

[17]*In Re Coordinated Pretrial Proceedings in Petroleum Products Antitrust Litigation,* 906 F.2d 432 (1990). The court observed that, given the system of branded franchising, the tankwagon prices are not of immediate significance to anyone other than the oil companies and their franchised dealers. Since the dealers were individually notified of the price changes, there appeared to be no legitimate business purpose served by the public dissemination.

Another private case (discussed more fully by Severin Borenstein as Case 13 in this book) involved claims that the major U.S. airlines used the computer system in which all fares are entered (and from which any fare for any airline can be retrieved by any other airline) to announce fare increases fourteen days in advance of their effective date. The plaintiffs' claim was that this practice allowed one airline to "signal" its desire to move to higher fares and to allow other airlines time to signal their assent or disagreement. This case was eventually settled without any of the substantive claims having been litigated.[18] Subsequent to the settlement of this case, the Justice Department filed a civil case under Section 1 on the Sherman Act on essentially the same basis, and the defendants consented to the elimination of certain of the identified practices.

Finally, in a matter brought by the FTC under Section 5 of the FTC Act, the principal manufacturers of infant formula were charged with exchanging certain information about their future conduct, which had the effect of reducing uncertainty and facilitating parallel conduct. In one instance, the information exchanged had to do with the terms on which future bids to a federal purchasing program would be made, and in the one matter that was litigated, the FTC was unsuccessful in establishing that the companies had acted unlawfully.[19] (There were also private cases involving the same or similar conduct.) Whether any of these cases represent harbingers of a renewed effort at applying the doctrine of facilitating practices will become clear only over time.

REFERENCES

Chamberlin, Edward H. *The Theory of Monopolistic Competition.* Cambridge, Mass.: Harvard University Press, 1933.

Cournot, Augustin. *Researches into the Mathematical Principles of the Theory of Wealth.* Translated by N. T. Bacon. Homewood, Ill.: Richard D. Irwin, 1963.

Hay, George A. "Oligopoly, Shared Monopoly, and Antitrust Law." *Cornell Law Review* 67 (March 1982): 439–481.

Posner, Richard A. "Oligopoly and the Antitrust Laws: A Suggested Approach." *Stanford Law Review* 21 (June 1969): 1562–1606.

Posner, Richard A. *Antitrust Law: An Economic Perspective.* Chicago: University of Chicago Press, 1976.

Scherer, F. M. *Industrial Market Structure and Economic Performance.* 2d ed. Skokie, Ill.: Rand McNally, 1980.

Scherer, F. M., and David Ross. *Industrial Market Structure and Economic Performance.* 3d ed. Boston: Houghton Mifflin Company, 1990.

[18]*In Re Domestic Air Transportation Antitrust Litigation,* DC NGa, no. 1:90-CV-2484 MHS & MDL no. 861, June 23, 1992.

[19]*FTC v. Abbott Laboratories,* 853 F. Supp. 526 (1994).

Stigler, George J. "A Theory of Oligopoly." *Journal of Political Economy* 72 (February 1964): 44–61.

Turner, Donald F. "The Definition of Agreement Under the Sherman Act: Conscious Parallelism and Refusals to Deal." *Harvard Law Review* 75 (February 1962): 655–706.

CASE 8

The Reasonableness of Horizontal Restraints: NCAA (1984)

Ira Horowitz

INTRODUCTION

From 1960 through 1981, the National Collegiate Athletic Association (NCAA) controlled the broadcast rights to its members' football games. These rights were packaged and sold to the highest bidder among the three major over-the-air television networks: ABC, CBS, and NBC. In 1982, the University of Georgia and the University of Oklahoma sought to reclaim control over their broadcast rights and filed suit in federal district court against the NCAA. They alleged that the associations' network contracts, which included a "recommended" price to be paid for a televised game as well as limitations on the number of games to be televised and designation of the specific games, violated the Sherman Act. Judge Juan C. Burciaga ruled in their favor,[1] and on appeal the U.S. Court of Appeals (Tenth Circuit) supported Judge Burciaga's decision.[2] In June 1984, on further appeal, the U.S. Supreme Court[3] held the NCAA's exclusive football telecasting plan to be in violation of Section 1 of the Act. One practical result of the successful suit is that fans can now spend fall Saturdays watching football from

Ira Horowitz was a consultant to the Universities of Oklahoma and Georgia in this case.

[1] *Board of Regents of the University of Oklahoma and the University of Georgia Athletic Association v. National Collegiate Athletic Association,* 546 F. Supp. 1276 (1982).

[2] *National Collegiate Athletic Association v. The Board of Regents of the University of Oklahoma,* 707 F.2d 1147 (1983).

[3] *National Collegiate Athletic Association v. Board of Regents of the University of Oklahoma,* 468 U.S. 85 (1984).

noon to night (and other nights of the week as well), rather than being restricted to a game or two.

Of particular interest, however, is the Supreme Court's decision in this case compared with its earlier *ASCAP* decision.[4] *ASCAP* involved the blanket licensing of copyrighted music by the American Society of Composers, Authors and Publishers (ASCAP) and Broadcast Music, Incorporated (BMI), which served as clearinghouses for owners and users. In *ASCAP* the Court held that "[n]ot all arrangements among actual or potential competitors that have an impact on price are per se violations of the Sherman Act or even unreasonable restraints."[5] The Court recognized that a cooperative arrangement might necessitate a price agreement in order to make the product available, and that efficiency-enhancing restraints that reduce transactions costs can be procompetitive. The former implies that a cooperative agreement may require a rule-of-reason assessment of "necessity"; the latter implies that a horizontal restraint may be beneficial to consumers.

In *NCAA* the Court further held that when the "necessity" assessment fails a rule-of-reason test and the restraint is not welfare enhancing, even without proof of market power a horizontal restraint affecting price is per se illegal. It left open to speculation just how a cooperative lacking market power can adversely impact price, output, and consumer welfare. The Court thus left open to debate and judicial attention whether there exists a general analytical framework for evaluating economic performance and market behavior that does not require a determination of who and what comprise the market. This chapter, in focusing on *NCAA,* highlights the relevant economic issues and suggests some answers for that debate.

BACKGROUND

Sports telecasts are a long-time television staple. Live collegiate football telecasts on fall Saturday afternoons fill a particularly important niche in television programming. In 1951, the NCAA was paid $1 million by NBC for an eight-date package of games. This fee compared favorably with the $0.7 million paid to the eleven National Football League (NFL) teams and the $4 million paid to the sixteen Major League baseball teams for all of their broadcast rights. By the fall of 1997, through an assortment of conference packages and individual-team arrangements, broadcasters were paying over $100 million to televise college football from the end of August through the New Year. Live college televised football has become a big-money enterprise.[6]

---

[4] *Broadcast Music, Inc. v. Columbia Broadcasting System, Inc.,* 441 U.S. 1 (1979).

[5] 441 U.S. 1, 23 (1979).

[6] For detailed discussions of how we have reached this point, see Hochberg and Horowitz (1973, pp. 113–118), Meyers and Horowitz (1995, pp. 687–697 and 700–708), and *Board of Regents of the University of Oklahoma and the University of Georgia Athletic Association* v. *National Collegiate Athletic Association,* 546 F. Supp. 1276, 1282–1291 (1982). Along with *Broadcasting & Cable* magazine, these are the principal sources for the data in this chapter.

The Special Problems of Leagues

Where league sports and money are involved, determining the division of the spoils becomes an imperative. This was true for the NCAA's early television packages; it is true for the current conference packages; and it holds for all sports leagues—college or professional—in their money-related activities. Groups of teams must therefore set up rules of governance that cover both their off-the-field and on-the-field activities. The interests of individual teams and their fans, however, do not necessarily mirror those of the league as a whole. A tenet of league sports is that fans prefer competitive games and seasons, though not when these are achieved by pervasive mediocrity. Another is that fans want their teams to win and to win often; in college football that means going undefeated. The rules of governance must therefore deal with the related problems of maintaining competitive balance, allowing the members of the league to maximize their joint profits by exploiting whatever market power adheres to the league when the teams operate as a collective, distributing that profit, and dealing with the reality that teams' markets are almost always disparate in terms of profit potential and that few teams are selfless where money is at issue.

League members, recognizing their joint interest in establishing rules to limit player remuneration, can usually think of some device such as a reserve clause that binds a player to a team in perpetuity, team salary caps, limited scholarships, and player drafts. But recognizing the profit-generating advantages of collusion, which for the NCAA meant pooling and selling members' television rights, and having the members cooperate in sharing the wealth while resisting the temptation to cheat or bolt, is something else. Getting the players to accept salary restraints and the government to accept de facto cartelization are also perennial concerns for which "maintaining competitive balance" is a frequent explanation aimed at mollifying the players, the government, and the fans. It may, however, simply be a cover for the exercise of market power.[7]

The NCAA and Televised Football

Television's initial growth came on the two coasts in the late 1940s. Participants in the 1951 NCAA convention were aware of the rise in college football attendance between the coasts, where few households could access televised football, and its wane in those areas where television was spreading. They drew the logical, if flawed, inference that live telecasts harm attendance. This led to approval of a virtual moratorium on live telecasts. The NCAA, faced with the rumored threat of an antitrust inquiry, adopted a program of regional telecasts of games that were not always of

---

[7] For the most recent theories of the economics of sports leagues, as well as references to earlier work, see Noll (1995), Quirk and Fort (1992), and Vrooman (1995).

interest to fans in those regions. NBC initially owned the rights, and live attendance continued to decrease. In 1954 the rights moved to ABC, and attendance increased, as it did every year thereafter through 1971. The simple inference that the telecasts aided attendance may also be flawed.

A policy of two-year packages began with a 1960–1961 deal in which ABC's $6.25 million bid topped NBC's $5.2 million bid. The games moved to CBS in 1962 and back to NBC in 1964, before finding their permanent home at ABC after it "bid" "15.5 million for the 1966–1967 rights. The word *bid* is in quotes, since the arrangement was really a marriage of convenience wherein the spouses pledged their troth, while agreeing to a biannual *renegotiation* of the living arrangements: the package price, the televised-game fees, the number of appearances permitted a team, and so forth.

Congress created an enhancement for the cartelization of television rights when it passed Public Law 87-331 in 1961.[8] The law allows professional teams to pool their rights in order to offer broadcasters a league package giving exclusive television coverage of their games. To deal with the potentially adverse effects of televised NFL games on college and high school football attendance, Congress inserted a stricture that effectively forbade Friday night and Saturday NFL telecasts during the normal high school and collegiate seasons. An indirect result of this stricture was that the two-year prototype package that the NCAA sold to ABC in 1960 guaranteed the network and its sponsors exclusivity over televised football on fall Saturdays. That exclusivity yielded a monopoly that did not go unexploited.

From one perspective, the NCAA was a cartel selling a limited number of games to ABC, thus giving it a virtual monopoly over live televised college football. This was the perspective of the University of Georgia, the University of Oklahoma and many of the other fifty-nine collegiate football powers that made up the College Football Association (CFA). These schools would eventually argue that they were being denied the opportunity to market and broadcast their games independently and that consumers were being denied their preferences through a restraint of trade.

From another perspective, the NCAA and its members had formed a joint venture to produce a television program to compete with other network programs. The NCAA and ABC eventually argued that the joint venture was the most efficient means of ensuring the cooperation of small sellers in the provision of a unique product, the television *program* "NCAA Football." The joint venture was their procompetitive sole means of producing a product that could effectively compete with other slightly differentiated products (other television programs). On the assumption that a package of choice NCAA games would be more attractive to networks and sponsors than would any one school's telecasts, "NCAA

---

[8] 77 Stat. 732.

Football" would *enhance* rather than restrain competition in the television-program market.

With many marriages the outsider wonders what the partners see in each other and why they stay together. In this case, however, the answers are apparent. The NFL and the neophyte American Football League (AFL) had sold their rights to CBS and to NBC, respectively. ABC needed college football to have *any* live football coverage. Otherwise, it could suffer both a direct opportunity (profit) loss and the indirect loss associated with the externalities that televised football might have on other network programming, either through promotion of other programs or through a lead-in effect, where perhaps half the viewers do not change stations at a program's conclusion.

For the NCAA, going with NBC or CBS risked sharing the network's attention and publicity with professional football, and this could translate into lower ratings that would lower the value of future broadcast rights; the NCAA sought to avoid that risk. The marriage made good sense, and the NCAA remained monogamous through 1981 (even though ABC has televised "Monday Night [NFL] Football" since 1970).

In 1976, the major football-playing schools outside of the Big Ten and Pac Ten conferences formed the CFA. These schools were dissatisfied with their limited telecast-and-revenue opportunities. The CFA's original intent was to promote the interests of these football powers within the NCAA structure. This intent eventually translated into wanting a bigger voice on television-related issues and a bigger share of a bigger revenue pie.

With its most recent ABC contract expiring in 1981, the NCAA began to consider seriously a "bigamy" option under which it would sell broadcast rights to both CBS and ABC. The joint contracts would yield $59 million in 1982 (up from $31 million in the previous four-year deal), rising to $72 million in 1985 for twenty-eight annual exposures (up from 24) to be equally divided between the networks. The choice of games selected for television would be coordinated so as to minimize the possibilities of simultaneous telecasts or having the networks get into a bidding war over any one game. At any given *time*, then, one network would monopolize live televised college football.

The only major over-the-air network without college football was NBC, so an NBC-CFA marriage was a natural. In August 1981 the CFA members ratified a contract with NBC that mirrored the earlier ABC-NCAA contracts, while yielding a higher income per CFA member than would the NCAA's two-network scheme.

This turn of events led the NCAA to threaten schools that went along with the CFA; the threats ranged from reprimands to expulsion. The Universities of Georgia and Oklahoma went to the courts and requested and were granted injunctive relief to prevent the NCAA from initiating disciplinary proceedings or from otherwise interfering with the agreement. Nevertheless, most CFA schools (28 of which initially either voted against the contract or abstained) were unwilling to go ahead with the plan, notwith-standing the NCAA's compliance with the injunction, and the NBC-CFA deal was off. But the CFA's battle to wrest its member's television rights out of the hands of the NCAA and return them to the schools had just begun, since the Universities of Georgia and Oklahoma were prepared to pursue fully their antitrust lawsuit against the NCAA.

THE ALLEGED ANTICOMPETITIVE ACTS AND THEIR ECONOMIC CONSEQUENCES

The ABC-NCAA contracts for 1978–1979 and 1980–1981 gave ABC exclusive network rights to college football. In 1978, for example, ABC was permitted twenty-three exposures (national plus regional telecasts) for a minimum aggregate fee of $29 million, and ABC was permitted twenty-two commercial minutes per telecast. The 1982–1985 network contracts were not substantively different, except in terms of the dollar amounts and CBS's participation. Exclusivity was maintained. The NCAA also contracted with TBS for exclusive live cablecasts for 1982–1983. These third-choice games would be carried on Thursday or Saturday evenings so as not to compete with the ABC or CBS telecasts. Again, exclusivity, at least in a given time slot, was preserved.

In principle, the fee paid to teams playing in a televised game was negotiable. Further, a school could elect not to televise its games, and/or it could take advantage of an "exception telecast" clause for any particular game that a network wanted, or it could simply strike out on its own and disregard the NCAA plan. In practice, however, negotiations never took place, and none of these options was feasible.

The District Court found that "[T]his so-called right to negotiate was clearly illusory."[9] By virtue of the NCAA contract, ABC was a monopsonist in the market for national broadcast rights for live college football games. The suppliers of a game that ABC wanted could either turn down the recommended fee or take it. The game would be played in any event. Since ABC wanted only the most attractive games, most of these games would have been sellouts by the time their being televised was announced. Thus, even had the participants believed that televising a game would harm actual attendance, the telecast would not ordinarily affect the ticket revenues. The only monetary loss would be in the parking lot and at the concession stands, and a sizable fraction of the potential attendance would have to stay home for this loss to exceed a fee of $250,000.

The "exception telecast" clause was not a viable option. A local broadcaster would be unwilling to outbid ABC for the right to broadcast to a market with relatively few television homes. The go-it-alone option

---

[9] 546 F. Supp. 1276, 1291 (1982).

entailed two insuperable complications: it takes two to play a game, and any attempt to go it alone would meet with sanctions and retribution from the NCAA. The risks simply overwhelmed the expected rewards.

The plaintiffs (the Universities of Gerogia and Oklahoma) saw in all of this two principal ways in which the competitive market was being superseded and the Sherman Act violated. First, by controlling its members' broadcast rights, the NCAA created a monopoly that (a) fixed the prices for televised games, (b) limited the number of telecasts, and (c) destroyed competition. Although approximately sixty games a year were telecast under the prevailing contract, even *more* would be telecast and *viewer preferences* would play a greater role if individual schools were free to televise their games.

Second, the controls effected two types of group boycott: (a) a threatened horizontal boycott of any school attempting to go it alone, ensuring an NCAA monopoly over televised college football; and (b) a vertical boycott of competitive networks and local broadcasters who were unable to bid for games that ABC did not want, which enhanced ABC's position in the television broadcast market vis-à-vis other broadcasters.

Price Fixing

Recognizing that price fixing harms consumers, whether the fixed prices are "reasonable" or not, the courts have made blatant price fixing a per se violation of Section 1 of the Sherman Act,[10] which prohibits every agreement that restrains trade. The per se approach, however, has not been sacrosanct. All business agreements, with or without a written contract, imply *some* restraint of trade. A franchiser, say, may literally restrain trade and fix prices, but these practices could be sound and efficient procedures that benefit consumers. Thus, the courts have occasionally accepted a rule-of-reason defense against allegations of an illegal price-fixing restraint.[11] The restraint is reasonable if its effect is to promote competition. The restraint is unreasonable if competition is not enhanced.[12]

Since defendants *always* have the option to attempt a rule-of-reason defense, at first blush the per se illegality of price fixing would seem to be rather meaningless. Precisely the opposite is true, however, because most illegal restraints fall into various categories of "naked restraints" that stifle competition.[13]

In *NCAA* the trial court had to decide the following: Should the negoti-

---

[10] See, for example, *United States v. Socony-Vacuum Oil Co.*, 310 U.S. 150 (1940), and *Arizona v. Maricopa County Medical Society*, 457 U.S. 332 (1982).

[11] See, for example, 441 U.S. 1 (1979) and *Continental T.V., Inc. v. GTE Sylvania, Inc.*, 433 U.S. 36 (1977).

[12] For an extensive discussion of these issues, see Scherer and Ross (1990, ch. 12).

[13] *The White Motor Company v. United States*, 372 U.S. 253, 263 (1963).

ating procedure for determining the price for a televised game be considered "price fixing"? If so, was the procedure "reasonable" in that it enhanced, rather than stifled, competition?

Monopoly Power and Output Restraints

The "monopolization" language of Section 2 of the Sherman Act led the Supreme Court in an early case to focus on *intent,* "because knowledge of intent may help the court to interpret facts and to predict consequences."[14] The determining factor is whether the actions are part of normal business practices, or whether their intent was to drive and exclude competitors from the market.[15] Defendants cannot argue that "because of the special characteristics of a particular industry, monopolistic arrangements will better promote trade and commerce than competition."[16] The concern is that the firm acquiring a monopoly will supply lower quantities and charge higher prices than would result under competition.

In *NCAA* the trial court had to decide the following: Did the NCAA's control of college football television constitute monopolization or the attempt to monopolize? If so, was this its intent? Finally, if the NCAA had monopoly power, could it limit output, and drive and exclude competitors from the market in violation of sections 1 and 2?

Group Boycott

Group boycotts are agreements among one group of traders to refuse to deal with others, and are per se Section 1 violations. A group boycott raises some difficult economic issues, because any decision to purchase solely from one seller implies a decision to not do business with any other(s).[17] Thus, the rule of reason has historically come into play in all but the most straightforward situations.

Rule-of-reason considerations are particularly germane where exclusive dealing is involved. If the NCAA's football package is viewed as the not-otherwise-available product of a joint venture, then its sale to the highest bidder merits rule-of-reason consideration. The reasonableness of any restrictions aimed at enhancing the product's ability to compete in the television-program market, and subsequent attempts to enforce the restrictions, must also be considered. If the NCAA is viewed as a cartel seeking to control televised college football, the applicability of the rule of reason is not as clear.

In *NCAA* the trial court had to decide the following: First, did the

---

[14] *Chicago Board of Trade* v. *United States,* 246 U.S. 231, 238 (1918).

[15] See, for example, *United States* v. *Standard Oil Co. of New Jersey et al.,* 173 Fed. 177 (1909), 221 U.S. 1 (1911), and *United States* v. *American Tobacco Co.,* 221 U.S. 106 (1911).

[16] *National Society of Professional Engineers* v. *United States,* 435 U.S. 679, 689 (1978).

[17] For an especially interesting discussion, see Posner (1976, pp. 207–211).

NCAA's television contracts constitute a per se illegal vertical boycott of broadcasters denied access to college football? Next, if schools that were refusing to cooperate with the NCAA were to be disciplined and denied television appearances, was this a per se illegal horizontal boycott? Finally, even if these actions were not illegal per se, would they fail a rule-of-reason test?

MARKET DEFINITION

Anticompetitive behavior must occur someplace and with respect to a particular product or service. In antitrust parlance these are the *relevant geographic* and *product markets,* and their determination is the problem of market definition. In *NCAA* it was readily agreed that the relevant *geographic* market was the entire United States. The relevant *product* market, however, became a matter of intense dispute. The plaintiffs proposed "college football television" as the relevant product; the defendant proposed "all television programming." Everybody agreed that the games had value only because they allowed sponsors to reach a select set of viewers. Thus the broadcasters' demand for college football is a derived demand stemming from sponsor's demands.

If the plaintiffs' product-market definition is accepted, the NCAA as the sole provider of televised college-football games was certainly a monopolist. Only the rule of reason and/or the NCAA's status as a voluntary association of not-for-profit academic institutions could save its football policy from being in violation of the Sherman Act. If the defendant's definition is accepted, the NCAA was the provider of perhaps 84 hours of programming a year out of about 7300 hours of total programming. The NCAA was thus comparable to the facilitator of a small joint venture selling a slightly differentiated product in an imperfectly competitive market in which it lacked market power.

The plaintiffs argued that college-football telecasts were unique, because most were provided on Saturday afternoons, their direct competition came only from grade-B movies and children's programs, and unlike prime-time television series that have residual value through eventual syndication in reruns, any game is a perishable good that has limited appeal once it has been played. The football audience was unique because of its age and income patterns compared with those of the audiences of other programs, including other sports telecasts.

The defendant countered that the buyers in the market are the sponsors, the sellers are the networks, the product being sold is commercial spots, and all commercial spots are fungible, with any differences attributable to demographics and the free market. By establishing *portfolios* of programs, sponsors showed that one program was substitutable for another. On average, a football sponsor allocated only 5.18 percent of its network advertising budget to NCAA football, indicating that the typical advertiser *must* be freely substituting other forms of programming; in essence, college football television is not unique!

The trial court noted, however, that while NCAA football accounted for only 0.44 percent of the total network programming time, the sponsors that spent over 5 percent of their budgets on it paid 2.5 times more per viewer to reach the football audience than it would cost to sponsor other network programs. The court inferred that college football television had "extraordinary appeal to advertisers," and that "[I]t is clear that in the minds of both the network and the advertisers, there is no close substitute for college football."[18] This finding meant that the (legal) ball game was essentially over.

THE NCAA'S DEFENSE

Rather than concede defeat, the NCAA argued that any anticompetitive acts were committed by the broadcasters, that its behavior comprised democratically chosen acts that had only the best on-the-field and off-the-field procompetitive intentions, and that any perceived restraints were ancillary to an overall regulatory scheme for collegiate athletics. Put otherwise, any acts for which the NCAA was directly accountable would pass a rule-of-reason test. The NCAA further argued that the plaintiffs had failed to demonstrate literal price fixing. If the problem was that its "recommended" prices were uniformly imposed, then ABC as the buyer was the price fixer. Moreover, televising sixty choice games a year is scarcely an output restriction. The NCAA defended its controls as designed to protect gate receipts, especially at smaller schools. These controls were just part of a general regulatory scheme aimed at preserving competitive balance and amateurism in collegiate athletics and protecting the health and well-being of the athletes.[19] Finally, the NCAA contended that the plaintiffs did not suffer antitrust injury.

THE DISTRICT COURT'S DECISION

The trial court dismissed the arguments that prices were not being fixed and that the plaintiffs did not suffer antitrust injury. It noted that there was no question that open bidding would have yielded much more than the

---

[18] 546 F. Supp. 1276, 1321–1322 (1982).

[19] For over a century colleges have found a way to support their student-athletes (Dealy, 1990). As television has become a very big revenue-generating business for a larger number of schools, their problem has become one of preserving it as a cash cow. Universities have an interest in preserving collegiate football as an amateur sport in that it permits them to place a ceiling on player "salaries."

$400,000 paid for a game between Oklahoma and Southern California that was carried by over 200 ABC affiliates, and much less than the $400,000 paid for a game between The Citadel and Appalachian State that was carried by four affiliates. The court found no merit in the arguments that ABC was responsible for any price fixing and that the NCAA would no longer recommend prices. The court did find merit in the *plaintiffs'* contentions that more games would have been telecast and viewer preferences better served without the restrictions. It also held that it was unrealistic to expect a school to bolt the NCAA or ignore its threats. The NCAA's argument that it lacked market power fell under the weight of evidence that it could manipulate the college-football television market and that it did so by excluding competition, restricting output, and dictating price.

As regards any deleterious effects of telecasts on attendance, the court dismissed the NCAA's studies as either outdated or flawed. That the NCAA permitted ten additional telecasts under the new pact and that games of the widest possible interest were always televised suggested to the court that the NCAA did not really believe its own arguments. As regards preserving competitive balance, the court viewed the tendency of the same schools to dominate in the wire-service polls year after year as suggesting that the controls were ineffective. Beyond that, the NCAA had other means of achieving all of its eminently commendable goals without resorting to additional television controls.

In particular, the court found as follows: (1) The NCAA exercised monopoly power in the relevant market of live college-football telecasts in the United States; (2) the NCAA-network contracts constituted per se illegal price-fixing agreements that restricted output; and (3) the NCAA had organized a group boycott via (a) a refusal to deal with any broadcaster with whom it had not been uniquely tied (vertical) and (b) threatened sanctions against any member that failed to adhere to its television plans (horizontal). The NCAA-network contracts were thus enjoined.

THE NCAA FIGHTS BACK

The NCAA did not go down without a fight. It first appealed the district court decision to the U.S. Tenth Circuit Court of Appeals.

The Court of Appeals

A 2-to-1 majority accepted the plaintiffs' relevant-market definition, which in essence compelled the finding that "the plan on its face suppresses product diversity and restricts output . . . and constitutes per se illegal price-fixing."[20] It also rejected the rule-of-reason defense, observ-

[20] 707 F.2d 1147, 1156 (1983).

ing that the anticompetitive aspects of the cartel arrangement outweighed any off-the-field procompetitive gains and that these gains in any case could be attained without impinging on the free market.

The Court of Appeals did not accept the trial court's group-boycott conclusions. As to the vertical boycott, the exclusivity aspect sought to raise the value of a network contract, but any network could bid. The fact that only one network was a successful bidder does not constitute a boycott or "an attempt by competitors at one level to foreclose competition by traders at the same level."[21] The court also held that the NCAA's power of expulsion did not by itself constitute a boycott, as it was not a naked attempt to exclude competition. This power was an enforcement mechanism within the purview of a voluntary association's activities.

When all was said and done, the plaintiffs still won the day.

The Supreme Court

The NCAA's last resort was an appeal to the Supreme Court, where it lost 7 to 2. The majority concurred with the earlier courts that the television plan restricted output, restrained the free market, and kept the schools from responding to consumer preferences. The dissenters accepted the NCAA's argument that its regulatory activities were essentially noneconomic, that its purposes and goals were notable and worthy, and that its television controls made sufficiently important contributions toward achieving these noble ends "to offset any minimal anticompetitive effects. . . ."[22]

A key finding of the Court majority was that the restraints were not per se illegal price fixing. Rather, it held that the NCAA and its members market a product, televised college football, that requires the preservation of on-the-field competition. This product differs from the seemingly comparable products offered by professional leagues, and its unique character widens the choice of both sports fans *and* student-athletes. No school is likely to adopt unilaterally the restraints required to preserve that unique character. Thus, the product can only be provided by mutual agreement, which implies that some horizontal restraints may be necessary and hence that any alleged antitrust violation requires a rule-of-reason analysis. The critical issues are whether the restraints are necessary to achieve a legitimate procompetitive goal.[23] This followed the Court's line of argument in *ASCAP,* where a majority opinion noted that individual compositions and the aggregating service offered through ASCAP's blanket licenses made

---

[21] 707 F.2d 1147, 1161 (1983).

[22] 468 U.S. 85, 136 (1984).

[23] The Court made clear that its welfare considerations extended to that of student-athletes and the preservation of collegiate amateur athletics. This extension implies that the broader terms *community* or *societal* welfare are more appropriate descriptors of the Court's concern than is the narrower and more common term *consumer* welfare. This concern further suggests the need to worry about the effects of a horizontal constraint on labor—the amateur athletes of the business world.

up a whole that is "truly greater than the sum of its parts." This whole is "to some extent, a different product" that is sold in a market "in which individual composers are inherently unable to compete effectively."[24] In such a market, even an arrangement that affects price might be reasonable and not per se illegal, because it might be necessary to the provision of the product. The *ASCAP* decision did not imply that the blanket-license arrangements did not violate the antitrust laws, "only" that the arrangements required a rule-of-reason assessment.

The NCAA, however, lacked an affirmative defense that would justify either the higher prices, lower outputs, and restricted viewer choice effected by its television plan, or the market power it acquired through its control of all television rights. The Court specifically noted that by allowing choice games to be telecast in competition with less attractive nontelevised games, the NCAA was undermining its argument that the plan sought to protect attendance. Moreover, the Sherman Act does not intend to inhibit such competition. The Court concluded that the plan restricted only some schools' broadcast revenues; there was no evidence that it promoted greater equality than could be achieved by restrictions on other revenue sources, such as ticket prices.

Ultimately, the majority turned to "the District Court's unambiguous and well-supported finding that many more games would be televised in a free market than under the NCAA plan"[25] and concluded that "[T]he finding that consumption will materially increase if the controls are removed is a compelling demonstration that they do not in fact serve any [such] legitimate purpose."[26] Most critically, the Court purposefully remarked that the "absence of proof of market power does not justify a naked restriction on price or output" and that such a restriction "requires some competitive justification even in the absence of a detailed market analysis."[27] In essence, the related issues of market definition and market power that have so often dogged Sherman Act litigation might henceforth be finessed when a restraint lacks "a plausible efficiency justification" (Muris, 1989, p. 861).

The majority, however, also asserted that (1) the trial court's detailed analysis showed that as a factual matter the NCAA did have the market power to glean supracompetitive prices in the college-football television market and that (2) the trial court had employed the correct market-definition test and had drawn the correct inferences as to both the appropriate market and the NCAA's market power from that test. Accordingly, the justices were not prepared to dismiss these inferences completely when evaluating the competitive effects of the NCAA's horizontal restraints.

The justices may have reasoned (implicitly) as follows. Standard tele-

---

[24] 441 U.S. 1, 21–22 (1979).

[25] 468 U.S. 85, 119 (1984).

[26] 468 U.S. 85, 120 (1984).

[27] 468 U.S. 85, 110 (1984).

vision fare and fall Saturday football telecasts are at best distant substitutes for prospective sponsors and are not at all substitutable for viewers as
a group. Let us accept, *arguendo,* that "NFL Football" and Saturday telecasts of "NCAA Football" are perfect substitutes for both sponsors and
fans, and that sponsors consider any other televised sports to be imperfect
substitutes for fall football. Even then, it is not credible to accept that by
preventing individual schools from televising their games, the NCAA had
not succeeded in reducing the number of telecasts and increasing their
price, while restricting viewer choice. A more credible view is that this
was the specific intent of the restraints. Finally, as in *ASCAP,* "NCAA
Football" could have been made available through the NCAA's *nonexclusive* control of the rights. The product just could not command as high a
price in whatever market is defined and regardless of the NCAA's power
in that market. The only proviso is that the market must have some economic validity.

THE AFTERMATH

NCAA effected major economic changes in college football telecasting
and provided legal reaffirmation of the usefulness of the rule of reason in
assessing horizontal restraints.

Televised College Football

When the Court ended the NCAA's control over college-football telecasts,
it replaced a monopoly with as many as 100 separate sellers—the Division
I football-playing schools—who could compete for the custom of numerous buyers, led by the three major over-the-air networks and trailed by
various national and regional cable systems, as well as local broadcasters.
The plaintiffs' economic experts had testified, and their attorneys had
argued, that such competition would expand consumer choice, increase
output, and reduce price. Whether the plaintiffs really believed that *they*
would be the ones to lose television revenues in a competitive market is
another matter.

Since 1984 the market has certainly worked with respect to output
and viewer choice. Saturday television audiences have typically had a
menu of college football games from which to choose. The market has
also worked with respect to the impact on price, perhaps to the unpleasant
surprise of the plaintiffs, as can be seen in the following figures:[28] After
the Supreme Court decision in the spring of 1984, the CFA and ABC
agreed on a $12 million package to be put in place that fall. The CFA also
agreed to a $9.2 million pact with ESPN. CBS paid $10 million for Big

---

[28] See Greenspan (1988) for an extensive discussion of the initial economic effects of *NCAA.*

Ten and Pac Ten games, and TBS got twelve Southeastern Conference (SEC) games for $6 million. The $37.2 million total is only slightly more than half of the $67 million that the NCAA contracts with ABC and CBS alone would have yielded. By 1985, the Big Ten, Pac Ten, and Atlantic Coast (ACC) conferences had all signed with CBS for two-year packages worth a total of about $12 million per year. Given the time to work things out, ABC and its new bedfellows, the CFA, agreed on a two-year package worth about $16 million per year for twenty-one games a year. ESPN contributed an additional $12.5 million to the CFA for a seventeen-game season. Thus, the major purchasers paid a total of around $40 million for major college-football telecasts—*less than half* the $90 million (or more) that the original NCAA contracts with ABC, CBS, and TBS would have yielded in 1985. Moreover, the market has continued to work through the late 1980s. From 1987 through 1990, ABC (Big Ten and Pac Ten), CBS (CFA), and ESPN (CFA) paid about $45 million for collegiate football, thereby paying less money while giving football fans a wider choice of games to watch.

As an ironic footnote to *NCAA,* when a pair of non-CFA members playing CFA teams were denied the right to televise those games, they brought charges against the CFA that were comparable to those that the CFA had brought against the NCAA.[29] And they won, despite the fact that the CFA's television controls were not nearly as tight as those of the NCAA. A subsequent suit against the CFA was nevertheless dismissed in Judge Burciaga's court.[30] In 1990, however, the Federal Trade Commission brought a complaint against the CFA and Capital Cities/ABC under Section 5 of the Federal Trade Commission Act, but the case was dismissed in 1994.[31] The CFA may have avoided a sack as a result of a ruling that as a nonprofit organization it was exempt from FTC regulation. What it was unable to avoid, however, was the realignment of teams and conferences due to the lure of higher television revenues that had initially led to *NCAA.*

In 1990, Notre Dame bolted the CFA and signed a five-year, $30-million contract with NBC for the exclusive rights to its home games. Over the next few years a number of football powerhouses altered their conference memberships and formed new alliances, or relinquished their independent status to join a conference, in pursuit of higher television revenues. Between over-the-air and cable conference packages, as well as through the sale of individual games on a pay-per-view basis, it is no longer unusual for even a medium-level Division I school to appear

[29] *Regents of the University of California* v. *American Broadcasting Co.,* 747 F.2d 511 (9th Cir. 1984).

[30] *American Association of Independent TV* v. *College Football Association,* 637 F. Supp. 1289 (W.D. Okla. 1986).

[31] *College Football Association,* No. 9242 (Federal Trade Commission, Sept. 5, 1990) (initiation) and No. 9242 (June 16, 1994) (dismissal).

regularly on television and earn millions of dollars in television rights. In 1996, ABC/ESPN alone televised over 150 games, and scores of other games were televised by CBS and various regional syndicators such as Jefferson Pilot. Nonetheless, the *total* that broadcasters pay for those rights is unlikely to be as great as would have obtained under an NCAA cartel, and not every school has profited. Viewer choice has in any event been expanded, and in June 1997 the CFA closed up shop, with the future of televised college football bright and secured.

Horizontal Restraints and the Rule of Reason

The future of the rule of reason is no less bright. In *NCAA* the Supreme Court reaffirmed its *ASCAP* view that agreement among competitors and horizontal restraints might under some circumstances be a necessary part of doing business in a competitive market. Offering an otherwise unavailable product to that market is an important case in point. The Court also reaffirmed that such agreements might be procompetitive, enhance efficiency, and benefit consumers, in which case they would pass a rule-of-reason test and not be considered per se illegal. Wholesale buying cooperatives[32] and service networks[33] are subsequent exemplars. Thus, the Court reaffirmed the need initially to apply a rule-of-reason analysis in assessing the merits of particular acts and agreements.

A horizontal restraint fails a rule-of-reason test if it is not essential to the conduct of business and if an alternative arrangement that is less likely to affect consumer welfare adversely is available. Passing this test is mandatory. A horizontal restraint also fails a rule-of-reason test if its likely result is a higher price; that is, if it is exclusionary and denies buyers acceptable and competitive lower-cost options. Passing this test, too, is mandatory. A horizontal restraint also fails a rule-of-reason test if it lacks clear transactions cost benefits that make the cooperative enterprise more efficient than any one of its components,[34] or if it lacks the potential to enhance consumer welfare in some other way. Passing this test is not mandatory because the restraint's effects might be neutral. Still, a passing grade helps to justify the restraint and place it in a more favorable light.

The Court went further in stating that once a market-restraining act or agreement fails a rule-of-reason test, a definitive determination of the relevant market and/or market power is unnecessary: the restraint is per se illegal. The Court, however, did not declare all cooperative agreements that are not efficiency enhancing, or procompetitive, or essential to the provision

---

[32] *Northwest Wholesale Stationers, Inc.* v. *Pacific Stationery & Printing Co.,* 472 U.S. 284 (1985).

[33] *Rothery Storage & Van Co.* v. *Atlas Van Lines, Inc.,* 792 F.2d 210 (D.C. Cir. 1986), *cert. denied,* 479 U.S. 1033 (1987); *Hassan* v. *Independent Practice Associates,* 698 F. Supp. 679 (E.D. Mich. 1988).

[34] Rubin (1990) discussed the role of transactions costs in managing business organizations, particularly in the context of antitrust and related issues.

of a good to be illegal per se. Thus, by implication, the Court had in mind agreements that are clearly anticompetitive and likely to effect higher prices, lower outputs, and restricted consumer choice in *some* market, and are thereby likely to impact consumer welfare adversely. But an anticompetitive act cannot have an anticompetitive consequence without individual market power or concerted behavior. Thus, by further implication, the Court had in mind only those restraints that adversely affect *some* market in which the cooperating parties doubtless have *some* market power. Only in this case is an explicit market definition and the coincident need to gauge market power unnecessary. Thus, the rule of reason is alive and well. So, too, are traditional antitrust market analysis and the concept of per se illegality.

And the sports leagues' rules of governance continue to result in disagreements among the teams, and between the teams and players, who do not hesitate to rely on external courts to resolve their internal conflicts. For example, teams have turned to the courts in both their successful[35] and their unsuccessful[36] attempts to relocate their franchises without league approval, and the leagues have relied on the courts in an effort to enforce the restraints that are imposed on individual members in marketing their products and services.[37] Players and coaches have also gone to court in an effort to minimize the restraints placed on their freedom of movement or other conditions of employment.[38] In *McNeil et al.* v. *NFL* the issue was whether the restraint was "reasonably necessary." More recently, a circuit court of appeals observed that a restraint might affect the *labor* market without having any anticompetitive effect on the *product* market.[39] Indeed, even as this is being written in the fall of 1997, Major League Soccer, which is organized as a single entity, allegedly to help generate public interest in soccer in the United States, is being sued by ten of its players on the grounds that it eliminates competitive bidding; it was established as a monopoly![40] The sports beat goes on.

REFERENCES

Dealy, Francis X., Jr. *Win at Any Cost.* New York: Carol Publishing Group, 1990.

Greenspan, David. "College Football's Biggest Fumble: The Economic Impact of the

---

[35] *Los Angeles Memorial Coliseum* v. *National Football League*, 726 F.2d 1381 (9th Cir. 1984), *cert. denied*, 469 U.S. 990 (1984).

[36] *National Basketball Association* v. *SDC Basketball Club, Inc.*, 815 F.2d 562 (9th Cir. 1987), *cert. dismissed*, 484 U.S. 960 (1987).

[37] *National Football League Properties Inc.* v. *Dallas Cowboys Football Club, Ltd.*, 922 F. Supp. 849 (S.D.N.Y. 1996).

[38] See *McNeil et al.* v. *NFL*, 790 F. Supp. 871 (8th Cir. 1992) in the former regard, and *Law* v. *NCAA*, 901 F. Supp. 1394 (D. Kan. 1995) in the latter regard.

[39] *Brown* v. *Pro Football, Inc.*, 50 F.3d 1041 (D.C. Cir. 1995).

[40] In *United States Football League* v. *National Football League*, 644 F. Supp. 1040 (S.D.N.Y. 1986), the NFL was held to be a monopoly in violation of Section 2, but one with which the USFL had aspired to merge.

Supreme Court's Decision in *National Collegiate Athletic Association* v. *Board of Regents of the University of Oklahoma.*" *Antitrust Bulletin* 33 (Spring 1988): 1–65.

Hochberg, Philip, and Ira Horowitz. "Broadcasting and CATV: The Beauty and the Bane of Major College Football." *Law and Contemporary Problems* 38 (Winter–Spring 1973): 112–128.

Meyers, D. Kent, and Ira Horowitz. "Private Enforcement of the Antitrust Laws Works Occasionally: *Board of Regents of the University of Oklahoma* v. *NCAA,* a Case in Point." *Oklahoma Law Review* 48 (1995): 669–709.

Muris, Timothy J. "The New Rule of Reason." *Antitrust Law Journal* 57 (1989): 859–865.

Noll, Roger. "The Economics of Sports Leagues." In *Law of Professional and Amateur Sports,* edited by Gary Uberstine. New York: Clark, Boardman and Callaghan, 1995.

Posner, Richard A. *Antitrust Law.* Chicago: University of Chicago Press, 1976.

Quirk, James, and Rodney D. Fort. *Pay Dirt: The Business of Professional Team Sports.* Princeton, N.J.: Princeton University Press, 1992.

Rubin, Paul H. *Managing Business Transactions.* New York: Free Press, 1990.

Scherer, F. M., and D. Ross. *Industrial Market Structure and Economic Performance.* 3d ed. Boston: Houghton-Mifflin, 1990.

Vrooman, John. "A General Theory of Professional Sports Leagues." *Southern Economic Journal* 61 (April 1995): 971–990.

CASE 9

Collusive Predation:
Matsushita v. *Zenith* (1986)

Kenneth G. Elzinga

INTRODUCTION

Within a few months of the Supreme Court's 5-to-4 opinion in *Matsushita* v. *Zenith*,[1] the case had become a widely cited and widely discussed decision of the Court. What the Supreme Court decided in only seventeen pages of written text came after millions of pages of documents had been examined and thousands of hours of labor had been expended before the litigation got to the nation's highest court. By antitrust standards, *Matsushita* v. *Zenith* was what lawyers call "a big case."

Justice Lewis Powell's Supreme Court opinion recognized that economic analysis merited an important role in the Court's reasoning process. Indeed, it is rare for the Court to place reliance on economic analysis to the extent that it did in this case. Four principles from the economists' tool kit have particular usefulness in assessing this case. They are the economic theory of predation, the theory of the cartel cheater, the law of one price, and the principle of alternative opportunity cost.

THE BACKGROUND OF THE LITIGATION

Some antitrust cases involve allegations of conspiracy. Some entail allegations of predatory pricing. *Matsushita* v. *Zenith* (hereafter *M* v. *Z*) was

Kenneth G. Elzinga served as a consultant to the Japanese television manufacturers in this case. Gratitude is expressed to David E. Mills for his input on this case study.

[1]The case originally was *Zenith* v. *Matsushita* at the district court: *Zenith Radio Corp. et al. v. Matsushita Electric Industrial Corp., Ltd., et al.*, 513 F. Supp. 1100 (1981). Upon the defendants' initial legal victory, the case was appealed by the plaintiffs, *Zenith Radio Corp. et al. v. Matsushita Electric Industrial Corp., Ltd., et al.*, 723 F.2d 238 (1983). After Zenith's victory at the initial appellate

about both conspiracy and predatory pricing. The plaintiffs charged that several companies that were supposed to be independent competitors entered a conspiracy to charge predatory prices in one market while collusively charging supracompetitive prices in another. Several laws were said to be violated by the defandants' behavior[2]; but the Sherman Act charges of a conspiracy to restrain trade and a collective attempt to monopolize were the focus of the action.

The Players

Matsushita v. *Zenith* was born in 1970 when National Union Electric Corporation (NUE) brought suit against a number of Japanese firms. NUE was the former Emerson Radio Company, a U.S. pioneer in the manufacture of radios and television receivers. Four years later, Zenith Radio Corporation filed a similar lawsuit against the same Japanese firms. The two actions were consolidated. The principal defendants were seven Japanese firms: Matsushita, Toshiba, Hitachi, Sharp, Sanyo, Sony, and Mitsubishi (hereafter the Japanese firms).[3] They are among the largest business corporations in the world. In 1974, the seven firms had combined sales of over $20 billion. Zenith and NUE are not "Mom and Pop" operations either: Zenith had sales of $910 million in 1974, and NUE had sales of $140 million.

The charges in *M* v. *Z* embrace the entire consumer electronics products industry: television receivers, radios, tape players, and stereo equipment. But the case was fought primarily over the relevant market of television receivers (hereafter televisions) in the United States.

Televisions are a consumer durable familiar to everyone. Originally the product of American and European inventors, the U.S. industry was the world leader in production volume and quality until the mid-1960s. The birth of the Japanese industry came largely through licensing arrangements and technical assistance from U.S. companies. American firms such as GE, RCA, Westinghouse, Western Electric, and Zenith, along with European firms such as Philips, were prominent exporters of licensed technology to Japan.

The basic charge against the Japanese firms was that they were engaged in a massive global conspiracy lasting more than two decades whose purpose was to destroy the American television industry. The alleged strategy had two prongs: (1) charging monopoly prices in Japan, the

---

level, the case went to the Supreme Court, *Matsushita Electric Industrial Corp., Ltd., et al.* v. *Zenith Radio Corp. et al.,* 475 U.S. 574 (1986). Throughout this article, the term *plaintiffs* refers to the original plaintiffs in the lawsuit: Zenith and National Union Electric Corporation.

[2]Sections 1 and 2 of the Sherman Act, Section 73 of the Wilson Tariff Act, Section 7 of the Clayton Act, the Robinson-Patman Act, and the Wilson Antidumping Act. The last law did not involve any conspiracy allegations.

[3]There were several other defendants, including subsidiaries of the Japanese firms and some American firms such as Sears, Roebuck. Sony was one of the original principal defendants. It settled with Zenith, but remained a defendant in the NUE half of the case.

defendants' home market, through a price-fixing conspiracy among the defendants there, and (2) using the monopoly profits made in Japan to subsidize below-cost, predatory pricing on export sales to the United States. Zenith and NUE claimed that, in the short run, U.S. producers like themselves were economically harmed by the predatory pricing and, in the long run, American consumers would end up paying monopoly prices on televisions after domestic competition was eliminated.

Predatory Pricing in the United States

Using monopoly profits made in one market to gain a monopoly position in another is a strategy often associated with some of the notorious trusts of an earlier industrial era. In *M* v. *Z*, the alleged predators were Japanese firms, and their war chest supposedly was derived from a cartelized home market largely shut off from outside competition.

The Mechanics of Predatory Pricing in *Matsushita* v. *Zenith*

Two Japanese organizations were said to form the heart of the export portion of the conspiracy: MITI (the Ministry of International Trade and Industry) and the JMEA (Japanese Machinery Exporters Association). Through MITI, an arm of the Japanese government, minimum prices, called "check" (or "reference" or "benchmark") prices, were established governing the sale to the United States of consumer electronic products, including televisions. Through the JMEA, the defendants allegedly adopted a "Five Company Rule" that limited each Japanese seller to only five wholesale customers in the United States. Under the Sherman Act it would be illegal for a group of competitors to agree upon minimum prices and to agree not to compete against each other for particular customers.[4]

The plaintiffs contended that not only were agreements made by the Japanese firms on the check prices but there were additional agreements to go below the check-price minimums. This disregard of the check prices was done, according to the plaintiffs, through secret rebates and discounts to U.S. customers. Zenith and NUE complained that these prices, or at least some of them, were artificially depressed and predatory.

There are, then, two antitrust issues running concurrently here: prices that are predatory in the U.S. television market, and a collusive agreement to put them there. The economic theory of predation sheds light on the first issue; the economic theory of cartels sheds light on the second.

---

[4]While both fixing minimum prices and dividing markets are Sherman Act offenses, it is not clear how rivals of firms adopting such behavior would be affected adversely by these practices. In fact, Zenith and NUE should have been the beneficiaries of such tactics, had they been carried out. If fixing minimum prices and dividing markets had constituted the plaintiffs' entire case, the district court would have denied them standing to sue because they would not have been injured parties but rather economic beneficiaries; 513 F. Supp. 1147–1148 (1981).

THE ECONOMIC THEORY OF PREDATION AND THE EVIDENCE

Predatory pricing is a conscious strategy of pricing below cost on a sustained basis to eliminate or discipline one's rivals in order to maintain or establish monopoly power. When this strategy is successful, rivals expire or cede pricing leadership to the predator. The upshot of successful predatory pricing is the monopolization of a market, to the detriment of consumers of that product or service. The topic of predatory pricing has been widely discussed in academic circles and has been a central allegation in several important antitrust cases that did not reach the Supreme Court in the decade prior to *M* v. *Z*.[5]

In many antitrust cases involving predatory pricing, courts typically examine evidence comparing a defendant's prices with its costs. The most famous methodology for comparing prices and costs considered by courts is adopted from the economic theory of the firm and was promoted in a 1975 article in the *Harvard Law Review*.[6] This method, now called the Areeda-Turner test, entails comparing an alleged predator's price with its average variable cost (as a proxy for marginal cost) and rests on the assumption that no seller normally will produce output if the market price is below the firm's out-of-pocket costs.[7] In the economic theory of the firm, the average variable cost curve is associated with the firm's shut-down point. In a mechanical application of this theory, a price below the shut-down point should cause the firm to cease operations.[8] If the firm chooses not to shut down, the inference is explored (or drawn) that the firm is engaging in predatory pricing.

Inherent in predatory pricing is that the predator must incur a short-run loss in order to impose losses on its prey. Zenith and NUE claimed that the Japanese defendants sold televisions in the United States at prices below cost. Partly because of the difficulty in estimating defendants' variable costs and partly because there was not a full trial on the merits, an

---

[5]The literature on predatory pricing is too large to cite comprehensively here. For a selective introduction to the topic and the ongoing debate, see Joskow and Klevorick (1979), Brodley and Hay (1981), Calvani and Lynch (1982), Isaac and Smith (1985), Shepherd (1986), Fisher (1987), Boudreaux, Elzinga and Mills (1995), and Areeda and Hovenkamp, (1996, pp. 221–465), as well as the references to the articles on price predation in footnote 20.

[6]Areeda and Turner (1975).

[7]As Areeda and Turner (1975, p. 733) put it: "Recognizing that marginal cost data are typically unavailable, we conclude that (a) a price at or above reasonably anticipated average variable cost should be conclusively presumed lawful, and (b) a price below reasonably anticipated average variable cost should be conclusively presumed unlawful."

[8]There are benign reasons a firm may price below average variable cost. The firm may be unloading inventory at distress prices; it may be a new seller engaging in promotional pricing; it may be a new firm whose output does not yet exploit expected lower costs due to a learning curve phenomenon; and its average variable cost curve may not reflect tax considerations that make pricing below this measure of cost profitable on a posttax basis.

Areeda-Turner type test was never used by the Court to examine the predation allegation.[9]

Predation as an Investment

In economic analysis, predation can be seen as having an investment-like character. One incurs significant costs, in the form of losses, during the period of predation. These losses are an investment in prospective monopoly profits. Justice Powell recognized this subtle facet of economic analysis when he wrote the following:

> The forgone profits [of predation] may be considered an investment in the future. For the investment to be rational, the conspirators must have a reasonable expectation of recovering, in the form of later monopoly profits, more than the losses suffered.[10]

Figure 9-1 illustrates and compares a predator's losses during predation and its profits during recoupment. Assume that the competitive, prepredation price is at a level of 100 and is represented by the distance *OH*. The total quantity sold per year at this price is also 100 and is represented by *OC*. Now suppose that the alleged predatory price of the Japanese sellers was equal to the distance *OF*, and assume that this unremunerative price caused some U.S. sellers to leave the industry and others to cut back their output such that U.S. sales were only *OA*. Assume further that the demand curve remains unchanged.

The total number of televisions consumers will buy during each year of predation is *OD*. Since U.S. producers have elected to produce only *OA* under the predatory conditions, the Japanese must produce the balance: *AD*. This means the Japanese firms' loss on each unit produced and sold is *FH*, the difference between the average competitive price *OH* (which is a proxy for long-run average costs, including a normal profit) and the predatory price *OF*. Thus the predators' losses in every year of predation are depicted by the product of *HF* × *AD* (the shaded rectangle).

Figure 9-1 can be used to assess the prospects for recoupment by the defendants. Assume that when predation is over, the U.S. competition is beaten back and continues to produce only *OA* units. This means the Japanese firms cannot consider the total demand curve as their own. They will raise prices during recoupment to maximize profits over the

---

[9]An economic expert for the plaintiffs opined that four of the Japanese firms had sold televisions in the United States at prices at least below average cost. The district court judge, for reasons not assessed here, ruled that this price-cost evidence was inadmissible on the grounds that the construction of the cost and price data was unreliable.

[10]475 U.S. 574, 588–589 (1986).

FIGURE 9-1 Predator's Predation Losses and Recoupment Gains.

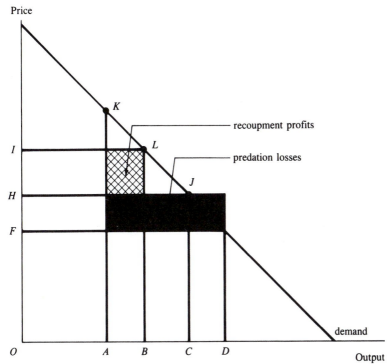

"residual" demand curve, which is that portion of the demand curve southeast of point *K*.[11]

The predators' profit-maximizing (monopolistic) price during recoupment is *OI*; their level of output is *AB*, which is the difference between the total demand *OB* at the recoupment price and the output *OA* of their U.S. rivals. The profit on each set is *IH*. The profit during each year of recoupment would be the product of *IH* × *AB* (the cross-hatched area). On the basis of Figure 9-1, a predatory pricing strategy would seem rational only if the value to the firm of the recoupment rectangle exceeded the cost to the firm of the loss rectangle. In the example shown (visually), this does not occur; but the rectangles represent only an annual benefit and cost. The predatory strategy, in its loss stage and recoupment stage, may take several years. Figure 9-1, therefore, is a heuristic device. A simple comparison of the rectangles, by itself, cannot reveal the full costs and benefits of predation because of the tactic's intertemporal dimension. But Figure 9-1 does illustrate key parameters of a predation strategy.

---

[11]The profit-maximizing price for the predators will be the midpoint of the segment *KJ* for a linear demand curve. Any price southeast of *J* on the demand curve could not be a recoupment option for the Japanese sellers if they were predators, since *J* itself shows the competitive price level. A price higher than *K* on the demand curve is not an option either. With the U.S. firms supplying *OA* already, nobody would pay such a price.

Present Value and Predation

Economic analysis teaches that a dollar tomorrow is worth less than a dollar today. Consequently, a rational predator recognizes that the profit rectangle during recoupment must more than offset the loss rectangle during predation in order to compensate the firm for the time-value of the funds employed. In a more careful analysis of predation, the discounted character of the losses would be compared with the future stream of monopoly profits.[12]

Whether the returns to investment in predation are sufficiently great to warrant the cost depends on how long and how far prices are below costs during the predation period, the rate of return the predator uses in making its investment decision, the reentry rate of rivals during the recoupment period, and the length of the recoupment period. In addition, the more inelastic is demand in the market, the better the prospects for a predator to be successful.

Using this analysis, Table 9-1 shows a series of conditions derived from the economic studies submitted by plaintiffs in *M* v. *Z*. The predatory price is expressed as a percentage of the prices that plaintiffs alleged would have prevailed, absent predation. For example, in column one, for color televisions, the entry "62" reflects the plaintiffs' contention that the average prices charged by Japanese firms during the period 1968 to 1975 were 62 percent of the but-for-predation price. Column two shows the same calculation for black-and-white receivers. Both columns reflect the deep discounting allegedly engaged in by the Japanese. Column one adopts plaintiffs' position that the period of predation ran at least from 1965 (when the Japanese first gained 5% of the market) to 1975 (the year after the cases were consolidated). Column two indicates that predation in

TABLE 9-1
Predation in Televisions

	Color Sets	Black-White Sets
Predatory price	62	58
Years of predation	10	13
Growth in demand	5%	-2%
Japanese beginning market share	5%	5%
Japanese ending market share	42%	17%
Recoupment price range	119–138	100–106
Years of recoupment	(∞)	*

*The alleged predatory pricing cartel could never recoup its predatory losses. Declining demand and increasing levels of non-Japanese imports and stable U.S. production levels would shrink Japanese sales to zero at prices above 100 percent of the open-market level by the tenth year of the recoupment period.

[12]This approach has been developed in Elzinga and Mills (1989). For a comparison of this approach with the Areeda-Turner test, see Elzinga and Mills (1994).

black-and-white sets purportedly endured for at least thirteen years. Given such deep discounting for such a long period, the losses (or magnitude of the investment in predation) would be enormous.

It would be unrealistic for the defendants to expect the output of U.S. television producers to fall immediately to zero under conditions of predatory pricing, if only because some consumers may prefer particular features of U.S. producers, such as cabinet styling, and some retailers who carry a full line of appliances made by a particular U.S. manufacturer may be slow to substitute a Japanese brand of television sets. For these reasons and others, there would be some lag before U.S. firms drastically reduced or ceased their television production because of predatory price levels. But if prices were in fact predatory, predators at a minimum could reasonably expect the output of U.S. firms not to expand during the predation period. If domestically produced output remained constant, as column one of Table 9-1 assumes, the Japanese would capture all television sales stemming from demand growth. This would have given the defendants 42 percent of the color market by 1975.

The demand for black-and-white sets was declining during the period under consideration. Column two's calculations ascribe to the Japanese producers their actual share of the black-and-white segment at the end of the predation period—17 percent. Japanese firms in the manufacturing sector at that time earned an average 12.2-percent rate of return on assets (Holland, 1984, Table 1-3, p. 9). If this approximates the alternative opportunity cost for the defendants of an investment in predatory pricing and if 1.2 is a reasonable estimate of the price elasticity of demand for televisions in the United States (Houthakker and Taylor, 1966, p. 130), the size of the putative losses of the Japanese firms can be compared with the prospective returns supposedly available to offset them. From this, one can estimate how long and at what level remunerative recoupment prices would have to be for predation to be worthwhile.

Table 9-1 shows the range of prices the Japanese could have expected to charge during the recoupment period and the duration of payment to make predation worth the candle. The analysis assumes that the rivals of the Japanese defendants sell the same number of televisions during the years of attempted recoupment as they did at the end of the predatory period. This assumption favors the prospect of the predation strategy's being successful, in that it means that the rivals of the predators do not expand their output even if monopoly prices were being charged by the Japanese producers. The table suggests that even under this assumption, recoupment is impossible for the Japanese firms in either of the television segments. If recoupment could go on for infinity, it would not pay off for the Japanese firms in color televisions because the huge initial losses swamp the modest price enhancement possible during recoupment. In the black-and-white segment, prospects are even worse. Because of declining demand, charging the best price it can for black-and-white sets (essentially, the competitive price) shuts the Japanese firms out of the market in ten years.

By the analysis reflected in Table 9-1, the pricing strategy imputed to the Japanese firms by the plaintiffs in *M* v. *Z* requires that the defendant firms act irrationally. Because the investment characteristics of the market do not support a predation theory, this suggests some other explanation of the events described (such as lower costs for the Japanese firms).

Market Power Prerequisite for Recoupment

Economic theory characterizes successful predation as a two-step sequence. The first step involves below-cost pricing to drive out or discipline rivals; exercise of the second step, recoupment, requires monopoly power. In antitrust enforcement, a firm's market share often serves as a proxy for its market power. A seller with a low market share in a market with several sellers cannot dictate market price unilaterally. A firm (or group of firms acting collusively) with a large market share may not have significant market power either if customers perceive other products or services as close substitutes, or if entry into the market is easy.

Notwithstanding the economic devastation supposedly inflicted upon U.S. firms, the Japanese defendants' combined market share (in terms of unit sales) of black-and-white and of color sets made to U.S. dealers never exceeded 50 percent.[13] Japanese-made color sets exported to the United States went from fewer than 700,000 units in 1968 to almost 4 million units by 1976. The numbers are impressive but not overwhelming. In 1965, the Japanese defendants supplied only about 10 percent of U.S. purchases of televisions; by 1970, the percentage had grown but was still under 30 percent.[14] If there were no collusion on export sales, a fortiori, the low market shares of individual Japanese firms would suggest that the defendants individually had no significant control over price. Indeed, Mitsubishi, in its biggest volume year in the United States, sold less than 1 percent of the black-and-white and color sets purchased in this country.[15]

While NUE and other U.S. television producers did exit the business, Zenith remained a prominent seller. In 1973, the year before the NUE and Zenith cases were consolidated, Zenith had 23.8 percent of the color television market, selling more sets in the United States than any other seller; Zenith was followed by RCA, another U.S. producer, which at that time had 20.1 percent of the U.S. color market.[16] Plaintiffs had difficulty

---

[13]513 F. Supp. 1100, 1322 (1981).

[14]513 F. Supp. 1100, 1251 (1981).

[15]513 F. Supp. 1100, 1285 (1981). Mitsubishi owned no manufacturing facilities in Japan, so it is not evident under the plaintiffs' theory of the case how it benefited from a predatory export cartel. It could not use gains from Japanese production to finance losses in the United States. In fact, it is a buyer of televisions (which it resells); it has no incentive to see the Japanese home market monopolized or to drive U.S. manufacturers out of business.

[16]513 F. Supp. 1100, 1255 (1981).

persuading the court that the Japanese firms, even collectively, ever gained monopoly power or had the prospect of gaining it to accomplish predation's second step. Economic reasoning persuaded the lower court that there was no reason to study or ascertain the height of any entry barriers in the television industry because of the low market shares held by the defendants.

Cheating in a Predatory Cartel

In the economic theory of the cartel, one of the most powerful concepts is that of the cheater. Cartel theory teaches that when a group of rivals collusively establishes price at the joint profit-maximizing level, it will be economically advantageous for any one seller to operate outside the cartel rather than within. Outside the cartel, a seller—the cheater—can enjoy the high cartel price but not be subject to the output limitation imposed on insiders that makes the high price possible.

Most cartels seek to maintain high prices. So the cheater typically is the firm that tries to sneak outside, shade prices, and clandestinely sell larger outputs. But in a predatory cartel, the cheater does the reverse. If firms have agreed to charge prices *below* cost, the cheater's incentive is to sell *less* than its share of the jointly mandated amount considered necessary to drive out the rivals. The cheater concept has powerful applicability in analyzing *M* v. *Z.*

Plaintiffs maintained that under the auspices of MITI, Japanese sellers collusively set check prices. The check-price minimums were to show the U.S. government that Japan wanted "fair competition" and should not be subject to tariffs and quotas that would be even more restrictive. Then, to circumvent the check prices, the Japanese sellers offered U.S. customers secret price cuts and rebates below these prices. Plaintiffs devoted some 2000 pages in their Final Pretrial Statement describing details of this "rebate scheme." The documentation is a powerful showing of the many ways by which buyers pay transaction prices lower than list prices. Zenith and NUE alleged that the prices the Japanese sellers netted after violating the check-price minimum were unremunerative.

The factual record surrounding the check-price violations actually is powerful evidence that these reference prices were not predatory because sellers sought additional sales at levels below them. It would be irrational (as a matter of economics) to want to sell "more than your share" at prices below cost, especially when such sales involved falsifying purchase orders, shipping documents, export validation forms, and U.S. Customs' invoices; entailed keeping double sets of books; and involved other types of concealment.[17]

---

[17]The Japanese sellers would secretly rebate to the customer the difference between the nominal price declared for export and import purposes and the actual transaction price quoted to the customer. These activities did not violate the antitrust laws, but they did expose the Japanese producers to other legal action by the U.S. Bureau of Customs and the U.S. Treasury Department.

It is logical to ask whether the secret rebates and clandestine discounts might not have been part of a concerted effort by the Japanese to move transaction prices down—perhaps without MITI's knowledge—to predatory levels. What is difficult to reconcile with such a conjecture is the eagerness with which Japanese sellers sought to expand their sales at prices below the check-price level, a level that allegedly was below production and marketing costs.[18] For example, an importer told Sharp (one of the seven principal defendants) that Sharp's competitors were rebating off the check prices and that if Sharp wanted any business, it must be prepared to lower its prices as well. Sharp obliged. When Matsushita was planning to acquire Motorola, a U.S. firm to which Sharp had sold televisions, Sharp requested Motorola executives not to tell Matsushita of its past rebates and deviations from the check prices.[19]

The only economic rationale for an eagerness to expand one's share of below-cost sales in a truly predatory cartel would be if a seller viewed its product line as being highly differentiated. If there were great customer inertia against switching brands, a cheating member of a predatory cartel might covet additional sales (even during the period of predation), knowing or believing that its new customers will not switch suppliers when prices are raised later to monopolistic levels.

Such a prospect does not square with consumer behavior in the television industry at the time of the alleged predation in *M* v. *Z*. Only Sony, among all the defendants, had significant brand recognition, and it sold at relatively high prices, not low prices. Large-scale buyers of Japanese televisions and other consumer electronics products, such as a K-Mart or a Woolco, who frequently attach their own "house brand" name to a product, do not become wedded to a particular manufacturer. Moreover, Japanese television manufacturers witnessed firsthand that American consumers were not locked in to their first television brand. Many switched from U.S. firms like Philco and Admiral to firms like Hitachi and Sanyo when they purchased their second television sets (or replaced their first).

The Economic Literature on Predatory Pricing

Legal opinions usually have many footnotes. But rarely are they references to economists. In *M* v. *Z*, the Supreme Court, to an extent not often seen, relied on economic studies of predation to influence its decision. Justice Powell mentioned the "consensus among commentators that predatory pricing schemes are rarely tried, and even more rarely successful."[20]

---

[18]Cartelization also implies not only concerted behavior but also similar behavior. Rebates were not offered to all customers, and the amount of rebates, when offered, varied between defendants and between customers of the same defendant. Such disparate behavior squares with independent rivalry more than joint conduct. 513 F. Supp. 1180, 1249 (1981).

[19]513 F. Supp. 1100, 1247, 1278 (1981).

[20]475 U.S. 574, 589 (1986). Some of the scholarly articles the Court cited are Easterbrook (1981), Koller (1971) and McGee (1958, 1980).

The word *consensus* is an apt one; *unanimity* would not have been. Most of the historical studies of alleged episodes of predatory pricing have shown the charges to be unfounded. They tend to support the prediction of economic theory that predatory pricing will be difficult because of the large losses a successful predator must somehow offset. Nonetheless, there are some economists who remain persuaded that predatory pricing is, in particular markets, a matter of serious antitrust concern.

THE LAW OF ONE PRICE

The economist's "law of one price" says that in competitive markets, sales of the same product will be at identical prices. Plaintiffs in *M* v. *Z* essentially argued: If a television set sells for $200 (in yen equivalent) in Japan, and the same set sells for $150 in the United States, sellers should increase supply in Japan and decrease supply in the United States (on the assumption that transportation costs are not substantial). In the process, by competitive arbitrage, only one price will result. If prices do not equilibrate, the argument continues, there must be a reason Japanese sellers do not expand sales in Japan (the home market conspiracy theory) and reduce sales in the United States (the predation theory). Capping off the argument is the closed Japanese market (for which there is much evidence), which prevents U.S. producers from accomplishing the arbitrage by increasing *their* shipments to Japan. The difficulty of obtaining retail and wholesale distribution appeared to be one of the main barriers to entry.

Plaintiffs offered evidence that compared defendants' home market prices for televisions with prices for U.S. export and argued that Japanese prices exceeded U.S. prices. Defendants claimed this evidence was marred because the economists' ceteris paribus conditions were not met in making the comparison: The sets were not identical in their engineering specifications, they were sold at different levels of distribution, and they bore different warranty and distribution costs in the two countries.

The lower court agreed with the defendants' economic analysis that these differences made the law of one price inapplicable. In fact, Japanese export sales to the United States did not have a lockstep relationship either to their own or to U.S. prices. Some of the defendants, notably Sony, charged relatively high prices in the United States.[21] Some charged relatively low prices. Moreover, relative prices varied among different models among the Japanese defendants themselves and in comparison with their U.S. rivals.

That Japanese firms often undercut established prices in the United States does not itself prove predation, since the Japanese were new entrants

---

[21]Sony was an awkward choice of firms for plaintiffs to group with the others. The prices charged by its profitable American distribution arm, Sonam, were considerably higher than both the check prices and the prices of Zenith and NUE sets. See 513 F. Supp. 1100, 1282 (1981). How Sony's high prices could injure American firms was never specified.

in the U.S. market, and the market is one where long-term cost reductions led price levels downward over time. In markets where economies of scale and learning-by-doing result in cost reductions, economic theory teaches that prices will trend downward. Frequently, such trends are led by the newer firms who are seeking to use low prices to help gain brand recognition, goodwill, and company reputation.[22]

Economists and Inferential Evidence

In the United States, price-fixing conspiracies often do not leave "smoking guns"—direct evidence in the form of a written agreement to charge joint profit-maximizing prices or a videotape of the conspiracy. Antitrust enforcement agencies often must use indirect or circumstantial evidence to prove price fixing. But in *M* v. *Z*, there was direct evidence that the Japanese firms had signed a document determining minimum export prices on television sales to the United States. Indeed, over time there were more than a dozen such agreements covering both black-and-white and color televisions.

This is the language of Article 8 of one such agreement (The Manufacturers' Agreements): "The parties to this agreement shall not offer for sale, make a contract for sale or deliver to export businessmen goods at prices lower than the prices specified in attached Schedule 2."[23] Signatories could sell at or above the check prices.

The defendants claimed that these agreements were mandated by the Japanese government through MITI and therefore were immune from U.S. antitrust prosecution by the "act of state" and "sovereign compulsion" doctrines. The plaintiffs contended that MITI did not compel joint action by the Japanese sellers and that MITI at best gave subsequent approval to business strategy initiated by the defendants.

Using economic reasoning, the district court recognized that Zenith and NUE (and other U.S. producers of televisions) could not be harmed by foreign firms setting minimum prices. Zenith, for example, should have been delighted if Hitachi were hamstrung by legal minimums. All Zenith would need to do to compete, assuming comparable quality and other terms, was charge a price less than the minimum to which Hitachi was bound.[24] Moreover, jointly setting minimum prices does not fit gracefully with the theory that prices are predatory.

---

[22]The combination of established brand recognition, high combined market shares, and import protection may explain the higher prices defendants enjoyed in Japan. Together, they controlled almost 95 percent of the Japanese market; but there is no credible evidence that transaction prices at the manufacturing level were higher in Japan. Higher prices at retail or wholesale in Japan relative to the United States probably are explained by higher distribution costs in Japan than in the United States.

[23]513 F. Supp. 1100, 1188 (1981).

[24]Paradoxically, MITI and the defendants claimed that the rationale behind the minimums was to limit the number of televisions exported to the United States, and thus the agreements represented a strategy by the Japanese to limit or prevent even more severe U.S.-imposed trade restrictions on Japanese goods through tariffs and quotas.

The Five Company Rule (limiting each favored seller to only five U.S. wholesalers) also was not compelling as evidence of predatory pricing. First, the rule did not always hold—several large American buyers, such as J. C. Penney, Sears, Roebuck, and Western Auto, purchased televisions from more than one of the seven Japanese sellers. Second, the rule was easily circumvented—a defendant could make its American subsidiary one of the five and sell to anyone in the United States through that subsidiary. Moreover, the rule could not have injured Zenith and NUE (or other U.S. producers). Indeed, if the Five Company Rule had constrained Japanese sellers, it should have made it easier for Zenith and NUE to sell to any particular domestic buyer, since that buyer allegedly was limited in its Japanese supply alternatives. From an economic perspective, the Five Company Rule runs contrary to the hypothesis of a low price export conspiracy. An organizer of a predatory cartel might have to say, "you *must* sell to these five" but not "you are *limited* to these five."

The Home Market Conspiracy

Price fixing in Japan supposedly was the means by which the Japanese sellers financed the sales of televisions at depressed prices in the United States. As sometimes happens in antitrust cases, as litigation commences from complaint to discovery, legal theories change. The district court noted early in its opinion that the war chest theory, which formed an important part of the plaintiffs' original charge, began to wane as the case progressed. By the time of the summary judgment, the judge wrote: "Little is said at this stage about 'war-chesting,' apparently because plaintiffs finally recognized that there is no evidence of it in the record."[25]

Earlier, in a controversial move, the lower court judge had rejected much of the written opinion of the plaintiffs' economic experts who contended that a home market conspiracy existed. These economists reviewed written materials that persuaded them, circumstantially, that a conspiracy existed. Much of this evidence was held to be untrustworthy and inadmissible. For example, one JMEA document contained this statement: "Thus, the businessmen involved have decided that, acting as one body, they will strive to maintain export order and, furthermore, to aim for steady expansion of exportation."[26] Economists for the plaintiffs saw such documents as evidence of conspiratorial intent. But the lower court judge interpreted

---

[25]513 F. Supp. 1100, 1129 (1981). Indeed, after surveying many of the documents concerning the meetings of Japanese executives about home market prices, Judge Becker concluded that discussions about home market prices were often discussions about how to maintain retailer margins, which may have lowered manufacturers' prices, and conversations about how prices were dropping in Japan to levels too low to enable manufacturers to break even. These were facts Judge Becker found difficult to square with the war chest theory. See 513 F. Supp. 1100, 1203–1204 (1981).

[26]513 F. Supp. 1100, 1231 (1981).

the document merely as expressing an intent to reduce trade friction between the United States and Japan. Moreover, he ruled that making judgments about conspiracy based on circumstantial evidence of this sort is not the task of an expert economist. Judges and juries are supposed to make such decisions. He dismissed much of the work of plaintiffs' economic experts as that of "conspiracyologists" and not the work of economists qua economists.[27]

The plaintiffs contended that parallel price discrimination was such strong inference of conspiracy that a trial was merited. The defendants argued that to go from a fact of sustained high prices in Japan and lower prices in the United States to the conclusion of conspiracy is not inference but speculation. The plaintiffs, it should be noted, never submitted any evidence of the rates of return made by Japanese defendants on home market sales. They argued that it should be sufficient to show a price difference.[28]

War Chests and Alternative Opportunity Costs

Economic analysis often proceeds from assumptions. At this juncture, let us assume that the Japanese firms *had* cartelized their home market and *were* making monopoly profits there. Let us assume, too, that the Japanese firms are considering a predation strategy in the United States. Plaintiffs in *M* v. *Z* argued that there is a connection or nexus between the circumstances in the two sets of assumptions: A successful television cartel in Japan renders more likely the adoption of a predatory campaign against the television industry in America. The profits from one market subsidize the other. This is the war chest theory of predation.

Economic analysis cautions against a quick adoption of such a theory. War chests, like everything else in the world of economics, do not come free. Their cost is the forgone profits that could have been earned by investing the purported monopoly profits made in Japan in some alternative endeavor. The alternative would include relatively riskless opportunities for the funds, such as government bonds. No rational firm would forgo a more certain and immediate stream of income for a riskier and more long-term prospect of gain unless the opportunities for the future gains are very attractive.

If predation were an attractive strategy, that is, if it were financially attractive as an investment relative to other risk-adjusted alternatives, then potential predators would adopt this strategy of export pricing independent of their home market position. In other words, if a predatory strategy (involving short-term losses) is a profitable investment because of an expected future monopoly position, it is attractive regardless of whether cartelizing in the home market (or any other market) also has proved profitable.

---

[27]513 F. Supp. 1100, 1138 (1981).

[28]513 F. Supp. 1100, 1205 (1981).

THE DISTRICT COURT DECISION

Judge Edward R. Becker, at the time serving on the U.S. District Court for the Eastern District of Pennsylvania, was the trial judge who in March of 1981 first decided *M* v. *Z*. It was his opinion that eventually was appealed to the Supreme Court. His decision was extraordinarily long, a reflection of the Brobdingnagian number of documents put before him. In 1980 alone, 114 briefs and memoranda were filed in *M* v. *Z*. In reaching his decision, Judge Becker relied heavily on his own economic analysis and the economic arguments placed before him. He ruled that "despite years of discovery, the plaintiffs have failed to uncover any significant probative evidence that the defendants entered into an agreement or acted in concert with respect to exports to the United States in any manner which could in any way have injured plaintiffs."[29] Judge Becker could find no evidence of admissible caliber that "refers or relates to the setting or coordination of export prices . . . or any other aspect of the 'export' component of the 'unitary' conspiracy claimed by plaintiffs."[30]

There were many documents that revealed meetings about home market conditions. But very few of these even contained reference to exports; those that did were to exports in general, not exports that were United States specific. There was some evidence that a Japanese trade association (the Electronic Industries Association of Japan) gathered and disseminated average prices of televisions sold for export, but no record of exchanges of current price information, much less agreement on prices or quantities of export. Absent evidence of this character, the plaintiffs' predation case becomes one requiring proof of predatory pricing by individual defendants. But none of these firms had enough market power, nor even the prospect of sufficient market power, to prey successfully in a unilateral fashion.

Notwithstanding the resources poured into this case, there never was a full trial on the merits. Judge Becker decided the case for the defendants on summary judgment. Summary judgment means that the judge read the pleadings in the case, heard oral argument, studied particularly the plaintiffs' Final Pretrial Statement, and determined what evidence of the plaintiffs would have been admissible if a trial were held. He then determined that, even if all of this admissible evidence were accepted as true and unrebutted by the defendants, the plaintiffs did not have a sufficient case, and there was no genuine need for a trial.

CONCLUSION

The U.S. Third Circuit Court of Appeals was unpersuaded that Zenith and NUE did not merit a trial. Essentially, the appellate court would have

---

[29]513 F. Supp. 1100, 1117 (1981).

[30]513 F. Supp. 1100, 1209 (1981).

admitted much of the evidence that Judge Becker held to be inappropriate, including the opinions and studies of economists employed by Zenith and NUE. The Supreme Court thought otherwise, albeit by a narrow majority.

While the predation strategy of the Japanese television producers does not make economic sense for monopolizing the television market alone, in theory one cannot rule out that a firm might prey in one market because the tactic generates spillover consequences—or reputational effects—in other markets. For example, if a firm operates in two markets and adopts a predation strategy in one, its behavior may deter new entry or supply expansion by rivals in the other market. If such a firm can establish a reputation as a reckless price-cutter in one market, and thereby deter otherwise prospective entrants from another market where it already has market power, then the payoff from entry deterrence in the second market must be weighed against the cost of predation in the first.[31]

When assessing predation strategies that seem, in hindsight, irrational, one also cannot dismiss the possibility that the would-be predator was mistaken: like the child whose eyes were bigger than his stomach. A firm that is pricing below cost may not realize how long it will take to push rivals from the market, and once having started, may keep trying, perhaps overestimating the amount of time it will then have in the recoupment period before monopoly prices attract new entry again.

In the case of the television market, not only is it clear that the payoff matrix did not support a predation theory for that market, there is no evidence that any reputation effects carried over into other markets for consumer electronic products. In the television market itself, concentration actually declined during the *Matsushita* litigation, and continued to decrease. The Herfindahl-Hirschman Index in 1976 was 1389; it was 1249 in 1985; and it was only 1027 in 1992. Retail prices for television sets have continued to decline in the post-*Matsushita* period as well.

Matsushita v. *Zenith,* from a purely legal perspective, is about the suitability of summary judgment—avoiding a full trial on the merits—in an antitrust case. If the facts about a case, as they are put forward by a plaintiff prior to a full trial on the merits, are not in accord with economic analysis (or "make no economic sense," as the Supreme Court put it bluntly), then a plaintiff's case may be dismissed without burdensome and costly trials being imposed on the defendant(s). This puts economic theory in the role of a filter, sorting out inappropriate cases from those worthy of a court's full consideration. *M* v. *Z* adds weight to the view that in antitrust, economic analysis matters. Moreover, *M* v. *Z* strengthens the view that vigorous price competition is so desirable and predatory pricing so rare that courts, to

---

[31]For a summary of reputation effects in the economic theory of predation, see Ordover and Saloner (1989, pp. 550–556). For an empirical critique of reputation effects, see Lott and Opier (1996).

ensure more of the former, should set a high standard of proof for allegations of the latter.[32]

REFERENCES

Areeda, Phillip E., and Herbert Hovenkamp. *Antitrust Law*. Boston: Little, Brown, Vol. III, 1996.

Areeda, Phillip E., and Donald F. Turner. "Predatory Pricing and Related Practices Under Section 2 of the Sherman Act." *Harvard Law Review* 88 (February 1975): 697–733.

Boudreaux, Donald J., Kenneth G. Elzinga, and David E. Mills. "The Supreme Court's Predation Odyssey: From Fruit Pies to Cigarettes." *Supreme Court Economic Review* 4 (1995): 5793.

Brodley, Joseph F., and George A. Hay. "Predatory Pricing: Competing Theories and the Evolution of Legal Standards." *Cornell Law Review* 66 (April 1981): 738–803.

Calvani, Terry, and James M. Lynch. "Predatory Pricing Under the Robinson-Patman and Sherman Acts: An Introduction." *Antitrust Law Journal* 51 (1982): 375–400.

Easterbrook, Frank. "Predatory Strategies and Counter-strategies." *University of Chicago Law Review* 48 (Spring 1981): 263–337.

Elzinga, Kenneth G., and David E. Mills. "Testing for Predation: Is Recoupment Feasible?" *Antitrust Bulletin* 34 (Winter 1989): 869–893.

Elzinga, Kenneth G., and David E. Mills. "Trumping the Areeda-Turner Test: The Recoupment Standard in *Brooke Group*." *Antitrust Law Journal* 62 (Spring 1994): 559–584.

Fisher, Franklin M. "On Predation and Victimless Crime." *Antitrust Bulletin* 32 (Spring 1987): 85–92.

Holland, Daniel M., ed. *Measuring Profitability and Capital Costs*. Lexington, Mass.: Lexington Books, 1984.

Houthakker, H. S., and Lester D. Taylor. *Consumer Demand in the United States*. Cambridge, Mass.: Harvard University Press, 1966.

Isaac, R. Mark, and Vernon L. Smith. "In Search of Predatory Pricing." *Journal of Political Economy* 93 (April 1985): 320–345.

Joskow, Paul L., and Alvin K. Klevorick. "A Framework for Analyzing Predatory Pricing Policy." *Yale Law Journal* 89 (December 1979): 213–269.

---

[32]It was this concern that provoked the Antitrust Division of the Department of Justice to be a party to this litigation, filing a brief as a friend of the Court. At the request of Zenith and NUE, the Antitrust Division in 1977 and 1978 investigated the plaintiffs' claims and found them without antitrust merit (Brief for the United States as Amicus Curiae Supporting Petitioners, 1985, p. 3). Charles F. Rule, who was Deputy Assistant Attorney General of the Antitrust Division in 1985, appeared before the Supreme Court in *M* v. *Z* and stated the Antitrust Division's fears that if Judge Becker's opinion were not upheld, the case would "offer strong encouragement . . . to beleaguered competitors seeking protection from the rigors of competition, and . . . that's precisely the wrong thing that the antitrust laws should do" (Rule, 1985, pp. 21–22).

Koller, Roland H. "The Myth of Predatory Pricing: An Empirical Study." *Antitrust Law & Economic Review* 4 (Summer 1971): 105–123.

Lott, John R., and Tim C. Opier. "Testing Whether Predatory Commitments Are Credible." *Journal of Business* 69 (July 1996): 339–382.

McGee, John S. "Predatory Price Cutting: The Standard Oil (N.J.) Case." *Journal of Law & Economics* 1 (October 1958): 137–169.

McGee, John S. "Predatory Pricing Revisited." *Journal of Law & Economics* 23 (October 1980): 289–330.

Ordover, Janusz A., and Garth Saloner. "Predation, Monopolization and Antitrust." In *Handbook of Industrial Organization,* vol. I, edited by Richard Schmalensee and Robert Willig. Amsterdam: Elsevier," 1989, pp. 537–596.

Rule, Charles F. Oral Argument: Official Transcript Proceedings Before the Supreme Court of the United States, Docket/Case No. 83-2004, November 12, 1985.

Shepherd, William G. "Assessing 'Predatory' Actions by Market Shares." *Antitrust Bulletin* 31 (Spring 1986): 1–28.

U.S. Department of Justice Antitrust Division. *Brief for the United States as Amicus Curiae Supporting Petitioners, Matsushita Electric Industrial Co. Ltd. et al. v. Zenith Radio Corp., et al.,* June 1985.

Predation by a Nondominant Firm: The Liggett Case (1993)

William B. Burnett

INTRODUCTION

In July 1984, Liggett Group, Inc., parent of Liggett & Myers Tobacco Company ("Liggett"), filed suit alleging predatory behavior by Brown & Williamson Tobacco Corporation ("B&W") for its conduct surrounding the introduction and marketing of generic cigarettes. Key allegations involved predatory pricing. Trial began five years later, in July 1989. In March 1990, after 115 days of hearings and 10 days of deliberations, the jury found that B&W had acted predatorily in its pricing of (and in other business conduct related to) generic cigarettes, and awarded damages of $49.6 million—$148.8 million after trebling. In August 1990, the trial judge granted a motion by B&W for judgment notwithstanding the verdict, set aside the jury verdict, and entered a judgment in favor of Brown & Williamson. Liggett appealed to the U.S. Fourth Circuit Court of Appeals, but that court affirmed the trial judge's opinion. Liggett appealed again, this time to the U.S. Supreme Court. In June 1993, the Supreme Court, while rejecting the reasoning of the Court of Appeals, upheld the dismissal of the case, relying heavily on the analysis of the District Court in granting judgment notwithstanding the verdict.[1]

William B. Burnett was an expert for Liggett Group, Inc. in this case. This article represents the views of the author and does not necessarily represent the views of Liggett Group Inc., its successors, or its counsel. While this chapter represents an overview of *Liggett* v. *Brown & Williamson*, it does not examine all of the major economic issues that were raised during the case, including the testimony of the author.

[1] *Liggett Group, Inc.* v. *Brown & Williamson Tobacco Corporation,* 748 F. Supp. 344 (M.D.N.C. 1990), aff'd 964 F.2d 335 (4th Cir. 1992). On appeal to the Supreme Court, the case was recaptioned to reflect a change in the ownership of Liggett Group, Inc.: *Brooke Group, Ltd.* v. *Brown & Williamson Tobacco Corporation,* 61 U.S.L.W. 4699 (1993).

In its starkest form, this is a case about the rationality and fact of predatory pricing in a highly concentrated, oligopolistic industry by a firm that was not the largest in its industry and did not have a dominant market share. In the 1970s and 1980s, there were only six domestic producers of cigarettes, and market concentration was very high. Liggett, the smallest firm in the industry and on the verge of failure in the late 1970s, introduced a no-name, generic line of cigarette products at a price significantly below that of any other product. The dramatic success of Liggett's generics provoked competitive reaction by B&W, the third-largest firm in the industry with a share of less than 12 percent (see Table 10-1). Liggett alleged that B&W priced its generic cigarettes below variable cost with the intention of either disciplining Liggett's generic pricing or driving the firm from the market.

Evaluating Predation Claims

Identifying instances of predatory pricing generally requires a two-step process. The analyst must isolate those market facts that demonstrate (1) that predatory pricing is rational or plausible behavior for the aggressor, and (2) that predatory pricing actually occurred. If predation is not rational, evaluation of claims of predatory behavior usually need go no further. If predation is plausible, however, analysis of the facts must determine whether it actually occurred.

The following definition of predatory pricing is adopted to isolate facts or conditions useful for distinguishing predatory conduct from aggressive but welfare-enhancing competitive behavior:

> Predatory pricing involves incurring losses by pricing below some measure of cost in the short run in order to exclude or discipline rivals in anticipation of recouping those losses in the future. Losses may be recouped through either the maintenance or establishment, and successful exercise, of market power.

TABLE 10-1
Cigarette Market Shares and Concentration

	1980	1984	1988
Philip Moris	30.9%	35.3%	39.3%
R. J. Reynolds	32.6	31.6	31.8
Brown & Williamson	13.7	11.3	10.9
American Tobacco	10.8	7.9	7.0
Lorillard	9.7	8.2	8.2
Liggett & Myers	2.3	5.7	2.8
Four-firm concentration ratio:	88.0	86.4	90.2
Herfindahl-Hirschman Index:	2421	2534	2799

Source: Plaintiff's exhibit 4285.

This definition of predatory pricing embodies serveral key assumptions or principles. First, predatory pricing cannot be a rational business strategy unless the predator has or is likely to gain market power. It can make no sense for a firm to suffer losses in the short run if it does not anticipate recouping those losses in the long run. Absent the successful exercise of market power, the aggressor firm that is incurring losses cannot expect to recoup any "investments" made in below-cost pricing. Second, the predator firm must either drive from the market the targeted, equally efficient rival or discipline that rival so that market prices remain at or rise to supracompetitive levels.

Third, short-run prices must be below cost, implying both losses by the predator on that product and likely losses for its targeted rival.[2] Fourth, predatory pricing involves immediate and certain short-run losses, in anticipation of uncertain future gains. The larger the short-run losses, and the farther in the future those losses are expected to be recouped, the less likely a predatory campaign makes sense. Only the present discounted value of the predator's future profits is relevant to their profit calculation. Profits in the distant future are worth little when discounted. Moreover, the farther in the future the losses are expected to be recouped, the greater the uncertainty surrounding future market events; therefore, application of a higher discount rate is appropriate. Fifth, the predator must have greater staying power than the target. If the firm that would incur the losses expects its target to "stay the course," it will not likely engage in predation.

LIGGETT AND THE GROWTH OF THE GENERIC CIGARETTE CATEGORY

In the late 1970s, Liggett, the smallest of the six U.S. cigarette manufacturers, was on the verge of liquidation. Its market share had fallen gradually for more than twenty years to reach 2.8 percent of domestic cigarette shipments by 1979 and only 2.3 percent in 1980. A cigarette company is not viable at this scale. Economies of scale in the manufacture and distribution of cigarettes extend to between 3 and 5 percent of domestic sales. Liggett had formulated a range of contingency plans for liquidation in the event that its sagging corporate fortunes could not be reversed, primarily through the introduction of new branded cigarette products.

In early 1980, TOPCO, a large wholesale grocery cooperative, inquired whether Liggett would produce a private label, or "generic," cigarette for TOPCO's grocery store members. In the hope of more fully utilizing its excess production capacity, Liggett agreed, expecting only to

---

[2] The appropriate measure of cost for evaluating predatory pricing claims has been the subject of vigorous debate. See Brodley and Jay (1981). For this case, price was compared with average variable cost, where average variable cost served as a proxy for marginal cost. See Areeda and Turner (1975). In other market settings, alternative measures of cost, including average total cost, varying measures of long-run costs, and others, may be appropriate.

manufacture modest volumes for a limited time, until it was able (as hoped) to introduce successful, new branded products. In the prior forty years, during which virtually all cigarettes were branded and sold at the identical "full revenue" price, no major cigarette manufacturer had attempted to sell a generic, low-priced product. There had been little, if any, systematic off-list discounting since the 1930s.

Liggett began shipping generics to TOPCO in mid-1980; the generics were profitable and exceeded volume expectations from the start. Later in 1980, Liggett began selling generic cigarettes to other customers, while setting up an extensive distribution network, separate and distinct from its branded sales organization, to sell and distribute the new product. Liggett generics grew rapidly and had a 0.9 percent share by 1982, and sales accelerated dramatically in 1983.

On January 1, 1983, the federal excise tax (FET) on cigarettes doubled from $0.80 to $1.60 per carton; all cigarette manufacturers increased the prices of branded cigarettes to (more than) reflect the increased tax. Liggett, however, absorbed the bulk of the tax increase and did not raise the price of its generics by the full extent of the tax increase. The wholesale list price "gap" between branded and generic cigarettes increased from $1.34 per carton in June 1982 to $2.38 per carton in December 1983; the percent difference in price increased from about 32 percent to 41 percent (see Figure 10-1).

FIGURE 10-1 The Percentage Differences between Branded and Generic Cigarettes.*

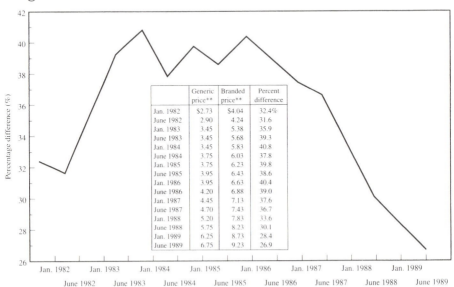

	Generic price**	Branded price**	Percent difference
Jan. 1982	$2.73	$4.04	32.4%
June 1982	2.90	4.24	31.6
Jan. 1983	3.45	5.38	35.9
June 1983	3.45	5.68	39.3
Jan. 1984	3.45	5.83	40.8
June 1984	3.75	6.03	37.8
Jan. 1985	3.75	6.23	39.8
June 1985	3.95	6.43	38.6
Jan. 1986	3.95	6.63	40.4
June 1986	4.20	6.88	39.0
Jan. 1987	4.45	7.13	37.6
June 1987	4.70	7.43	36.7
Jan. 1988	5.20	7.83	33.6
June 1988	5.75	8.23	30.1
Jan. 1989	6.25	8.73	28.4
June 1989	6.75	9.23	26.9

* Based on Liggett branded and generic prices.
** Price per carton.

The price gap at retail also increased substantially, and generic sales continued to accelerate rapidly. Liggett generics grew from 5.8 billion cigarettes (0.9 percent of all cigarette sales) in 1982 to 23.9 billion cigarettes (4.0 percent of all cigarette sales) in 1984. Liggett's share of total cigarette sales increased from 2.9 percent to 4.8 percent between 1982 and 1983, and then to 5.7 percent in 1984. The success of Liggett's generics thus injected new life into a failing company, in addition to introducing price competition into the industry for the first time in more than forty years.

Brown & Wiliamson's Generic Response

The increasing sales of Liggett generics came at a crucial time for B&W and, to varying degrees, other producers. Total cigarette sales in the United States peaked in 1981, at 627 billion "sticks," and then began a steady decline, falling to about 600 billion sticks in 1984 and to 558 billion sticks in 1988, or roughly 1.65 percent per year. Further, B&W's established, branded products had been gradually declining in share for more than a decade. The firm's market share fell from about 17.5 percent in 1973 to 14.4 percent in 1979. Liggett's increasing generic sales accelerated and exacerbated the decline in branded cigarette sales by the larger manufacturers. B&W thus confronted a declining market share in a shrinking market, the effect of which was intensified by the shift in sales from branded products to Liggett's generic cigarettes.

Moreover, B&W's consumer switching studies evaluating the losses of each firm's branded sales to generics showed that B&W was one of two principal "losers" to Liggett generics, disproportionately contributing about 21 percent of the almost 17.9 billion units gained by Liggett. As B&W's share of all cigarette sales was then about 12 percent, the firm contributed to generics an amount equal to about 1.7 times its market share. For each of the larger producers, such lost sales resulted in very large profit margin losses on branded products that were directly attributable to the growth of Liggett's generics. For example, estimating the actual and potential unit and dollar losses attributable to generic growth, B&W wrote in March 1984:

> B&W's contribution to generics is disproportionately high. Specifically, B&W contributes about 70% more than its fair share volume to generics. B&W losses account for about 21% of generics' gains. In 1983 B&W lost about 3.7 billion sticks to generics, a variable margin loss of over $50MM. By 1988, this loss could total 18 billion sticks and about $350MM lost variable margin.[3]

Subsequent to Liggett's introduction of generics, B&W's share of all cigarettes continued its historic decline, falling from 14.4 percent in 1979

---

[3] PX-5. PX indicates "Plaintiff's Exhibit," or documents introduced into evidence at the trial.

to 11.5 percent in 1983, during which time its unit sales fell even more rapidly, reflecting both declining industry sales and a falling share, from about 88.5 billion units to 68.5 billion units (about 6.2% per year). B&W's motivation to retain or regain unit sales was further bolstered by the need to utilize fully its new world-class production facility at Macon, Georgia, which was being phased into production.

In late 1983, B&W formed a task force of senior executives to evaluate the effects of generic cigarettes on that firm and to make recommendations concerning the possible launch of a generic cigarette product to compete with Liggett's. After five months of study, B&W's task force characterized Liggett's unprecedented and threatening competitive move and the effects it could have on branded cigarette prices and profits as follows:

> This is the first time that a manufacturer [Liggett] has used pricing as a strategic marketing weapon in the U.S. since the depression era. At that time, when economic conditions were more severe than at present, low price brands captured approximately 23% of the market before the dominant manufacturers dropped their prices on full priced brands, thereby limiting the low price entries to 10%–14% market share during the 1930s. . . .

> If the economy segment were to grow to 25 to 30 percent of the total market, manufacturers as a last resort may reduce list prices of full margin products in an attempt to repeat the action of the 1930's.[4]

The response of the major tobacco companies to low-priced cigarette introductions in the 1930s led to their conviction for attempted monopolization under sections 1 and 2 of the Sherman Antitrust Act. B&W did not wait until generics' share reached 25 percent but introduced a generic of its own, the first shipments of which were made in July 1984.

In June and July 1984, B&W first offered to sell generic products at a list price equal to Liggett's ($3.75 per carton for 85-mm cigarettes), with volume rebates (discounts off wholesale list price) of up to $0.30 per carton. No sales were transacted at this price. Liggett immediately responded by offering rebates as well, adopting a policy of matching B&W's rebates to within about $0.07 per carton, usually maintaining a net price (list price less rebates) slightly higher than B&W's offer. After several rounds of increasingly deep rebate offers by both firms in June and July of 1984, B&W was selling generics at rebate levels of between $0.40 and $0.80 per carton, depending on the number of cartons purchased per quarter.

Discounts increased still further in December 1984, and again several times in 1985. On average, B&W discounts totaled about $0.62 per carton in 1984 and about $0.82 per carton in 1985. These were large and dramatic

---

[4] PX-12. For discussion of cigarette pricing behavior in the 1930s, see Nichols (1949) and Tennant (1950).

figures when compared with 1984 list prices of $3.75 per carton (85-mm cigarettes); the rebate's significance is further highlighted when the $1.60 per carton FET is deducted from the list price, yielding B&W gross revenues after deduction of federal taxes of $2.15 per carton. B&W's net realizations from generic sales, after all deductions for discounts and taxes, were $1.53 and $1.41 per carton in 1984 and 1985, respectively. Against this backdrop of aggressive price cutting and other business conduct, Liggett filed suit against B&W in July 1984, alleging predatory pricing and other unfair business practices.[5]

LIGGETT'S CLAIM OF PREDATION

Liggett's theory of the case, which was largely derived from and supported by B&W documents, alleged that firms in the highly concentrated cigarette industry tacitly colluded to raise branded cigarette prices and profits above competitive levels.[6] All cigarette manufacturers, including B&W, benefit from the avoidance of competition and have supranormal profits to protect on the sale of branded products. Liggett, the smallest firm and on the verge of failure, took the unprecedented step of introducing a generic product—at a discounted price. Its incentives differed materially from those of the other manufacturers. Liggett generics would take branded sales from all larger manufacturers but would not "cannibalize" or materially reduce its own very small share of branded sales. B&W observed in March 1984: "Generic growth represents volume erosion for all competitors. Unchallenged, L&M will continue aggressive segment development since it has virtually no stake in the branded, full price segment."[7]

As alleged by Liggett, B&W priced its product below variable cost to reduce Liggett's competitive initiatives in low-price cigarettes and to slow the growth rate of generics. B&W cut prices by offering volume rebates as opposed to reducing list prices, expecting that price cuts implemented in this manner would not be reflected in reduced prices to consumers, thus increasing the branded-generic price gap. After an interval of below-cost pricing, B&W hoped to reduce the price gap either by imposing such significant losses that Liggett would raise generic prices, *or* by seizing control of the generic category and then raising prices itself. B&W also hoped to induce Liggett to reduce its marketing intended to make consumers

---

[5] Predatory pricing claims were filed under Section 2(a) of the Clayton Act, as amended by the Robinson-Patman Act, 15 U.S.C. Section 13(a); claims involving B&W's copying of Liggett's generic packages were filed under the Lanham Trade-Mark Act, 15 U.S.C. Section 1125(a). Similar claims were made under various state common law and statutory unfair trade practice provisions.

[6] There were no allegations of overt or explicit collusion among firms in the industry. All allegations and evidence involved tacit collusion.

[7] PX-5.

more aware of generics, believing that both these reductions would slow or reverse the growth in generic sales.

Predation by a Firm with a 12-Percent Share

Predation by a firm with a share of only about 12 percent does not fit the textbook model of predation by a dominant firm, but that model does not consider potential predatory behavior in a highly concentrated market characterized by tacit collusion. Indeed, by focusing on single-firm market share as the sole indicator of monopoly power, the textbook model conceals the critical factor that makes predation "rational" or "plausible"—the existence or possible attainment of *market power* (not simply market share), which can exist in highly concentrated oligopolies as well as in single-firm monopolies. Participants (individually or in concert) in a well-functioning, tacitly collusive oligopoly may profit from targeting and disciplining a price-cutting rival, thereby enjoying long-run increased or sustained supranormal prices and profits.

While B&W might well have wished to share the costs of its predatory campaign with its rivals, such joint action is both difficult to implement and strictly proscribed by Section 1 of the Sherman Act. Liggett's case made no claim that B&W explicitly cooperated or colluded in any manner with the other cigarette manufacturers. Rather, B&W was said to have made an independent cost-benefit calculation demonstrating that the reduced revenues of a price-cutting campaign would be substantially smaller than the large losses (as much as $350 million to $398 million) it alone might suffer if the generic category continued to grow. Joint action was unnecessary.

The Use of Volume Rebates to Cut Price

According to Liggett, B&W priced below variable cost not by reducing list prices but by offering very large, cumulative volume rebates. Indeed, in its internal documents, B&W recognized that cigarette industry prices at retail are determined by the list prices charged by manufacturers. As a practical matter, rebates and discounts granted by manufacturers to wholesalers were rarely passed on to retailers and, therefore, not reflected in lower retail prices. Similarly, volume discounts granted to private label customers were not reflected at retail. B&W believed that wholesale and private label customers would shift among generic suppliers on the basis of the discounts granted, in essence "pocketing" the volume discounts. B&W could, therefore, discount its generics and lure wholesale and private label accounts away from Liggett without increasing the retail branded-generic price gap, thereby fueling generic growth. But, if Liggett also offered rebates and retained its wholesale customers, it would suffer substantially reduced revenues if not outright losses.

In addition to the "pocketing" of rebates, wholesaler and retailer pricing behavior played yet another important role in B&W's plan. When a large manufacturer raises its list price, wholesalers raise the prices of all competing cigarettes, *whether or not the other manufacturers have raised the list prices of substitutable cigarettes.* A manufacturer therefore gains little by failing to take list price increases when one of the larger firms does so. As the sole producer of generics, Liggett was able to keep generics priced below branded cigarettes, and wholesalers did not raise Liggett generic prices when branded prices were raised. B&W believed, however, that if it gained a significant (one-third) share of the generic category, it could increase the price of its generics and that wholesale distributors would then also increase Liggett's generic prices. Alternatively, if Liggett retained the large majority of generic sales, and sustained significant losses over time, it might be forced to raise prices itself.

"Win-Win/Lose-Lose"

A key B&W objective was to reduce the branded-generic price gap. Volume discounts, in conjunction with the pricing features described above, might accomplish this in either of two ways—termed the "Win-Win/Lose-Lose" aspect of the B&W plan.

Liggett had two possible responses to B&W's volume rebate offers. It could choose not to offer comparable discounts, in which event a significant number of wholesalers and private label accounts would switch to B&W and give B&W a significant position in the generic segment. Since wholesalers would raise the price of Liggett-supplied generics if B&W raised its generic price, B&W would be in a position to raise generic prices generally and narrow the price gap. B&W wins; Liggett loses. Alternatively, Liggett could choose to grant comparable rebates or discounts and likely maintain a large portion of generic sales—but also incur the lion's share of the losses. Not capable of sustaining large losses for very long and remain the principal seller of generics, Liggett would be forced to raise generic list prices, narrowing the price gap. B&W wins; Liggett loses.

In actuality, Liggett chose to (almost) meet B&W's volume discounts. One year after the price war began, Liggett, unable to sustain continued losses on generics, raised the list price. Five months later, B&W followed, and the list price gap began to narrow. From spring 1984 (prior to B&W's generic introduction) through 1985, the gap (measured as the percent difference between branded and generic prices) was 38 to 40 percent. In 1986 it began a steady downward drift, reaching only 27 percent by June 1989 (see Figure 10-1).

B&W's generic plan and the win-win/lose-lose scenario directly address several issues critical to predatory pricing theory. First, in the dominant-firm model, the larger predator firm loses a greater amount during the period of below-cost pricing than does its target. Such a large loss makes recoupment, after the predatory campaign has ended, far less likely. However, by forcing Liggett to respond via volume rebates so as not to rapidly lose its generic volume, B&W's *offer* to sell generics below cost forced the great bulk of the losses onto Liggett, the target. Thus, in the period of recoupment, B&W had less to recoup than would a dominant firm that was targeting a smaller rival.

Second, if B&W succeeded in narrowing the price gap, its recoupment was likely to be rapid and certain rather than distant and uncertain. B&W's branded cigarettes were already priced above competitive levels; every branded unit lost to Liggett generics constituted an immediate loss of substantial margins and profits. If the rate of loss of *branded* sales could be reduced, as a consequence of its conduct with respect to *generics,* B&W's recoupment would be rapid. Without price cutting in the generic category, B&W's losses would have been even greater. This "simultaneous recoupment," as it was termed at the trial, meant that price-cutting "investments" made at a specific time were recouped very quickly by reducing the number of branded sales that would have been lost absent these investments. From B&W's perspective, the margin and profit losses at issue were tremendous. In May 1984 B&W estimated that, if it did nothing with respect to generics, it might lose as much as $398.2 million in profits on branded cigarettes for the period 1984 through 1988.[8] After imposing the bulk of the losses on Liggett, B&W had only to slow the rate of growth in generics by a small amount to justify its modest investment.

Finally, the B&W plan reflected its understanding of Liggett's inability to weather a sustained attack on its generics. Liggett was a subsidiary of the large, diversified British firm Grand Metropolitan, PLC. Liggett, however, did not have strong support from its parent. Grand Met had originally purchased Liggett in a hostile takeover in order to acquire its liquor distribution business and had long sought to sell the cigarette division. Although Grand Met financed Liggett's losses for the first twelve to eighteen months of B&W's attack, it placed limits on its support. Liggett's success in generics in the early 1980s had made the firm's cigarette business a more attractive investment. B&W was well aware that its generic launch and off-list price discounting had prevented Liggett from completing a leveraged buyout and that, if Grand Met were to sell Liggett, the losses on generics had to be limited or stopped. This could have been done by either (1) eliminating the volume rebates (and accompanying losses) and therefore ceding generic volume to B&W after which B&W could raise generic prices (half of win-win for B&W), or (2) raising the list price of generics, which B&W would follow (the other half of win-win for B&W). In both cases, Liggett would lose, having given up control of the category either by allowing B&W to sell

[8] PX-12. Brown & Williamson's measure of loss was stated in terms of "trading profit"; trading profit is net revenue (after taxes and discounts) less manufacturing cost, marketing expenditures, manufacturing overhead expenses, and profit sharing.

more generics or by raising generic prices. In fact, Grand Met allowed Liggett to remain an active participant in the price war for about a year, after which Liggett began to raise generic prices. By the end of 1985, the price gap began to narrow.

THE PLAUSIBILITY OF PREDATION, AND PRICING BELOW COSTS

The theory of predation (and of Liggett's case) requires that prices charged for and profits earned on the sale of branded cigarettes be above competitive levels. In the absence of noncompetitive prices and profits, B&W would have had no interest or motivation to target Liggett to prevent expansion of the generic category. If profits were not above competitive levels, industry firms could not have hoped to recoup any investments in predatory behavior. In the cigarette industry, characterized by high market concentration but not single-firm market dominance, such recoupment requires that the firms successfully coordinate behavior to raise prices above competitive levels and to avoid destabilizing forms of nonprice competition that threaten the maximization of joint profits.

Branded Cigarette Prices and Profits

In addition to statements in B&W documents and testimony by both B&W and Liggett executives that cigarette industry profits were greater than in most other manufacturing industries, Liggett's analysis focused on several categories of economic evidence, each of which is addressed vey briefly below.

High Market Concentration

Firms in highly concentrated markets recognize their mutual interdependence and may tacitly coordinate their behavior to maintain prices and profits above competitive levels. While the existence of high concentration does not prove or establish that firms in the industry successfully maintain prices above competitive levels, such concentration increases the probability that firms will be able to succeed in maintaining these prices. In fact, market concentration in the manufacture and sale of cigarettes was and remains very high. Four firms sold more than 88 percent of all cigarettes in the United States, and only a handful of consumer product markets exhibit higher levels of concentration.

List Price Leadership

In highly concentrated markets, successful efforts to avoid competition may require firms to adopt forms of business conduct that maintain prices above competitive levels in the face of changed supply and demand conditions. Price leadership, in which one firm announces a price increase and others follow the price leader, is one such mechanism. A strong pattern of price leadership has been documented in the cigarette industry since the 1930s.[9] In recent years, the manufacturers' pattern was one of leader-follower, in which one of the larger firms would announce a price increase that, within several weeks, other manufacturers would follow. The pattern was not perfect, but it was highly regular. In the ten years preceding 1989, price increases usually occurred twice a year, and list prices for all branded, full-revenue products have been virtually identical.

Price Changes Inconsistent with Cost and Demand Changes

In both competitive markets and in monopolies where the firm or firms maximize short-run profits, prices generally will move with and reflect changes in costs and demand. For example, when costs rise, firms will generally increase prices, but by less than the increase in costs (reflecting the magnitude of the elasticity of demand), and profit margins fall. If prices and margins do not reflect cost and demand changes, there is reason to believe that the firms have discretion over the prices charged and that effective competition does not prevail. There were several instances when cigarette price changes did not reflect cost or demand shifts. In 1982, for example, when the FET on cigarettes increased by $1.60 per carton, prices (and profits) actually increased by more than the tax increase. Similarly, throughout the 1974–1988 period generally, while B&W's share and sales were declining, and while cigarette sales in general were falling, B&W's prices and profit margins rose significantly.

In a competitive market, declining demand (for both the firms and the market) and rising costs would have placed downward pressure on margins and profits earned by B&W. Moreover, even in single-firm monopolies or oligopoly settings where the firms jointly maximized short-run profits, margins would have fallen, not risen. Yet in the cigarette industry, prices, margins, and profits all rose. It is possible that, when faced with declining demand and increasing costs, the cigarette companies discovered that, as they raised prices, quantity demanded did not fall by as much as had been anticipated; that is, the realization that the elasticity of demand was even lower than previously believed led the firms to raise prices even further above competitive levels than in the past. The ability to raise prices in the face of rising costs and declining demand is not consistent with the existence of effective competition.

Profits Above Competitive Levels

If firms in an industry successfully engage in tacit collusion, maintaining prices above competitive levels, then properly measured and evaluated

---

[9] See Tennant (1950) and Nichols (1949). Patterns of price leadership are often very complex and difficult to detect.

rates of return will be greater than average for firms of the same risk class unless firms in the industry compete away such high profits by allowing nonprice competition to "get out of hand."[10] The cigarette companies have earned returns far above those of companies in similar markets. For the period 1979 to 1985, the accounting profits of firms in the tobacco industry exceeded those in the food and kindred products sector (food sector) of the U.S. economy by about 50 percent. Moreover, examination of the firms' individual line of business returns established that accounting profit rates on cigarette business activities in the United States generally exceeded those for any other line of business by very large amounts—roughly twice those of other lines of business in the food sector.[11]

Significant Entry Barriers

If entry into a market is easy and likely to occur rapidly with prices and profits above competitive levels, there will be no monopoly profits to protect, or to attempt to earn, and predation will be generally implausible. Entry into the cigarette industry has been difficult, requiring a long period of time and a very large investment. Scale economies require an efficient, profitable firm to have sales of at least 3 to 5 percent of industry output. The typical "successful" new brand introduced between 1970 and 1985 achieved a share of only about 1 percent, and there were only a handful of "major winners," securing shares of more than 3 percent. Indeed, most new brands failed outright. When added to the product portfolio of an existing firm, a new brand with a share of only 1 or 2 percent may well be profitable, but that same new brand would result in losses for a new entrant that had not achieved minimum efficient scale.

Liggett as a Maverick Firm

An individual firm can play a key role in driving competition in many industries, particularly in highly concentrated markets where prices and profits are above competitive levels. In that environment, one firm can engage in competitive strategies that materially affect its competitors; large-share rivals often cannot ignore such "maverick" behavior. As perceived by its rivals, Liggett played such a role, introducing generics in 1980 and taking significant sales and profits from other manufacturers, who sold only full-revenue, branded cigarettes. These actions motivated the larger firms to target Liggett in a program intended to prevent yet wider availability of generics and to reduce the dollar spread between generic and branded prices. Clearly recognizing the dangers involved, B&W stated in March 1984: "Stipulating that the industry's interests—other than L&M's—would

---

[10] See, for example, Posner (1976).

[11] It is possible that accounting rates of return above competitive levels are sufficiently biased so that such comparisons are inappropriate. The high returns earned by cigarette companies are not attributable to either risk or investment in intangible assets, such as marketing expenditures.

be far better served had generics never been introduced, they are an immediate and growing threat to all other manufacturers. Competitive counteractions are essential and inevitable."[12]

BROWN & WILLIAMSON'S GENERIC PRICING

Having addressed whether predation was rational or plausible, because existing producers had supracompetitive profits to protect and defend, Liggett's analysis then required that prices were actually set at predatorily low levels for a substantial time. Analysts testifying for both Liggett and B&W adopted the Areeda-Turner standard, which requires that prices be set below variable costs.[13] That standard, which for ease of computation substitutes variable costs for marginal costs, is taken as proof that prices were set to reduce competition. Adoption of this standard is premised on the belief that no profit-maximizing firm will price below variable (marginal) cost except to harm a competitor and competition.[14]

Liggett's Data on Prices and Costs

In addition to B&W's repeated statements reflecting its intention to target Liggett's generics, calculation of B&W's actual generic prices and costs demonstrated, according to Liggett, that the firm was indeed pricing below variable cost.[15] Table 10-2 presents data on B&W revenues and variable costs per carton for the period July 1984 through December 1985. Net revenues were equal to gross revenues or total invoice charges (less "prompt payment" terms) from the sales of generics, less the $1.60 per carton FET and two categories of rebates, plus an interest credit on the rebate payments. Brown & Williamson paid two types of rebates to its customers: the cumulative volume discounts discussed above, and, in 1985, a "direct account incentive program" (DAIP) rebate. The cumulative volume discounts paid by B&W on generics were actually collected from its customers with the payment of each invoice, but then rebated to those customers at the end of each calendar quarter. The DAIP rebates were paid on the basis of the total value of B&W cigarettes, including both branded and generic products,

---

[12] PX-5.

[13] See Areeda and Turner (1975). For other approaches to diagnosing predatory pricing, see Joskow and Klevorick (1979) and Williamson (1977). For summaries and critiques of the various predatory pricing tests, see Brodley and Hay (1981) and Hay (1981).

[14] While the cost standard adopted is drawn from Areeda-Turner, the overall analysis of the industry, encompassing far more than just prices and costs, is very similar to that advocated by Scherer (1976).

[15] Brown & Williamson documents repeatedly state that the firm was willing to "spend full variable margin" in the effort to dislodge Liggett as the trade's major source of generics. If B&W did spend "full variable margin," then, according to its own accounting conventions, it would have priced the product below variable cost.

TABLE 10-2
Brown & Williamson Generic Cigarette Revenues and Variable Costs,
July 1984–December 1985

	18 months: July 1984–December 1985 (per carton)[a]		
Gross paid sales including excise tax	$3.802		
Less excise tax	1.600		
Net sales		$2.202	
Less rebates:			
Trade rebates	$0.750		
DAIP rebates	0.043		
Interest credit on rebates	(0.014)		
Total: Rebates		$0.779	
Net revenues per carton			$1.422
Less variable costs:			
Variable manufacturing cost	$1.039		
Leaf LIFO expense (adjusts leaf to current cost)	(0.010)		
SUI revaluation	0.020		
Freight, cartage, and insurance	0.071		
Total: Manufacturing cost and freight		$1.119	
Promotional costs	$0.028		
Direct selling costs	0.017		
Displays	0.066		
Retailer payments	0.181		
Generic leverage program	0.030		
Total: Selling costs		$0.322	
Variable overhead	$0.100		
Carrying costs	$0.140		
Manufacturing variances	$0.040		
Total: Overhead, carrying costs and variances		$0.280	
Average variable costs per carton			$1.721
Excess of average variable costs per carton over net revenues per carton (loss)			($0.298)

[a]Numbers do not add due to rounding.

Source: Plaintiff's exhibit 3967A.

purchased during the year and were paid only if the customer bought B&W generic cigarettes. The DAIP rebates were accrued throughout the year but paid annually. The "interest credit" entry in Table 10-2 reflects the interest B&W earned on the rebate monies before rebate payments were made to customers.

Table 10-2 also reflects assessment of the following costs of production and distribution. Variable manufacturing costs included the value of leaf tobacco, cigarette paper, flavorings, packaging, and factory labor cost used to produce generics. "Leaf LIFO expense" is an inventory valuation entry that adjusted the cost of raw materials from their acquisition expense to replacement or economic cost. The entry "SUI revaluation" was a technical inventory revaluation implemented in spring 1995 subsequent to a formula change. Freight, cartage, and insurance reflected the cost of outbound freight to move cigarettes from the manufacturing facility to customers.

There were five categories of selling costs. Promotional costs were associated with selling aids such as "battle kits" that were used by salespeople in making presentations to customers. Direct selling costs reflected the salaries and related expenses of six regional sales managers who had no selling responsibilities except for generics. Display expenses reflected the cost to B&W of the racks that hold cigarettes in retail outlets. Retailer payments were costs associated with payments to retailers made in the form of off-price "stickers" and coupons affixed to generic packages and redeemed by the retailer at the checkout counter.

The generic leverage program was a promotional program involving both branded and generic cigarettes that was instituted in November and December 1984. If a customer purchased one carton of generic cigarettes over and above his or her average weekly purchase, he or she would receive two $1.50 stickers that would be placed on B&W branded products. The customer thus received stickers for branded cigarettes, but only if the customer bought a larger quantity of generics. Sales of both branded and generic cigarettes benefited from this program. Since three cartons of cigarettes were involved in each transaction (an increase of purchases of one generic carton yielded stickers for two branded cartons), one-third of the cost of the program was allocated to generics.

B&W also calculated a category of manufacturing costs termed "manufacturing overheads," which included both fixed and variable components. Variable costs in manufacturing overheads included such expenses as the hourly wages of a shift supervisor, maintenance expense (a portion of which is dependent on the rate of operation of a machine), and utilities that vary with output.

All manufacturing activities involve carrying costs. Money is typically expended before a product is sold, including investments in working capital and accounts receivable that are implicit but real costs of doing business. Most firms do not calculate an interest-carrying charge on the funds tied up in their business activities because, in part, it is not particularly large. For tobacco manufacturers, however, such costs are large because leaf tobacco is a significant component of cost and is usually aged in inventory for a long period (two years or more). Brown & Williamson specifically calculated an inventory "carrying cost" that reflected the implicit interest costs of holding inventories of leaf tobacco and other inputs, as well as finished goods. Finally, Brown & Wiliamson's data for manufacturing costs are "budgeted" or "standard costs." Those estimated costs must be adjusted, or "brought back to actual," by calculating manufacturing variances (reflecting the difference between budgeted and actual costs).

During the eighteen-month period from July 1984 to December 1985, B&W sold 50.1 million cartons of generic cigarettes at an average price of $3.80 per carton, but realized net revenues of only about $1.42 per carton after deducting taxes and rebates. The firm's estimated variable costs were about $1.72 per carton. B&W priced its generics below variable cost by a total of $14.96 million, or $0.298 per carton. Liggett's calculations showed that B&W priced below variable cost in every month from July 1984 to December 1985 by amounts ranging from $0.081 to $0.813 per carton. Moreover, the amount by which B&W priced below cost remained substantial throughout the period; in December 1985 it priced below variable cost by more than $0.34 per carton, equaling or exceeding its losses in any other month in 1985.

B&W's costs were evaluated in detail for the entire period for which data were available. For some new products, firms lose money during introductory periods on such outlays as advertising and promotion. Such losses may have nothing to do with predation. Why, then, was it appropriate to evaluate only the first eighteen months of B&W's generic prices and costs? The first reason is highly pragmatic. Responding to B&W's arguments that producing additional data was both burdensome and unnecessary, the trial judge limited production of most data to the period ending in December 1985. Limiting attention to this period, however, is appropriate for a product such as generic cigarettes. With regard to many new products, the costs that cause losses are those associated with spending on intangible assets, such as advertising, that are believed to have long-lived effects; that is, they are expected to generate revenues in future periods. For generic cigarettes, spending on intangibles was insignificant. There was effectively no advertising. Most of the introductory "costs" were really price cuts—either in the form of rebates to distributors or stickers and coupons to consumers. Price cuts are not the sort of costs typically treated as long-lived investments. Moreover, B&W documents specifically stated that none of its introductory expenses was an investment.

BROWN & WILLIAMSON'S ANALYSIS AND DEFENSES

B&W argued that Ligget had failed to prove several important aspects of its case. Their key objections are summarized below.

Evidence of Supracompetitive Pricing

B&W witnesses either contested the significance or disputed the sufficiency of Liggett's evidence regarding supracompetitive pricing and profits. B&W did not contest the fact that industry concentration was quite high, but observed (correctly) that its mere existence did not prove that firms had coordinated behavior so as to raise prices and profits. B&W also observed, again correctly, that one cannot infer the existence of a collusive agreement from the existence of barriers to entry. B&W further argued that the analysis of price-cost changes and profits was inadequate—that the information available was insufficient to establish any premise.

More substantively, B&W argued that the accounting returns relied on by Liggett to estimate cigarette profitability were seriously flawed because of the failure to account for risk and intangible assets. B&W believed that the industry was more risky than other food and related product industries, largely because of the potential effects of health litigation and possible expanded government intervention. Moreover, B&W argued that accounting measures of cigarette profits were biased, not reflecting the "intangible" value of brand names. B&W also objected to accounting data that may have understated the value of all assets, particularly leaf tobacco inventories. B&W did not attempt to estimate the magnitude or significance of these potential biases on the cigarette companies' profits.

B&W witnesses also disputed the significance of list price leadership and uniformity. Liggett's analysis was faulted for focusing on only one dimension of competition and ignoring other widely used competitive tools. Because the tobacco companies compete vigorously via shelf payments, new product introductions, coupons, and other selling tools, B&W believed that list price leadership had little if any competitive significance.

Finally, B&W argued that viewing Liggett as a disruptive competitive force, because it had introduced low-priced cigarettes, was inappropriate, becasue Reynolds had done the same and rapidly increased sales of its products. According to B&W, there was no shortage of firms willing to engage in aggressive, competitive behavior.

In sum, B&W contended that, individually or as a group, the characteristics adduced by Liggett to establish the existence of monopoly power in the cigarette industry were inconclusive.

Pricing Below Cost

While B&W witnesses assessed various aspects of Liggett's calculations of generic prices and costs, B&W did not place great weight on rebutting the contention that its generic prices were below variable costs. The firm did, however, vigorously contest the relevance of the price/variable cost test for generic cigarettes, seeking rather to estimate the overall profitability of its decision to introduce its own generic cigarettes. Specifically, B&W argued that, if it had not entered generics, its costs of producing *branded* cigarettes would have been lower as a result of changes in its tobacco inventories and the way they would have been valued; lower cost for its leaf tobacco inventories would have resulted in higher profits and a greater corporate tax liability. By maintaining its corporate volumes and inventories because it began to sell generics, B&W avoided this increase in tax liability. The firm argued that this reduction in taxes should be viewed as a credit to the introduction of generics that offset any losses (including losses resulting from below-cost pricing) on generics.

This "LIFO Decrement Tax Avoidance" calculation went well beyond any existing analysis of predation. A key objection to predatory pricing is that it results in inefficient resource allocation for the product whose price is first set below marginal or variable cost and then later set above marginal cost. The fact that B&W could reduce taxes on profits earned from the sale of branded cigarettes, while attributing this reduced tax liability to generics, was not relevant to the efficiency with which generics were produced. The argument also implicitly assumed that pricing below cost on generics was the only manner in which B&W could have maintained corporate volumes so as to avoid a reduction in leaf inventories. B&W, however, had a wide range of alternatives available to it, including attempting to increase the sales of its existing branded products, introducing new products, or, indeed, selling generics at a price greater than variable cost, with the intention of increasing industrywide sales of generics rather than simply replacing Liggett as the primary industry supplier of generics. Moreover, such a benefit would not be available to a firm if it did not have tax liabilities that would be affected by the inventory adjustment. Thus, if a firm manufactured only the product being evaluated, and therefore did not have profits on other products to use as offsets, it could not avail itself of this argument and defense.[16]

Market Definition and Liggett's Alternatives

B&W presented a wide variety of additional arguments to rebut Liggett's theory and evidence. Witnesses for both Liggett and B&W agreed that the relevant market within which to evaluate competition and the effects of B&W's product introduction was the manufacture and sale of all cigarettes. Despite focusing heavily on generics, Liggett did not assert that they constituted a separate, distinct market. Indeed, the fact that they grew at the expense of branded products was direct and compelling evidence of substitution and that they were therefore in the same market. Moreover, the products were manufactured on similar if not identical equipment, from highly similar raw materials, and were or could have been sold through the same sales force and retail outlets.

Describing the dominant-firm model of predation, B&W claimed that prices and costs typically are and should be evaluated within the entire market in which predation was alleged; it is not appropriate to compute prices and costs only for some subset of the products. If the market were all cigarettes, evaluation ought to be made with respect to all cigarettes. According to B&W, Liggett had inappropriately evaluated only generics.

---

[16] Liggett also disputed the actual calculations of such tax savings.

Moreover, as demonstrated by Liggett's own data and analysis, B&W's overall cigarette operations were highly profitable; B&W had not priced below variable costs for all cigarettes, and therefore had not violated the Areeda-Turner standard. B&W also argued that applying the Areeda-Turner test only to generics ignored the existence of "branded generic" products—advertised name-brand products sold at generic-level prices. According to B&W, had its predatory campaign succeeded in inducing Liggett to raise generic prices, all that consumers of generics would have needed to do was to switch to the similarly low-priced branded generics, which had not been the target of predatory pricing.

Again, according to B&W, Liggett's attempt to assert that the market encompassed all cigarettes while evaluating prices and costs only for generics confused issues for yet another important reason. If all cigarettes was the proper market, then Liggett had a competitive option that would have allowed it to avoid losses on generics while continuing to sell cigarettes. Because all cigarettes are in the same market, which implies that the products are substitutable, B&W claimed that all Liggett need have done when B&W began to sell below cost was to substitute the sale of other cigarette products in other categories for its sales of generics. B&W suggested that Liggett could have abandoned the generic category, let B&W "bathe in its own blood," and then reentered the generic category when B&W ceased offering to sell at such low prices.

B&W's presentation relied largely on the textbook dominant-firm model of predation. Liggett, however, never asserted that each or all of those features applied to the cigarette industry or to B&W's conduct in generics. Moreover, Liggett's analysis specifically explained how and why it differed from the dominant-firm model yet still embodied the necessary elements of a predation model. At the most fundamental level, a predatory firm targets another equally efficient firm in order to raise consumer prices in the long run. Thus, the proper focus should be on pricing that has the potential or actual effect of allowing the aggressor firm(s) to raise prices in the long run. In markets where products are similar or homogeneous, the Areeda-Turner standard would generally apply to all products. B&W's assertion that it was improper to apply the price/variable cost test only to generics was inconsistent with the fact that cigarettes are differentiated products and that changing prices or promotional activities in one category or segment of the market might well have effects on others, although those effects would likely be muted or slow to occur. Just as competitive moves in menthols would yield delayed but pronounced effects on nonmenthols, competitive actions in generics did have material effects on branded products, *but they did not occur immediately.* Cutting prices on generics had isolated short-term effects on Liggett that were not rapidly transmitted to other segments of the industry. Price cutting, however, did induce Liggett to change its pricing behavior and over time resulted in a reduction of the branded-generic price gap.

Recognizing that cigarettes are differentiated products highlights the relevance of applying the Areeda-Turner test only to generics. Because of the differentiation of cigarette products, Liggett's generic sales could be targeted. The effects of charging below-cost prices via rebates on generics could be limited to this one category, without having those low prices spread to and affect prices and sales of branded products. Because Liggett's generic sales could be targeted, and that behavior had the potential to force Liggett to raise the price of low-priced generics, it was appropriate to apply the Areeda-Turner test only to that category.

Moreover, recognizing that cigarettes are differentiated products also highlights the limits of B&W's "bathe in its own blood" analysis. Had Liggett been able to move to another segment of the market to avoid B&W's pricing campaign, it might never have introduced generics. Liggett had been unsuccessful in introducing new branded products for many years. There is no reason to believe that, having been targeted in generics, it was any more likely to succeed now than in the past. Although B&W's assertion that Liggett could have avoided the effects of predatory pricing might make sense in a market where product differentiation was less important, the premise was implausible in the cigarette industry.

Finally, B&W argued that Liggett's claims were illogical because, if Liggett were driven from generics, consumers could simply purchase the widely available, low-priced, branded generic products sold by several of the large producers, and prices would not be affected. In the short run, branded generics did provide a ready alternative to Liggett's "real," unbranded product. Liggett's analysis, however, was that the larger manufacturers would have been better able to raise the price of branded generics than would be possible with generics alone; that is, once Liggett was disciplined and had raised prices, branded generic prices would simply be "managed" up. This is, in fact, what occurred. By mid-1989, the price gap between generics, branded generics, and full-revenue, branded products had been reduced to about 27 percent.

OUTCOME OF THE CASE

After 115 days of hearings and 10 days of deliberations, the jury returned a verdict in Liggett's favor, finding that B&W possessed market power and had engaged in below-cost pricing that likely harmed Liggett and competition. Despite having agreed to send the case to the jury in the first place, the trial judge, relying on evidence and analysis available to him before the case was sent to the jury, reversed the decision and dismissed the case. The judge's ruling did not dispute the potential for recoupment by a firm with a 12-percent share in a concentrated oligopoly. He did, however, criticize the economic evidence adduced by Liggett to establish that prices were set at supracompetitive levels, in part because that evidence and data were inconsistent with testimony by Liggett executives, who had denied both that the industry was characterized by tacit collusion and that the firms in the industry earned excessive profits.[17] Moreover, the judge believed that the availability of branded generics at prices lower than full-revenue brands negated any effect that B&W's actions may have had on Liggett.[18]

Liggett appealed to the Fourth Circuit Court of Appeals, which affirmed the judge's dismissal of the case, but for reasons different from those advanced by the District Court. The Appeals Court decision asserted that only an actual monopolist or explicit cartel rationally would engage in predation because a single firm could never be *certain* that its rivals would not mistake the disciplining, below-cost pricing for aggressive competitive behavior.[19] Liggett appealed to the Supreme Court in November 1992, and the Court agreed to hear the case. In June 1993, by a 6-to-3 vote, the Supreme Court dismissed the case.[20] In so doing, however, the Court rejected the certainty standard enunciated by the Court of Appeals and relied on analysis similar to that of the District Court. Thus, despite finding that (1) the cigarette industry was one of the most profitable in the United States; (2) B&W documents provided a sound basis for concluding that B&W entered the generic category with the intent to engage in anticompetitive behavior; and (3) there was evidence of below-cost pricing on generic cigarettes, the Supreme Court determined that B&W (contrary to the firm's own beliefs) could not rationally expect to recoup any of its alleged predatory investments.

The Supreme Court erred (in this author's view) at several key points in its analysis. After correctly stating the proposition that Liggett's case relied on recoupment by B&W of its predatory investment in below-cost pricing on generics (thereby protecting high-profit, branded cigarette sales), the Court asserted that a necessary element of Liggett's case was that there be recoupment through supracompetitive, coordinated pricing on low-priced cigarettes. This was not so. What was necessary was that Liggett have a greater incentive to maintain a lower price for generics than

[17] The judge had before him the testimony both of Liggett executives and of Liggett's expert economist on at least three occasions prior to this ruling: at a motion for summary judgment, at the time of a motion to dismiss at the end of Liggett's case, and at the conclusion of the entire trial, before the case went to the jury. In each instance, the judge allowed the case to proceed, and ultimately to reach the jury, before reversing field. Moreover, the questions and testimony on which he based this ruling are highly suspect. Liggett executives were asked questions embodying terms with which they, as businessmen, were unfamiliar, or they interpreted those terms differently from economists. For example, while an economist uses the term "tacit collusion" to reflect the ability of firms to raise prices without overt collusion, business executives focus on the "collusion" portion of the phrase and deny that they have engaged in such illegal, "collusive" behavior.

[18] For the judge's complete ruling, see *Liggett Group, Inc.* v. *Brown & Williamson Tobacco Corporation,* 748 F. Supp. 344 (M.D.N.C. 1990).

[19] *Liggett Group, Inc.* v. *Brown & Williamson Tobacco Corporation,* 964 F.2d 335 (4th Cir. 1992).

[20] *Brooke Groupe Ltd.* v. *Brown & Williamson Tobacco Corporation,* 61 U.S.L.W. 4699 (1993).

would the other firms. Since Liggett had nothing to lose by expanding the generic category, while each of the other firms stood to cannibalize its own sales, Liggett had the incentive to maintain a lower price for generics than did the other firms. Moreover, while B&W may not have recouped its losses on generics through higher postpredation prices on those products (which was neither proved nor disproved at the trial), the only form of recoupment necessary to the theory of the case involved stemming lost sales and profits on branded cigarette volumes.[21]

Finally, in finding that there was no evidence of harm to consumers, the Court placed significant weight on the fact that low-priced cigarette unit sales increased very rapidly even after B&W's price-cutting efforts; in the face of such rapid and dramatic growth in low-priced cigarette sales, the Court wondered, how could there have been any harm to consumers? Such rapid growth, however, is not so surprising when viewed in relation to the stunning increase in branded cigarette prices over the period. Prices for branded cigarettes rose from $6.43 per carton in January 1986 to $9.23 per carton in June 1989 (about the time the trial began); by mid-1992 they had reached $13.25 per carton. Thus, branded cigarette prices rose by 43 percent between 1986 and mid-1989 and by another 43 percent between 1989 and 1992. Prices more than doubled for the period overall. Viewed in the context of these dramatic and unprecedented price increases, the fact that low-priced cigarette sales did not grow even more is the real issue.

Before this matter, the courts had been raising the standards of proof required to extablish predatory pricing; the *Liggett* case raised the standards yet higher. Documentary evidence of an intention to engage in predatory behavior, even coupled with clear evidence of below-cost pricing, will not sustain a predation claim. A plaintiff must offer a *simple* explanation regarding how an alleged predator might expect to benefit from its behavior. While the complexity of the plaintiff's theory articulated in *Liggett* might have accurately captured the underlying complexity of competition in the cigarette industry, it also complicated the presentation, understanding, and acceptance of the theory itself.

POSTSCRIPT

Sales of discounted cigarettes, priced at less than "full-revenue" or branded prices, grew significantly in the years just after the initial *Liggett* trial in 1990. Does this mean that B&W's behavior had no effect on pricing in the cigarette industry, or in the behavior of Liggett & Myers, or that

---

[21] The majority opinion also asserted that no evidence had been introduced at trial to the effect that the prices analyzed (list prices) reflected true differences between the net prices (list prices less all discounts) paid by consumers—that is, that list prices did not reflect transactions prices. This point was addressed on several occasions at trial, and thus was an issue before the jury for review. Justice Stevens' dissent quotes one passage from the trial transcript reflecting such analysis.

Liggett's analysis was incorrect and B&W's conduct had no anticompetitive effect on industry prices? Not necessarily. While discounted cigarette sales grew, prices on branded cigarettes continued to rise, and the average price realized for all cigarettes, including both full-revenue and discounted products, increased rapidly until April 1993, when the large firms cut branded prices in order to narrow the price gap between branded and generic cigarettes.

Even after this realignment of prices, some recent analysts (including, in a different proceeding, the staff of the Federal Trade Commission) have observed: (1) that the cigarette industry is characterized by effective (albeit imperfect) price coordination that has resulted in prices above the competitive level; and (2) that the extent to which the industry has successfully raised prices has been adversely affected by the success of smaller fringe firms, including primarily Liggett, in pursuing competitive policies that bar more effective coordination by the larger firms. In fact, by 1996 Liggett's share had fallen to less than 2 percent of domestic cigarette sales, and industry observers were repeatedly questioning the firm's viability. Despite the firm's shrinking and tenuous market position, the FTC staff continued to attribute to Liggett a key role in maintaining prices at levels below those that would otherwise prevail:

> . . . Liggett remains the only firm of significant size [1.9 percent share] that has an appreciably older brand portfolio in terms of premium-brand life cycles and a primary commitment to the discount segments of the cigarette market. This makes Liggett one of the most significant constraints on higher industry pricing today.[22]

Thus, even this recent analysis would seem to confirm Liggett's claim that the larger firms had supranormal prices and profits to defend, and that Liggett's disruptive generic pricing made it an obvious target for the other companies.

REFERENCES

Areeda, Phillip, and Donald Turner. "Predatory Pricing and Related Practices Under Section 2 of the Sherman Act." *Harvard Law Review* 88 (February 1975): 697–733.

Brodley, Joseph, and George Hay. "Predatory Pricing: Competing Economic Theories and the Evolution of Legal Standards." *Cornell Law Review* 66 (1981): 738–803.

Federal Trade Commission. *Competition and the Financial Impact of the Proposed Tobacco Industry Settlement.* Staff Report. Washington, D.C.: Federal Trade Commission, 1997.

---

[22] Federal Trade Commission Staff Report (September 1997), p. 13.

Hay, George. "A Confused Lawyer's Guide to the Predatory Pricing Literature." In *Strategic Predation and Antitrust Analysis,* edited by Steven Salop, 155–202. Washington, D.C.: Federal Trade Commission, 1981.

Joskow, Paul L., and Alvin K. Klevorick. "A Framework for Analyzing Predatory Pricing Policy." *Yale Law Journal* 89 (December 1979): 213–269.

Nichols, William. "The Tobacco Case of 1946." *American Economic Review* 39 (May 1949): 284–296.

Posner, Richard. *Antitrust Law: An Economic Perspective.* Chicago: University of Chicago Press, 1976.

Scherer, F. M. "Predatory Pricing and the Sherman Act: A Comment." *Harvard Law Review* 89 (1976): 869–889.

Tennant, Richard B. *The American Cigarette Industry: A Study in Economic Analysis and Public Policy.* New Haven, Conn.: Yale University Press, 1950.

Williamson, Oliver E. "Predatory Pricing: A Strategic and Welfare Analysis." *Yale Law Journal* 87 (December 1977): 284–340.

CASE 11

Antitrust and Higher Education: MIT Financial Aid (1993)

Gustavo E. Bamberger and
Dennis W. Carlton

INTRODUCTION

In 1991, the U.S. Department of Justice's Antitrust Division ("the Government") sued the Massachusetts Institute of Technology ("MIT") and the eight colleges and universities in the "Ivy League"—Brown University, Columbia University, Cornell University, Dartmouth College, Harvard College, Princeton University, the University of Pennsylvania, and Yale University. According to the Government, the nine schools violated Section 1 of the Sherman Act by engaging in a conspiracy to restrain price competition for students receiving financial aid. The Government claimed that the schools conspired on financial aid policies in an effort to reduce aid and thereby raise their revenues.

The schools responded that the Sherman Act did not apply to them because they are not-for-profit institutions. Furthermore, they justified their cooperative behavior by explaining that it enabled them to concentrate aid only on those in need and thereby helped the schools to achieve their socially desirable goals of "need-blind" admission coupled with financial aid to all needy admittees. Without collective action, the schools argued, there would be less financial aid available to needy students, with a resulting decrease in the number of lower-income students attending those schools.

Dennis Carlton testified as an expert witness on behalf of MIT. Gustavo Bamberger assisted in the development of the economic analysis underlying Carlton's testimony. This chapter is based in part on Carlton et al. (1995). We thank Greg Pelnar for his assistance and John Kwoka, William Lynk, and Larry White for helpful comments.

All of the Ivy League schools signed a consent decree agreeing to stop the challenged cooperative activity. MIT refused to sign and went to trial. In September of 1992, MIT was found to have violated the Sherman Act.[1] Government investigations against several schools outside of the Ivy League continued. Soon after the trial ended, Congress passed the Higher Education Act of 1992, allowing colleges and universities to engage in certain cooperative conduct aimed at concentrating aid only on needy students. In September of 1993, the Court of Appeals overturned the District Court's verdict and ordered a new trial.[2] The Government subsequently dropped all investigations against other schools and reached a settlement with MIT that allows MIT to engage in most of the conduct that the Government had challenged.

This case raises several interesting and important issues about the treatment of not-for-profit institutions under the antitrust laws. Should the antitrust laws apply to not-for-profits, and if so, how? Specifically, how should the application of the antitrust laws to not-for-profit firms differ, if at all, from their application to for-profit firms?

This chapter describes the economics of not-for-profit schools and the schools' actions that were challenged by the Government, with the economic arguments and evidence relied on by each side. It then discusses the findings of the District Court and the Court of Appeals. It also summarizes the settlement reached by MIT and the Government. It concludes with a discussion of the issues raised by this case and more recent developments in the application of the antitrust laws to not-for-profit institutions.

THE ECONOMICS OF NOT-FOR-PROFIT SCHOOLS

In the standard models of firm behavior used by economists, firms are assumed to have a simple objective—maximize profits. These profits are enjoyed by the owner or owners of the firm. A not-for-profit firm, however, typically is barred from paying out any profits it may earn (and there are no "owners" to whom profits could be paid). In the United States, not-for-profit firms typically are organized under IRS Regulation 501(c)3.[3] This regulation legally constrains the actions of a not-for-profit firm, specifically preventing the disbursement of any excess revenues over costs. Under the IRS code, private donations made to a not-for-profit institution can be deducted from the donor's taxable income and thus reduce the donor's tax. In this way, both the donor and the general tax-paying public support not-for-profit institutions.

Although not-for-profit firms are relatively rare in the U.S. economy,

---

[1] *U.S. v. Brown University, et al.,* 805 F. Supp. 288 (E.D. Pa. 1992).

[2] *U.S. v. Brown University, et al.,* 5 F.3d 658 (3rd Cir. 1993).

[3] MIT and the other Ivy League schools are 501c(3) corporations.

several sectors of the economy are dominated by not-for-profits. Most higher education in the United States is provided by not-for-profit institutions. These institutions are either public, such as state universities, or private not-for-profit schools. In addition to most institutions of higher education, most religious and cultural institutions are not-for-profit. Similarly, most hospitals in the United States are organized as not-for-profits.[4]

Not-for-profit firms often are created to achieve (or attempt to achieve) a particular goal or goals that the firm's founders believe are socially desirable.[5] Some not-for-profit firms, such as educational institutions, solicit donations. Donors who would be reluctant to donate to a for-profit firm for fear that the owners would simply keep the donation do not face that concern in the case of not-for-profits because of the legal constraint on distributing funds.[6] Because for-profit firms may not have incentives to achieve certain goals that are considered socially desirable, not-for-profit firms can be viewed as a response to a "market failure."[7]

In the case of colleges and universities, the institution likely is interested in achieving various goals. For example, colleges and universities typically are thought to be interested in:[8]

- providing a quality education
- enhancing the general welfare of its students
- enhancing the general welfare of its faculty and administrators
- sponsoring high-quality and innovative research
- providing innovative teaching programs
- satisfying alumni and other potential donors' preferences[9]

Because these institutions have various goals (not all of which are mutually consistent), it is difficult to specify precisely the "objective function" of the institution—that is, it is difficult to specify what exactly a particular school is attempting to maximize.

The not-for-profit nature of schools explains many school practices that would be unusual in a for-profit world. Schools maintain many prohibitions on transactions that would be inefficient in a profit-maximizing context. For example, schools such as MIT and the Ivys do not allow students to buy admission (or at least there is no formal procedure for doing

---

[4]See Hansmann (1980) and Lynk (1995).

[5]However, some not-for-profit firms may be formed to maximize the profits of other firms. For example, a not-for-profit trade organization likely takes actions intended to increase the profits of the firms it represents.

[6]Of course, donors are concerned that their donations will be well spent.

[7]See Hansmann (1980, p. 845).

[8]See, for example, Hopkins (1988).

[9]The MIT Alumni Association filed a brief in support of MIT in this case.

so) if they have poor grades. It seems likely that MIT and Harvard as well as many other schools could abandon need-blind admissions and profitably auction off their last five admission spots without a material decline in either their reputation or quality of the student body, but with a significant increase in revenue.[10] Since constraints on trading are generally undesirable, the behavior of schools can be reconciled with reasonable behavior only because of the complicated nature of each school's not-for-profit objective function.[11]

THE CHALLENGED CONDUCT

The history and development of the challenged conduct was not a disputed issue during the trial. Unlike most alleged price-fixing cases, both sides agreed on the basic facts.

In the 1950s, members of the Ivy League met to discuss the desirability of not bidding for "star" athletes. These meetings were called "Overlap meetings" (because they discussed students who were admitted to "overlapping" schools), and the schools participating in the meetings were called the "Overlap schools." Schools adopted the rule that no athlete could receive aid beyond that justified by financial need, and financial need was calculated according to a common formula. The meetings soon took up the issue of whether such a rule was sensible for nonathlete students. The schools reasoned that if they were forced to bid for star students who had no financial need, the schools would have less money to give out to other students who had such need. Before the 1950s, few schools had significant scholarship programs, and the Ivys were accessible primarily to the wealthy.[12] The purpose of the Overlap meetings, according to the participating schools, was to concentrate scarce financial aid only on needy students to enable such students to attend.

A student's aid package consists of two components. One is called "self help," which represents what a student contributes and is based on loans or jobs that the school may provide or help the student gets.[13] The other is grants (also known as scholarships), which are outright gifts to students. For most schools, grants and scholarships come primarily from either the Government (primarily through Pell grants) or the institution itself. A student pays for his or her education from grants, self help, and "family contribution." The sum of the first two categories is the student's

---

[10]It is undoubtedly true that many schools do show preference to alumni and large donors and that this is a rough way of "selling" admission. MIT gives applicants of alumni and donors no preference.

[11]See Rothschild and White (1993) for a discussion of other school practices that are inconsistent with profit maximization.

[12]See Clotfelter (1991).

[13]There often may be a subsidy component to a loan that a student receives.

aid package. The sum of the last two categories is what the student pays to the school (Figure 11-1). The Overlap schools reached agreement with each other on the family contribution for commonly admitted students seeking financial aid, so that regardless of which Overlap school a student was admitted to, the student's family contribution was identical. (Notice that even if gross tuition levels differed among schools, the Overlap schools equalized family contribution.) Some Overlap schools reached agreement on the division of the aid package between self help and grants, whereas others—including MIT—did not.

The number of schools participating in Overlap meetings grew over time. By the 1970s, there were regular meetings among the Ivys plus MIT and fourteen other prestigious schools.[14] The schools participating in Overlap meetings: (a) agreed to give aid based only on need; (b) agreed on a common methodology to define need; and (c) met to discuss individual cases of commonly admitted students.[15]

At the Overlap meetings, a listing of commonly admitted students was circulated among the schools together with each school's proposed

FIGURE 11-1 The Sources of Students' Tuition Payments.

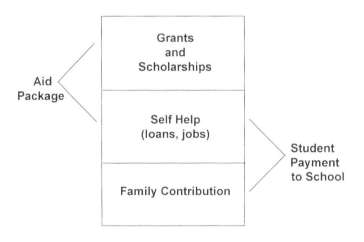

[14]The Ivys and MIT met together. The other fourteen schools also met together and some of these schools also met with certain members of the Ivy/MIT group. The other fourteen Overlap schools were Amherst College, Barnard College, Bowdoin College, Bryn Mawr University, Colby College, Middlebury College, Mount Holyoke College, Smith College, Trinity College, Tufts University, Vassar College, Wellesley College, Wesleyan University, and Williams College.

[15]A valid inquiry is whether the Overlap schools could have market power in view of their small share of total undergraduate enrollments in the United States (less than 1%). For example, the total undergraduate enrollment of all the Overlap schools was less than that of the total undergraduate enrollments of the Universities of Illinois, Michigan, and Wisconsin. If the Overlap schools lacked market power, it would be hard to explain why the Overlap process existed.

family contributions for each student. In cases of significantly differing proposals (ones that differed by more than several hundred dollars), the schools would discuss their justification for the family contributions and would agree to compromise on a common figure or (less often) agree to disagree. There were initial disagreements on about 10 to 20 percent of the commonly admitted students applying for financial aid.[16] The initial disagreements usually arose either because schools had different information (e.g., if an applicant had an older sibling at a school, one school could have more complete information than another about family finances) or because the schools had varying degrees of sophistication in analyzing complicated financial holdings (e.g., the treatment of a low reported income that took advantage of various tax shelters).

ECONOMIC ARGUMENTS AND EVIDENCE

The Government's Claims

According to the Government, there was little need for economic evidence in this case—the undisputed facts were enough to condemn MIT's conduct under Section 1 of the Sherman Act. The Government offered five arguments. First, the Government argued that the Sherman Act applied to MIT's financial aid policies because the collecting of fees from students and their families is a commercial activity governed by the antitrust laws. According to the Government, "financial aid is a discount from the list price that is offered to certain customers. Universities grant discounts in their own self-interest, just as do other businesses that compete in the market place."[17] The Government also argued that "[t]he selling and discounting of educational services involves a fundamentally commercial aspect of the higher education industry."[18]

Second, the Government argued that because MIT's financial aid policies constituted commercial activity, "MIT's status as a 'non-profit' corporation does not shield its anticompetitive conduct from the Sherman Act"[19] and that the "higher education industry" has no antitrust immunity.[20]

---

[16]See Dodge (1989).

[17]Memorandum of Law in Support of Government's Motion for Summary Judgment, Civil Action No. 91-CV-3274, United States District Court for the Eastern District of Pennsylvania, ("Government's Memorandum"), at 87.

[18]Government's Memorandum, at 86. The Government distinguished the "commercial nature" of MIT's financial aid policies from the issues involved in *Marjorie Webster Junior College, Inc.* v. *Middle States Association of Colleges and Secondary Schools, Inc.,* 432 F.2d 650, 654 (D.C. Cir.), *cert. denied,* 400 U.S. 965 (1970), which, according to the Government, stood for "the fairly unremarkable proposition that non-commercial activities, not related to pricing, are outside the scope of the Sherman Act" (at 92).

[19]Government's Memorandum, at 88.

[20]Government's Memorandum, at 92.

Instead, the Government contended that an analysis of a challenged practice "must focus on the conduct in question, not on the nature of the industry involved or the organizational form of the actors."[21]

Third, given that the challenged conduct constituted commercial activity, the Government argued that the Overlap process was "garden variety price fixing."[22] The purpose of the price fix was to agree on the number and amount of discounts (grants) from list price (tuition) that the schools would offer. However, the Government did not allege a conspiracy to fix the list price, that is, the gross tuition level charged by the schools.[23]

Fourth, the Government further claimed that the inevitable consequence of the collective behavior of the Overlap schools was to increase the schools' net tuition revenues.[24] Indeed, the Government argued that even in the absence of evidence that average net tuition actually rose, the consequences of the school's actions were so inevitable that the conduct should be condemned as a per se violation of the antitrust laws.[25] The Government argued that "[t]he critical issue in applying the per se rule is whether the court has had experience with the type of restraint in question, not whether it has had experience in a particular industry."[26] According to the Government, although the terminology used by MIT and the Ivys differed from that used in most industries, it was easy to translate that terminology into "standard economic terms":

> "Tuition, Room and Board" and other compulsory charges is the list price of college attendance; "financial aid" and "merit scholarships" are selective discounts offered to some students. The "family contribution" is the net price for college attendance, that is, the list price minus the discount. By agreeing to fix family contributions . . . and to ban merit scholarships, MIT and the Ivy League institutions have engaged in a trade practice that the courts have experience with and have prohibited time and time again—price fixing.[27]

---

[21]Government's Memorandum, at 91.

[22]District Court Trial Transcript, at 725.

[23]The Government's theory implied that the schools increased revenues by colluding on the net tuition charged to needy students, but not to rich students. The Government did not explain why conduct allegedly intended to extract higher tuition payments ignored the students with the most money.

[24]The Government did not allege that the challenged conduct reduced the schools' output. For example, the Government did not claim that the Overlap process had reduced enrollments at the Overlap schools.

[25]Conduct that courts have found almost always harms competition is condemned as a per se violation without any analysis required of the effect in the specific case at hand. Conduct that might or might not harm competition is analyzed under a "rule of reason," where analysis of the effects of the conduct determine its legality. (In practice, however, the distinction between per se and rule-of-reason analyses often is not sharp.)

[26]Government's Memorandum, at 82.

[27]Government's Memorandum, at 84.

Finally, the Government argued that "social policy" justifications for the challenged conduct were irrelevant even under the rule of reason: "[N]o justification for price-fixing is allowed and no analysis of the specific factors involved in a particular industry is required."[28] According to the Government, the Supreme Court "has consistently rejected social or quality-based justifications for anticompetitive conduct" under the rule of reason.[29]

MIT's Position

Unlike most defendants in a price-fixing case, MIT did not dispute that it engaged in the challenged conduct—MIT readily admitted that it met with the other Overlap schools and discussed financial aid packages for individual students. However, MIT vigorously disputed the Government's characterization of its conduct as an attempt to raise net tuition revenues.

MIT had four responses to the Government. First, MIT argued that, as a threshold matter, the challenged conduct did not constitute "trade or commerce" and thus was not proscribed by the Sherman Act. MIT argued that it and the other Overlap schools "engaged in Overlap to advance educational access and socioeconomic diversity and to maximize the effective use of private charitable funds. In so doing, they neither sought nor obtained any financial or commercial benefit," and therefore MIT's conduct should not be subject to the antitrust laws.[30] Furthermore, MIT argued that because the actual cost of an MIT undergraduate education exceeded the total revenue received from every student (even those receiving no financial aid), all grants of financial aid constituted a form of charity, not a reduction from "list price." Thus, according to MIT, the conduct at issue "involved the coordinated distribution of private, charitable funds to qualified but needy students to help them defray the expenses of an education at MIT."[31]

MIT argued that the legislative history of the Sherman Act showed that it was not intended to apply to the charitable activities of not-for-profit educational institutions. For example, in 1890 Senator Sherman argued that there was no need to amend his proposed act to exempt temperance unions:

> I do not see any reason for putting in [an exclusion for] temperance societies any more than churches or schoolhouses or any other kind of moral or educational associations that may be organized. Such an association is

---

[28]Government's Memorandum, at 79.

[29]Government's Memorandum, at 79.

[30]Massachusetts Institute of Technology's Brief in Opposition to the Antitrust Division's Motion for Summary Judgment ("MIT's Brief"), at 44.

[31]MIT's Brief, at 40.

> not in any sense a combination or arrangement made to interfere with interstate commerce . . . I do not think it is worth while to adopt the amendment [relating to] temperance societies. You might as well include churches and Sunday schools.[32]

Second, MIT argued that if the court decided that the Sherman Act did apply to the challenged conduct, that conduct should not be condemned as a per se violation but instead should be analyzed under the rule of reason. MIT argued that the per se rule should be applied only to types of conduct where "a court can look back upon unambiguous judicial experience demonstrating that the challenged practice is a 'naked restraint of trade with no purpose except stifling of competition.' "[33]

MIT argued that the court did not have unambiguous judicial experience with the type of challenged conduct because the firms acting collectively were not-for-profit institutions, whereas most antitrust cases involve for-profit firms. According to MIT, the court should not condemn conduct practiced by not-for-profits simply because that same conduct when practiced by for-profit firms would harm competition. That is, even though the court's experience shows that when profit-maximizing firms meet to set price, they almost always intend to increase prices and profits (and thereby harm consumers), the same is not necessarily true when not-for-profit schools meet to set financial aid policy collectively.

In particular, MIT argued that the Government's claim that net tuition revenues inevitably would increase as a consequence of the collective action was wrong as a matter of economic theory. Even if the Government's argument generally were true for profit-maximizing firms, it was not true for not-for-profit firms. Because not-for-profit firms maximize a multiattribute objective function, it simply is not possible to predict inevitable consequences from cooperative price setting. As a matter of economic theory, the cooperative efforts of the Overlap schools could indeed be to conserve their financial aid so as to achieve their stated goal of enabling greater numbers of needy students to attend their schools.

Third, MIT argued that the challenged conduct was justified on "social welfare" grounds that the Government endorsed. In particular, MIT argued that the challenged conduct was needed to conserve aid for only the truly needy and claimed that the Overlap conduct helped the Overlap schools achieve their goals of need-blind admissions with a guarantee of full aid if admitted. Moreover, the schools believed that their policies were entirely consistent with the Federal Government's financial aid policy. With minor exceptions, federal money can be given *only* to needy students. A meritorious high-income student generally cannot receive any federal aid. Moreover, students receiving any federal aid usually cannot receive supplemental awards from a school beyond demonstrated financial need.

---

[32]MIT's Brief, at 40 (citations omitted).

[33]MIT's Brief, at 58, citing *White Motor Co. v. United States*, 372 U.S. 253, 263 (1963).

MIT pointed out that the Government seemed specifically to endorse collective behavior by MIT and the Ivys when used to make aid decisions for student-athletes. The consent decree signed by the Ivys provided that:

> Nothing in this Final Judgment shall prevent defendants that are members of a common athletic league from: (1) agreeing to grant financial aid to recruited athletes or students who participate in athletics on the sole basis of economic need with no differentiation in amount or in kind based on athletic ability or participation, provided that each school shall apply its own standard of economic need.[34]

MIT argued that if the Government believed that such agreements were reasonable for athletes, it made no sense to argue that similar agreements were per se illegal when applied to nonathletes.[35]

Finally, MIT argued that if the challenged conduct were evaluated under the rule of reason, the empirical evidence showed that the Overlap agreements produced no antitrust harm. MIT argued that the economic rationale for a per se rule against collective price setting is that price typically rises as a result of the collective action. Because this underlying rationale does not apply necessarily to not-for-profit schools, MIT claimed that the only way to determine whether the collective agreements on aid raised price is to study what happened as a result of the agreements. MIT's expert economist performed such a study and found no statistically significant basis for the claim that the collective action raised average net tuition per student at the Overlap schools.[36] Thus, MIT argued that the statistical evidence did not support the Government's hypothesis that the collective action inevitably must have increased the Overlap schools' net tuition revenues.[37]

MIT's expert investigated through a multiple regression analysis whether average net tuition per student was higher at schools that engaged in the challenged conduct. A multiple regression analysis is a well-accepted standard statistical procedure used to examine the factors influencing a variable of interest, such as average net tuition per student. Through a multiple regression analysis, it is possible to isolate the effect of a single variable in a complex factual environment containing multiple variables. In the regression analysis offered by MIT, other characteristics of a school that could affect average net tuition per student in addition to

---

[34]MIT's Brief, at 78 (quoting consent decree entered into by the Ivy League schools).

[35]Similarly, the Government has not opposed the NCAA's collective enforcement of limits on athletic aid packages.

[36]The Government's expert economist agreed that average net tuition per student was the appropriate variable to study.

[37]In the typical alleged price-fixing conspiracy, the conspiring firms are accused of raising price and restricting output. Because a school's "output" is multidimensional, measuring the effect of Overlap on output is difficult. The Government provided no evidence nor made any claim that the challenged behavior reduced the Overlap schools' output.

participation in the Overlap collective agreement were accounted for. For example, whether a school is a private or public institution or whether a school has a religious affiliation could influence average net tuition. By accounting for these other factors, an analyst can obtain estimates of the effect of Overlap membership on the average net tuition per student charged by a school.

The variables used to explain average net tuition per student at a particular school were:

1. Whether the school had a religious affiliation (this variable is labeled NONRELIG in the regression analysis)

2. Percentage of students scoring more than 700 on the SAT verbal or math test (SAT)

3. Real state per-capita disposable income in the state where the school is located (YDPC)

4. Percentage of applicants accepted (PCTACC)

5. Percentage of undergraduates not receiving need-based aid (PCT-NOAID)

6. Percentage of class completing a degree (COMPDEG)

7. Type of school, as determined by the Carnegie Foundation for the Advancement of Teaching (DOCTOR1, DOCTOR2, RSRCH1, RSRCH2)

8. Real endowment per full-time equivalent student (ENDOW)

9. Whether mandatory fee information was unavailable (FEEMISS)

10. Whether the school was MIT or in the Ivy League (IVY)

11. Whether the school was one of the non-Ivy League Overlap schools (NONIVY)

The analysis was based on annual data for each of these variables for the years 1984–1990 for approximately 160 private schools. Adding public schools to the analysis did not have a substantial impact on the results.[38]

MIT's expert analyzed yearly data as well as an average over the entire 1984–1990 period, and found that the results were unambiguous— there was no statistically significant evidence that membership in Overlap was associated with higher average net tuition per student. A typical result is presented in Table 11-1, which shows, for example, that

---

[38]Experiments with different models and estimation techniques found substantially similar results—the Overlap conduct did not result in statistically significant higher average net tuition per student at the Overlap schools, holding constant school characteristics.

TABLE 11-1
Weighted Average Net Tuition Regression Results, 1984–1990
(standard errors in parentheses)

Intercept	2299.47
	(2429.07)
IVY	−322.42
	(678.72)
NONIVY	130.37
	(463.81)
RSRCH1	1042.21
	(435.09)
RSRCH2	1062.57
	(514.05)
DOCTOR1	545.66
	(551.02)
DOCTOR2	−1143.27
	(493.21)
FEEMISS	−540.82
	(294.78)
PCTACC	−27.89
	(11.97)
PCTNOAID	43.58
	(9.44)
SAT	2.31
	(11.16)
YDPC	0.36
	(0.07)
COMPDEG	45.68
	(16.64)
NONRELIG	1343.18
	(250.19)
ENDOW	−5.95
	(3.77)
R^2	0.726
Number of Observations	162

1. All else equal, MIT and the Ivy League schools charged slightly *less* than non-Overlap schools (i.e., the estimated coefficient on IVY is negative but not significantly different from zero).

2. All else equal, schools that were not religiously affiliated charged, on average, roughly $1350 more than schools that were religiously affiliated (i.e., the estimated coefficient on NONRELIG is about 1350).

3. Highly selective schools were more expensive, all else equal, than less selective schools. For example, a school that accepted 25 percent of its applicants charged roughly $1400 more on average than a school that accepted 75 percent of its applicants (i.e., the coefficient on PCTACC times 50 equals about 1400).

Thus, MIT argued that the evidence provided no statistically significant support for the Government's position that the Overlap agreements raised the average net tuition per student charged by the Overlap schools.[39]

THE RESULTS

The District Court

After a ten-day bench trial, the District Court for the Eastern District of Pennsylvania found that MIT had violated Section 1 of the Sherman Act. The court rejected MIT's contention that the challenged conduct did not constitute commercial activity: "[t]he court can conceive of few aspects of higher education that are more commercial than the price charged to students."[40]

Although the court accepted the Government's position that the Overlap conduct affected commerce and thus was susceptible to attack under the Sherman Act, the court refused to find the Overlap process per se illegal. The court observed that "[m]erely because a certain practice bears a label which falls within the categories of restraints declared to be per se unreasonable does not mean a court must reflexively condemn that practice to per se treatment."[41]

The court did not, however, undertake an in-depth rule-of-reason analysis of the Overlap conduct. Instead, the court ruled that the challenged conduct should be examined using an abbreviated rule-of-reason analysis. The court deemed that a full-scale rule-of-reason analysis was not needed because the Overlap conduct was "so inherently suspect" that "'no elaborate industry analysis'" was required to demonstrate its anticompetitive character.[42]

The court ruled that "[since] the Ivy Overlap Agreements are plainly anticompetitive, the Rule of Reason places upon MIT 'a heavy burden of

[39] At trial, the Government's economist presented regression studies that he claimed showed that the Overlap conduct did increase average net tuition per student at those schools. These results were based on a small subset of the data used in MIT's analysis. MIT argued that the Government's studies were flawed statistically.

[40] *U.S. v. Brown University, et al.*, 805 F. Supp. 288 (E.D. Pa. 1992), at 298.

[41] *U.S. v. Brown University, et al.*, 805 F. Supp. 288 (E.D. Pa. 1992), at 299.

[42] *U.S. v. Brown University, et al.*, 805 F. Supp. 288 (E.D. Pa. 1992), at 303, quoting *FTC v. Indiana Fed'n of Dentists*, 476 U.S. 447, 459, 106 S.Ct. 2009, 2018 (1986).

establishing an affirmative defense which competitively justifies this apparent deviation from the operations of a free market.'"[43] The court held that evidence that the challenged conduct did not affect the prices charged by the Overlap schools did not provide an affirmative defense for the conduct. "Even accepting MIT's premise that Overlap was revenue neutral [i.e., did not affect average net tuition per student], to say that a restraint is revenue neutral, by itself, says nothing of its procompetitive virtue."[44]

The court rejected MIT's justifications for Overlap and concluded:

> The court is not to decide whether social policy aims can ever justify an otherwise competitively unreasonable restraint. The issue before the court is narrow, straightforward and unvarnished. It is whether, under the Rule of Reason, the elimination of competition itself can be justified by non-economic designs. The Supreme Court has unambiguously and conclusively held that it may not.[45]

The Court of Appeals

Both the Government and MIT appealed certain portions of the District Court's ruling. In September 1993, the Court of Appeals for the Third Circuit ruled (by a 2-to-1 majority) that the District Court had erred in several respects and remanded the case to the District Court for retrial.[46]

The Court of Appeals first examined whether the challenged conduct constituted trade or commerce. The Court of Appeals upheld the District Court's finding and ruled that providing educational services in return for payment (whether discounted or not) is a commercial activity that subjects MIT to the antitrust laws. However, the Court of Appeals noted that "[a]lthough MIT's status as a nonprofit educational organization and its advancement of congressionally recognized and important social welfare goals does not remove its conduct from the realm of trade or commerce, these factors will influence whether this conduct violates the Sherman Act."[47] Thus, the Court of Appeals ruled that the social goals of MIT's policy were relevant in an antitrust analysis.

The Court of Appeals also addressed whether the District Court erred by using a rule of reason, instead of a per se, approach in evaluating

---

[43]*U.S.* v. *Brown University, et al.,* 805 F. Supp. 288 (E.D. Pa. 1992), at 304, quoting *NCAA* v. *Board of Regents of the University of Oklahoma, et al.,* 468 U.S. 85, 113, 104 S.Ct. 2948, 2966 (1984).

[44]*U.S.* v. *Brown University, et al.,* 805 F. Supp. 288 (E.D. Pa. 1992), at 304.

[45]*U.S.* v. *Brown University, et al.,* 805 F. Supp. 288 (E.D. Pa. 1992), at 305.

[46]In dissent, Judge Weis argued that the Sherman Act should not apply to the challenged conduct because MIT was a not-for-profit firm and argued that the District Court should have granted judgment in favor of MIT.

[47]*U.S.* v. *Brown University, et al.,* 5 F.3d 658 (3rd Cir. 1993), at 668.

Overlap.[48] The Court of Appeals upheld the District Court's ruling that Overlap was not per se illegal and held that Overlap's "alleged pure altruistic motive and alleged absence of a revenue maximizing purpose contribute to our uncertainty with regard to Overlap's anti-competitiveness, and thus prompts us to give careful scrutiny to the nature of Overlap, and to refrain from declaring Overlap per se unreasonable."[49]

The Court of Appeals disagreed with the District Court's ruling that the effect of Overlap on average net tuition per student was irrelevant. The Court of Appeals ruled that "the absence of any finding [by the District Court] of adverse effects such as higher price or lower output is relevant, albeit not dispositive, when the district court considers whether MIT has met [its burden of establishing an affirmative justification for Overlap]."[50]

The Court of Appeals also ruled that the District Court erred by not investigating more fully MIT's procompetitive and noneconomic justifications for the Overlap conduct. The Court of Appeals noted that MIT had proffered procompetitive economic justifications for Overlap. For example, the Court of Appeals explained that if Overlap increased consumer choice (by allowing needy but able students to attend MIT who otherwise would not have attended), then "rather than suppress competition, Overlap may in fact merely regulate competition in order to enhance it, while also deriving certain social benefits. If the rule of reason analysis leads to this conclusion, then indeed Overlap will be beyond the scope of the prohibitions of the Sherman Act."[51] The Court of Appeals ruled that "[t]he nature of higher education, and the asserted pro-competitive and pro-consumer features of the Overlap, convince us that a full rule of reason is in order here."[52]

Finally, the Court of Appeals held that "[e]ven if anticompetitive restraint is intended to achieve a legitimate objective, the restraint only survives a rule of reason analysis if it is reasonably necessary to achieve the legitimate objectives proffered by the defendant."[53] If, on remand, the District Court found that MIT could persuasively justify Overlap, then the Government would have an opportunity to prove that a reasonable but less restrictive alternative existed that could meet Overlap's objectives.

The Settlement

The new trial called for by the Court of Appeals did not take place because the Government and MIT reached a settlement in December of 1993.

---

[48]MIT argued that the District Court erred by not using a full-scale (as opposed to an abbreviated) rule-of-reason analysis; the Government argued that the District Court erred by not finding Overlap to be per se illegal.

[49]*U.S. v. Brown University, et al.,* 5 F.3d 658 (3rd Cir. 1993), at 672.

[50]*U.S. v. Brown University, et al.,* 5 F.3d 658 (3rd Cir. 1993), at 624.

[51]*U.S. v. Brown University, et al.,* 5 F.3d 658 (3rd Cir. 1993), at 677.

[52]*U.S. v. Brown University, et al.,* 5 F.3d 658 (3rd Cir. 1993), at 678.

[53]*U.S. v. Brown University, et al.,* 5 F.3d 658 (3rd Cir. 1993), at 678–679.

Under the terms of the settlement, MIT and other schools are allowed to engage in Overlap-type behavior, including pooling of student information. Agreements not to give merit aid and to use common principles to determine aid are allowed, but discussions about individual students' financial aid are not. Audits to detect schools that deviate significantly from the agreed-upon common principles for awarding aid are allowed.

DISCUSSION

Economic Efficiency

To many economists, the economic content of the antitrust laws is simple: prevent inefficiency.[54] Did Overlap affect economic efficiency? If the Overlap process left the schools' revenues and class size unchanged and prevented the use of merit aid at those schools, then the Overlap process likely transferred income that otherwise would have gone to meritorious nonneedy students toward other students. The Overlap conduct also probably resulted in a different allocation of students to schools than otherwise would have occurred—a larger number of needy students attended the Overlap schools.[55]

There is no necessary inefficiency generated by Overlap; instead, its major effect is better characterized as income redistribution.[56] The Government argued that there was a class of consumers harmed by the Overlap conduct—namely, meritorious high-income students. But if Overlap primarily redistributed income, then for every winner, there was an equal loser. There is no necessary efficiency loss from income transfers.

The general hostility that most economists (including us) have toward

---

[54]Others have argued that efficiency should not be the sole goal of the antitrust laws. See, e.g., Lande (1989) and Pitofsky (1979).

[55]The schools claimed that Overlap allowed them to obtain a diverse group of students. As a general matter, it is unclear how to determine whether one mix of students is more efficient than an alternative mix because there is no unambiguous agreement on what "output" a school should be trying to achieve. As a theoretical matter, it is possible to justify the Overlap conduct on the basis of efficiency in matching. Suppose that students care about the quality of their classmates. Then given the quality attributes of each person, one can ask whether competition can achieve the optimal allocation of students to schools. This problem is similar to one posed by Koopmans and Beckmann (1957) and studied by Roth and Sotomayer (1990). (See also Telser, 1978.) These studies show that unconstrained competition cannot always achieve an optimal allocation. This finding can provide a possible theoretical justification for limitations on the use of prices and for cooperative assignment of students to schools. We are unaware of any empirical attempts to examine this potential justification. (See Hansmann and Klevorick, 1993.)

[56]If the Government were correct and the Overlap conduct had raised the schools' revenues, then the cooperative action would seem similar to a cartel. Even here, the not-for-profit schools could argue that they differ from a profit-maximizing cartel because any increased revenues that they receive are more likely to be spent on desirable causes. Except perhaps in unusual cases, the enforcement problem associated with determining whether the increased revenues were spent productively strike us as so great that it would not be desirable to allow such a defense even for not-for-profit institutions. Moreover, the danger of the cooperative agreement's causing inefficiency increases as average net tuition per student rises.

cooperative price setting in the profit-maximizing sector should not lead to an automatic condemnation of a practice that is focused primarily on equity concerns and appears to have few if any efficiency consequences and that would never arise (at least, for the motives claimed by MIT) in the profit-maximizing sector.[57] No cartel of profit-maximizing firms would cooperate *solely* to redistribute income among its customers.

If one articulates goals for the antitrust laws other than economic efficiency, one can justify condemning many practices. For example, if one assumes that the antitrust laws guarantee unrestricted competition under all circumstances, then by assumption the Overlap conduct violates this goal. But that standard would condemn many practices generally viewed as procompetitive. For example, policies that reduce information costs or that allow a manufacturer to use vertical restrictions on distributors to encourage the provision of services often are considered procompetitive. Yet in each case some individuals may be harmed. Consumers with low search costs or consumers with no need for service would benefit if the antitrust laws forbade such policies, even if, overall, consumers gain from these policies. Thus, any sensible antitrust policy must involve some balancing of harms and benefits to consumers.

Social Goals

Was the Overlap conduct necessary to meet MIT's and the other schools' social goals? In particular, does assisting needy students require collective action, or would it be possible for each school to meet the same goal by unilaterally implementing its own financial aid policy?

MIT presented expert testimony that without Overlap, competition for star students would break out in the future and financial aid to needy students would be reduced.[58] The adverse consequences of such an effect on the needy could be especially pronounced in light of recent trends in financing higher education.[59] Federal support for higher education declined substantially since its high point in the 1970s. For example, real federal aid (grants plus loans) per enrolled undergraduate student dropped by about 15 percent between 1975 and 1988 (see Table 11-2). Real federal grants per enrolled undergraduate student fell by about 60 percent over the same time period. Furthermore, the real cost of a college education increased by almost 40 percent during the same period. The combined effect of reductions in total aid and increases in tuition caused the real price paid per student to rise by at least 50 percent between 1975 and 1988. To offset

---

[57]Even in the profit-maximizing sector, cooperation can sometimes be efficient, e.g., among firms in a network industry. See Carlton and Klamer (1983). Cooperation among competing (profit-seeking) teams in a sports league also may be efficient; see, e.g., Noll (1982).

[58]The demise of Overlap apparently led to some bidding for students by at least some former Overlap members. See, for example, Carlson and Shepherd (1992, p. 569).

[59]See McPherson and Schapiro (1991) for a detailed study of financing trends.

TABLE 11-2
Ratio of Aggregate Merit Aid to Need Aid by Carnegie Classification[a]

Carnegie Classification	Number of Schools	1984 Ratio Merit Aid to Need Aid	1989 Ratio Merit Aid to Need Aid
Research I	11	0.1467	0.1730
Research II	8	0.1880	0.1946
Doctoral I	4	0.1426	0.2139
Doctoral II	9	0.3032	0.3758
Liberal Arts I	40	0.0759	0.1313
Total	72	0.1339	0.1800

[a]Based on schools with available information.

Sources: *Peterson's Annual Survey of Undergraduate Institutions* and the Carnegie Foundation for the Advancement of Teaching.

the decline in federal grants and aid, states and schools have expanded their grant and aid awards. The data in Table 11-3 show that merit aid has generally become increasingly important as a fraction of institutional aid. As schools grant more aid, they grant it increasingly to meritorious non-needy students. In recent years, several schools (including Brown University and Smith College, former participants in Overlap) have announced that they will no longer maintain "need-blind" admissions policies.[60]

Did Overlap achieve its goal of increasing access of the needy to Overlap schools? It is difficult to measure quantitatively whether Overlap did achieve its social goal, and little systematic evidence was presented at trial. Ideally, one would want evidence on the family income of entrants to examine whether Overlap affected the income distribution of its entrants by allowing a larger number of needy students to attend. Though such income data are not available in sufficient detail to perform a study, data are available on the percentage of the entering class that is black or Hispanic, a variable that likely is roughly related to income. Although these percentages are only rough proxies for income, they should provide some indication of Overlap's effect.

Studies performed by the authors found evidence that Overlap increased black enrollment by a statistically significant amount.[61] The magnitude indicates that for the typical school, Overlap increased black enrollment to about 5 percent during the period 1984–1990 from the about 3 percent that would otherwise be predicted. These results provide indirect evidence to support MIT's claim that Overlap did achieve its social goal.

[60]See Lubman (1994) and Stout (1992).

[61]See Carlton, Bamberger, and Epstein (1995).

THE ANTITRUST REVOLUTION

TABLE 11-3
Sources of Financial Aid to Students
(In millions of 1998 dollars)

	Total Federal, State, and Institutional Aid	Total Federal Aid (Grants and Loans)	Federal Grants	Institutionally Awarded Aid	Undergraduate Enrollment (in 1000s)	Real Education Price Index[a]
1963–64	2,269	893	456	1,160	Not Available	Not Availabl
1975–76	23,269	19,036	15,240	3,155	10,880	100.0
1984–85	22,331	17,272	6,701	3,667	12,305	116.6
1988–89	26,661	19,063	7,126	5,156	13,116	138.1

[a]Real Education Price Index equals CPI for personal and educational expenses divided by all items CPI.

Sources: Clotfelter (1991). Table 4.4.; *Statistical Abstract of the United States* (1991), Tables 263 and 769.

The evidence is weaker for Hispanics than for blacks that Overlap improved access.[62]

Recent Developments

The relevance of the difference between for-profit and not-for-profit firms in an antitrust analysis has emerged as a factor in other contexts. For example, in 1996, the Federal Trade Commission (FTC) filed suit to block a proposed merger between two not-for-profit hospitals in Grand Rapids, Michigan.[63] The District Court denied the request.[64] First, the court found that the usual assumptions made in an analysis of a proposed merger of for-profit firms should not apply automatically to an analysis involving not-for-profit firms. Second, the court relied on empirical evidence that mergers of not-for-profit hospitals do not lead generally to price increases.[65] Finally, the court ruled that the fact that some consumer groups could be harmed by the proposed merger should not automatically lead it to block the merger if other groups of consumers could benefit significantly from the merger.

[62]Although these results provide evidence that Overlap did increase access to these schools, it is not clear that the collective setting of financial aid awards by a group of schools is an optimal way for society to ensure access to higher education.

[63]*FTC v. Butterworth Health Corporation and Blodgett Memorial Medical Center,* (W.D. Mi., Southern Division, 1996). The not-for-profit status of hospitals also was considered in (among other cases) an earlier hospital merger challenged by the U.S. Department of Justice. See *U.S. v. Carilion Health System,* 707 F. Supp. 840 (W.D. Va., 1989), discussed by Eisenstadt in this volume, Case 2.

[64]The FTC appealed the District Court's ruling. The Court of Appeals for the Sixth Circuit affirmed the District Court in July of 1997.

[65]The court relied on the writings and testimony of William Lynk. Lynk and Lexecon were retained by the defendants.

Not-for-Profits and Antitrust Law

If Overlap did provide the needy with increased access to the Overlap schools, then it would seem that such an effect could be relevant to MIT's defense under a rule of reason.[66] But is such a defense possible under the antitrust laws?

The antitrust laws and most economists generally are hostile to collective price setting. In numerous cases, the Supreme Court has not allowed profit-maximizing firms to justify their cooperative actions to set prices on the basis of reasonableness of the prices that have been set.[67] Only when the collective actions generate unusual efficiencies has the Court allowed collective price setting.[68] Although it is possible to label the greater access of the needy to Overlap schools as an unusual efficiency and thereby fit this case within existing antitrust precedent, we think it clearer to ask and answer the question of whether the antitrust laws leave room for a not-for-profit firm to use the achievement of social goals as a valid defense for collective behavior.

The most relevant precedent is *Professional Engineers,* where the Court struck down an agreement by a not-for-profit trade association that restricted price competition for the stated purpose of assuring quality.[69] The trade association, composed of profit-maximizing members, promulgated restrictions on bidding to raise price and increase safety. In that case, the Court's concern was clearly that, as a result of the agreement, price

---

[66] A related question is whether MIT or the Government should have the burden of proving the effect of Overlap on access of the needy to schools. In *NCAA* v. *Board of Regents of University of Oklahoma, et al.,* 468 US 85 (1985), the Court ruled that the NCAA bore "a heavy burden" to prove the procompetitive effects of its action because of the elevated price and reduced output of its actions. See the discussion by Horowitz in this volume (Case 8). Here the evidence does not support such overall adverse price and output effects, so it is unclear whether MIT should bear such a "heavy burden."

[67] See, e.g., *U.S.* v. *Trans Missouri Freight Assoc.,* 166 US 290 (1897), *U.S.* v. *Addyston Pipe & Steel Co.,* 175 US 211 (1899), *U.S.* v. *Trenton Potteries Co.,* 273 US 392 (1927), and *U.S.* v. *Socony Vacuum Oil Co.,* 310 US 150 (1940).

[68] *Broadcast Music Inc. et al.* v. *CBS et al.,* 441 US 1 (1979). The Supreme Court does not characterize its decision in this way but instead says that the price action was "ancillary" to the production of a new product. Indeed, in other cases, the Supreme Court specifically states that it will not consider efficiency in a "price fixing" case. Such a view simply replaces the question of whether there are unusual efficiencies with the question of what is "price fixing" and what is "ancillary."

[69] *National Society of Professional Engineers* v. *U.S.,* 435 US 679 (1978). The Supreme Court has recognized the distinction between for-profit and not-for-profit firms in applying the antitrust laws. See, e.g., *Goldfarb* v. *Virginia State Bar,* 421 US 773, 788–9, n. 17 (1975). It is unclear how much of this distinction has been preserved after *Professional Engineers.* See Justice Blackmun's concurring opinion in *Professional Engineers.* The dissent by Justices White and Rehnquist in *NCAA* recognizes explicitly the need for schools to be able to defend their conduct by referring to non-economic goals.

would be raised to all consumers. The Court suggested that any ethical rule with an overall anticompetitive effect is forbidden.[70]

We believe that there are two features of the MIT case that distinguish it from *Professional Engineers*. First, unlike *Professional Engineers*, there was no alleged output restriction and, as already described, no finding of a price effect. Second, the membership of the Overlap group, unlike the trade association, consisted of not-for-profit firms.

With no effect on total output or average price, the achievement of desirable social goals can, we believe, provide an economic defense of MIT's conduct without violating the logic of existing antitrust precedents.[71] We believe that this result is sensible because these 501(c)3 institutions receive that special status in return for the performance of valuable social goals presumably not achievable through competition of profit-maximizing firms.[72] Indeed, if the achievement of a social goal is not a justification under the rule of reason for competing not-for-profits to engage in collective action—and only the more traditional justification of improved efficiency is recognized—then no collective action of competing not-for-profits is likely possible under the antitrust laws, because economists' notions of improved efficiency usually will not apply to collective action of not-for-profits engaged in aspects of income redistribution or achievement of social goals.[73]

REFERENCES

Carlson, D., and G. Shepherd. "Cartel on Campus: The Economics and Law of Academic Institutions' Financial Aid Price Fixing." *Oregon Law Review* 71, no.3, (Fall 1992): 563–629.

Carlton, D., G. Bamberger, and R. Epstein. "Antitrust and Higher Education: Was There a Conspiracy to Restrict Financial Aid?" *Rand Journal of Economics* 26 (Spring 1995): 131–147.

Carlton, D., and J. Klamer. "The Need for Coordination Among Firms with Special Reference to Network Industries." *The University of Chicago Law Review* 50 (Spring 1983): 446–465.

Clotfelter, C. "Financial Aid and Public Policy." In *Economic Challenges in Higher Education*, edited by C. Clotfelter, R. Ehrenberg, M. Getz, and J. Seigfried. Chicago: University of Chicago Press, 1991.

---

[70]See the concurring opinion of Justice Blackmun in *Professional Engineers*, who does not endorse such a suggestion.

[71]If there were an output restriction or elevated average price, *Professional Engineers* would condemn the behavior.

[72]For profit-maximizing firms and perhaps for not-for-profits composed of profit-maximizing members, the achievement of social goals would not seem an appropriate defense for collective price setting because the achievement of social goals is not what those firms are intended to do.

[73]For a different view, see Salop and White (1991); Morrison (1992); Carlson and Shepherd (1993); and Shepherd (1995).

Dodge, S. "Overlap Group Makes Aid Process Fairer Targets of Inquiry Argue." *Chronicle of Higher Education*, October 11, 1989, p. A32.

Hansmann, H. "The Role of Nonprofit Enterprise." *Yale Law Journal* 89 (April 1980): 835–901.

Hansmann, H., and A. Klevorick. *Competition and Coordination in Markets for Higher Education.* New Haven, Conn.: Yale University Press, 1993.

Hopkins, D. "The Higher Education Production Function: Theoretical Foundations and Empirical Findings." In *The Economics of American Universities: Management, Operations and Fiscal Environment,* edited by Stephen Holnack and Eileen Collins. Albany State: University of New York Press, 1998.

Koopmans, T., and M. Beckmann. "Assignment Problems and the Location of Economic Activities." *Econometrica* 25 (Janurary 1957): 53–76.

Lande, R. "Chicago's False Foundation: Wealth Transfer (Not Just Efficiency) Should Guide Antitrust." *Antitrust Law Journal* 58 (1989): 631–644.

Lubman, S. "The Tradition of Need-Blind Admissions Is Starting to Die." *Wall Street Journal,* January 5, 1994.

Lynk, W. "Nonprofit Hospital Mergers and the Exercise of Market Power." *Journal of Law and Economics* 38 (October 1995): 437–461.

McPherson, M., and M. Schapiro. *Keeping College Affordable.* Washington, D.C.: The Brookings Institution, 1991.

Morrison, R. "Price Fixing Among Elite Colleges and Universities." *University of Chicago Law Review* 59 (Summer 1992): 807–835.

Noll, R. "The U.S. Team Sports Industry: An Introduction." In *Government and the Sports Business,* edited by R. Noll. Washington, D.C.: Brookings Institution, 1982.

Pitofsky, R. "The Political Content of Antitrust." *University of Pennsylvania Law Review* 127, no. 4 (April 1979): 1051–1075.

Roth, A., and M. Sotomayer. *Two-Sided Matching: A Study in Game Theoretic Modeling and Analysis.* Cambridge: Cambridge University Press, 1990.

Rothschild, M., and L. White. "The University in the Marketplace: Some Insights and Some Puzzles." In *Studies of Supply and Demand in Higher Education,* edited by C. Clotfelter and M. Rothschild. Chicago: University of Chicago Press, 1993.

Salop, S., and L. White. "Antitrust Goes to College." *Journal of Economic Perspectives* 5 (Summer 1991): 193–199.

Shepherd, G. "Overlap and Antitrust: Fixing Prices in a Smoke-Filled Classroom." *Antitrust Bulletin* 50 (Winter 1995): 859–884.

Statistical Abstract of the United States. Washington, D.C.: Government Printing Office, 1991.

Stout, H. "Education: Many Colleges Face More Cuts on Basic Services." *Wall Street Journal,* August 3, 1992.

Telser, L. *Economic Theory and the Core.* Chicago: University of Chicago Press, 1978.

CASE 12

Joint Venture Membership: Visa and Discover Card (1993)

David S. Evans and
Richard L. Schmalensee

INTRODUCTION

Visa is a joint venture of financial institutions that persuade consumers to use credit cards with the Visa name (the issuing function), persuade merchants to accept those cards (the acquiring function), and process transactions involving those cards using a shared network. Two years after Dean Witter Financial Services Group (then owned by Sears, Roebuck and Co.)[1] successfully launched the Discover Card in 1986, it sought membership in Visa. Visa refused and then passed a rule—Bylaw 2.06—that expressly excluded issuers of Discover or American Express cards from Visa membership. In May 1990, Dean Witter bought a Visa membership as part of its purchase of the defunct MountainWest Savings and Loan from the Resolution Trust Corporation. When Dean Witter tried to issue a Visa card through its new bank, Visa invoked Bylaw 2.06 and refused to print the cards. Dean Witter sued in federal district court. It claimed, among other things, that Visa's Bylaw 2.06 was an unreasonable restraint of trade that violated Section 1 of the Sherman Act.

A jury agreed with Dean Witter. They would have required Visa to accept Dean Witter (and presumably American Express) as members. The

David S. Evans and Richard Schmalensee were retained by Visa, USA in this litigation, and Richard Schmalensee offered expert testimony. They thank Stephen Bomse and Laurence Popofsky for numerous valuable conversations and Howard Chang and Daniel J. Hassan for effective assistance.

[1] After the trial Sears spun off its Dean Witter subsidiary, which then merged with Morgan Stanley in 1997. Throughout this chapter, we refer to Dean Witter as the plaintiff for simplicity.

Tenth Circuit Court of Appeals reversed the decision. It rejected Dean Witter's arguments that Visa had market power and that Visa's Bylaw could have a substantial effect on competition in the relevant market. It accepted Visa's arguments that Bylaw 2.06 was reasonably related to Visa USA's operation and no broader than necessary. After reviewing briefs written by Robert Bork (supporting Dean Witter) and Phillip Areeda (supporting Visa), among others, the Supreme Court declined to hear Dean Witter's appeal.

The *MountainWest* case added fuel to debates regarding standards for evaluating the conduct of joint ventures and on the proper roles of evidence on efficiencies and on consumer harm in that context. This case also illustrates how different approaches to the analysis of market power can lead to opposite results. Dean Witter argued, and the trial court and jury accepted, that Visa had market power because its members collectively had a large share of the relevant market. Visa argued, and the Tenth Circuit accepted, that Visa's exclusion of Dean Witter could not have an appreciable effect on prices or output because card issuing is an almost atomistically competitive market.

In this chapter we describe the payment card industry, describe the progression of *MountainWest* from the trial court to possible review by the Supreme Court, discuss the arguments presented by both sides at trial, and then examine the ultimate resolution of the case by the Tenth Circuit.

INDUSTRY BACKGROUND[2]

The parties stipulated that the relevant antitrust market consists of payment cards that could be used in a variety of merchant locations throughout the United States. From the standpoint of the consumer and merchant, payment cards provide a straightforward service. The consumer pays with the card and gets a bill some weeks later, which he or she pays in full or in part depending on the type of card (charge or credit) and preference for financing the transaction. The merchant runs the card through a terminal and receives payment into its depository account generally one to three days later.[3] Competition in the payment card industry takes place at two levels: the system level and the issuer level.[4]

Competition Between Systems

There are four major payment card systems in the United States: American Express (started in 1958), Visa (1966), MasterCard (1966), and Discover

---

[2]For further details see Evans and Schmalensee (1993).

[3]A small and decreasing fraction of transactions is still paper based.

[4]There is also competition in the payment card industry for signing up merchants and processing merchant transactions. We do not discuss this competition further because it was not an issue in the case.

(1986).[5] Each system consists of a "brand" and a "network" for processing transactions between consumers using cards of that brand and merchants that accept those cards. "And they don't take American Express"—the well-known Visa ad—is an example of the competition that takes place at the system level. There are two types of systems: Open systems consist of many members issuing cards and acquiring transactions on a shared network; closed systems consist of a single entity that issues all cards and acquires all transactions on a proprietary network.

Visa and MasterCard are open systems. Visa is a joint venture of financial institutions that issue Visa cards to consumers and acquire transactions from merchants who accept Visa cards. It operates pursuant to a system of rules, adopted by its board of directors, that govern and facilitate operation of its interdependent financial exchange network. Aside from administering this system of rules, it also (1) maintains computer networks for processing transactions between cardholders, the bank whose name appears on the cardholder's card ("the issuing bank"), merchants, and the merchant's bank ("the acquiring bank"); (2) establishes brand image; and (3) conducts research and development for the benefit of members. Its members are individually responsible for setting prices and other terms and conditions for card holders and merchants.

There are several important differences between Visa and a typical firm. Visa earns no profits and pays no dividends. Visa provides services for its members, and they in turn use those services as inputs into their own credit card businesses. The members elect the Board of Directors, which must approve major decisions at Visa. Visa members, including those who serve on the Board, compete with each other in issuing cards and acquiring transactions from merchants.

MasterCard is also a joint venture of financial institutions and operates much like Visa. Until the mid-1970s, Visa and MasterCard had different members. That changed in 1976 when the U.S. Department of Justice refused to support Visa's request to support its exclusion of MasterCard members.[6] Faced with significant antitrust exposure, Visa and MasterCard allowed dual membership and soon had almost completely overlapping membership. Although duality, as this pattern of membership is called, reduces incentives for system competition in advertising or product development, the organizations act differently because of different membership shares (and resulting influence on decisions), because members cannot have representatives on both boards, and because the managements of the two associations have incentives to compete with each other. Relatively poor performance by one of the associations is likely to lead issuers to emphasize the other's brand in their marketing

[5] Two other card systems—Diner's Club and Carte Blanche—have a small share of cards issued in this country. Both of these systems were owned by Citibank during the period under discussion here.
[6] See Baker and Brandel (1988, pp. 23ff) and *Worthen Bank and Trust Co. v. National Bank-Americard Inc.*, 185 F. 2d 119 (1973).

Discover and American Express are closed systems and, unlike Visa and MasterCard, are organized as traditional businesses with shareholders, a board of directors elected by those shareholders, and management appointed by the board. Discover operates the computer systems and backroom operations necessary for completing the following essential steps of any card transaction: (a) verifying credit when the customer presents the card to a merchant; (b) crediting the value of the transaction less service charge (i.e., less the merchant discount) to the merchant's account; (c) debiting the value of the transaction to the consumer's card account; and (d) billing and subsequent collection of card balances. Discover shapes brand image through product development and advertising, and it engages in research and development to enhance card products and features as well as the system for processing transactions. Finally, Discover—unlike the Visa system but like the Visa members—issues cards to consumers, signs up merchants to take its cards, processes transactions from those merchants, and determines all prices and other terms and conditions affecting cardholders and merchants. American Express operates in a similar way.

The payment card systems compete by making their brands more appealing to consumers and merchants. For example, system decisions affect various aspects of card processing (e.g., the speed of approval and fraud detection) that in turn affect the value of the payment card brand to consumers and merchants. Similarly, by encouraging relatively low merchant discounts—the price merchants have to pay Visa banks for each transaction—Visa built a high rate of merchant acceptance.[7] American Express maintained relatively high merchant discounts and had a lower rate of merchant acceptance. Its charge card appealed to a segment of consumers that some merchants were willing to pay high merchant discounts to attract. In the mid-1980s, Visa began its hugely successful "And they don't take American Express" advertising campaign. It appears that this campaign curtailed the growth of American Express cards and encouraged American Express to lower its merchant discount to increase merchant acceptance.

In addition to the four main systems described above, there are two additional card brands in the United States: Diner's Club and Carte Blanche. Diner's Club was bought by Citibank in 1981, and Carte Blanche was bought by Citibank in 1978. Both have been niche products in the United States for some time.[8] A large portion of Diner's Club cards, for example, are simply corporate accounts at travel agencies.

Table 12-1 shows the shares of the payment card systems based on

---

[7]Visa itself does not determine the merchant discount. It does, however, determine the "interchange fee" that acquiring banks pay issuing banks as a percentage of each transaction, and the interchange fee places a floor on the merchant discount. The legality of collective determination of interchange fees was upheld in the *NaBanco* case: *National Bancard Corp. (NaBanco)* v. *VISA USA, Inc.,* 596 F. Supp. 1231 (S.D. Fla. 1984), *aff'd,* 779 F.2d 592 (11th Cir.), *cert. denied,* 479 U.S. 923 (1986).

[8]Diner's Club is successful in some foreign markets. For example, it has the largest share of the Greek payment card market.

TABLE 12-1
Market Share of Major Brands by Charge Volume, 1991

Visa	41.9%
MasterCard	25.8%
American Express	24.6%
Discover	5.4%
Diners/Carte Blanche	2.2%
HHI:	3060

1991 charge volume data that were presented at trial. Visa has the largest share, 41.9 percent, followed by MasterCard, American Express and Discover. The Herfindahl-Hirschman Index (HHI) at the system level is 3060 based on charge volume.

Competition at the Issuer Level

For brand positioning, research and development, and operation of the computer systems that, among other things, determine how long the consumer has to stand around waiting for his or her card to be approved, the system level is where competition occurs. For the prices, card attributes, and other features that are directly relevant to the cardholder, competition occurs at the issuer level. That is because Visa and MasterCard have about 6000 members, each of whom independently sets prices and other card features. These issuers compete with each other and with cards issued by Discover and American Express.

Table 12-2 lists the largest twenty issuers of payment cards as of 1990 based on transaction volume. The largest single issuer of payment cards was American Express with a 24.6 percent share; Discover was the third largest issuer with a 5.4 percent share. The largest ten issuers accounted for approximately 58 percent of the payment card market in 1990.[9]

Entry and exit at the issuer level within MasterCard and Visa are relatively easy. The open membership policies of Visa and MasterCard permit entry by both traditional financial institutions and financial institutions that specialize in issuing credit cards, many of which are owned by or affiliated with nonbanks such as retailers, investment firms, insurance companies, and automobile manufacturers. As shown in Figure 12-1, substantial entry took place into the Visa system between 1981 and 1991. The existence of markets for card issuers' portfolios has made exit easy as well, since exiting issuers can sell their portfolios to entering or expanding issuers.

---

[9]The HHI based on transaction volume was approximately 850. The HHI based on outstanding balances was approximately 450.

TABLE 12-2
Top Twenty Issuers of Payment Cards, 1990
(Based on Charge Volume)

Issuer	Volume ($ billions)	Market Share (%)
1 American Express	$88.30	24.6
2 Citicorp	$40.30	11.2
3 Discover	$19.40	5.4
4 First Chicago	$12.95	3.6
5 Chase Manhattan	$11.36	3.2
6 MBNA Corp.	$11.04	3.1
7 Bankamerica Corp	$10.40	2.9
8 Wells Fargo	$4.80	1.3
9 AT&T Universal	$4.40	1.2
10 The Bank of New York	$4.01	1.1
11 USAA Fed. Savings	$3.95	1.1
12 Manufacturer's Hanover	$3.69	1.0
13 NCNB Corp.	$3.46	1.0
14 Security Pacific Corp.	$3.28	0.9
15 Chemical Banking Corp.	$2.90	0.8
16 First Deposit Bank	$2.75	0.8
17 Marine Midland Bank	$2.73	0.8
18 Seafirst Bank	$2.68	0.7
19 Household Intl	$2.55	0.7
20 Colonial National	$2.50	0.7

Source: *Nilson Report,* March 1991, issues 495, 496.

FIGURE 12-1 Number of Visa Issuers.

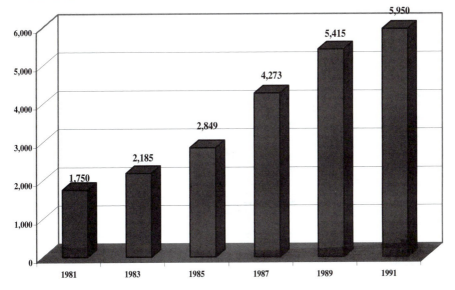

Portfolio sales enable issuers to recover the capital value of having developed relationships with a set of creditworthy consumers.

Through the expansion of payment card issuers and the entry of new ones, output of the payment card has grown rapidly over the years. Figure 12-2 shows the growth of output measured by transactions. Figure 12-2 also shows that real prices have not increased.[10] During this time, the quality of payment cards improved dramatically because they became more widely accepted by merchants, the waiting time at merchants for acceptance declined, and cards offered more features such as credits toward frequent flier programs.

Accounting profits have fluctuated over time with the state of the economy and other aspects of the industry evolution. Profits were relatively low in the late 1970s and early 1980s during inflation and a credit crunch and were relatively high in the late 1980s as interest rates (and thus a significant portion of the costs of financing consumer credit) declined and credit card usage expanded rapidly. Figure 12-3 shows the trend.

More controversy surrounds the measurement and interpretation of economic profits. Lawrence Ausubel argues that the payment card industry has had relatively high economic profits that have persisted in the face of entry.[11] It is thus, he contends, a paradox—an almost atomistically com-

FIGURE 12-2 Real Price Index Versus Charge Volume for Visa and Master-Card Credit Cards (1992 Dollars).

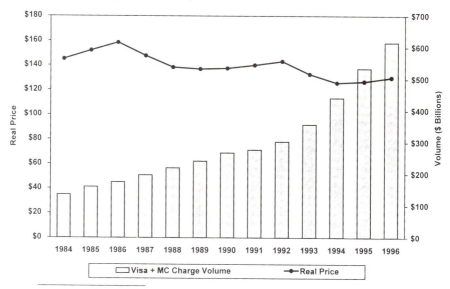

[10]The real price is based on the real cost of annual fees, service fees, and finance charges. It is based on transactions for only the Visa and MasterCard systems. For a discussion of real prices see Evans, Reddy, and Schmalensee (1997b).

[11]Ausubel (1991).

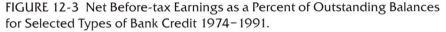

FIGURE 12-3 Net Before-tax Earnings as a Percent of Outstanding Balances for Selected Types of Bank Credit 1974–1991.

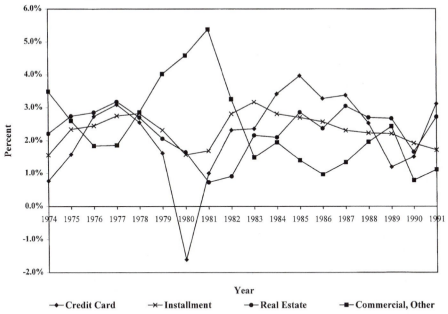

Sources: Federal Reserve Banks (1991); and Canner and Luckett (1992).

petitive industry in which the firms earn supracompetitive profits. His explanation for this phenomenon is that consumers are irrational—they think they are going to pay off their credit card debts, but do not, thereby enabling payment card issuers to charge high interest rates despite the availability to the consumer of other alternatives. Stewart Myers and Carlos LaPuerta, who were experts for Visa, have noted that payment card credit is more risky than many other lines of credit because it is not secured.[12] They find that conservative adjustments for risk reduce estimated rates of return in the unusually prosperous period analyzed by Ausubel almost to competitive levels. Similarly, Myers and LaPuerta argue that Ausubel estimated extremely high rates of return on portfolio sales because he ignored the investment in identifying creditworthy customers—by buying a card portfolio the purchaser avoids the cost of having to prospect for creditworthy customers and the seller realizes a return for identifying customers and ascertaining their payment patterns. Finally, at the level of theory, Ausubel's model does not explain why competition in annual fees, which consumers are not likely to misperceive, does not suffice to eliminate excess profits.

Ausubel also pointed to "sticky" interest rates as evidence that the

---

[12]LaPuerta and Myers (1997).

payment card industry does not function as competitively as economists would expect on the basis of its structure. It takes some time for card rates to respond fully to changes in market rates.[13] However, the cost of funds comprises only 41.5 percent of the variable cost of a payment card operation.[14] Other major costs are processing costs and the costs of fraud and bad debt. Given this, it is not surprising that card rates do not fluctuate in tandem with market rates.[15]

To summarize, there is no controversy that at the issuer level the payment card industry has a highly competitive structure. There is some controversy over whether this structure has resulted in the performance that one would expect from a highly competitive industry.

LEGAL AND PROCEDURAL BACKGROUND

Sears and its Dean Witter subsidiary considered entering the payment card industry in the early 1980s.[16] Sears was the largest payment card issuer as a result of its store card—$11.6 billion outstanding in 1984 (the second largest issuer, Citibank, had only $4.4 billion)[17]—and had extensive experience in evaluating the creditworthiness of prospective cardholders and processing transactions. Dean Witter considered two different methods of entering: joining the open payment card systems or starting its own system. After detailed internal review, it decided to start its own: the Discover Card, which it first issued nationally in 1986. While this strategy was widely derided by observers, it proved remarkably successful. Dean Witter incurred substantial initial losses as it spent money prospecting for cardholders and increasing merchant acceptance. But the Discover Card soon turned into a highly profitable product and garnered 6.6 percent of all credit card outstandings less than five years after its start.

In the face of the first new system entry in a decade, Visa responded in a number of ways. For example, it encouraged its members banks not to let their merchant terminals take Discover Cards, which forced Dean Witter to develop its own terminals.

Dean Witter, in turn, applied for Visa membership in late 1988. Visa's board rejected this application. At the same time, the Visa board adopted Bylaw 2.06 that denied membership to

[13]Stavins (1996).

[14]Visa USA, *Profit Analysis Report*, quarter ending June 30, 1992; includes both issuing and acquiring.

[15]See, for example, Raskovich and Froeb (1992). For a discussion to the contrary, see Calem and Mester (1995).

[16]See *SCFC ILC, Inc. v. VISA U.S.A., Inc.*, 819 F. Supp. 956 (D. Utah 1993), pp. 5ff for more details.

[17]DeMuth (1986), p. 223.

> any applicant which is issuing, directly or indirectly, Discover cards or
> American Express cards, or any other cards deemed competitive by the
> Board of Directors; an applicant shall be deemed to be issuing such cards
> if its parent, subsidiary or affiliate issues such cards.[18]

Dean Witter complained but did not sue.

A year later Dean Witter purchased the assets of an insolvent thrift institution, MountainWest Savings and Loan in Utah, from the Resolution
Trust Corporation (RTC). Those assets included a Visa membership and a
small payment card portfolio. Dean Witter intended to use this membership to launch Prime Option, a Visa card to be issued nationally. MountainWest requested the printing of 1.5 million Prime Option Visa cards
without letting Visa know that it was now owned by Dean Witter. A small
Utah thrift preparing a major national launch piqued Visa's curiosity.
When its investigation revealed Dean Witter's ownership, Visa refused to
print the cards. In January 1991, Dean Witter filed a lawsuit in the Federal
District Court for the District of Utah, complaining that Visa had violated
Section 1 of the Sherman Act among other things, and sought damages
and a permanent injunction ordering Visa to admit MountainWest as a
member.

Several skirmishes took place before a trial on the merits of the case
commenced. Dean Witter moved for a preliminary injunction to allow it to
launch Prime Option. The District Court agreed, but the Tenth Circuit reversed. Congress then appeared to come to Dean Witter's rescue, passing a
law requiring the continuation of contracts with thrifts after their subsequent takeover and sale by the RTC. Dean Witter sought summary judgment under the new statute, but the District Court refused because Dean
Witter did not comply with all the terms and conditions of the original
contract—Bylaw 2.06 in particular—as required by the statute. Visa, for
its part, sued Dean Witter for fraud, violation of Section 7 of the Clayton
Act, and other miscellaneous claims.

After the judge denied both parties' motions for summary judgment,
the trial began in October 1992. Dean Witter's Sherman Act claim was
tried by a jury, and Visa's Clayton Act counterclaim was tried by the judge
only. The nonantitrust claims and damages were to be tried later.

After a three and one-half week trial, the jury found for Dean Witter.
Visa asked the judge to overturn the jury verdict and had some hope for
optimism. In oral arguments after the verdict, the trial court judge had
said, "I would have hung the jury before I would have come back with that
verdict" (transcript, p. 1592).

Nonetheless, on April 1, 1993, the judge denied Visa's motions for a
decision in its favor or for a new trial. He rejected Visa's proposed legal
standard and concluded that under the correct standard the jury did have a

---

[18]See Visa U.S.A, Inc., "By-Laws/Operating Regulations," May 1, 1992, p. 7.

reasonable basis, given the evidence, for reaching their conclusion. He also ruled against Visa on its Clayton Act claim, finding that the harm from reduced intersystem competition was not sufficient to outweigh the benefits from increased intrasystem competition through Dean Witter becoming a Visa issuer.

Visa appealed. In September 1994, a three-judge panel of the Tenth Circuit decided in Visa's favor. The Tenth Circuit refused Dean Witter's motion for a rehearing, and the Supreme Court declined to hear Dean Witter's appeal.

THE PARTIES' ARGUMENTS

When do the antitrust laws compel a joint venture (e.g., Visa) to admit a direct competitor? That was the key question raised in the legal proceedings described above. Dean Witter thought the answer was:

> A joint venture that (a) has a large share of the relevant market and (b) cannot show that the exclusion is necessary for the efficient operation of the joint venture must admit any applicant for membership. Moreover, admission into an open joint venture or network joint venture is presumptively efficient.[19]

Dean Witter argued that Visa had a large share of the relevant market and that Visa's efficiency justifications were mere pretexts for an anticompetitive exclusion.

Visa thought the answer was:

> A joint venture may have to admit a direct competitor only if its participation in the joint venture is essential for competition in the relevant market. Moreover, forced admission is presumptively bad because it is tantamount to the forced sharing of property with a competitor—a policy that would reduce the long-term incentives for the creation of property through investment and innovation.[20]

Visa argued that Dean Witter had demonstrated its ability to compete in the relevant market through its successful Discover Card and that it should not get to use Visa's property just because it could compete better that way. It also argued that letting Dean Witter into the tent would allow Discover to gain competitive intelligence on its system competitor, to free-ride on Visa investments and innovations, and to disrupt competitive decision making.

---

[19]See Responding Brief of Appellee MountainWest, 10th Circuit Court of Appeals, October 15, 1993; also see Carlton and Frankel (1995a) and Pratt et. al. (1997).

[20]See Opening Brief of Appellant Visa U.S.A., Inc., 10th Circuit Court of Appeals, and Evans and Schmalensee (1995).

In addition to these polar opposite legal views, the two parties had quite opposing views of the economic effects of exclusion on intrasystem and intersystem competition. Dean Witter claimed that its Prime Option Card would expand output and would cause lower prices as a result of increased intrasystem competition and that its presence in Visa would not have any significant effect on intersystem competition. Visa argued that Prime Option would have a negligible effect on intrasystem competition because of the highly unconcentrated structure at that level but that Dean Witter's presence in Visa would hinder intersystem competition. We now consider Dean Witter's and Visa's arguments in more detail.

Dean Witter's Case

Background

According to Dean Witter, Visa's members collectively control over 70 percent of the relevant antitrust market—general purpose payment cards in the United States. The Visa joint venture has two important characteristics. First, it is a network in which firms work interdependently to provide a service. As with many networks, the value of the network service increases with the number of network participants; economists say there are "positive network externalities." Payment cards are more valuable to merchants if more consumers hold those cards and are more valuable to consumers if more merchants accept those cards. Second, it has been an open joint venture. Historically, virtually any financial institution could join the Visa system. It made sense that Visa was open because it was more "efficient" with more members—more members, more positive network externalities.

Before passing Bylaw 2.06, Visa did not demand exclusivity. It allowed members to issue MasterCards beginning in 1976. Citibank, which issues Visa cards, owns two competing payment card systems—Diners Club and Carte Blanche. Visa's exclusion of Dean Witter was therefore not only historically unprecedented, it was discriminatory and unfair. Existing members could issue competing cards (MasterCard in the case of all members and additionally Diners Club and Carte Blanche in the case of Citicorp). As Dean Witter's trial attorney put it in his closing arguments,

> based on the rules that the Visa member banks have decided to set for themselves you're not disqualified from Visa simply because you offer a competing card. . . . [T]hose are the rules that Visa members have chosen to play by. . . . Those should be the same rules that apply to everybody in the market in particular in this case the same rules that apply to Dean Witter and MountainWest. [Tr. 2673–2674]

Dean Witter executives testified that they had planned to enter the payment card industry by first introducing its proprietary Discover Card and then adding their own Visa and MasterCard.[21] Indeed, Dean Witter's president testified that it would not have launched the Discover Card had it known it could not later introduce a Visa card.

Market Power

When Dean Witter sought to become a Visa member, Visa exercised market power through its collective rule-making ability. According to Dean Witter, a proper measure of this market power is the aggregate share of the relevant market held by the members who adopt rules. Collectively, the members who adopted Visa Bylaw 2.06 had a 45.6-percent share of the payment card market through their membership in Visa and an additional 26.4-percent share of the payment card market through their dual membership in MasterCard, for a total market share of 72-percent, all based on transaction volume. Visa therefore had market power because its members who adopted the exclusionary rule collectively had a 72-percent market share. This high market share gave Visa's members significant incentives to keep interest rates and profits high.

Dean Witter's market power theory was explained by its economic expert:

> . . . we have a collective rule, By-Law 2.06, and that led me to look at then [sic] collective share. . . . I found that the collective share was very large, and as a consequence my conclusion was that the collective rule was an exercise of market power. It is an exercise of market power because the members of the Visa association acting collectively have both the incentive and the ability to exercise that market power. They have the incentive because this market share was large and they want to protect that market share. And they also have the incentive because since this is large, if they can keep prices up or from falling they can make a lot of money. . . . [T]here is nothing here that can prevent the exercise of market power. . . . (Tr. 1594–1595)

The economic proposition that apparently underlies this testimony is that the aggregate market share is a predictor of the effect of an exclusionary rule, adopted by a collective of firms, on output and prices in the relevant market. A joint venture with a large market share has an incentive to adopt an exclusionary rule because it can thereby prevent prices (and profits) from falling as a consequence of entry by new participants within the joint venture. Only competition outside the joint venture could prevent this effect from taking place. Dean Witter argued that competition from nonbank cards (e.g., Discover and American Express) was not sufficient because, for example, the Discover Card is considered a "second card" for most consumers, to be carried only after they have first obtained a Visa or

---

[21]The claim that Dean Witter intended to add a Visa card was never mentioned in pretrial proceedings or discovery and was hotly disputed by Visa.

MasterCard. It is this economic proposition that became the focus of the Tenth Circuit decision.

Aside from the high market share, Dean Witter's economic expert cited three other key pieces of evidence to support the claim that Visa has market power. First, Visa's members, especially its top-ten issuers, have enjoyed "high profits" for many years. For example, a Visa consulting study was cited that found: "The 'quick and dirty' analysis determined that [Visa] Members have received a high return on their historic investment, considering the extremely high profitability of Members' credit card businesses in recent years" (plaintiff's exhibit 761). For procedural reasons, Dean Witter's economic expert was precluded from testifying on whether payment card issuers earned "excess profits," that is, additional profits that exceed the level required for a normal rate of return.[22]

The second piece of evidence was that substantial entry had taken place in the payment card industry.

> And there was substantial entry but that substantial entry continued over a full decade. And what we know now is that there are still large firms that are announcing that they are coming into this market and that suggests to me that profits are remaining high in this market. (Tr. 1605)

Thus the fact of substantial entry was taken as evidence that Visa and MasterCard members had high profits that were not competed away through entry.

The third piece of evidence was that payment card issuers engaged in price discrimination. Two examples of prices discrimination were offered: (1) prices have declined subsequent to entry by issuers but not to all cardholders and (2) issuers were willing to waive card fees for cardholders who called to close their accounts (Tr. 1658–1659).

Competitive Effect of Bylaw 2.06

Dean Witter argued that Bylaw 2.06 harms competition and consumers by providing an "enormous disincentive for firms that might enter the market by developing new proprietary cards" and excluding a "large low cost new Visa Card" (Tr. 1592). According to the "disincentive theory," Bylaw 2.06 reduced the incentives to start a new proprietary card because the entrant would not be able then to issue Visa cards. Existing Visa issuers were discouraged from starting their own proprietary systems because they

---

[22]The Ausubel studies cited above were not discussed by Dean Witter's expert. However, the results of these studies were introduced by Dean Witter through their cross-examination of Visa's expert. Visa's expert noted that Ausubel had focused on a short period of time and that profits were lower before that period and were heading down at the end of that period. He also noted that if Ausubel were right, the payment card market exhibits supracompetitive profits with almost atomistic competition and entry. Adding another firm to the fray would be unlikely to remedy that problem.

would have to leave Visa (i.e., sell off their portfolios) to do so. Dean Witter argued that the fact that no proprietary system had been started since the enactment of Bylaw 2.06 was evidence of this disincentive.[23]

Dean Witter's economic expert argued that the top-ten issuers of Visa cards had been slow to change their prices in response to the substantial entry that had taken place during the 1980s. That fact, along with the existence of "high profits" and "price discrimination," led him to conclude that entry by Prime Option, as a "large, low cost Visa card" (TR. 1603), would reduce prices. Consumers would benefit from Prime Option's low-priced card, and this option would place pressure on other issuers to lower their prices as well.

Possible Benefits of Bylaw 2.06

Dean Witter also considered whether Bylaw 2.06 provided any economic benefits that could offset the economic harms described above. The expert found no basis for believing that Bylaw 2.06 would decrease costs to members. He then examined whether Bylaw 2.06 was necessary to prevent outsiders from "free-riding" on the joint venture. The fact that Visa had operated as an open joint venture was critical to his conclusion that free-riding was not a concern:

> Visa is an open association. It was completely open until the passage of the amendment to bylaw 2.06. It remains open except for those firms that are targeted in that bylaw. Firms come into this association all the time. The firms in the association remain profitable and output has increased in this market as firms have entered under this open rule. And for all those reasons I conclude that output has increased, it has not gone down, and there is not a free-riding problem in this market with entry. (Tr. 1669)

Summary of Dean Witter's Evidence

In rejecting Visa's motion for a directed verdict or a new trial, the judge provided a useful summary of Dean Witter's evidence.[24]

1. Testimony of Sears' [economist]. . . . on the appropriateness of calculating Visa USA's market power by aggregating the individual market shares of Visa USA and MasterCard; and his conclusion that Visa USA exercised market power through its collective power to make rules; and testimony about "the presence of high profits."[25]

---

[23]See Responding Brief of Appellee MountainWest, 10th Circuit Court of Appeals, October 15, 1993.

[24]For the Appeals Court summary see *SCFC ILC, Inc. v. Visa USA, Inc.*, 36 F.3d 958, 962 (10th Cir. 1994).

[25]*SCFC ILC, Inc. v. Visa U.S.A., Inc.*, 819 F. Supp. 956, 985 (D. Utah 1993).

2. Dean Witter's president, Phillip Purcell's, testimony that had Sears known that developing the Discover Card would disqualify it from Visa USA entry, it would not have placed a new proprietary card in the market.[26]

3. Testimony that no new proprietary card had been introduced in the relevant market since Bylaw 2.06 was enacted although memberships in Visa USA and MasterCard increased.[27]

4. Testimony that Prime Option "would be a low-cost card which would be supported by powerful marketing and advertising strategies on a national level."[28]

5. Testimony by Sears' executives that Discover Card, in the face of Prime Option's entry, would remain an aggressive competitor.[29]

6. Testimony that intersystem competition would not be harmed "because Prime Option Visa was designed to reach that part of the market that Discover does not reach."[30]

7. Testimony that "Sears would benefit significantly from issuing Prime Option Visa as opposed to Prime Option Discover or another proprietary card."[31]

Visa's Case

Background

While Visa responded to the arguments presented above, it placed a great deal of weight on the importance of property rights. As Visa saw it, their members had engaged in significant innovation and investment to develop the Visa system. The Visa brand name, and the rights to use this brand name and the other Visa property associated with it, belonged to Visa. Thus, unless Visa were declared an essential facility and sharing its property were deemed essential to competition, Visa alone had the right to decide who it was going to share its property with. Discover was a successful system competitor. Visa decided that it did not want a system competitor in the tent. Dean Witter, in Visa's view, was trying to trespass on its property.

Visa tied this property rights argument to what Philip Areeda (1990) has described as the "macro level" implications of antitrust policy. Forcing

[26]Ibid., 986.
[27]Ibid., 986.
[28]Ibid., 986–987.
[29]Ibid., 987.
[30]Ibid., 987.
[31]Ibid., 988.

Visa to share its property with a competitor not only harmed Visa, it reduced the incentives for other firms to come together and engage in innovation and investment through the joint-venture form of organization. Joint-venture property would be less immune to encroachment by competitors and therefore less valuable to prospective investors and innovators.

According to Visa's legal argument—which, despite its rejection by the trial court, was the subtext for much of the Visa testimony and summations—the property of joint ventures should be treated no differently from that of a single firm. Single firms are required to share their property only under extreme circumstances—generally only when access to that property is "essential" for competition—and joint ventures should be required to do so only under those same extreme circumstances. Membership in Visa was not essential for Dean Witter to compete—it was already in the relevant antitrust market with its Discover Card. And, since the payment card market was highly competitive, granting Dean Witter membership was not essential to competition either.

Thus, Visa argued—explicitly to the court and implicitly to the jury— that it should not be required to admit Dean Witter even if it had market power and if the other facts alleged by Dean Witter were true. Visa should be no more required to admit Dean Witter than McDonald's should be required to admit a Burger King franchisee or than Microsoft should be forced to integrate a competitor's product in Windows. The courts generally do not second-guess decisions by businesses on what to do with their property— even if that business is a monopolist—except possibly when that property is "essential" for other firms to compete. The courts should not second-guess joint ventures like Visa either.

Market Power

Market power in antitrust analysis refers to the ability of a firm (or group of firms) to increase price (or reduce output) significantly above competitive levels.[32] Visa and its economic expert argued that the entry of another issuer into a highly unconcentrated and competitive market would not result in a significant increase in price or reduction in output. As discussed above, the payment card industry has over 6000 issuers, an HHI below 500, and easy entry at the issuer level. Dean Witter estimated that Prime Option would achieve a 5-percent share of the payment card market in seven years. As a relatively small firm in a highly competitive industry, its entry was unlikely to have any discernible effect on prices even if, as claimed by Dean Witter, it was a low-cost card.[33]

---

[32]Carlton and Perloff (1994, p.8).

[33]Moreover, the actual effect of the exclusion is the difference between the quantity of output that would be added as a result of Dean Witter's issuing a Prime Option Visa card and the quantity of output that would be added as a result of Dean Witter's pursuing its next best alternative— perhaps another brand of Discover Card or further investment in Discover.

The aggregate market share of Visa issuers is not an appropriate measure of market power according to Visa. In and of itself, that share provides little economic information on whether the exclusion of a competitor would have a significant effect on price. For example, the exclusion of only a small quantum of output, no matter how large a share the excluding entity has, cannot possibly have any effect on price or output. Conversely, the exclusion of a large quantum of output could have a large effect on price or output even if the excluding entity does not have a dominant market share. Price effects depend on what is added to or subtracted from a market, not on the aggregate share of the firms making the decisions.

The aggregate market share would be an appropriate measure of market power if Visa had agreed to fix prices. But there was a fundamental mismatch between the measure of market power proposed by Dean Witter and the alleged anticompetitive practice being addressed. As Visa's economic expert testified,

> . . . if they had . . . done collective rule making that had fixed prices or fixed fees or fixed features, that would have been an exercise of market power. But they didn't. The case is not . . . about price fixing by Visa. They passed bylaw 2.06 and they presumably also agreed on the lunch menu at the annual meeting. The question is not might they have done something . . . , but did what they did actually affect competition or harm consumers. (Tr. 2285–2286)

Visa did not agree that other evidence cited by Dean Witter established the existence of market power. "High" accounting profits do not establish supracompetitive economic profits. Moreover, even supracompetitive economic profits over a short period of time do not necessarily establish that there is any market imperfection. High short-term profits can result from short-term market developments, such as a spurt of demand or a sudden reduction in input costs. There was rapid expansion of the use of payment cards following the end of the 1981–1983 recession. Finally, Visa cited a Federal Reserve Bank study that found that credit card profitability was lower than other bank lending for the longer period 1974–1991.[34]

The fact of entry is ordinarily taken as the best evidence that entry barriers are low. Low entry barriers make markets more competitive, since entry reduces and may eliminate the ability of incumbent firms to exercise market power. So, Visa argued, it was odd that Dean Witter would point to entry as evidence of market power.[35]

---

[34]Canner and Luckett (1992, p. 661); and Federal Reserve Banks (1991).

[35]In pretrial motions, Dean Witter argued that prices fell after AT&T entered the payment card market with its own Visa and MasterCard program in early 1990. This claim was supported by trade press observations that AT&T's entry with a no-annual-fee card had forced other issuers to reduce or eliminate annual fees as well. Visa's economic expert prepared an econometric study of the effect of AT&T's entry on the average real cost to consumers of using credit cards and found no evidence that AT&T's entry was correlated with a reduction in that cost. Annual fees accounted for only about 10%

Finally, while price discrimination is evidence that a market is not perfectly competitive in the textbook sense, economists recognize that price discrimination, like imperfect competition, is widespread in the economy. Price discrimination alone, without more, proves essentially nothing.[36]

Competitive Effects of Bylaw 2.06

Visa argued that the primary effect of repealing Bylaw 2.06 would be to reduce intersystem competition. The admission of Dean Witter into the Visa system would have resulted in a partial integration of Discover and Visa (and presumably MasterCard). If Dean Witter were a significant Visa issuer, it would have a seat on the Visa Board of Directors and as a result of that, and its projected size, would have influenced Visa decisions. In particular, it would be in a position to influence Visa decisions concerning competition with Discover.

Visa argued that there was no evidence that Bylaw 2.06 was a disincentive for the entry of proprietary systems. Dean Witter did not identify any prospective entrant who was deterred as a result of the Bylaw or any firm that indicated it might be deterred. There was no evidence that any member of Visa had contemplated starting a proprietary system. Between 1966 when Visa and MasterCard both started and 1989 when competing systems were excluded from membership, only one proprietary card system was started—Discover in 1986. The fact that no proprietary system was started between 1989 and 1992, the time of trial, did not show that there was a disincentive. There was testimony that starting a proprietary system was a highly risky and expensive undertaking. Given that entry through Visa or MasterCard is much easier, it is not surprising that most entrants have chosen that course of action.

Finally, Visa argued that Dean Witter was not excluded from the relevant antitrust market at all. It could not issue Prime Option under the Visa "brand," but it could issue Prime Option under the Discover "brand." Both brands were in the market as defined by both sides. If Prime Option were a particularly innovative product desired by consumers, in principle it could be attractive if issued through the proprietary Discover system. Dean Witter presented no evidence that access to the Visa brand was necessary for the success of Prime Option, only that it would have been helpful.

---

of the average real cost at the time of AT&T's entry; they were trending downward before AT&T entered and continued to do so after AT&T entered. Dean Witter's economist did not mention AT&T in his testimony, and Visa therefore chose not to present the results of its own rebuttal study. The effect of AT&T's entry on payment card prices has taken on somewhat a life of its own after trial. The Visa study was summarized in Evans and Schmalensee (1993). Carlton and Frankel (1995b) then claimed that the entry of AT&T and GM resulted in a statistically significant reduction in annual fees. We have argued that the Carlton-Frankel work is flawed [Evans, Reddy, and Schmalensee (1997)].

[36]For a discussion of price discrimination as a common practice see Carlton and Perloff (1994, ch. 11) or Scherer and Ross (1990, ch. 13).

Benefits of Bylaw 2.06

Visa witnesses identified several benefits of Bylaw 2.06. As discussed above, Bylaw 2.06 preserved intersystem competition by erecting a wall between system competitors. Visa executives testified at trial that duality had resulted in a reduction in competition between Visa and MasterCard and that Dean Witter's participation in Visa would tend to reduce competition between Visa/MasterCard and Discover. They also testified that Bylaw 2.06 prevented a system competitor from obtaining valuable information from Visa through its participation in Visa business decisions and through its receipt as a member of confidential data. Apparently, Dean Witter thought that by becoming a member it could curtail Visa competition with the Discover Card and learn more about a system competitor.[37]

Mismatches

According to Visa, the antitrust problem identified by Dean Witter and the remedy it proposed were inconsistent with each other. The essential antitrust problem was that Visa allegedly had market power derived from its ability to engage in collective rule-making. According to Dean Witter, the extent of that problem—the degree of market power—was properly measured by the aggregate shares of the members involved in that collective rule-making. Dean Witter's proposed remedy was the admission of Dean Witter and, if it wished, American Express to Visa. Under that remedy, Visa could be forced to raise the aggregate shares of its members to 100 percent of the market, thus increasing the system's market power. As Visa's economist put it, ". . . if [Dean Witter's] diagnosis is right, then [Dean Witter's] prescription would make things worse. It is like my doctor saying to me as he does every once in a while that I'm a little bit too heavy and so I should eat a lot more ice cream" (Tr. 2331).

There was also a fundamental mismatch between Dean Witter's argument that Bylaw 2.06 discourages the entry of proprietary systems and its argument that Bylaw 2.06 should be repealed so that proprietary systems could join Visa. If the market problem is that there are too few proprietary systems, the solution should be to *close* the door at Visa—not to *open* the door more as desired by Dean Witter. Closing the door would encourage companies like AT&T and GM to start their own proprietary systems (AT&T had considered doing so). Keeping the door largely open encourages firms to enter as Visa issuers, not as proprietary systems.

THE APPEAL TO THE TENTH CIRCUIT

After losing the jury verdict and failing to convince the District Court to declare a mistrial or overrule the jury, Visa appealed to the Tenth Circuit.

[37]See Opening Brief of Appellant Visa U.S.A., Inc., 10th Circuit Court of Appeals, p. 15.

Both parties sought to frame the appeal in terms of the proper legal rule toward joint ventures. Visa argued that it should not have to admit Dean Witter unless Dean Witter could prove that it could not compete successfully without access to Visa's property. Dean Witter argued that joint ventures should not be allowed to impose membership conditions that have the purpose and effect of restraining competition and that are not ancillary to any legitimate purposes of the association.

After summarizing the existing case law, the appellate court set the stage for a rule-of-reason analysis that ultimately imposed the burden on Dean Witter to show that the Bylaw would harm consumers:

> We do not read the Court's precedent involving joint ventures to imply any special treatment or differing antitrust analysis. Indeed, aside from clarifying the inappropriateness of automatically invoking *per se* scrutiny of a joint venture's alleged antitrust violation, the Court has not articulated a different rule of reason approach. . . . To be judged anticompetitive, the agreement must actually or potentially harm consumers. . . . That concept cannot be overemphasized and is especially essential when a successful competitor alleges injury at the hands of a rival.[38]

Dean Witter ultimately lost because the court rejected the collective rulemaking analysis proffered by Dean Witter. The court found that "it is not the rule-making *per se* that should be the focus of the market power analysis, but the effect of those rules—whether they increase price, decrease output, or otherwise capitalize on barriers to entry that potential rivals cannot overcome"[39] (APP. 24–25). The court noted that there was no evidence presented (other than the unconvincing aggregate market share analysis) that the Visa rule had any anticompetitive effects on consumers. The court went on to say

> Thus, without any eye on effect, the very exercise of rule-making became the factual basis for rule of reason condemnation of Bylaw 2.06. Consequently, rule-making was not only divorced from its functional analysis but also from the facts of the case. . . . We believe the evidence cited by the district court to conclude Visa USA possessed market power is insufficient as a matter of law. [That] conclusion set the path for its uncharted journey upon a landscape of speculation, conjecture, and theoretical harm. The consequence is the finding of liability based on tendentious and conclusory statements, none of which amounts to evidence of restraint of trade. [In a footnote the court remarked] Sears' disincentive argument [regarding Bylaw 2.06 and the entry of new systems] provides the widest array of speculation. . . .[40]

---

[38]*SCFC ILC, Inc. v. Visa USA, Inc.,* 36 F 3d 958, 964–965.

[39]Ibid., 968.

[40]Ibid., 968–969.

The court also rejected Dean Witter's view that, in effect, Visa had to show that the "selective exclusion imposed by Visa's Bylaw 2.06 is ancillary to Visa's legitimate purpose as an open industry association."[41] The appellate judges observed that the Bylaw does not bar Dean Witter access to the payment card market and pointed out that there was no evidence that the Bylaw precluded Dean Witter from introducing Prime Option through Discover or any other means. They did not believe that the Sherman Act required the admission of Dean Witter into Visa so that it could compete more effectively. But the court stopped short of an explicit endorsement of Visa's "essential facility" standard for forced admission to a joint venture.

CONCLUSION

Business A, which competes with Business B, decides that it could make more money if it could sell B's product line in addition to its own. Business B says no. Can Business A make a claim under Section 1 of the Sherman Act? The general answer is clearly no, and this answer does not depend on whether Business B has market power, whether it let Business C sell the product line three days before, or whether it says that it would like to drive Business A into the dirt. Businesses do not have to share their property with anyone, let alone direct competitors, except under highly restrictive circumstances.

How then did Dean Witter's claim—which has almost exactly this fact pattern—survive summary judgment? The answer lies in the courts' long-standing hostility to joint ventures. Joint ventures are typically agreements between competitors, and it is well known that such horizontal combinations can do bad things: cartels can fix prices; trade associations can set standards that can block entry; and colluding firms can sometimes exclude competition by locking up essential inputs.[42] The courts therefore scrutinize joint ventures more closely than they do other forms of business organizations. Dean Witter could fashion an antitrust claim only because Visa was organized as a joint venture, and Dean Witter could therefore argue that Visa's exclusionary rule was enacted by a horizontal combination of competitors.

This higher level of scrutiny is somewhat paradoxical, since there is generally more competition when firms operate through a joint venture than when they merge. That is especially true for joint ventures that share input production and costs but then compete in output markets. If Visa and MasterCard had organized themselves as proprietary systems (e.g., with member banks having equity shares) in which members did not compete with

---

[41]Ibid., 971.

[42]See Kwoka (1994) for a discussion of the antitrust issues involved in the joint venture of GM and Toyota for manufacturing automobiles.

each other, there would have been far less competition in the payment card industry than there is today. This is not to say that joint ventures cannot provide a vehicle for anticompetitive behavior, but so can trade associations, industry conferences, and Sunday golf outings.

Not content with just having gotten to court, Dean Witter wanted (and needed) an even higher standard of scrutiny to win its case: a joint venture with a large market share would have to admit all comers unless it could show that exclusion was necessary for efficiency. And if it was admitting other new members or had recently done so, the exclusion of any applicant was presumptively not efficient. According to this view, large, open joint ventures must admit all applicants even if they are direct competitors of the venture. That view was rejected by the Tenth Circuit. Had the Tenth Circuit instead accepted Dean Witter's arguments, it would have made joint ventures, especially joint ventures that had admitted members in the past because of network externalities, a second-class form of business organization with attenuated property rights. Such a ruling would discourage the formation of joint ventures and would encourage resorting to mergers to exploit gains from cooperation.

Although its imagery could use work, the Tenth Circuit reached a sensible conclusion concerning Dean Witter's proposed revision to joint venture antitrust law and the result it would have required:

> Given Visa USA's justification the bylaw is necessary to prevent free riding in a market in which there was no evidence that price was raised or output decreased or Sears needed Visa USA to develop the new card, we are left with a vast sea of commercial policy into which Sears would have us wade. To impose liability on Visa USA for refusing to admit Sears or revise the bylaw to open its membership to intersystem rivals, we think, sucks the judiciary into an economic riptide of contrived market forces. . . . The Sherman Act ultimately must protect competition, not a competitor, and were we tempted to collapse the distinction, we would distort its continuing viability to safeguard consumer welfare.[43]

REFERENCES

Areeda, Phillip E. "Essential Facilities: An Epithet in Need of Limiting Principles." *Antitrust Law Journal* 58 (1990): 841–853.

Ausubel, Lawrence M. "The Failure of Competition in the Credit Card Market." *The American Economic Review* 81 (March 1991): 50–81.

Baker, Donald I., and Roland E. Brandel. *The Law of Electronic Fund Transfer Systems.* New York: Warren, Gorham & Lamont, 1988.

Calem, Paul S., and Loretta J. Mester. "Consumer Behavior and the Stickiness of

---

[43]*SCFC ILC, Inc. v. Visa USA, Inc.*, 36 F. 3d 958, 972.

Credit-Card Interest Rates." *The American Economic Review* 85 (December 1995): 1327–1336.

Canner, Glenn, and Charles Luckett. "Developments in the Pricing of Credit Card Services." *Federal Reserve Bulletin* 28 (September 1992): 652–666.

Carlton, Dennis W., and Alan S. Frankel. "The Antitrust Economics of Credit Card Networks." *Antitrust Law Journal* 63 (1995a): 228–248.

Carlton, Dennis W., and Alan S. Frankel. "Antitrust and Payment Technologies." *Federal Reserve Bank of St. Louis Review* 77 (November/December 1995b): 41–54.

Carlton, Dennis, and Jeffrey Perloff. *Modern Industrial Organization.* 2nd ed. New York: HarperCollins, 1994.

DeMuth, Christopher C. "The Case Against Credit Card Interest Rate Regulation." *Yale Journal of Regulation* 3, no. 2 (Spring 1986): 201–247.

Evans, David S., Bernard J. Reddy, and Richard Schmalensee. "Did AT&T & GM Affect Credit Card Pricing?" N.E.R.A. Working Paper, 1997.

Evans, David S., and Richard Schmalensee. *The Economics of the Payment Card Industry.* Cambridge, Mass.: N.E.R.A., Inc., 1993.

Evans, David S., and Richard L. Schmalensee. "Economic Aspects of Payment Card Systems and Antitrust Policy Toward Joint Ventures." *Antitrust Law Journal* 63 (1995): 861–898.

Federal Reserve Banks. "Functional Cost Analysis: 1991 National Average Report."

Kwoka, John E., Jr. "International Joint Venture: General Motors and Toyota (1983)." In *The Antitrust Revolution: The Role of Economics,* edited by John E Kwoka, Jr., and Lawrence J. White, 46–75. 2d ed. New York: Oxford University Press, 1994.

LaPuerta, Carlos, and Stewart C. Myers. "Measuring Profitability in the Credit Card Business." Mimeo, January 7, 1997.

Pratt, William, James Sonda, and Mark Racanelli. "Refusals to Deal in the Context of Network Joint Ventures." *The Business Lawyer* 52 (1997): 531–557.

Raskovich, Alexander, and Luke Froeb. "Has Competition Failed in the Credit Card Market?" U.S. Department of Justice, Economic Analysis Group Discussion Paper, June 12, 1992.

Scherer, F. M., and David Ross. *Industrial Market Structure and Economic Performance.* Princeton, N.J.: Houghton Mifflin, 1990.

Stavins, Joanna. "Can Demand Elasticities Explain Sticky Credit Card Rates?" *New England Economic Review* (July/August 1996): 43–54.

Visa USA. *Profit Analysis Report,* quarter ending June 30, 1992.

Visa U.S.A. Inc. "By-Laws/Operating Regulations," May 1, 1992.

CASE 13

Rapid Price Communication and Coordination: The Airline Tariff Publishing Case (1994)

Severin Borenstein

A firm announces a price increase and shortly thereafter its competitor announces its own increase to the same price level. Is that price fixing? Most antitrust economists and lawyers would say no. What if the announcements are made and changed rapidly? What if each firm makes many announcements before they settle down at identical prices? Finally, what if the prices being announced are to take effect at some future date so that no sales actually take place at these prices while the announcements are being made? This is a gray area of the antitrust laws. While an agreement among competitors to fix prices is per se illegal, computer technology that permits rapid announcements and responses has blurred the meaning of "agreement" and has made it difficult for antitrust authorities to distinguish public announcements from conversations among competitors.

These were some of the issues that were raised in the U.S. Department of Justice's investigation of the major U.S. airlines and the Airline Tariff Publishing Company (ATPCO), which is owned by the airlines and disseminates price change information to airline and travel agent computer systems. The investigation began in 1991, and the resulting case was settled with a consent decree in March 1994. The case never went to trial and, therefore, it set no formal precedent. Still, the legal pleadings, negotiations, and the final consent decree indicate some of the difficult antitrust issues that are raised by rapid price announcements as well as the impact of new communication technologies on those issues.

Severin Borenstein consulted for the U.S. Department of Justice in this matter. For helpful comments and discussions, I am grateful to Dennis Carlton, Rob Gertner, Rich Gilbert, John Kwoka, Carl Shapiro, and Larry White.

THE AIRLINE INDUSTRY IN THE EARLY 1990s

From the time of airline deregulation in 1978 through the early 1990s, the airline industry was in a state of nearly constant upheaval. At the time of deregulation, the U.S. domestic jet air travel market included about twenty competitors ranging from small regional carriers to the largest national and international airlines. Immediately following deregulation, many startup airlines entered the domestic market. Concentration at both the national and the route level fell in the first five years following deregulation. Most of the startups were small regional airlines. Under the financial pressure of competition, few were ever able to turn a profit. By the mid-1980s, airlines were folding faster than new ones were entering, and many were disappearing through merger. A merger wave in the middle and late 1980s, along with more exits during that time, raised the Herfindahl-Hirschman Index for domestic air travel from 854 at the beginning of 1985 to 1074 at the beginning of 1990.

Two of the most important and unforeseen developments in the industry following deregulation were the airlines' moves to hub-and-spoke networks and their increased sophistication in pricing and marketing their products. The hub system created a natural area of dominance for a carrier. Since most cities do not have sufficient traffic to support hubs for two different carriers, a typical big-city airport is likely to be dominated by a single airline. From its hub, an airline would offer nonstop service to many or most of the country's other large cities and many small cities in the region of the hub. Such a network also lends itself naturally to offering change-of-plane service between airports for which the hub is a convenient intermediate stop. These routings could compete with nonstop service offered by a carrier that has a hub at one of the end-point airports. For instance, while Northwest was the only carrier to offer nonstop service between its Detroit hub and Los Angeles, it had less than 60 percent of the traffic in that market. The remaining traffic flowed over competing carriers' hubs: with Continental, changing planes in Denver; with American, changing planes in Chicago; with United, changing planes in Denver or Chicago; with Delta, changing planes in Salt Lake City.

The major carriers also became very sophisticated in marketing and pricing their products following deregulation. They developed customer loyalty plans that reinforced their dominance at their hubs. These included frequent flyer programs and travel agent commission override programs (TACOs). TACOs are effectively "frequent booker" programs for travel agents: Agents are rewarded for directing a high proportion of their bookings to the airline. Airlines also offered corporate discount programs that rewarded a corporation for concentrating its air travel with just one airline. The debate about the efficiency versus market power enhancement properties of these programs is still active, but there is general agreement that these programs led to greater airport concentration.[1]

Believing that hubs delivered significant competitive advantages, and forecasting continued growth in the industry, the remaining carriers in the late 1980s invested heavily in new equipment. The world's largest producer of jet aircraft, Boeing, reported record sales, and the delivery lag on some aircraft grew to many years. Carriers continued to establish new hubs in ever smaller cities, including Dayton, Raleigh-Durham, and Kansas City. By early 1990, however, it was apparent that the industry had overinvested in aircraft capacity. Demand was not expanding as rapidly as expected, and hubs at smaller airports were frequently turning out to result in more costs than benefits to the hub carrier. As the 1990–1991 recession hit and the Gulf War reduced even domestic air travel demand, newspapers reported that fleets of commercial aircraft were being grounded and stored in the Mohave desert. Many carriers went into financial distress and a number entered Chapter 11 bankruptcy proceedings: Eastern (1989), Continental (1989), Braniff (1989), Pan Am (1991), America West (1991), Midway (1991), and TWA (1992). As a whole, the industry reported record losses in 1990, 1991, and 1992.

AIRLINE PRICING

By the time the ATPCO investigation began in 1991, airlines had developed very sophisticated systems for setting fares, determining the number of seats available at each price, and disseminating this information to customers, travel agents, and other airlines. On a single route, such as Minneapolis-Atlanta, a carrier was likely to have more than a dozen different fares available at a time, and to have still more listed fares that were unavailable because no seats had been allocated to that fare category.

ATPCO is a central clearinghouse for distribution of fare change information. Each day airlines send to ATPCO information on new fares to be added, old fares to be removed, and existing fares to be changed. At least once a day, ATPCO produces a compilation of all industry fare change information and sends that computer file, which includes thousands of fare changes, to a list of recipients. The list includes, among others, all of the major airlines and all four of the computer reservation systems (CRSs) in the United States—Sabre, Apollo, Worldspan, and System One. Each CRS company operates a networks of computers that travel agents and airlines use to access flight, fare, and seat availability information on virtually any airline in the world. Thus, information sent to the CRS becomes available to consumers, travel agents, and all other airlines by the following morning.

---

[1]For a description of market power that might result from these loyalty plans and increasing hub concentration, see Borenstein (1992). For an alternative view, see Carlton and Bamberger (1996).

To follow the ATPCO case, it is important to understand the information that is transmitted by ATPCO. Fare information that airlines submit to ATPCO includes a fare basis code (a "name" of the fare), the origin and destination airports, the price, first and last ticket dates, first and last travel dates, and any restrictions on the use of the fare (e.g., advance purchase; minimum stay; blackout dates; type of consumer who can buy it, such as clergy; or a specific routing or set of flights to which the fare applies). First and last ticket dates indicate when the carrier or a travel agent can sell tickets on the fare, while first and last travel dates indicate the range of dates on which travel can occur under the fare. By setting a future first ticket date on a new fare or setting a future last ticket date on an existing fare, a carrier could announce a fare increase, but delay its implementation until a specific future date. This ability to pre-announce price increases became a central focus of the investigation.

Ticket and travel dates, and all restrictions, are submitted as a "footnote" to the fare. Each footnote has a "footnote designator," which is a name for the footnote. Footnotes do not follow a numerical order, but are simply given footnote designators by the submitting airline. The use of fare basis codes and footnote designators as possible modes of communication also became a focus of the investigation.

"COMPETITIVE" PRICING IN IMMEDIATE-RESPONSE OLIGOPOLY MARKETS

While the ATPCO case involved a complex set of institutions and markets, one of the issues at its core was quite basic: When a small number of firms selling a homogeneous good can monitor one another's prices and respond to changes almost immediately, what is the likely outcome? In such a case, collusive pricing can result even without any sort of explicit communication among the firms. Acting unilaterally, each firm recognizes that price cuts will be matched immediately, so cutting price makes sense only if the firm would prefer an equilibrium in which all firms charged the new lower price. This greatly reduces the incentive to compete on price.

In recent work, Gertner (1994) has explored the outcome in such a market when firms have different costs and capacity constraints. His work, which is motivated by and refers frequently to the airline industry, concludes that if firms are not too different, the outcome in immediate-response markets will still be close to the collusive outcome and the price will be dictated by the firm that prefers the lowest price. This occurs because higher-cost firms have nothing to offer a low-cost firm in return for its agreeing to a price above its own profit-maximizing levels. Of course, if the firm that prefers the lowest price differs across markets, there may well be room for trades in which each firm agrees to a higher price than it would like in one market in return for increasing price closer to its preferred level in another market. Gertner also finds that if firms differ sufficiently in costs or other attributes, one firm may be able to sustain a lower price than others with none wanting to change its price given the prices charged by others. This result relies on the lower-cost firms' having a capacity constraint. In such a case, the higher-cost firms are better off allowing the low-cost firm to fill its capacity and then selling to the remaining demand than matching the price of the lower-cost firm and gaining a higher market share. Thus, even though the airlines differed in costs and other attributes, the ability to monitor one another's prices closely and respond very quickly could still result in prices well above the competitive level.

This line of economic research, however, has a mixed message for antitrust. On the one hand, low-cost monitoring and quick response raise concern that prices will end up at supracompetitive levels and will harm consumers. On the other hand, this may happen without any further facilitating circumstances—that is, without any actions that are clearly in violation of antitrust laws. It is not an antitrust violation for a firm unilaterally to charge high prices. Not only does such a circumstance present a dilemma for the prosecution of an antitrust case, it also makes it difficult to devise a remedy to the situation. Neither "charge lower prices" nor "stop responding to the actions of other firms" are realistic remedies under the antitrust laws (though the former is the basis for much of economic regulation).

THE JUSTICE DEPARTMENT'S CASE

On December 21, 1992, the U.S. Department of Justice filed antitrust charges against ATPCO and eight major airlines.[2] The complaint charged that the airlines, through ATPCO, had colluded to raise price and restrict competition in the airline industry. The Justice Department argued that the airlines had carried on detailed conversations and negotiations over prices through ATPCO. It pointed to numerous instances in which one carrier on a route had announced a fare increase to take effect a number of weeks in the future. Other carriers had then announced increases on the same route, though possibly to a different fare level. In many cases cited, the airlines had iterated back and forth until they reached a point where they were announcing the same fare increase to take effect on the same date. In cases where one airline did not announce that it would post the same fare increase as the others, the increase generally did not take place. In such situations it was common for carriers to "roll" their fare increases—that is, to move the effective date further into the future, in order to give the carrier that had not announced a matching fare increase more time to do so.

---

[2]The airlines were Alaska, American, Continental, Delta, Northwest, Trans World, United, and USAir.

The DOJ garnered this information simply from the records of the ATPCO. It also had documents from each airline's daily internal fare change reports, which included phrases of the nature "we are waiting to see if [carrier name] is going to go along with our proposed increase," "we are abandoning the increase on [city1]-[city2] because [carrier name] has not matched," and "[carrier name] is now on board for the [date] increase to [fare level] on [city1]-[city2]." The DOJ argued that the announcement of fares that are to take effect at a later date allowed the airlines to negotiate over prices without ever offering those prices to the public. While none of the announcements was binding, such "cheap talk" can still aid collusive behavior.[3]

The DOJ's case also was based on patterns of multimarket coordination that it claimed to have identified. The complaint argued that the carriers were using fare basis codes and footnote designators to communicate to other airlines linkages between fares on different routes. A typical example of the allegation went something like this: Say that airline A1 has a hub at city C1 from which it serves a route to city C3 with nonstop flights, as illustrated in Figure 13-1. Airline A2 has a hub at C2, which is between C1 and C3. Airline A2 is offering a relatively low fare in the C1-C3 market with service that requires a plane change at C2. This low fare is siphoning customers from the nonstop service that A1 offers on the route. A1 would like A2 to raise its fare on the C1-C3 route.

If that were the whole story, however, A1 would not have much ability to bribe or coerce A2. However, A2 serves C2-C4 with nonstop service, and A1 offers change-of-plane service on that route over its hub at C1—exactly the reverse of the previous situation. A1 could strike a deal with A2 in which each carrier agrees not to undercut the other's nonstop service with its own fares that require a plane change at its own hub.

FIGURE 13-1 Carriers with Overlapping Networks.

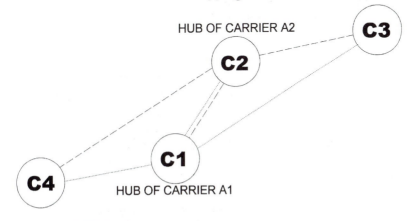

HUB OF CARRIER A2

C3

C2

C1

C4

HUB OF CARRIER A1

---

[3]See Farrell and Rabin (1996) for a thorough discussion of the effects of cheap talk on collusion.

The DOJ argued that in such situations the ATPCO system of fare basis codes and footnote designators offered the sort of sophisticated communication necessary to spell out and agree upon such a deal. Here's one way the DOJ said it would work: A1 would institute a new fare on C2-C4 that undercut A2's fare on that route, and A1 would give this new fare the same or a similar fare basis code as A2 was using for the fare A1 was unhappy with on C1-C3, thus signaling to A2 the connection between the two fares. A1 would then put a short last-ticket date on this new fare, indicating that it would be available for only, say, two weeks. It would also put in a fare on the C2-C4 route that matched A2's current fare and would give that fare a first-ticket date that was the same as its last-ticket date for the cheaper fare. A1 would then wait to see if A2 got the message. If it did, A2 would put a last-ticket date on its fare on C1-C3 that was the same as the last-ticket date A1 had put on its cheap C2-C4 fare and would add a new fare that matched A1's fare on C1-C3 and had the same date for its first-ticket date. If that happened, then two weeks hence each carrier, without further action, would raise its fare on the other's nonstop route so that it was no longer undercutting the nonstop route with change-of-plane service.

If A2 did not get the message or respond in the way that A1 wished, A1 could roll forward its last-ticket date on its cheap C2-C4 route. By refiling the fare with a different last-ticket date, A1 could also make sure that this fare again showed up on A2's daily list of new fares, just in case A2 had overlooked it the previous time.

The DOJ argued that the combination of future first-ticket dates and fare basis codes or footnote designators that allowed an airline to highlight a link between two fares on different routes made it much easier than it would otherwise be for two airlines to "negotiate" over fares on different routes. With these facilitating devices, the Department asserted, the airlines could make clear the "trades" they were offering: raising price on one route in return for a rival raising price on another route.

THE AIRLINES' DEFENSE

While under Section 1 of the Sherman Act blatant price fixing has been found to be per se illegal, in reality there are many cases that do not fit that mold. Often, as in the ATPCO case, the action under scrutiny is not secret meetings of executives in smoke-filled rooms. In this case, no face-to-face meetings were alleged. Rather, the airlines were accused of making very frequent statements that amounted to a negotiation over price. The statements were also made in public insofar as travel agents and others with access to a CRS could follow the rounds of announced future price changes. The basis of the Supreme Court's view that blatant price fixing is per se illegal is that there is no credible argument that such behavior could benefit consumers or competition. The airlines asserted that there was a clear argument that the actions at issue could benefit consumers, so that any examination should be under a rule-of-reason standard.[4]

The airlines responded to the specific DOJ charges by pointing out that all firms price in response to the actions of their competitors. They argued that each carrier was acting in its own independent best interest when it raised price. It would be unrealistic to think that a carrier would set its fares without considering the response that they could anticipate from other airlines. Once it was recognized that it is legitimate for an airline to consider the likely response from it competitors, the airlines argued that the DOJ allegations were indistinguishable from competitive behavior. A carrier probably would not want to cut price if all its competitors would match. Likewise, an airline will not be able to make a price increase "stick" if other airlines keep their prices at a lower level.

One can draw a parallel with a market that is undeniably competitive, such as the wheat market. For the price of wheat to increase, some seller must be the first to raise its price. It will do so in the belief that the competitive equilibrium price is higher than the current level. If it is incorrect, then most other wheat sellers will not follow, and the first firm will lose all or most of its sales. It then will be forced to reduce its price again. It has done nothing anticompetitive, but rather has engaged in a normal part of the price discovery process in a competitive market. As recently as June 1993, the Supreme Court found in *Brooke Group Ltd. v. Brown & Williamson Tobacco Corp.* that such parallel pricing is likely to occur in competitive or oligopolistic markets without collusion.[5] In a slightly earlier case, the Supreme Court had stated that "conduct that is as consistent with permissible competition as with illegal conspiracy does not, without more, support an inference of conspiracy."[6]

The defendants argued not only that the observed parallel price movements were consistent with competition, but that pre-announcements of price increases were in the interest of consumers. Far from being devices for price fixing, the airlines asserted that such advanced warnings to consumers were a device for creating consumer benefits and maintaining goodwill. They submitted hundreds of affidavits from travel agents praising the airlines' policy of advanced notice on price rises and making dire predictions if such notices were eliminated. The travel agents said that consumers became very angry when the price of a ticket increased between the time that the traveler reserved the seat and actually purchased the ticket. Many agencies reported having programs to notify their loyal

---

[4]Carlton et al. (1997) make this argument persuasively.

[5]See *Brooke Group Ltd. v. Brown & Williamson Tobacco Corp.,* 61 U.S.L.W. at 4703. Also see Case 10 by William Burnett in this volume.

[6]*Matsushita Electric Industrial Co. v. Zenith Radio Corp.,* 475 U.S. 574, 597 n. 21 (1986). Also see Case 9 by Kenneth Elzinga in this volume.

customers of pending fare increases that were likely to affect them. It was clear that the travelling public was used to receiving plenty of warning of fare increases and that, *holding fare levels constant,* they would prefer to continue to get advanced notice of increases.

The airlines supported their argument that consumers value information of future price increases by introducing evidence about the bookings "surge" that had occurred prior to some price increase. They focused on a few incidents in 1991: heavily advertised fare wars that ended at a certain date, a date that had been widely publicized in advance. The airlines showed that bookings surged just before the end of these "sales" and then fell substantially in the days following the price increase. In one of these incidents, the surge had been so dramatic and the demand for bookings so great as to cause the Sabre CRS, the largest in the United States, nearly to crash on the night before the discounts expired.

The airlines also defended advanced notice of price increases by pointing out—in an argument reminiscent of the *Ethyl* case—that airlines engaged in such advanced warnings on monopoly routes as much as on competitive routes.[7] This demonstrated, the airlines argued, that the primary consideration in pre-announcing fare increases was maintaining goodwill with consumers, not signaling to competitors.

Further, the defendants argued, the price-fixing theory was refuted by the fact that airlines didn't pre-announce price decreases. They pointed out that there is no goodwill justification for delaying a price decrease in order to give advanced warning rather than putting it in place immediately. On the other hand, they contended, price cuts are very destabilizing to cartels, so a member of a price-fixing conspiracy would be as, or more, concerned with getting the approval of its fellow conspirators for a price decrease as for a price increase. Thus, if airlines were to use advanced notice of price changes to support a price-fixing conspiracy, they would be more inclined to preannounce decreases.

The airlines recognized that documents received by the DOJ in the discovery process had indicated a few occasions in which one carrier had retaliated against another's incursion into its area of dominance by cutting fares on routes dominated by the aggressor airline. They argued, however, that this was a natural part of the competitive process. If other carriers hit you where it hurts, you turn around and hit them back where it hurts them. This wasn't multimarket price fixing; it was aggressive, perhaps excessively macho, competition. If on a few occasions a pricing analyst got carried away with the conflict analogy, that was certainly not evidence of price fixing. Furthermore, if a carrier knows that another airline is likely to respond aggressively and to expand a fare war beyond a single market, it

---

[7]In the *Ethyl* case, one of the defendants demonstrated that the practices it had been accused of engaging in to facilitate collusion were the same practices that it had used decades earlier when it was the only producer of the gasoline additive. *E.I. DuPont de Nemours & Co. v. FTC,* 729 F.2d 128 (1984). Also see Case 7 by George Hay in this volume.

is only natural for it to be less inclined to initiate a fare cut even if it would otherwise like to. The point, the defendants argued, was still that all of this behavior was undertaken unilaterally by each airline, that no agreement was solicited or accepted.

All of the defendant airlines protested that they had never used fare basis codes or footnote designators to signal connections between fares or to communicate information to other airlines that might support price fixing. The few cases in which a fare basis code was found to contain the two-letter code of a rival airline were argued to be anomalies that did not constitute a pattern of collusive behavior. The airlines also explained that it was often easier to give certain fares the same footnote designators when they were likely to have the same restrictions for the foreseeable future or to give different footnote designators to fares with the same restrictions if it was believed likely that the restrictions on one would become different from the restrictions on the other.

Two other factors, the airlines asserted, made price fixing untenable in the airline industry. First, not all of an airline's prices were public. Airlines regularly cut special deals with large corporations. In return for a guaranteed amount of traffic from the corporation or share of the firm's business, an airline typically would offer some percentage rebate on all tickets. The size of that rebate was kept secret. Any carrier could cheat on a collusive agreement with these rebates and faced a low probability of detection. Second, airlines could not monitor how many seats a carrier was making available at each fare it published. An airline could effectively cut its prices by making a large number of seats available at its lower published fares. A competing airline could never be sure of the exact mix of passengers and fares that another carrier was serving.

Finally, the airlines argued that common sense didn't support the price-fixing story. The airlines were experiencing the largest annual losses in their history. Major airlines had recently entered Chapter 11, and two of the largest preregulation carriers, Pan Am and Eastern, had been liquidated. New entry had nearly stopped since the middle of 1990, further indicating that the industry was not offering firms an attractive return on investment. If there was price fixing, it certainly wasn't making the airlines rich.

THE JUSTICE DEPARTMENT'S RESPONSE

While the DOJ continued to argue that the case could be prosecuted as a per se violation of Section 1 of the Sherman Act, both sides pursued arguments that would be relevant only under a rule-of-reason standard. The Department recognized that some consumers may have benefited from pre-announcement of fare increases. Rather, it argued that such benefits were likely to be very small in comparison to the opportunity that pre-announcement afforded airlines to coordinate price increases.

Furthermore, the DOJ argued that consumers also were often misled by last-ticket dates. A DOJ study found that about half of all last-ticket dates placed in the CRS systems turned out to be inaccurate. In some cases, they were rolled forward until all airlines on a route had announced the same increase, with only the last announcement being correct. In many cases, they were simply withdrawn if competing carriers did not go along. (On rare occasions, the increase was implemented sooner than the last-ticket date suggested.) Consumers who bought tickets sooner than they would have liked, due to pre-announced increases that never actually occurred, were made worse off by these announcements.

The airlines' "surge" data turned out to be less persuasive than appeared to be the case at first. The airlines had submitted surge data for only the largest and most highly publicized sales in the recent past. These were not the pre-announced increases that most concerned the DOJ, because the heavy advertising that accompanied these last-ticket dates made it very difficult for the carriers to "negotiate" through numerous changes in the dates and fares. The airlines did not supply surge data for more typical unadvertised increases or ones that came about after a number of different announced last-ticket dates and subsequent changes.

The Justice Department agreed that pre-announcement of price decreases would indeed be powerful evidence that they were being used for collusion, but argued that the absence of such announcements simply could be due to the airlines' awareness that such behavior would assure an antitrust investigation. The practice of pre-announcing price increases could still be a device intended to facilitate collusion. Similarly, while the use of pre-announcements on monopoly routes indicates that such announcements are not valueless to consumers, it does not indicate the predominant reason for use of pre-announcements on competitive routes.

The DOJ also suggested that the airlines had available a ready substitute for advanced notices of fare increases, one that did not raise the antitrust issues that were the focus of this case: The airlines could guarantee a fare for some period of time after a traveler made a reservation. The guarantee could be for a few days, a week, or longer. Implementing such a system would not be trivial, however, since airline reservation systems were programmed only to ticket at the price effective at the time the ticket was purchased. A price-guarantee system would require that the computers maintain a record of the price in effect at the time the reservation was made. Opinions differed with regard to the cost of implementing such a program. Many of the airlines also argued that it would not substitute for pre-notification of price increases, as many customers would still be angry if they waited longer than the price guarantee period and found themselves facing an increased fare.

Finally, even if all last-ticket dates were accurate and if fare guarantees could not viably replace them, a simple "back-of-the-envelope" calculation indicated that the total savings to consumers from early warning of price increases was likely to be very small. Here's how such a calculation could be done: Assume that on a typical route, price increases were implemented once every sixty days (which is more often than actual) and that a typical fare increase is 5 percent. Assume that advanced notice of the increase caused a full day of bookings that would have occurred after the increase to instead take place before. For an increase that is not advertised outside the CRSs, this is a very large surge effect. This would mean that one-sixtieth of consumers would receive a savings of 5 percent due to the advanced notice of price increases, or an average savings of slightly less than 0.1 percent per traveler on the route. Of course, those consumers who missed the fare increase date due to the absence of pre-announcement would be unhappy about paying the increase, but for the entire group of travelers on the route, the average savings is likely to be extremely small. If the pre-announcements aided collusion to any noticeable extent, it is likely that consumers would benefit from their elimination.

Two points were made in response to the assertion that discounting to corporations made collusion implausible. First, even if sales to corporations remained competitive because of secret discounting, there was no reason to think that this disciplined prices to all other consumers. Corporate discount tickets accounted for less than 10 percent of volume on nearly all routes, so this still left a large proportion of the market subject to the collusive prices. Second, the corporate discounts were mostly discounts off list prices. In the short run, with these discount agreements in place, any increase in the list price would be reflected proportionally in the discounted prices as well. Of course, in the longer run, if the market for corporate discount passengers were competitive, list price increases would be largely offset by greater proportional corporate discounts.

The issue of seat availability is a complex one. Airlines expend a great deal of effort to try to figure out the proportion of seats their competitors sell at each published fare, but they are not entirely successful. At any point in time, however, they can see whether a competitor has any seats available at a given price—in airline parlance, whether a "bucket" is open or closed. Thus, if one carrier attempts to cheat on a collusive price by offering a greater number of seats at lower listed prices, competitors can observe that it is keeping a low-price bucket open and can keep their own corresponding bucket open as well. This is not a perfect substitute for knowing a competitor's total sales in each bucket, but it means that no airline can secretly undercut its rivals by having a low price available when others don't.

The Justice Department argued that profit levels were not relevant to the investigation. DOJ investigators pointed out a number of cases in which the colluding firms were in poor financial health. While collusion is likely to raise profits compared with the same market without collusion, there are many cases in which colluding firms lose money. In the ATPCO case, it was noted that the airlines had made massive investments in capacity just before the 1990–1991 recession hit, leaving them with aircraft that were depreciating without even providing services. Besides the costs of holding excess capacity, the existence of that capacity lowered each firm's marginal cost of serving a given route, thus putting downward pressure on prices. This is part of the normal economics of markets with large fixed capital investments. Though excess capacity depresses prices and causes firms to report losses, economists agree that this is the efficient economic response to such situations. Even if firms colluded in such a situation—and the desire to do so is likely to be great—they may not be able to raise prices to the point that they can cover the cost of all prior investment errors.

FASHIONING A REMEDY AND NEGOTIATING A SETTLEMENT

As the Justice Department continued the investigation in 1992, a question hung over the case: If the Department could prove its case and prevail at trial, what remedy should it seek? Parallel price movements of competing firms are not generally illegal. DOJ was reluctant to pursue a settlement that would place such restrictions on how or how often firms could change their prices. Through the discussions with the defendants and the memos written by each side, the case came to focus on two issues: the pre-announcement of price increases and the alleged use of fare basis codes and footnote designators to communicate linkages between prices on different routes. It became apparent to all involved in the case that rapid information transmission was inherent in the computer technology in use in the industry. The DOJ would not easily be able to prevent airlines from "proposing" fare increases and then withdrawing those fares relatively quickly if competitors didn't match.

Instead, the Department decided to pursue remedies that it hoped would make it more costly and less effective to use the system for collusive bargaining. First, the DOJ proposed the elimination of last-ticket dates except in situations in which the carrier was engaged in significant advertising through newspapers, television, radio, or other media intended to inform consumers of the last-ticket date. The idea was that such announcements are clearly aimed at consumers, and making changes to such information after it is advertised is costly and potentially harmful to the carrier's reputation. (Later in negotiations between the airlines and the DOJ, it was agreed that carriers could also post a last-ticket date if it was only to match the last-ticket date of another carrier, which had advertised that date.) Likewise, airlines would not be able to pre-announce prices that would go into effect in the future, that is, they could not use future first-ticket dates. Thus, an airline could advertise "Sale Ends November 30," but could not say what the price would be after November 30.

Some airlines argued that requiring a carrier to advertise a sale in print, television, or other media would raise the cost of running a sale and would thus discourage price cutting. There was, however, no requirement of advertising to run a sale, only to put a last-ticket date on the sale. An airline was free to cut its price for any period of time it liked without advertising. It could not, however, put a last-ticket date on the fare in its listing with ATPCO unless it also communicated in some direct fashion to consumers. It was also unclear what sort of a short-term sale an airline would want to run without advertising. The point of cutting price is to increase sales as much as possible to make up for the lower price a firm receives from those who would have bought even at the high price. A sale without advertising seems more likely to decrease revenue from those who would have bought at the high price while minimizing the increase in total sales.

The other major condition of the proposed remedy was on the use of fare basis codes and footnote designators. The Justice Department proposed that these codes could contain only the basic information they were said to contain: abbreviations that indicated fare class, minimum stay or advanced purchase, and other restrictions. In the course of the case, examples had come to light in which one carrier had put the two-letter airline code of another in a fare that appeared intended to retaliate against that competitor. Similarly, the DOJ's proposed remedy restricted the use of footnote designators to make them more generic and less able to convey information about the connection between different fares. A carrier would be required to use the same footnote designator for *all* its fares that had footnotes with identical information: such as first and last travel dates. Carriers generally had many footnote designators that pointed to footnotes containing the same information. In addition, carriers would not be allowed to list footnote designators that pointed to "empty" footnotes, ones that had no further information about the fare. This practice had also been observed during the investigation in situations where it appeared to be used to identify connections between fares on different routes.

THE CASE FILING AND PARTIAL SETTLEMENT

On December 21, 1992, the DOJ filed the case accusing all eight of the airlines under investigation of price fixing through the ATPCO. As it often does, the DOJ had, prior to filing, engaged in lengthy informal discussions of the case and settlement talks with the defendants. Thus, along with filing the case, the Justice Department also announced a settlement with United Airlines and USAir. Under the settlement, the airlines did not admit guilt on any of the charges, but they agreed to abide by the DOJ's proposed remedies. In particular, United and USAir agreed to stop announcing most price increases in advance of the date on which they took effect. Instead, most price increases would have to take effect at the time they were announced.

Under the Tunney Act, a settlement of a government antitrust case such as this one must be approved by a federal court. The idea behind the Tunney Act was to ensure that the government didn't cut a backroom deal with specific defendants in return for favors. The court must review the settlement, hear arguments from all interested parties, and determine that the settlement is in the public interest.

At the Tunney Act hearing, which took place shortly after the settlement with United and USAir was reached, the other accused airlines argued strongly against the settlement. Their arguments were essentially the same as they had used in responding to the government's investigation: first- and last-ticket dates are for the purpose of informing consumers and give significant benefits to them; airlines act unilaterally but are of course influenced by the prices that other carriers' charge; the evidence did not support the feasibility or practice of collusion in this market; and any signaling or attempt to coerce competitors to raise price was an anomaly.[8]

In responding to these filings, the DOJ examined the airlines' incentive for making such an argument. The Justice Department argued that if the airlines' pleading was accurate, they would have no incentive to oppose restrictions being placed on their competitors, United and USAir, in the use of first- and last ticket dates and other complex information transmission through ATPCO. The DOJ argued that accepting the nonsettling airlines' arguments would imply that they would gain a significant competitive advantage versus United and USAir. In fact, two of the nonsettling carriers stated that they would not accept the proposed settlement for themselves, because it would put them at a competitive disadvantage against other airlines that were not part of the case.[9] If this were true, the DOJ argued, one would expect the other airlines to be happy to see United and USAir subjected to these restrictions.

In contrast, DOJ submitted, if the techniques that United and USAir had agreed to cease using had been part of a system of price coordination, one would indeed expect the nonsettling airlines to fight it. If these facets of ATPCO filings had supported coordinated behavior, the inability of United and USAir to use them would be nearly as harmful to the other airlines as if they had been forced to accept these restrictions on their own behavior. Thus, their arguments against the settlement with United and

---

[8]Some of the airlines also argued that the proposed settlement could raise fare levels. If airlines found it more difficult to raise prices, they might be less inclined to experiment with lower fares, because it would be difficult to return to the pre-discount level. Of course, this same argument applies to nearly any impediment to collusion: if firms cannot collude as easily as previously, they might be less inclined to start a price war. The argument is not logically inconsistent, but there does not appear to be any evidence that impeding collusion reduces aggressive price competition.

[9]In a pleading shortly after the settlement with United and USAir, Delta stated that it had not discontinued the use of first- and last-ticket dates because if it did so, it "would be at a competitive disadvantage with respect to the remaining airlines that would be operating under no similar restriction." TWA made a similar argument. Joint Response of the Airline Tariff Publishing Company, Alaska Airlines, Inc., American Airlines, Inc., Continental Airlines, Inc., Delta Air Lines, Inc., Northwest Airlines, Inc., and Trans World Airlines, Inc., to the Court's order of May 24, 1993, requesting information, June 28, 1993, p. 10.

USAir may have undermined the procompetitive case the other defendants had made for the suspect behavior.

THE FINAL SETTLEMENT AND ITS EFFECTS

Despite the protests of the other defendant carriers, the settlement with United and USAir was accepted by the courts under the Tunney Act. Shortly after, the other six defendants entered further negotiations with DOJ. On March 17, 1994, a final settlement of the ATPCO case was announced. The other six airlines agreed to nearly the same restrictions as had United and USAir. The consent decree is to last for ten years, until 2004. Until that time, these airlines cannot use footnote designators and fare basis codes to convey anything but the most basic information; they cannot link different fares with special codes; and they cannot preannounce price increases except in the case of widely publicized sales.

While the settlement restricts behavior that the DOJ believed facilitated the communication of information that supported collusion, it does not restrict the fares that a carrier can offer or when the carrier can begin or end their availability. This was made clear in a memorandum filed with the settlement at the request of American Airlines. Two examples detailed in the memo make clear the freedom that airlines still have and the difficult antitrust issues that remain. The DOJ, as part of the settlement, accepted that neither of the following scenarios would constitute a violation of the consent decree:

> *Scenario 1: At noon on Friday Airline A transmits 10% fare increases on certain city-pairs to ATPCO. The increased fares become available for sale through CRS at 5 p.m. that same day. On Saturday, Airline B transmits 5% increases to ATPCO on the same city-pairs. Airline A withdraws its 10% fare increases on Sunday when it learns that competing airlines have not offered matching fares for sale. Airline B withdraws its 5% increased fares. The following week, on Friday, Airline A raises its fares 5% on those city-pairs where Airline B had raised its fares 5% the previous week. On Saturday, Airline B matches Airline A's 5% fare increases, and both Airlines thereafter offer those fares for sale.*

> *Scenario 2: Airline A offers for sale a low fare (e.g., $101) for travel on a route that is important to Airline B. Airline B matches the $101 fare for travel on the same city-pair and also offers for sale a $101 fare for travel on a city-pair that is important to Airline A. Airline B withdraws both $101 fares after one day. Airline A then withdraws its initial $101 fare the next day.*

The DOJ stated that these scenarios involved the offering of bona fide fares for sale that are available to consumers at the time they are published. Because they involved a change in the carrier's economic behavior in the marketplace, and were not intended solely to communicate a carrier's planned future fare changes, the DOJ agreed that they would not be forbidden under the consent decree.

Beyond clarifying the settlement, these scenarios also described the way that prices have been set in the industry since shortly after the December 1992 settlement with USAir and United. Since that time, the airlines have implemented most of their fare changes on weekends, when a very small share of tickets are actually sold because most travel agencies are closed. It is now common for an airline to post price increases on a Friday afternoon, which then become available in the CRSs on Saturday morning. If its competitors in the markets do not match the increase by Sunday afternoon, the airline withdraws the increase Sunday night, so that the original lower prices are in effect on Monday morning.[10] If its competitors match, the higher fares remain in effect.

The ATPCO case raised some of the most subtle and challenging issues in enforcement of Section 1 of the Sherman Act, the cornerstone of U.S. antitrust law. Unfortunately, because the case never went to trial, the ATPCO case set no legal precedent. Furthermore, because the remedy fashioned addressed only institutional aspects of the airline industry, today it provides little guidance as to where in the gray area of Section 1 legitimate communication ends and price fixing begins. It did, however, clarify the DOJ's willingness to pursue cases of coordinated pricing through rapid communication, as well as the types of arguments that are likely to arise in such cases.

REFERENCES

Borenstein, Severin. "The Evolution of U.S. Airline Competition." *Journal of Economic Perspectives* 7 (Spring 1992): 45–73.

Carlton, Dennis, and Chip Bamberger. "Airline Networks and Fares." Unpublished manuscript, 1996.

Carlton, Dennis W., Robert H. Gertner, and Andrew M. Rosenfield. "Communication Among Competitors: Game Theory and Antitrust." *George Mason Law Review* 5 (Spring 1997): 423–440.

Farrell, Joseph and Matthew Rabin. "Cheap Talk." *Journal of Economic Perspectives* 10 (Summer 1996): 103–118.

Gertner, Robert H. "Tacit Collusion with Immediate Response: The Role of Asymmetries." Unpublished manuscript, 1994.

Hirsch, James S. "Fliers Discover They Don't Fare Well on the Weekends." *Wall Street Journal*, July 30, 1993, B1.

---

[10]See Hirsch (1993).

PART 3

Vertical and Complementary Market Issues

The Economic and
Legal Context

Vertical and complementary market issues—the business relationships and market structures that affect suppliers (sellers), customers (buyers), and otherwise related firms—have been troublesome areas for both economics and antitrust law. Incomplete analysis and excessive attention to form over substance have, in the past, marred economic and legal thought in this area, with the consequence that false or minor threats to competition have often been subject to attack, while more valid competitive problems have sometimes been ignored.

In the past thirty years, however, there has been a blossoming of sophisticated economic analysis and legal thought concerning such relationships, and these developments have had substantial effects on antitrust enforcement policies, court opinions, and the state of antitrust law. These developments have not been unidirectional. One branch of thought (often associated with the "Chicago School" of economics and legal thinking) has tended to treat vertical and complementary market mergers and arrangements as almost always benign or beneficial. This way of thinking was especially influential on antitrust policy in the late 1970s and the 1980s. But, almost simultaneously, a "counterrevolution" in economic and legal reasoning has led some analysts to be more wary of vertical and complementary market arrangements as potential inhibitors of competition under some circumstances. The case studies here in Part 3 are testaments to these sophisticated and varied developments.

ECONOMIC THEORY

For a better understanding of vertical arrangements, a discussion of a few key concepts is warranted.[1] One useful concept is vertical integration: the

---

[1]Useful overviews can be found in Katz (1989) and Perry (1989).

combining of two or more vertically related production processes under the auspices of one ownership-and-control entity. There are at least two ambiguities that immediately arise: First, any given production process is capable of being divided into narrower, vertically related processes that, in principle if not in practice, could be handled by separate entities in a supplier-customer relationship to each other.[2] Second, though vertical relationships are frequently referenced in terms of "upstream" and "downstream," these relationships can easily be reversed. For example, though manufacturers typically sell their goods to distributors and retailers (who in turn sell to the public), the former could as easily (and sometimes do) "buy" distributional and retailing services from the latter (e.g., paying a fee or commission) while retaining ownership of the goods until they are sold to the public.[3] What is "upstream" and what is "downstream"?

These ambiguities have important implications. First, there is no inherently "natural" level of vertical integration. Instead, various levels of vertical integration (or, conversely, of vertical specialization) are likely to arise according to the efficiency and profitability that firms perceive from various arrangements. In turn, these outcomes are likely to be driven by the state of technology, entrepreneurial expertise, factor costs, and many legal arrangements (e.g., tax laws), as well as any opportunities for exploiting market power through vertical integration. Second, there is no inherently "natural" direction of flow of intermediate goods and services in the production processes that create finished products that are sold to final users. Instead, the direction of the flows will be determined by many of the same idiosyncratic technological and institutional features of an economy.[4]

Vertical integration can occur through the merging of two previously independent entities or through the de novo expansion of an existing firm into vertically related areas.

At the opposite pole from vertical integration is the interaction of buyers and sellers in a spot market, with one-at-a-time transactions. In between these two extremes is a wide range of vertical arrangements, agreed to by both parties, that limit the behavior of one or both and that thereby, in essence, achieve partial degrees of vertical integration. These arrangements include long-term contracts, franchising, licensing, tying, exclusive dealing, requirements contracts, full-line forcing, territorial restraints, and resale price maintenance. Many of these same arrangements arise in the

---

[2]In essence, any production process can be divided into a set of "make or buy" decisions, with the "make" decision implying vertical integration and the "buy" decision indicating otherwise.

[3]Equivalently, a farmer can sell his wheat to the local grain elevator (storage) operator (who in turn sells to the flour mill); or the farmer can rent space from the elevator operator while retaining ownership of the wheat.

[4]Despite the ambiguities, we will (for simplicity and because of their familiarity) use the terms *upstream* and *downstream* in the discussion that follows. However, since vertically related components are usually complements in the production process, an alternative approach is simply to refer to and deal with them as complements. See Economides and White (1994).

case of entities that are related, but not necessarily in a traditional vertical sense. Their products or production processes may be complementary, giving rise to similar opportunities and incentives to engage in tying, requirements contracts, bundling, and so on.

Before the 1960s there had been little rigorous economic analysis and little understanding of these practices or of vertical integration itself. The general attitude toward them was, at best, one of ambivalence: a recognition that they could contribute to efficiency, but also a strong suspicion (sometimes borne of confusion between form and function) that they were frequently the tools for the creation or enhancement of market power, primarily through "foreclosure": the fear that the vertically integrated entity would favor itself (i.e., its vertically integrated affiliates), thereby disadvantaging its rivals (cutting them off from suppliers or distributors) and enhancing its own market power.[5]

More recent analyses have shed much better light on these practices of partial or complete vertical integration and have shown that they can represent efficient reactions to market imperfections, such as externalities, free-riding, informational limitations, and the limitations of formal contract arrangements.[6] Resale price maintenance, for example, may be a way by which a manufacturer can induce point-of-sale services from its retailers, each of whom might otherwise be tempted to free-ride on the services of the others. Territorial restraints may allow a manufacturer to avoid duplication of selling effort and free-riding among its geographically dispersed retailers. Exclusive dealing may be a way that manufacturers can achieve focused efforts by their retailers and prevent free-riding by other manufacturers. Long-term contracts provide both parties with greater levels of certainty, which can be valuable for planning and investment. Tying can be a means of ensuring quality and improved overall performance of a product or service. Franchising and other licensing arrangements can allow the originators of an idea to extend its use and maintain quality control over its use, without the necessity of engaging in the direct production (in which they may have little relevant expertise) themselves. Vertical integration itself is a way of securing greater control over production processes, internalizing externalities, and overcoming informational deficiencies. Under some circumstances, it is also a way of overcoming the problem of "successive monopoly" or "double marginalization"[7]: When an upstream firm with market power sells an item to a downstream firm, the former will include its profit margin in its price; this causes the downstream firm to "see" its input costs as being excessively high, which in turn will cause its prices to be inefficiently high.

---

[5]See, for example, Kaysen and Turner (1959, pp. 120, 126, 133, and 159); see also White (1989).

[6]See, for example, Telser (1960), Posner (1976), Klein et al. (1978), White (1981), Marvel (1982), Williamson (1983), Klein and Saft (1985), Klein and Murphy (1988), O'Brien and Shaffer (1992), Innes and Sexton (1994), Deneckere et al. (1996), and Butz (1997).

[7]See Tirole (1988, ch. 4).

At the same time, however, these practices may be vehicles for the enhancement of market power or the more effective exploitation of that power.[8] Many of the practices can be used to practice price discrimination, which will increase profits (but with social welfare consequences, in terms of creation of deadweight loss, that are ambiguous[9]); for example, territorial exclusivity arrangements may make it easier for a manufacturer to charge higher prices in some areas (where demand is perceived to be less elastic) than in others. Other practices may raise barriers to entry or otherwise raise costs to actual or potential rivals. Exclusive dealing arrangements, by allowing a manufacturer to restrict the access of other manufacturers to its retailers, may raise costs to its rivals or may make entry difficult, if the supply of retailing services is an important bottleneck for that line of products; long-term contracts may achieve the same end. The tying of a complementary product (e.g., a manufacturer's insistence on the purchase of a complementary item, such as spare parts or servicing) may allow it to raise prices for the combined package.[10] Under certain circumstances, some of these practices may simply be a cover for horizontal collusion among manufacturers or retailers, either to raise prices directly or to raise entry barriers to potential rivals.[11] Complete vertical integration itself may raise entry barriers or enhance market power. A dominant upstream firm may be able to disadvantage its upstream rivals by integrating downstream and reducing the latter's access to distribution (or equivalently, a dominant downstream firm may integrate upstream and disadvantage its downstream rivals by reducing their access to suppliers).

These uses of vertical practices or structure to achieve anticompetitive ends require the actual or potential presence of market power (individually or collectively), including impediments to entry in the areas affected.[12] Accordingly, benign consequences can be presumed in many circumstances in which market power is absent, creating "safe harbors" for policy. If an individual seller's market share is such that market power is unlikely, and joint exercise of market power with other sellers is unlikely (or none of the other sellers is engaging in the practice), then any vertical arrangement between that seller and its downstream customers (including a manufacturer's resale price maintenance agreement with its retailers, or its own entry into retailing) is unlikely to have anticompetitive

---

[8] See, for example, Burstein (1960a, 1960b), Vernon and Graham (1971), Hay (1973), Schmalensee (1973), Warren-Boulton (1974), Westfield (1981), Salop and Scheffman (1983, 1987), Scherer (1983), Comanor (1985), Comanor and Frech (1985), Aghion and Bolton (1987), Salinger (1988), Hart and Tirole (1990), Ordover et al. (1990), Whinston (1990), and Rasmusen et al. (1991).

[9] See Schmalensee (1981) and Kwoka (1984).

[10] See the discussion by Jeffrey MacKie-Mason of the *Kodak* case, Case 16 in this volume.

[11] Resale price maintenance, for example, appears to have acquired a bad image among many economists largely because it was a vehicle for horizontal price fixing among pharmacists and other small retailers during the 1930s.

[12] The presence of economies of scale is also often a component of the models that demonstrate the potential anticompetitive effects of vertical arrangements.

consequences. This approach thus calls for closer analysis only when the entity in question may be able to exercise market power individually or the practice appears among a group of firms who may be able to exercise market power collectively.

This approach depends critically on a correct delineation of the appropriate market for the determination of market shares and the potential for market power. Unfortunately, the market definition paradigm established by the 1982 *Merger Guidelines* is useful primarily for assessing the possibility of the *prospective* exercise of market power consequent to a *proposed* merger; it has far less value for establishing the relevant market's boundaries when market power is suspected of already being exercised (e.g., a firm that is already employing a vertical restraint). To understand this point, it is important to remember that a monopolist maintains prices at levels at which some potential customers (who would buy at lower, competitive prices) have turned to alternatives; in essence, the monopolist maintains prices at levels that bring it into competition with rivals that would likely not be considered to be in the market if prices were at lower (competitive) levels.[13] This dilemma of delineating the relevant market in situations where market power is already being exercised is one that has not yet been satisfactorily resolved for antitrust policy.

ANTITRUST LAW

A broad range of the antitrust laws' provisions has been used to attack vertical and complementary market arrangements. The Sherman Act's Section 1 language of "contract, combination . . . or conspiracy in restraint of trade . . ." has been used to challenge resale price maintenance arrangements and territorial restrictions and other nonprice restraints. The Act's Section 2 language of "monopolize" has been used to challenge vertical restraints and vertical integration itself. The Clayton Act's Section 3 specifically forbids contracts imposing a restraint whereby the customer "shall not use or deal in the goods . . . supplies, or other commodities of a competitor of the lessor or seller" where the effect "may be substantially to lessen competition or tend to create a monopoly." In addition, Section 7 of the Clayton Act has been used to challenge mergers between vertically related firms.

---

[13]In antitrust analysis, this is frequently described as the "cellophane" problem, referring to the 1956 case that focused on the question of whether Du Pont had a monopoly over cellophane. The defense claimed (and the Supreme Court agreed) that the appropriate market for analysis was "flexible wrapping materials," in which Du Pont's cellophane had only a small share. But, if Du Pont did have a monopoly over cellophane, it would have maintained prices at high enough levels so that some of its potential customers would instead be buying other flexible wrapping materials and there would be significant cross-elasticities of demand at the elevated cellophane price. See *U.S. v. E. I. Du Pont de Nemours and Co.*, 351 U.S. 377 (1956); see also Stocking and Mueller (1955).

For the discussion that follows, it is useful to classify the antitrust treatment of vertical and complementary market relationships into four areas: vertical integration, restraints involving prices, territorial restraints, and other nonprice restraints.

Vertical Integration

Section 2 of the Sherman Act has been used, albeit sparingly, to attack vertical integration that appeared to promote or enhance market power. The 1911 *Standard Oil*[14] decision resulted in vertical dissolution (e.g., oil pipelines being separated from refineries) as well as horizontal dismemberment (refineries in different geographic regions were separated into independent companies). The 1948 *Paramount*[15] case resulted in the separation of movie exhibition (theaters) from distribution and production. The Federal Trade Commission's suit against the integrated petroleum companies,[16] filed in 1973 but dismissed in the early 1980s, was aimed in part at their vertical integration. The Justice Department's *AT&T* case[17] was largely based on the theory that AT&T's vertical integration encompassing local exchange service, long-distance service, and equipment manufacturing, when buttressed by local and national economic regulation, created competitive distortions. Also, the 1980s investigations of airlines' computerized reservation systems by the Civil Aeronautics Board and then the Department of Transportation[18] was an important effort to come to terms with a new (vertically related) technology in a recently deregulated industry.

Section 7 of the Clayton Act has been used to prevent vertical integration through merger. Even before Section 7 was strengthened in 1950, the Department of Justice (DOJ) was able successfully to challenge a substantial stock ownership position by General Motors in its major supplier of paints and finishes, Du Pont.[19] In the heyday of the antitrust enforcement agencies' merger-prohibition victories of the 1960s, vertical mergers (as well as horizontal mergers) were regularly challenged and stopped.[20] The DOJ's 1968 *Merger Guidelines* devoted a quarter of that document to vertical mergers, specifying the market shares of the supplier and of the customer in their respective markets that would generate a challenge by the DOJ to the merger.

---

[14]*United States* v. *Standard Oil Co. of New Jersey et al.*, 221 U.S. 1 (1911).

[15]*United States* v. *Paramount Pictures Inc., et al.*, 334 U.S. 131 (1948).

[16]*In the matter of Exxon Corporation et al.*, docket no. 8934, complaint filed January 24, 1973.

[17]For a discussion, see Noll and Owen (1994).

[18]See Guerin-Calvert (1994).

[19]*United States* v. *E. I. Du Pont de Nemours and Co. et al.*, 353 U.S. 586 (1957).

[20]See *Brown Shoe Co.* v. *United States,* 370 U.S. 294 (1962); *Reynolds Metals Co.* v. *Federal Trade Commission,* 309 F.2d. 223 (1962); and *Ford Motor Co.* v. *United States,* 405 U.S. 362 (1972).

By the 1980s and 1990s, however, the new economics developments were reflected in the enforcement policies of the two antitrust agencies. The DOJ's 1982 and 1984 *Merger Guidelines* devoted less than a fifth of their lengths to vertical mergers, and their tone was far less hostile than that of the 1968 version; the 1992 *Merger Guidelines* did not mention vertical mergers at all. Few such cases were brought by the enforcement agencies.[21] The Federal Trade Commission (FTC) initiated but then dismissed its challenge to the integrated petroleum companies. At the same time, however, as the *AT&T* case indicated, the DOJ was prepared to "litigate to the eyeballs"[22] a challenge to vertical integration under some circumstances.[23] Also, as two of the cases in this part indicate,[24] the FTC in the mid-1990s was sufficiently concerned about the vertical aspects of some mergers that it was prepared to examine them closely and insist on some remedial provisions.[25]

Resale Price Maintenance

In the 1911 *Dr. Miles Medical Co.*[26] case, the Supreme Court declared that resale price maintenance (RPM) was a per se violation of the Sherman Act's Section 1 prohibition of "every contract, combination, . . . or conspiracy in restraint of trade. . . ." That view has been repeated in a series of decisions, including the important 1984 *Monsanto*[27] decision, discussed by Frederick Warren-Boulton in this Part (Case 15). This per se approach means that RPM is treated in the same way that horizontal price fixing among competitors is treated: If a plaintiff can convince a judge or jury that the defendant engaged in RPM, the plaintiff wins; any evidence that the defendant might offer as to its small market share or the efficiencies of the practice are irrelevant.

In 1937, the Congress passed the Miller-Tydings Act, which legalized RPM—"fair trade"—on a state-option basis. It appears that most of the sentiment supporting the legalization of RPM came from small retailers, who saw RPM as a way of checking the spread of larger retailers (since

---

[21]See White (1985) for a discussion of one of the few vertical mergers that was challenged by the DOJ.

[22]This was a statement by William Baxter, the Assistant Attorney General for Antitrust in 1981, at a crucial point in the litigation; see Temin (1987, p. 230).

[23]The Bell Atlantic-NYNEX Merger case, discussed by Steven Brenner in Case 5 of this volume, had some of the same vertical issues, but much of antitrust concern in that case was the horizontal issue of Bell Atlantic as a potential competitor into NYNEX's local service areas.

[24]See Case 18 by Philip Nelson and Robert Stoner and Case 19 by Stanley Besen and colleagues.

[25]It is interesting to note that both of the mergers discussed in this Part had aspects that made their structures similar to the *AT&T* problem: Time Warner is extensively involved in local regulated monopoly cable television franchises; Lockheed Martin sells much of its output to the U.S. Department of Defense, which places regulation-like limits on the profits that its suppliers can earn.

[26]*Dr. Miles Medical Co. v. John D. Park and Sons Co.*, 220 U.S. 373 (1911).

[27]*Monsanto Co. v. Spray-Rite Service Corporation*, 465 U.S. 752 (1984).

the latter would be forbidden from selling at lower prices than the former); in essence, this was providing a legal cover for horizontal price fixing among the retailers. This exemption from the application of the Sherman Act was repealed by Congress in 1975, however, and *Dr. Miles Medical Co.*'s per se prohibition still stands as prevailing law. However, in 1997 the Supreme Court declared that cases involving vertical *maximum price fixing* (e.g., the manufacturer specifies a maximum price, above which a retailer is not allowed to stray) should be judged under a rule of reason.[28]

The new economic developments, though, influenced enforcement policy in the 1980s in this area as well, and the two enforcement agencies did not bring any cases challenging unilateral imposition of RPM by an upstream entity on its downstream distributor.[29] The two agencies would likely challenge any RPM arrangement that they believed to be a cover for a collusive horizontal price-fixing agreement, however, and private antitrust challenges to perceived RPM arrangements are still a potent enforcement force.

Territorial Restraints

The legal area of territorial vertical restraints represents one of the major turnarounds of the Supreme Court, at least partially in response to the new economic developments.[30] In 1963, in response to the DOJ's challenge to White Motor's imposition of territorial (and customer classification) restraints on its distributors, the Court said, in essence, "We're not sure about these practices," and declined to condemn them as per se violations of Section 1 of the Sherman Act.[31] Four years later, in response to the DOJ's challenge to similar restraints by Schwinn, the Court had become "sure" and condemned them as per se offenses.[32] But in 1977, the Court reversed itself and declared in the *GTE Sylvania*[33] case that these practices should be judged under the more lenient rule-of-reason approach, in which the relative

---

[28]*State Oil Co.* v. *Khan*, 66 L.W. 4001 (1997). This decision overruled an earlier Supreme Court decision, *Albrecht* v. *Herald Co.*, 390 U.S. 145 (1968), which had declared maximum RPM to be a per se violation in the tradition of *Dr. Miles Medical Co.*

[29]Also, the DOJ entered an amicus brief in the *Monsanto* case, urging the Supreme Court to reassess its position on RPM. And the DOJ and the FTC entered a joint amicus brief in *State Oil Co.* that urged the Court to adopt the rule-of-reason approach for maximum RPM that the Court did indeed choose.

[30]Indeed, it is this turnaround in the area of territorial restraints that keeps alive the hope by those who are sympathetic to RPM as a device that can be used to enhance efficiency that the Supreme Court will eventually reverse its *Dr. Miles Medical Co.* position on RPM and, at least, substitute a "rule-of-reason" requirement for its current per se illegal approach. The Court's 1997 turnaround on maximum RPM in *State Oil Co.* will surely fan those hopes further.

[31]*White Motor Co.* v. *United States*, 372 U.S. 253 (1963).

[32]*United States* v. *Arnold, Schwinn and Co. et al.*, 388 U.S. 365 (1967).

[33]*Continental T.V.* v. *GTE Sylvania*, 433 U.S. 36 (1977); for a discussion of the case, see Preston (1994).

advantages and disadvantages of the practice need to be weighed. This tolerant view was echoed by the Court in its 1984 *Monsanto* decision, although that decision simultaneously reiterated the Court's hostile view of RPM.

Enforcement policy has embraced this new tolerance. In 1985, the DOJ issued a set of *Vertical Restraints Guidelines,* which indicated that the DOJ would be unlikely to challenge these arrangements in settings where market power was unlikely to be present.[34] There apparently have been no enforcement agency challenges to these practices, though private challenges are still present.

Other Nonprice Restraints

Until the mid-1970s, the Supreme Court and the antitrust enforcement agencies showed a general hostility to tying, exclusive dealing, and other nonprice vertical restraints that could be challenged under Section 2 of the Sherman Act and Section 3 of the Clayton Act. Since then, however, the Court has been moving toward greater tolerance and leniency. The Court's rejection of tying claims in the 1984 *Jefferson Parish*[35] case (see William Lynk's discussion in Case 14 in this Part) is indicative of this new tolerance, although the Court (by a narrow 5-to-4 vote) declined to move tying from a per se violation category to a rule-of-reason category. However, in what may be a major departure, in the 1992 *Kodak*[36] case the Court declined to grant summary judgment to Kodak, which was accused of tying repair services to the sale of its high-speed photocopy machines (see the discussion by Jeffrey MacKie-Mason and John Metzler in Case 16 in this part); Kodak was subsequently found guilty of tying by a jury, and the verdict was upheld by the Ninth Circuit Court of Appeals.

Enforcement has here also embraced this new tolerance readily, and the DOJ's 1985 *Vertical Restraint Guidelines* again provided a wide area of forbearance for situations where market power is unlikely to be exercised. However, in 1994 the DOJ challenged Microsoft's use of vertical restraints and negotiated a consent decree in which Microsoft agreed to cease the practice (see Richard Gilbert's discussion in Case 17 in this part). And private antitrust plaintiffs continue to bring challenges to a wide variety of vertical restraints.[37]

THE CASES

Though the Supreme Court continues to label tying as a per se violation of the antitrust laws, the Court has also found exceptions to a strict application

[34] These *Vertical Restraints Guidelines* were withdrawn in 1993, however.

[35] *Jefferson Parish Hospital District No. 2 v. Edwin G. Hyde,* 466 U.S. 2 (1984).

[36] *Image Technical Service, Inc., et al. v. Eastman Kodak Co.,* 504 U.S. 451 (1992).

[37] As MacKie-Mason and Metzler note, there have been six other Circuit Court decisions in private cases in the mid-1990s on just *Kodak*-like issues alone.

of the per se approach. William Lynk's discussion of the *Jefferson Parish* case, decided by the Court in 1984, highlights the ambiguities of determining the presence of tying and distinguishing it from the similar phenomenon of exclusive dealing (which is subject to a rule-of-reason approach). Lynk also indicates the crucial roles played by market delineation and by the Court's determination that the defendant did not have market power in leading the Court to decide that the defendant was not engaged in illegal tying in this case. Though the Court was unanimous in its decision that the defendant was not guilty, only a narrow majority of five justices (out of nine) wanted to keep the per se standard; the minority announced that it was ready to adopt a "rule-of-reason" approach.

Resale price maintenance represents the area where the Supreme Court has maintained the toughest stance toward vertical practices, insisting on a per se standard. The 1984 *Monsanto* case gave the Supreme Court an opportunity to reexamine the legal issues surrounding RPM. Frederick Warren-Boulton provides the details of this case and sets out the arguments as to why RPM generally, as well as the specific behavior of Monsanto that was at issue, may be procompetitive and socially beneficial, despite the Court's adverse decision.

The Supreme Court had another opportunity to examine tying when it decided the *Kodak* case in 1992. As Jeffrey MacKie-Mason and John Metzler indicate, Kodak was accused of tying repair services to its sale of high-speed photocopy machines. Early in the fact-finding process, Kodak moved for summary judgment: In essence, Kodak was arguing that even if all of the facts gathered by the plaintiffs were accepted as true, the plaintiffs could not as a matter of law win their case. The Court decided that Kodak had not satisfied its burden at that stage of the proceedings, so the lawsuit continued. Kodak subsequently lost a jury trial, and the Ninth Circuit Court of Appeals upheld that jury verdict. Throughout this proceeding, the questions of market delineation were important: Were high-speed photocopiers a separate market? Should sales and repair services be considered to be separate markets, or were they fundamentally a linked system? Was Kodak constrained by competition and the knowledge and sophistication of its customers in its pricing of the composite bundle of copier and repair services? Or did it have the flexibility and capability to charge higher prices and extract higher profits in the repair market?

Microsoft accounts for over 80 percent of the operating systems sold on PCs and over 90 percent of the operating systems on Intel-based PCs. In 1994 the DOJ challenged Microsoft's contracts with its customers (the PC manufacturers) and with the suppliers of complementary components (software developers), arguing that these vertical arrangements raised the costs of Microsoft's rivals in operating systems and raised barriers to entry. Microsoft acceded and signed a consent decree agreeing to modify the contracts so as to make them less restrictive. The Department did not, however, address the vertical integration between operating system and software applications that has been the source of many of Microsoft's software application rivals. Their legal challenge to the consent decree held up its final approval by the district court for almost a year. Richard Gilbert lays out the pro's and con's of this case, pointing toward the continuing controversy and litigation that are likely to continue to surround Microsoft and its vertical practices. One such example is the DOJ's October 1997 claim that Microsoft had violated the consent decree by bundling its Internet browser with its Windows 95 operating system and requiring the PC manufacturers to accept them as a bundle.

Since the end of the Cold War in the late 1980s, the U.S. defense budget has been shrinking as a percentage of U.S. gross domestic product, implying a shrinking of markets for defense contractors. One important response by the defense industry has been a breathtaking series of mergers. As Philip Nelson and Robert Stoner note in their discussion of the 1995 merger of Lockheed and Martin Marietta, thirty-five notable mergers occurred in the years 1994–1997 alone. These mergers have often presented both horizontal and vertical issues. The Defense Department has encouraged much of this consolidation as a necessary rationalization and cost-reducing process, and usually feels that it can maintain an adequate amount of competition among contractors even when only two are left in the field. But the vertical issues, as Nelson and Stoner demonstrate, can be thorny. In the case of Lockheed Martin, horizontal issues did not prove to be troublesome; but the FTC was concerned about the confidential (proprietary) information that the merged firm might learn from its (vertically related) suppliers and customers that it might then use to favor its own (vertically related) subsidiaries, and the FTC's consent order included provisions that the FTC hoped would reduce such possibilities.

In 1996 the FTC, after a twelve-month investigation, approved the merger of Time Warner and Turner Broadcasting. As the discussion by Stanley Besen and his four coauthors indicates, both horizontal and vertical issues were raised by this case. In the former area, there was competitive overlap between some of the programming services of the two organizations. In the latter area, the FTC was concerned that the Time Warner cable systems (Time Warner is the nation's second-largest operator of cable systems, serving about 15 percent of all subscribers) would unduly favor Turner's programming services and disadvantage other programming services and was also concerned that TCI (the nation's largest cable television operator, serving 25 percent of all subscribers), which owned 23 percent of Turner, would become a 9-percent owner of Time Warner (and could become an 18 percent owner); this latter link might further raise the barriers to new entry in programming services and also raise the barriers to alternative systems of program distribution, such as direct broadcasting from satellites. In the consent decree that accompanied its approval of the merger, the FTC addressed only these vertical issues and placed restrictions on the behavior of the merged entity that the FTC hoped would limit the likelihood of market foreclosure.

These six studies, written by economists who participated in each case, provide illuminating discussions of the useful role that economics arguments played in these important antitrust cases.

REFERENCES

Aghion, Phillippe, and Patrick Bolton. "Contracts as a Barrier to Entry." *American Economic Review* 77 (June 1987): 388–401.

Burstein, Meyer L. "The Economics of Tie-In Sales." *Review of Economics and Statistics* 42 (February 1960a): 48–73.

Burstein, Meyer L. "A Theory of Full-Line Forcing." *Northwestern University Law Review* 55 (1960b): 62–95.

Butz, David A. "Vertical Price Controls with Uncertain Demand." *Journal of Law & Economics* 40 (October 1997): 433–459.

Comanor, William S. "Vertical Price-Fixing, Vertical Market Restrictions, and the New Antitrust Policy." *Harvard Law Review* 98 (March 1985): 983–1002.

Comanor, William S., and H. E. Frech III. "The Competitive Effects of Vertical Agreements." *American Economic Review* 75 (June 1985): 539–546.

Deneckere, Raymond, Howard P. Marvel, and James Peck. "Demand Uncertainty, Inventories, and Resale Price Maintenance." *Quarterly Journal of Economics* 111 (August 1996): 885–914.

Economides, Nicholas, and Lawrence J. White. "Networks and Compatibility: Implications for Antitrust." *European Economic Review* 38 (April 1994): 651–662.

Guerin-Calvert, Margaret. "Vertical Integration as a Threat to Competition: Airline Computer Reservation Systems (1992)." In *The Antitrust Revolution: The Role of Economics*, edited by John E. Kwoka, Jr. and Lawrence J. White, 432–468. 2d ed. New York: Oxford University Press, 1994.

Hart, Oliver, and Jean Tirole. "Vertical Integration and Market Forclosure." *Brookings Papers on Economic Activity: Microeconomics* (1990): 205–276.

Hay, George A. "An Economic Analysis of Vertical Integration." *Industrial Organization Review* 1 (1973): 188–198.

Innes, Robert, and Richard Sexton. "Strategic Buyers and Exclusionary Contracts." *American Economic Review* 84 (June 1994): 566–584.

Katz, Michael L. "Vertical Contractual Relations." In *Handbook of Industrial Organization*, edited by Richard Schmalensee and Robert Willig, 655–721. Amsterdam: North-Holland, 1989.

Kaysen, Carl, and Donald F. Turner. *Antitrust Policy: An Economic and Legal Analysis.* Cambridge, Mass.: Harvard University Press, 1959.

Klein, Benjamin, Robert A. Crawford, and Armen A. Alchian. "Vertical Integration, Appropriable Rents, and the Competitive Contracting Process." *Journal of Law & Economics* 21 (October 1978): 297–326.

Klein, Benjamin, and Kevin M. Murphy. "Vertical Restraints as Contract Enforcement Mechanisms." *Journal of Law & Economics* 31 (October 1988): 265–297.

Klein, Benjamin, and Lester F. Saft. "The Law and Economics of Franchise Tying Contracts." *Journal of Law & Economics* 28 (May 1985): 345–361.

Kwoka, John E., Jr. "Output and Allocative Efficiency Under Second Degree Price Discrimination." *Economic Inquiry* 22 (April 1984): 282–286.

Marvel, Howard P. "Exclusive Dealing." *Journal of Law & Economics* 25 (April 1982): 1–25.

Noll, Roger G., and Bruce M. Owen. "The Anticompetitive Uses of Regulation: *United States* v. *AT&T* (1982)." In *The Antitrust Revolution: The Role of Economics,* edited by John E. Kwoka, Jr., and Lawrence J. White, 328–375. 2d ed. New York: Oxford University Press, 1994.

O'Brien, Daniel P., and Greg Shaffer. "Vertical Control with Bilateral Contracts." *Rand Journal of Economics* 23 (Autumn 1992): 299–308.

Ordover, Janusz, Garth Saloner, and Steven C. Salop. " Equilibrium Vertical Foreclosure." *American Economic Review* 80 (March 1990): 127–142.

Perry, Martin K. "Vertical Integration: Determinants and Effects." In *Handbook of Industrial Organization*, edited by Richard Schmalensee and Robert Willig, 183–255. Amsterdam: North-Holland, 1989.

Posner, Richard A. *Antitrust Law: An Economic Perspective*. Chicago: University of Chicago Press, 1976.

Preston, Lee E. "Territorial Restraints: *GTE Sylvania* (1977)." In *The Antitrust Revolution: The Role of Economics*, edited by John E. Kwoka, Jr., and Lawrence J. White, 311–327. 2d ed. New York: Oxford University Press, 1994.

Rasmusen, Eric, Mark Ramseyer, and John Wiley, Jr. "Naked Exclusion." *American Economic Review* 81 (December 1991): 1137–1145.

Salinger, Michael. "Vertical Mergers and Foreclosure." *Quarterly Journal of Economic* 103 (May 1988): 345–356.

Salop, Steven C., and David T. Scheffman. "Raising Rivals' Costs." *American Economic Review* 73 (May 1983): 267–271.

Salop, Steven C., and David T. Scheffman. "Cost-Raising Strategies." *Journal of Industrial Economics* 36 (September 1987): 19–34.

Scherer, F. M. "The Economics of Vertical Restraints." *Antitrust Law Journal* 52 (1983): 687–707.

Schmalensee, Richard. "A Note on the Theory of Vertical Integration." *Journal of Political Economy* 81 (March/April 1973): 442–449.

Schmalensee, Richard. "Output and Welfare Implications of Monopolistic Third-Degree Price Discrimination." *American Economic Review* 71 (March 1981): 242–247.

Stocking, George W., and Willard F. Mueller. "The Cellophane Case and the New Competition." *American Economic Review* 45 (March 1955): 29–63.

Telser, Lester G. "Why Should Manufacturers Want Fair Trade?" *Journal of Law & Economics* 3 (October 1960): 86–105.

Temin, Peter. *The Fall of the Bell System: A Study in Prices and Politics.* New York: Cambridge University Press, 1987.

Tirole, Jean. *The Theory of Industrial Organization.* Cambridge, Mass.: MIT Press, 1988.

Vernon, John M., and Daniel A. Graham. "Profitability of Monopolization by Vertical Integration." *Journal of Political Economy* 79 (July/August 1971): 924–925.

Warren-Boulton, Frederick R. "Vertical Control with Variable Proportions." *Journal of Political Economy* 82 (July/August 1974): 783–802.

Westfield, Frederick M. "Vertical Integration: Does Product Price Rise or Fall?" *American Economic Review* 71 (June 1981): 334–346.

Whinston, Michael. "Tying, Foreclosure, and Exclusion." *American Economic Review* 80 (September 1990): 837–859.

White, Lawrence J. "Vertical Restraints in Antitrust Law: A Coherent Model." *Antitrust Bulletin* 26 (Summer 1981): 327–345.

White, Lawrence J. "Antitrust and Video Markets: The Merger of Showtime and the Movie Channel as a Case Study." In *Video Media Competition: Regulation, Economics and Technology,* edited by Eli M. Noam, 338–363. New York: Columbia University Press, 1985.

White, Lawrence J. "The Revolution in Antitrust Analysis of Vertical Relationships: How Did We Get from There to Here?" In *Economics and Antitrust Policy*, edited by Robert J. Larner and James W. Meehan, 103–121. New York: Quorum, 1989.

Williamson, Oliver E. "Credible Commitments: Using Hostages to Support Exchange." *American Economic Review* 73 (September 1983): 519–540.

CASE 14

Tying and Exclusive Dealing:
Jefferson Parish Hospital v. *Hyde* (1984)

William J. Lynk

INTRODUCTION

Tying—a producer's decision to link the sale of one product or service to another—is a frequent phenomenon in the marketplace. It has also posed difficult antitrust issues for the courts. An important tying case that was ultimately decided by the Supreme Court in 1984—*Jefferson Parish Hospital* v. *Hyde*—provides a good illustration of these difficulties.

JEFFERSON PARISH: THE FACTS

In the late 1960s, Jefferson Parish,[1] Louisiana, decided to build a new hospital, and in 1971 it opened the East Jefferson Hospital in the New Orleans suburb of Metairie. Shortly before commencing operations, the hospital contracted with Roux & Associates, a recently formed firm of anesthesiologists, to provide for all of the hospital's anesthesia requirements. The hospital was to provide all of the necessary space, equipment, supplies, and, subject to Roux's approval, nurses. Roux, in turn, was to provide all of the anesthesiologists. The hospital apparently prospered; by 1980 over 10,000 surgical operations per year were performed there.

The dispute that eventually resulted in this case began in July of 1977, when Dr. Edwin G. Hyde approached the hospital for privileges. Dr. Hyde

William J. Lynk served as an economic consultant to counsel for Jefferson Parish Hospital during the Supreme Court phase of this case. Dennis Carlton, Frank Easterbrook, and the editors provided extremely helpful comments, but bear no responsibility for any remaining errors or omissions.

[1]A parish in Louisiana is the same as a county in most other states.

was a board-certified anesthesiologist, and Dr. Hyde wanted to practice anesthesiology at East Jefferson Hospital. The hospital's board of directors denied Dr. Hyde's application, indicating that to grant him privileges would be inconsistent with its intent to use only Roux for anesthesia services. Dr. Hyde then sued under, among other laws, Section 1 of the Sherman Act, seeking an injunction that would compel his admission to the medical staff.

Dr. Hyde and East Jefferson Hospital had their day in court not once, but three times. In 1981, the U.S. District Court for the Eastern District of Louisiana heard all of the evidence—testimony and documentary exhibits—and considered the arguments of each side's lawyers. The District Court denied Dr. Hyde's request, first finding that East Jefferson Hospital lacked any significant monopoly power in hospital services and then reasoning that therefore its contract with Roux was competitively innocuous.[2]

Dr. Hyde appealed, and in 1982 the same evidence led the Fifth Circuit Court of Appeals to the opposite conclusion. The Court of Appeals found that the hospital *did* have monopoly power and that its contract with Roux & Associates constituted a "tying arrangement," one in which the patient was forced to use Roux's anesthesia services if he or she wanted to use East Jefferson's operating rooms.[3] Concluding that that was per se illegal, the Court of Appeals reversed the District Court.

East Jefferson Hospital then appealed to the Supreme Court, which accepted the case for review. Both parties subsequently filed briefs with the Court, joined by amicus curiae ("friend of the court") briefs from interested groups (among others, the American Society of Anesthesiologists, siding with Dr. Hyde, and the American Hospital Association and the U.S. Department of Justice, siding with East Jefferson Hospital). Reversing the Appellate Court's reversal of the District Court, the Supreme Court found in favor of the hospital in its relationship with Roux & Associates.[4]

Jefferson Parish has for over a decade been the leading Supreme Court case on the commercial practice of tying.[5] But *Jefferson Parish* is also a case regulating the permissible range of a hospital's competitive conduct, and to understand it requires at least a stylized understanding of the way in which hospitals compete.[6] Therefore, this chapter first sketches some of the peculiarities of hospital competition and then outlines some of

---

[2]513 F. Supp. 532 (E. D. La. 1981).

[3]686 F.2d 286 (5th Cir. 1982).

[4]466 U.S. 2 (1984).

[5]*Jefferson Parish Hospital District No. 2* v. *Edwin G. Hyde,* 466 U.S. 2 (1984). The Supreme Court amplified its views on tying in the 1992 *Kodak* case, but, perhaps because *Kodak* was confounded with legal and evidentiary issues apart from the analysis of tying as such, *Jefferson Parish* continues to this day to be cited for legal authority on tying. See *Eastman Kodak Co.* v. *Image Technical Services, Inc.,* 112 S.Ct. 2072 (1992), discussed by Jeffrey MacKie-Mason as Case 16 in this volume.

[6]Feldstein (1988, pp. 213–251) and Phelps (1992, pp. 220–280) outline some of the basics of the hospital industry.

the essentials of tying and exclusive dealing as they apply in that context. After those preliminaries, the chapter explains the economic theories and evidence stressed by the litigants and reports their reception by the Court. It concludes with some observations on tying and its treatment under the law.

HOW DO HOSPITALS COMPETE?

The process begins with a typical consumer of hospital services—say, a patient whose medical condition would be improved by surgery. The patient must choose a surgical specialist who will perform the surgery and who in turn must choose the hospital at which the surgery will be performed. The next choice, also generally made by the surgeon rather than the patient, is the array of specific complementary inputs necessary for the surgery; this could include a radiologist to do the preoperative X-rays, a backup surgeon and a team of nurses to assist in the operation, and an anesthesiologist to keep the patient sedated. Only after all of these inputs have been selected will the surgical operation be performed.

A surgical operation is a complex bundle of complementary inputs. Because each input is essential for surgery, there is no demand for any one of these providers' services unless there is a corresponding supply of each of the other providers' services. By extension, the demand for any one provider's service is enhanced by a greater supply—that is, a lower price or higher quality—of the other providers' services.

To set the stage for the *Jefferson Parish* case, it is useful to divide physicians into two camps: admitting physicians and hospital-based physicians. "Admitting physicians" are defined loosely as those physicians (frequently surgeons) who are responsible for the management of the patient's overall course of treatment, including the selection of the hospital. Depending on the patient's illness, admitting physician specialties could run the range from general practice to neurosurgery.

"Hospital-based physicians," on the other hand, never admit patients, or at least not in their capacity as hospital-based physicians. The medical specialists in pathology, radiology, and anesthesiology probably best exemplify the concept. Their job is to be ready on the sidelines to assist the patient-generating "rainmaker"—the admitting physician—with their specialized skills and expertise. Although they may often be more intensively trained in their own medical specialties than are the admitting physicians in theirs, in this analytical framework the hospital-based physicians fall into the same category as the nursing staff and the pharmacy: just one more support input, whose supply the hospital must ensure if it wants to keep the admitting physicians happy.

How does a hospital compete in this sort of environment? It has become an industry bromide to say that "hospitals don't compete for patients, they compete for doctors." The implication is that, since patients usually pick doctors rather than hospitals, the patient admissions will come automatically if the hospital attracts many doctors to its admitting staff. But this answer raises the next question: How, then, does the hospital compete for doctors?

A common, and accurate, answer is that the hospital does so not only by improving the quality of the facility itself, which is under the hospital's direct administrative control, but also by attaching to itself an attractive constellation of all of the *other* complementary inputs that the doctor considers in making the patient-admitting decision but that are not under the hospital's direct control. The hospital competes in the first instance by increasing its own attractiveness: for example, by keeping the operating rooms spotless, the food tasty, and the technological gadgetry extensive and up-to-date. But, as noted above, this by itself is not sufficient; even a state-of-the-art hospital and an assembly of crackerjack admitting surgeons will be hamstrung if the pathologist fumbles the lab tests or all of the anesthesiologists are out playing golf. So the hospital competes further by doing what it can to ensure the reliable and high-quality supply of all of the *other* independent inputs that must be affiliated with it before it can do its job.

For purposes of antitrust analysis, there is a straightforward "buyer and seller" characterization of these relationships. In essence, the hospital "buys" the services of the hospital-based physicians and "sells" its own package of services to the admitting physician. In this framework, the anesthesiologist is an upstream input supplier to the hospital, and the admitting physician (acting as an agent of the patient) is the downstream customer of the hospital. This model of the market process is illustrated in Figure 14-1.

At issue in *Jefferson Parish* is the role that the hospital plays as intervenor between the hospital-based anesthesiologists and the admitting physicians, a role that varies depending on how the hospital chooses to attract its anesthesiologists. At one extreme, the anesthesiologists may be hospital employees, a practice more common forty years ago but relatively rare today. At the other extreme, for an "open-staff" hospital, any qualified anesthesiologist can apply for privileges to be available to the surgeon, thus making his relation to the admitting physician similar to that of the hospital. Finally, for a hospital that arranges for anesthesia through exclusive contract, the contracting firm of anesthesiologists serves at the pleasure of the hospital, just as an individual employee anesthesiologist would, with the distinction that the money received by the anesthesia firm typically comes directly from the patient without passing through the hospital's treasury.

These differences among the alternative ways in which a hospital intermediates the access of the admitting physicians to the hospital-based physicians were what caused the *Jefferson Parish* controversy. They also

FIGURE 14-1 A Model of Hospital Market Relationships.

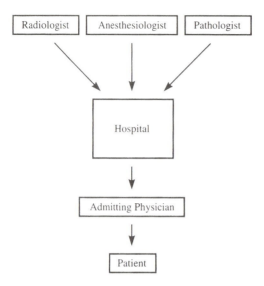

create an analytical issue—the distinction between the practice of tying and the practice of exclusive dealing—that the next section explains.

TYING AND EXCLUSIVE DEALING

Tying

Tying and exclusive dealing are forms of vertical restraint that appear frequently in business relationships. Economic analysis shows them to be somewhat related, but antitrust law has treated them in importantly different ways.

Tying is a practice whereby the seller of product A will sell A only on the condition that the buyer also purchase product B. A is referred to as the "tying product" and B as the "tied product." Most of the tying cases in the legal literature concern "requirements tie-ins," in which the buyer can get product A only if he agrees to purchase all of his requirements of B from the seller. For example, at one time a customer could lease an IBM tabulating machine only by also purchasing all of the necessary punch cards from IBM.[7]

---

[7] *International Business Machines Corp.* v. *U.S.*, 298 U.S. 131 (1936). IBM would only lease, not sell, its tabulating machines and would terminate the lease of any customer found evading the tie-in.

The other principal type of tie-in is a "package tie-in," also called "product bundling." Here the seller defines the product as one unit of A plus one unit of B and will not sell the A component separately. For example, a consumer who buys a Chrysler automobile (product A) gets it with a Chrysler car radio (product B), regardless of whether he or she wants to purchase a radio from a different vendor or even wants a radio at all.[8]

Why tie?[9] There are a number of benign, or at least neutral, explanations for tying. One is that it helps ensure quality; for example, surgeons engage in a form of requirements tying when they insist on using a favorite brand of sutures. Another explanation is that tying lowers transaction costs; for example, automobile manufacturers engage in package tying every time they make some features standard equipment, thereby reducing the number of separate options. In such circumstances, tying ordinarily raises no serious concerns about competitive issues.

There are also less benign explanations for tying, explanations that stress the profitable exploitation of monopoly power. Most prominent among these is tying as a form of price discrimination. Here we must suppose that (1) the seller has monopoly power in product A, the tying product; (2) customers differ in the level of their demands for A; and (3) their demands for product B, the tied product, are correlated with their demands for any given quantity of A. In the earlier IBM illustration, IBM (assumed to have a monopoly in tabulating machines) could have set a single profit-maximizing price, and each customer would pay the same amount per machine. But customers with high demands for tabulating services typically use the tabulating machine more intensively and therefore use more punch cards. So if IBM produces (or buys from a supplier) punch cards, ties them to the sale of its machines, and marks up the price of the cards (with an offsetting price cut on the machines themselves), it will increase its profit from the simple monopoly level to a discriminating monopoly level, by effectively charging higher prices to the more intensive machine users.[10]

Exclusive Dealing

Exclusive dealing is a conceptually distinct practice, although as we will see it can be related to tying. It occurs when a buyer agrees to purchase all of its requirements of a product from a single seller. The initiative for an

---

[8] This practice has in fact generated a number of antitrust complaints; for example, *Town Sound and Custom Tops, Inc.* v. *Chrysler Motors Corp.*, 959 F.2d 468 (3rd Cir. 1992) (Chrysler radios), and *Heatransfer Corp.* v. *Volkswagenwerk, A.G.*, 553 F.2d 964 (5th Cir. 1977) (Volkswagen air conditioners).

[9] For a more extensive discussion of tying, see Carlton and Perloff (1994, pp. 467–479) or Scherer and Ross (1990, pp. 565–569). Its earliest comprehensive treatment is probably Bowman (1957), who credits Aaron Director with developing much of the underlying theory.

[10] At the time of the 1956 antitrust case, IBM's revenues from the cards were one-third of its revenues from the machines. Note that under this method of price discrimination, IBM does not need to identify in advance the customers with high demands for tabulating services.

exclusive dealing arrangement may come from either the seller—who may refuse to sell except on an exclusive basis—or the buyer—who may offer exclusivity to a seller if the seller offers favorable terms.

Why deal exclusively? Here, too, there is no single explanation, and under different circumstances exclusive dealing may have different effects.[11] Economically beneficial explanations often stress the property rights incentives for long-term investment that are fostered by a grant of exclusivity. To illustrate, suppose that a hospital and its radiologists would benefit if the radiologists upgraded the department, but that after the radiologists incurred the necessary sunk costs, the hospital would likely admit numerous additional radiologists to the staff. The resultant dilution of the original radiologists' gains could make the entire sequence unprofitable to the radiologists, and the improvement in quality likely would not be undertaken. But a properly structured contract that prohibits such postcontractual opportunism might permit a deal to be struck, which the absence of exclusive property rights would have prevented.

Exclusive dealing also has its share of "dark side" explanations. Perhaps the most common is that it is a way for sellers to foreclose their competitors' access to customers (or, symmetrically, for buyers to foreclose their competitors' access to input suppliers). As an illustrative story, suppose that the manufacturer of a popular brand of shampoo informs all of the salons to which it sells that it will no longer deal with them unless they use its shampoo exclusively. The salons would rather offer a variety of shampoos, but, forced to choose between the popular brand only or the lesser brands only, each agrees (because it is more profitable) to exclusivity. This cuts off the other shampoo manufacturers' access to the salons and thus increases further the popular brand's share of shampoo sales. Exclusive dealing has much in common with vertical integration and is often characterized as integration through contract rather than through ownership.

THE LEGAL TREATMENT OF TYING AND EXCLUSIVE DEALING

Tying and exclusive dealing are typically treated as distinct phenomena in the economics literature, but the two practices often appear in tandem. Consider a hypothetical example of a common industrial practice. Ford solicits bids for its next year's requirements of tires, and after the bidding, it selects Goodyear as its exclusive supplier. Ford also refuses to sell its new cars without tires; if the consumer wants to buy a Ford, the consumer must also buy the Goodyear tires that come with it. Another tire manufacturer—say, Firestone—may be unhappy with this outcome, but what is the source

---

[11]See Carlton and Perloff (1994, pp. 838–839) or Scherer and Ross (1990, pp. 563–564). Klein, Crawford, and Alchian (1978) and Marvel (1982) provide a more extensive investigation of the subject.

of its unhappiness? Firestone's basic problem is that it does not have practical access (for the term of the contract) to Ford purchasers. But its complaint against Ford could be framed either as opposition to Ford's exclusive dealing—Firestone wants a piece of the action at the factory floor—or to Ford's tying of tires to cars—Firestone wants the business it could get if Ford purchasers could put Firestone tires on their cars (and, of course, have the cost of the Goodyears deleted). In principle, elimination of either practice would give Firestone a chance for some of the business that instead is exclusively Goodyear's.

Although tying and exclusive dealing often arise together, they need not do so in all circumstances. Ford might instead have bought tires from scores of suppliers, without dealing exclusively, and still engaged in tying tires to cars. Conversely, if Ford's independent dealers routinely offered customers a "tire delete" option (perhaps because they also sold tires on the side), then from the consumer's point of view (if not the dealer's) the Ford-Goodyear arrangement would be exclusive dealing but not tying.

The distinction between tying and exclusive dealing is less clear when a hospital enters into an exclusive contract for the provision of hospital-based physician services. If a hospital patient could bring along his favorite anesthesiologist for his surgery, that would eliminate the tying, but it would also necessarily eliminate the exclusivity of the anesthesiology contract. And if another anesthesiologist could obtain staff privileges side-by-side with the contract anesthesiologists and offer his services to patients, that would eliminate the exclusive dealing, but it would also gut the tying arrangement. In short, the disputed practice in *Jefferson Parish* involved both tying and exclusive dealing.

As a matter of economic analysis, this distinction should be only a detail. Whether we call the practice tying, call it exclusive dealing, or call it a banana, the elements of the practice are comprehensible and imply certain economic studies to determine whether the practice is injurious to consumer welfare. In effect, the terminology is not critical to the economic analysis.

Jefferson Parish, however, was not an abstract exercise in economic analysis. It was a lawsuit tried in a U.S. Federal District Court, and there the standards by which legality is judged depend importantly on whether the hospital's exclusive contract is treated as a tying case or as an exclusive dealing case. Tying arrangements up to the time of *Jefferson Parish* (and, we will see, after it) have been judged per se illegal, at least once certain important factual preconditions have been proved. (The most important of these preconditions is that the defendant possess monopoly power in the tying product.) In contrast, exclusive dealing, like other forms of vertical integration, is judged under the rule of reason.[12] Thus, because of the divergence of

---

[12]Other cases, both before and after *Jefferson Parish,* have treated factually similar contracts primarily within a vertical exclusive dealing framework; see, for example, *Dos Santos* v. *Columbus-Cuneo-Cabrini Medical Center,* 684 F.2d 1346 (7th Cir. 1982), and *Collins* v. *Associated Pathologists, Ltd.,* 884 F.2d 473 (7th Cir. 1988).

legal standards in judging tying and exclusive dealing, the parties in this case had an obvious interest in characterizing the challenged practice in different ways.

THE PARTIES' ECONOMIC ARGUMENTS

As could be expected, the plaintiff and the defendant offered substantially different economic analyses to buttress their respective positions in the case.

Dr. Hyde's Position

Dr. Hyde, the plaintiff, sought to establish a number of factual propositions that together would imply that East Jefferson Hospital's contract with Roux & Associates was a per se illegal tying arrangement. The plaintiff also sought to show that the arrangement at issue actually had stifled competition and injured consumer welfare, evidence that would be relevant if the court treated it as a rule-of-reason case.

First, Dr. Hyde wanted to establish that this case was about tying, and not about exclusive dealing. The plaintiff identified three findings that would put the hospital's contract into the tying pigeonhole. The first was that there were in fact two separate products involved, not just one.[13] This, it was said, was obvious on its face. The service provided by the hospital was the maintenance of the surgical operating room, and the service provided by Roux was the provision of anesthesia. The separateness of these services was suggested by the presence of other hospitals in the New Orleans area where anesthesia was provided independently, and billed independently, by anesthesiologists with nonexclusive staff privileges.[14] In fact, Dr. Hyde himself had active privileges in anesthesia at Lakeside, another Metairie hospital.[15] So, the argument concluded, there were two inherently separate products—operating rooms and the professional services of anesthesiologists—that did not need to be bundled together.

That established, Dr. Hyde's next element was to show that the two separate products were in fact tied. On this there was no serious dispute: If a patient wanted surgery at East Jefferson Hospital, he got his anesthesiology from Roux & Associates, or he didn't get it at all. Access to East Jefferson was the tying product, and Roux's anesthesia was the tied product.

The final element that Dr. Hyde needed to establish was that East Jefferson Hospital possessed monopoly power in the tying product. This was a troublesome issue for Dr. Hyde. When the District Court found against

---

[13]Brief for the Respondent, pp. 42–46.

[14]Ibid., p. 42.

[15]Ibid., p. 31.

him, it did so largely because it found that the hospital lacked monopoly power; and when the Appellate Court went the other way, its principal basis was a finding that the District Court was wrong, and that the hospital *did* have monopoly power. In both of those decisions, and in the appeal to the Supreme Court, the principal focus of the monopoly power inquiry was the extent of the relevant geographic market for hospital services and East Jefferson's share of it. The plaintiff's argument urged the Supreme Court to affirm the Appellate Court's finding on this point.[16] That, in the plaintiff's argument, was by itself sufficient to declare the arrangement a violation of the Sherman Act, but the argument went on to detail some of the actual adverse competitive consequences supposedly caused by the arrangement. Among them were that (1) since Roux had a "monopoly" of the anesthesia that flowed through East Jefferson Hospital, patients at that hospital were deprived of their freedom to choose their own anesthesiologist; (2) patients were provided with lower-quality care (for example, anesthesia administered by nurse anesthetists rather than by M.D. anesthesiologists); and (3) patients were subjected to higher prices for anesthesia.[17] These consequences, it was argued, flowed from the complete elimination of "intrahospital" competition within East Jefferson Hospital, allowing the anesthesiologists there to become sluggish and unresponsive to consumer preferences.[18] And not only were consumers injured, but Roux's competitors were too; Dr. Hyde, denied access to East Jefferson Hospital, found part of his market foreclosed.[19] Thus, Dr. Hyde's story was simple. The defendant hospital had a monopoly of, or monopoly power in, a market for hospital services. Other complementary input suppliers—for example, anesthesiologists—did not have such power, or would not have it without the hospital's conduct. But the hospital had in effect bootstrapped its monopoly power in hospital services into monopoly power in anesthesia, by tying the latter to the former. It was this incremental monopoly power that was said to injure consumer welfare, for all of the usual reasons.

East Jefferson Hospital's Position

The defendant hospital, not surprisingly, saw things differently and argued (among other things) for a completely different analytical approach to the case. In the hospital's view, this case was fundamentally about exclusive

---

[16]Ibid., pp. 36–38.

[17]Ibid., pp. 20–29. The argument about higher anesthesia prices was weak, in view of the complete absence of empirical evidence presented to the District Court and the Appellate Court's finding that "[I]t is true that the tying of anesthesia services to operating rooms in the instant case did not lead to a higher charge for anesthesia services." 686 F.2d 286, 291 (5th Cir. 1982).

[18]Brief for the Respondent, pp. 30–36.

[19]Ibid., pp. 32–34.

dealing, and if tying was involved at all, it was only as a tangential by-product.[20] After all, the hospital pointed out, a patient's choice of anesthesiologist at any one hospital is *always* limited—even at open-staff hospitals, the number of anesthesiologists with staff privileges was comparable to the number in the Roux group—yet no one would consider that a tying arrangement. Instead, said the hospital, limitation of anesthesiologist choice was a simple fact of life, and all that this case concerned was the way in which the "chosen few" at East Jefferson Hospital were chosen.

If this was so, the hospital argued, then Dr. Hyde was looking at the wrong market. Dr. Hyde had focused on the market in which the patient received the hospital's service and, whether tied or untied, the services of other complementary providers. That may be a market, said the hospital, but it is not the market that is directly affected by the exclusive contract. Instead, the directly affected market is the one in which anesthesiologists (and other hospital-based physicians) seek out hospital staff positions.[21] That market, the affected market, is essentially national in scope—the statistics in evidence showed that hospital-based physicians are extraordinarily mobile—and no hospital has monopoly power in it.

The hospital offered an analogy to the earlier *Tampa Electric* case.[22] In that case, Tampa Electric, a Florida public utility, entered into a long-term exclusive contract with a Tennessee supplier of coal, and the competitive effect of the contract's foreclosure of other coal suppliers was at issue. There, it was irrelevant that every resident of Tampa bought electricity from Tampa Electric alone; the directly affected market was not the one in which Tampa Electric sold its output, electricity, but rather the geographically broader one in which it bought one of its inputs, coal. Analogously, in the present case, the directly affected market was not the one in which the hospital sold surgical output, but rather the one in which it "bought" (that is, selected) anesthesiology inputs.

The hospital also denied the idea that the contract should be treated as tying because, as a practical matter, there really were not two separate products involved here, at least not in any meaningful sense.[23] A hospital stay, in this characterization, is just one single, albeit complex, product. If a patient cannot have a hospital surgical stay without all of the necessary inputs, then what sense does it make to treat each of the inputs as a separate product? Moreover, to treat this arrangement as tying is to treat virtually every product as tying. By way of examples, a consumer cannot ordinarily buy a car without getting the engine, or a razor without getting the blade. These, and virtually all, products are really just bundles of individual components, and the reason they are sold as bundles is that it is efficient to allocate some of the packaging to the seller.

---

[20]Brief for the Petitioners, pp. 43–45; Reply Brief for the Petitioners, pp. 2–5.

[21]Brief for the Petitioners, pp. 34–39.

[22]Ibid., pp. 35–36; *Tampa Electric Co. v. Nashville Coal Co.*, 365 U.S. 320 (1961).

[23]Brief for the Petitioners, pp. 39–42.

East Jefferson conceded that it was possible to characterize the contract as a tying arrangement. But the hospital argued that even if its exclusive contract *did* in some sense tie separate anesthesia services to hospital services, and even if it *did* enjoy monopoly power in a hospital services market, the contract could not logically be explained through any of the standard economic scenarios by which tying could be used to enhance monopoly profits. In particular, the hospital pointed out (and Dr. Hyde did not dispute) that, unlike our earlier IBM example, operating-room access and anesthesia were used in essentially fixed proportions.[24] This observation alone sweeps away the standard price-discrimination explanation for tying, and it also wipes out the applicability of all of the analytically interesting variable-proportions input-substitution explanations for tying.[25]

In fact, the hospital asserted, anticompetitive tying in this case would be illogical even if anesthesia *were* used in price-responsive variable proportions. For one reason, since the hospital has the ability to charge the patient separately for every individual element of treatment that he receives, including time spent in the operating room and the use of anesthesia itself, the hospital could *already* balance the relevant price ratios; a tie-in of Roux's professional services adds nothing.[26] Furthermore, a tie that resulted in Roux and his associates' being paid more than a competitive price actually would reduce the hospital's profit, since the demand for the hospital's own services is net of the price paid for all of the other inputs (including physicians' services) that are complementary to a hospital stay.[27] In addition, as to the point that competition among anesthesiologists practicing within East Jefferson Hospital was extinguished, the hospital's rejoinder was that competition for the contract itself had supplanted contemporaneous patient-by-patient competition.[28] Competition in anesthesia was vigorous, and the hospital had simply chosen to take advantage of it in its own way.

All of these arguments, the hospital pointed out, are wholly applicable to a hospital with monopoly power. But it would have been imprudent to ignore or concede the monopoly power issue—the Appellate Court's reversal of the District Court had hinged on it—and the hospital did neither. It argued that the statistics cited by the Appellate Court showed that East Jefferson Hospital in fact competed in a market that was geographically broader than just East Jefferson Parish.[29] There were only two relevant statistics in the record on which such a determination could be made. One was that, from East Jefferson Hospital's point of view, it got only 70 percent of its admissions from residents of East Jefferson Parish, and thus 30

---

[24]Ibid., p. 22.

[25]See, for an early and elegant example, Vernon and Graham (1971).

[26]Brief for the Petitioners, pp. 21–22.

[27]Ibid., pp. 22–23.

[28]Ibid., pp. 37–39. The point is similar to that made in Demsetz (1968) and Baumol, Panzar, and Willig (1982).

[29]Brief for the Petitioners, pp. 30–34.

percent from other parishes. The other statistic was that, from the patient's point of view, only 30 percent of the hospitalized residents of East Jefferson Parish went to East Jefferson Hospital, and 70 percent went to some other hospital, either in Jefferson or in some other parish. (The equality of the percentage pairs is a coincidence.) On that basis, said the hospital, the District Court had been justified in including the adjoining East Bank of Orleans Parish within the market. In that market, which included New Orleans, East Jefferson Hospital competed with over twenty hospitals and had a share (based on all patient admissions) of just 9.0 percent, far below any level suggestive of monopoly power.[30]

THE ECONOMIC ANALYSIS OF THE SUPREME COURT

It is hard to distill "the economic analysis" in a decision as divided as *Jefferson Parish*. Five justices signed the majority opinion, written by Justice John Paul Stevens, while four justices filed a concurring opinion, written by Justice Sandra Day O'Connor, that agreed with the result of the majority opinion but disparaged its reasoning.

The Majority Opinion

The controlling majority opinion of the Court ultimately found in favor of East Jefferson Hospital, ruling that its contract with Roux & Associates did not violate the Sherman Act. This does not mean that the Court agreed with all of the hospital's arguments, of course. For example, the hospital had denied that there really were two separate products at issue.[31] But the Court rejected the hospital's conception of a single product:

> Unquestionably, the anesthesiological component of the package offered by the hospital *could* be provided separately and *could* be selected either by the individual patient or by one of the patient's doctors if the hospital did not insist on including anesthesiological services in the package it offers to its customers. As a matter of actual practice, anesthesiological services are billed separately from the hospital services petitioners provide.[32]

The Court indeed found two elements that might qualify the arrangement for an *economic* definition of tying: Two separate products, with one tied to the other. But not all tying qualifies for *legal* condemnation as tying. For that, Dr. Hyde had to prove a key third element: monopoly

---

[30]Ibid., Appendix B.

[31]"Petitioners argue that the package does not involve a tying arrangement at all—that they are merely providing a functionally integrated package of services." 466 U.S. 2, 18 (1984).

[32]466 U.S. 2, 22 (1984) (emphasis added).

power in the tying product, which was the most prosaic issue in the case and had been the principal issue of disagreement between the District Court and the Appellate Court. And on this issue, it was East Jefferson, not Dr. Hyde, that carried the day.

As noted above, the empirical evidence in the record on the extent of East Jefferson Hospital's relevant geographic market and on its share of such a market was skimpy. On this slim factual base, the Court simply held that there was no basis to find that the hospital had monopoly power in hospital services, the tying product.[33] Without that factual predicate, the contract could not be condemned on a per se basis.

The Supreme Court's finding was not based solely on its own reading of the record. It also pointed out that the Court of Appeals opinion would have had the same reading, but for that court's inappropriate injection of "market imperfection" minutia into the analysis:

> The Court of Appeals . . . recognized that East Jefferson's market share alone was insufficient as a basis to infer market power, and buttressed its conclusion [of market power] by relying on "market imperfections" that permit petitioners to charge noncompetitive prices for hospital services: the prevalence of third party payment for health care costs reduces price competition, and a lack of adequate information renders consumers unable to evaluate the quality of the medical care provided by competing hospitals. 686 F.2d, at 290. While these factors may generate "market power" in some abstract sense, they do not generate the kind of market power that justifies condemnation of tying.[34]

In a way, this dismissal of industry-specific "factors" is ironic. Hospital and medical defendants had for years argued that the special characteristics of medicine called for correspondingly special (and lenient) treatment under the antitrust laws. For years, the Supreme Court regularly replied that such characteristics created no special absolution under the law.[35] In *Jefferson Parish,* the Court completed the loop by noting that no special thumbscrews were called for either.

East Jefferson Hospital may not have escaped the clutches of the tying characterization, but it did at least win on its view of the correct relevant market for analysis of the exclusive dealing aspects of the contract. The majority held that Dr. Hyde would not have prevailed under that approach to the case either:

---

[33]"East Jefferson's 'dominance' over persons residing in Jefferson Parish is far from overwhelming." 466 U.S. 2, 26 (1984).

[34]466 U.S. 2, 27 (1984).

[35]See, for example, *Goldfarb* v. *Virginia State Bar,* 421 U.S. 733 (1975); *National Society of Professional Engineers* v. *U.S.,* 435 U.S. 679 (1978); *National Gerimedical Hospital and Gerontology Center* v. *Blue Cross of Kansas City,* 452 U.S. 378 (1981); and *Arizona* v. *Maricopa County Medical Society,* 457 U.S. 332 (1982).

> [T]he burden of proving that the Roux contract violated the Sherman Act
> . . . necessarily involves an inquiry into the actual effect of the exclu-
> sive contract on competition *among anesthesiologists*. . . . Without a
> showing of actual adverse effect on competition, respondent cannot make
> out a case under the antitrust laws, and no such showing has been made.[36]

In other words, if we have a tying case, we look downstream from the
hospital in Figure 14-1, and if we have an exclusive dealing case, we look
upstream. Either way, in this case the hospital wins.

THE CONCURRING OPINION

Suppose that East Jefferson Hospital *had* been found to have monopoly
power. The majority's analysis would seem to suggest that in that event,
the hospital would have been liable because tying in the presence of monopoly power is (still) per se illegal. This strikes many economists as a triumph of formalism over logic: The effects of tying on consumer welfare
are theoretically ambiguous, and tying is sometimes necessary to obtain
the beneficial effects of exclusive dealing. If this is so, then how can tying
be thrown into the same category as naked price fixing, a practice so obviously and always harmful to consumer welfare that it may be condemned
without question?

The concurring minority apparently had a similar reaction. The minority would have dumped entirely the per se treatment of tying and would
have required a plaintiff in a tying case to prove not just that there was a
tie-in, but also that it in fact caused competitively injurious effects. The
minority observed that although per se treatment sounds simple—"If they
did it, they're guilty"—when the treatment is applied to tying, it still requires a complex and laborious determination of monopoly power in the
tying product. But, once that intensive factual investigation is completed,
any resultant evidence of procompetitive effects is completely suppressed,
even if it shows the tie to be wholly beneficial to consumer welfare.[37] The
concurrence went on to assert that the only circumstances under which
tying could be competitively objectionable would be those in which the
practice would create market power in the market for the tied product.
This is a questionable proposition; tying can in theory injure consumer
welfare in the tying product market irrespective of perfect competition in
the tied product market. However, the proposition may be consistent with
the principle that a monopolist is free to exploit its monopoly power in

---

[36]466 U.S. 2, 29, 31 (1984) (emphasis added).

[37]"The '*per se*' . . . tying doctrine incurs the costs of a rule of reason approach without achieving its benefits: the doctrine calls for the extensive and time-consuming economic analysis characteristic of the rule of reason, but then may be interpreted to prohibit arrangements that economic
analysis would show to be beneficial." 466 U.S. 2, 34 (1984).

whatever way it sees fit (so long as it has come by the monopoly power legally), but is no more allowed to monopolize a second market than anyone else is.

Since the concurrence also found in favor of East Jefferson's contract, the hospital won 9-to-0 on liability. The minority identified an additional reason why the contract did not create a tying arrangement: They agreed with the hospital's "one product" view of the case:

> [T]here is no sound economic reason for treating surgery and anesthesia as separate services. Patients are interested in purchasing anesthesia only in conjunction with hospital services, so the Hospital can acquire no *additional* market power by selling the two services together.[38]

The point might be read as an endorsement of the "one unified product" view of the world when two components of the final product are consumed in essentially fixed proportions.[39]

SOME OBSERVATIONS ON THE ECONOMICS OF *JEFFERSON PARISH*

Though economic issues were prominent in this case, there were significant omissions in the use of economic evidence and in the treatment of some economic questions.

Market Definition, Market Share, and Market Power

The judicial analysis of *Jefferson Parish* suffered from the absence of explicit expert economic testimony at the trial court level. There were, to be sure, statistics and testimony placed in the record that had economic significance, but neither party introduced an economist to try systematically to assemble, analyze, and interpret the relevant economic data and evidence. Thus, by the time it was necessary to shape and support the economic arguments for presentation to the Supreme Court, the effort was hampered by the absence of clearly framed and focused empirical evidence within the citable trial record.

Perhaps nowhere was this more evident than in the assessment of the relevant geographic market. Data had been available on patient origin and destination patterns in the New Orleans metropolitan area. These data could have been used, for example, to identify specifically the hospitals most

---

[38]466 U.S. 2, 43 (1984).

[39]Note that with (1) fixed proportions, (2) a monopoly of product A, and (3) a competitive supply of product B, the final product price (of A + B) is the same whether the monopolist ties B to A or not.

directly in competition with East Jefferson Hospital. But that analysis would have to have been introduced during the initial trial in 1980; by the time of the final appeal, the record on the extent of the geographic market was limited to the two bare summary percentages discussed earlier.

In a tying case, the market definition question is factually important because the market power issue is legally important. Roughly put, the per se rule in tying seems generally to be: No power, no harm; no harm, no foul. If a seller has rivals who can bundle or unbundle their products as they (or as the customers) wish, then the seller has little or no leeway to sustain a pattern of product packaging (e.g., tying) that the customer dislikes.

Empirical evidence aside, the Court made at least a modest contribution to the legal treatment of the question, "Does a given market share imply market power?" In particular, it brushed aside a number of supposed "market imperfections"—here, high information costs and low price sensitivity—as a basis for finding market power when the plain fact of a low market share would imply otherwise. But it was less direct in clarifying what level of market power is required for what sort of antitrust violation. When economists use the term *market power*, they usually mean only that a firm has the ability profitably to elevate market price above the competitive level.[40] But a market share sufficient to confer this ability may be insufficient to allow a firm profitably to impose a tying restriction. The reason is that the conventional explanation for monopoly tying (e.g., the earlier IBM example) implies price discrimination, and it may take a significantly higher market share to make price discrimination stick than it does to exercise simple nondiscriminatory market power.

To illustrate, consider a firm with a 60-percent share of a market for a perfectly homogeneous good, with the other 40 percent supplied by rivals who are at capacity (i.e., their collective supply curve is vertical). Assume that the firm has and exercises conventional market power: Market price is significantly above the level we would see if the firm produced at price equal to marginal cost. Can the firm profitably price discriminate, by tying or by any other means? If it tries to do so, it will raise the price to the customers with relatively inelastic demands and lower it to the customers with elastic demands. But in response, all of its inelastic customers will flock to its rivals, and all of its rivals' elastic-demand customers will come to it. If 60 percent or more of the prior market demand was from elastic-demand customers, then the only effect of the attempt to discriminate is to reallocate customers by their intensity of demand, and the attempt will fail.[41]

---

[40]See, for example, Landes and Posner (1981).

[41]The key assumption here is that the product is homogeneous, so that interfirm cross-elasticities of demand are very high. If the firm's output is instead differentiated from all others, then even in this example discrimination might work. When Phlips discusses "discriminating oligopolists," he warns that "This [concept] may cause some surprise, given that only *monopolists* are supposed to price discriminate, according to the standard literature." But in some cases, he observes, "[D]uopolists, oligopolists, and small competitors in *differentiated* markets can price discriminate."

Thus, different degrees and types of market power are necessary for different types of competitive conduct. A clarification of this "sufficient market power" point with respect to tying—as some courts have done with respect to predatory pricing—would have been useful, although perhaps not necessary to resolve *Jefferson Parish.*

Economic Interest

One essential economic point that the Supreme Court never considered was the economic interest of the tying seller in the provision of the tied product. If, in our earlier illustration, monopolist IBM increases its profits by tying overpriced punch cards to tabulating machines, it does so by collecting for *itself* the markup or overcharge on the cards. It is impossible for IBM to increase its assumed monopoly profits by tying overpriced punch cards if it simply requires machine purchasers to buy their cards from, say, International Paper. (This is so whether IBM or International Paper sets the card price.) If cards are a complement to machines and are sold by independent vendors in which IBM has no financial stake, then IBM's interests are best served if cards are supplied at the competitive price. In practice, this means that if IBM for some reason "ties" someone else's cards to its tabulating machines—for example, by requiring its customers to purchase cards directly from International Paper—then its interests would be best served by an agreement from International Paper to sell at the competitive price in return for being named the sole card vendor.

But this feature of the IBM case applies directly to the *Jefferson Parish* case. If a given hospital maximizes profits, then whether the hospital has monopoly power or not, we may assume that it sets every element of its own prices at the profit-maximizing level. But the hospital recognizes, in principle, that patients are influenced not only by the hospital bill as such, but also by the bills of the hospital-based physicians affiliated with the hospital. Ignoring the information cost issue (as did the Supreme Court), we would expect that patients would shun the hospital just as much for a $1000 increase in the hospital-based physician's bill—the radiologist who reads the X rays, the pathologist who runs the lab tests, the anesthesiologist who sedates the patient—as for a $1000 increase in the hospital's bill.[42] The only difference is that in the first case, the hospital gets none of the gain. It is notable, given this, that East Jefferson retained

---

Phlips (1981, pp. 16, 39; emphasis modified). The key distinction, of course, is whether the firm's control over its own price—measured by the elasticity of demand for the firm's output—comes from a large share of a homogeneous product market, or instead from the sale of a significantly differentiated product.

[42]This point is discussed explicitly and at some length in *Todorov* v. *DCH Healthcare Authority,* 921 F.2d 1438 (11th Cir. 1991).

complete discretion over the level of fees that Roux charged its patients for anesthesiology.[43]

Thus, we see that the premise upon which tying theory was applied to this case is flawed. Anticompetitive tying involves a monopolist of one product increasing its profits through the tie of a second product over which it does not initially have a monopoly; this practice is not likely to involve the channeling of that profit into someone else's pocket. The fundamental logical problem with *Jefferson Parish,* and indeed most other hospital privileges cases involving exclusive contracts, is that the proffered theory implies that the hospital is voluntarily acting against its own interests by conferring a gratuitous benefit on the contracting physicians.

Although the Supreme Court has not spoken on this issue in tying, some courts have found that the theory of anticompetitive tying makes no economic sense if the defendant has no financial interest in the tied product. For example, when a developer of condominiums insisted that purchasers also take the services of a specified but independent property management firm, the Seventh Circuit Court of Appeals declined to find an illegal tie-in because of an absence of financial interest in the tied product.[44] The absence of a coherent economic theory of competitive injury is sometimes enough to get a lawsuit dismissed; as the Supreme Court noted in a later case, "[I]f the claim is one that simply makes no economic sense— [plaintiffs] must come forward with more persuasive evidence to support their claim than would otherwise be necessary."[45] As a counterpoint, a later anesthesia privileges case provided a theory (and facts) that avoided this flawed economic logic.[46] St. Peter's Hospital, the only hospital in an isolated town, had canceled Mr. Tafford Oltz's anesthesia privileges (he was a nurse anesthetist) in order to benefit the incumbent M.D. anesthesiology group, which promptly raised its fees by a handsome increment once Mr. Oltz left town. Why, the theorist asks, would the hospital do such a thing? Because, the *Oltz* court found, the M.D. anesthesiologists had threatened the hospital with a boycott. The hospital would not have wished for this circumstance; it was doing fine with both providers. But faced with the choice of just the M.D. anesthesiologist group or just Mr. Oltz,

---

[43]Brief for the Petitioners, p. 3. The plaintiff responded that this discretion was less than absolute, stressing the hospital's consultation with Roux in the process of fee determination. Brief for the Respondent, pp. 8–9.

[44]*Carl Sandburg Village Condominium Association* v. *First Condominium Development Co.,* 758 F.2d 203 (7th Cir. 1985). The opinion noted, however, that the interest of the tying seller in the tied seller need not be limited to outright ownership; commissions or kickbacks, for example, might be enough. In a later hospital exclusive-privileges case, the Fourth Circuit rejected any characterization of the exclusive contract as a tying arrangement because "the lack of the hospital's economic interest in the tied product is sufficient to defeat [the] tying claim. . . ." *White* v. *Rockingham Radiologists,* 820 F.2d 98 (4th Cir. 1987).

[45]*Matsushita Electric Industrial Co.* v. *Zenith Radio Corp.,* 475 U.S. 574 (1986). See the discussion by Kenneth Elzinga, Case 9 in this volume.

[46]*Oltz* v. *St. Peter's Community Hospital,* 861 F.2d 1440 (9th Cir. 1988).

the hospital's economic interest in setting up an anesthesia monopoly coincided with the anesthesia group's. Thus, under those circumstances, there was no irrationality inherent in the hospital's anticompetitive tying of an independent group's anesthesia services to its own hospital services.

POSTSCRIPT

Two post-1984 developments since *Jefferson Parish* bear mention. One concerns hospital exclusive contracting, the economic activity at issue. The other concerns tying, the legal doctrine at issue.

At the time that the Court was deciding *Jefferson Parish,* there were no solid statistics on the actual extent of exclusive contracting for the services of hospital-based physicians. Available studies of the frequency of hospital contracts with physicians did not distinguish between exclusive and nonexclusive arrangements, so the Court had no way of knowing whether its decision affected most hospitals or only a handful. But in 1984, the year the Supreme Court decided *Jefferson Parish,* the American Hospital Association added a carefully focused question to its annual survey to determine the prevalence of this practice. The results were surprising: Exclusive contracts with hospital-based physicians were the norm, not the exception.[47] The percentage of hospitals with exclusive arrangements varied by physician service:

Pathology	62.3%
Radiology	59.9
Emergency	48.7
Anesthesiology	30.2
Any specialty	73.4

Thus, postdecision information showed that the contracts that the *Jefferson Parish* decision affected were widespread and, correspondingly, widely affected by the decision. However, those who had thought that *Jefferson Parish* would settle the law in this area in a way that would reduce litigation were proved incorrect; the volume of hospital exclusive contract lawsuits has risen substantially since 1984.[48]

These same data have been analyzed further to investigate the monopolization theme of hospital exclusive contracts.[49] Loosely stated, the hypothesis was that if "bootstrapping" a hospital's monopoly power to benefit the

---

[47]The findings of the survey are reported in Morrisey and Brooks (1985).

[48]See the dozens of such cases cited in *BCB Anesthesia Care, Ltd.* v. *Passavant Memorial Area Hospital Assoc.,* 36 F.3d 664 (7th Cir. 1994).

[49]Lynk and Morrisey (1987).

hospital-based physician was an important reason for exclusive contracts, then we ought to see relatively more of these contracts in highly concentrated hospital markets, where hospitals might have monopoly power. But the data do not support that hypothesis. Instead, the finding was that

> [T]here is no support for the contract monopoly or market power explanation. . . . [W]e find essentially no relation between concentration and the weighted frequency with which hospitals adopt hospital-based physician exclusive contracts. . . . We conclude that, whatever the diverse reasons why, under certain circumstances, hospitals and hospital-based physicians find it in their mutual interest to contract exclusively, conferring market power on the favored specialist does not appear to be one of them.[50]

The other subsequent development concerns the legal treatment of tying, regardless of the industry in which it is found. The Supreme Court recently revisited the subject in the *Kodak* case.[51] Some observers thought that this might be the case in which the Court finally abandoned the per se rule in tying cases. Because of turnover on the Court since *Jefferson Parish,* the potential for change seemed high.

The change never came. Both the majority opinion and the dissent in *Kodak* took it as settled precedent that tying was a per se offense, implying liability if the requisite market power in the tying product is found. The dissent (by Justice Antonin Scalia) noted in passing that a rule-of-reason analysis would be preferable, but that the disposition of the case did not require a renewal of that debate. Thus, as matters still stand, the economic analysis of tying in a legal setting remains truncated by the per se presumption of liability once the necessary predicate factual conditions are established.

REFERENCES

Baumol, William J., John C. Panzar, and Robert D. Willig. *Contestable Markets and the Theory of Industry Structure.* New York: Harcort Brace Jovanovich, 1982.

Bowman, Ward S. "Tying Arrangements and the Leverage Problem." *Yale Law Journal* 67 (November 1957): 19–36.

Carlton, Dennis W., and Jeffrey M. Perloff. *Modern Industrial Organization.* New York: HarperCollins College Publishers, 1994.

Demsetz, Harold. "Why Regulate Utilities?" *Journal of Law & Economics* 11 (April 1968): 55–65.

Feldstein, Paul J. *Health Care Economics.* New York: John Wiley & Sons, 1988.

---

[50]Ibid., p. 413.

[51]*Eastman Kodak Co. v. Image Technical Services, Inc.,* 112 S. Ct. 2072 (1992); see the chapter by MacKie-Mason and Metzler (Case 16) for further discussion.

Klein, Benjamin, Robert G. Crawford, and Armen A. Alchian. "Vertical Integration, Appropriable Rents, and the Competitive Contracting Process." *Journal of Law & Economics* 21 (October 1978): 297–326.

Landes, William M., and Richard A. Posner. "Market Power in Antitrust Cases." *Harvard Law Review* 94 (March 1981): 937–996.

Lynk, William J., and Michael A. Morrisey. "The Economic Basis of Hyde: Are Market Power and Hospital Exclusive Contracts Related?" *Journal of Law & Economics* 30 (October 1987): 399–421.

Marvel, Howard P. "Exclusive Dealing." *Journal of Law & Economics* 25 (April 1982): 1–25.

Morrisey, Michael A., and Deal C. Brooks. "The Myth of the Closed Medical Staff." *Hospitals* 59 (July 1, 1985): 75–77.

Phelps, Charles E. *Health Economics.* New York: HarperCollins Publishers, 1992.

Phlips, Louis. *The Economics of Price Discrimination.* Cambridge: Cambridge University Press, 1981.

Scherer, F. M., and David Ross. *Industrial Market Structure and Economic Performance.* Boston: Houghton Mifflin, 1990.

Vernon, John M., and Daniel A. Graham. "Profitability of Monopolization by Vertical Integration." *Journal of Political Economy* 79 (July/August 1971): 924–925.

CASE 15

Resale Price Maintenance Reexamined: *Monsanto* v. *Spray-Rite* (1984)

Frederick R. Warren-Boulton

INTRODUCTION

On August 31, 1968, the Monsanto Company, a major U.S. manufacturer of chemical products, declined to renew its distributorship with the Spray-Rite Service Corporation, a small Iowa herbicide distributor whose net revenue from sales of Monsanto herbicides in 1968 had been about $16,000. Sixteen years and millions of dollars in legal costs later, the Supreme Court upheld a Federal District Court's award of $10.5 million to Spray-Rite.[1]

Monsanto Co. v. Spray-Rite Service Corp. is really two stories. The first is a legal saga that exemplifies many of the worst characteristics of private antitrust cases. But the Monsanto case is also the story of the ongoing attempt to transform antitrust into rational public policy.

THE ECONOMICS OF RPM

Resale price maintenance (RPM), or "fair trade," is the practice whereby an upstream entity (e.g., a manufacturer) specifies a minimum price (or sometimes a maximum price) to which a downstream entity (e.g., a retailer) is required to adhere in its sales efforts. Note immediately that the manufacturer is not the direct beneficiary of this action, since RPM specifies the retail price, whereas the manufacturer's profits are determined by its wholesale price. In essence, once the wholesale price is given, RPM specifies a retail margin.

Frederick R. Warren-Boulton was a consultant for Monsanto at the District Court stage of this case.

[1]*Monsanto Co. v. Spray-Rite Service Corp.*, 465 U.S. 752 (1984).

How might RPM be anticompetitive? Two possible explanations hinge on RPM's being a cover or facilitating device for horizontal price fixing or a horizontal cartel. One possibility is a cartel among manufacturers that cannot observe each others' wholesale prices but can observe retail prices. They may collectively fear that "price wars" among their retailers may tempt individual manufacturers among them to cut wholesale prices surreptitiously, thereby undermining the cartel. Resale price maintenance would prevent these price wars.

Alternatively, RPM might be motivated by a dealer cartel (among a group of dealers that collectively have market power, if they could succeed in colluding) that find that they cannot collude without external help. Accordingly, they ask one or more manufacturers to enforce their cartel by establishing RPM.

These cartel-motivated views of RPM, supplemented by a general notion that RPM had to be anticonsumer because it meant higher prices, were prevalent until the 1960s. They were reinforced by the experience of the 1930s, in which political pressures by small retailers (especially druggists) led to individual states' passing of fair trade laws for intrastate commerce and to the Congress's passing of the Miller-Tydings Act of 1937, which permitted RPM on a state-option basis for goods involved in interstate trade that were sold in the relevant state.

This general view of RPM as anticompetitive and harmful to consumers began a slow process of reversal when Telser (1960) laid out the first of the "free-rider" efficiency explanations for RPM. Telser began by pointing out that a manufacturer would appear only to lose from a higher retail margin. Any supranormal return to the retailer acts as a tax on the product, appropriating revenue that could have gone to the manufacturer. Using RPM to impose a higher retail margin could be in the manufacturer's interest only if the higher retail margin were somehow necessary to induce retailers to provide services that were worth more to consumers than they cost the retailers.

One example[2] of this phenomenon, suggested by Telser, is the provision of information or other services at the point of sale, for which the retailer cannot charge a separate fee. Suppose the following: A manufacturer of a complicated item—for example, a stereo receiver—believes that its product is best sold if the retailer provides a great deal of point-of-sale service, such as information, demonstration models, and the opportunity to hook up the receiver with many other combinations of stereo components, even if this high level of retailing services is costly and means that the receiver will carry a higher retail price than in the absence of these services. But retailers usually find it difficult to charge a separate fee for these services. Under these circumstances, some retailers would be tempted to

---

[2] There have been a number of elaborations on Telser's theme since 1960; for a recent contribution that has references to earlier studies, see Butz (1997).

establish the equivalent of catalog stores, urging their customers to obtain the necessary information and demonstrations at a neighboring full-service retailer and then to return to the catalog store, which could sell the product for less (because the catalog store did not have the extra costs of providing the information and the demonstrations). In essence, the catalog retailer would free ride off the full-service retailer; however, the full-service retailers would then lose sales, no one would want to be a full-service retailer of that product, and the manufacturer's sales would suffer.

One solution for the manufacturer would be for it to insist that all of its retailers provide a full range of services; but policing their provision of service may be difficult. An alternative would be to establish a system of RPM. By insisting that all retailers sell at the same minimum retail price, the manufacturer would eliminate the price advantage of the catalog retailer, thereby reducing the free-riding problem. In essence, by restricting price competition among its retailers, the manufacturer would be virtually forcing its retailers to compete among themselves on the basis of service (since, with prices uniform among the retailers, improved service would presumably be the means by which the retailer would attract and retain customers). If it is easier for the manufacturer to police the RPM scheme than to police a direct insistence on the provision of retailer service, then RPM could be the manufacturer's preferred method.[3]

At first glance, even the unilateral imposition of RPM by a manufacturer may appear to be anticompetitive. After all, the manufacturer is restraining price competition among its retailers. But if the manufacturer is correct in its judgment that a high level of retail service is best for selling the product, this outcome should generally mean enhanced satisfaction for consumers.[4] As another way of seeing this point, consider that the manufacturer could vertically integrate, establish its own retail outlets, specify the retail price of the product sold by these outlets, and instruct its own retail employees to provide a high level of retail service in conjunction with the sales of the product. Would this latter situation generally be considered anticompetitive? Resale price maintenance, in essence, achieves the same outcome.

THE LEGAL TREATMENT OF RPM

In contrast with the changed economics perception of RPM, the legal treatment of RPM has remained harsh. In the 1911 *Dr. Miles Medical* case,[5] the

[3]This could be true if it were easier for the manufacturer to verify instances of off-price sales—perhaps in response to other retailers' complaints—than to verify instances of the lack of adequate service.

[4]For arguments that even unilateral RPM may not be in the interest of most consumers, see Scherer (1983), Comanor (1985), and Comanor and Kirkwood (1985). For a criticism of these arguments, see White (1985).

[5]*Dr. Miles Medical Co. v. John D. Park & Sons Co.*, 220 U.S. 373 (1911).

Supreme Court declared RPM to be a per se violation of Section 1 of the Sherman Act; that is, this form of vertical restraint was placed in the same category of condemned practices as horizontal price fixing among competitors (and, indeed, RPM is frequently characterized as "vertical price fixing"). Eight years later, in the 1919 *Colgate* case, the Supreme Court appeared to open a major loophole for RPM, declaring,

> In the absence of any purpose to create or maintain a monopoly, the act does not restrict the long recognized right of a trader or manufacturer engaged in an entirely private business, freely to exercise his own independent discretion as to parties with whom he will deal. And, of course, he may announce in advance the circumstances under which he will refuse to sell.[6]

Thus, it appeared that a manufacturer could legally enforce an RPM program by simply announcing the expected retail prices in advance and refusing to deal with any retailer who did not adhere to those prices. But the Court quickly closed the loophole, consistently finding in subsequent cases[7] that manufacturers' efforts to enforce RPM among their dealers constituted agreements between the manufacturer and the dealers and hence were violations of the Sherman Act, consistent with Dr. Miles Medical. In a long line of cases since then, the Court has repeatedly reaffirmed its condemnation of RPM as a per se violation.[8] The Court in 1968 even condemned RPM in a situation in which a newspaper attempted to impose *maximum* resale prices on its distributors.[9] In 1997, the Court reversed itself on this last point and unanimously declared that maximum RPM should be judged under the rule of reason; the Court specifically stated, however, that "arrangements to fix minimum prices . . . remain illegal per se."[10]

The Supreme Court has not been nearly as consistently harsh with respect to nonprice vertical restraints—for example, a manufacturer's instructions to retailers of its products as to where they may locate or in which geographic areas they may sell. Here, after condemning these practices as a per se violation in 1967,[11] the Court in 1977 reversed itself and declared them instead to be subject to the rule of reason.[12] This disparity in legal treatment is striking, since the economic logic underlying the two

---

[6]*United States* v. *Colgate Co.,* 250 U.S. 300, 307 (1919).

[7]See *United States* v. *Schrader's Son, Inc.,* 252 U.S. 85 (1920); *Frey & Sons, Inc.* v. *Cudahy Packing Co.* 256 U.S. 208 (1920); and *FTC* v. *Beech-Nut Packing Co.,* 257 U.S. 441 (1922).

[8]See *United States* v. *Bausch & Lomb Optical Co.,* 321 U.S. 707 (1944); *United States* v. *Parke, Davis & Co.,* 362 U.S. 29 (1960); and *Simpson* v. *Union Oil Co.,* 377 U.S. 13 (1964).

[9]*Albrecht* v. *Herald Co.,* 390 U.S. 145 (1968).

[10]*State Oil Co.* v. *Khan,* 66 L.W. 4001, 4005 (1997).

[11]*United States* v. *Arnold, Schwinn and Co.,* 388 U.S. 365 (1967).

[12]*Continental T.V.* v. *GTE Sylvania,* 433 U.S. 36 (1977).

forms of vertical restraint is fundamentally similar, and both (since they restrain competition among the retailers of a manufacturer's product) are likely to cause retail prices of the relevant product to be higher than in the absence of the practice.[13]

THE CASE

Monsanto is a major American manufacturer of chemical products, including agricultural herbicides.[14] During the 1960s, several companies, including Monsanto, Geigy, Stauffer, Eli Lilly, DuPont, and Rohrer AmChem, developed a new generation of weed killers for use on corn and soybeans. Previous herbicides were sprayed on weeds after the weeds were grown and had already injured the crops. The new "preemergent" herbicides prevented this damage by killing weed seeds before they germinated.

By 1968, the leading producer of corn herbicides was Geigy, whose Atrazine brand held a 70-percent market share, while Monsanto's Randox (introduced in 1956) and Ramrod (introduced in 1966) brands accounted for 15 percent of the corn herbicide market. In soybean herbicides, where the two leading firms held market shares of 37 percent and 33 percent, Monsanto's market share was only 3 percent.

Monsanto marketed its herbicides primarily through about 100 independent distributors who resold to retail dealers, including feed stores and farm implement dealers, who in turn resold to farmers. Each distributor was assigned a geographic "area of primary responsibility," but that assignment was nonexclusive: authorized distributors could sell herbicides of other manufacturers; distributors could sell outside their assigned area of primary responsibility; and Monsanto assigned approximately ten to twenty distributors to each area.

Between 1957 and 1968, one of those distributors was the Spray-Rite Service Corporation. Spray-Rite was a small family business whose owner and president was also its sole salaried salesman. Spray-Rite bought herbicides from Monsanto and other manufacturers and resold them to retail dealers and farmers in northern Illinois and adjacent areas. In 1968, 90 percent of Spray-Rite's sales volume came from herbicide sales. Spray-Rite was the tenth largest of the approximately 100 distributors of Monsanto's primary corn herbicide. Monsanto's products, however, accounted for only about 16 percent of Spray-Rite's $3.4 million in total sales in 1968; Geigy's Atrazine corn herbicide accounted for 73 percent of Spray-Rite's herbicide sales. Spray-Rite was a low-margin, high-volume operation that even characterized itself as a "brokerage house." Spray-Rite sold

---

[13]See White (1981).

[14]Monsanto's sales in 1974 were about $3.5 billion, with about 10% of those sales accounted for by its agricultural chemical products group.

primarily to large seed-corn companies, large sprayers, and large dealers; 30 percent of its 1968 sales were made to one large seed-corn company, De Kalb, and only six customers combined accounted for nearly 75 percent of its total sales of Monsanto products.

In 1967, faced with a flat market share in corn herbicides and a declining market share in soybean herbicides, Monsanto decided to change its marketing strategy in order to stress dealer education. Herbicide application is technically complex and risky. The optimal application depends on location, soil, weather, and weed type, and selecting an inappropriate herbicide or misapplying an appropriate one can result in an ineffective application or even serious crop damage. Monsanto relied upon its distributors to educate the dealers, who in turn would provide individual farmers with specific technical advice on the optimal selection and application of its herbicides.

In September 1967, Monsanto informed each of its distributors, including Spray-Rite, that for the upcoming 1967–1968 season it would appoint distributors for only one-year terms and that authorized distributorships would expire automatically unless renewed by Monsanto. Renewal would depend on compliance with six criteria, including the following:

> Is the Distributor's primary activity the solicitation and distribution of agricultural chemical products to dealers? . . .
>
> Is the Distributor willing and capable of carrying out Monsanto's technical programs at both the Dealer and Farmer levels with properly trained personnel? . . .
>
> Can the Distributor be expected to "exploit fully" the potential markets for the Goods in the Distributor's area of primary responsibility? (plaintiff's exhibit no. 196)

In October 1968, Monsanto declined to renew its contract with Spray-Rite and four other distributors. After its termination by Monsanto, Spray-Rite continued to purchase some Monsanto products from other distributors. In 1969, its total sales increased by 52 percent to $5.2 million, although its sales of Monsanto products declined. Spray-Rite also reported its first net loss on herbicide operations since 1965. In 1970, total sales fell to $2.4 million, and net losses rose to over $91,000. While sales recovered and losses fell in 1971, by 1972, with sales down to $1.4 million and losses over $75,000, Spray-Rite went out of business.

In the meantime, jolted by a 30-percent fall in sales in 1968, Monsanto had taken several other marketing actions. First, it tried to push dealer education directly: It hired additional sales personnel to work with dealers, established herbicide training schools for dealers and for distributor personnel, offered cash bonus payments to distributors that sent salesmen to training classes, and offered distributors price discounts on herbicides resold to dealers who attended Monsanto's technical programs. Second, it changed its shipping policies to encourage distributors to develop the market in their areas of primary responsibility. Beginning in 1968, it permitted distributors to pick up products only at Monsanto warehouses within each distributor's area and provided free deliveries of products to the distributor or its customers only within that area. A distributor that resold the product outside its primary area had to pay the additional shipping costs. Third, it reduced the prices charged to its distributors as well as the suggested resale prices. While this reduced the suggested distributor profit margin from 11 percent to 7 percent, Monsanto also offered price discounts, rebated to the distributor at the end of the season, on orders purchased early in the season. Fourth, in 1969, it introduced its "third-generation" corn and soybean herbicide, LASSO.

The combined effect was dramatic. Monsanto's share of the corn herbicide market went from 15 percent in 1968 to 28 percent in 1972; its market share in soybean herbicides went from 3 percent in 1968 to 19 percent in 1972. These increases came largely at the expense of the firms with the largest market shares. In corn herbicides, Geigy's share fell from 70 percent in 1968 to 52 percent in 1972. In soybean herbicides, the combined share of the two leading firms (Eli Lilly and AmChem) fell from 70 percent in 1968 to 55 percent in 1972. During the same period, total use of corn and soybean herbicides grew by approximately 15 percent and 75 percent, respectively.

The District Court

In 1972, Spray-Rite sued Monsanto for violating Section 1 of the Sherman Act, alleging that Spray-Rite had been terminated as part of a conspiracy to fix the resale price of Monsanto herbicides and that the termination, combined with a post-termination boycott by Monsanto and its distributors and the use by Monsanto of such nonprice vertical restraints as areas of primary responsibility and dealer compensation and shipping programs, had eventually forced Spray-Rite out of business. Spray-Rite's case thus consisted of three separable factual allegations: (1) Its termination was pursuant to an RPM conspiracy among Monsanto and some of its distributors; (2) Monsanto's nonprice policies were pursuant to that conspiracy; and (3) Monsanto and some of its distributors conspired to boycott Spray-Rite after the termination.

On the first and most important allegation, Monsanto denied ever engaging in RPM and contended that it had decided unilaterally not to renew Spray-Rite's distributorship because of the latter's failure to satisfy Monsanto's announced criteria for renewal. Monsanto also argued that Spray-Rite failed to prove the existence of an agreement among Monsanto and any of its distributors to terminate Spray-Rite because of its price cutting and pointed out that price cutting by other, nonterminated distributors was widespread. But Spray-Rite was able to show that Monsanto was concerned about the resale prices of its herbicides, that Monsanto had agreed that its company-owned outlets would not undercut its suggested retail prices, that Monsanto had received price complaints about Spray-Rite from other distributors, that Monsanto representatives had informed Spray-Rite of those complaints and requested that prices be maintained, and that Monsanto terminated Spray-Rite subsequent to those complaints but without ever having discussed with Spray-Rite the distributorship criteria that were the alleged basis for the action. In addition, evidence was introduced that, subsequent to Spray-Rite's termination, Monsanto had advised price-cutting distributors that if they did not maintain the suggested resale price they would not receive adequate supplies of Monsanto's new herbicide, LASSO.

On the boycott allegation, Spray-Rite was able to deliver testimony from Monsanto employees and from distributors that Monsanto had threatened to terminate distributors who sold to Spray-Rite. Finally, with respect to Monsanto's nonprice policies, Spray-Rite did not argue that Monsanto's promotional programs and distribution policies were illegal under the *Sylvania* rule-of-reason standard. Indeed, it agreed that Monsanto had become a more effective competitor after their introduction. Spray-Rite did argue, however, as the court eventually instructed the jury, that it was per se unlawful for a manufacturer to utilize customer or territorial restrictions as part of a comprehensive price-fixing plan or boycott and that the jury could consider the effect of Monsanto's distributor compensation programs as circumstantial evidence of the conspiracy to boycott.

These three allegations were reformulated by the court and given to the jury as three special interrogatories:

1. Was the decision by Monsanto not to offer a new contract to plaintiff for 1969 made by Monsanto pursuant to a conspiracy or combination with one or more of its distributors to fix, maintain, or stabilize resale prices of Monsanto herbicides?

2. Were the compensation programs and/or areas of primary responsibility and/or shipping policy created by Monsanto pursuant to a conspiracy to fix, maintain, or stabilize resale prices on Monsanto herbicides?

3. Did Monsanto conspire or combine with one or more of its distributors so that one or more of those distributors would limit plaintiff's access to Monsanto herbicides after 1968?

The jury responded "yes" to each interrogatory and returned a general verdict against Monsanto.

Damages

Spray-Rite argued that a herbicide distributor needed to carry a "full line" of different products because dealers and farmers wanted to buy all their herbicides from one seller. Access to Monsanto's products was thus essential for survival. The combination of Monsanto's 1968 termination of Spray-Rite, the post-termination boycott, and Monsanto's post-termination compensation programs, delivery policies, and territorial restrictions forced Spray-Rite out of business in 1972. Further, the conspiracy to impose RPM and boycott Spray-Rite was the only event of substance that would have affected Spray-Rite's actual or potential business after 1968. It would thus be reasonable to expect that, in the absence of the alleged conspiracy, the relationship from 1969 to 1978 between Spray-Rite's total sales and the total corn and soybean herbicide sales in the region would have been the same as it had been from 1963 to 1968. Extrapolation of sales and profits to 1978 brought the latter to a grand total of about $3.3 million.

Alternative calculations of Spray-Rite's damages, more favorable to Monsanto, would have yielded considerably smaller figures. But the jury accepted Spray-Rite's estimates and apparently rounded them up to $3.5 million, which the court then trebled.

Strategy

The jury can hardly be blamed, however, for this decision. *Monsanto* was argued as a per se case; the jury was not to wonder if Monsanto's actions benefited either its customers or society in general. As the Supreme Court later noted, Monsanto's lawyers never argued that a rule-of-reason standard should apply to RPM, nor did they dispute Spray-Rite's contention that any nonprice practices instituted as part of an RPM conspiracy should also be subject to per se treatment.

Monsanto's trial strategy was to argue the case on as narrow grounds as possible. The appropriateness of a per se standard for RPM was never disputed, which meant that a potential opportunity to argue RPM as a rule-of-reason case was missed: The facts of the case provided strong support for an efficiency explanation for RPM and no support for any inference that RPM had been part of a price-fixing conspiracy by either dealers or manufacturers.

For a litigator, however, that same evidence of the social desirability of RPM carried several dangers. First, to the extent that RPM is a rational, profit-maximizing, appropriate, efficient, and effective response to free-riding by distributors, it is also a more likely response. Spray-Rite's factual allegations thus become more plausible, and it becomes harder to convince the jury that RPM never occurred. Second, the attorney's goal is to win, putting the interests of his or her client first and ignoring any potential social or precedential impact of the case.

Third, any trial attorney has limited resources, and any jury has a limited ability to absorb information; putting on a rule-of-reason case could distract attention or resources away from other lines of defense. Finally, it can be difficult for attorneys to evaluate the potential for a defense that removes them from strictly legal and evidentiary issues where they are sure of their competence and places them in the unknown, speculative, uncertain, and uncontrollable world of economics.

Balanced against these dangers from a rule-of-reason strategy were only limited benefits. The jury might have been persuaded that any use of RPM by Monsanto was in the public as well as the private interest, and this might have countered some of the natural sympathy for a small, local businessman and his family in their battle against a huge corporation. But even after the recent decision in *Sylvania,*[15] the probability that *Monsanto* would be the case in which the Supreme Court would finally reverse its long-standing position on the per se illegality of RPM must have seemed small. The social gain from using *Monsanto* as a vehicle for such a reversal was an externality appropriately ignored by Monsanto's legal staff. It was thus left to the Department of Justice, whose friend-of-the-court (amicus brief) program was designed precisely to respond to the social externalities that private attorneys would ignore, to use *Monsanto* to argue for an end to the per se treatment of RPM.

In retrospect, however, the decision to forgo a rule-of-reason defense at the district court level may have been expensive for both Monsanto and for society. The use of a per se strategy meant that the full evidentiary record that was needed to support a rule-of-reason argument before the Supreme Court case was never developed. In addition, the Supreme Court was able to argue that the failure to raise the issue at the District Court level meant that the Court was not required to reach the broader issue in *Monsanto.*

The Court of Appeals

Monsanto appealed, arguing that there were errors in the District Court judge's charge to the jury, that there was insufficient evidence to support the verdict, and that the District Court made several erroneous evidentiary rulings. The United States Court of Appeals for the Seventh Circuit found none of these arguments persuasive and affirmed the judgment of the District Court.[16]

The principal nonfactual issue was evidentiary: Monsanto argued that evidence of price complaints coupled with evidence of termination in response to those complaints should be insufficient to prove the existence of an RPM agreement. The Court of Appeals disagreed, stating, "We believe . . . that proof of termination following [rephrased in the subsequent paragraph in the opinion as "in response to"] competitor complaints is sufficient to support an inference of concerted action."[17]

---

[15]*Continental T.V.* v. *GTE Sylvania,* 433 U.S. 36 (1977).

[16]*Spray-Rite Service Corp.* v. *Monsanto Co.,* 684 F.2d. 1226 (1982).

[17]684 F.2d 1226, 1238, 1239 (1982).

Monsanto also argued that its promotion and distribution policies should be tested under the *Sylvania* rule-of-reason standard. The Court of Appeals held, however, that *Sylvania* did not limit the Supreme Court's earlier holding in *Sealy*[18] that otherwise lawful vertical restrictions imposed as part of an unlawful scheme to fix prices are per se illegal and that *Sylvania* applies only if there is no allegation that the territorial restrictions are part of a conspiracy to fix prices.

The Supreme Court

On petition from Monsanto and from the Department of Justice (DOJ) as amicus curiae, the Supreme Court granted certiorari. The petitioners presented three central questions to the Supreme Court. The first two were evidentiary: What evidence is sufficient to infer that nonprice restraints are so connected to an RPM scheme that they should be treated under a per se rather than a rule-of-reason standard, and what evidence is sufficient to infer that a dealer has been terminated as part of a conspiracy to impose RPM? The third question was presented only by the Department of Justice: Should RPM be per se illegal?

On the first question, both Monsanto and the DOJ seized on a statement by the Court of Appeals that *Sylvania* applies to nonprice restraints only if there is no "allegation" that those restraints are part of an RPM conspiracy. Both Monsanto and the DOJ argued that, given the potentially procompetitive benefits from nonprice restraints that the Supreme Court had recognized in *Sylvania*, a "mere allegation" that such restraints were part of an RPM scheme should be insufficient for per se treatment. Even evidence that nonprice restraints have had an effect on price should not be sufficient. As the DOJ's amicus brief pointed out, nonprice restrictions that prevent free-riding and encourage dealers to provide more or higher-quality point-of-sale services can be expected to result in higher retail prices. If the value of those additional services to consumers is greater than the increase in the retail price, however, consumers will be better off and will respond to the increase in both price and quality by buying more of the product. Thus, the critical evidentiary distinction between a procompetitive vertical restraint and an anticompetitive increase in either the manufacturer's wholesale price or the dealer's margin is its effect on quantity: The former results in an increase in the quantity sold, the latter in a decrease.

The Supreme Court disposed of this question in a footnote, stating that the lower court's language could be read to say that a plaintiff must prove, as well as allege, that the nonprice restrictions were in fact part of a price conspiracy. Monsanto had conceded that if the nonprice practices were proved to have been instituted as part of a price-fixing conspiracy, they

---

[18]*United States v. Sealy*, 388 U.S. 350 (1967).

would be subject to per se treatment. Since the jury had found that the nonprice practices were created by Monsanto pursuant to a conspiracy to fix resale prices, Monsanto's argument was reduced to the proposition that the jury did not have sufficient evidence to support this finding. Monsanto had failed to make that argument at the Court of Appeals, and, since that court did not address the point, the Supreme Court declined to reach it, stating only that "nothing in our discussion today undercuts the holding of *Sylvania* that non-price restrictions are to be judged under the rule of reason."[19]

A second question, which did interest the Supreme Court, was whether a per se unlawful vertical price-fixing conspiracy could be inferred solely from evidence that a manufacturer had received price complaints from a distributor's competitors and later did not renew the distributor's contract. Monsanto and the DOJ argued that the Appeals Court's holding that "termination following competitor complaints is sufficient to support an inference of concerted action" was incorrect. It undermined the Sherman Act's crucial distinction between collective and unilateral conduct by permitting a jury to infer conspiracy from normal marketplace behavior that was fully consistent with unilateral conduct. Manufacturers routinely terminate distributors unilaterally for being unwilling or unable to promote or service their product in the way desired by the manufacturer. Indeed, one indicator of that failure may be the distributor's pricing strategy. Even a manufacturer that is making no effort to control the resale price may have good reasons for closely monitoring the operations of price-cutting dealers. In doing so, the manufacturer is likely to be helped by complaints from rival dealers, especially if those dealers believe that they are losing sales because the price-cutting dealer is free-riding on their efforts. Neither parallel desires nor evidence of communication, by themselves or in combination, provides sufficient evidence to imply collusion between a manufacturer and one or more dealers. Further, the practical effect of a "termination that follows complaints" standard for inferring collusion could be virtually to immunize dealers from terminations once a competitor had complained.

The Supreme Court began its approach to the evidentiary standard in Monsanto by reiterating the two central themes of the legal approach to vertical restraints—the distinction between concerted and independent action, and the distinction between concerted action to set prices and concerted action on nonprice restrictions. The Court acknowledged that the economic effects of vertical arrangements, whether concerted or unilateral, price or nonprice, are often similar or identical. The Court did not, however, proceed from this observation to conclude that these distinctions were invalid as the basis for choosing between a rule-of-reason or a per se standard. The Court concluded that for the per se approach of vertical price restraints,

---

[19]465 U.S. 752, 761, fn. 6 (1984).

> something more than evidence of complaints is needed. There must be evidence that tends to exclude the possibility that the manufacturer and non-terminated distributors were acting independently. . . . The antitrust plaintiff should present direct or circumstantial evidence that reasonably tends to prove that the manufacturer and others "had a conscious commitment to a common scheme designed to achieve an unlawful objective, . . . a unity of purpose or a common design and understanding, or a meeting of minds in an unlawful arrangement."[20]

The Court thus rejected the Court of Appeal's evidentiary standard of termination following complaints. The new standard, however, was not enough to save Monsanto. Applying the new standard to the facts of this case, the Court concluded that "there was sufficient evidence for a jury to have concluded that Monsanto and some of its distributors were party to an 'agreement' or 'conspiracy' to maintain resale prices and terminate price cutters" and affirmed the judgment of the lower court.[21]

The third question presented to the Court in the DOJ's amicus brief was potentially the most important: Should RPM be per se illegal? The amicus brief argued that the Court should take this opportunity to do what it had never done: analyze RPM in terms of its actual economic effects. It pointed out that a manufacturer who wished only to raise the resale price could and would do so simply by raising its own price to the distributor and that preserving or increasing the downstream margin may be a more efficient way to achieve procompetitive effects than various nonprice restraints judged under a rule of reason. The brief went on to cite control of the free-rider problem as a major beneficial effect of RPM and argued that the evidence in *Monsanto* pointed to this as the explanation for Monsanto's conduct. Finally, the brief argued that the conditions under which any adverse competitive effects (i.e., a manufacturer or dealer horizontal cartel) from RPM might occur are readily ascertainable.[22]

While some of the justices showed a keen interest in the question during oral argument, the Supreme Court's opinion ducked the question, stating only in a footnote that:

> Certainly in this case we have no occasion to consider the merits of this argument. This case was tried on per se instructions to the jury. Neither party argued in the District Court that the rule of reason should apply to a vertical price-fixing conspiracy, nor raised the point on appeal. In fact, neither party before this Court presses the argument advanced by amici.

---

[20]465 U.S. 752, 764 (1984).

[21]465 U.S. 752, 765 (1984).

[22]Necessary conditions for RPM to facilitate manufacturers' collusion include high concentration, barriers to entry, and industrywide use of the practice. Necessary conditions for RPM to be a disguised dealer cartel include market power by dealers in the resale market and some price inelasticity for the product of the manufacturer or group of manufacturers coerced by dealer pressure.

We therefore decline to reach the question, and we decide the case in the context in which it was decided below and argued here.[23]

Justice Brennan, in a concurring decision, did, however, provide one explanation by stating that,

> As the Court notes, the Solicitor General has filed a brief in this Court as amicus curiae urging us to overrule the Court's decision in *Dr. Miles Medical Co.* v. *John D. Park & Sons Co.,* 220 U.S. 373 (1911). That decision has stood for 73 years, and Congress has certainly been aware of its existence throughout that time. Yet Congress has never enacted legislation to overrule the interpretation of the Act. Because the Court adheres to that rule and, in my view, properly applies *Dr. Miles* to this case, I join the opinion and judgment of the Court.[24]

The history of Congress's views of RPM is a long and complex one. The amicus brief for the United States argued that Congress's views on RPM had varied over the years, that in repealing the broad per se legality afforded by the Fair Trade Laws (the Miller-Tidings and McGuire Acts) in 1975 Congress did not specify that RPM be treated as per se illegal, and that determination could properly be assumed by the Court.

But Congress had made its recent views extremely clear in resolutions, committee hearings, and, most strikingly, in passing a statute to prohibit the Justice Department from urging in its oral argument before the Court in *Monsanto* that the per se treatment of RPM be altered.[25] The Court was surely aware of these views.

AN ECONOMIC ANALYSIS OF *MONSANTO*

Turning now to economic diagnostics, can we discern from the available evidence the "true" reason and effects of Monsanto's actions? For all practical purposes, the answer is yes. But the ability of the Court or any observer to diagnose this case correctly is severely hindered by the legal structure under which it was brought.

First, Monsanto was not appropriately an antitrust case at all: If anything, this was a contract dispute between a manufacturer and a distributor that was transformed into an antitrust case by the combination of a per se standard and the prospect of treble damages. In general, the ability of

---

[23]465 U.S. 752, 762, fn. 7 (1984).

[24]465 U.S. 752, 769 (1984).

[25]"None of the funds appropriated . . . may be used for any activity the purposes of which is to overturn or alter the per se prohibition against resale price maintenance in effect under Federal antitrust laws." Public Law No. 98-166 (1983), sec. 510. This law was passed after the DOJ had submitted its written amicus brief but before the DOJ's oral argument before the Supreme Court in *Monsanto*.

courts to resolve such contract disputes efficiently requires that the parties provide information on explicit or implicit contracts and address any violations directly. Costuming such disputes as antitrust claims leaves some valid contract claims unaddressed while other efficient contracts are heavily penalized, thus reducing the incentives of firms to enter into efficient contracts.

To this author's knowledge, Spray-Rite never asserted that Monsanto had violated an explicit or implicit contract. In general, however, distributors' legal claims of violations of implicit contracts by a manufacturer may be economically defensible. For example, Spray-Rite could have reversed the free-rider argument against Monsanto by asserting that it (Spray-Rite) had invested a considerable effort over ten years in building up an understanding and acceptance of Monsanto's products among a group, however small, of major customers; that as a result, sales of Monsanto products to these customers had become a highly profitable business; and that Monsanto's decision to terminate Spray-Rite was simply a naked seizure of Spray-Rite's investment. Termination would allow Monsanto to appropriate that investment directly by making those sales through its vertically integrated sales system. Alternatively, Monsanto could assign such highly profitable customers to its other distributors, extracting in return either additional distributor services or a lower average distributor margin. Thus, instead of Spray-Rite's free-riding on the efforts of Monsanto or of other distributors, Monsanto was attempting to free ride on Spray-Rite.

Second, even if this were appropriately an antitrust case, the application of the per se rule meant that only by accident would a court discover the cause and effects of Monsanto's decision to terminate Spray-Rite. If *Monsanto* had been judged under a rule-of-reason standard, it would not have been sufficient to show that Monsanto had agreed with other distributors to impose a minimum distributor margin and had terminated Spray-Rite for price cutting. Under the *Sylvania* standard, Spray-Rite would have had to show that RPM by Monsanto had an anticompetitive effect. Under a per se standard, however, all that mattered was whether Monsanto had done the deed, not why or with what effect.

The absence of any incentive for Spray-Rite to establish the cause or effect of RPM by Monsanto placed Monsanto in a dilemma. Monsanto, of course, vigorously denied ever engaging in RPM—a response that could only be expected but one that may also have prevented much valuable information from ever appearing. As the DOJ's amicus brief later put it,

> It is true that Monsanto has denied engaging in resale price maintenance; but the per se unlawful status of that practice has been universally assumed by courts for so long and the consequences of being adjudged to have engaged in the practice are so severe—treble damages and possible

felony prosecution—that few antitrust defendants can be expected to concede participating in such an agreement, a concession that is necessary as a matter of litigation strategy if they wish to argue that the practice was procompetitive. For 70 years, then, it has been unlikely that the per se status of resale price maintenance would be placed directly in issue by an antitrust defendant.

Monsanto did, of course, go to some efforts to argue that its real goal was to improve dealer education and increase customer services. The strategy, however, appears to have been more to provide an explanation for Monsanto's behavior that might be taken by the jury to be an alternative to—or even perhaps mutually exclusive with—RPM, rather than an attempt to justify RPM.

The per se treatment of RPM thus forced both parties to adopt litigation strategies under which a number of important factual questions were neither asked nor answered. Nevertheless, a great deal is clear beyond a reasonable doubt. First, both of the standard anticompetitive scenarios—dealer collusion and manufacturer collusion—can be ruled out. With respect to dealer collusion, there was evidence that other distributors complained to Monsanto about price cutting by Spray-Rite. As noted, however, such dealer complaints are both routine and explicable on other grounds. There was no evidence of any concerted effort by a group of distributors to force Monsanto to raise the retail margin against its will. It might be argued that an explicit agreement among distributors would not be essential if a few large distributors each accounted for a large proportion of the sales of one or more relatively small and powerless manufacturers. But the large number of actual or potential distributors, the absence of any entry barriers into distribution, and the enormous size discrepancy between manufacturers and distributors of herbicides would render incredible any scenario of unilateral threats by dealers against an unwilling manufacturer. The evidence from both structure and conduct show clearly that any RPM in this case was inspired and enforced by the manufacturer.

It is also clear that any RPM was imposed unilaterally by Monsanto. Again, no evidence was introduced, nor any allegation made, that Monsanto imposed RPM as part of an agreement among manufacturers aimed at facilitating oligopolistic price coordination. Collusion among herbicide manufacturers would not be implausible. The available data showed that in 1968, both the corn and the soybean herbicide markets were highly concentrated.[26] But there was no evidence of the kind of pricing behavior that RPM is alleged to prevent: retail price shading that induces retaliatory wholesale price cuts by manufacturers. Most important, there was no evidence or

---

[26]All indications are that corn and soybean herbicides are separate product markets. Even using only the available market share data, the HHI was over 5125 in corn herbicides and over 2822 in soybean herbicides.

allegation that RPM was being imposed industrywide or even by a group of firms with a sizable share of the market.[27] Moreover, Monsanto was apparently the least likely instigator of any attempt at collusion. In 1968, Geigy dominated the corn herbicide market, while in soybean herbicides Monsanto's 3-percent market share made it a fringe firm in that market. Resale price maintenance seems to have appealed more to small fringe firms than to the large firms that might be expected to have had an interest in "stabilized prices."

The ease with which the only two anticompetitive scenarios can be dismissed allows us to rule out any potential for an anticompetitive effect from the use of RPM by Monsanto and should have been enough to dismiss the case under a rule-of-reason analysis. But both Monsanto and the DOJ argued that the available facts in *Monsanto* not only demonstrate the absence of the necessary conditions for an anticompetitive effort but also provide considerable positive evidence that Monsanto's vertical practices were procompetitive and beneficial to consumers.

The most dramatic evidence is the very large increase in Monsanto's share of the market between 1968 and 1972, from 15 percent to 28 percent in corn herbicide and from 3 percent to 19 percent in soybean herbicide. With much of those increases coming at the expense of the leading firms, concentration fell significantly in both markets.[28] Unfortunately, we do not know how much of the increase in Monsanto's market shares to ascribe to Monsanto's introduction of its "third-generation" herbicide, LASSO, in 1969.

Monsanto could also point to a significant fall in the relative prices of its products. Between 1967 and 1979, while an index of Monsanto herbicide prices rose by 23 percent, prices of all agricultural chemicals increased by 53 percent, the CPI rose by 119 percent, and the overall indexes of prices received and paid by American farmers rose by 147 percent and 149 percent, respectively. Again, however, little if any of this fall in Monsanto's relative prices could be ascribed to Monsanto's new distribution policies. A number of critical patents expired after 1975—notably Geigy's Atrazine patent in 1976 and AmChem's Amibem patent in 1978—and some price cutting to deter postexpiration entry was expected by 1972.

Both Monsanto and the DOJ as amicus argued that the relevant model was Telser's "free-riding on special services" model. Indeed, Monsanto appeared to provide almost a textbook example of the free-rider scenario: a complex product, where the provision of complete and accurate presale information is crucial, sold by a discounting broker. Curiously, however, to this author's knowledge no evidence was ever presented of

---

[27]One Monsanto document reported that "Stauffer, DuPont, and Elanco have sold on a Fair Trade policy. Elanco [the division of Eli Lilly that produced Treflan] dropped Fair Trade in about 1968." (Monsanto's Corn/Soybean Product Area Business Plan 1970–1975. Plaintiff's exhibit 13a.) Of these three, only Treflan accounted for a sizable market share.

[28]The HHI fell from over 5125 to over 3488 in corn herbicides, and from over 2822 to over 1886 in soybean herbicides.

even one uninformed farmer or dealer who had been educated in the benefits of Monsanto's product by a full-service distributor and who then purchased Monsanto herbicides from Spray-Rite at discount prices. Perhaps there were instances of such postservice but presale switching, but Monsanto decided not to introduce them at trial for fear of emphasizing the pricing aspects. Thus, while the standard free-riding story cannot be entirely dismissed because we cannot be certain that no significant postservice/presale switching occurred, it seems dubious at best.

What does emerge clearly is Monsanto's concern that Spray-Rite was selling too little rather than too much and in particular was refusing to attract new, smaller customers in its area of primary responsibility. Monsanto's criteria for renewal, its partial vertical integration into distribution, its shipping policies, and its complex pricing and payment system for distributors all point to a concern with the intensive margin and a concerted effort to increase Monsanto's market share by pushing distributors to develop new customers and expand purchases by past customers.

Why was this necessary? Why could not Monsanto simply establish a wholesale price and sell to anyone interested in buying? Why could Monsanto not rely on competitive downstream distributors and dealers to make the same decisions Monsanto would have if it were vertically integrated and controlled those decisions directly? In other words, why did the price system fail? The usual reason given is Telser's free-riding story. But the free-riding story does not fit this particular set of facts very well.

The concern with and attempts to influence decisions by competitive downstream firms appears almost ubiquitous among manufacturers who have "market power" or even just a differentiated product, even if presale services are not priced separately or are easily free-ridable. This points to a much broader market failure than free-riding. Simply put, whenever an input or intermediate product is sold at a price above marginal cost, an inefficiency can arise because socially incorrect information and commands are being provided to the downstream market. There is a considerable literature on the effects of upstream pricing above marginal cost when market power is also exercised independently downstream. Such "successive monopoly" conditions give rise to incentives for vertical integration or for partial forms of vertical control such as setting maximum resale prices. The result is an increase in joint profits and a decrease in prices to consumers. Thus, vertical control under successive monopoly conditions is unambiguously socially beneficial.[29] In addition, even when the downstream stage is competitive, if the monopolized input can be used in variable proportions with competitively supplied inputs, the upstream firm has an incentive to integrate vertically (or use other vertical practices, such as tying arrangements) to control the input proportions decision.[30] In these models, the competitively

[29]For a review of that literature, see Warren-Boulton (1978).

[30]See Vernon and Graham (1971), Hay (1973), Schmalensee (1973), Warren-Boulton (1974, 1978), Mallela and Nahato (1980), and Westfield (1981).

supplied inputs and the monopolized inputs are net substitutes, and the upstream firm's problem is that when it sets its price above its marginal cost, independent downstream firms are induced to use too much of the competitive inputs relative to monopolized inputs.

In the manufacturer-distributor context, however, inputs provided at successive stages appear to be net complements. When the manufacturer of a differentiated good sets the wholesale price above marginal cost, the independent distributor or retailer will "underprovide" complementary downstream services, whether those services are shelf space for breakfast cereal or blue jeans, or complete inventories and presale information to customers in the case of agricultural herbicides.

The manufacturer has several alternatives. First, it can vertically integrate downstream into retailing and provide those enhanced services directly. Second, it can establish complex nonlinear pricing and subsidy schedules that raise the return to the dealer at the margin without raising the average dealer return (i.e., lower the inframarginal return and raise the marginal return). Third, it can make an all-or-nothing offer: Either the dealer provides specific services (e.g., to small herbicide customers in its area of primary responsibility) that would not be profitable by themselves to the dealer, or the dealer is terminated. Of course, the threat to terminate is meaningful only if termination would preclude profitable sales to other customers—perhaps that dealer's share of large and well-informed herbicide users in the dealer's area of primary responsibility, to whom large sales can be made at relatively low cost and at resale margins protected by the manufacturer through threats of dealer termination.[31] All three strategies have the same effect, and Monsanto appears to have tried all three, searching for the most effective and least-cost combination.

Whichever form or combination of forms of vertical control is used to achieve the manufacturer's goal, both consumer and total welfare from such an expansion of downstream services would appear to be substantially greater. Even in the short run, the manufacturer and marginal consumers clearly gain, while, given the endogeneity of the wholesale prices, inframarginal consumers—the large and well-informed purchasers—may gain or lose. The effects seem to be analogous to first-degree price discrimination. In the long run, given the ex ante competitive conditions that are likely to prevail at the research and development stage, any increase in potential manufacturer profits will be dissipated in the form of additional expenditure on research and development, leading to a large number and variety of such products.

This is a far cry from a practice that invariably has a pernicious effect on competition and lacks any redeeming competitive virtue for which the rule of per se illegality was intended. Clearly, in the history of antitrust cases brought against anticompetitive practices, *Monsanto*, and, almost

---

[31]See Klein and Murphy (1988).

without exception all cases involving resale price restraints unilaterally imposed by a manufacturer, are false positives.

Unfortunately, while the first and the second strategies are generally legal by themselves, under legal current doctrine attempting the third can expose a manufacturer to the possibility of very large penalties. This is a triumph of form over function.

The uncertainty and arbitrariness of such a legalistic distinction between price and nonprice forms of vertical control have imposed large transaction costs on society, including the legal costs of the many manufacturer-dealer contract disputes transformed into RPM cases. But the major cost must be the cost of acts committed and the forgone benefits of acts not undertaken by those threatened by such sanctions. In the former category is a bias toward nonprice forms of vertical control, such as vertical integration—surely a paradoxical result of a legal standard apparently motivated in part by a political desire to protect small business. In the latter category are the downstream services not provided and the output not produced and sold or perhaps not even developed.

THE LEGACY OF *MONSANTO*

In *Monsanto,* a jury found sufficient evidence to conclude that Monsanto had been conducting an illegal RPM program, and the Court of Appeals and then the Supreme Court both affirmed. The plaintiff won, and RPM continued to be condemned as a per se violation of Section 1 of the Sherman Act. Yet, ironically, *Monsanto* has come to be considered a substantial victory for the defendant's bar.

This paradoxical outcome stems from the standard of proof that the Supreme Court enunciated in its opinion: "Permitting an agreement to be inferred merely from the existence of complaints, or even from the fact that termination came about 'in response to' complaints, could deter or penalize perfectly legitimate conduct. . . . Thus, something more than evidence of complaints is needed."[32] The Court found enough "more" in *Monsanto* to affirm the jury's conclusion, but the standard itself tightened the criteria that had been used by the Court of Appeals. In addition, subsequent to the decision a number of dealer termination cases, in which RPM allegations were based largely or solely on evidence of complaints followed by termination, were dropped by the plaintiffs. And in 1988 the Supreme Court in *Sharp*[33] extended even further the evidentiary burden on plaintiffs in RPM cases.[34]

[32]465 U.S. 752, 763, 764 (1984).

[33]*Business Electronics Corp.* v. *Sharp Electronics Corp.,* 485 U.S. 717 (1988).

[34]*Sharp* held that termination of a dealer following complaints about such dealer's pricing is not per se illegal absent evidence that the manufacturer and the nonterminated distributor agreed to set or maintain prices at a specific level.

The decade following *Sharp* was a relatively quiet one for antitrust policy with respect to RPM. Despite congressional expressions of displeasure with the Supreme Court's tightening of the evidentiary burdens on plaintiffs in *Monsanto* and *Sharp*, no legislation overturning these decisions was ever passed.

In 1997, however, the Supreme Court reversed course with respect to *maximum* RPM. In *State Oil Co.*[35] the Court unanimously declared that maximum RPM should be judged under a rule-of-reason standard, overturning the per se standard for maximum RPM that it had established in the 1968 *Albrecht* case.[36] Though the Court indicated that this decision did not change its per se rule for minimum RPM, this new flexibility shown by the Court may eventually inspire it to revisit the RPM question more broadly and adopt a broader rule-of-reason approach.

REFERENCES

Butz, David A. "Vertical Price Controls with Uncertain Demand." *Journal of Law & Economics* 40 (October 1997): 433–459.

Comanor, William S. "Vertical Price-Fixing, Vertical Market Restrictions, and the New Antitrust Policy." *Harvard Law Review* 98 (March 1985): 983–1002.

Comanor, William S., and John B. Kirkwood. "Resale Price Maintenance and Antitrust Policy." *Contemporary Policy Issues* 3 (Spring 1985): 9–16.

Hay, George A. "An Economic Analysis of Vertical Integration." *Industrial Organization Review* 1 (1973): 188–198.

Klein, Benjamin, and Kevin M. Murphy. "Vertical Restraints as Contract Enforcement Mechanisms." *Journal of Law & Economics* 31 (October 1988): 265–298.

Mallela, P., and B. Nahala. "Theory of Vertical Control with Variable Proportions." *Journal of Political Economy* 88 (October 1980): 1009–1025.

Scherer, F. M. "The Economics of Vertical Restraints." *Antitrust Law Journal* 52 (1983): 687–707.

Schmalensee, Richard. "A Note on the Theory of Vertical Integration." *Journal of Political Economy* 81 (March/April 1973): 442–449.

Telser, Lester G. "Why Should Manufacturers Want Fair Trade?" *Journal of Law & Economics* 3 (October 1960): 86–105.

Vernon, J. M., and D. A. Graham. "Profitability of Monopolization by Vertical Integration." *Journal of Political Economy* 79 (July/August 1971): 924–925.

[35]*State Oil Co. v. Khan*, 66 L.W. 4001 (1997).

[36]*Albrecht v. Harold*, 390 U.S. 145 (1968). A number of amicus briefs in *State Oil Co.* (including a joint brief by the DOJ and the FTC) urged the Court to adopt a "rule of reason" standard for maximum RPM; opposing amicus briefs urged the court to maintain its per se standard even for these cases (apparently fearing that this might be an opening wedge for the Court eventually to apply a rule of reason standard in all RPM cases).

Warren-Boulton, Frederick R. "Vertical Control with Variable Proportions." *Journal of Political Economy* 82 (August 1974): 783–802.

Warren-Boulton, Frederick R. *Vertical Control of Markets: Business and Labor Practices.* Cambridge, Mass.: Ballinger, 1978.

Westfield, F. M. "Vertical Integration: Does Product Price Rise or Fall?" *American Economic Review* 71 (June 1981): 334–346.

White, Lawrence J. "Vertical Restraints in Antitrust Law: A Coherent Model." *Antitrust Bulletin* 26 (Summer 1981): 327–345.

White, Lawrence J. "Resale Price Maintenance and the Problem of Marginal and Inframarginal Customers." *Contemporary Policy Issues* 3 (Spring 1985): 17–22.

CASE 16

Links Between Vertically Related Markets: Kodak (1992)

Jeffrey K. MacKie-Mason and
John Metzler

"The difficulty of obtaining parts, technical information and diagnostic software has effectively kept 3rd party service suppliers out of the advanced equipment service market"[1]

"Both IBM and Xerox will sell spare parts, but we do not. This makes it more difficult for a third party to service our copiers."[2]

INTRODUCTION

In 1987 seventeen small companies filed an antitrust lawsuit against the Eastman Kodak Corporation ("Kodak"). These companies, several of them literally "mom and pop" operations, had been trying to compete with Kodak for contracts to provide maintenance service to end customers who owned expensive, durable Kodak photocopier or micrographics equipment. Eleven years later, there have been two District Court opinions, two from the Ninth Circuit Court of Appeals, and one from the Supreme Court. A second, partial District Court retrial has been ordered on part of the damages calculation, and Kodak may yet appeal its guilty verdict to the Supreme Court one more time. Entire conferences have been devoted to the antitrust economics issues raised by *Kodak,* and numerous articles have been published in both

Since 1994, MacKie-Mason has served as expert economist for the plaintiffs, and testified at trial. Metzler assisted in the economic analysis.

[1] Trial Exhibit (hereafter, "Exh.") 99 at 6762, a Kodak report on micrographic service.

[2] Exh. 649 at 1315–1316, a Kodak internal document.

legal and economics scholarly journals. Since the initial Supreme Court opinion in *Kodak,* there have been at least seven closely related Appeals Court opinions, and they stand in sharply divided conflict. *Kodak* is one of the most significant antitrust cases of the last decade or two. It is also one of the most controversial, and the controversy is far from resolved.

In this chapter we report on the history and status of *Kodak,* fully aware that the legal proceedings may not yet be finished. We focus on the economic issues. Although there is still sharp disagreement on the antitrust *policy* that should be followed in response to the economic issues, there is now a fairly broad agreement about the structure, assumptions, and results of the basic economic theories. After summarizing the relevant factual and procedural background, we describe the theories. We then describe the economic analyses presented by the parties in court. We close by discussing several issues in the law and economics of antitrust that *Kodak* raises, but that have implications far beyond cases about durable equipment and maintenance.

MARKET BACKGROUND[3]

This case concerned Kodak practices relating to parts for, and maintenance service on, micrographic equipment and high-volume copiers. These machines are "durable" goods: goods that are purchased with the expectation of gaining utility from them for an extended period of time. ("Consumption" goods are purchased for the one-time utility that they provide.) Many durable goods, perhaps most, require ongoing maintenance for continued utility. For example, a copier with a burned-out light bulb generates little utility beyond that of an ordinary countertop.

Specialized terms have been developed to describe the markets in which these goods are sold. Consider a car, as an example: because the utility derived from the car is what brings consumers into these markets, the market in which the car is sold is the "foremarket" or "primary" market. Demand for maintenance is composed entirely of consumers of the primary market good: consumers don't demand brake service if they don't own a car. Therefore, we refer to the market for maintenance goods as the "aftermarket."[4]

Micrographics

Micrographics equipment is used for creating, filing, retrieving, viewing, and printing microforms. Microforms include microfiche, microfilm (for example, with back issues of *The New York Times*), and, for secret agents,

---

[3] In the interest of space we do not provide specific citations to the trial evidence to support most of these background facts.

[4] Foremarkets and aftermarkets do not exist only for equipment and maintenance. For example, we could have a computer operating systems foremarket and application program aftermarkets.

microdots. These are variations on the same basic idea: using optics and fine-grained film, it is possible to expose an image of printed matter onto film at a greatly reduced size, thereby reducing storage space. With another set of optics, the film image can be enlarged to the original size, then viewed or printed.

Kodak invented this process in the late 1920s. Over the last seventy years, micrographics equipment has developed to encompass cameras, film processors, film duplicators, readers (that enlarge microfilm for viewing or printing), COM (computer output to microfilm, devices that "print" to microfilm rather than paper), and CAR (computer automated retrieval, largely software/hardware combinations to automate handling large libraries of microfilm). Kodak remained a significant manufacturer and seller in most of these equipment categories.

Photocopiers

Kodak began manufacturing and selling high-volume photocopiers in the mid-1970s. These are large machines, weighing hundreds of pounds and generally selling for tens of thousands of dollars. High-volume photocopiers can handle from 60,000 to over one million copies per month.

Maintenance

Both copiers and micrographic equipment require extensive, ongoing maintenance, consisting of service labor and parts. In this case, essentially all maintenance calls included a service component, and many, perhaps most, required parts as well. Labor and parts are not required in fixed proportions. Among other things, they can vary due to the choice between part repair and replacement, and the use of preventive maintenance.

Kodak established a national network of service technicians to provide maintenance on its copiers, and another technician network for maintenance of its micrographics equipment. Kodak advertised the quality of its maintenance.

By the early 1980s, there were many, small independent service organizations (ISOs) providing maintenance on Kodak micrographic equipment. There were a few ISOs servicing Kodak photocopiers.

These ISOs typically provided maintenance at prices 15 to 30 percent below those of Kodak. They provided service generally of the same quality as Kodak's, some better, some worse (that was also true within Kodak's service). They at times provided customized maintenance options Kodak would not provide.

The "Parts Policy"

In 1985 Image Technical Services (ITS) had won a large contract from the Computer Service Corporation (CSC) for micrographics maintenance.

Kodak had been servicing CSC's equipment for about $200,000 per year with a four-hour guaranteed response time. ITS submitted a bid of $150,000 with the same four-hour response time guarantee. Kodak countered by lowering its bid to $135,000. ITS came back with a bid of $100,000 and agreed to put a service technician on-site full time.[5]

Shortly thereafter, Kodak instituted a policy of no longer selling parts for either copier or newly introduced micrographics equipment to ISOs.[6] This was clearly a change in practice for micrographics. Kodak had previously sold parts to anyone who ordered them and seemed to support the small ISOs. Kodak agreed that this was a change in policy, but claimed that the policy applied only prospectively: Kodak would refuse to sell parts only for equipment models introduced after the policy was announced.

It is not clear whether the change in *practice* on copier parts sales was also a change in policy. Kodak had previously sold copier parts to some ISOs and had referred the ISOs to Kodak's in-house technician help line for assistance. Kodak claimed such sales were unintentional.

Over time, Kodak increasingly policed its no-parts sales policy. It began tracking parts sales to ensure that equipment owners were not purchasing more than they would reasonably need for the equipment that they owned. Kodak required prospective parts purchasers to provide proof of ownership of the equipment model for which they were ordering parts. It additionally required, for copier parts, certification that the customer had a Kodak-trained employee to effect the repairs. Kodak also required customers to agree to not resell parts.

PROCEDURAL HISTORY

The Initial Case, and the Motion for Summary Judgment

In April 1987, ITS and several other ISOs filed suit against Kodak in Federal District Court, Northern District of California. The suit alleged that Kodak used its monopoly over parts to monopolize the service markets for its copiers and micrographics equipment; that Kodak had conspired with its outside parts suppliers to preclude ISO access to parts, thereby monopolizing the service market; and that Kodak had tied its service labor to parts, thereby harming competition in the service market. These actions were alleged to violate Sections 1 and 2 of the Sherman Act.

Very early in the fact-finding process, Kodak moved for "summary judgment."[7] Kodak argued there was no allegation that it had market

---

[5] Trial Transcript (hereafter, "Tr.") at 1213–1215.

[6] The record is not clear on whether the policy was implemented in 1985 or 1986. It was not much enforced, if at all, prior to mid-1986.

[7] "Summary judgment" is granted when the Court is persuaded that, even if all disputed facts are resolved in favor of the nonmoving party, the nonmoving party cannot, as a matter of law, win the case. Essentially, it is a way to avoid wasting Court resources. See below.

power in the equipment markets. Kodak claimed that equipment consumers had many alternatives available to them and made purchase decisions based on the total cost of ownership,[8] and thus any attempt by Kodak to extract higher profits from maintenance customers would result in equipment customers' taking their business elsewhere. Thus, because it could not have service market power, Kodak argued that as a matter of law it could not be found guilty of tying or monopolizing service markets. The judge agreed, and granted summary judgment.[9]

The ISOs appealed to the Ninth Circuit Court of Appeals, claiming that Kodak's arguments were purely theoretical. Various market imperfections could break the link between higher aftermarket prices and reduced foremarket sales, preventing foremarket competition from sufficiently disciplining aftermarket market power. The Ninth Circuit granted the appeal, overturned the summary judgment order, and remanded the case for trial.[10]

Kodak appealed to the Supreme Court, which ruled in 1992. The Court agreed with the Ninth Circuit, and remanded the case for trial in district court.[11]

It is important to recognize that the Supreme Court did *not* find that Kodak had illegally monopolized or tied. Nor did it find that parts and service were necessarily relevant markets. The Supreme Court found only that Kodak had not carried its burden of proof for summary judgment. Kodak had failed to convince the Court that economic theory proved that it was impossible for Kodak to be guilty. Rather, the Supreme Court concluded that the ISO's economic theories were plausible, and that Kodak's guilt or innocence hinged on the interpretation of the *facts* in the case: a trial would be required.

The Trial

On June 19, 1995, the jury trial of *ITS* v. *Kodak* began in District Court. The trial involved sixty-three witnesses giving twenty-seven days of testimony. At the close of evidence, the plaintiffs dropped the tying claims. Therefore, the only claims presented to the jury were that Kodak had monopolized the service markets for its high-volume copies and micrographics equipment. The alleged monopolizing acts were the restrictive parts policies, which leveraged Kodak's parts monopolies into service monopolies. The jury deliberated for thirteen days and returned a unanimous guilty verdict. Kodak was held liable for $24 million in damages, trebled to $72 million. On February 15, 1996, the District Court issued a ten-year

---

[8] "Total cost of ownership" is the present discounted (expected) value of all costs associated with owning and using the machine, including future maintenance costs. This is also called "life cycle" analysis.

[9] 1988 WL 156332 (N.D. Cal.).

[10] 903 F.2d 612 (9th Cir. 1990).

[11] 504 U.S. 451 (1992).

injunction requiring Kodak to sell parts to ISOs at nondiscriminatory prices.[12]

Kodak appealed to the Ninth Circuit Court of Appeals with three interesting economic points: Can Kodak be required to sell patented parts and copyrighted service software and manuals? Can "all Kodak parts" be a relevant market, despite the lack of substitutability between two different parts? Can a firm be convicted of monopolizing its *aftermarkets* without first being found to have obtained supracompetitive *systems* profits or prices?

On August 26, 1997, the Ninth Circuit ruled. The Court rejected these three Kodak arguments and upheld the plaintiffs' verdict on all liability issues.[13]

ECONOMICS OF AFTERMARKET MARKET POWER

The central economic feature of *Kodak* was the dispute over theories of market power in aftermarkets. Kodak argued before the Supreme Court that primary market competition, as a matter of economic theory, precludes anticompetitive aftermarket actions. After the Supreme Court rejected this argument, Kodak argued at trial that the *presumption* should be that aftermarket power was unlikely and that Kodak's circumstances were consistent with this presumption. We refer to this as the "systems" theory. The plaintiffs argued that there are several theories showing commonplace circumstances under which a durable goods manufacturer could monopolize its aftermarkets. Therefore, they argued, there should be no presumption against aftermarket power. Further, the plaintiffs presented facts to demonstrate that Kodak both had and exercised market power. To present the arguments put forth on each side, we will use a very simple model of firm profits from a foremarket and an aftermarket.

Whereas a firm competing in a single good has only a single price lever, a firm participating in foremarkets and aftermarkets considers both prices (p^f, p^a) when maximizing profits.[14] The firm chooses these to

---

[12] *Image Technical Service, Inc., et al.* v. *Eastman Kodak Co.*, C 87-1686 (January 18, 1996) and *Image Technical Service, Inc., et al.* v. *Eastman Kodak Co.*, 1996-2 Trade Case (CCH) para. 71,624 (N.D. Cal) (Feb. 28, 1996).

[13] The court required a new trial to recalculate a portion of the damages because the damages expert and the fact witnesses did not sufficiently link some of the damages to the antitrust violation. *Image Technical Service, Inc., et al.* v. *Eastman Kodak Co.*, 1997-2 Trade Case (CCH) para. 71,908 (9th Cir. 1997).

[14] Whether firms compete in prices ("Bertrand") or quantities ("Cournot") is not important here; we discuss "price" competition for convenience. However, a focus on just price alone (or just quantity) *is* an important simplification. Consumers consider factors beyond just price when products are differentiated. Such differentiation is particularly true with "service" type goods: two service programs might differ in technical quality, response time, flexibility of contract terms, provision of manufacturer-independent advice, and so forth. Kodak surveys showed that typical customers rated several factors as more important than price when choosing a service provider (see Exh. 264).

maximize profits (π), which, on the assumption of constant costs (c^f, c^a) are:[15]

$$\pi \quad = \pi^f + \pi^a$$
$$= (p^f - c^f) q^f (p^f, p^a) + (p^a - c^a) q^a (p^f, p^a)$$

We assume that the quantities demanded for each product depend on *both* prices, that is, $q^f = q^f(p^f, p^a)$. That is, if the price of service rises, we generally expect the demand for primary market equipment to fall. This linkage between goods across markets is the essential feature of aftermarket economics. Most of the disputes can be summarized as arguments over how strong that link is under various factual circumstances.

We start by assuming that foremarkets and aftermarkets are perfectly competitive: $p^f = c^f$ and $p^a = c^a$. We are interested in whether a firm can increase its profits by acquiring market power in its aftermarket while its foremarket remains competitive. Thus, we are asking if a firm can profit overall by raising p^a above c^a. That is, the basic disagreement is whether, starting from competitive pricing, the sign of $\partial \pi^f / \partial p^a + \partial \pi^a / \partial p^a$ is positive or negative.

Economists on both sides agree that under most circumstances aftermarket profits can be increased, $\partial \pi^a / \partial p^a > 0$, but that there will be a simultaneous decline in foremarket profits, $\partial \pi^f / \partial p^a < 0$, because increasing p^a increases the overall cost of owning equipment and forward-looking buyers will reduce their equipment purchases. The debate, then, is about whether $\partial \pi^f / \partial p^a$ is sufficiently negative to offset monopoly aftermarket profits, and thus make aftermarket monopolization unprofitable overall.

Economists writing since the Supreme Court opinion, including at least one who testified for Kodak at trial, have mostly agreed that there are circumstances under which aftermarket monopolization can be profitable overall; that is, $\partial \pi^a / \partial p^a > - \partial \pi^f / \partial p^a$.[16] We shall briefly describe some of the theories, in order to frame the facts and economic arguments presented at trial.

Preliminaries

Under what conditions might we expect foremarket competition to protect aftermarket consumers? That is, when might the total effect, $\partial \pi / \partial p^a$, be zero or negative, so that aftermarket monopolization is not attractive?

[15] Typically, aftermarket sales associated with a given foremarket sale will occur over a period of time. Therefore, what we refer to as aftermarket prices (for consumers) and profits (for firms) are actually discounted streams of future expenditure and profits, respectively.

[16] See, e.g., Chen and Ross (1993); Borenstein, MacKie-Mason, and Netz (1995); and Shapiro (1995). There is yet another dispute, which is that under some circumstances even if it is profitable overall to monopolize an aftermarket, social welfare may be harmed only a little, or even improved, and thus legal antitrust intervention might be inappropriate. See footnote 26 below.

First, it is at least necessary that there be some "local" market power, which we define as $\partial \pi^a / \partial p^a > 0$. That is, the firm must have the ability to raise aftermarket price above the competitive level and earn additional aftermarket profits, ignoring the effect on foremarket profits. This requirement implies two necessary conditions: There must be some protectable aspect to the aftermarkets, and some form of switching costs related to the primary market good.

Protectable aftermarkets mean that there are limited substitutes for, and limited entry into, the equipment manufacturer's aftermarket.[17] If aftermarket substitutes are widely available at competitive prices, say from independent parts manufacturers or service providers, increases in p^a will merely result in the firm's equipment customers making their aftermarket purchases from another supplier. That would imply $\partial \pi^a / \partial p^a \leq 0$.

Similarly, if equipment owners can costlessly change from their existing equipment to a competitively priced alternative, a service price increase would induce consumers to sell their equipment and buy the alternative brand of equipment and service. It must be costly for current equipment owners to switch to another brand of equipment if the manufacturer is to have aftermarket power. There are two basic types of switching costs: inefficient used equipment markets, and complementary sunk investments that are specific to the given brand of primary good. An inefficient used equipment market means the seller of a used primary market good cannot expect to recover the full economic value of the good when he sells it. This could be due to a lemons problem or to other causes.[18] We will refer to these as "financial" switching costs. Financial switching costs are coterminous with the economic life of the specific piece of equipment: once a machine has zero economic value, there is no financial cost of switching to a new brand.

Switching costs from complementary investments arise when a firm needs to make investments in addition to the equipment and aftermarket good in order to utilize the equipment *and* these investments are of little value with any other brand of equipment. The classic example of complementary investment is custom applications software written for a specific operating system—switching to a new operating system requires rewriting the applications. Other switching costs include training and familiarization, conversion of data and archival file formats, custom configuration of peripherals, development of new relationships with expert, sales, and service personnel, and so forth. We refer to these as "technological"

---

[17] This implies that the primary market is monopolistically competitive or a differentiated product oligopoly. It is difficult to conceive of protectable aftermarkets in combination with truly homogeneous primary market goods: If there are no differences among primary market goods, how can a given aftermarket good work only with one "brand" of the primary market goods?

[18] See Akerlof (1970). However, even a perfectly functioning used-equipment market might not eliminate financial lock-in resulting from installed base opportunism. See the text below.

switching costs. Technological switching costs can extend beyond the economic life of an individual piece of equipment.[19]

The level of total switching costs puts an upper bound on the amount of surplus a firm can extract by exercising aftermarket power. Any attempt to extract the current owner's surplus in excess of the cost of switching results in the equipment owner's switching brands. However, there are situations where switching costs are large and this constraint might not be significant. When switching costs are significant, we say consumers experience *lock-in*.[20]

If aftermarkets are not protectable and switching costs are negligible, then we would generally expect no local aftermarket power, $\partial \pi^a / \partial p^a < 0$, and the systems theory would prevail.

Necessary Conditions for the Systems Theory

When a durables manufacturer has local aftermarket power ($\partial \pi^a / \partial p^a > 0$), systems theory proponents argue that linkage to a competitive foremarket will protect locked-in aftermarket consumers from monopoly exploitation. That is, $\partial \pi^f / \partial p^a$ is sufficiently large and negative so that a foremarket profit loss offsets the aftermarket profit gain. The argument is that either switching costs are low, so that current equipment owners can switch at low enough cost to constrain sufficiently the manufacturer's aftermarket power, or that new customers (and repeat customers upgrading or replacing their equipment) will see the high aftermarket prices and demand lower equipment prices to compensate, or will purchase elsewhere. What conditions are necessary to establish a sufficiently strong linkage between foremarkets and aftermarkets? Three have received the most attention: sufficient, low-cost information; effective simultaneity of foremarket and aftermarket purchases; and competitive foremarkets for equipment. We explain each in turn.

Sufficient, Low-Cost Information

The systems theory assumes that consumers are aware of aftermarket prices, make reasonable assumptions about their own future demand for the aftermarket goods corresponding to each primary market good, and use this information when making price comparisons. Thus, consumers are aware when a given primary market supplier charges supracompetitive prices in the aftermarket, and take their custom elsewhere.

---

[19] This can lead to the confusing situation where future equipment purchases should properly be analyzed as aftermarket purchases: The choice of which primary market good to buy in the future is contingent on which is purchased today. Thus, technological switching costs increase competition in new product markets but reduce competition in mature markets. With new markets, firms compete vigorously to get a large base of locked-in customers; in mature markets, most customers are already significantly locked-in to a brand. See Klemperer (1987).

[20] For more on switching costs and lock-in, see Farrell (1985), Porter (1985), and Williamson (1985).

Effective Simultaneity

Aftermarket goods and services are typically purchased later than foremarket equipment. Yet the systems theory requires that an increase in aftermarket prices be accompanied by an offsetting decrease in foremarket profits. This linkage requires what we call "effective simultaneity"; that is, the markets must operate as if the foremarket and aftermarket purchasing decisions were being made simultaneously. Systems theory proponents suggest several ways in which effective simultaneity might be obtained. First, product lifetimes might be sufficiently short that current equipment owners will soon be purchasing new equipment, and will expect that, if charged high current aftermarket prices, they will be charged high prices in the future. (Note that this argument assumes low or nonpersistent *technological* switching costs, since these can lock in repeat purchasers beyond the life of their current equipment.) Second, the ratio of new potential buyers to existing owners may be sufficiently large that high current aftermarket prices will dissuade sufficient new buyers, because they expect to be charged high aftermarket prices. (This argument requires that the firm not be able to price discriminate openly between new and old buyers.) Both approaches assume that a firm's pricing reputation is important because consumers consider the firm's past pricing.

Another approach to obtaining effective simultaneity is through warranties and long-term aftermarket contracts purchased at the time of equipment purchase. Similarly, the availability of rental or lease agreements that include the aftermarket good or service might restrain a firm's aftermarket power by reducing lock-in.[21] These arguments received little attention in *Kodak* (and similar cases) because aftermarket contracts extending for the full life of the equipment were never offered by Kodak.

Competitive Foremarkets

The third premise of the systems theory that durable manufacturers cannot have aftermarket power is that the equipment foremarket be competitive. The linkage argument requires that an attempt to charge high aftermarket prices will be foiled by strong competition in the foremarket.

Theories of Market Power in Aftermarkets

Kodak proposed to the Supreme Court that as a matter of *law,* on the basis of the systems theory, the Court should hold that it was not *possible* for Kodak to have aftermarket power, and thus should dismiss the case without a full factual inquiry. Various economists—some involved in the case, some not—responded by showing that under plausible circumstances *any* of the necessary conditions of the systems theory might not hold and that

---

[21] However, these protect only against financial, not technological lock-in.

the conclusion about lack of market power in the aftermarkets would then change. We shall now briefly describe the main theoretical challenges to the systems theory.

Installed Base Opportunism (IBO)

One theory disputes the assumption of *effective simultaneity.* For at least some customers, there is *not* simultaneity: those who already own equipment, and who are not about to replace it. Even if the other assumptions hold, the manufacturer could practice what is known as *installed base opportunism:* After customers are locked in, surprise them by raising aftermarket prices above the competitive level.[22] Competition in the foremarket may force the firm to discount new equipment sales to offset the aftermarket price increase, thereby earning zero economic profits on new sales, but due to competition the firm was *already* earning zero profits on all customers. Now the firm gets excess profits equal to the total switching costs faced by its installed base. IBO will be especially attractive for mature and declining product lines, in which most revenues are from locked-in, rather than new, customers.

Costly Information

Consumers will rationally forgo complete life-cycle cost analysis if *sufficient low-cost information* is not available. Costly information also mitigates the effectiveness of reputation and thus undercuts the *effective simultaneity* assumption.[23] Since maintained durables often have lives of seven, fifteen, or even more years, and may have parts lists thousands of items long, obtaining sufficient information about future costs, and future user needs, can be quite difficult. In addition, both durables and their aftermarket goods and services may be highly differentiated. This means that a complete analysis requires extensive information gathering about each of the various models and brands considered, as well as about many features other than price. Indeed, many aftermarket products, for example, maintenance or software, have significant "experience" components: Potential buyers have great difficulty knowing their value ex ante.[24]

Imperfect Foremarket Competition

Another critique of the broad applicability of the systems theory relaxes the assumption of perfectly competitive equipment markets. Markets for expensive durable equipment are often quite concentrated; and even if

[22] Salop (1993) applied IBO theory to *Kodak.* The theory had been applied previously in other contexts. See, e.g., Williamson (1985).

[23] The plaintiffs presented this theory to the Supreme Court; Shapiro has discussed it (1995).

[24] For some background on experience goods, see Tirole (1988, pp. 294–295) and references, and Carlton and Perloff (1994, pp. 601–602) and references.

they are not, there is often a substantial degree of product differentiation. Thus, we see the conditions for monopolistic competition, with each firm facing a downward-sloping residual demand curve.[25]

When foremarkets are not competitive, it will be generally true that a manufacturer can increase its profits further by monopolizing the aftermarket. Klemperer (1987) has shown that in an oligopolistic market with switching costs, the collusive output level can occur in a noncooperative equilibrium. Several authors have pointed out that one way in which aftermarkets can be used to increase foremarket profits is through price discrimination. Suppose that customers are heterogeneous in the utility they derive from the good and its aftermarket. This heterogeneity is not observable in the primary market. The heterogeneity is, however, related in some manner to the consumer's demand for the aftermarket good. This allows the equipment manufacturer to use aftermarket purchases as a metering device if it has an aftermarket monopoly, and thereby to extract additional profits.[26]

Pure Version of Systems Theory Fails

Borenstein, MacKie-Mason, and Netz (1995) present a model that is based on precisely the assumptions of the systems theory, and show that even then there will generally be supracompetitive aftermarket pricing, and harm to consumer (and overall) welfare. The main point is that when firms cannot sign complete contracts for aftermarket products that cover the full life of the durable good, and all contingencies, then *effective simultaneity* will generally be an *approximation,* and there will be at least some room to profit from the slippage.

The intuition is not hard: As soon as the firm has some locked-in customers, it can earn at least some monopoly profits by charging a supracompetitive aftermarket price. Due to foremarket competition it may lose some foremarket profits and need to lower equipment prices, but the firm was only earning competitive (zero) profits before and the cost of a small aftermarket price change at the margin is zero, or small compared with the aftermarket profit gain. That is, given switching costs and lock-in, a rational firm will always want to extract at least some of the aftermarket

---

[25] In high-volume copiers, Kodak and Xerox produced about 90% or more of all units sold during the relevant years. Not only was the market concentrated, but between them, each had several models, and each model differed on three or more salient dimensions.

[26] Chen and Ross (1993) have modeled the use of aftermarkets for price discrimination. They note that price discrimination itself has ambiguous welfare effects: The firm unambiguously increases its profits, but combined producer plus consumer welfare can either increase or decrease. Indeed, Hausman and MacKie-Mason (1988) have shown that price discrimination can even lead to a Pareto improvement if new markets are opened or economies of scale are significant. However, these concerns do not undermine the basic point: When a firm has foremarket power and can use the aftermarket to meter, it *will* earn higher profits due to aftermarket monopolization, contrary to the systems theory. It is still necessary to show antitrust *injury* from the profitable monopolization effort before winning a case.

monopoly profit, even if foremarket competition prevents it from extracting all of the profit. The result does not require the surprise element of the IBO theory.

The consumer harm could be much larger if, for example, aftermarket monopolization reduces desirable product differentiation (such as variety in service terms or quality), or eliminates innovation that might have occurred in a competitive aftermarket (Borenstein, MacKie-Mason, and Netz, 1995). Since this theory shows that the systems theory never holds completely, and that the magnitude of harm depends on the facts, it directly challenges the view that aftermarket monopolization should be strictly or even presumptively legal as a matter of law.[27]

THE ARGUMENTS PRESENTED IN THE SUPREME COURT AND IN TRIAL

Supreme Court

It bears repeating that *Kodak* came to the Supreme Court as the result of Kodak's motion for summary judgment. This has two implications for the outcome: All questions about disputed facts were resolved for the non-moving party (the ISOs), and the moving party had to demonstrate that it could not be found guilty under any reasonable interpretation of the facts of the case. As the Supreme Court noted in its decision, the motion was heard early in the discovery of the case: The Court had a slim factual record upon which to base its decision.

Kodak argued that it faced substantial equipment competition in both copiers and micrographic equipment. Kodak claimed that it competed with Xerox, Canon, and others in copiers. It listed Canon, Anacomp, Bell & Howell, 3M, and others among its micrographics equipment competitors. Kodak argued that, given this equipment competition, any attempt by it to abuse its aftermarket customers would have a ruinous impact on its equipment sales: It could not *profitably* exploit whatever market power it had in its aftermarkets. Therefore, parts and service could not be distinct relevant markets for antitrust, and Kodak could not be guilty of tying or monopolization.

Under the case law, even if Kodak tied or monopolized, it might not be guilty if it had legitimate business justifications. Kodak asserted three pro-competitive business justifications: desire to provide quality maintenance, desire to control its inventory costs, and desire to prevent the ISOs from "free-riding" on Kodak's investments in equipment, parts and service.

The ISOs countered that customers were not perfectly informed and

---

[27] European Union law essentially presumes aftermarket monopolization is harmful—firms are required to sell parts. See Reed (1992).

they faced high switching costs. Therefore, even if equipment markets were competitive, aftermarket customers might not be protected from abuse. The ISOs also argued that there was evidence that Kodak had engaged in IBO. Thus, they relied on two of the theories that undo the systems theory.

The Court rejected Kodak's argument in a detailed opinion. The Court noted that Kodak's theory required factual assumptions about the real world[28]; Kodak's theory was not compelling on purely theoretical grounds[29]; and Kodak's theory, rather than being supported by evidence in the record, was contradicted by the record.[30] Furthermore, the ISOs presented plausible explanations for why Kodak's theory didn't explain the evidence.[31]

Trial

The case at trial was somewhat different than the case argued before the Supreme Court. This difference stemmed in large part from the plaintiffs' discovery that Kodak had substantial market shares in what were very concentrated foremarkets.

Although this case involved copiers and various micrographics equipment, we will concentrate on the analysis of copiers. At the end, we shall briefly describe some differences in the micrographics part of the trial.

Plaintiffs

The plaintiffs made three main arguments at trial: first, that Kodak had monopoly power over repair parts, and leveraged this power to maintain and extend a service monopoly; second, to rebut Kodak's main defense, that Kodak in fact had significant market power in the foremarkets; third, also in rebuttal to Kodak, that several factors sufficiently broke any linkage between foremarkets and aftermarkets.

Market Definition: The plaintiffs argued there was a relevant market for the repair parts needed for Kodak copiers. The evidence indicated

---

[28] "Kodak's proposed rule [that "equipment competition precludes any finding of monopoly power in derivative aftermarkets" (504 U.S. 451 at 466, citing Kodak's Brief at 33)] rests on a factual assumption about the cross-elasticity of demand in the equipment and aftermarkets. . . ." *Kodak,* 504 U.S. 451 at 469. That is, the Court recognized that the strength of the linkage depended on the factual circumstances of the case.

[29] "Thus, contrary to Kodak's assertion, there is no immutable physical law—no 'basic economic reality'—insisting that competition in the equipment market cannot coexist with market power in the aftermarkets." *Kodak,* 504 U.S. 451 at 471. Borenstein, MacKie-Mason, and Netz (1995) showed later that even Kodak's idealized conditions, stated in Justice Scalia's dissent, imply at least some market power in aftermarkets.

[30] *Kodak,* 504 U.S. 451 at 472.

[31] *Kodak,* 504 U.S. 451 at 473.

that many Kodak-copier parts had no substitutes at all: they were unique to Kodak copiers. Furthermore, there were substantial costs involved in switching to another high-volume copier brand, indicating that customers would have an inelastic response to a significant increase in the price of Kodak copier parts. Last, there were barriers to entry into production of Kodak parts. Evidently a single firm controlling access to the parts could profitably raise prices substantially.

The "all parts" nature of the parts market definition was a departure from a strict interpretation of the DOJ/FTC *Guidelines* methodology. It resulted in clustering complements within the same relevant market. For example, fuser rollers and image loops were both in the relevant market. The plaintiffs argued that "all parts" were a relevant market based on the "commercial realities" of the case: If parts demanders could not get, for example, fuser rollers, they would have no demand for image loops. Kodak's parts manager testified that one would need "an assured supply of parts" to be in the service business.[32] Most customers would deal only with service providers who had an assured source of supply for all parts. Additionally, Kodak's policy applied to all parts, not just specific parts.

The switching costs that were relevant for parts were equally relevant for service labor, as were the theories undercutting the systems theory. Thus, a single firm controlling all service could profitably raise price substantially, and service was a relevant market.

Last, the plaintiffs argued that there was a relevant market for high-speed, high-volume (HV) photocopiers. Customer (deposition) testimony, internal Kodak documents, and industry sources all strongly suggested that there was a distinct HV copier market and that it was a duopoly comprising Kodak and Xerox. This led the plaintiffs to define the HV copier market using copier speed, volume capability, and durability measures.[33]

Market Power: The plaintiffs contended that Kodak had market power in the parts market. Kodak had patents on various critical parts and refused to provide the specifications on others. There were entry barriers to parts production apart from the patents—in particular, significant minimum efficient scale.[34] Because a potential service competitor required access to all parts to compete, these restraints were sufficient to conclude that Kodak had monopoly power in the parts market.

---

[32] Tr. at 5585. Kodak used 9942 different parts in one year to service its installed base of copiers. It used 6430 different parts for servicing its micrographics equipment. Tr. at 5558–5559.

[33] The plaintiffs used two measures of copier speed (reproducing single-sided, single-page documents and two-sided, multipage documents), rated monthly copy volume, and weight (to reflect durability). Some Japanese copiers with high single-page speeds were offered by the early 1990s; these units still fell far short of the Kodak and Xerox offerings in the other characteristics. See Tr. Ex. 724–726, 744, 752, 753.

[34] A copier parts manufacturer testified that, for most parts, he would need to be supplying parts for 2000 or more machines, roughly 5% of Kodak's installed base, to generate a sufficient return on design and tooling investments (ignoring technical and patent difficulties). Tr. at 818–820, 825–827.

Kodak also allegedly had market power in the service market. Kodak's market share was 98 percent.[35] There was evidence that Kodak restricted service contract options[36] and engaged in significant price discrimination across service customers.[37]

The plaintiffs also argued that the equipment market did not discipline the exercise of market power in the aftermarkets. One significant piece of evidence was that Kodak did *not* engage in systems pricing. Whereas systems pricing requires that customers paying above-average service prices pay below average prices for their equipment and vice versa, there was essentially no statistically significant correlation between the prices customers paid for equipment and the prices they paid for maintenance. What the data showed was that customers paid widely different systems prices on a total-cost-of-ownership (TCO) basis.[38]

Plaintiffs gave serveral reasons for this unlinking:

- There were significant switching costs across copier brands.[39] In addition, shortly after introducing its parts policy Kodak increased switching costs within the Kodak service market by quadrupling the inspection and restoration fees it charged for Kodak to begin servicing a copier bought from or previously serviced by someone other than Kodak.[40]

- Several equipment customers testified that they did not engage in TCO. A Kodak saleswoman indicated that her "TCO" proposals for customers included at most an initial few years of service, while the equipment generally lasted much longer.[41] Kodak's expert testified that the inclusion of later renewal agreements was necessary for TCO calculations to be correct.[42]

- Kodak had market power in the equipment market. Kodak and Xerox were essentially the only suppliers in the high-volume copier equipment market.[43] There was also extreme price discrimination across equipment purchasers.[44]

The plaintiffs showed that when ISOs could obtain access to parts they could compete with Kodak for service contracts with lower prices

---

[35] Exh. 730. This left the ISOs with one-fourth to one-twentieth the share held by ISOs in some other high-tech industries. Kodak's expert said that Kodak's share was 90% (Tr. at 4573:11–16).

[36] Exh. 215. For example, ITS offered CSC an on-site technician, but Kodak did not.

[37] Exhs. 238, 239.

[38] See Exh. 743.

[39] Exh. 735. See also Plaintiff's Expert Report on Liability Issues for a more detailed analysis.

[40] Exh. 742. This action made it riskier to try ISO service: If a customer was not satisfied with the ISO, it would be very expensive to return to Kodak service.

[41] Tr. at 4511–4517.

[42] Tr. at 4587–4589.

[43] Exh. 748. The Herfindahl-Hirschman Index for high-volume copiers was over 3100.

[44] Some customers paid 1.7 to 2.3 times as much for a given equipment configuration as did other customers purchasing the same quantity.

and comparable quality. Kodak's own documents recorded that the parts policy helped Kodak exclude competition (see the quotes at the opening of this chapter). Therefore, the plaintiffs argued, Kodak's parts policy was used to maintain and extend its service monopoly.

IBO: Installed base opportunism was a prominent, though not the only, theory presented to the Supreme Court. It was not the central theory at trial for copiers, but the plaintiffs did present IBO evidence. Such evidence was more prominent for micrographics. Several customers testified that after a few years on Kodak maintenance, the price increased significantly. Additionally, a Kodak saleswoman testified that *renewal* maintenance agreement terms were more limited and less attractive than for agreements purchased at the time of equipment sales.[45] Thus, although there was not a specific date on which Kodak raised prices to *all* current owners of Kodak equipment, there was evidence that IBO was applied customer by customer. Further, earlier standard industry practice had been to permit independent service. Both IBM and Xerox had sold parts for their copiers. Kodak had sold parts for its micrographic equipment. Therefore, when Kodak implemented a policy to refuse parts sales, and thus stunted the development of ISOs as the market matured, customers were surprised to find that ISOs could not get parts, and prices were higher than they *would* have been, even if they did not rise in nominal terms.[46]

Kodak

Kodak's expert testimony closely paralleled its Supreme Court case. This meant that it followed a significantly different framework from the plaintiffs' presentation. Kodak asserted the *presumption* that equipment competition precluded profitable abuse of aftermarket power and therefore "systems" were the relevant market.

Market Definition: Consequently, Kodak's market definition effort focused strictly on the copier equipment market. It claimed that the market was for copiers with a multicopy speed greater than 60 cpm. By ignoring throughput and durability, Kodak argued that there was significant competition in the 1990s. Kodak also argued that the plaintiffs' price discrimination evidence did not indicate market power in a concentrated market, but rather hard customer bargaining in a vendor-competitive environment.[47]

Market Power in the Aftermarkets: Kodak's experts then addressed whether this competitive equipment market would adequately protect Ko-

---

[45] Tr. at 4511–4517.

[46] ISOs, when they could get parts, offered service at prices that were about 15 to 30% less than Kodak; and when Kodak competed head-to-head, it cut prices drastically. See, e.g., Exh. 729.

[47] Tr. at 4634, 4669–4670.

dak's aftermarket customers.[48] They presented hypothetical examples to suggest that Kodak would lose profits from lost future systems sales if it overcharged aftermarket customers.[49] They asserted that it was reasonable to expect that Kodak would lose future sales if it exploited aftermarket power because a significant part of both its micrographic and copier sales were made to existing customers,[50] but they offered no direct evidence that repeat purchasers were responsive to aftermarket practices.

Kodak's copier expert suggested that switching costs were not significant. He did not analyze them in detail because he had concluded that it would not be profitable for Kodak to exploit lock-in even if it did exist.[51]

Kodak argued that information costs were also not significant. They presented evidence that several publications were available that gave guidance on how to conduct TCO as well as giving independent, if anecdotal, pricing information. Additionally, information cost effects were mitigated by the high proportion of repeat purchasers: because such customers would be able to spread any costs of performing TCO over their several purchases, they would have lower information costs per equipment unit. Kodak's experts also noted that Kodak had spent considerable money developing an automated quote system that included pricing on initial service contracts. They argued that Kodak wouldn't have done this if either it was counting on customer ignorance or customers hadn't regularly asked for such TCO information.[52]

Kodak also pointed out that equipment manufacturers typically have large aftermarket shares. Kodak "invented" the Kodak aftermarket, inherently having a 100-percent share at the inception of the aftermarket. Thus, Kodak's "monopoly" share in the market was not the result of Kodak's parts policy, but was instead a natural effect of Kodak's having created the market.[53]

Business Justifications: Kodak claimed several procompetitive business justifications for its parts policy. Kodak argued that it had chosen to

---

[48] Kodak's economic expert on copiers believed that the systems *theory* was dispositive: he testified that merely knowing that Kodak had to compete with Xerox would have been sufficient for him to conclude that Kodak could not harm its aftermarket customers. (Tr. 4515:23–4516:3.)

[49] Exh. 3697 and Tr. at 4603–4608. However, the exhibit was based on the *assumption* that Kodak would lose all future systems sales to this customer. This is the exact assumption that the Supreme Court refused to accept as dispositive, demanding instead that the facts be examined. Kodak presented a similar exhibit in its micrographics presentation, using the same underlying *assumption*. Exh. 3768 and Tr. at 6010–6014, and 6323–6325.

[50] Seventy-five percent of Kodak's copier sales between 1986 and 1994 were to past or current owners of Kodak copiers. Exh. 3695. In micrographics, somewhere between 68% and 90% of purchases from 1990 to 1994 were to past or current owners of Kodak equipment. Exh. 3733 and Tr. at 5999–6000.

[51] This conclusion was based on Exh. 3697. See fn. 49 and related text.

[52] Tr. at 4592–4593.

[53] Kodak's expert presented evidence on other industries, including IBM copiers, in which ISOs had only a 5% market share. The IBM copier example is particularly apropos because IBM was required to sell parts for its equipment to anyone who asked. Tr. at 4578, Exh. 3693, 3692.

compete in the equipment market by adopting a strategy of providing high-quality maintenance. This and the avoidance of finger-pointing were reasons to prevent ISOs from servicing Kodak equipment.[54] Kodak claimed that it also needed to be the sole service provider so that it could control its parts inventory costs. Kodak argued that the ISOs were free-riding on its investment in developing maintenance methods, tools, and parts. Last, Kodak argued that its patents gave it the explicit right to refuse to sell patented parts.

Jury Findings

The jury returned a unanimous verdict against Kodak. On the basis of the written instructions from the judge to the jury (and on the written opinion of the Ninth Circuit, which reviewed the case), we can infer[55] that the jury concluded:

a. Equipment, parts, and service were distinct relevant markets.

b. Kodak had a parts market monopoly.

c. Kodak levered its parts monopoly to monopolize service.

ANTITRUST AND ECONOMICS AFTER *KODAK*

Kodak raises interesting issues about the role of economics in antitrust analysis that transcend the economics of aftermarkets. We shall briefly describe two here; space is too limited for a more thorough treatment. First, should a plausible but relatively untested economic theory be sufficient, as a matter of law, to prevent a case from getting to a factual determination by a jury? Second, having gotten to the jury, where does the plaintiff's burden of proving the relevant market with *partial* equilibrium evidence in a *general* equilibrium world end?

Government intervention in markets, even when intended to correct market failures, is itself costly, and subject to error. The summary judgment procedure exists in part to balance the costs of intervention with the benefits of antitrust enforcement. A party can move for summary judgment on the basis that it will prevail as a matter of *law,* even if the facts are all interpreted in the other party's favor. Kodak made a somewhat novel motion for summary judgment: It claimed that on the basis of an *economic theory,* it would be impossible to show that Kodak had market power even if the plaintiffs had the facts right. If the plaintiffs could not establish

---

[54] Finger-pointing was described as the customer's inability to distinguish between poor service and poor equipment. Thus, Kodak claimed, it had the right to control service because poor service could harm Kodak's equipment reputation.

[55] Juries, unlike judges, do not issue written opinions to support their decisions, but the jury was instructed by the judge that it had to make specific findings on several questions before it could conclude that Kodak was guilty.

market power, Kodak would prevail. The question raised is whether courts should rely on a novel, untested economic theory to conclude that despite the facts, the plaintiffs would not be able to demonstrate market power.

When dealing with questions such as market power, courts necessarily rely on economic theories. However, it is our view that there should be a strong presumption against granting summary judgment on the basis of a theory that has not been well tested in previous cases, or for that matter in the economics literature. Kodak's theory had a superficial plausibility, and was endorsed by Justice Scalia in his dissent to the majority Supreme Court position. However, as shown above, economic research since *Kodak* has established that the plaintiff's alternative theory is sound, and *additional* theories have been published and accepted under which market power in an aftermarket could exist.[56] When an opposing party offers a plausible alternative theory, judges are called on to evaluate the competing theories for correctness and appropriateness to the alleged factual setting, and since this is not their area of expertise, the risk of judicial error is high.

The second question, we think, is fundamental to the practice of antitrust economics: When it is impossible to do a complete, general equilibrium analysis of market interactions, how far does the burden of proof on the plaintiffs extend? Kodak argued in trial and in its appeal to the Ninth Circuit that since higher service profits might be offset by lower equipment profits under systems competition, the *plaintiffs* were obligated to show that *combined* profits were above competitive levels. Only then, Kodak argued, would the ability profitably to monopolize a service market be established; that is, only if Kodak *did* earn combined monopoly profits would plaintiffs have shown that it had market power.[57] This is a difficult proof issue that we believe requires a policy judgment. Should it be the plaintiff's burden to prove that systems competition *did not* protect consumers from antitrust harm, or should it be the defendant's responsibility to prove that systems competiton *did* protect consumer welfare?[58]

---

[56] Indeed, one of Kodak's expert economists at trial had published an article acknowledging the theoretical correctness of four of the alternative theories (Shapiro, 1995).

[57] "Plaintiffs never kept their implicit promise to the Supreme Court to prove that Kodak could profit by exploiting its installed base. . . . Plaintiffs never addressed Kodak's system pricing or profitability." Eastman Kodak Company, Appellant's Opening Brief to the Ninth Circuit Court of Appeals, 12 April 1996, p. 45.

[58] Kodak relied on a passage in the Supreme Court's summary judgment decision for authority on this burden of proof argument: "In the end, of course, Kodak's arguments may prove to be correct. It may be that its parts, service, and equipment are components of one unified market, or that the equipment market does discipline the aftermarkets so that all three are priced competitively overall." *Eastman Kodak Co.* v. *Image Tech. Servs., Inc.,* 504 U.S. 451 (1992), p. 486. From the passage and its context in the opinion, it is not evident that the Supreme Court was saying that *plaintiffs* had to establish that overall system profits were possible, rather than the defendant proving that they were not. The Ninth Circuit held that under the standard for review, the plaintiffs had presented sufficient evidence to support the jury's finding, and did not address Kodak's legal argument that this passage imposed a burden on plaintiffs. *ITS, Inc., et al.* v. *Eastman Kodak,* Ninth Circuit, 26 August 1997, slip op. p. 10627.

405

In an ideal world, we would assess all interactions between a hypothetical monopolization and other markets. If, taking into account all interactions, it would not be possible for a defendant to harm overall social welfare, then we would not find it guilty of an antitrust violation. But a complete, general equilibrium analysis will almost never be possible, yet clearly it is not consistent with antitrust policy to bar all plaintiffs from court because they are unable to perform such an extensive analysis. In general, all market definition analyses are partial equilibrium in nature.

Consider an example. Suppose Kodak asserted that by charging supracompetitive service prices, enough disgruntled customers would stop buying Kodak film products that Kodak overall would not be able to earn supracompetitive profits. (Most micrographic equipment in this case requires film, and Kodak, of course, also sells other film.) Should plaintiffs also have the burden to prove that film profit losses do not outweigh service profit gains?[59] What if Kodak proposed an even more remote linkage? Where should the line be drawn?

The question raised about burden of proof and the proper bounds for practicing market definition apply generally. Plaintiffs practice, and courts permit, "reasonable" partial equilibrium analysis. However, this provides only general guidance. How far the plaintiff has to go is a policy question for Congress or the courts.

POSTSCRIPT: DEEP CONFLICT IN THE LOWER COURTS

There have been at least seven Circuit Court opinions on aftermarket cases since *Kodak*, and the results are deeply divided on a fundamental issue. Three, we believe, clearly misread *Kodak*.[60]

These three opinions turned on the same question: Was the allegation of installed base opportunism the crucial issue in *Kodak*? The First, Sixth, and Seventh Circuits have now each held that a *surprise* change in policy is necessary for a finding of a separate aftermarket that can be monopolized

---

[59] This is not so farfetched. Kodak argued at trial that the line should be drawn not just around its equipment and complementary service, but around every product Kodak produced that a service customer might buy. Tr. at 6010–6014. Thus, Kodak argues for a presumption of "systems" wherever there are complementary products *and* that Kodak's "reputation" is sufficiently important to make a wide range of superficially unrelated products effectively complements: Kodak couldn't overcharge micrographic service customers because they might, someday, be a prospective buyer for Kodak copiers.

[60] The three we believe are in error are: *Lee* v. *Life Ins. Co. of North America*, 23 F.3d 14 (1st Cir.), cert. denied, 513 U.S. 964 (1994); *PSI* v. *Honeywell*, 104 F.3d 811 (6th Cir.), cert. denied (1997); and *Digital Equipment Corp.* v. *Uniq Digital Techs., Inc.*, 73 F.3d 756 (7th Cir. 1996) (writ of cert. pending as of this writing). The other four are *Kodak* itself in its second visit to the Ninth Circuit; *United Farmers Agents* v. *Farmers Ins. Exchange*, 89 F.3d 233 (5th Cir. 1996); *Allen-Myland* v. *IBM*, 33 F.3d 194 (3rd Cir. 1994); and *Virtual Maintenance* v. *Prime Computer*, 11 F.3d 660 (6th Cir. 1993). Note that in two opinions, the Sixth Circuit is in conflict with itself.

when the foremarket is competitive.[61] Each has dismissed a plaintiff's claims, because there was no evidence or allegation of IBO.

The Supreme Court did not write that IBO was a single, special circumstance that permitted aftermarket power. The Court wrote:

> The fact that the equipment market imposes a restraint on prices in the aftermarket by no means disproves the existence of power in those markets. . . . Thus, contrary to Kodak's assertion, *there is no immutable physical law*—no "basic economic reality"—insisting that competition in the equipment market cannot coexist with market power in the aftermarkets.[62]

The Court emphasized that "marketplace realities" and market imperfections, such as high information costs and lock-in from switching costs, "could create *a less responsive connection* between service and parts prices and equipment sales."[63]

The *Kodak* Court made specifically the point that we described in the theoretical section above: The key factor in whether aftermarket power is possible is the strength of the link between the foremarket and aftermarket responses to supracompetitive aftermarket pricing. The Court noted that *every* monopolist faces some constraints on its prices; the crucial question was the cross-elasticity between the aftermarket and the foremarket: How strong is the link?

This is the key factual issue for market definition in *all* antitrust cases. For example, slide rules can, to a degree, substitute for computers: Is the linkage strong enough that consumers are protected from computer monopolization by slide-rule competition? The Court agreed with the plaintiffs that the connection could be sufficiently weak due to IBO. The Court also stated that switching costs and high information costs could make the connection sufficiently weak. In short, the Court stated that *one theory* under which the systems view could fail is IBO; it did not state that this is the only theory. This point has been reinforced by the post-*Kodak* economic literature. Even one of Kodak's own expert economists has published an article in which four different theories are identified under which there is an opportunity to behave monopolistically in aftermarkets, with a reduction in consumer welfare (Shapiro, 1995).

There is a general, consistent economic theme here: Firms wish to maximize profits, and thus would like to act like monopolists given the opportunity. However, only sometimes are monopoly profits possible. The crucial economic question is what market constraints there are on a firm's ability to charge supracompetitive prices or otherwise earn excess profits

---

[61] For example, the Sixth Circuit held "that an antitrust plaintiff cannot succeed on a Kodak-type theory when the defendant has not changed its policy after locking-in some of its customers." *PSI v. Honeywell,* 104 F.3d at 820.

[62] *Kodak,* 504 U.S. at 471 (emphasis added).

[63] *Kodak* 504 U.S. at 473 (emphasis added).

at the expense of consumers. When studying behavior in an aftermarket, one such market constraint may be the effect that aftermarket pricing has on foremarket profitability. This link should be analyzed in an aftermarket case. But there are any number of different circumstances under which the link is not sufficient to prevent monopoly harm. Simple but incomplete economic theories should not provide antitrust immunity for entire classes of potentially harmful behavior. If plaintiffs in a case have a plausible alternative theory of aftermarket power, and allege facts consistent with the theory, the case should proceed to trial, as did *Kodak*.

REFERENCES

Akerlof, G. "The Market for 'Lemons': Quality Uncertainty and the Market Mechanism." *Quarterly Journal of Economics* 84 (August 1970): 488–500.

Borenstein, S., J. MacKie-Mason, and J. Netz. "Antitrust Policy in Aftermarkets." *Antitrust Law Journal* 63 (Winter 1995): 455–482.

Carlton, D., and J. Perloff. *Modern Industrial Organization.* 2nd ed. New York: HarperCollins, 1994.

Chen, Z., and T. Ross. "Refusals to Deal, Price Discrimination, and Independent Service Organizations." *Journal of Economics and Management Science* 2 (Summer 1993): 593–614.

Farrell, J. GTE Laboratories Working Paper 85-15, 1985.

Hausman, J., and J. MacKie-Mason. "Price Discrimination and Patent Policy." *RAND Journal of Economics* 19 (1988): 253–265.

Klemperer, P. "Markets with Consumer Switching Costs." *Quarterly Journal of Economics* 102 (May 1987): 375–394.

Porter, M. *Competitive Advantage.* New York: Macmillan, 1985.

Reed, C. "EC Antitrust Law and the Exploitation of Intellectual Property Rights in Software." *Jurimetrics Journal* 32 (Spring 1992): 431–446.

Salop, S. "Kodak as Post-Chicago Law and Economics." Unpublished manuscript, presented at ALI-ABA "New Directions in Antitrust Law," January 21–23, 1993.

Shapiro, C. "Aftermarkets and Consumer Welfare: Making Sense of Kodak." *Antitrust Law Journal* 63 (1995): 495–496.

Tirole, J. *The Theory of Industrial Organization.* Cambridge, Mass.: MIT Press, 1988.

Williamson, O. *The Economic Institutions of Capitalism.* New York: Free Press, 1985.

CASE 17

Networks, Standards, and the Use of Market Dominance: Microsoft (1995)

Richard J. Gilbert

INTRODUCTION

On July 15, 1994, the Department of Justice brought a complaint against the Microsoft Corporation alleging violations of Sections 1 and 2 of the Sherman Act. The complaint alleged that Microsoft used exclusionary and anticompetitive contracts to market its personal computer operating system software and thereby unlawfully maintained its monopoly of personal computer (PC) operating systems and unreasonably restrained trade. Simultaneous with the filing of the complaint, Microsoft and the Department of Justice entered into a consent decree in which Microsoft agreed to abide by certain restrictions in its licensing arrangements.[1] The consent decree enabled the Department of Justice to remedy anticompetitive practices, permitted Microsoft to agree to those remedies without admitting antitrust liability, and avoided a likely protracted trial. After a year of legal wrangling, the consent decree was formally approved by the courts on June 16, 1995.

This chapter provides a brief history of the federal antitrust investigation of Microsoft leading to the consent decree. It then describes the allegations of anticompetitive conduct in the government's complaint and summarizes key provisions of the consent decree. It chronicles the judicial skirmish between the U.S. District Court, the Department of Justice, and

Richard Gilbert was Deputy Assistant Attorney General for Antitrust Economics in the U.S. Department of Justice during the Microsoft investigation that led to the 1994 consent decree. The discussion in this chapter is based on public information and does not reflect the views, opinions, or deliberations of the Department of Justice. The author is grateful to Glenn Woroch and the editors of this volume for helpful comments.

[1]The text of the consent decree is in *United States* v. *Microsoft Corp.*, 1995-2 Trade Cases para. 71,096 (D.D.C. 1995).

Microsoft over the proposed consent decree, and discusses the issue of "monopoly leveraging" that was raised in that debate.

The growth of the IBM PC platform and the ascent of Microsoft is a textbook example of the importance of proprietary standards and network externalities. The company began in 1975 as a partnership between Bill Gates and Paul Allen, then 19 and 21 years old, respectively. Their original business plan focused on the development of computer languages for the new microcomputers. Microsoft entered the operating system business in 1980 at the behest of IBM, which was looking for an operating system for its new IBM PC personal computer. Microsoft developed a disk operating system called MS-DOS, based in part on another operating system, 86-DOS, which it acquired from Seattle Computer Products for the reported sum of $50,000 (Wallace and Erickson, 1992). IBM licensed MS-DOS from Microsoft, which retained the ownership rights.[2] The rest, as they say, is history. The combination of the popularity of the IBM personal computer platform and the key role of the operating system in defining the standards for applications and for new operating system improvements propelled Microsoft into one of the greatest commercial success stories of all time. Microsoft became a publicly traded corporation in 1986 with revenues of approximately $200 million and a net income of $39 million. By 1996, Microsoft's revenues had soared to $8.67 billion. In the same year, Microsoft's net income was $2.19 billion, which represents a compound annual growth rate over the ten-year period of almost 50 percent per year. In September 1997, Microsoft had a market capitalization of $160 billion.

The magnet for antitrust scrutiny of Microsoft was (and continues to be) its market power in personal computer operating systems—the software that controls the operation of a computer by managing the interactions among the computer's central processing unit, memory, and peripheral devices. Table 17-1 shows shipments of personal computer operating systems for 1991–1993, the years immediately preceding the Department of Justice (DOJ) complaint. Microsoft's share of all operating systems exceeded 50 percent, and its share of IBM-PC compatible operating systems exceeded 70 percent in this time period.[3] These shares likely understate Microsoft's market influence because IBM's PC-DOS was a virtual clone of MS-DOS, which IBM licensed from Microsoft. Together, these two products accounted for about 90 percent of the sales of IBM-compatible

---

[2] Several reasons have been suggested as to why IBM licensed rather than bought the operating system for its IBM PC, and in the process lost control of key software standards. The IBM PC was on an aggressive development schedule, and licensing was a quick way to acquire the necessary software. Licensing also demonstrated IBM's commitment to an open platform (although the BIOS and other components were proprietary to IBM). Another suggested explanation is that IBM was wary of allegations of trade secret theft, the risk of which was minimized with a license. (Wallace and Erickson, 1992)

[3] The Microsoft Windows product available in this time period required MS-DOS or an MS-DOS compatible operating system, and thus is not counted separately in these figures.

TABLE 17-1
New Shipments of Personal Computer Operating Systems (000's)

Company	Operating System	1990	1991	1992
Microsoft	MS-DOS	11,648	13,178	18,525
IBM	PC-DOS	3,031	3,003	2,315
DRI/Novell	DR-DOS	1,737	1,819	1,617
IBM	OS/2	0	0	409
Other IBM-PC compatible		186	288	389
Subtotal: IBM-PC compatible		16,602	18,288	23,255
Apple	Macintosh	1,411	2,204	2,570
UNIX	UNIX	357	582	797
Other	NEC, etc.	5,079	4,628	4,458
Total		23,449	25,702	31,080

Source: Bernstein (1993)

PC operating systems in 1992. Digital Research's DR-DOS (subsequently acquired by Novell) accounted for most of the remainder, although IBM's OS/2 was perceived at that time as a formidable potential competitor. As of June 30, 1993, approximately 120 million PCs in the world utilized MS-DOS.[4]

Microsoft's dominant market share, the high barriers to entry for vendors of new operating systems, and the high costs to consumers if they attempt to switch to other computer platforms together imply that Microsoft has substantial power to determine prices in the market for IBM-compatible personal computer operating systems.[5] Barriers to entry in the market for IBM-compatible PC operating systems include the considerable time and expense required to develop, test, and market a new PC operating system[6] and the difficulty of convincing independent software developers to write applications for a new operating system, which is necessary for market success. The latter reflects the importance of network externalities for market structure and competition in this industry.

[4]The installed base of personal computers running Windows software was about 50 million in 1993.

[5]IBM-compatible personal computer operating systems are operating systems that support the x86 class of microprocessors, which includes Intel 286, 386, 486, and Pentium microprocessors, as well as compatible microprocessors manufactured by other companies.

[6]IBM was reported to have spent more than $1 billion to develop, test, and market its OS/2 operating system (Computer Business Review, 1997).

BACKGROUND OF THE FEDERAL ANTITRUST INVESTIGATIONS OF MICROSOFT

The Federal Trade Commission (FTC) initiated an antitrust investigation of Microsoft in June 1990. The initial stimulus for the FTC probe was a November 13, 1989, joint announcement by IBM and Microsoft that described their development efforts for new graphically based PC operating systems. The announcement outlined a plan in which Microsoft would design its Windows operating system as a platform for low-end systems, while reserving high-end features for IBM's OS/2 operating system (Sherer and Fisher, 1991). The alleged agreement between Microsoft and IBM raised competitive concerns because it had elements of a market division between two actual (or potential) competitors. However, the FTC had little time to contemplate the competitive effects of the IBM-Microsoft development strategy because whatever cooperation there was between the two companies in the development of operating systems soon dissolved. By early 1991, Microsoft was promoting Windows as a fully featured operating system, and IBM was promoting its yet to be released OS/2 operating system as a competitive alternative to Windows (Zachmann, 1991). The two companies were clearly on separate, competing tracks to develop and market the next generation of graphically based PC operating systems.[7]

Once the antitrust probe was under way, the FTC heard a panoply of allegations that Microsoft's success was not solely the product of its business acumen and the power of network externalities. Critics asserted that Microsoft had engaged in anticompetitive conduct that was designed to eliminate competition in PC operating systems and applications. In response to these concerns, the FTC expanded its investigation into other areas of Microsoft's conduct, including whether Microsoft used its dominance in operating systems to coerce original equipment computer manufacturers (OEMs) and computer distributors to purchase other Microsoft products and whether Microsoft leveraged control over information flows between its operating systems and applications groups to disadvantage competitors.

In response to these claims, after three years of investigation, the FTC's legal staff recommended that the Commission bring a case that focused on Microsoft's licensing practices with its OEMs.[8] However, the recommendation failed to win the majority vote of the commissioners required

---

[7]An additional complaint lodged against Microsoft was that its flip-flop with IBM over OS/2 created confusion among application software developers that advantaged Microsoft's applications. For example, a senior executive at WordPerfect claimed that WordPerfect was nine months late in getting to market with its Windows product because it had bet on OS/2 instead of Windows, initially with Microsoft's encouragement (Fisher, 1991, p. 21).

[8]The FTC economics staff did not recommend that the Commission file a case against Microsoft (Lopatka and Page, 1995).

to bring a case. In February of 1993 the Commission (with one member re-cused) deadlocked in a 2-to-2 vote, which ended the investigation.

Soon after the FTC's vote, the Antitrust Division of the Department of Justice, in an unusual but not unprecedented action, continued the investigation of Microsoft. The Division's investigation was far reaching and had the benefit of the work product of the FTC. In addition, the DOJ issued twenty-one Civil Investigative Demands (subpoenas for information) to Microsoft and third parties, interviewed more than 100 people at roughly eighty companies, and deposed twenty-two individuals including Microsoft's chairman and other key executives. The DOJ's investigation alone consumed approximately 14,000 attorney hours, 3650 economist hours, and 5500 paralegal hours. Together, the DOJ and the FTC accumulated approximately one million pages of documents related to the Microsoft investigation (Bender, 1995).

MICROSOFT'S LICENSING PRACTICES

The Department of Justice investigation culminated in a complaint against Microsoft that focused on Microsoft's licensing arrangements with original equipment manufacturers of PCs and on Microsoft's nondisclosure agreements with independent software developers. The general thrust of the complaint was that Microsoft had engaged in several practices that had the effect of promoting a de facto exclusive dealing arrangement with its OEMs and with independent software developers. The licensing practices identified in the DOJ complaint are:

- long term contracts
- large minimum commitments
- the "per-processor" contract
- overly restrictive nondisclosure agreements

Simultaneous with the U.S. consent decree, Microsoft and the European Economic Commission (EEC) entered into a substantially similar consent decree. The EEC had investigated allegations of Microsoft's licensing arrangements in Europe that were similar to the allegations in the United States. Microsoft, the Department of Justice, and the EEC entered into joint negotiations over the terms of an acceptable settlement, which enabled Microsoft and the antitrust authorities to deal with the competition issues at a global level. Global coordination of competition policy is obviously desirable for markets, such as computer software, that are international in scope. In these markets, international differences in permissible licensing arrangements risk incurring large transaction costs on firms and ultimately harming consumers. By allowing Microsoft to deal with competition allegations at a global level, the jointly coordinated consent decree represented a major positive development for international antitrust policy. We will first describe the competitive concerns associated with these licensing practices, followed by a summary of the prohibitions on Microsoft's conduct specified in the consent decree.

Long-term Contracts with Large Minimum Commitments

Economic theory illustrates how a firm can employ long-term contracts with large minimum commitments to maintain a monopoly. Suppose that a firm, such as Microsoft, sells its product to a large number of buyers, who make independent purchase decisions. In the Microsoft case, the consumers are OEMs. A large number of OEMs sell IBM-compatible PCs, although a few account for a disproportionately large share.

The seller may charge prices that substantially exceed competitive levels if the firm can foreclose the entry of competitors. This could be accomplished by entering into long-term contracts with minimum commitments that bind customers to make their purchases from the firm. The difficulty with this strategy is that the firm must convince customers to accept the long-term contracts, even though customers would benefit from the competition created by the entry of rival suppliers. In the Microsoft situation, why would OEMs agree to purchase most or all of their operating systems from Microsoft, if by doing so they foreclose entry of new operating systems and thus deny themselves the benefit of competition?

Rasmussen, Ramseyer, and Wiley (1991) provide an answer. They show that consumers, acting independently, may voluntarily sign contracts to purchase from a firm at monopoly prices, even though each consumer would prefer to purchase from an entrant at a lower price.

This result can occur if each OEM believes that it is too small to have an effect on the demand that is available for a new operating system. In that case, no OEM would have an incentive to reject a long-term contract from Microsoft, because its rejection would have no impact on the likelihood of entry. Thus a rational OEM, anticipating that its purchase decision will have no effect on entry, would be better off buying from Microsoft, even at an elevated price.[9] Segal and Whinston (1996) refine the Rasmussen analysis and show that a monopolist may profitably use long-term contracts to foreclose entry under a wide range of circumstances.

Contracts can impede entry if the number of customers who are free to exercise choice of a supplier is less than the minimum scale required for profitable entry. Short-term contracts are less likely to deter entry because shorter contracts imply that more customers are free to negotiate with a new supplier at any date. Short-term contracts do not guarantee that customers will choose a new supplier when they have the opportunity to exer-

---

[9]This assumes the consumer enjoys some surplus at the monopoly price.

cise choice. As discussed above, buyers, acting independently, may resign themselves to purchase at monopoly prices if they believe that their purchase decisions cannot affect the state of competition in the market. However, the number of customers who are free to choose is larger when contracts have short durations, and thus the likelihood is greater that an entrant can assemble a large enough demand to be profitable.

Minimum commitments obligate the consumer to purchase from the incumbent supplier. If the minimum commitment is large, there is little demand available for an entrant during the term of the contract, and thus the purchase obligation, in combination with the contract term, can successfully impede entry. Microsoft's minimum commitment obligations often were 50 percent or more of an OEM's expected sales. The terms of these licenses often were in excess of three years, and some were for as long as five years. These are long terms relative to the product cycle of computer software. In addition, Microsoft often would credit unused balances on a customer's minimum commitment obligation if the customer would agree to a new long-term contract. Otherwise, such balances came due and payable. The effect of this practice was to extend the duration of the contract life, since most customers would rather roll forward their unused balances into a new contract than have to pay off their current obligation.

For Microsoft's exclusive dealing provisions to have an anticompetitive effect, they must succeed in foreclosing entry of competing operating systems, or at least substantially increase the height of entry barriers, and thereby raise the price or reduce the quality of operating systems that are available to consumers. To accomplish this, the demand available to a new entrant as a consequence of Microsoft's licensing practices must be less than the minimum efficient scale of entry. In *Jefferson Parish Hospital District No. 2* v. *Hyde,* 466 U.S. 2 (1984), a concurring Supreme Court opinion by four justices recognized that exclusive dealing is an unreasonable restraint on trade only when a significant fraction of buyers or sellers are frozen out of a market by the exclusive deal.[10] The concurring justices then went on to find, without engaging in a detailed analysis of the market, that the exclusive contract (which foreclosed 30% of the market) was not an unreasonable restraint of trade because there was no likelihood that the exclusive contract would unreasonably enhance market power.[11]

There are procompetitive reasons for the use of long-term contracts with minimum commitments. Long term contracts and minimum commitments provide assurance that a new product (such as Microsoft's Windows

---

[10]The case involved a five-year exclusive contract between a hospital and a firm of anesthesiologists. The majority opinion in *Jefferson Parish* addressed the contract as a tied sale rather than as an exclusive dealing contract. See the discussion by William Lynk (Case 14) in this volume.

[11]Note that courts have upheld practices that effectively operate as partial exclusive dealing arrangements—partial requirements contracts, minimum purchase requirements, and sales quotas—on the basis that they do not preclude competing sellers from selling to the buyers on whom the partial exclusive dealing requirements have been imposed.

95) will achieve sales objectives. This assurance helps to promote investment in the new product by Microsoft, by software companies that develop complementary applications, and by the OEMs that market the computer systems. From the OEM's perspective, a long-term contract provides
a reliable source of supply and may also provide protection against future
price increases. Moreover, even if Microsoft's contracts had the effect of
committing existing OEMs to use only Microsoft's products, this would
not prevent the entry of competing operating system products if the minimum efficient scale of entry for an OEM that specializes in an alternative
operating system (e.g., Apple) is sufficiently small.

The "Per-Processor" Contract

The most publicized aspect of Microsoft's licensing arrangements was the
"per-processor" contract. Microsoft licensed its operating system software
under three types of contracts. The "per-copy" contract charged the customer (usually an OEM) a fee for each copy of the operating system software that the customer installed on a machine. Under a "per-processor"
contract, the OEM paid Microsoft a fee for each sale of a computer system
that used a designated microprocessor, such as the Intel 80486 microprocessor, whether or not the system was sold with a Microsoft operating
system. Microsoft also offered a third contracting alternative, the "per-system" contract, which allowed the OEM to designate a particular computer
model and charged the OEM for each unit of the designated model that it
sold. Under the per-system contract, the OEM had the option of paying
Microsoft only for sales of computers that were shipped with Microsoft
operating systems. For example, the OEM could designate a model number, for example the Alpha 486/33i, that was sold with IBM's OS/2 operating system and was exempt from a Microsoft royalty. By contrast, under
the per-processor contract, the OEM was obligated to pay Microsoft for
sales of all computers that included the designated microprocessor. Thus,
if the Intel 486 microprocessor was included in the OEM's contract, the
OEM would have to pay Microsoft a royalty on each sale of the Alpha
486/33i.

Typically, Microsoft's unit royalty was highest on the per-copy contract. Microsoft tended to offer its larger OEMs the best prices on a per-
processor contract, and over time the share of Microsoft's operating system products that were licensed under the per-processor contract increased
substantially. Table 17-2 shows the percentage of MS-DOS units sold
under per-processor licenses. The share increased from about 20 percent
in fiscal year 1989 to 60 percent in fiscal year 1993. The percentage of
Windows sales to OEMs under the per-processor license was 43 percent in
FY 1993.

The per-processor contract has certain features in common with
entry-deterring contracts described by Aghion and Bolton (1987). They

TABLE 17-2
Percentage of MS-DOS Units Sold Under Per-Processor Licenses

Fiscal Year	Percentage
1989	20
1990	22
1991	27
1992	50
1993	60

Source: DOJ Competitive Impact Statement.

consider a market in which a buyer and an established seller enter into a contract that calls for the buyer to pay a price, p, if the buyer makes a purchase from the established seller, and to pay a penalty, f, if the buyer purchases from any other seller (a "take-or-pay" contract). The penalty tilts competition in favor of the established firm, since the effective cost of a purchase from another firm is $p_e + f$, where p_e is the firm's per-unit price. In the per-processor contract, the purchase price and the penalty are the same. Aghion and Bolton show that if the buyer (the OEM) and the established seller (Microsoft) bargain over contract terms without the participation of other sellers, then the buyer may agree to a contract that would foreclose the entry of a potentially more efficient rival.

However, the per-processor contract also can be characterized in more innocent ways. The contract can promote economic efficiency by discouraging piracy of Microsoft's operating system. Under a per-copy or per-system contract, an OEM could sell a machine without an operating system and avoid paying a royalty to Microsoft. The OEM could pass some of these savings on to the buyer of the computer system, who could obtain an operating system perhaps by illegal means. The quantitative significance of this alleged efficiency is questionable. Abetting software piracy clearly would put an OEM at risk as a vendor of Microsoft products. Moreover, Microsoft sells only operating system upgrades in the retail channel, so a consumer would face obstacles in obtaining a Microsoft operating system for a "naked" machine.

Focusing on the pricing effects of the per-processor contract, one can argue that it does not have the inefficient entry-deterring consequences that Aghion and Bolton identify. Aghion and Bolton consider competition between firms selling identical products, whereas sellers of computer software typically compete in the attributes that the products offer to consumers (they are "differentiated" products). To see how the per-processor contract affects competition between differentiated operating systems, let u be the value that the OEM places on the Microsoft operating system (as measured by the price it can command for a Microsoft equipped system). Similarly, let v be the value that the OEM places on an alternative operating system, and let p_e be the per-unit price of the alternative operating system. Under the per-processor contract, the net value to the OEM of selling an additional computer with a Microsoft operating system is $u - p$, where p is the per-processor fee. The net value to the OEM from selling a computer with a rival operating system is $v - p_e - p$. An OEM may benefit from the use of a competing operating system if $v > u + p_e$. In contrast, the use of the alternative operating system is socially optimal if and only if $v > u + (c_e - c_m)$, where c_e and c_m are the marginal costs of the rival and Microsoft operating systems.

If we ignore the typically small short-run marginal costs of computer software, the use of an alternative operating system would be socially optimal only if $v > u$. Under this assumption, the distortion in the OEM's decision is caused not by Microsoft's take-or-pay contract, but rather by the entrant's choice of a strictly positive per-unit price. Thus, to achieve a level playing field, the per-processor contract forces the vendor of the rival operating system to compete by offering the OEM a contract with a zero marginal price (i.e., a fixed-price contract).

Competition with fixed fees may seem efficient when the low marginal cost of operating system software is taken into account. Efficient pricing in the short run calls for prices to equal marginal cost, which is close to zero for software (particularly for software that is distributed through OEMs, thereby reducing marginal distribution and selling expenses). However, this result ignores important longer-run dynamics of the software market. Extending work by Segal and Whinston (1997), Gilbert and Shapiro (1997) show that contracts of the per-processor type can distort economic efficiency by reducing incentives for rival vendors to invest in their software products. The per-processor fee extracts some of the profits that an entrant could earn in the form of a payment to Microsoft, a part of which Microsoft may pass on to the OEM. The reduction in the profit of the entrant reduces the incentive for the entrant to invest. In this way, the per-processor fee has negative consequences for competition in the long run, even if it arguably has some benefits by forcing vendors to compete with very low marginal prices in the short run.

Microsoft's Nondisclosure Requirements

The Department of Justice complaint also alleged that Microsoft interfered with competition by imposing excessive nondisclosure requirements on independent developers of application software programs. The success of an operating system depends on the application programs that will run under the control of that system. Both Microsoft and independent software developers have an interest in cooperating during the development (beta test) stage of the operating system. Microsoft benefits by expanding the number of compatible application programs, and independent software vendors benefit by having a head start in the release of their products.

There is a legitimate role for nondisclosure agreements. Microsoft cannot involve application writers in its beta test without disclosing some confidential information about the structure and design of its product. However, Microsoft's nondisclosure agreements in connection with its Windows 95 beta test prevented at least some independent software developers from working with competitors of Microsoft for more than a year, which is a long time in the fast paced computer industry. Microsoft's nondisclosure agreements had the effect of encouraging application developers to be exclusive to the Microsoft operating system by imposing high costs on developers who would choose to write programs for another system. The theory of penalty clauses is applicable to Microsoft's nondisclosure conditions and leads to the similar conclusion that the nondisclosure conditions raise the cost of entry for developers of rival operating systems.

THE CONSENT DECREE

The consent decree (also called the Final Judgment) applies to Microsoft's current and predecessor versions of MS-DOS, Windows, Windows for Workgroups, and to successor versions of these products, including Windows 95 (the "covered products"). Excluded from the decree are Microsoft's network server products, Windows NT Workstation and Windows NT Advanced Server, neither of which had a significant share of the relevant market at the time (Competitive Impact Statement, p. 8).

The decree limits the duration of Microsoft's license agreements with OEMs for any covered product to one year, with OEMs having an option to renew the license for up to one additional year on the same terms and conditions as the original license. It also states that Microsoft shall not enter into any license agreement containing a minimum commitment.

The decree limits the duration of a nondisclosure agreement (NDA) for the pre-commercial release of any covered product to the lesser of (a) the commercial release of the product covered by the NDA, (b) a public disclosure authorized by Microsoft of information covered by the NDA, or (c) one year from the date of the disclosure of the information covered by the NDA. In addition, NDAs for the covered products may not restrict persons from developing software products that would run on competing operating systems, provided that such development efforts do not disclose or use any Microsoft proprietary information.

The decree prohibits Microsoft from entering into per-processor licenses, but does permit per-copy and per-system licenses. If Microsoft offers a customer a per-system license, the decree requires that the license agreement include a statement that explains the rights of the customer to include or exclude computer systems from the license agreement. In particular the required statement includes the warning that "As a Customer, you may create a 'New System' at any time that does not require the payment of a royalty to Microsoft unless the Customer and Microsoft agree to add it to the License Agreement." This clearly distinguishes a per-system license from a per-processor license, which would require the customer to pay the same royalty to Microsoft for every system the customer sells that contains a covered CPU.

The decree prohibits "lump sum pricing," defined as a royalty payment for a covered product that does not vary with the number of copies licensed or sold. However, the decree explicitly permits Microsoft ". . . to use royalty rates, including rates employing volume discounts, agreed upon in advance with respect to each individual OEM. . . ." Microsoft and an OEM may develop nonbinding estimates of projected sales, and Microsoft may charge royalties that depend on these projections. Thus the decree does not prohibit price discrimination or volume pricing incentives.

The decree includes certain provisions that, in the words of the Competitive Impact Statement, ". . . go beyond the alleged exclusionary practices in order to ensure that Microsoft's future contracting practices— not challenged here because not yet used—do not unreasonably impede competition." These parts of the decree prohibit Microsoft from engaging in tied sales or from restricting the freedom of an OEM to license, purchase, use, or distribute a non-Microsoft product. These provisions became the subject of a separate dispute over Microsoft's licensing practices involving its internet browser, as discussed below.

The decree's treatment of volume discounting met with some criticism on the theory that Microsoft can use volume discounts to force OEMs to purchase desired minimums, for example by using "cliff pricing" in which the marginal (or even average) price of the operating system declines precipitously if an OEM's purchases exceed a threshold level (Baseman et al., 1995). Indeed, a contract may include financial incentives that have the economic effect of promoting exclusive dealing. However, volume discounts also can be procompetitive.[12] The Competitive Impact Statement explained that, "The Department ultimately concluded that it would not require provisions in the Final Judgment to attempt to proscribe in advance the various means by which Microsoft could attempt to structure volume discounts as a means to thwart competition rather than as a means of promoting competition . . . ," in part because there was no evidence that Microsoft had structured its volume discounts to achieve anticompetitive ends. The Competitive Impact Statement also expressed that the Department stood ready to initiate an antitrust action should Microsoft adopt anticompetitive volume discount structures in its future licensing agreements.

---

[12]It has been argued that volume discounts have no efficiency advantage relative to uniform prices for an intermediate good such as an operating system (Baseman et al., 1995). However, this argument is valid only under restrictive assumptions. There are a wide range of conditions under which volume discounts may be beneficial. For example, Microsoft could employ volume discounts (with procompetitive results) to encourage OEMs to sell computers that use a new operating system, such as Windows 95 or Windows 98.

THE HEARING

Antitrust consent decrees proposed by the Department of Justice are not legally binding until approved by a court, which must evaluate the decree under the public interest standard specified in the Tunney Act. The Microsoft consent decree went before Judge Stanley Sporkin of the U.S. District Court for the District of Columbia. Judge Sporkin called for a hearing on the decree and requested that the Department of Justice and Microsoft respond to several questions. These included:

1. Why the consent decree should not cover all of Microsoft's operating system products

2. How the proposed consent decree would restore competitive balance to the operating systems market

3. Why the decree should not be amended to include provisions that would
   a) establish a wall between the development of operating systems software and the development of applications software at Microsoft
   b) bar Microsoft from engaging in the practice of "vaporware"
   c) require Microsoft to disclose all instruction codes in its operating system software designed to give Microsoft an advantage over competitors in the applications software market

Both the Department of Justice and Microsoft argued that many of Judge Sporkin's questions covered issues that were not properly addressed in a Tunney Act proceeding. The Tunney Act, they argued, permitted the court to review the adequacy of the consent decree in light of the anticompetitive conduct that was alleged in the complaint. The Department of Justice, not the court, has the discretion to define the case it wishes to prosecute. The Department of Justice chose not to bring a case alleging that Microsoft had engaged in anticompetitive product pre-announcements ("vaporware").[13] Similarly, the Department of Justice did not allege in its complaint that Microsoft had used its market power in operating systems to harm competition in markets for applications software. Consequently, both the Department of Justice and Microsoft maintained that the items in part (3) of Judge Sporkin's questions exceeded the court's authority in evaluating the adequacy of the proposed consent decree.

Even under the parties' interpretation of the scope of the Tunney Act review, valid issues remained with respect to parts (1) and (2) of Judge

---

[13]Product pre-announcements can have anticompetitive effects by causing consumers to wait for the introduction of a new product rather than switch to another, available product. See, for example, Katz and Shapiro (1985) and Farrell and Saloner (1986). Whether such announcements constitute an antitrust violation depends on whether the announcements are knowingly false and whether they have the effect of monopolizing a market.

Sporkin's list. As discussed above, the proposed consent decree excluded Windows NT Workstation and Windows NT Advanced Server because Microsoft did not, at the time, have substantial market power in markets for network server products. With respect to restoring competitive balance to the operating systems market, the position of the Department of Justice was that eliminating Microsoft's anticompetitive licensing practices would remove artificial barriers to the entry of competing operating systems, and thus restore a level competitive playing field.

In response to Judge Sporkin's concerns, a lively debate ensued as to whether the proposed consent decree was an adequate remedy for Microsoft's anticompetitive practices. A focus of this debate was the interaction between Microsoft's conduct and the effect of Microsoft's installed base of users in maintaining its market power. A memorandum of unnamed amici curiae (literally, "friends of the court") argued that Microsoft's installed base of users had increased more than six-fold from 1988 to 1995, that this increase in its installed base was the result of anticompetitive licensing practices, and that Microsoft's large, unlawfully acquired installed base allows Microsoft to displace competing operating system and application software products, including competing products with greater functionality. The memorandum's thrust was that it was not enough to stop Microsoft's anticompetitive licensing practices. The damage to competition was achieved by unlawfully expanding Microsoft's installed base: "Contrary to the assertions of the Assistant Attorney General, the relief proposed by the Government, a cessation of further anticompetitive practices, will not restore competition to the X86 operating system market because of the 'network effects' present in the market."[14] Thus, the memorandum to the court concluded that "Microsoft's installed base and share of the applications market is so large that its products are 'locked-in' and true competition can be restored only through truly massive forces or structural relief."[15]

With respect to the claim that Microsoft had amassed its installed base using anticompetitive licensing practices, the Department noted that Microsoft did not employ the per-processor license until 1988 and that the share of OEMs subjected to anticompetitive licensing practices was relatively insignificant as late as 1991. Thus, the Department argued that the growth of Microsoft's installed base was largely the result of the success of the IBM-compatible PC platform and not of the licensing practices challenged in the government's complaint. The Department of Justice argued that its proposed consent decree was a timely and expeditious means to address the potential effects of Microsoft's licensing practices on the emergence of future competition in operating systems, particularly IBM's OS/2, which had features that substantially differentiated it from

---

[14]Memorandum of Amici Curiae in opposition to Proposed Final Judgment, *U.S. v. Microsoft*, CA 94-1564 (ss), p. 84.

[15]Ibid., p. 76.

Microsoft's DOS and Windows products. The Department's economics expert underscored this point, stating that "Microsoft's anticompetitive licensing practices, although a significant impediment to the use of the OEM distribution channel by competing operating system suppliers, made only a minor contribution to the growth of Microsoft's installed base."[16]

Judge Sporkin was unimpressed, and on February 15, 1995, ruled that the proposed consent decree was not in the public interest (*United States* v. *Microsoft Corp.,* 159 F.R.D. 318 (D.D.C.) (1995)). The government and Microsoft appealed. In an expedited proceeding, the Court of Appeals for the D.C. Circuit heard oral argument two months after the District Court's decision and issued its decision two months later. The Court of Appeals found that the District Court had exceeded its authority under the Tunney Act, ordered approval of the proposed consent decree, and removed Judge Sporkin from the case (*United States* v. *Microsoft Corp.,* 56 F.3d 1448 (D.C. Cir. 1995) (Anderson, 1996).

MONOPOLY LEVERAGING

Although the DOJ complaint did not address many of the competitive allegations raised by Judge Sporkin, those allegations do raise important economic and legal issues. We will briefly discuss some of the broader concerns about Microsoft's use of its economic power in operating systems to affect competition in application programs.

All application software has to communicate with the computer's operating system to perform essential functions such as memory management, interaction with other programs, and communication with the computer's peripheral devices. Detailed information about the operating system is necessary for application programs to function effectively, and it is likely that Microsoft application software developers enjoy a lead time advantage in access to important operating system information. For example, advance information about Microsoft's Windows operating system gives Microsoft application developers a head start in producing Windows-compatible programs and helps to ensure that their programs function efficiently and seamlessly with other programs. In addition, Microsoft's rivals have complained that they cannot learn the details of the operating system or encourage Microsoft to introduce desired features in the operating system without revealing confidential information about their products.[17]

While much can be said of the benefits that accrue to Microsoft from its ownership of the operating system, there are also valid business reasons that restrain Microsoft from fully exploiting its informational advantage. A

---

[16]Declaration of Kenneth Arrow.

[17]"By far the most nagging ISV [independent software vendor] complaint about Microsoft is its notorious reputation of evaluating third-party technology, then announcing surprisingly similar, competing products" (Fisher, 1991).

broad array of compatible application programs enhances the value of the operating system, and therefore an operating system vendor has an economic incentive to promote compatibility.[18] The success of Microsoft's Windows depended on convincing large numbers of application software developers to write programs that would run under the Windows platform.

The legal hurdle to a successful monopoly leveraging claim depends in part on the required proof of competitive impact.[19] The U.S. Supreme Court has held that evidence of an adverse competitive impact on adjacent markets is not sufficient to establish a monopoly leveraging claim. Instead, the law requires evidence of actual or likely monopolization.[20] In 1993, Microsoft's unit share of application software for Windows/DOS operating systems was 44.6 percent for spreadsheets (Table 17-3) and 39.0 percent for word processors (Table 17-4). Given the state of competition in software application markets in the early 1990s, a legal challenge that Microsoft had leveraged its operating system monopoly into markets for application software likely would have been difficult to justify at that time.[21] Of course, the law would not protect Microsoft from other conduct, such as the tying of the sale of operating systems to the purchase of application

TABLE 17-3
1993 Windows/DOS Spreadsheet Shipments

	Units (millions)	Share (%)
Microsoft Excel	3.3	44.6
Lotus 1-2-3	1.6	21.6
Borland Quattro Pro	1.0	13.5
Other	1.5	20.3
Total	7.4	100.0

Source: Computer Industry Forecasts, third quarter 1994, no. 39 (1994), p. 92.

[18]Whinston (1990) notes that a monopolist that sells a product that is complementary to other products does not have an incentive to foreclose entry into the complementary products. Whinston's model is highly simplified, and there are likely many reasons, including price discrimination and the erection of barriers to entry, why Microsoft may choose to extract supracompetitive profits from applications as well as operating system software.

[19]Note the crucial distinction in antitrust law and economics between effects on *competitors* and effects on *competition*. It is conceivable that Microsoft's control of the operating system has disadvantaged its competitors. However, this is not of primary concern if the conduct has not adversely affected competition among software developers and thus increased the quality-adjusted prices that consumers pay.

[20]*Spectrum Sports, Inc.* v. *McQuillan*, 506 U.S. 447 (1993) (Section 2 [of the Sherman Act] makes the conduct of a single firm unlawful only when it actually monopolizes or dangerously threatens to do so). See Kattan (1994) and Blair and Esquibel (1995) for discussion of the legal doctrine of monopoly leveraging.

[21]Application markets did show signs of increasing concentration at that time. For example, Microsoft was enjoying a very large share of shipments of application suites (software bundles) in 1993.

TABLE 17-4
1993 Windows/DOS Word Processor Shipments

	Units (millions)	Share (%)
Microsoft Word	3.2	39.0
Word Perfect	3.7	45.1
Lotus Ami Pro	0.6	7.3
Other	0.7	8.5
Total	8.2	100.0

Source: Computer Industry Forecasts, third quarter 1994, no. 39 (1994), p. 92.

software, or predatory pricing, which courts have held are anticompetitive abuses of market power.

If analysis of Microsoft's conduct established that the company had unlawfully used its market power in operating systems adversely to affect competition in applications, the question remains whether feasible remedies exist to eliminate the anticompetitive effects. Microsoft's control of the operating system is an example of control over an input that is necessary for effective competition. Such inputs are sometimes called "bottleneck" or "essential" facilities (if they are in fact essential to production). There are two basic approaches to deal with anticompetitive effects that may result from the control of such facilities, which I refer to as the "separation model" and the "conduct model."[22]

The separation model has been applied in the deregulation of industries that possess natural monopoly assets. The consent decree in *U.S.* v. *AT&T* separated local telephone service, which was considered to have natural monopoly characteristics that required continued regulation, from long-distance service, for which competition was considered to be easier to achieve. In the natural gas industry, deregulation required pipeline companies to unbundle the sale of unregulated natural gas from the provision of regulated pipeline carriage. A similar approach is being followed in some electricity deregulation efforts that require the unbundling of the generation of electricity from the provision of transmission and distribution services. In the case of Microsoft, separation could take the form of a physical divorcement of Microsoft's operating system assets from its application program assets, similar to the divestiture by AT&T of its local telecommunications business.[23]

The separation of operating systems from application programs would

---

[22]See Gilbert and Shapiro (1996) for a discussion of the economic implications of compulsory access to essential facilities.

[23]Separation of natural monopoly from competitive services, either functionally through governance rules or through corporate divestiture, does not eliminate the need for regulation, but rather changes the locus of regulation to the price of and conditions of access to the natural monopoly.

require intensive oversight. Basic questions such as "What is an operating system?" and "What is an application?" raise vexing legal and technical issues, and these are only necessary antecedents to ensure that access to the operating system is provided under nondiscriminatory terms. Moreover, the existence of regulation often provides opportunities for rent-seeking and strategic behavior that is contrary to the objective of economic efficiency.

The second approach to the control of bottleneck or essential facilities is the conduct model. The conduct model entails defining the boundaries of permissible conduct and information flows within the company in an attempt to control abuses from the control of the monopoly facility without requiring physical divorcement of those facilities. An example would be a requirement to maintain "firewalls" that constrain the flow of information between Microsoft's operating system and application software activities. The antitrust agencies sometimes apply the conduct model in vertical mergers or joint ventures that pose competitive risks from control of bottleneck facilities, but for which structural separation is not a feasible remedy because it would negate the efficiency gains from the transaction.

As in the separation model, an effective conduct remedy would require diligent enforcement. If the boundaries of permitted conduct are not clear, rival firms can strategically manipulate enforcement of the decree to serve their own ends, sometimes with anticompetitive consequences. Similarly, a conduct decree may have anticompetitive consequences if the decree proscribes conduct that is necessary to achieve efficiencies.

THE BROWSER WARS

On October 20, 1997, the Department of Justice filed suit alleging that Microsoft violated certain provisions of the consent decree. Section IV(E)(i) of the consent decree prohibits Microsoft from entering into any operation system licence that is ". . . expressly or impliedly conditional upon the licensing of any other . . . product." Microsoft required OEMs to license Microsoft's Internet browser, called Internet Explorer, as a condition for obtaining a Windows 95 operating system license. The Department of Justice sought an injunction against Microsoft to cease this practice and sought damages of $1 million for each day that the violation continued.[24]

Microsoft's defense focused on a part of Section IV(E)(i) that states ". . . this provision in and of itself shall not be construed to prohibit Microsoft from developing integrated products." Microsoft argued that Windows 95 was designed to include Web browsing functionality and that

---

[24]"Petition by the United States for an Order to Show Cause Why Respondent Microsoft Corporation Should Not Be Found in Civil Contempt," *United States of America* v. *Microsoft Corporation*, U.S. District Court for the District of Columbia, Civil Action No. 94-1564. The DOJ also complained that Microsoft's nondisclosure agreements deterred companies from providing information about Microsoft's business practices to the government.

Windows 95 and the Internet Explorer are an integrated operating system software product, even if they can also be viewed as separate products.[25] The DOJ countered that Microsoft had packaged and marketed Internet Explorer as a separate product, and that the bundling of Windows 95 and Internet Explorer was a deliberate attempt by Microsoft to leverage its operating system monopoly to gain advantage over competing Web browsers, particularly Netscape's Navigator.[26] On December 11, 1997, Judge Jackson of the District Court issued a preliminary injunction ordering Microsoft to offer OEMs a Windows 95 product without the Internet Explorer.[27] Microsoft immediately appealed this order.

The DOJ's case raises issues that are larger than whether Microsoft's bundling of Internet Explorer and Windows 95 is in violation of the consent decree. Windows 98 (the next Windows upgrade) may escape the technical reach of the consent decree by including an Internet browser as an integral part of the operating sustem. However Windows 98 will not obviate competitive concerns about product bundling. Joel Klein, Assistant Attorney General of the Antitrust Division, made clear the weight of these issues by stating in connection with the consent decree complaint, "Even as we go forward with this action today, we also want to make clear that we have an ongoing and wide-ranging investigation to determine whether Microsoft's actions are stifling innovation and consumer choice."[28]

Determining the boundaries of anticompetitive product bundling is crucial to competition policy, in the software industry and in other industries. Product bundling, whether it takes the form of a tie-in sale or the creation of an integrated product from previously separate products, raises competitive concerns typically addressed under the topic of monopoly leveraging.[29] The competitive issues raised by this type of conduct are extraordinarily complex, but we can be certain that Microsoft and the browser wars will stimulate new thinking on the subject.

CONCLUDING REMARKS

The Microsoft investigation attracted much attention for many reasons. It was a competitive inquiry into an industry that in little more than a decade

---

[25] "Memorandum in Opposition to Petition of the United States for an Order to Show Cause Why Respondent Microsoft Corporation Should Not Be Found in Civil Contempt," *Op. Cit.* Microsoft also argued that permitting OEMs to choose whether or not to license Internet Explorer would destroy the benefits of a common operating system platform, in effect using network externalities to defend its licensing practices.

[26] "Reply Brief of Petitioner United States of America," *Op. Cit.*

[27] "Memorandum and Order," *Op. Cit.* (Dec. 11, 1997).

[28] USDOJ press release, October 20, 1977.

[29] These issues are addressed in other important antitrust cases such as *Jefferson Parish v. Hyde* and *ITS v. Kodak*. See discussion of these cases in Chapters 14 and 16 of this book, by William Lynk and by Jefferey MacKie-Mason and John Metzler, respectively.

metamorphosed from hobby toys into the engine of the modern information economy, with much of that growth under the direction and control of Microsoft. It is an industry characterized by network externalities, installed base effects, and increasing returns, all of which raise formidable challenges for the proper role of antitrust policy. For an antitrust case, it was high drama.

In the end, the consent decree negotiated between Microsoft and the Department of Justice was structured around a classical remedy to a narrow complaint. The allegation was that Microsoft had engaged in de facto exclusive dealing, which erected artificial barriers to entry by vendors of competing operating system products. Although Microsoft's "per-processor" license attracted the most public attention, this analysis suggests that the duration of Microsoft's licenses and the large minimum commitments were at least as important.

Those opposed to the proposed decree argued that it failed to address significant anticompetitive conduct by Microsoft and that it ignored the crucial features of increasing returns economics in the market for operating systems. With respect to the first point, the Department of Justice duly noted that the consent decree addressed only the conduct that was alleged in the complaint and that the settlement did not prevent the government from bringing a complaint on other conduct in the future. With respect to increasing returns, as Lopatka and Page (1995, p. 352) note, "For the amici, the theory [of network externalities] proves too much by establishing for them the inevitability of Microsoft's monopoly." There was no doubt as to the significance of increasing returns in this industry. The government's case was not predicated on the inevitability, or lack thereof, of the emergence of a single operating system standard for IBM-compatible PCs. Instead, the government drew a sharp distinction between whatever natural barriers to entry may exist in the industry and the artificial barriers to entry created by Microsoft's licensing practices. In a rather conventional application of the antitrust laws, the government crafted a complaint and reached a settlement that addressed these artificial barriers.

REFERENCES

Aghion, Philippe, and Patrick Bolton. "Contracts as a Barrier to Entry." *American Economic Review* 77 (June 1987): 388–401.

Anderson, Lloyd. *"United States* v. *Microsoft,* Antitrust Consent Decrees, and the Need for a Proper Scope of Judicial Review." *Antitrust Law Journal* 65, no. 1 (1996): 1–40.

Baseman, Kenneth, Frederick Warren-Boulton, and Glenn Woroch. "Microsoft Plays Hardball: The Use of Exclusionary Pricing and Technical Incompatibility to Maintain Monopoly Power in Markets for Operating System Software." *Antitrust Bulletin* 40, no. 2 (Summer 1995): 265–315.

Bender, David. "The Microsoft Antitrust Wars." In *Intellectual Property Antitrust* (G-414), edited by David Bender. Practising Law Institute, 1995, pp. 319–363.

Bernstein, Sanford C. "FTC Investigation of Microsoft." Bernstein Research, January 1993.

Blair, Roger D., and Amanda K. Esquibel. "Some Remarks on Monopoly Leveraging." *Antitrust Bulletin* (Summer 1995): 371–396.

Computer Business Review. "OS/2 — Blind Loyalty to a Lost Cause?" *Computer Business Review* 5, no. 3 (March 1, 1997).

Farrell, Joseph, and Garth Saloner. "Installed Base and Compatibility: Innovation, Product Pre-announcements, and Predation." *American Economic Review* 76 (December 1986): 940–955.

Fisher, Susan E. "FTC Investigation Unearths Many Microsoft War Stories." *PC Week* 8, no. 20 (May 20, 1991).

Gilbert, Richard, and Carl Shapiro. "Economic Analysis of Unilateral Refusals to License Intellectual Property." *Proceedings of the National Academy of Sciences of the United States of America* 93, no. 23 (November 12, 1996): 12749–12755.

Gilbert, Richard, and Carl Shapiro. "Antitrust Issues in the Licensing of Intellectual Property: The Nine No-Nos Meet the Nineties." *Brookings Papers on Economic Activity: Microeconomics* (1997): 283–336.

Kattan, Joseph. "The Decline of the Monopoly Leveraging Doctrine." *Antitrust* 9 (1994): 41–49.

Katz, Michael, and Carl Shapiro. "Network Externalities, Competition and Compatibility." *American Economic Review* 75 (June 1985): 424–440.

Lopatka, John E., and William H. Page. "Microsoft, Monopolization, and Network Externalities: Some Uses and Abuses of Economic Theory in Antitrust Decision Making." *The Antitrust Bulletin* (Summer 1995): 317–370.

Rasmussen, Eric, J. Mark Ramseyer, and John Wiley. "Naked Exclusion." *American Economic Review* 81 (December 1991): 1137–1145.

Segal, Ilya, and Michael Whinston. "Naked Exclusion and Buyer Coordination." Harvard Institute of Economic Research, Discussion Paper 1780, 1996.

Segal, Ilya, and Michael Whinston. "Exclusive Dealing and Specific Investments." Technical Report, Harvard University and University of California Berkeley, 1997.

Sherer, Paul M., and Susan E. Fisher. "FTC Probe Incites Microsoft Criticism: Inquiry Keys on IBM Partnership." *PC Week* 8, no. 11 (March 18, 1991).

Wallace, James, and Jim Erickson. *Hard Drive: Bill Gates and the Making of the Microsoft Empire.* New York: Harper Business, 1992.

Whinston, Michael. "Tying, Foreclosure and Exclusion." *American Economic Review* 80, no. 4 (1990): 837–859.

Zachmann, William F. "This Means War . . . (IBM and Microsoft Corp. Increasingly Conflict)." *PC Magazine* 10, no. 18 (October 29, 1991): 105.

CASE 18

Defense Industry Rationalization: Lockheed Martin (1995)

Philip B. Nelson and
Robert D. Stoner

INTRODUCTION

In recent years there have been a series of large defense mergers. Thirty-five of the more notable mergers are listed in Table 18-1.[1] As a consequence, the number of large contractors supplying two-thirds of military procurement has fallen from seventeen in 1989 to thirteen in 1993 and to only five in 1997. While a large number of smaller defense contractors remain, there is little doubt that there has been significant industry consolidation.

The 1995 merger between Lockheed Corp. and Martin Marietta Corp. took place against the backdrop of this contraction. That merger, which formed Lockheed Martin, illustrates the policy issues with which the Department of Defense (DOD) and antitrust authorities must grapple. As is explained in more detail below, this merger was motivated by the economic pressures that were spawned by the decline in defense spending. While major customers, such as the DOD and National Aeronautics and Space Administration (NASA), supported the merger, some competitors and subcontractors opposed it.[2]

Philip B. Nelson and Robert D. Stoner were retained by Lockheed to analyze its merger with Martin Marietta. The authors would like to thank David Beddow, Raymond Jacobsen, and Richard Parker for helpful comments.

[1]The consolidation since 1994, which has involved some very large mergers, is sometimes termed the "second wave" of consolidation, with an earlier set of more generally modest transactions in the 1980s referred to as the "first wave."

[2]Hughes Aircraft and TRW filed public comments with the FTC. There probably were some nonpublic complaints. However, some observers have speculated that competitor responses were milder than one might have expected because competitors planned future mergers of their own. See, e.g., *Wall Street Journal*, "Martin Marietta and Lockheed Near Accord with FTC," December 21, 1994, p. B10.

TABLE 18-1
Notable Merger and Acquisition Cases, 1994–1997

Acquirer	Acquiree	Value (Millions)	Year
Loral	IBM Federal Systems	$1,575,000	1994
Northrop	Grumman	$2,100,000	1994
Martin Marietta[a]	*Greneral Dynamics Space Systems*	$209	1994
Westinghouse Elec Sys	Norden Systems	$100	1994
Northrop Grumman	Vought	$130	1994
Allied Signal	Textron Lycoming	~ $375	1994
Litton	Teledyne Electronic Systems	N/A	1994
Hughes	CAE Link	$1,707	1995
Alliant Techsystems	*Hercules Aerospace*	$466	1995
Lockheed	*Martin Marietta*	> $9,000	1995
Rolls Royce	Allison Gas Turbine	$525	1995
Tracor	Lundy Tech Center	$7	1995
Loral	Unisys Defense Operations	$862	1995
Litton	Imo	N/A	1995
E-Systems	Raytheon	$2,300	1995
General Dynamics	Bath Iron Works	$300	1995
GM Hughes	Magnavox Electronic Systems	$370	1995
Litton	Hughes-Delco Inertial Systems	~ $70	1995
Allied Signal	Northrop Grumman Precision	~ $50	1995
Logicon	Geodynamics	$32	1996
Litton	Sperry Marine	$160	1996
GM Hughes	*Litton-Itek*	$26	1996
Litton	*PRC*	$425	1996
Northrop Grumman	Westinghouse Electronic Systems	$3,600	1996
General Dynamics	*Teledyne Vehicle Systems*	N/A	1996
Lockheed Martin	*Loral*	$9,500	1996
Raytheon	Chrysler Technologies	$455	1996
Southwest Marine	Continental Maritime	N/A	1996
GEC-Marconi	Hazeltine	$110	1996
Tracor	Cordant	$65 – $80	1996
Boeing	*Rockwell Aerospace & Defense*	$3,025	1996
Litton	SAIT Division of SAIC	N/A	1996
General Dynamics	Lockheed Martin Armament & Defense Systems	$450	1997
GM Hughes	Alliant Techsystems Marine Systems Group	$141	1997
Raytheon	Texas Instruments Defense Business	$2,950	1997
Boeing	*McDonnell Douglas*	$13,300	1997
GM Hughes Defense Business	Raytheon	$9,500	1997
Announced / Under Review			
Lockheed Martin	Northrop Grumman	N/A	N/A

[a]Italicized merger and acquisition cases involved consent decrees.

Source: Update of list from Defense Science Board (DSB) Task Force on Vertical Integration and Suppliers Decisions.

Complainants advanced two specific arguments. First, competitors were concerned that the combined firm controlled components of weapon systems that would allow it to foreclose rivals from competing for the weapon system itself. This control was thought to result both from Lockheed Martin's production of key components and from the exclusive contracts that it had with suppliers of key components. Second, there was concern that, through the merger, there would be information flows between vertically related businesses within Lockheed Martin that would allow the merged firm to obtain proprietary information about its competitors.

After review, the Federal Trade Commission (FTC) determined that the merger should be allowed to proceed, subject to minor changes that were designed to address certain of these vertical issues. No major horizontal competitive problems were identified, so no divestitures of competing businesses were required.

MERGERS IN DECLINING INDUSTRIES

The rash of defense mergers is not a random event. Rather, this major change in industry structure is a response to dramatic changes in industry demand. Specifically, the end of the Cold War has allowed Congress to make significant cuts in the DOD budget. The fluctuation in defense spending over time is shown in Figure 18-1. Real DOD outlays (procurement, RDT&E,[3] or total outlays) peaked during periods of war (e.g., Vietnam War) and when government authorities felt that it was important to respond to Cold War pressures (e.g., the build-up under the Reagan administration). Figure 18-1 also shows that the overall defense budget declined by about 31 percent between 1987 and 1997 in real terms. Not surprisingly, expenditures on national defense as a percentage of gross domestic product have also been falling (Perry, 1996, p. B-4).

The recent decline has had a more significant impact on defense contractors than one might think looking only at total DOD expenditures. As Figure 18-1 indicates, the procurement budget (which is the portion of the budget that goes to the purchase of products from defense contractors, rather than military salaries) has declined by almost 58 percent during the same eleven-year period. This is a somewhat sharper decline than that for DOD expenditures as a whole.

Because the end of the Cold War came unexpectedly quickly, the cuts in DOD procurement materialized at a time when defense expenditures were high and expected to continue for some time. As a result, budget cuts led to substantial amounts of excess capacity. For example, plants that used

---

[3]RDT&E stands for research, development, test, and evaluation.

FIGURE 18-1 Department of Defense Outlay by Title.

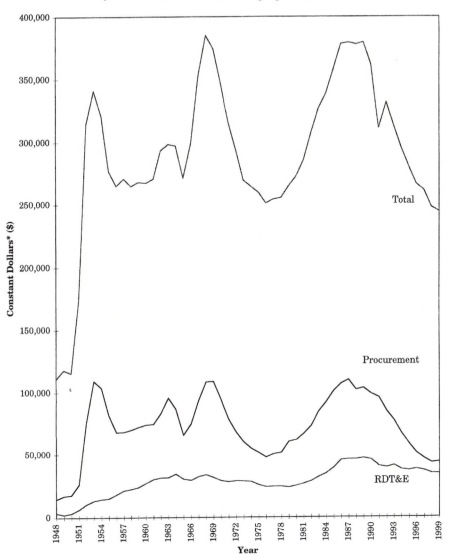

* Constant dollars are FY 98 dollars.

Source: National Defense Budget Estimates - FY 1998, Office of the Under Secretary of Defense (Comptroller).

to manufacture thousands of missiles per year are now producing a few hundred. Similarly, R&D laboratories that were funded to develop multiple
new missile systems that were to be built in the near future are now being
asked to develop fewer systems with more distant delivery dates.

The resulting excess capacity could, in principle, be resolved by exits from the business, redeployment of assets,[4] or mergers. Mergers may have advantages in terms of optimal consolidation and asset retirement. In particular, where fixed and sunk costs are a relatively large proportion of overall costs, capacity reduction is difficult and costly. In the short run, firms will continue to operate assets that are making some contribution to fixed costs. Where these assets represent sunk investments, their value cannot be easily recouped upon exit. As a consequence, assets may not be retired optimally from the standpoint either of minimizing cost or preserving long-run competition. In contrast, mergers may speed the transition to a new equilibrium, allowing efficiencies to be reaped both in terms of short-run cost savings and long-run industry performance. By merging two defense businesses that have similar production and/or distribution efforts, it is possible to shed redundant overhead (including managers, support staff, and sales forces) and to consolidate production and product development efforts at "centers of excellence." This may allow the realization of economies of scale and scope at R&D and production facilities as well as the freeing of resources through the closure of unneeded facilities.

While mergers may generate significant efficiencies, they may also lead to anticompetitive price increases. By consolidating horizontal control over key assets, mergers may facilitate coordinated interactions or the exercise of unilateral market power. They may also present vertical concerns, such as the threat of foreclosure.

The defense industry is not unique in presenting the antitrust agencies with difficult trade-offs attendant to industry rationalization. However, a number of factors suggest that merger may be a particularly appropriate economic response to demand declines in the defense industry. First, national security concerns require the United States to maintain the technical expertise that is needed to design and produce advanced weapons systems.[5] Accordingly, it is important to ensure that the process of industry consolidation will occur rapidly enough to maintain industry incentives to innovate and to maintain R&D capability. In declining industries, firms may be focusing on short-term survival, which requires cost cutting that may jeopardize long-run technical capabilities. For example, technology specialists may be allowed to leave the industry, leading to a significant erosion in firm and industry capabilities. As a result, there are national security interests in encouraging and overseeing the consolidation of the industry to preserve

---

[4]Another strategy is to find ways to redeploy the excess capacity. Specifically, some defense contractors moved toward using their defense assets to produce commercial products (see e.g., Department of Defense, 1995). However, this redeployment of assets is not always possible since the know-how and technical structure of the defense assets is not always suited for commercial markets. Often, defense assets are designed to make smaller volume production runs of higher quality products, making it difficult to produce commercially cost-competitive products on the defense line.

[5]As has been pointed out by Robert Pitofsky, the current FTC Chairman, "We're not just dealing with shoes or tennis balls or steel or oil. We're talking about national defense." *New York Times*, "Reshaping the Arms Industry," August 31, 1994, p. D5.

state-of-the-art knowledge that might be lost if consolidation occurred based on a series of price competitions for specific contracts.

Second, unlike many other customers, the DOD is often committed to covering the overhead of defense contractors. As a result, the presence of significant excess capacity not only raises per unit costs, but increases prices.[6] Specifically, under cost-plus contracts a decline in production rates can lead to very large increases in the prices that DOD pays, since DOD is obligated to cover the contractors' fixed (overhead) costs, which will be spread over substantially fewer units. This means that unless defense contractors can shed unneeded capacity, DOD will have to pay higher prices for the goods and services that it procures. This problem can worsen over time. The failure of a defense contractor to shed unneeded capacity to keep costs competitive will lead to lost bids, which implies that the firm may have even fewer sales, causing its per unit costs to rise even further. These increased costs imply that the firm may be even less well positioned in the future to offer competitive bids, suggesting that the firm may face a "downward spiral" if it does not find a way to cut costs and remain competitive.

Third, defense industry contracting procedures may inhibit the outbreak of price wars that could hasten the optimal exit of assets. In many industries, excess capacity has often brought price wars, as firms are willing to sell products at prices well below total costs in order to cover their variable costs and at least some portion of their fixed costs. This can hasten exit and provide needed industry consolidation, perhaps with less merger activity. Because the presence of cost-plus contracts and other contracting procedures reduce the likelihood of price wars in defense, merger-induced consolidation may be more necessary to ensure prompt movement to the new equilibrium.

Because of these potential cost savings, DOD has supported the rationalization of the industry through merger. This support is reflected in speeches and reports. In addition, DOD has undertaken substantive changes in policies, such as changes in accounting rules, to encourage mergers. For example, in July 1993 then-Undersecretary of Defense John Deutch wrote a memo promising that the industry's postmerger restructuring expenses (e.g., the transitional costs incurred to close down redundant facilities) would be reimbursable under DOD contracts (Sapolski and Gholz, 1997).

Consistent with the view that recent defense mergers have largely been a response to the need for industry rationalization, the antitrust authorities have challenged very few defense mergers, and virtually none of the largest ones. Many have been allowed to proceed without any modifications at all, since the antitrust review revealed no anticompetitive

---

[6]In more typical industries subject to competition, short-run prices will not necessarily cover overhead costs, although long-run prices must.

effects.[7] Some, mostly smaller ones, have been stopped because they were found to be anticompetitive,[8] although this has happened less than a half-dozen times during the last twenty years when there were more than 300 defense industry mergers (Defense Science Board, 1994, p.1). Others have been allowed to proceed after the merging parties undertook some sort of "fix" that addressed the anticompetitive issues that were identified by the government authorities.[9] The next section discusses the specific steps that the antitrust authorities have used to analyze recent defense mergers, and the growing role of the DOD in that analysis.

ANTITRUST ANALYSIS OF DEFENSE MERGERS

Under Section 7 of the Clayton Act, mergers are illegal if their effect "may be substantially to lessen competition, or [to] create a monopoly." Under this and other antitrust laws, the two antitrust authorities (FTC and Department of Justice) have the final word on whether a defense merger is to be challenged in Federal District Court. The DOD nonetheless has an important role in the antitrust review of defense mergers. As the key customer, DOD provides the antitrust authorities with its perspective on key issues, including the strength of different competitors, the likelihood that DOD would turn to foreign suppliers, the realism of efficiency calculations that are submitted by the merging parties, and national security concerns that are raised or solved by the merger. In fact, it is likely that the FTC and the Department of Justice will not reject a merger that is strongly supported by the DOD.

---

[7] For example, General Dynamics' sale of its fighter business to Lockheed was allowed to proceed without any "fixes" after the FTC studied the transaction.

[8] Illustrative defense mergers that were stopped through litigation include: (1) Grumman's acquisition of LTV (which was stopped because it was found to lessen competition substantially in the carrier-based aircraft, major airframe subassemblies, and nacelles (engine housings) markets. (*Grumman Corp.* v. *LTV Corp.*, 527 F. Supp. 86 (E.D.N.Y.), aff'd. 665 F.2d. (2d Cir. 1981)). (2) PPG Industries' acquisition of Swedlow Inc. (which was stopped because it was found to reduce competition in the "high technology aircraft transparencies" market) (*FTC* v. *PPG Industries, Inc.* 628 F. Supp. 881 (D.D.C.), aff'd. in part, 798 F.2d 1500 (D.C. Cir. 1986)). (3) Imo Industries Inc.'s attempted acquisition of Optic-Electronic Corporation (which was stopped because the firms were believed to be the two most cost-competitive producers of particular image intensifier tubes used in night vision devices) (*FTC* v. *Imo Industries* §69,943 at 68,555 (D.D.C. Nov. 22, 1989) (redacted memorandum opinion)). (4) Alliant Techsystems Inc.'s attempted acquisition of Olin Corporation's Ordinance Division (which was stopped because the two contractors were competing in an upcoming multiyear procurement of 120-mm ammunition which was designed to reduce the number of suppliers from two to one) (*FTC* v. *Alliant Techsystems Inc.*, 808 F. Supp. 9 (D.D.C. 1992)).

[9] For example, General Dynamics was allowed to sell its launch vehicle business to Martin Marietta after Martin Marietta agreed to construct "firewalls" that would limit the flow of information between its launch vehicle business and its satellite business. The Lockheed-Martin Marietta merger also falls in this category.

Horizontal Mergers

In 1995, when the Lockheed-Martin Marietta merger was approved, horizontal mergers were evaluated using the standards identified in the 1992 *Merger Guidelines*. The general question that is asked is whether the merger is likely to harm customers that buy a particular product by increasing prices or lowering product quality.

While the basic analytical framework of the 1992 *Merger Guidelines* is used to evaluate defense mergers, there are characteristics of defense markets (besides national security issues) that affect the analysis. For example, the Defense Science Board (DSB) Task Force points out (Defense Science Board, 1994):

> The basis for a finding that mergers in non-defense industries are illegal is usually that they facilitate coordinated interaction. That might be true with mergers in the defense industry involving standardized products (tents, uniforms, certain components of weapons systems), but the risk of anticompetitive effects from coordinated interaction with respect to mergers involving producers of sophisticated weapons systems is likely to be small. The systems themselves are complex and heterogeneous, and cost positions and technical capabilities of competing firms vary greatly, making it difficult to reach tacit agreements that would benefit all sellers. Also, cartels are difficult to implement when competition occurs through bids for large multi-unit, multi-year procurements.

The Task Force found that a significant source of potential horizontal competitive concern in defense mergers is that:

> Competition also can be lessened through unilateral effects, particularly when the merging firms account for more than 35% of the market. The greatest risk of unilateral anticompetitive effects is presented when the only two competitors in a product market propose to merge to monopoly, or the two lowest cost and therefore most efficient firms propose to merge. Mergers in those situations will need to be carefully reviewed.

With respect to the analysis of efficiencies, the Task Force concluded that:

> A broad range of efficiencies may be taken into account by the enforcement agencies in the exercise of prosecutorial discretion, and are sometimes taken into account by courts. Efficiencies will not carry much weight if they can be achieved through less anticompetitive means than mergers (for example, a temporary teaming arrangement), and must be demonstrated by clear evidence. In the situation where a merger between the only two firms in a market is proposed, a "winner-take-all" competition between the firms will almost always be preferable to a merger. A merger to monopoly could be preferable only in special circumstances

and when the net benefit of efficiencies is greater than the anticompetitive effect.

The DSB Task Force also concluded that:

> DOD should alert the enforcement agencies to proposed mergers and joint ventures that it believes are essential to national security and the agencies [DOJ and FTC] are likely to give the Department's substantiated views on this issue significant weight.

In sum, the analysis of horizontal overlaps between merging defense contractors involves an assessment of whether DOD's prices are likely to rise as a result of the transaction. When DOD perceives that a merger will generate significant efficiencies and that it will benefit from these efficiencies through lower prices, DOD is likely to support the proposed merger even if postmerger concentration levels exceed *Merger Guideline* levels. Moreover, the DOJ and FTC will also support this type of efficiency-enhancing merger. Indeed, as a practical matter, the antitrust agencies are unlikely to challenge a defense merger that is supported by DOD, since DOD is the principal customer.

Vertical Mergers

While the initial DSB Task Force stated "It is conceivable that vertical mergers and joint ventures (i.e., between customers and suppliers) could be anticompetitive, but threats to competition by those sorts of transactions are less likely to lead to problems" (Defense Science Board, 1994, p. 7, n. 3), there has been substantial recent concern about vertical mergers. Indeed, a second DSB Task Force was assembled to study vertical integration and the policy toward vertical mergers. The second DSB Task Force identified seven cases in which vertical concerns led the antitrust authorities to require the merging parties to make adjustments in their merger to address vertical problems that had been identified (Defense Science Board, 1997, p. 32).

As is true for horizontal mergers, vertical mergers are analyzed by the antitrust authorities using guidelines. For vertical mergers, the relevant guidelines are the 1984 *Merger Guidelines.* These guidelines indicate that the antitrust authorities are concerned with two basic problems that vertical mergers may raise: (1) increased barriers to entry, and (2) the facilitation of collusion. In addition, it has become evident that the DOD and antitrust authorities are concerned that vertical mergers may weaken suppliers of inputs (as vertically integrated firms turn to internal sources of supply) and may allow the merged firm to obtain access (through its newly acquired downstream or upstream presence) to a competitor's proprietary information.

The notion that a vertical merger may deter entry is based on the possibility that a merger may allow a firm to obtain control over a critical component that is needed by rivals for an upcoming contract and that this control can be used to prevent rivals from competing effectively for that contract. This concern involves not only entry into the market in general, but the use of control over key technologies to block competitors from bidding on particular upcoming contracts (either by denying competitors access to the technology or by charging a prohibitive price for the technology). According to the DSB Task Force, DOD is particularly concerned about input markets involving products or technologies that are essential to the achievement of improved performance levels for key weapons systems and where the number of suppliers is, or may drop below, three.[10] The notion that a vertical merger may facilitate collusion is based on the concern that vertical linkages will allow horizontal competitors to exchange information that will make it easier to coordinate their competitive activities. Key questions that will be asked are:

> Do the merging parties together represent the preeminent technical capability in important discriminating product or technology areas? Can they prevent other firms from entering the market by enforcing patent rights or denying them access in other ways? How much time and investment is required for other firms to either remain in the business or to become serious competitors to the vertically integrated firms' sub-tier business? Are firms that now depend on access to important or discriminating product or technology areas expressing concern about the effects of the merger and/or acquisition?

The DSB Task Force expressed the view that vertical mergers may be problematic if they lead vertically integrated defense contractors to prefer their internal sources of supply, weakening independent suppliers (Defense Science Board, 1997, p. 3). In the extreme, the fear is that some efficient independent suppliers may be forced to exit.

The concern that vertical integration may give firms access to proprietary information is based on the observation that firms often have to share detailed technical information about their products with firms that either use their product or that are supplying inputs into their products. For example, in the defense industry it may be necessary for a satellite manufacturer to provide detailed design specifications to the launch vehicle manufacturer that will launch the satellite. If a large defense contractor that has a subsidiary that manufacturers satellites acquires a launch vehicle manufacturer, rival satellite manufacturers may be concerned that the launch

---

[10]Defense Science Board (1997, pp. x, xvi). Examples of key product and technology areas that have been identified by the DSB Task Force are high-temperature and specialty materials (low observable materials, single/grown crystal metallics), diode-pumped lasers, focal plane arrays, missile seekers, fire-control systems, monolithic microwave integrated circuits, and large-scale composite structures.

vehicle subsidiary will transmit proprietary information to its satellite subsidiary, allowing the satellite subsidiary to "free ride" on a competitor's valuable proprietary information.[11]

The Formation Of Lockheed Martin

To understand the antitrust issues raised by this merger, it is useful to describe the structure of both Lockheed and Martin Marietta before their combination. We then discuss the horizontal and vertical issues that were examined and ultimately resolved by the Federal Trade Commission.

Firm Backgrounds

Lockheed

At the time of the merger, Lockheed was one of the largest defense contractors, with over $13 billion in sales (having grown from about $7.7 billion in 1984) (Lockheed, 1993 *Annual Report*, p. 26). Lockheed was particularly strong in aeronautical systems, producing fighter bombers (F-16 and a share of the F-22) and special mission aircraft (e.g., C-130, U-2, F-117A, P-3). In 1993, its Aeronautical Systems division experienced a significant increase in sales (from $2.9 billion in 1992 to $6.0 billion in 1993) due to its acquisition of General Dynamics' tactical aircraft business. However, that increase did not permanently reverse the ongoing decline in business. For example, in 1994 there was a 19 percent decrease in the Aeronautical Systems' order backlog due to a decrease in the number of new government orders.

Lockheed's Missiles & Space Systems segment was a major supplier of missiles, satellites, and launch vehicles. With respect to missiles, Lockheed was the prime contractor on the Trident II, a submarine-launched missile, and the Theater High Altitude Area Defense (THAAD) program, which was intended to be a system that could intercept theater ballistic missiles at a long range.

Lockheed was a major satellite contractor (building both defense and communications satellites). For example, it contributed the spacecraft ("bus") for Motorola's Iridium TM/SM global communication satellites and the Milstar communications satellite for the U.S. Air Force.

Lockheed's launch vehicle business involved both the provision of launch vehicles (the LLV) that it would manufacture and a marketing agreement with Russian launch vehicle suppliers. Lockheed's LLV was being designed to launch small satellites into low earth orbit. Larger satellites could

---

[11]Even without the antitrust authorities' intervention, it is common to have contractual clauses that create firewalls that will prevent the flow of information.

be launched by the Lockheed-Khrunichev-Energia International (LKEI) partnership.

The Lockheed Missiles & Space Systems segment was experiencing declining sales at the time of the merger. Specifically, its sales peaked at slightly above $5 billion in 1990 and had fallen to just over $4 billion by 1993. As its 1994 10-K form points out: "Missiles and Space Systems programs continue to experience reductions in funding and, in some cases, terminations by various government customers" (p. 19).

Lockheed's Electronic Systems segment participated in both defense and commercial markets. It developed and manufactured radio systems, infrared and electrooptical countermeasures, mission planning, surveillance, automated test equipment, antisubmarine warfare systems, microwave systems, avionics, and computer graphics equipment. Unlike the larger business segments, this segment was facing stable to increased order backlogs.

Lockheed's Technology Services segment provided support for the space shuttle. It also managed the Idaho National Engineering Laboratory and provided a variety of other environmental and facilities management services. This small segment of the firm's business was growing in 1994.

Martin Marietta

Like Lockheed, Martin Marietta was one of the largest defense contractors, having sales of $9.4 billion and earnings of $450 million before the merger. Because a number of its businesses did not overlap with those of Lockheed, the FTC's investigation focused on Martin Marietta's Electronics Group and its Space Group.

Martin Marietta's Electronics Group primarily developed electronic systems for precision guidance, navigation, detection and tracking of threats, missiles, armaments, aircraft controls and subsystems, and secure communications systems. In particular, Martin Marietta was viewed as a leader in certain electronics components (e.g., fire-control systems, such as LANTIRN, which provides night vision for aircraft and helicopters).

Martin Marietta's Space Group designed and produced spacecraft, launch vehicles, supporting ground systems, electronics, and instrumentation. In particular, it developed and supplied such products as Titan/Atlas launch vehicles, military/civil/commercial satellites, and the external fuel tanks for the space shuttle. To some extent this business grew through acquisition. For example, Martin Marietta acquired G.E.'s Aerospace division (a major satellite business) in November 1992 for around $3 billion (Janes, 1993–1994, p. 582). Similarly, it merged General Dynamic's Atlas launch vehicle business with its Titan business in 1994. However, other parts of the business grew internally over the years.

Reasons For The Transaction

As was outlined above, defense markets were contracting. This was placing financial pressures on Lockheed and Martin Marietta. Lockheed responded to these pressures by focusing its attention on its most promising businesses (including an effort to grow its commercial satellite and launch vehicles businesses) and by reviewing its strategic options (Lockheed, 1994 10-K, pp. 19–20). In particular, Lockheed was looking for acquisition candidates that fit with its existing business, as is evidenced by its acquisition of the General Dynamic's military aircraft business. Without a merger such as the Martin Marietta merger, Lockheed expected that it might have to undertake a major "downsizing" and take a pretax write-off of $200 million.[12]

Martin Marietta was pursuing a similar strategy. As its 1993 *Annual Report* indicates, it had acquired General Dynamic's launch vehicle business and GE's aerospace and jet engines businesses and planned to

> continue to seek acquisition opportunities that further position Martin Marietta for the future in its core markets. As in the past, however, our interest will focus on acquisitions that promise a strategic fit with Martin Marietta, enhance growth, are appropriately priced and assure long-term value to the Corporation's stockholders.[13]

Martin Marietta tried to acquire Grumman in 1994, but Northrup outbid it.[14] In sum, as Martin Marietta's and Lockheed's annual reports indicate, both firms were seeking to merge with other firms that had complementary businesses.

As the preceding description of Martin Marietta's and Lockheed's businesses suggests, their businesses were complementary. Specifically, their businesses involved similar skills and know-how, suggesting that they could expect to realize significant cost savings if they merged.[15] For example, the firms' satellite and launch vehicle businesses were a good strategic fit. By combining the firms' businesses, they could realistically expect to compete more effectively in the growing and competitive commercial satellite business, through the combination of their skills and through the realization of economies of scale. More generally, the firms could expect to shed redundant costs (e.g., eliminate redundant satellite production facilities, headquarters, sales forces, managers, and support staff) and spread overhead over larger volumes.

Many of the efficiencies that motivated the merger are reflected in

---

[12]"Lockheed Warns of Missiles & Space Fallout from Merger Legal Battle," *Aerospace Daily*, November 14, 1994, p. 227.

[13]Martin Marietta, *1993 Annual Report*, p. 2.

[14]*New York Times*, "Reshaping the Arms Industry: The Overview," August 31, 1994, p. A1.

[15]As the 1995 Lockheed Martin *Annual Report* (p. 5) indicates, the merger and subsequent consolidation was expected to lead to economies of scale and corporate-wide synergies.

Lockheed Martin's June 26, 1995, announcement of a major postmerger, corporate-wide consolidation. This consolidation was projected to yield $1.8 billion in *annual* savings, with *one-time* transition costs of around $1.7 billion dollars (Lockheed Martin Fiscal 1995 10-K, p. 1). As a result, the consolidation of Lockheed's and Martin Marietta's businesses was expected to generate savings having a present value in excess of $10 billion. The consolidation (which calls for adjustments over a five-year period ending in 1999) involves the closing of at least twelve facilities and laboratories, as well as twenty-six duplicative field offices in the United States and abroad. Through the consolidation, Lockheed Martin will eliminate 12,000 positions and 7.7 million square feet of excess capacity.

Given these efficiencies, it is not surprising that DOD supported the merger. As one DOD official indicated when they announced approval of the Lockheed-Martin Marietta merger,

> This is what we wanted to happen. We have a substantial amount of over-capacity in the defense industrial base, with space launch being the most obvious example. . . . To the extent that we can consolidate through mergers such as Lockheed Martin, we may well avoid the shutdown of a key portion of the base.[16]

Horizontal Issues

Although both Lockheed and Martin Marietta were very large defense companies active in many of the same general defense segments, there was limited overlap between the two companies. Indeed, in many areas there was no overlap at all. For example, Lockheed was a significant aircraft manufacturer and Martin Marietta was not. Similarly, Martin Marietta had ship and submarine systems (e.g., sonar) that Lockheed did not offer.

Nonetheless, there were overlaps, for example, in launch vehicles, satellites, and defense electronics. However, many of these overlaps were not competitively significant, either because the firms' products differed or because other defense contractors were viable competitors.

Satellite Overlap

Satellites are purchased by the military, civil government (e.g., NASA and National Oceanic and Atmospheric Administration (NOAA)), and commercial organizations (e.g., telecommunication companies). While commercial expenditures were stable or rising,[17] DOD expenditures for satellites began to decline in 1994 (falling from over $3.5 billion in 1993 to under

---

[16]*Defense News,* December 4, 1994, p. 3.

[17]Commercial satellite revenues grew from $550 million in 1988 to $1.3 billion in 1992, fell in 1993, but grew to $1.4 billion in 1994 (Department of Commerce, 1992, p. 41-1; 1993, p. 27-1; 1994, p. 28-1).

$2 billion in 1995).[18] This put some pressure on smaller military satellite manufacturers and led industry observers to expect some consolidation.

There are numerous types of satellites (e.g., communications, early warning (detect missile launches), navigation (such as global-positioning satellites), geodesy (measure earth's surface), meteorology, surveillance, nuclear test/radiation detection, and experimental). Satellite programs typically involve a prime contractor (who usually provides the satellite "bus") and others who contribute parts to the "payload."[19] As a result, firms that manufacture satellites and/or parts of satellites may be selling very different products that do not compete. For example, a firm offering a "bus" for a communications satellite is not competing with a firm that is designing a "payload" for a surveillance satellite.

A review of historical satellite programs and anticipated projects reveals that Lockheed and Martin Marietta (or the GE business it acquired) were prime contractors on a number of historical military and civil satellite contracts. For example, Martin Marietta (GE) won a Defense Satellite Communications System (DSCS) contract, a Defense Meteorological Satellite Program (DMSP) contract, a naval global-positioning satellite contract (NAVSTAR GPS), a communications contract (ACTS), a meteorological contract (NOAA), and remote sensing/earth observation contracts (e.g., EOS, Landsat) (Janes, 1993–1994). Similarly, Lockheed was a prime contractor on the Military Strategic & Tactical Relay (MILSTAR) program and a remote sensing/earth observation contract (Seasat).

Lockheed and Martin's satellite activities were largely complementary. Although there were some potential satellite contracts on which the merging firms might have bid as competitors, other firms were also well positioned to bid. Significant satellite competitors included Hughes, TRW, Boeing, Space Systems/Loral, and GTE. Some of these firms, such as Hughes, Space Systems/Loral, and GTE, were leading suppliers of commercial satellites, which gave them volume that would help them cover their fixed costs and lower the price they could bid for military business. As a result, there was a basis for the antitrust authorities to conclude that the merging firms faced significant competitors, particularly if the key customers (DOD and NASA) did not express concern over the merger. In addition, given the declining demand for defense satellites, there was reason to believe that a merger would generate efficiencies by allowing the merging firms to reduce their overheads and to preserve valuable know-how that might otherwise be lost.

Launch Vehicle Overlap

Launch vehicles are used by military, civil, and commercial organizations to launch satellites. There are two basic types of vehicles: expendable

---

[18]Euroconsult (1994, pp. 26, 27, 242); Department of Defense Budget, fiscal year 1995; Congressional Record, August 13, 1994.

[19]A satellite bus is the main body of the spacecraft that houses the payload. It helps place the payload in final orbit, helps maintain it in the desired orbit, and supplies power to the satellite.

launch vehicles (ELVs) and reusable launch vehicles (e.g., Space Shuttle). Launch vehicles differ with respect to their designs, which affects where they can be launched and the size of the payload they can place in different orbits. For example, some are small, single-stage vehicles that can place only light satellites into low earth orbit. Others are large, multistage vehicles that can place heavier satellites in geosynchronous earth orbits.[20]

DOD's budget authority for expendable launch vehicles (procurement of vehicles plus funding of R&D) grew during the 1980s, peaking in 1987 when it was over $1 billion. Between 1988 and 1995, budget authority was typically below $850 million, except for 1994 when unusually high R&D expenditures pushed the budget authority above $1 billion. While commercial revenues from large-capacity commercial launchers fell between 1990 and 1991, they grew between 1991 and 1994. In 1994, they reached $580 million.

Both Lockheed and Martin Marietta supplied expendable launch vehicles.[21] Lockheed offered heavy lift launch vehicles through its LKEI partnership, which used Russian Proton launch vehicles.[22] Lockheed was also developing its LLV launch vehicle that was capable of lifting modest weights (2200 to 4000 pounds for initial versions and up to 8500 pounds for later versions) into low earth orbit (Teal, 1994). At the time of the merger, the LLV had not had a successful launch, although it was scheduled to launch at least one commercial payload in 1995.[23] Martin Marietta supplied Titan and Atlas launch vehicles that came in a variety of sizes, only one of which, the Atlas E, overlapped in capability with the LLV.

While it may appear that Lockheed's LLVs would compete with the Atlas E, this competition was limited by two key facts: (1) the Atlas E was in limited supply[24] and (2) the Atlas E focused on polar orbits rather than equatorial or other orbits, since it had to be launched from Vandenberg Air Force Base (California) (Isakowitz, 1991, p. 3).

With respect to the potential competition between the Russian Protons and the generally heavier Atlas and Titan launch vehicles, it was unlikely that defense satellites would be launched on the Russian vehicle for national security reasons. With respect to commercial launches, if one expanded the market to include foreign suppliers, there were significant foreign launch vehicle companies besides the Russians that would have to be included in

---

[20]Geosynchronous orbits are circular orbits that are approximately 22,300 miles and that appear to hover over a fixed longitude.

[21]Public complaints by Hughes Aircraft and TRW did not focus on this horizontal issue. Instead, they focused on the vertical implications of allowing Lockheed Martin to have a significant position in both launch vehicles and satellites. These vertical issues are discussed below.

[22]Russian Proton launch vehicles were capable of lifting 44,100 pounds to low earth orbit from Tyuratam (Isakowitz, 1991, pp. 2–3).

[23]The initial postmerger test of this small launch vehicle in 1995 was unsuccessful. 1995 Lockheed Martin *Annual Report*, p. 2.

[24]There were only seven remaining Atlas Es, which were dedicated to particular programs (Isakowitz, 1991, p. 186).

the relevant market. Of these competitors, Ariane (a French company) was a particularly important alternative. Moreover, the Space Shuttle is capable of launching a variety of types of satellite.[25] As a result, the antitrust authorities had good reason not to be concerned about the horizontal launch vehicle overlap. Moreover, the consolidation of the launch vehicle operations could lead to significant synergies. For example, redundant launch crews could be consolidated to reduce costs.

Defense Electronics Overlap

Lockheed and Martin Marietta were both active in defense electronics. With respect to Lockheed, its Sanders and Canadian divisions had active defense and commercial electronics businesses. They were developing automated test systems, surveillance systems, target acquisition systems, fire-control systems, tactical airborne radar, avionics subsystems, training/simulation equipment, and countermeasures. Martin Marietta focused mostly on weapons systems such as targeting systems, command and control modules, and radar systems. Often, the firms were in somewhat different niches, supplying products that did not compete. For example, while both firms produced radar, Lockheed provided X-band radars that have a narrow focus and are used to do such things as fire control (aiming a weapon), while Martin Marietta provided S-band radar that has a much wider span, such as AWAX. In some cases where there was some competition between the firms (e.g., automated test systems, countermeasures, signal processing, and training/simulation devices), other firms were significant competitors, often with stronger positions than at least one of the merging parties.[26] In other cases where there might appear to be a horizontal overlap, such as the next generation countermeasure systems and flight control program (INEWS), the firms were on the same team and thus were not competing. As a result, serious competitive issues were not raised by defense electronics overlaps.

Conclusion

As the preceding discussion suggests, the horizontal overlaps were not particularly significant. This fact was reflected in the FTC Consent Agreement for the Lockheed-Martin Marietta merger, which did not force any divestitures and which focused on vertical issues.

Vertical Issues

The Lockheed-Martin Marietta merger raised a number of vertical issues that were particularly worrisome to competitors. Specifically, competitors

---

[25]The Space Shuttle can launch satellites up to 53,700 pounds into low earth orbit and 13,000 pounds into geosynchronous orbit (Isakowitz, 1991, p. 3).

[26]For example, both firms were involved in Integrated Defensive Electronics Countermeasures (IDECM), which is a new electronics countermeasure system that is designed to protect the Navy's F-18 E/F aircraft against radar and infrared threats. However, numerous other firms were well positioned to bid on this program.

were concerned that Lockheed Martin could use proprietary information or leverage obtained through the acquisition to grow at their expense. As a result, competitors encouraged the FTC to intervene. The most significant vertical issues involved three areas.

Low-Altitude Navigation and Targeting Infrared for Nightvision (LANTIRN)

One of the competitors' and FTC concerns involved the vertical integration that resulted from combining Lockheed's military aircraft business with Martin Marietta's LANTIRN system. As its name suggests, LANTIRN is a navigation and targeting system that is contained in a dual pod that is externally mounted on aircraft.

LANTIRN was viewed by the FTC as a key component of military aircraft that was supplied only by Martin Marietta. Before the merger, Martin Marietta (which was not a significant military aircraft manufacturer) had an incentive to design LANTIRN so that it could be used by all aircraft manufacturers, including both Lockheed and Lockheed's competitors. The FTC's concern was that, after the merger, Lockheed Martin could modify or upgrade LANTIRN in ways that would prevent rival aircraft manufacturers from competing.

The FTC also believed that the merged firm was in a position to obtain access to information about Lockheed's aircraft competitors through its work on the LANTIRN navigation and targeting systems that were installed on competitor aircraft. It was feared that the proprietary information that was obtained through these vertical relationships would benefit Lockheed Martin's military aircraft division after the merger, lessening competition in military aircraft.

The FTC resolved the two vertical concerns that were raised by LANTIRN by ordering Lockheed to take remedial actions. First, the FTC ordered Lockheed Martin not to make changes in LANTIRN that would discriminate against other aircraft manufacturers unless these changes were necessary to compete against foreign suppliers. Moreover, any changes that were made would have to be approved by DOD. Second, the FTC required Lockheed Martin to impose a firewall that prevented the flow of proprietary information, without the written consent of the proprietor, between its military aircraft division and the division that produced the LANTIRN. It also required Lockheed Martin to use only third-party proprietary information that it obtained through LANTIRN in its capacity as the LANTIRN provider.

Satellites/Launch Vehicles

Hughes and TRW, which competed with Lockheed and Martin Marietta in the manufacturing of satellites, expressed the concern that Lockheed Martin would use its control over launch vehicles to advantage itself in satellite competitions. They made three specific arguments. First, they were concerned that proprietary technical information about Hughes and TRW satellites that was shared with Lockheed Martin's launch vehicle operation might be given to Lockheed Martin's satellite business. Second, they believed that Lockheed Martin might redesign its launch vehicles so that it would be more costly to launch a competitor's satellite than a Lockheed Martin satellite. Third, they raised the possibility that Lockheed Martin might charge discriminatory higher prices to launch competitor's satellites than they charged to launch Lockheed Martin satellites.

The FTC appears to have dismissed the second two concerns, since they were not addressed in the FTC Order. One reason may be that the FTC did not perceive that the merger changed the structure of the launch vehicle or satellite markets in ways that created or significantly increased the problems that Hughes and TRW identified. As was explained above, the merger did not significantly reduce the options that the satellite competitors had. Moreover, on the basis of the public comments, it does not appear that TRW or Hughes advanced any examples of Martin Marietta's using its premerger control over Atlas or Titan launches to advantage its satellite business. As a result, it is likely that the FTC dismissed these two matters because it had no evidence to support them.

The FTC did express concern about Lockheed Martin's use of confidential information that it obtained about its rivals' businesses through the operation of its launch vehicle and satellite businesses. A 1994 FTC Order that was signed by Martin Marietta when it acquired General Dynamics' Space Systems Division had dealt with the scenario in which Lockheed Martin's launch vehicle division might share confidential information that it obtained from rival satellite manufacturers with Lockheed Martin's satellite business. As a result, the FTC Order for the Lockheed-Martin Marietta merger focused on controlling the flow of any confidential information that Lockheed Martin's satellite business obtained about rival launch vehicle manufacturers when it used their launch vehicles. Specifically, the FTC required Lockheed Martin to impose firewalls between its satellite business and its launch vehicle business that prevented its launch vehicle business from obtaining proprietary information.

Space Based InfraRed System (SBIRS)

A third vertical concern involved Space Based Early Warning Systems, which are satellite systems used to provide early warning and attack assessments for theater and strategic missile defense. One of these early warning systems was the SBIRS. At the time of the merger, both Lockheed and Martin Marietta were competing on separate teams for the SBIRS contract. Each had teamed with a different sensor provider (Lockheed with Hughes, Martin Marietta with Northrup Grumman), which were two of the leading sensor providers that could meet the needs of the SBIRS program. Since the merging parties' agreements with these partners were exclusive, the FTC was concerned that they were positioned to block other competitors from obtaining access to this key technology.

To address the risk that Lockheed Martin could block entry into Space Based Early Warning System competitions through its contracts with sensor providers, the FTC ordered Lockheed Martin to free both Hughes and Northrup Grumman so that each could support rival teams for any Space Based Early Warning System contracts (including SBIRS), as well as Lockheed Martin. Specifically, it required Lockheed Martin not to enforce the exclusivity provisions in either the Lockheed/Hughes or the Martin Marietta/Grumman Teaming Agreements. The purpose was to increase the number of competitors for SBIRS.

Conclusion

As the preceding discussion suggests, the FTC was concerned about some vertical issues that were raised by the formation of Lockheed Martin. Rather than jeopardize and/or delay the multi-billion dollar merger, Lockheed Martin agreed to certain behavioral restrictions and contractual modifications that the FTC believed addressed their concerns.

SUMMARY

The decline in the defense budget placed significant financial pressures on defense contractors. These pressures led to a large number of defense mergers, including the merger between Lockheed and Martin Marietta. While the defense contractors benefited because the mergers improved their ability to compete for future contracts and lowered their costs for existing contracts, the DOD also benefited. As Deputy Defense Secretary John Deutch indicated in testimony before Congress:

> Properly done, . . . restructuring can save the Department [DOD] and the taxpayer billions of dollars. But without those savings we will be unable to obtain the defense systems we need at the prices we can afford. Therefore, the Department has begun to promote the rational downsizing of the defense industry. . . .
>
> In many instances the most effective restructuring comes from a combination of businesses in merger or acquisition. . . . The potential savings from those combinations could run in billions of dollars. . . .
>
> If we do not allow those restructurings to take place we will pay dearly in the form of higher prices for the defense systems that we need and reduced capability for the forces that we field.[27]

The series of defense mergers that have occurred over the last five years or so have caused a significant structural shift in industry supply. For

---

[27]Hearings of the House Oversight and Investigations Subcommittee, July 27, 1994.

example, in 1987, 3,665,000 workers were employed in the defense industry. Since then, the number has fallen each year. By 1998, employment is projected to fall to 2,050,000, which reflects a 44-percent drop from 1987.[28] Not surprisingly, the defense mergers have also been increasing the capacity utilization rates at defense plants.

As Secretary of Defense William Perry indicated in his annual report to the President and the Congress (Perry, 1996, p. 74), "To date, DOD has found substantial savings in case after case." While the savings that are being realized often are below early estimates, they are nonetheless significant.[29] DOD is clearly saving billions of dollars, and social costs are being reduced by even more.[30]

While these savings have come at the cost of some decline in competition, careful antitrust reviews appear to have successfully protected the key consumer. As the Lockheed Martin case suggests, when DOD and the antitrust authorities have perceived that there are competitive issues, they have arranged specific business restrictions and contract changes (including divestitures) to address them (Perry, 1996, p. 74). In general, as the DSB Task Force on Vertical Integration and Supplier Decisions points out (Defense Science Board, 1997, p. 32), "The remedies ordered by the antitrust agencies appear to be effective; no evidence, either from the antitrust agency's follow-ups, or the Department's ongoing interactions with firms, suggests otherwise."

REFERENCES

Defense Science Board (DSB) Task Force. *Report of the Defense Science Board (DSB) Task Force on Antitrust Aspects of Defense Industry Consolidations, 1994.*

Defense Science Board (DSB) Task Force. *Report of the Defense Science Board (DSB) Task Force on Vertical Integration and Supplier Decisions, 1997.*

Department of Commerce. *U.S. Industrial Outlook,* 1992, 1993, 1994.

Department of Defense. *Dual Use Technology: A Defense Strategy for Affordable, Leading-Edge Technology,* February 1995.

Euroconsult. *World Space Markets Survey.* 1994.

Government Accounting Office, *Defense Restructuring Costs: Projected and Actual Savings From Martin-Marietta Acquisition of GE Aerospace,* September 1996.

Sapolski, H., and E. Gholz. "Indefensible Defense Costs." *The Wall Street Journal Interactive Edition,* July 11, 1997, p. 1.

---

[28]Ibid., Table 7-6.

[29]The Deputy Secretary of Defense testified in mid-1994 that early estimates from recent defense mergers indicated that projected savings would range from one and one-half to seven times the projected adjustment costs. Some subsequent studies have found savings in the low end of this range. (See, e.g., Government Accounting Office, 1996, p. 4.)

[30]See, e.g., Office of Secretary of Defense (1997), which indicates that DOD's share of the reported savings over five years from six mergers is $3.23 billion.

Isakowitz, Steven J. *International Reference Guide to Space Launch Systems.* Washington, D.C.: American Institute of Aeronautics and Astronautics, 1991.

Janes Information Group. *Janes Space Directory.* Arlington, Va.: 1993–94.

Office of Secretary of Defense. *Report on the Effects Of Mergers in the Defense Industry*, March 1997.

Perry, William J., Secretary of Defense. *Annual Report to the President and the Congress*, March 1996.

Teal Group Corp. *World Space Systems Briefing Book.* Fairfax, Va.: 1994.

CASE 19

Vertical and Horizontal Ownership in Cable TV: Time Warner-Turner (1996)

Stanley M. Besen
E. Jane Murdoch
Daniel P. O'Brien
Steven C. Salop
John Woodbury

INTRODUCTION

After a twelve-month investigation, the Federal Trade Commission in 1996 approved, subject to certain conditions, the merger of Time Warner and Turner Broadcasting, creating, in the words of the merging parties, "a global media organization with the world's foremost combination of news, entertainment, information resources and distribution systems."[1] The FTC alleged that the merger was potentially anticompetitive because of (a) a horizontal overlap between the cable program services of the merging entities, (b) a vertical linkage between the Turner program services and the Time Warner cable television systems, and (c) the participation in the transaction of TCI, the nation's largest cable television operator, which was a major

The authors served as consultants to the attorneys who represented TCI before the FTC in the Time Warner-Turner merger. Because of space limitations, some issues related to the merger have been abbreviated, and some issues have not been addressed at all. The authors would like to thank Jonathan Baker, Christopher Bogart, Kathy Fenton, Robert Joffe, and Joe Sims for their helpful comments on earlier drafts. Of course, the views expressed here are the authors' own and do not necessarily reflect those of TCI or any of the other participants in the merger.

[1] "Time Warner Inc. and Turner Broadcasting System, Inc. Agree to Merge, Creating the World's Foremost Media Company." Press release of Time Warner, September 22, 1995.

owner of Turner and which became an owner of Time Warner, the second largest cable operator, as a result of the merger.[2]

Time Warner was a large, diversified company with ownership interests in magazine, book, and music publishing; the Warner Brothers motion picture studio; the WB broadcast television network; a large number of cable television systems; and five cable television program services, including, most prominently, Home Box Office (HBO), the largest and most successful premium cable service. Most of Time Warner's cable interests were held through Time Warner Entertainment, a partnership with US West in which Time Warner had a 75-percent ownership share.

Turner Broadcasting owned a number of cable television program services, including TBS, TNT, CNN, and the Cartoon Network, as well as a television broadcast station (WTBS), the Atlanta Braves baseball team, the Atlanta Hawks basketball team, and some movie studios. Ted Turner owned a major interest in Turner Broadcasting, and the transaction would make him Time Warner's largest individual shareholder with an ownership stake of about 10 percent. The merger resulted in Time Warner's adding the stable of Turner services to its ownership of HBO and its other program services. Moreover, it combined Time Warner's extensive cable system ownership with the Turner services.

A number of major cable television system operators, including Time Warner, TCI, Comcast, and Cablevision Systems, held ownership interests in Turner[3] that would become holdings in Time Warner as a result of the merger. TCI held its interest through its Liberty subsidiary. Although Liberty was traded on the stock market separately from TCI, the FTC treated them as a single entity. Thus, TCI's 23-percent ownership interest in Turner would become an approximately 9-percent ownership interest in Time Warner. TCI would now have a financial interest in Time Warner's cable systems and program services. Table 19-1 summarizes the major cable interests of Time Warner, Turner, and TCI at the time of the transaction.

TCI also entered into an agreement with Turner (the Program Service Agreement) that specified the terms under which TCI would carry the various Turner program services. The Agreement committed TCI to carry the services for twenty years in return for a price equal to 85 percent of the average price paid by other cable operators.

A BRIEF HISTORY OF THE CABLE TELEVISION INDUSTRY

Cable television initially developed as a means to deliver television broadcast signals via antennas, microwave towers, and cables to consumers. The

---

[2]For a statement of the FTC's views, see Federal Trade Commission, *Analysis of Proposed Consent Order to Aid Public Comment,* September 12, 1996.

[3]Time Warner had previously owned 23 percent of the Turner shares.

TABLE 19-1
Cable Subscribers and Program Service Ownership Interests
(By Company, 1996)

	Time Warner	TCI	Turner
Cable Subscribers	12,100,000	16,009,000	na
National Video Program Services (ownership share)	Cinemax (100%) Comedy Central (50%) Court TV (33.3%) E! (50%) HBO (100%)	BET (17.5%) Court TV (33.3%) Discovery (49%) Encore (90%) E! (10%) Faith & Values (49%) The Family Channel (20%) Fit TV (20%) HSN (80.4%) International Channel (50%) Intro TV (100%) NewSport (33%) Prime Network (33%) QVC (43%) Q2 (43%) Request TV (47%) Starz! (90%) TLC (49%) Viewer's Choice (10%)	Cartoon (100%) CNN (100%) Headline News (100%) TBS (100%) TCM (100%) TNT (100%)

Sources: Paul Kagan Associates, Inc., *Economics of Basic Cable Networks*, 1997, pp. 48–50; 1996, pp. 39–40; 1993, p. 38. NCTA, *Cable Television Developments* 21, no. 1 (Spring 1997): 14.

relationship between broadcasting and cable was initially symbiotic, with cable systems providing either improved reception of local television signals or service to rural areas without broadcast television stations, thereby increasing station viewership and advertising revenues. Eventually, however, cable systems found that they could sell the reception of "distant" television broadcast signals to urban viewers who wished to augment the broadcast service they could receive over the air. Thus began the transformation of cable, from offering an improved antenna to becoming the source of a wide array of programming not available to over-the-air viewers.

Because distant signals competed for viewers and advertising revenues, television broadcasters complained to the Federal Communications Commission (FCC) that cable threatened their economic viability, or at least their ability to satisfy FCC-imposed public interest obligations. Responding to these complaints, the FCC initially prohibited the importation of distant television signals into larger markets and required cable systems to carry local broadcast signals. Until the early 1970s, the restrictions on the carriage of distant signals effectively confined the growth of cable television mainly to rural areas with little or no over-the-air television service.

In a further effort to protect television broadcasters from cable competition, the FCC imposed limits on the programming that cable systems could provide to their subscribers. In particular, the FCC prohibited the offering of series programs of any type, severely constrained the sporting events that could be carried, and permitted movies to be shown only if they were less than two or more than ten years old. These "antisiphoning" restrictions were adopted to prevent the migration of the most popular types of broadcast programming to cable.

Notwithstanding these restrictions, HBO, which was then majority-owned by Time and subsequently became a wholly owned subsidiary, began offering uncut, commercial-free movies in 1972 as a "premium" service to cable systems in return for a portion of the fees that these cable systems collected from their subscribers. However, FCC rules, combined with the high cost of using ground-based communications systems to deliver the service to individual cable systems, initially limited HBO largely to New York City. This changed when a young Time executive named Gerald Levin identified what would subsequently prove to be an historic opportunity. Noting that new FCC rules permitted a reduction in the size of "receive-only" satellite dishes, Levin convinced Time to use satellites to deliver HBO to cable systems across the country. This delivery system dramatically reduced the costs of distribution and made it economical for HBO to reach cable systems throughout the United States.

Equally important for HBO's subsequent growth was a 1977 Court of Appeals decision that overturned the FCC's restrictive "antisiphoning" rules, thus permitting HBO to obtain the rights to a much wider array of movies.[4] The consequences were dramatic. In 1979, HBO had only about 2 million subscribers; by 1996, it had more than 18 million subscribers and was the leading pay-per-channel service, with access to virtually all cable households.

Although the FCC began to relax its distant-signal restrictions in 1972, widespread carriage was still confined by the high cost and limited availability of the ground-based microwave relay systems that were then in use. Another young entrepreneur, Ted Turner, identified a way out of this difficulty. Turner, then the owner of a small independent UHF broadcast station in Atlanta (and former America's Cup winner), arranged to place the signal of his station on a satellite, thus making it available to any

---

[4]*Home Box Office* v. *FCC*, 567 F.2d 9 (D.C. Cir. 1977), cert. denied, 434 U.S. 829 (1978).

cable system with a receiving dish. Although copyright laws prevented Turner from collecting payments from the cable systems that retransmitted the signal of what became WTBS, Turner could obtain revenues from national advertisers because the reach of his Atlanta station now extended to the entire country. This, in turn, permitted Turner to acquire more expensive programming, and the "superstation" concept was born.

Turner demonstrated that "basic" services as well as "premium" services could take advantage of satellite delivery.[5] Subsequently, Turner Broadcasting launched the Cable News Network (CNN). CNN offered the first competitive challenge to the news organizations of the three major broadcast networks. Moreover, because CNN was not a retransmitted broadcast signal, Turner could charge cable operators directly for the service as well as receive revenues from national advertisers. Along with HBO, CNN helped transform cable from primarily a rural service that retransmitted broadcast signals into a nationwide service that offered programming unavailable on broadcast television. By the time that the FCC eliminated its remaining distant-signal carriage limitations in 1980, cable was poised to offer its subscribers a wide range of basic and premium services.

As long as cable was confined by FCC regulation primarily to rural areas, the entities that operated cable systems were relatively small. Indeed, during this period, cable systems were generally not viewed as attractive investments. Nonetheless, a number of entrepreneurs, apparently anticipating the eventual removal of regulations and the improved economic prospects that such deregulation promised, began to build or acquire large numbers of cable systems. In 1976, the ten largest multiple system owners, or MSOs, together served about 37 percent of all cable subscribers. By 1996, that figure had grown to almost 74 percent.

A key player in this growth was a third young entrepreneur, John Malone, who had earned a Ph.D. in operations research and had also published an article in the first issue of what would become a leading economics journal (*The Bell Journal of Economics and Management Science*). Malone's company, Telecommunications, Inc. (TCI) would eventually become the largest of these MSOs. In 1976, when the rapid growth of TCI under the leadership of Malone and Robert Magness began, TCI had only about 500,000 subscribers, or less than 5 percent of all cable households in the United States. By the time of the Time Warner-Turner merger, TCI had over 16 million subscribers, or about 25 percent of all cable households, and held ownership interests in a number of significant cable program service providers, including 23 percent of Turner Broadcasting.

Table 19-2 illustrates some of the dramatic changes that occurred in the cable industry beginning in 1976. Between 1976 and 1996, basic

---

[5]Basic services are offered as a package in return for a single price, while premium services are offered on an "à la carte" basis, although discounts are generally offered when more than one premium service is taken.

TABLE 19-2
History of Cable Growth 1976–1996

	1976	1986	1996
Total subscribers (millions)[a]	10.8	37.5	61.7
National cable video program networks[b]	4.0	68.0	162.0
Percent of systems with channel capacity greater than 12[c]	23.4	74.1	95.3[d]
Percent of systems with channel capacity greater than 30[c]	na	51.3	81.3[d]
Percent of subscribers having access to systems with channel capacity greater than 30[c]	na	73.7	98.2[d]

[a]Warren Publishing, Inc., *Television & Cable Factbook,* vol. 64, 1996, pp. 1–80.
(Numbers are as of January 1 of each year.)

[b]NCTA, *Cable Television Developments* 21, no. 1 (Spring 1997): 6.
(Numbers are as of year-end; superstations included.)

[c]*Television & Cable Factbook,* 1976–1997. Published by Television Digest, Inc., 1976–1987; and by Warren Publishing, Inc., 1988–1997. (Nonreporting systems were excluded from these calculations.)

[d]Numbers are as of October 1, 1996.

subscribership (i.e., the number of households purchasing the lowest-price package of services) rose by a factor of six, and the number of systems offering more than twelve channels to subscribers quadrupled. During the same period, the number of nationally distributed satellite programming services rose from 4 to 162. Importantly, the major urban areas became profitable to wire for cable service, which greatly increased the subscriber base for new programming services.

As the number of cable programming services increased, vertical integration by large MSOs into the development and ownership of cable networks became more prevalent. Warner Cable partnered with Viacom in launching MTV and with American Express in starting The Movie Channel. Viacom, which was at the time a major cable television system operator, also launched a number of the most popular cable services on its own, including Nickelodeon and Showtime. Viacom later acquired The Movie Channel from Warner-Amex (White, 1985). TCI launched Encore and Starz!, and its equity and experience helped launch Black Entertainment Television and the Discovery Channel, among other services.

When Turner Broadcasting experienced financial difficulties in the mid-1980s, a number of cable operators, including Time Warner and TCI, provided financial support in return for ownership interests. This support proved critical, enabling Turner to return to profitability. Turner expanded the number of program services it offered and was one of the major sources of programming to cable at the time of the proposed merger with Time Warner.

By the mid-1990s, TCI held interests in ten national program services including BET, Court TV, The Discovery Channel, Encore, and QVC, and had interests in a number of regional sports services as well. Although most of these services were operated by others, the growing involvement of TCI in the development and distribution of cable programming networks led to complaints by competing program services that TCI had used its position as the largest cable operator to favor the program services in which it had ownership interests by refusing to carry competing services on its cable systems. Similar charges were leveled against Time Warner, the second largest cable operator.

Although about half of the most popular services were not vertically integrated with large MSOs, the substantial amount of vertical integration that did exist gave rise to two antitrust concerns, often called "vertical foreclosure" (Riordan and Salop, 1995). First, vertically integrated MSOs might refuse to carry rival program services on their own cable systems. There are substantial economies of scale in creating a cable network because it is expensive to produce or purchase the programming that will be shown and to obtain access to satellite transport, but costs do not vary much with the number of cable systems that carry the service, or the number of viewers that subscribe. To survive, a network must reach a certain minimum number of subscribers at specified prices, a level that is referred to as "minimum viable scale" (MVS). The failure of a vertically integrated MSO to carry rival services might weaken these rivals and prevent them from reaching MVS. This could reduce the competition faced by the integrated MSOs' program services, thus enabling those services to raise their prices to other cable operators. Because it typically is more expensive to provide higher quality programming, the MVS for networks with broad appeal like ESPN or CNN is arguably higher than the MVS for a smaller, "niche" competitor, such as the Home & Garden Network or CNNfn.

Second, vertically integrated cable operators might deny their own program services to new competitors such as direct broadcast satellites (DBS) and local telephone companies. The result might be to weaken these competitors by reducing the attractiveness of their service offerings and thus permitting the integrated cable operators to raise their cable subscriber fees. In addition, some observers expressed misgivings about the control exercised by large vertically integrated MSOs in the "marketplace of ideas." From this perspective, the growth of these MSOs was undesirable because it reduced the number of independent media "voices."

The extent to which vertically integrated cable operators fail to carry rival services has always been controversial. In the authors' view, considerable empirical evidence indicates that vertically integrated cable operators do not generally disfavor basic program services in which they do not have ownership interests, and that any disadvantage for the premium services is quantitatively small. On the latter point, for example, one recent study using 1989 data found that HBO's rival Showtime was carried 37 percent less frequently on Time's cable systems than on other similar but unintegrated systems. However, this seemingly large carriage shortfall on

Time's systems reduced Showtime's subscriber access by only about 2.6 percent of the total cable subscriber universe. Similarly, other evidence suggests that cable operators did not deny affiliated programming to competing distribution technologies (Klein, 1989).

Concerns also were raised about monopoly power by cable operators, including concerns that cable rates were rising rapidly. Although the cable industry argued that these increases were justified by the substantial growth in the number of program services that subscribers were receiving in return for the higher rates, Congress enacted the 1992 Cable Act, which resulted in the regulation of virtually every aspect of the cable industry. In addition to mandating the regulation of basic cable rates and limiting the national share of cable subscribers that may be reached by any single cable operator to 30 percent, Congress also instructed the FCC to implement rules to deal directly with the two vertical foreclosure concerns.

To prevent vertically integrated cable operators from denying access to their cable systems by rival *program services,* the FCC adopted "channel occupancy" rules. These regulations prevent a cable operator from devoting more than 40 percent of its activated channels (up to a maximum of seventy-five channels) to nationally distributed program services in which it has an "attributable" ownership interest, usually defined as an interest of at least 5 percent. In addition, FCC rules prohibit discrimination by a cable system in favor of its affiliated program services. They also prohibit a cable operator from demanding a financial interest in a programming service as a condition of carriage and from "coercing" a programming service to provide exclusivity against other distributors. Finally, each system must be prepared to lease up to 15 percent of its capacity to unaffiliated programmers on a nondiscriminatory basis at rates and terms set by the FCC.

To prevent vertically integrated MSOs from denying access to popular programming services by rival *distributors,* the FCC adopted a number of "program access" rules. These rules effectively ban any exclusive distribution arrangement with cable operators, prohibit discrimination by vertically integrated programming services against competing distributors, and seek to prevent a cable system from "unduly or improperly" influencing an affiliated program service's price and terms of sale to unaffiliated distributors.

Attacks on vertical integration were not made solely by Congress and the FCC. In the 1980s, Viacom was sued over MTV's limited exclusivity for certain popular music videos. Viacom itself brought a suit that claimed that Time had limited its carriage of Viacom's premium services, Showtime and The Movie Channel, in order to provide a competitive advantage to HBO. In the 1990s, Viacom sued TCI, claiming that TCI could credibly threaten to prevent the entry of a new program service by refusing to carry the service if the entrant did not agree to grant TCI an ownership interest. All of these suits were eventually resolved by negotiated settlements.

THE FTC'S CONCERNS

Large mergers are reviewed in advance by the Federal Trade Commission or the Department of Justice for possible antitrust violations. The proposed Time Warner-Turner merger was reviewed by the FTC. The transaction raised competitive concerns for the FTC in both the cable program services and cable program distribution markets.[6] The FTC feared that the combined firm might be able to exert market power in the sale of programming to other cable distributors and create barriers to entry into both cable program services and cable distribution. As a majority (3-to-2) of the FTC Commissioners put it:

> The proposed merger and related transactions among Time Warner, Turner, and TCI involve three of the largest firms in cable programming and delivery—firms that are actual or potential competitors in many aspects of their businesses. The transaction would have merged the first and third largest cable programmers (Time Warner and Turner). At the same time, it would have further aligned the interests of TCI and Time Warner, the two largest cable distributors. Finally, the transaction as proposed would have greatly increased the level of vertical integration in an industry in which the threat of foreclosure is both real and substantial.[7]

These views can be classified into four specific competitive concerns: (1) the anticompetitive effects of TCI's ownership interest in Time Warner; (2) elimination of competition in cable program services; (3) creation of barriers to entry into cable program services; and (4) creation of barriers to entry for alternative video distributors. We discuss these four allegations in turn.

TCI's Ownership Interest in Time Warner

As a result of the Time Warner-Turner merger, TCI's approximate 23-percent ownership interest in Turner would become about a 9-percent ownership interest in Time Warner, with no legal barriers to prevent TCI's interest from later increasing to about 18 percent. The FTC contended that this ownership would permit TCI to influence Time Warner's competitive decisions and would also affect TCI's own competitive behavior. The FTC apparently felt that TCI's financial interest in Time Warner would reduce the incentives of the two firms to compete vigorously in the market for cable programming, particularly affecting competition between HBO and TCI's premium movie service, Starz!.

---

[6] For a statement of the FTC's views, see Federal Trade Commission, *Analysis of Proposed Consent Order to Aid Public Comment*, September 12, 1996.

[7] Separate Statement of Chairman Pitofsky and Commissioners Steiger and Varney, *In the Matter of Time Warner Inc.*, p. 1. Although a majority of the FTC opposed the merger as originally proposed, the combination was eventually approved after the merging parties accepted certain conditions imposed by the Commission. These conditions are discussed below.

The FTC also was concerned that TCI's ownership interest in Time Warner could facilitate coordinated vertical foreclosure by the two firms. Even if Time Warner and TCI did not coordinate their behavior, the FTC apparently believed that, as a large shareholder in Time Warner, TCI would have the incentive to refuse carriage to new program services that compete with services owned by Time Warner in order to raise barriers to entry. In particular, the FTC expressed concern that TCI might refuse to carry new twenty-four-hour news channels like Fox News and MSNBC that potentially would compete with CNN.

Eliminating Competition in the Cable Program Services Market

The FTC was concerned that the acquisition of Turner by Time Warner would eliminate competition between the program services owned by these two major competitors, thus giving Time Warner the power to raise the prices of these services. The FTC specifically contended that after the acquisition, Time Warner and Turner would have ample *unilateral* market power in a relevant market composed of all cable networks, defined as basic and premium services but excluding retransmitted broadcast stations. Unilateral market power differs from market power that is based on collusion in that it can be exercised without the cooperation of other suppliers. According to the FTC, Time Warner would control over 40 percent of this alleged "market" after the merger, a level of dominance that raises concerns under the DOJ/FTC *Merger Guidelines,* especially where, as the FTC contended, there are significant barriers to entry facing new cable networks. In addition, the FTC argued that the parties would be able to enhance the barriers to entry facing new cable networks by refusing to carry competing new networks, as discussed in the next section.

The FTC contended that competition would be particularly restrained among a limited group of networks that it referred to as "marquee" networks. According to the FTC, cable operators require access to a small number of highly popular services such as HBO, CNN, the Disney Channel, and ESPN to retain existing subscribers, or to expand their base of subscribers. The FTC also believed that barriers to entry to becoming a marquee network are particularly high and that the merged firm would control a large number of such networks. Thus, the FTC believed that the merger would permit Time Warner to raise the prices to cable operators for the Turner and Time Warner marquee networks.

Raising Barriers to Entry into Cable Program Services

TCI and Time Warner each own a large number of cable systems. TCI serves about 25 percent of all cable subscribers, and Time Warner serves about 15 percent. Although cable systems generally do not compete with one another because they serve different geographic areas, access to some minimum number of subscribers is no doubt essential for the survival of new cable programming networks. According to the FTC, by denying access to their subscribers, a combination of Time Warner and TCI could raise substantial barriers to entry to new program services by making it difficult or impossible for such services to gain the minimum number of subscribers to be viable over the long term, or to gain the larger number of subscribers that the FTC asserted was essential to achieve marquee network status. The FTC argued that if entry barriers were raised in this way, the Time Warner and Turner program services would gain market power over cable operators and cable subscribers.

The FTC's concern was particularly focused on twenty-four-hour cable news channels. Shortly after the Time Warner-Turner merger was announced, MSNBC and Fox News indicated their intention to enter. However, it was not clear whether these networks would be able to survive, let alone compete effectively with CNN or other marquee services. The FTC believed that access to the Time Warner and TCI cable systems was essential to the viability of these new cable networks.

The FTC also believed both that Time Warner would have the incentive to refuse to carry these competitors in order to protect the dominance of CNN, and that Time Warner would not carry an additional news network unless it was forced to do so. According to the Commission, if these competitors failed, CNN would be able to maintain, or even raise, the high per-subscriber fees it charged cable operators while retaining its viewing audience and the advertising revenues that it attracted. The FTC also felt that TCI, as a significant shareholder in Time Warner, would have carriage incentives similar to those of the Time Warner systems and that the Program Service Agreement between TCI and Turner would reinforce these incentives by committing TCI's limited channel capacity to the carriage of the Turner services, thereby reducing TCI's ability to carry competing news channels. The Commission also apparently believed that the twenty-year term of the Agreement was far longer than the industry norm and that the additional length did not yield any added efficiencies.

Raising Barriers to Entry Facing Alternative Multichannel Program Distributors

At the time of the transaction, cable had become the prevalent form of multichannel television distribution, with over 90 percent of all households capable of receiving cable service and 60 percent actually subscribing. Moreover, very few areas were served by more than a single cable operator. The potential for entry and the expansion of existing competitors came from two primary sources: DBS and local telephone companies. The FTC argued that Time Warner and TCI, as large cable operators, would have incentives to raise barriers to entry to these new entrants to maintain their cable monopolies. According to the FTC, the transaction could facilitate creation of entry barriers into distribution in three complementary ways.

First, the FTC believed that Time Warner could refuse to provide access to its marquee networks to the new entrants or could charge them discriminatorily high prices. According to the Commission, if these entrants did not have access to HBO and CNN, for example, they would be unattractive to subscribers. Similarly, if the entrants had to pay substantially more for their programming than did Time Warner cable systems, their costs would be higher and so their entry would be less attractive. In either case, Time Warner's cable subscriber base, and the profits earned from its cable systems, would be protected.

Second, the FTC similarly felt that TCI would have the ability and incentive to raise barriers to the entry of DBS and the telephone companies. Although TCI might have had comparable incentives to protect TCI systems before the Time Warner-Turner transaction, the FTC apparently feared that its ownership interest in Time Warner would create additional incentives for TCI to protect the Time Warner cable systems as well.

Third, the long-term Program Services Agreement for TCI carriage of the Turner services gave TCI a discount from the price that others would pay for the same services. The FTC felt that this provision might disadvantage entrants that competed with TCI systems.

THE MERGING PARTIES' ANSWERS TO THE FTC CONCERNS

The merging parties disagreed with the FTC's analysis. At the outset, they pointed out that well-recognized efficiencies from vertical integration could be expected to flow from combining the Turner programming services and the Time Warner cable systems. The parties noted that vertical mergers can eliminate the necessity for negotiation and execution of vertical contracts, reduce the associated risk and uncertainty, and discourage opportunistic behavior after contracts have been signed. In the context of the Time Warner-Turner merger, the parties expected that the combination would make it easier for Turner to secure carriage commitments for, and thus reduce the launch costs of, new program services. The parties also noted that Turner Broadcasting's fragmented ownership structure made it difficult for Turner to utilize its assets efficiently because a small number of owners could effectively veto important initiatives.

The parties went on to challenge the FTC's general presumption that this transaction created the equivalent of a merger among Time Warner, TCI, and Turner. They argued that TCI would be a small and noninfluential shareholder of Time Warner with no incentives to sacrifice its own profits to protect the profits of Time Warner. Indeed, they pointed out that

TCI's share in Time Warner would be substantially smaller than its share in Turner prior to the Time Warner-Turner merger.

With respect to the FTC's four specific competitive concerns, the parties contended that the FTC's arguments were deficient. This conclusion was also shared by two of the five FTC Commissioners. As Commissioner Azcuenaga argued in her dissenting statement:

> [T]he majority adopts a highly questionable market definition, ignores any consideration of efficiencies and blindly assumes difficulty of entry in the antitrust sense in the face of overwhelming evidence to the contrary. The decision of the majority also departs from more general principles of antitrust law by favoring competitors over competition and contrived theory over facts.

TCI's Partial Ownership of Time Warner

The transaction provided TCI with a 9-percent ownership stake in Time Warner, and TCI could in principle increase its ownership interest to about 18 percent. These facts apparently suggested to the FTC that the Time Warner-Turner merger would effectively also combine the interests of Time Warner and TCI. However, the parties argued that this inference was false.

A complete merger creates common *control* over and identical *financial interests* between two previously independent firms. TCI's partial interest in Time Warner, however, would not exhibit these properties. First, TCI's interest in Time Warner would be much smaller than it would be in a complete merger. Second, TCI could exercise no control over Time Warner since, as part of the transaction, TCI's shares were to be nonvoting. In addition, TCI officers and managers were not permitted to discuss Time Warner operations with Gerald Levin. Thus, although the transaction would give TCI a significant ownership position in Time Warner, TCI would have no control, or even influence, over the competitive decisions of Time Warner because of the way in which the merger was structured. Of course, Time Warner would have no ownership interest in, or ability to control, TCI.

Even if TCI's ownership stake in Time Warner were passive, so that Time Warner's behavior would be unaffected by TCI's ownership interest, this financial interest could theoretically change *TCI's* own unilateral economic incentives. For example, the financial interest could reduce the incentives of TCI program services to compete with those owned by Time Warner. Similarly, it could reduce the incentives of TCI cable systems to carry cable program services that compete with Time Warner's networks. However, the parties argued that, even at the 18-percent maximum possible ownership level, TCI's financial interest in Time Warner would not be large enough to significantly affect its behavior in the relevant markets.

To illustrate this analysis, consider the FTC's concern in the context of competition between Time Warner and TCI program services. As a general economic matter, when one firm takes a partial ownership interest in a rival, its unilateral incentives to increase its price (or restrict its output) may be enhanced. This is because a price increase (or output restriction) will increase the profits of the rival, profits in which the investing firm is entitled to share.

These unilateral incentives can be explained in more detail by comparing the impact of a price increase on the aggregate earnings of a firm before and after it obtains a partial ownership interest in a rival. When a firm increases its price, it loses some sales to competing firms. The direct impact on its profits involves two elements: (1) the profits foregone on those lost sales, and (2) the increased profits on the sales retained at the higher price. In the absence of an ownership interest in a competing firm, the firm chooses its price to maximize profits by balancing these two factors. This is the point at which marginal revenue and marginal cost are equated.

When a firm holds a partial financial interest in a rival firm, however, its earnings also are affected by a third element: the profits earned by the rival. In particular, when the firm raises its price, the profits of the rival increase because the rival obtains some of the sales lost by the firm. As a partial owner of the rival, the firm obtains a share of these increased profits. Thus, the ownership share gives the firm an economic incentive, which is not present if the two firms remain independent, to sacrifice some of its own profits in order to increase the profits of its rival. Starting from an initial price that maximizes its own profits, the firm has an incentive to raise its price to the level where, at the margin, its share of any additional increased profits flowing to the rival just equals the associated reduction in its own profits.

The effect of the partial ownership on the unilateral incentives of the firm depends on the size of the firm's ownership share in the rival, its own market share, the market share of the rival, and the degree of the firm's influence or control over the rival.[8] The role of each of these factors is as follows:

- *Magnitude of ownership share:* The greater is the firm's ownership stake in the rival, the greater is its incentive to raise its price. This is because a higher ownership share entitles the firm to a larger percentage of the rival's increased profits that result from any price increase.

- *Market share of the firm:* The greater is the firm's market share, the greater is its incentive to elevate price above the competitive level. This is

---

[8] It also depends on the extent of consumer substitution to other firms outside the market, the entry of new firms, fringe expansion, and synergies created by the ownership interest, all of which could reduce the adverse competitive impact of the partial ownership interest. In this matter, the substitution would be to new cable networks, over-the-air broadcast television, and video cassette rentals.

because a higher market share means that the higher price will be obtained for more units of output. Thus, there will be a larger increase in profits caused by any price increase.

- *Market share of the rival firm:* Similarly, the greater is the market share of the rival in which it has an ownership interest, the greater is the firm's incentive to raise its price. This is because a higher market share of the rival means that the resulting higher market price will be obtained for more units of the rival's output. Thus, there will be a larger increase in the profits of the rival in which the firm will share.

- *Degree of influence or control by the firm over the rival:* If the firm also can influence the rival to raise its price in response to its own price increase, this will further increase the anticipated profits from the price increase. In contrast, if the financial interest conveys no control, but instead is passive or "silent," the firm's incentive to raise prices will be weaker because it cannot be certain of the rival's response to its price increase.

To gauge the magnitude of the effect of the partial ownership interest, it is useful to have an index, or summary statistic, that measures the combined effect of these four factors. In a complete merger, the Herfindahl-Hirschman Index (HHI) of concentration is often calculated. The HHI is the sum of the squared market shares of all firms in a market. The higher is the value of the postmerger HHI, the more concentrated is the market after the merger, and the more likely are prices to exceed competitive levels. Similarly, it is assumed that the greater is the increase in the HHI caused by the merger, the greater is the expected price increase resulting from the merger, ceteris paribus.

Of course, the change in the HHI would be a poor indicator of the competitive effect of TCI's partial interest in Time Warner, since TCI would have a smaller share and less control than it would have in a complete merger. A better concentration index for this transaction would account for this partial ownership interest and the absence of TCI's control over Time Warner's management. A "modified" Herfindahl-Hirschman Index (MHHI) has been developed to account for these effects (Bresnahan and Salop, 1986). In a complete merger, the change in the HHI is twice the product of the market shares of the merging firms, or $2S_1S_2$. If the transaction instead involves the acquisition of a partial ownership interest that is "silent" (i.e., that involves no management control), the resulting change in the MHHI equals the partial ownership share times the product of the market shares of the two firms, or $\sigma S_1 S_2$, where the ownership share is denoted by the symbol σ.

Comparing these two changes shows the dramatic difference between a complete merger and the acquisition of a small, silent financial interest. A complete merger between a firm with a 5-percent market share and one with a 50-percent market share produces a change in the HHI of 500 points (i.e.,

$2 \times 5 \times 50$). In contrast, if the smaller firm acquires a 10-percent *silent financial interest* in the larger firm, the corresponding change in the MHHI is only 25 points (i.e., $0.10 \times 5 \times 50$).

The difference between the changes in the HHI and the MHHI arises from the difference between the factors that are used to multiply the products of the merging firm's shares. The product of the market shares is multiplied by 2 in calculating the HHI to take into account the fact that each firm is effectively a half-owner of the other and has full control over its output. The product of the market shares is multiplied by the partial ownership share in calculating the MHHI to take into account the fact that one firm has a partial ownership interest in its rival and neither firm has any control over the output of the other.

This MHHI analysis can be applied to TCI's financial interest in Time Warner. Recall that TCI owns a premium movie service, Starz!, that competes with Time Warner's movie services, HBO and Cinemax (hereafter, "HBO"). One of the FTC's concerns was that TCI might have an incentive to sacrifice some of the profits of Starz! by raising its price in order to increase HBO profits, in which TCI now has an ownership interest. In addition, the FTC might have been concerned that Time Warner's management would take the separate interests of its owners, including TCI, into account in determining HBO's competitive behavior. However, this concern was likely to be mitigated by the fact that TCI's ownership interest would be silent.

To calculate the MHHI in this transaction, recall that TCI received at most a 9-percent financial interest in Time Warner in exchange for its interest in Turner. Time Warner owned approximately 75 percent of Time Warner Entertainment (TWE), which owns HBO (and most of the Time Warner cable systems). As a result, TCI effectively would obtain a 6.75-percent ownership interest in HBO (i.e., 75% of 9%) as a result of the merger, or even less if Time Warner issued more shares. We treat this interest as silent.

On the basis of the annual revenues of the premium movie services at the time of the merger, the shares of HBO and Starz! were about 68 percent and 2 percent, respectively, in a narrow hypothetical market limited to "premium cable movie services" that included Showtime and The Movie Channel (both owned by Viacom) in addition to HBO and Starz!. On the assumption of a 6.75-percent silent financial interest by TCI in HBO,[9] the transaction increases the MHHI by only 9.2 points (i.e., $.0675 \times 68 \times 2$).

---

[9] TCI also argued that its nominal interest in Time Warner overstated its effective financial interest because it lacked control over the disposition of Time Warner profits. On this issue see, e.g., Jensen (1986). TCI may have been compensated for this increased agency risk by paying a lower price for the Time Warner stock than it received in the transaction or may buy in the future. However, the issue here is not the riskiness of Time Warner stock generally, but whether TCI would find prudent the transfer of *additional* revenues from TCI to HBO *in the future* by sacrificing profits in Starz! that it otherwise would control.

This increase is far less than the 50 points that represents a "safe harbor" under the Merger Guidelines on the grounds that "mergers producing an increase in the HHI of less than 50 points, even in highly concentrated markets post-merger, are unlikely to have adverse competitive consequences and ordinarily require no further analysis."[10]

Even if it were assumed that the market share of Starz! would rise to 10 percent at Showtime's expense, the change in the MHHI would still fall short of 50 points ($.0675 \times 68 \times 10 = 45.9$). Finally, even if TCI were to buy more Time Warner stock up to the maximum level of about 18 percent, so that TCI's partial ownership interest in HBO were to rise to 13.4 percent (i.e., 75% of 18%) and Starz!'s share of premium movie revenues were to rise to 10 percent, the change in the MHHI would still be only 91.1 points (i.e., $.134 \times 68 \times 10$). Under the *Merger Guidelines*, increases in the HHI of fewer than 100 points often indicate that no significant competitive problems exist. TCI contended that these figures showed that, far from approximating a merger, the TCI stock ownership in Time Warner would have virtually no effect on TCI's incentives to compete with Time Warner, even in this narrow hypothetical market.[11]

Elimination of Competition Between Time Warner and Turner Broadcasting Program Services

As discussed above, the FTC apparently was concerned that after the transaction Time Warner would control over 40 percent of an alleged market composed of all nonbroadcast cable programming. Under the *Merger Guidelines*, this market share would raise significant competitive concerns, on the assumption that there were barriers to entry. The FTC contended that barriers to entry were substantial, particularly for marquee networks, and that the transaction would actually raise these barriers.

The FTC staff argued that basic and premium services should be placed in the same market because they are alternatives available to the cable operator for attracting subscribers and thus compete for "shelf space" on cable systems. Time Warner (and the dissenting FTC Commissioners) disagreed with the FTC majority's contentions. They argued that the FTC's market definition, which combined basic services like CNN and ESPN with premium services like HBO and Showtime, and which excluded broadcast television and prerecorded video entertainment, was inapposite. Basic services are sold to cable systems which, in turn, package them for sale to subscribers. By contrast, premium services are sold to cable subscribers on an optional à la carte basis. Time Warner also argued

---

[10]U.S. Department of Justice and Federal Trade Commission, *Horizontal Merger Guidelines*, April 2, 1992 (revised April 8, 1997), Section 1.51 (c).

[11]Of course, even a large increase in the MHHI might not have been sufficient to demonstrate an anticompetitive effect, since competition in a broader product market, entry, and product repositioning could also defeat an attempt to raise prices.

that premium services like HBO face more competition from video cassette rentals than from basic services like CNN and TNT, which, in turn, face their greatest competition from television broadcasters, so that a market that comprises only basic and premium cable services is either too large or too small.

Time Warner further argued that barriers to entry were low, pointing to evidence that the number of cable networks had increased from 106 to 129 in 1995 alone and that 30 new cable networks were set to launch in 1996. The FTC majority countered by asserting that no network that had entered since 1991 had obtained a substantial market share. In the words of the majority, "the launch of a new 'Billiards Channel' or 'Ballet Channel' or the like will barely make a ripple on the shores of the marquee channels through which Time Warner can exercise market power." However, it is noteworthy that Fox News attained substantial penetration in a short period of time after the merger, including substantial penetration on TCI systems that had agreed to carry Fox News before the FTC decision.

Time Warner also criticized the marquee network product market definition. It argued that there was no evidence of any cable operator ever playing CNN and HBO off against one another in order to obtain a better deal. As for the fear that Time Warner would bundle HBO with Turner services after the merger, Time Warner pointed out that there was no evidence that premium and basic services had ever been bundled by Time Warner or by Viacom, which controlled premium services like Showtime and The Movie Channel and basic services like MTV and Nickelodeon. Nonetheless, the FTC was apparently concerned about less formal types of bundling in which, say, Time Warner might insist on higher prices for CNN from those cable operators that declined to take HBO, without explicitly linking these prices in their offerings (Baker, 1997).

Raising Barriers to Entry into Program Services

According to the FTC, Time Warner would have the incentive to deny carriage on its cable systems to competing services in order to protect the dominance of Turner services like CNN. Similarly, the Commission argued that TCI's ownership stake in Time Warner, coupled with the long-term carriage agreement for Turner networks, would eliminate TCI's incentive and ability to carry competing services such as twenty-four-hour news services like Fox News and MSNBC. Time Warner and TCI disagreed, arguing that they had neither the incentive nor the ability to prevent the entry of rival cable networks that their cable subscribers desire.

Time Warner and TCI made three general points. First, they argued that as cable operators, they had the incentive to carry the cable networks that their subscribers most wanted. Behaving otherwise would reduce the profits they earned as cable operators and leave them vulnerable to entry by alternative distributors. In this regard, they analyzed the incentives and introduced evidence that Time Warner and TCI had not refused to carry competing networks in the past.

Second, they argued that even if Time Warner and TCI refused to carry these competitors of CNN, the entrants could still survive and prosper if they were carried on other systems. In short, they argued that carriage on Time Warner and/or TCI cable systems was not "essential" to the successful entry of new program services.

Third, they argued that even if a few entrants were deterred, CNN and other Time Warner networks would not have the power to charge noncompetitive prices because they compete in a broad program service market that includes broadcast television and video cassette rentals, as well as many other cable program services. Thus, even if certain other cable networks were unable to enter, CNN could not charge noncompetitive prices, which would eliminate any incentive for Time Warner to deter such entry.

We focus here on the alleged potential for the foreclosure of competing news networks that figured prominently in the FTC's concerns. The FTC's theory required that TCI and Time Warner be willing to deny carriage to a news service that their subscribers desire (say, Fox News) in order to raise barriers to entry. Of course, by denying carriage to a desirable network, TCI and Time Warner necessarily would reduce their profits as cable operators. (This assumes that a cable system that was not integrated with a rival program service otherwise *would* carry the new entrant.) However, according to the FTC's theory, the resulting sacrifice in profits would be more than offset by the firms' share of the increased profits that Time Warner services, say CNN, would earn from deterring the entry of the new competitor.

We have already discussed why TCI's small ownership share in Time Warner tends to limit TCI's incentives to engage in behavior that increases Time Warner's profits at the expense of its own. Moreover, TCI pointed out that its agreement to carry CNN and other services actually enhanced TCI's incentives to promote competitive entry. This is because the price it would pay to Time Warner for CNN under the Program Service Agreement was tied to the price CNN charges other cable operators. Thus, if CNN gains power to increase the price it charges to other cable operators, the price to TCI will also increase.

Because TCI's stake in cable program distribution is so much larger than its ownership share in CNN, TCI substantially benefits from lower, not higher, prices for CNN. An increase in the price of CNN reduces TCI's profits on the approximately 25 percent of total cable subscribers that TCI serves, but TCI receives only 6.75 percent of CNN's increased profits through its ownership share in Time Warner. Put somewhat differently, a CNN price increase reduces TCI's profits on the 25 percent of subscribers it might be said to "own" through its cable systems, and increases its profits on the 6.75 percent of CNN subscribers that it might be said to "own" through its interest in Time Warner. Thus, the analysis shows a substantial *loss* to TCI from an increase in the price of CNN.

This substantial difference between TCI's subscriber share and its CNN ownership share provides the simplest explanation of why a unilateral denial of carriage by TCI would prove unprofitable.[12] However, a number of other factors further reduce the profitability of this behavior and reinforce the view that it would be in TCI's overall interest to offer carriage to cable program services that its subscribers value.

First, if TCI failed to carry a rival service that its subscribers value, subscribership to its systems would likely fall below what it otherwise would have been, or its cable prices would have to be reduced, or both, resulting in lower profits from sales to subscribers. Subscriber losses would also reduce local advertising revenues that would otherwise have been obtained by TCI's cable systems. Second, an increase in the price of CNN might permit services in which TCI or Time Warner do *not* have ownership interests to raise their prices. Because TCI is a buyer of these services, this would reduce the profits of its cable systems. Third, Time Warner program services in addition to CNN would suffer a reduction in profits as a result of any reduction in the number of TCI subscribers. By virtue of its ownership share in Time Warner, TCI would bear a portion of those profit reductions in addition to the similar profit reductions experienced by all other services in which TCI has an ownership interest.

One could analyze Time Warner's incentives in a similar way. Although Time Warner would initially benefit from eliminating competition to CNN from another twenty-four-hour news service, those benefits would be offset by the factors just discussed. Moreover, Time Warner argued that the FTC's analysis of Time Warner's incentives made a second implausible assumption—that if Time Warner denied carriage to a new cable network entrant, the denial would significantly disadvantage the entrant.

Time Warner also argued that many services do not require access to the entire cable universe to succeed. If Time Warner failed to carry these services, this "foreclosure" would not create a substantial competitive disadvantage for these services, nor would it be likely to drive these services below minimum viable scale. Moreover, Time Warner's incentive to engage in a foreclosure strategy is further reduced by the imminent growth in channel capacity that soon will result from digital technology. Time Warner's cable operations will be demanding more program services to fill these additional channels. Finally, Time Warner also observed that the rapid growth of the high-powered DBS services (DirecTV and EchoStar) provides an increasingly important alternative to distribution on the Time Warner (or other) cable systems. To the extent that Time Warner were to

---

[12] This analysis of TCI's incentives was reinforced by the announcement during the FTC investigation that TCI had agreed to carry Fox News on TCI cable systems in exchange for a payment of $10 per subscriber.

refuse to carry services desired by its subscribers, its subscribers could switch to the DBS services carrying those services.

TCI and Time Warner also argued that they had not disfavored rival networks in the past. As already noted, studies of the effects of vertical integration in the cable industry indicate that vertically integrated operators, including TCI and Time Warner, have typically carried programming services in which they lack an ownership interest. Moreover, in the few cases in which TCI and Time Warner do carry unaffiliated services less frequently than do other cable operators, the extent of the noncarriage on the TCI and Time Warner systems has only a trivial effect on the subscriber universe to which the service has access. Indeed, TCI and Time Warner also argued that MSO ownership interests in programming have enhanced the array of services available to consumers.

Finally, the FTC's theory assumed that CNN would be able to raise its prices in the event that entry by competing twenty-four-hour news networks was deterred. This assumes that competition is limited to twenty-four-hour news services. The parties argued that, at a minimum, competition also involves other news sources, particularly those available on the over-the-air television networks (ABC, NBC, CBS, and Fox). In this alleged market, the share of viewers accounted for by CNN is relatively small. (In the advertising market, CNN clearly competes with broadcast news and other programs that attract similar demographics and has a tiny share of advertising on news programs.) Indeed, even the FTC's marquee network theory is premised on the assumption of competition among marquee networks that offer diverse programming, not on competition limited to twenty-four-hour news services.

Barriers to Entry Facing Alternative Multichannel Video Program Distributors

The FTC was also concerned that the transaction would raise barriers to entry facing new distributors, such as DBS operators and telephone companies. In particular, the Commission argued that, after the merger, Time Warner and TCI would have increased incentives to deny access to their own program services to rival distributors, thus limiting the competition faced by their own cable systems.

The parties argued that this concern was unfounded for several reasons. First, the program services owned by Time Warner, Turner, and TCI face intense competition from other networks, so that rival distributors could obtain programming from other sources if the merging parties denied them programming. Second, the parties sacrifice revenues when they refuse to sell their services to other operators, and these losses are unlikely to be offset by significant gains to their cable system operations, especially if there are rival program services. Third, FCC regulations already prohibit discrimination against rival distributors by severely limiting the ability of a cable operator to obtain exclusive program carriage rights and by constraining differences in the prices that can be charged to competing operators. Fourth, the parties argued that a long-term pricing agreement between TCI and Time Warner for the Turner services was needed to prevent either side from behaving opportunistically by demanding large price changes in the future. Finally, the parties argued that the discounts received by TCI represented a legitimate volume discount that was permitted under FCC rules because of TCI's large subscriber base.

THE SETTLEMENT AND CONSENT DECREE

In August 1996, about one year after the transaction was announced, the FTC and the parties settled the case and agreed to a consent decree. The decree permitted the merger to go forward subject to certain modifications. The decree was not particularly draconian. As discussed in more detail below, it did not require Time Warner to divest itself of ownership of any Turner networks, nor did it require TCI to sell its Time Warner stock. Instead, it simply enjoined certain conduct, mandated other conduct, and limited the number of additional shares in Time Warner that could be acquired by TCI. Although the settlement with the government required certain relatively minor modifications to the transaction, it also eliminated the risk that the entire transaction might be enjoined by a court. (For an interesting exchange about the relative bargaining power of the government and the merging parties in negotiating consent decrees, see Baer (1997) and Sims and Herman (1997).)

Limiting TCI's Ownership Interest in Time Warner

As a result of the consent decree, TCI's ownership interest in Time Warner, including the interests of TCI's major shareholders, was capped at approximately 9 percent of the fully diluted shares. By limiting the number of additional shares that TCI could acquire, the FTC sought to ensure that TCI's financial interest in Time Warner remained too small to affect its incentives and ability to significantly influence Time Warner's behavior after the merger.

Restrictions on Service Bundling

The consent decree did not require Time Warner to sell any of the Turner networks to alleviate the horizontal competitive concerns discussed above. Instead, it forbade Time Warner from bundling the sale of Time Warner premium services and Turner basic networks. Under this provision, Time Warner cannot require a cable system to take (say) CNN or CNNI as a condition of buying HBO. Nor can Time Warner require that a cable system that wants CNN or Headline News also carry a Time Warner premium service such as HBO or Cinemax.

Removing Barriers to Entry into Cable Program Services

The consent decree dealt with entry barriers in two ways. First, Time Warner agreed to offer carriage by the year 2001 to one new, independent twenty-four-hour news network on cable systems that served at least 50 percent of Time Warner subscribers. Time Warner eventually chose to carry MSNBC to fulfill its obligations under this provision. Second, the decree required Time Warner and TCI to terminate the long-term Program Service Agreement for the Turner services and limited the length of subsequent carriage contracts to five years. Although the parties could renegotiate their agreement, they would be forced to wait until after a six-month "cooling off" period, effectively separating those negotiations from the Time Warner-Turner merger.

Protecting Program Access by Competing Distributors

The consent decree prohibited Time Warner from discriminating against competing operators in the distribution of the current set of Turner services. Although this provision tracks the nondiscrimination rules in current FCC regulations, the FTC apparently believed that it could enforce the provisions of the decree more effectively than the FCC. In addition, through termination of the program service carriage agreement with TCI, that potential source of discrimination was eliminated.

POSTSCRIPT

Time Warner and Turner merged shortly after the final consent decree was approved, but the controversy over the transaction did not end there. To satisfy its requirement to carry an additional news service, Time Warner had agreed to carry MSNBC. Shortly after, Fox filed suit against Time Warner to require carriage of Fox News Network and to undo the transaction. Fox's antitrust claims tracked the FTC's vertical foreclosure concerns about the need for carriage on Time Warner cable systems for Fox News Network to survive and compete effectively with CNN. However, the suit went considerably further than the FTC in that Fox contended that carriage on Time Warner's New York City cable system was itself essential to Fox News because it provided access to a large number of advertising and media executives who live and work in New York.

Fox also enlisted the aid of New York City Mayor Rudolf Giuliani, who proposed to air Fox News on the public access channels that were allocated to the city under the Time Warner cable franchise, an action that

Time Warner successfully blocked in court. However, with the trial of the antitrust issues looming, the parties eventually settled the suit, and Time Warner agreed to carry the Fox News Channel. There were no public statements about what Time Warner received in return. However, press reports cited a lucrative carriage deal in which Fox paid Time Warner for carriage of the Fox News Channel. Press reports also mentioned approval by Fox's parent, News Corporation, of the continuing carriage of Major League Baseball by WTBS after the conversion of that station to a basic cable service, approval of which was apparently required under Fox's contract with Major League Baseball. Moreover, Time Warner was given channel capacity otherwise claimed by the City of New York that it could use to carry Fox News and add other commercial services.

REFERENCES

Baer, William J. "Reflections on Twenty Years of Merger Enforcement Under the Hart-Scott-Rodino Act." *Antitrust Law Journal* 65 (Spring 1997): 825–863.

Baker, Jonathan B. "Unilateral Competitive Effects Theories in Merger Analysis." *Antitrust* 11 (Spring 1997): 21–26.

Bresnahan, Timothy F., and Steven C. Salop. "Quantifying the Competitive Effects of Production Joint Ventures." *International Journal of Industrial Organization* 4 (December 1986): 155–175.

Jensen, Michael C. "Agency Costs of Free Cash Flow, Corporate Finance, and Takeovers." *American Economic Review* 76 (May 1986): 323–329.

Klein, Benjamin J. "The Competitive Consequences of Vertical Integration in the Cable Industry." Mimeo, June 1989.

Riordan, Michael H., and Steven C. Salop. "Evaluating Vertical Mergers: A Post-Chicago Approach." *Antitrust Law Journal* 63 (Winter 1995): 513–568.

Sims, Joe, and Deborah P. Herman. "The Effect of Twenty Years of Hart-Scott-Rodino on Merger Practice: A Case Study in the Law of Unintended Consequences Applied to Antitrust Legislation." *Antitrust Law Journal* 65 (Spring 1997): 865–904.

White, Lawrence J. "Antitrust and Video Markets: The Merger of Showtime and the Movie Channel as a Case Study." In *Video Media Competition: Regulation, Economics, and Technology,* edited by E. M. Noam. New York: Columbia University Press, 1985.